WALTER LYNWOOD FLEMING LECTURES

IN SOUTHERN HISTORY

LOUISIANA STATE UNIVERSITY

THE WHITE HOUSE LOOKS SOUTH

FRANKLIN D. ROOSEVELT,

HARRY S. TRUMAN,

LYNDON B. JOHNSON

WILLIAM E. LEUCHTENBURG

LOUISIANA STATE UNIVERSITY PRESS

BATON ROUGE

PUBLISHED WITH THE ASSISTANCE OF THE V. RAY CARDOZIER FUND

DESIGNER: Andrew Shurtz
TYPEFACE: Adobe Caslon
TYPESETTER: The Composing Room of Michigan, Inc.

LIBRARY OF CONGRESS CATALOGING-IN-PUBLICATION DATA
Leuchtenburg, William Edward, 1922–
The White House looks south : Franklin D. Roosevelt, Harry S. Truman,
Lyndon B. Johnson / William E. Leuchtenburg.
p.   cm. — (Walter Lynwood Fleming lectures in southern history)
Includes bibliographical references and index.
ISBN: 0-8071-3079-6 (hardcover : alk. paper)
1. Roosevelt, Franklin D. (Franklin Delano), 1882–1945.   2. Truman, Harry S., 1884–1972.
3. Johnson, Lyndon B. (Lyndon Baines), 1908–1973.   4. Presidents—United States—
Biography.   5. United States—Politics and government—20th century.   6. Southern States—
Civilization—20th century.   7. Southern States—Politics and government—1865–1950.
8. Southern States—Politics and government—1951–   9. Regionalism—United States—
History—20th century.   10. Regionalism—Southern States—History—20th century.
I. Title.   II. Series.
E747.L48   2005
973.91′092′2—dc22   2004029192

FOR JEAN ANNE

Counselor in Perplexity

Comfort in Sorrow

Companion in Joy

CONTENTS

ACKNOWLEDGMENTS

This book originated in the Walter Lynwood Fleming Lectures in Southern History that I delivered at Louisiana State University in Baton Rouge. I am indebted to the members of the LSU history department and the editors of the LSU Press for making that occasion such a congenial one. Those lectures have been greatly expanded as a consequence of research in more than four hundred manuscript collections and over two hundred oral histories in every southern state as well as elsewhere in this country and abroad, and at every archive I have been gratified by the unfailing collegiality and expertise of skilled and gracious archivists. Numbers of generous scholars have gone out of their way to share their wisdom with me. I think especially of Edward Ayers, Tony Badger, Kenneth J. Bindas, James Cobb, Travis Dayhuff, Robert Dallek, Robert H. Ferrell, the late Frank Freidel, Alonzo L. Hamby, Stephen Keadey, Richard Kirkendall, Franklin Mitchell, David Moltke-Hansen, James Peacock, the late Jordan Schwarz, and Timothy Thurber. I have benefited greatly from the perceptive counsel of David Goldfield, whose writings have contributed so much to our knowledge of the modern South, and the insightful comments of Lizabeth Cohen after I presented some of my findings to a faculty colloquium when I was a visiting professor at Harvard. I am grateful, too, for the assistance of Thomas Devine, Ethan Kytle, and Brian Steele. I have had the good fortune of being able to draw upon well over a hundred unpublished dissertations, essays, and conference papers, and I would like to pay special tribute to their authors. Most of this work will never appear in print, but these scholars, many of them young men and women at the start of their careers, have made invaluable contributions.

My greatest debt, once again, is to my wife, Jean Anne, who accompanied me to remote archives; offered, always disarmingly, any number of brilliant suggestions; and who prepared and edited the manuscript in a way that encouraged, cheered, and inspirited me.

THE WHITE HOUSE
LOOKS SOUTH

PROLOGUE

Every time I try to say what this book is about I get interrupted. "What are you working on now?" an acquaintance asks. Two sentences, I figure, is all anyone wants to hear. "It's on three twentieth-century presidents and the South," I begin. I never get to add the second sentence. "Don't tell me who they are, I know," the inquirer interjects. "Jimmy Carter, Bill Clinton, and, oh yes, going back a long way, Woodrow Wilson."

Actually, it is none of these, but I have no trouble understanding the supposition. Jimmy Carter ran for the White House as a peanut grower with a pronounced Georgia drawl. When the Arkansas governor Bill Clinton teamed up with Al Gore of Tennessee, the tandem was called "the Bubba Bubba ticket." Woodrow Wilson, who, as a boy in Augusta saw thousands of Confederate soldiers march by to meet Sherman's invaders, cherished "the delightful memory of standing, when a lad, for a moment by General Lee's side and looking up into his face." No one could doubt that these men were as down South as grits and country ham.[1]

When I reveal my altogether different choices—Franklin Delano Roosevelt, Harry S. Truman, and Lyndon Baines Johnson—eyebrows rise. Johnson, it is acknowledged, has a certain credibility as a southerner. At least, he came from a state that seceded from the Union. But Texas, and especially the Johnson hill country, seems as much western as southern. Truman's Independence, Missouri, the starting point for the Oregon Trail, also faced west as well as south. And FDR? How could a man born and raised in New York's Hudson River valley be regarded as, in any respect, southern? Why in the world would I pick these three?

For good reason. When Lyndon Johnson eyed a presidential nomination, no one ever let him forget that he was a son of Dixie, and hence unacceptable.

Harry Truman grew up in a home that glorified the Confederacy and in a town imbued with racist assumptions he never entirely forsook. Franklin Roosevelt, as a consequence of his many stays in Warm Springs, frequently thought of himself as a Georgian and was viewed by others as at least an "adopted son."

Granted, the three men do not have the credentials of the Wilson-Carter-Clinton trio, but that is precisely their appeal to me. Each had one foot below the Mason-Dixon line, one foot above. Their intimate ties to the South gave them an understanding of, and empathy for, the section denied a Calvin Coolidge or a Gerald Ford. Living in southern or quasi-southern communities schooled them. FDR, for one, learned the fundamentals of the cotton culture in Georgia's Meriwether County. At the same time, the three men viewed the South from a national, or at least northern, perspective. Each of them drew on familiarity with, and acceptance in, the South to nudge it toward changing its institutions and attitudes, especially with regard to race.

Ambiguity about place also opens up the possibility for reinventing oneself, and, at different periods, both Franklin Roosevelt and Lyndon Johnson did that. In the 1920s, at a time when his career was in eclipse, FDR laid claim to being not only a New Yorker, but also a Georgian, someone the South need not fear, a consideration that would prove of no small importance in his quest for the presidency in 1932. Johnson, on the other hand, recognizing that identification as a southerner put him at a disadvantage in seeking national office in the 1950s, tried on a new persona as a westerner, liberated from a Confederate past. As a border-stater, Truman was in the enviable position of alienating neither North nor South, and hence of finding acceptance in national politics. For Harry Truman, place was destiny.

II

The White House Looks South rests on six premises: that, at a time when historians are preoccupied with race, class, and gender, not enough attention is given to place; that, in a period of increasing homogenization, section is still salient; that, in an era when social history is in vogue, political history is of abiding importance; that, in contrast to the assertion that the state is merely a superstructure, the state is capable of acting autonomously and affecting profoundly people's lives; that, though the impact of social forces is enormous, individuals continue to be change-makers; and, more particularly, that certain American presidents have made a difference. Each of these propositions is out of fashion, or at least energetically contested.

Almost all observers agree that globalization has brought about "a peculiarly modern malaise called placelessness," in the phrase of a literary critic. "Never in history . . . have man's relationships with place been more numerous, fragile and temporary," asserted Alvin Toffler in *Future Shock*. "We are witnessing a historic decline in the significance of place to human life." Ivy League colleges, he noted, have eliminated, or sharply diminished, geographical diversity as a criterion for admission, since place has come to matter so little, especially when people move constantly about the country. "The rootlessness of most Americans has undermined our sense of place," Joseph Persky has contended. "We have been so numb to our surroundings that few of us perceive ourselves as part of a community at all."[2]

Commentators bemoan the tedious uniformity of the American scene. "Visually, there is little difference between the superhighways and streetscapes of Ohio and Alabama," Jack Temple Kirby has remarked. "The cars, gasoline stations, subdivision architecture, glass-faced office towers, and gaudy fast-food stands are the same." Another critic has said, "The only thing that keeps parts of Seattle, Washington, from looking exactly like Route 1 in Saugus, Massachusetts, is the looming presence of Mount Rainier (when Seattle's weather is clear enough to allow it to be seen), which developers have not yet figured out how to standardize or obliterate." More mordantly, Walker Percy, noting that "Americans ricochet around the United States like billiard balls," wrote, "Places are consumed nowadays. The more delectable the place, the quicker it is ingested, digested, and turned to feces."[3]

Scholars have highlighted this perception. Michel Foucault has noted the "devaluation of space" by historians, who regard space as "undialectical" and "immobile," and, after scrutinizing recent writing in the field, the geographer John Jakle was struck by "the lack of spacial orientation displayed in all but a few historical works." Some social scientists actually welcome the advent of placelessness. Sociologists rejoice in the "overthrow of the tyranny of geography," and a geographer looks forward to the prospect "that the perception of place that has dominated us since pre-history will be lifting. . . . We will witness increasing negation of the significance of place."[4]

Geographers keep watch on the disappearance of the distinctions that have been central to their life's work. One of them has asserted that the "ageographical city," defined as "a city without a place attached to it," is "particularly advanced in the United States," in "the disaggregated sprawl of endless new suburbs without cities; and in the antenna bristle of a hundred million rooftops from Secaucus to Simi Valley, in the clouds of satellite dishes pointed at the same geosynchronous blip." The notion of "placelessness," however, as the geographer Edward Relph points out, is not simply descriptive. "Placelessness," he explains, "describes both an environment without significant places and the underlying attitude which does not acknowledge significance in place."[5]

Some historians, social scientists, and men and women of letters, though, dispute the assumption that place has lessened in importance. "Space and place permeate the grand acts as well as the ordinary events of American life," write Wayne Franklin and Michael Steiner in their seminal essay on the need to "reground" American studies. "It is the rare human issue that is truly spaceless." One behavioral scientist found that "people's sense of both personal and cultural identity is intimately bound up with place identity. . . . 'Losing one's place' may often trigger an identity crisis." The U.S. Constitution, a scholar has asserted, "is as much a geographical document as a political one; it is as much the product of geosophical perspectives of the Founders and their adversaries as of their political philosophies." Robin Weeks, commenting on "a renewed or persistent sense of place" in the 1970s and 1980s, stated, "We hunger for this sense of place in our architecture, music, films, food, and whatever linguistic, demographic, and economic realities the cliometricians may point to." In 2003 Peter Stearns, noting that social history "has almost always been highly place-specific," offered a new challenge to the field: "geography."[6]

Emphasis on place may suggest a covert conservative agenda because of an implicit valuing of continuity, but the radical Welsh novelist and critic Raymond Williams has written:

> A new theory of socialism must now centrally involve *place*. Remember the argument was that the proletariat had no country, the factor which differentiated it from the property-owning classes. But *place* has been shown to be a crucial element in the bonding process—more so perhaps for the working class than the capital-owning classes—by the explosion of the international economy and the destructive effects of deindustrialization upon old communities. When capital has moved on, the importance of place is more clearly revealed.[7]

For centuries the literati have been sensitive to the pertinence of place. "Consult the genius of the place in all," said Alexander Pope. In *Studies in Classic American Literature*, D. H. Lawrence declared: "Every people is polarized in some particular locality, which is home, homeland. . . . The spirit of place is a great reality." More recently, Lawrence Durrell maintained that "human beings are expressions of their landscapes," and the literary critic Denis Donoghue wrote, "Poets would do better to turn away from time toward space, from history toward geography, topography, landscape, place." Wallace Stegner concluded: "The mind never loses the impression of the place that shaped it. Why else did Ibsen and Joyce, self-exiled from their native countries and hating them heartily, never write about anything but Norway and Ireland, and in the terms that their upbringing had made inescapable: Ibsen as a Northern Protestant moralist and Joyce as an inverted Jesuit?"[8]

Two writers have spoken with uncommon grace about the subject. In a poignant passage, Annie Dillard says: "When everything else has gone from my brain—the President's name, the state capitals, the neighborhoods where I lived, and then my own name and what it was on earth I sought, and then at length the faces of my friends, and finally the faces of my family—when all this has dissolved, what will be left, I believe, is topology: the dreaming memory of land as it lay this way and that." And Eudora Welty, in one of her illuminating essays, observes: "Place absorbs our earliest notice and attention, it bestows on us our original awareness; and our critical powers spring up from the study of it. . . . It never really stops informing us, for it is forever astir, alive, changing, reflecting, like the mind of man itself. One place comprehended can make us understand other places better. Sense of place gives equilibrium. . . . Carried off we might be in spirit, and should be, when we are reading or writing something good; but it is the sense of place going with us still that is the ball of golden thread to carry us there and back and in every sense of the word to bring us home."[9]

Place, remarked the historian Frank Vandiver, reflecting Eudora Welty's sentiments, "is a vital touchstone to the understanding of Southerners." He added: "They *belong* somewhere, or have. Fast travel and shifting job patterns may uproot most remaining authentic Southerners. If that happens, I suspect *place* will be fulfilled by longing. 'Who's your family? Where are you from?' These are still big questions in the South." The literary critic Scott Romine began a recent essay by writing, "Of the several stock answers to the perennial question, 'What is southern literature?' the importance of 'place' (or the presence of 'sense of place') surely ranks near the top of the list." He added, "Place is, after all, what the deracinated Yankees don't have." In a similar vein, James Cobb, one of the most gifted interpreters of the modern South, has pointed out:

"Like country music and the blues, the South's rich autobiographical literature clearly stresses the importance of place. From Will Percy and William Faulkner to Richard Wright, Willie Morris, Ann Moody, Albert Murray, and Eudora Welty . . . Southern writers have consistently emphasized their connection with place. . . . Harry Crews even subtitled *A Childhood*, his vivid reminiscence, *The Biography of a Place*. In keeping with this tradition, Charlayne Hunter-Gault called her 1992 memoir *In My Place*."[10]

Charlayne Hunter-Gault has offered her own testimony. Though her life was in danger when she became one of the first two black students at the University of Georgia, she found: "The hot, sultry Athens summer brought an unexpected gift: the evocative sights, sounds, and smells of my small-town childhood, the almost overpowering sweet smell of honeysuckle and banana shrub seducing buzzing bumblebees and yellow jackets; the screeching cries of crickets emanating from every shrub and bush; clouds of black starlings producing shadows wherever they flew over the dusty red-clay haze. This was the part of the South that I loved, that made me happy to be a Southerner, that left me unaffected by the seamier side." Similarly, the African-American novelist and poet Margaret Walker, who has called Mississippi the "epicenter" of her life, has said, "Warm skies and gulf blue streams are in my blood."[11]

IV

Unsurprisingly, commentators who maintain that place is no longer pertinent believe that sections, too, have evaporated. "By the 1940s and '50s, regionalism had become a dirty word for a generation of intellectuals newly committed to a faith in the 'seamlessness' of American culture," Michael Steiner has written. Regionalism had come to be "perceived as the belletristic pipe dream of a few Southerners and Westerners longing for the better days of hardy folk and noble savages." As the age of Roosevelt was drawing to an end, a writer in the *American Economic Review* alleged that the regionalists had failed to transmute "the Mr. Hyde of sectionalism into the Dr. Jekyll of regionalism." Jane Jacobs dismissed regional planners as sentimentalists who sought to create synthetic communities "where Christopher Robin might go hoppety-hoppety on the grass." More than four decades ago, Paul Goodman asserted that "any regional differences that once existed have vanished into the sameness of Hilton hotels and Hertz drive-yourself cars." In the Cold War era, writers stressed not distinctions within America, but rather the contrast between a united country and enemy states. Remarking on "the wintry demise of regionalism" during these years, Richard Maxwell Brown pointed out that even at the University of North Carolina, where Howard Odum had won a considerable following, his regional approach no longer flourished. "Today," Bruce Clayton has remarked, "it is hard to remember how brightly Howard Odum's star once blazed." A 1973 article on former presidents of the American Sociological Association reported that close to half of recent Ph.D.s in the field had never heard of him. "By 1969," Brown concluded, "regionalism was largely out of fashion as a scholarly and cultural enterprise."[12]

Arbiters of belles lettres take an especially harsh view of regionalism. Even in the heyday of Constance Rourke, many thought it an inferior genre. In 1937 a literary critic scoffed that "regionalism . . . would probably hold that the Heavenly Muse does herself over, with protean variability, each time that she crosses a state line." By the 1960s essayists were writing that "'regionalist,' with its heavy connotative carry-over from 'provincial,' or 'sectional,' or 'local-color,' had significations of 'mediocre,' 'quaint,' and, literarily-speaking, 'second-rate,'" and concluding "that the region, the state, the nation, the political entity or the geographical entity no longer demands the first loyalty of most people."[13]

These sentiments would have come as a shock to Frederick Jackson Turner, who, from the 1890s into the 1930s, was America's most influential historian. The United States, he maintained, should be thought of as a "congeries of geographic regions," with the course of the nation determined by "the outcome of the interaction of the various sections." There was "no more enduring, no more influential force in our history," he said, "than the formation and interplay of the different regions of the United States." Relations between sections, he contended, "are to the United States what international relations are to Europe." Sectionalism, he believed, had a more profound impact than even ideological polarities. "The triumph of Bolshevism or capitalism," he asserted, "would still leave a contest of sections." Turner's contentions received support from Sir William Beveridge, who at the end of a month's tour of the United States, remarked, "If I had to sum up my impressions, I should . . . choose a parody from Pirandello: 'Six Americas in search of a Faith.'" The regions, he declared, displayed "profound divisions of race and history with opposed economic interests, with different ways of life and thought."[14]

Turner believed that sectionalism, far from diminishing because of an impetus toward homogeneity, would become more intense. In a paper delivered in 1907, he prophesied, "As the nation reaches a more stable equilibrium, a more settled state of society, with denser populations pressing upon the means of existence, with this population no longer migratory, the influence of the diverse physiographic provinces which make up the nation will become more marked." The passage of time did not shake that conviction. Less than a decade before Franklin Roosevelt took office, Turner foresaw that "as the years go on and the United States becomes a settled nation, regional geography is certain to demand at least the same degree of attention here as in Europe," and that as the sections matured, "their differences, and even their antagonisms" would magnify.[15]

Frederick Jackson Turner's ideas, however, have long since fallen out of favor. "During the 1930's and afterward," noted Richard Hofstadter, "as though someone had opened the floodgates, a consistent and relentless flow of Turner criticism swept through the historical profession." In 1948 Arthur M. Schlesinger Jr., today regarded as one of the sharper critics of Charles A. Beard, praised Beard as one who had "done more than any other single historian to free American history from what seem to me the simplicities of Turnerism." A generation later, Turner's often admiring biographer Ray Allen Billington wrote that "if Turner's paper on 'The Significance of Sections' was confused, so was Turner himself." When Turner maintained "that sectional divisions would continue to deepen," Billington went on, "he was flying in the face of common sense." In the wake of nationalizing forces such as industrialization, urbanization, and the expansion of the national government in the age of Franklin Roosevelt, "the sectionalism that had bulked so large a generation before was forgotten. . . . Turner's sectional thesis was . . . discredited by the end of the 1950s." As recently as 1987, William Cronon, Turner's heir at the University of Wisconsin, said of his predecessor's sectional paradigm, "It didn't work."[16]

Some of Turner's most trenchant critics, though, conceded that his insights may not have been exhausted. Billington said of Turner's sectional thesis: "Its fate should not be interpreted to mean that the hypothesis lacked some significance or that it will not regain respectability among future historians." A generation ago, Hofstadter noted that "in the past ten years or so . . . there has once again appeared a disposition to revive Turnerism in a chastened form." Though he thought that Turner had been excessive, he acknowledged that "it was certainly useful to warn that under modern nationalized conditions historians might fail to see the importance of sectionalism in the past." With characteristic fairmindedness and breadth of vision, Hofstadter concluded: "But there is still more than this to be said for him: many of his substantive assertions will have their durability. Here it is important to remember that not all the returns are in, that the work of discovery still goes on; each of the past several decades has been marked by some new turning in the course of historical thought; there is good reason to believe that this process will be continued, that in its course some old ideas will be revived, and some recent ones will prove not very viable after all."[17]

Turner would have found gratifying the resurgence of interest in regionalism over the past generation. "In a nation as vast and diverse as ours," David Potter asserted in 1968, "there is really no level higher than the regional level at which one can come to grips with the concrete realities of the land." Not until the next decade, though, did the signposts of renewal become manifest. "By the early 1970s," David Goldfield has observed, "there were indications in urban historiography that a broader regional approach that combined elements of both the Annalistes and the Chapel Hill group was emerging." Two books, in particular, buttressed the growing sense of the salience of region: Raymond D. Gastil's *Cultural Regions of the United States* (1975) and Joel Garreau's freewheeling *The Nine Nations of North America* (1981). Garreau prefaced his volume by saying, "I found the United States impossible to understand when it was presented to me as one great place, three thousand miles long, fifteen hundred miles deep, 3,615,122 square miles in area, ending mysteriously at some lines on the other side of which were voids called Canada and Mexico." At the end of the twentieth century, James Cobb reported, "Although the South had a clear head start, regional studies centers were sprouting from Maine to Arizona. . . . Across the nation, scholars were absorbed in collecting, cataloging, and emphasizing their region's supposedly distinctive cultural artifacts and traits."[18]

Some of the most thoroughly researched work in political history reads like Turner redivivus. "Sectional competition—grounded in a geographical division of labor between the economically advanced northern core and the underdeveloped southern and eastern periphery—has been and remains the dominant influence on the American political system," Richard Bensel has contended. "Sectional stress appears to be primordial." In an important study, Elizabeth Sanders, noting that social scientists assume that "acrimonious contests over the distribution of wealth" result from "an ideological or class-based struggle," maintained that, on the contrary, the American political system brings about "more bitter struggles over issues of regional redistribution than over issues involving social classes," in good part because of "the territorial basis of elections." An analysis of Bill Clinton's bid for the presidency concluded that localism and regionalism "are just as important to the formation of voters' preferences as issues and party affiliation," and as recently as 2003 Thomas Sugrue asserted, "To understand the peculiarities of America's liberal state requires that we bring the local back in."[19]

Section looms large in virtually every discussion of the South, which, in the view of one historian, may be perceived like Quebec, "as an island of regionalism in the sea of a loosely-knit nation-state." In his introduction to a book on southern autobiography, J. Bill Berry declared that "the idea of region cuts across worn paths to reach central questions including race, class, and gender." The renowned southern literary critic Cleanth Brooks said, "What has been happening in the South is analogous to what has been happening everywhere else: Thomas Hardy's Wessex, Dylan Thomas's Wales, W. B. Yeats's Ireland, Robert Frost's New Hampshire—all of them point to the powerful emergence of the province in the literature of our time." If the South abandoned its commitment to regionalism, he declared, it would be committing "spiritual suicide."[20]

v

For the past generation, scholars have been reporting the eclipse of political history by social history. In his introduction to a fine overview published in 1980, Michael Kammen wrote, "It seems fair to say that political history is no longer the focal point for historical scholarship," and the following year Peter Smith declared, "The new concern is with the daily lives of ordinary people, a trend that offers a clear prognostication for political history in the 1980s: there will not be much of it." Since "social historians had all but forsaken the study of politics," commented Sean Wilentz in writing of the historiography of nineteenth-century America, "Andrew Jackson . . . virtually disappeared from what had once been called the Age of Jackson." Graduate students working on topics such as the Jefferson presidency feared that no department would hire someone who had chosen to write a dissertation on a dead white male politico. "In its recent assessment of the prospects and achievements of American history," Paul Goodman pointed out in 1984, "*Reviews in American History* published no essay on the field of political history, an omission that probably escaped notice of many readers, or, if it did not, went unlamented."[21]

Nothing revealed so well the priorities in the guild as the programs of the annual conventions. Hugh Graham calculated that more than half the presentations at the 1970 meeting of the Organization of American Historians dealt with political regimes. "American historians still wrote about and listened to papers about presidents, Congress, Supreme Court decisions, wars, and diplomacy," he stated. Two decades later, such subjects accounted for only 12 percent, while social history absorbed 75 percent. At the very time that "the state had grown like Leviathan, . . . the ability of our political historians to understand and explain the behavior of the modern American state was not just being overwhelmed—it was disintegrating from within."[22]

Graham's figures provide the underpinning for an often-heard complaint. In 1981 Eric Foner, though he applauded the activities of social historians, commented: "The theme of last year's Organization of American Historians convention was 'To Study the People.' Its nearly one hundred panels included papers on everything from the boll weevil to Chicano murals, while virtually ignoring national politics, as if this were irrelevant to 'the People's' experience." A *New York Times* reporter assigned to the 1988 American Historical Association (AHA) convention was startled to come upon panels not in the tradition of Gibbon and Michelet, but on topics such as "Sodomy and Pederasty among 19th-Century Seafarers." More than a decade later, Anthony Badger found nothing changed. Political historians, he noted, "felt particularly betrayed by their professional organizations. They searched in vain for sessions on political history at the annual meeting and found themselves invisible in the pages of the *Journal of American History*, which published articles that were far more likely to talk about washing machines and cinema than elections and public policy."[23]

Recently, one of the foremost political historians, Joel Silbey, reported that "the subject . . . is holding on by its fingertips," and the historian Lewis Gould wrote: "Hard as it now may be to believe, there was a time not so long ago when political history stood astride the profession as the dominant form of inquiry. But the buzz of yesteryear has faded, and the study of presidents, parties, and elections is now seen as slightly disreputable, a guilty pleasure for its practitioners and irrelevant for historians concerned about the deeper problems of social and cultural events. Periodic efforts to reestablish the relevance of politics by 'bringing the state back in' have not yet rehabilitated this down-at-the-heels branch of the discipline."[24]

I have muttered many of the same gripes myself, and have joined in efforts to revamp the programs at the annual conventions, but, in truth, the demise of political history has been exaggerated. As Steven Gillon noted perceptively, "Political history's relative decline appears precipitous because of its previously inflated position in the profession." Though Badger, who holds the Mellon chair at Cambridge University, has recognized that history "from the bottom up" is the *dernier cri*, he has also remarked that it was "difficult for a British observer to sympathize fully with the political historians' lament. It was not easy to picture prizewinners and holders of distinguished chairs such as Bill Leuchtenburg, Alan Brinkley, Laura Kalman, and James Patterson as marginalized outsiders or a persecuted minority."[25]

Moreover, informed Americans continue to gobble up books on presidents, as the popularity of David McCullough's biographies of Harry Truman and John Adams attests, and to demonstrate in other ways a lively interest in affairs of state. "Ironically, while professional historians are abandoning 'old-fashioned' political history, the public is embracing it," Gillon has pointed out. "If you want to get an appreciation of what most interests the public, flick on the *History Channel* some evening or pick up a copy of the *New York Times* bestsellers' list. The public is fascinated by great political leaders and major national events. Traditional political history may be out of fashion in the nation's leading universities, but it is thriving in the heartland."[26]

There is, in fact, considerable evidence of a renascence within as well as outside the profession. When a few of us organized a session on political history at the 1995 annual convention of the Organization of American Historians, which I agreed to chair, we expected a tiny turnout. Instead, hundreds showed up. Every seat was occupied, and large numbers stood for two hours on all sides of the room and far out into the hotel corridor. In 2001 the Smithsonian Institution's National Museum of American History, a temple of folk culture, surprised Washington by putting on a 9000-square-foot exhibit on the U.S. presidency. Though only ticket-holders could enter, it drew "wall-to-wall people at all hours," the political scientist Michael Nelson observed. He added that, despite absurdly president-centric displays, the show might be "a sign of good things to come in historical studies. Traditional political history, so popular at the grass roots, has been bereft of academic regard in recent years. Establishing a beachhead in the country's leading museum of American history is a powerful step back from exile."[27]

Much of the most ardent support for a revival has come from an unexpected source: social historians. "Like all successful revolutionists just after the new regime is installed," remarked Sean Wilentz, "social historians looked at each others' work and grimaced." When countless localized studies failed to provide a Rosetta stone, thoughtful historians sought to puzzle out what had gone wrong. "Everyone who comments on social history's fragmentation," wrote Alice Kessler-Harris, "agrees that it somehow lost its path as a result of its disconnection from politics." The editor of the leading journal in social history, Peter Stearns, who had once expressed the hope that the history of menarche would be given the same recognition as the history of monarchy, confessed, "Some of us have erred . . . in unduly neglecting the political side," and said of his fellow social historians, "We are so concerned with the anonymous and the diurnal that we are chary to discuss elite policy actors—like the historian who once proclaimed with pride that he could write a history of Illinois without mentioning Lincoln."[28]

Some of the criticism had a bite to it. Eugene Genovese and Elizabeth Fox-Genovese chided social historians for "a philistine disregard of the centrality of politics. . . . By bypassing political history they wistfully find themselves . . . bypassing everything essential to the development of human society."[29] In Britain, a prominent social historian, Tony Judt, insisted that a "consequence of the divorce of political from social history is the insulting denial to people in the past of their political and ideological identity. . . . Strangely, then, modern social history fails at its first hurdle—the proper and sympathetic account of *people*. . . . This sort of 'history with the politics left out' is inimical to the very enterprise of social history."[30]

Political scientists, who a generation ago were in the thrall of model building with no timeline, have been flocking toward history. In the 1950s and 1960s, one political scientist has noted, "ahistorical behavioralism" dominated the field, but "since the 1960s, history has returned to American political science." To explain why they had chosen "Restoring the State" as the theme of the 1981 American Political Science Association convention, Theodore Lowi and Sidney Tarrow said, "We want to recognize that the state and the institutions of public control should be brought back . . . to the center of political science." Mavericks launched *Studies in American Political Development* in 1986, and another periodical, *Journal of Policy History*, just three years after. In 1990 a Section on Politics and History was created in the American Political Science Association, and within two years it counted over five hundred members.[31]

Buoyed by social historians and political scientists, political historians— some of them, at least—are speaking with more confidence. In a manifesto in *History Teacher*, Myron Marty asserted: "We must squarely address the issue of a common core in our teaching of history. There *is*, I believe, a body of knowledge that ought to be the subject of study in the classrooms. . . . There are some things in this body of knowledge that all Americans ought to know. At the heart of it is political history." Mark Leff, affirming that "government and the public sphere have actually mattered in people's lives," foresaw "a resurgent role for political history," and in an essay on "the need for synthesis," Thomas Bender declared that "politics, power, public life . . . remain a viable scaffolding for a synthetic national history." As recently as September 2002, the editor of a special issue of the *Journal of American History* wrote, as though it were the accepted wisdom, "History, we know, is always political," and in 2003 editors of an imaginative collection of essays in the field began the book with the bold assertion, "We are now in a moment when American political history is flourishing."[32]

VI

Over several decades, public officials, political scientists, and historians have downplayed the relevance of the state. "Government," said Jimmy Carter in his second annual address to Congress, "cannot eliminate poverty, or provide a bountiful economy, or reduce inflation, or save our cities, or cure illiteracy, or provide energy." His successor, Ronald Reagan, insisted in his inaugural address that "government is not the solution to our problem; government *is* the problem," and Bill Clinton announced, "The era of big government is over." Historians have come to view the state as of only marginal interest, for it was little more than a reflector of external interests. In 1971 Gordon Craig observed: "The functions of the state have proliferated so vastly, and its impact upon almost every phase of its subjects' lives has become so obvious, that one might have expected young historians to be fascinated by this process of aggrandizement and to wish to study it in all its details. Instead, an increasing number act as if the state had somehow or other withered away." The editor of the *Journal of American History* summed up the situation in 1994: "The faith that government would or should respond to demands by the excluded for inclusion and representation in public policy—which inspired historians from Carl Becker to Arthur M. Schlesinger, Jr., or William Leuchtenburg, for example—no longer centers history." Political institutions, he declared, had lost their relevance.[33]

Numbers of scholars, however, have registered a vigorous dissent. "The state . . . is an abstraction," wrote Murray Edelman, "but in its name men are jailed or made rich on oil depletion allowances and defense contracts, or killed in wars." In his presidential address to the Economic History Association, Lance Davis asserted, "If we are to understand economic history, we must be able to . . . explain the behavior of the government sector." One of the foremost students of corporatism in America, Ellis Hawley, has noted that "formulations in which the state is viewed as a mere extension of . . . interest-group interaction, social organization, or ongoing class struggle have not held up well." In keeping with the teachings of Max Weber, scholars such as Hawley saw bureaucrats not as puppets on strings manipulated by power blocs but as men and women capable of autonomous action. "A more satisfactory answer can be had if pride of place in the story is given to state institutions as they are operated by public officials," Hawley maintained. The greatest stir, however, was created by Theda Skocpol, who ignited a controversy by publishing a call to arms with the catchy title, "Bringing the State Back In."[34]

A good many historians, while welcoming the added attention given to the private realm, object to paying so little heed to government. In a thoughtful essay in *Daedalus* in 1984, Alan Brinkley commented: "However appropriate it might be to study earlier centuries by isolating social structures from political developments, by looking at communities in isolation from the larger, public world, it is virtually impossible to do so in the twentieth century. In the modern era, public events are not ephemera; they are often among the central realities of everyday life. No individual, no community in modern America, can live an isolated, unbroken life, insulated from the behavior of the state or national economic institutions."[35]

Scholars of this persuasion point out that millions of Americans are keenly aware of what is happening in Washington. One thinks of the state as being much more pervasive in Europe than in the United States, but a comparative study found that a larger proportion of Americans said that the national government had a great effect on their daily lives than did citizens of the United Kingdom, Germany, and Italy. Asked which aspect of the nation they felt proud of, 85 percent of American respondents said governmental and political institutions, in contrast to 46 percent in the United Kingdom, 7 percent in Germany, and 3 percent in Italy. Furthermore, no other feature of American life came close; the next nearest, the economic system, drew only 23 percent and "physical attributes of the country," the favorite among Italians, just 5 percent. The terrible events of September 11, 2001, may well have intensified these feelings. Shortly afterward, a *Newsweek* columnist wrote: "The idea that politics was unimportant and that government didn't matter seems almost absurd in the light of last week's events. . . . The state is back, and for the oldest Hobbesian reason in the book—the provision of security."[36]

To illustrate the centrality of government in American life, historians, social scientists, and novelists have pointed to the imposing presence of the courthouse in U.S. communities. "The courthouse," a geographer has stressed, was "often the grandest and most ornate building in the county, standing alone in the middle of the square. . . . The square recapitulates the history of the town.

The courthouse was its reason for being, its first central function, the seat of its creator." In his sprawling epic, *Raintree County*, the novelist Ross Lockridge wrote: "In the years when there was no court house in the middle of the Square, Esther and everyone else had felt as if a sacred object containing the innermost meaning of life in Raintree County had lost its tabernacle. But as the New Court House had begun to rise, slowly the feeling of security returned. . . . Here were the County Commissioners, the Clerk, the Treasurer, the Judge. . . . Somewhere in these odorous, secret rooms reposed the State."[37]

The courthouse had an especially vital place in the South. Often, it gave a village its name: think of Appomattox Courthouse. North Carolina, a historian has noted, created a county "solely for the purpose of erecting a courthouse," and in this building for decades planters and farmers met to settle their differences with no class distinctions observed. There the Notables shared common benches with poor rural folk. John Brinckerhoff Jackson, remarking that "the county courthouse . . . was an institution which played a unique role in the lives of country people in the South," adds: "It continues to play an important role in every community where Southern influence has been strong. That is to say, it is a familiar feature of that part of the American landscape everywhere south of the Ohio River and more or less south of the Red River. . . . On the other hand the courthouse does not amount to much, socially speaking, in the East and the North and throughout the High Plains." The South, he concludes, "could hardly have survived without that gathering place, that center of sociability."[38]

More than anywhere else in the country, "courthouse politics" reigned in the South. The anthropologist Conrad Arensberg, viewing the American county seat as the rural counterpart of the European baroque capital, saw it as drawing "planter and field- or house-hand from the fat plantations, free poor whites or Negro from the lean hills and swamps, for the pageantry and the drama of Saturdays around the courthouse, when the courthouse, the jail, the registry of deeds, and the courthouse square of shops and lawyers' row made a physical center of the far-flung community." In a study of St. Helena Parish, Louisiana, another anthropologist observed: "Until quite recently, it was difficult to travel through a county without being required by the route system to pass before the courthouse. . . . The importance of the functions and people arrayed around the square is impressed upon all travelers, but most importantly upon the citizens."[39]

No one captures this so well as William Faulkner, who in his 1951 novel, *Requiem for a Nun*, set forth the origins of his mythical town "Jefferson." His character Peabody explains, as the town is laid out: "We're going to build a school . . . soon as we get around to it. But we're going to build the courthouse today." Several pages later, Faulkner writes: "But above all, the courthouse: the center, the focus, the hub; sitting looming in the center of the country's circumference like a single cloud in its ring of horizon, laying its vast shadow to the uttermost rim of horizon; musing, brooding, symbolic and ponderable, tall as cloud, solid as rock, dominating all: protector of the weak, judiciate and curb of the passions and lusts, repository and guardian of the aspirations and the hopes."[40]

VII

Historians from Karl Marx to Fernand Braudel have discounted the capability of individuals to be change-makers. The "great man" theory has been a particular object of scorn. To Voltaire's contention that "almost nothing great has ever been done in the world except by the genius and firmness of a single man" and to Thomas Carlyle's claim that "the history of what man has accomplished in this world is at bottom the History of the Great Men," social determinists such as Friedrich Engels countered that if Napoleon Bonaparte had not arrived on the scene, someone just like him would have. "During the twentieth century," Sidney Hook observed, "the overwhelming majority of historians have been in unconscious thralldom to one or another variety of social determinism," with figures such as Alexander, Caesar, and Peter the Great no more than "expressions" or "instruments" of underlying forces.[41]

That presumption has not gone unanswered. Noting that historians were insisting that decisions were brought about not by individuals but by the social structure, Walter Karp derided those who waited "like Micawber for someone to 'fully' explain how the 'social structure' caused President Johnson to bomb North Vietnam after that same social structure failed six years earlier to do anything of the kind to President Eisenhower." Eric Nordlinger has dismissed the belief that policymakers do not act autonomously but are merely creatures of social imperatives as "surrealistic," and Don Higginbotham, writing of George Washington, has said, "If . . . he was a product of history, he also drove history. . . . A country's destiny can be shaped by a great man rather than by impersonal socioeconomic forces." In a book published in 2004, Alonzo Hamby asserts: "Individuals, acting within the limitations of the world in which they live, make history. Neither the New Deal nor Nazism nor 'Tory socialism' were foreordained in their societies. They reflected the efforts of strong and capable political leaders."[42]

Sidney Hook offered the most sustained rebuttal in his classic study, *The Hero in History*. "Men can and do make their own history," he maintained, though that capacity is conditional. Columbus elicits admiration as an intrepid explorer, he observed, but the New World would have been discovered by Europeans if he had never lived. Furthermore, the time must be ripe. "There is no good reason to believe that if a man with the biological endowment of Newton or Raphael or Napoleon had been born in early prehistory he would have rediscovered fire or created magnificent ornaments and paintings or achieved renown as a warrior." (Similarly, I acknowledge that if Franklin Roosevelt, Harry Truman, or Lyndon Johnson had entered the White House in a different year, say 1924, they would have had negligible impact on the South or the country.) Nonetheless, Hook stated, there are "situations in which a gifted man of good or evil genius can so profoundly affect men and events that he becomes an event-making man." We have reason, he concluded, to be "gratified that the assassin's bullet missed President Roosevelt in 1933."[43]

VIII

For more than half a century, historians have derided "the presidential synthesis," a phrase coined by Thomas Cochran in a widely noted article in the *American Historical Review* in 1948 to warn against arranging a narrative of the American experience, with its multifarious socioeconomic aspects, according to which men chanced to be the White House incumbents. He urged historians to eschew "a false emphasis on colorful individuals and exciting events," and concentrate instead on secular trends that could not be cabined by arbitrary four-year terms. "The precise social effect of the rapid rise of the corporation from 1850 to 1873 . . . cannot be measured," he declared, "but the social scientist is reasonably sure that it is of more importance than the presidential aspirations of Horatio Seymour."[44]

Cochran's admonition seems only common sense to historians who believe that excessive attention is focused on the Oval Office. Both Jordan Schwarz and Tony Badger have objected to conflating Franklin D. Roosevelt and the New Deal, since many of the economic policies of the 1930s were set not by FDR but by Congress or the bureaucracy. "Historians know as much as they need to know about the life of Franklin D. Roosevelt," Badger contends. Asked by *American Heritage* in 1988 to name the most overrated figure in U.S. history, Robin Weeks responded: "Nearly any of the Presidents (a group by whom we tend to organize our textbooks, as though their years somehow defined time for us) who actually did virtually nothing. Even to discuss Chester Arthur or Millard Fillmore is to overrate them."[45]

The generation of social historians who came of age in the 1960s found the notion of privileging the president preposterous. They denied that one could understand an issue such as civil rights by examining the actions of national leaders. Politicians, they insisted, never take initiatives but act only when grassroots pressure compels them to respond. Hence, one should avert attention from the White House and concentrate instead on social movements. Summing up the state of the field for the AHA in 1990, Eric Foner asserted, "The old 'presidential synthesis' . . . is dead (and not lamented)."[46]

In a book published in 1999, though, Russell L. Riley still found it necessary to deplore the "now-longstanding inclination in American political culture to inflate presidential achievement." He observed that "towering above the District's tidal basin flats, visible for miles as the capital's highest structure, is a granite and marble obelisk erected to the memory of George Washington," near tributes to Lincoln and Jefferson, and found an "asymmetry" in this "commitment of such spacious parkland to the memory of three figures." Furthermore, "Mt. Rushmore, carved out of the Black Hills of South Dakota, repeats the pattern nearly a continent away, in a fashion at least suggestive of the stone monuments keeping silent watch over Easter Island. Pilgrims flock to these hills just as they do to national sepulchers on the Potomac." He regretted that Americans, like primitive folk awestruck by idols, "are . . . a nation of presidency worshipers."[47]

Riley ended the volume by endorsing what Warren Harding said at the dedication of the Lincoln Memorial in 1922. On that occasion, Riley contended, Harding was voicing "an enduring verity of American politics" when he reminded his audience that "Abraham Lincoln was no superman," but like Washington "a very natural human being, with the frailties mixed with the virtues of humanity. There are neither supermen nor demi-gods in the government of kingdoms, empires, or republics." In those words, Harding was echoing what his predecessor, William Howard Taft, had said only a short time before, "The President cannot make clouds to rain and cannot make the corn to grow, he cannot make business good." In keeping with this view, Democrats from Carter to Clinton have retreated from the FDR-Truman-LBJ conception of the White House. One commentator titled an article on Bill Clinton, "Honey, I Shrunk the Presidency." Still, as recently as 2003, a speaker on a panel, "State-of-the-Field: Political History" at the annual convention of the Organization of American Historians in Memphis found it necessary to call for fresh thinking to "move us out of the presidential synthesis."[48]

A number of historians continue to believe that who is chosen president can make a difference, and, at critical moments, a considerable difference. It mattered that voters chose Thomas Jefferson rather than John Adams, Abraham Lincoln instead of Stephen Douglas (or later George McClellan), Theodore Roosevelt and not Alton Parker. If Floridians had correctly marked a few more butterfly ballots for Al Gore in 2000, Iraq would not have been invaded. The most striking example, however, is the train of events set off by the defeat of Herbert Hoover by Franklin Roosevelt, who barely survived a challenge from decidedly more conservative rivals at the 1932 Chicago convention. Badger, despite his reservations about employing a biographical approach to understanding the 1930s, takes pains to state: "I do not argue that there could have been a New Deal without Roosevelt. It is difficult to imagine the frantic excitement in Washington between 1933 and 1936 if John Nance Garner, Albert Ritchie or Newton Baker had been elected in 1932."[49]

To social historians studying folk attitudes toward institutions, the reverence expressed by so many U.S. citizens for the presidency must seem compelling. "The personal response of ordinary Americans to the patrician from Hyde Park is extraordinary," Badger has observed. "It is reflected in the crowds that lined the streets to see him, the thousands and thousands of letters painfully scrawled, often in pencil, on scraps of paper to the White House, the listening figures for the fireside chats, and the pictures of the President on the walls of sharecropper shacks. Industrial workers and African-Americans clearly identified with, and voted with great loyalty for, a man who could not have come from a more different background." FDR is not alone in eliciting this veneration. Franklin Forts has pointed out that "although many Americans heap ridicule on . . . the resident of 1600 Pennsylvania Avenue, each year millions of these very same citizens flock to our nation's capital to connect with the American past and secure their place in the larger narrative of this nation. In the shrines of American identity— the Lincoln Memorial, the Jefferson Memorial, and the White House, to name a few—we find affirmation of our American selves and the hope that as long as the nation lives and endures, we live and endure."[50]

IX

Some critics may raise a different objection to my enterprise—that there is no such thing as the South. They find the very assumption chimerical. "Regions,"

Donald Meinig states, "are abstractions, they exist in our minds," and Richard Gray asserts, "The South is an imagined community." W. Fitzhugh Brundage has stated, "The relative importance attached to one region or another reflects only the historical narratives told about it, not any inherent, 'objective' significance. . . . The historical South that exists today is the consequence not of some innate regional properties, but of decades of investment, labor, and conscious design by individuals and groups of individuals who have imagined themselves as 'southerners.'"[51]

Others maintain that what is familiarly called "the South" is too heterogeneous to constitute a discrete entity. "Nearly all who use 'South' bootleg into the usage an assumption that the term is singular, the region firm and regular," Jack Temple Kirby observes. "In fact South has always been plural." In an essay on southern distinctiveness, Larry J. Griffin asks: "When we talk about 'the South,' . . . which South, exactly, are we talking about? The glittering Sun Belt, franchise-laden South of Houston, Atlanta, Nashville, Charlotte, or the rural, small-town and disappearing South of coalminers in eastern Kentucky, sharecroppers in the Mississippi Delta, textile workers in small Carolina towns throughout the Piedmont? In our definitions of southerners, do we include the Chinese in Mississippi and the Cherokee in Georgia? The Cuban Americans in Miami and the forty thousand or so Hispanics in Nashville? The Cambodians in Atlanta and the Vietnamese along the Texas Gulf Coast?"[52]

These probing questions come from esteemed students of the South, but most writers pay them no nevermind. "The South is another land," said W. J. Cash. "Now and then . . . there have arisen people, usually journalists or professors, to tell us that it is all a figment of the imagination. . . . Nobody, however, has ever taken them seriously. And rightly." David Moltke-Hansen has observed, "The South is an imagined community, but it embodies more than invented traditions." That eleven states seceded from the Union and created a new country is not a "construct." The novelist Reynolds Price has remarked, "I can travel from Durham, North Carolina, to Jackson, Mississippi, which is a distance of 800 miles, and find that people are still speaking almost exactly the same dialect that I have grown up with and known all my life, whereas I can go from Durham . . . to Philadelphia, a distance of 400 miles, and find them speaking an utterly different dialect." After acknowledging the difficulty of defining "the South" (Bakersfield, California, is southern whereas Virginia suburbs have been penetrated by northerners), John Boles nonetheless wrote that "most students of the South accept the truth that there really is something different about Dixie."[53]

I find the conclusions of my colleague John Shelton Reed convincing. In an entry titled "Southerners" in the *Harvard Encyclopedia of American Ethnic Groups*, he pointed out that former Confederates became "Americans against their will, a fact that has a great deal to do with their persistence as an identifiable group" with "their own flag, anthem, and holidays," and in the course of a meticulous survey published in 1983, he learned that "nearly all Southerners have some mental construction labeled 'Southerner,' some degree of regional consciousness." Recently, he added: "Sure it's a concept, and you can deconstruct it in various ways. But it's there on the ground too. And the fact that there are people who, when you ask them, say, 'Hell, yes, I'm a southerner,' is every bit as much a fact as the kudzu that's growing in your backyard. . . . You know, the South's there. Southerners are there. . . . You kick them, you hurt your toe."[54]

By "the South" I mean the eleven states of the former Confederacy plus Kentucky. (Statistical aggregates omit Kentucky.) Even though Kentucky did not secede, it seems, in a number of respects, as "southern" as Tennessee, which did. In the 1970s the *New York Times* commented: "Many Louisvillians say 'you-all,' yet insist that the city is not Southern, since it was a Union stronghold in the Civil War. Yet what is it now? Certainly the people here seem warmer than in the Middle-West, quicker than in the Deep South and decidedly less likely to push you onto the subway tracks (if there were any here) than some New Yorkers are." Kentucky has seventy-two tributes to the Confederacy but only two to the Union, though considerably more than twice as many Kentuckyians fought for the North. On Jefferson Davis's birthday Todd County crowns a hoop-skirted Miss Confederacy, who is required to give a proper answer to the question, "What will you do while holding the title to promote and defend Southern heritage?"[55]

My definition excludes Oklahoma, which both the 1938 New Deal study, *Report on Economic Conditions of the South*, and the modern *Congressional Quarterly Almanac* regard as southern. I recognize that two of the most important civil rights decisions arose in the state. In 1915 the Supreme Court, in a unanimous ruling, invalidated Oklahoma's "grandfather clause," an effort to deny the franchise to African Americans so flagrant that it embarrassed even white supremacists, and as recently as 1950 the Court sternly rebuked the state for its shabby scheme to maintain the essence of Jim Crow by isolating a black graduate student in the classroom, the library, and the cafeteria.[56] Nonetheless, Oklahoma, in its politics and its economy, seems to me more middle border than southern. It is hard to imagine a Mike Monroney, a Fred Harris, or a Carl Albert conniving with the Dixie bloc to sustain a filibuster. This land of the Osage and the Kiowa, of amber fields of grain and grazing cattle, of short grass and Dust Bowl Okies, of prairie dogs and coyotes, resembles Nebraska more than Louisiana. Not every Sooner rode in a surrey with a fringe on top, but in Oklahoma the wind does come sweeping down the plain.

Though the dispute over how to define "southern" has been frequently aired, the meaning of "national" has all too easily been taken for granted, and I have tried not to do that. As the Charleston-born literary critic Louis Rubin once shrewdly commented: "When I went up to the University of Pennsylvania for a few years, back in the mid-fifties, I found a rather curious thing. When we . . . talked about experience in the South— . . . we called it Southern. . . . Up there they talked about experience in Pennsylvania, but they didn't call it Eastern: they called it American. They assumed that anything their writers did or thought was American. All other kinds of writers were offshoots, regional offshoots." Similarly, David Carlton has observed that the emergence of "a South *perceived* to be distinctive was . . . constructed as a mirror image of what in fact may have been an even more distinctive region, the manufacturing belt." A thoughtful Alabama editor has offered a different insight. "In the South we have forgotten that we were Americans before we ever thought to be Southerners," H. Brandt Ayers has pointed out. "Southerners—Jefferson, Madison, John Marshall—conceived the design of our democracy and found the words to describe it."[57]

X

Some may raise a final objection: that I am irredeemably disqualified from writing a book about the South since I was born, not just in the North, but in Brooklyn, and, still worse, to parents who grew up in Hell's Kitchen. In Faulkner's *Absalom, Absalom!* Quentin Compson, asked by his Canadian roommate in college what shaped southerners, responds, "You cant understand it. You would have to be born there." Once upon a time, though no longer, I could relate to a literary critic reared in Abe Lincoln's town, Springfield, Illinois, who wrote, "Whenever I go south, my feet feel welcome but my head keeps looking around for the deportation notice." Having grown up watching movies such as *I Am a Fugitive from a Chain Gang*, I thought, only partly in jest, that if I ever had a run-in with a cold-eyed Mississippi sheriff, I would call my consul, like a former president of the Southern Historical Association, Carl Degler, who confessed, "As an urban-bred adult becoming increasingly interested in southern history, I still thought of the South as almost a foreign country." I don't care for stock car racing; I can't imagine why anyone would want to eat a Moon Pie or sip Dr. Pepper; and, though I don't say this out loud, I think much too much is made of Elvis. And Billy Graham.[58]

I am prepared to believe, accordingly, that certain nuances of southern folkways may escape me. The short story writer Mary Hood has remarked:

> Suppose a man is walking across a field. To the question "Who is that?"
> a Southerner would reply by saying something like "Wasn't his grand-
> daddy the one whose dog and him got struck by lightning on the steel
> bridge? Mama's third cousin—dead before my time—found his railroad
> watch in that eight-pound catfish's stomach the next summer just above
> the dam. I think it was eight pounds. Big as Eunice's arm. The way he
> married for that new blue Cadillac automobile, reckon how come he's
> walking like he has on Sunday shoes, if that's who it is, and for sure it
> is." A Northerner would reply to the same question (only if directly
> asked, though, never volunteering), "That's Joe Smith." To which the
> Southerner might think (but be much too polite to say aloud), "They
> didn't ask his name, they asked who he *is*!"[59]

The humorist Roy Blount, who enjoys ribbing people from away, has written: "If a Northern visitor makes it clear to Southerners that he thinks it would be typical of them to rustle up a big, piping hot meal of hushpuppies and blackstrap, Southerners will do that, even if they were planning to have just a little salad that night. Then the visitor will ask how to eat hushpuppies and blackstrap. . . . The strictly accurate answer is that nobody in his or her right mind eats these two things together, in any way at all. But that isn't a sociable answer. So Southerners may say, 'First you pour your plate full of the molasses, and then you crumble up your hushpuppies in it, and then you take the *back* of your spoon and. . . .' Southerners will say things like that just to see whether it is still true that Northerners will believe anything. About the South."[60]

I have, though, had an association with the South which began in 1935 when, as a boy of twelve, I earned enough tutoring neighborhood kids in New York to take a nine-hour Greyhound bus trip to Washington, where I made a point of crossing the Key Bridge into Virginia so that I could set foot in the South. Over the ensuing period of nearly seventy years, I have been drawn south for the most diverse reasons: to vacation in Florida over my boys' spring breaks from grade school and high school; to birdwatch at refuges from the Outer Banks on the Atlantic to High Island on the Gulf of Mexico; to march with Martin Luther King in Montgomery; and to make annual baseball pilgrimages to spring training with a group of friends, including at least one authentic southerner, Lee Smith. I have done archival research in every southern state (for this book, I have worked in more than 240 of these collections), and I've lectured at venues from the University of Virginia in Charlottesville to The Citadel in Charleston to Baylor University in Waco. *The White House Looks South* originated in three lectures delivered over the course of two days in Baton Rouge.

For over a quarter of a century, I have made my home in the South, first as a Fellow, and then Mellon Senior Fellow, at the National Humanities Center in Research Triangle Park, North Carolina, and later, for two decades, as William Rand Kenan, Jr. Professor of History at the University of North Carolina at Chapel Hill. During that time, I also taught for a decade at Duke Law School, with Walter Dellinger and John Hope Franklin, and, as visiting professor, at the College of William and Mary and the University of Richmond. It did not take long for me to cotton to southern ways, though I concede that I started with the enormous advantage of being able to say with one Virginian that "sour mash is just mother's milk to me."[61] No New Year's Day goes by now without blackeyed peas and collards, even if they are eaten with a grimace. At first, it seemed odd to hear the mountain range I knew so well pronounced "Appalatchin," but in a short while "Appalaychin," which is how I had heard it for so long, grated on my ears. Southern hospitality quickly became a vivid reality to me. Before I had taught my first class in Chapel Hill, I was invited to be the speaker on University Day that October, and one Sunday morning I picked up the *Raleigh News and Observer* to find that I was "Tar Heel of the Week."

It is conceivable, though I would not press the claim, that there may be a benefit in not being embedded in regional identity. "It appears that someone has to stand at a certain remove from his culture in order to see it as something that can be dealt with, accepted or rejected by an act of the will, analyzed and *used*," John Shelton Reed has observed. It was while an expatriate in Europe that Pat Conroy, summoning up memories of his Carolina sea island boyhood, began his novel *The Prince of Tides* with four arresting words: "My wound is geography"; then added, "It is also my anchorage, my port of call." Similarly, reflecting on the North of England, Alan Sillitoe recalls that he wrote his first novel "a thousand miles from the actual streets in which it took place, and several years distant in time—which I think enabled me to see things all the more clearly. A sense of place for a writer also involves a sense of distance." Furthermore, Elizabeth Hardwick has observed, "Many persons who have been in residence in the South for years, decades even, would not describe themselves as southern." She cites Edgar Allan Poe as evidence that "not every creative mind living in the region has found itself engaged by that condition." Poe's "years in Virginia and Maryland do not appear to have been a moral or aesthetic definition. His true home was far away: in Romantic poetry, dark landscapes, brilliant researches and puzzles. . . . Southernness is more a decision than a fate."[62]

A 1967 panel of literary critics noted how much it could matter that a writer was *of* but not *in* the South. Just as James Joyce wrote his great works about Dublin not while living there but in Zürich, Paris, and Trieste, so William Styron summoned forth his homeland from a house in Connecticut. "As you think back across the Southern writers whom we would include in the group that we discuss in this renascence," commented Hugh Holman, "was there one of them who did not achieve somehow a physical distancing and detachment before he was able to begin actually producing the work about the South which his fame rests on at the present time?" Similarly, Louis Rubin, though not fully accepting Holman's premise, acknowledged, "In each case there's a tremendous detachment along with a tremendous sense of identification, and both attitudes have to be there."[63]

With each passing year, however, my own sense of disengagement diminishes. I now identify with a northerner who has written, "It was almost fifty years ago when I first saw the highway signs that read US 1-South, but my heart still leaps up when I see them, just as it did then," and with another onetime Yankee, Peter Applebome, who says he "hasn't lived in the North for twenty-one years, doesn't want to go back, and has come to the point where Southerners look normal and Yankees seem weirdly out of touch—among them, people who actually thought Michael Dukakis could be elected president of the United States." I agree, too, with most of what he goes on to write: "Like countless people before me, I know I've been seduced. The weather is warmer, the people nicer, the traffic milder (well, don't hold me to this one), the prices lower, the pace of life saner, the greenery lusher, the history richer." Lastly, I identify once again with Carl Degler who, in his presidential address to the Southern Historical Association, remarked, "It is true that one southern-born past president of this Association has denominated me an 'honorary Southerner,' but he also added that 'they are often the worst kind.'"[64]

In sum, I am in, but not of, the South—like my three protagonists.

FRANKLIN D. ROOSEVELT

ONE

FDR: GEORGIA SQUIRE

I

To present Franklin Delano Roosevelt as, in any respect, southern seems absurd. Born and reared on a Hudson River estate far removed from the Tombigbee or the Pee Dee, he came to the White House from a state capitol so far north that it was within a few hours' drive of the Canadian border. No bluebonnets or palmettos graced the fir-clad slopes of the Adirondacks; neither Louisiana heron nor scarlet ibis glided over Albany or Poughkeepsie. While Confederate belles were knitting garments for the brave boys in gray, the young girl who would be FDR's mother sewed a muslin shirt for a Union soldier, and Franklin himself later remembered seeing in his grandfather's library "a lithograph of . . . mile after mile of vessels headed South to be sunk at the mouth of a Confederate harbor."[1]

Yet Franklin Roosevelt not only came to think of himself as southern, but was frequently so perceived. Sometimes he would refer to Georgia as his "other" state, and southerners would call him an "adopted" son, but on occasion he seriously thought of himself as a native, and not a few Georgians accepted his characterization. "He was the only liberal, big-city Democrat who was warmly received by his political partners in the South," Hugh Gallagher has pointed out. "They always saw him as a Southerner." To be sure, Roosevelt, even during the many years of long stays in the South, spent most of his time above the Mason-Dixon line, and when he said "we," he could easily slip back into meaning "we of the North." Nonetheless, his Georgia sojourn helped shape, in important ways, his conception of his task in the White House. And in the course of his long presidency, Roosevelt, operating on the premise that he knew the region as only a native could, yet also seeing it from a national perspective, would help bring about such significant transformations that the South in 1945 was a quite different place from what it had been in 1933.[2]

II

Though Roosevelt had consanguineal ties to the South, his real relationship to the region began in 1924 when, afflicted by polio, he first went to Bullochville (soon to be renamed Warm Springs), a spa hamlet in Meriwether County, Georgia, to which a century before John C. Calhoun had repaired. In Savannah in 1933, he would speak "of all that Georgia means to me personally, through my long association with this State and also through the kinship which my wife and my children bear to the early settlers who participated with Oglethorpe in the founding of civilization on this portion of the Atlantic seaboard." But it was the illusory hope that at Warm Springs he might swim his way back to full use of his legs that first drew him to reside in the South, and so congenial did he find that experience that by the spring of 1926 he had plunged nearly two-thirds of his fortune in the purchase of a rundown resort there. He was to be intimately involved with the little Georgia community ever after.[3]

Roosevelt never forgot how Warm Springs received a partially paralyzed Yankee. When he arrived at the depot on an October night in 1924 on the milk train, a delegation of villagers, including the mayor, turned out to welcome him; he found his larder stocked with food and a cord of logs for his fire. Almost every evening one of his neighbors would poke in his head and ask, "Do you need some kindling-wood? Can I get you some eggs tomorrow?" They arrived laden with gifts: country hams, quail, bouquets of flowers. Without that kind of hospitality, he later attested, "this place would not have been possible. . . . I was all alone down here." The warmth of these southerners made him "want to come back, and that is why the following spring I came back, and the influx of people began." He contrasted these encounters with his visit to a New England town where no one ever said "Howdy."[4]

He quickly learned to cherish the Georgia countryside, which he toured in his specially built roadster, the top down, on dusty byways shouting out "Hiya, neighbor!" In one high-spirited letter, he told of driving his Ford flivver over the 5-mile scenic avenue up to Pine Mountain and of his delight in the Georgia weather: "warm and bright, the peach blossoms coming out." At another time, he wrote an aunt, "You would love the . . . truly languid southern atmosphere of the place!" He came to savor Brunswick stew, Country Captain (a curried chicken dish, his favorite), cornbread, and hush puppies, even to stomach possum. One source of moonshine on the banks of the Flint River became known as "Roosevelt's still" because he was alleged to have driven there when he needed corn liquor for a party. In 1927, in a speech at the Biltmore Hotel in Atlanta, Roosevelt praised Warm Springs as "this garden spot" he hoped would attract people from the rest of the country. "If they are constituted like me," he said, "they will fall in love with Georgia and claim it as another home and claim its men and women as their kinfolk."[5]

Georgia returned the affection. "To the friendly farming folk of Georgia's red hills, he was 'neighbor Roosevelt,'" wrote a southern reporter. He added: "They 'took' to him. 'Took' to this 'Yankee' who was part-time Georgia 'Cracker.' He was invited into their homes, where he ate at their tables such typically Southern food as collards, turnip greens, black-eyed peas and cracklin' bread, sliced to hold slabs of butter. He cultivated a taste for barbecue, sizzling from the pit and dripping with hot sauce. And this adopted son of Georgia learned, too, the thrill that accompanies possum hunts. Hounds baying at their prey from the foot of a tree. Lanterns causing fantastic shadows to dance through the pitch dark woods."[6]

Over the next two decades, Roosevelt journeyed thirty-nine times to Warm Springs. (By contrast, he went back to his summer retreat at Campobello in New Brunswick only thrice.) In just one year for the rest of his life did he fail to come to Georgia, and that was in the midst of World War II. Though Warm Springs was often referred to as FDR's "second home," it was, as Kenneth Davis noted, "a happier place for him than Hyde Park. . . . He was the master of his house and land in Georgia as he could never be of the house and land at Crum Elbow while his imperious mother lived." In like manner, another biographer, Geoffrey Ward, has said: "Warm Springs was his creation: he was its most eagerly sought-after resident, the laughing, vigorous center of things. It's hard to communicate all that he meant to the people there. His example sustained and inspired them, but they sustained him, too, and throughout his life he would return as often as he could to be among them."[7]

Roosevelt, who had started out concerned only with operation of the spa, delved more deeply into Georgia soil as proprietor of a 1750-acre farm at Pine Mountain, "one of the last, futile upward acts of defiance by the dying Appalachians." On these hilly fields, he cultivated novelties such as scuppernong, a variety of muscadine grape. "No cotton, though," he told his manager, for Georgia needed to be weaned away from one-crop agriculture. (Roosevelt, Henry Wallace would later note in his diary, "was very, very sensitive to cotton problems. . . . 'You may know about corn and hogs,' he'd say to me, 'but I know about cotton.'") Instead of contributing to the cotton surplus, he experimented with everything from goats to loblolly pine to pure-bred cattle, none of it profitable but all of it instructive. Running the farm not only taught him a lot, but also encouraged him to identify with the southern grower.[8]

Georgia kept alive his aspirations for public office too. In an article published by the *Atlanta Journal* in the fall of 1924, not long after the disastrous Democratic convention at Madison Square Garden where Tammany bully boys reviled southern delegates, a political writer said: "Mr. Roosevelt has made a great hit with the people of Warm Springs who have met him, and they are extending him a hearty welcome as a prospective regular visitor. A number of Georgia's public men have also called to pay their respects and extend greetings. Georgians who attended the Democratic national convention have been especially cordial, because they appreciate the interest Mr. Roosevelt showed in them, and his courtesy in apologizing, as an Al Smith leader, for unfortunate and embarrassing incidents in connection with the convention."[9]

For eight weeks in the spring of 1925, at a time when many elsewhere in the country had written him off as a cripple who was yesterday's news, Georgia gave him the opportunity to remind people of his presence when he was invited to be a newspaper columnist. At a dinner party in 1937, the president remembered, "I substituted for Tom Lawless on the *Macon Telegraph* in 1925 when he was sick. The first week my column was splendid. The second week it wasn't so good and by the third week it was punk." Still, he said, "The observations I wrote for Tom Lawless set forth the original thinking I had on the New Deal."[10]

Within a short time after his arrival, reporters and Georgia politicians had beaten a path to his door, though the nearest paved road was 10 miles away. "I think every organization in Georgia has asked me to some kind of party," he wrote his mother. Though he went south not for political reasons but in pursuit of health, he was, as the historian Frank Freidel later observed, "so wholeheartedly and joyously a political man that politics inevitably followed him, and at Warm Springs he established himself not only as a valiant polio fighter but also as something of a Georgia farmer-politician." Eventually, journalists were to call his white clapboard hilltop cottage in Warm Springs "the Little White House."[11]

Franklin Roosevelt further authenticated his credentials as a Georgian by pointing to the background of his wife, who, one of her biographers has written, "considered herself . . . half-Rebel." Georgia's Bulloch Hall, an eleven-room 1840 mansion in Roswell on the Chattahoochee that was the home of Eleanor's grandmother, had kept nineteen slaves, including a "little black shadow" for each white child. Grandmother Bulloch's brother was exiled to Europe for a year after killing his little black shadow in a fit of rage. Martha Bulloch was a fierce Confederate partisan who, from her home in the Roosevelt town house in Manhattan, smuggled supplies to the South. One of her brothers, dispatched to England on a secret mission, designed and launched the fearsome Confederate raider *Alabama* on which another brother served. As enemies of the Union, the two brothers were excluded from the postwar amnesty and spent the rest of their days as outcasts, banned from returning to their native land. Sherman hardened the family's anti-Yankee convictions when, on his march to the sea, his forces looted the Bulloch plantation. Though Eleanor Roosevelt stayed at Warm Springs as little as possible, in good part out of dislike of its endemic racism, she adored *Gone with the Wind* because Tara, which has been said to have been modeled on Bulloch Hall, reminded her of the Georgia family home she visited.[12]

So quickly did Roosevelt make a place for himself that Georgians came to regard him as one of them. In the 1920s, there was even talk of running him for governor of Georgia. At a possum supper during FDR's second term as governor of New York, his Georgia neighbor, Judge H. H. Revill, plump as Friar Tuck, called FDR not only the country's greatest Democrat but the first citizen of Meriwether County. (At Warm Springs, Roosevelt indulged in a running gag with the judge in which, with mock-superciliousness, he would preen himself on his high ranking as a statesman, and the judge, staring him down, would say, "You will please bear in mind that you didn't get anywhere until you came out of the North to Georgia, and then people realized that you must have pretty good sense.") In 1930 *Georgia,* a magazine sponsored by the State Chamber of Commerce, listed him in a group of prominent Georgians, and in the spring of 1933 a newspaper caption identified him as "Roosevelt, Georgia Farmer."[13]

Well before then, Roosevelt had come to perceive himself as a Georgian. When he returned to Georgia in the fall of 1933, he told a Savannah crowd that he was "glad to come back again to his own state." He addressed the people of Savannah as "you, my neighbors," and later that month referred to "you, my neighbors of Warm Springs and Meriwether County." In the years to come— in a talk in Alabama in 1939, at an off-the-record meeting in 1940, and many other times—he alluded to "my State of Georgia." As a Georgian, he could lay claim to being a southerner. In one address he spoke of "*Our* South," and when he was about to spring the surprise of his appointment of Hugo Black of Alabama to the U.S. Supreme Court, he hinted to a southern associate that his choice was "someone from *our* part of the country."[14]

In January 1933 in the Tennessee Valley, he made a number of remarks revealing an eager, even overeager, desire to identify himself with the South and its history. At Sheffield, Alabama, he began with the salutation, "My friends," then added, "I think I can almost say, 'My neighbors,' because, from my little cottage at Warm Springs, from Pine Mountain which lies back of it, I can look into Alabama." By the time he reached Montgomery, all doubt had vanished; he started his comments there, "My friends and *neighbors* of Alabama." It was, he told the gathering, "a great privilege to me to stand in this sacred spot where a great American took oath of office as the President of the Confederacy." He went on to state:

> As some of you may know, one of the Roosevelts married into a Georgia family and I can remember, as a small boy, that two very distinguished gentlemen, intimately connected with the Navy of the Confederacy—mind you, this was in the 80's—came to New York to visit the Roosevelt family. Because those two brave and distinguished officers had fought in the Navy of the Confederacy, there were some Roosevelts who still regarded them as "Pirates."
>
> Now, that is hard to understand by the younger generation . . . and I am glad to know that my own daughter who is with me today and all the rest of my children and all of the younger generation just laugh heartily at hearing brave officers of the Confederate Navy referred to as pirates.

Having gotten off that ham-handed tribute to the South, Roosevelt continued more felicitously: "I am particularly happy, as one who is about to occupy another White House, to have had the privilege of seeing the first White House of the Confederacy as I turned the corner to come here to the Capitol. . . . I shall always regard this as a red-letter day. . . . I have had the opportunity to come here and stand where Jefferson Davis once stood." In the course of paying homage to the president of the Confederacy, Roosevelt, instead of talking, as most northerners would have, of the "Civil War," referred to "the war between the states." Alabama Congressman Lister Hill, who witnessed the performance, said jubilantly: "After being treated as the red-headed step child of the Nation for all these years, the South is indeed to have a new deal."[15]

Roosevelt could relate easily to white southerners because he shared their outlook toward Reconstruction. Even before Claude Bowers published *The Tragic Era,* with its lurid allegations of misrule by carpetbaggers, scalawags, and blacks, Roosevelt wrote him, "That period from 1865 to 1876 should be known as America's Dark Ages." After perusing Bowers's account of how, as the result of politicians' "wading in the muck" and "masses . . . moving crazily," "the Southern people literally were put to the torture," Roosevelt, writing from Warm Springs, informed the author: "Since I have been down here for the last two weeks at least a dozen good people have spoken to me about 'The Tragic Era,' and they have not been confined to Georgians or southerners. The book, more than any other book in recent years, had a very definite influence on public thought." As president, Roosevelt continued to voice these views. In 1937 he declared:

> Today, old and young alike are saddened by the knowledge of the bitter years that followed the war—years bitter to the South because of economic destruction and the denial to its population of the normal rights of free Americans—years bitter to the North because victory engendered among many the baser passions of revenge and tyranny.
>
> We must not deny that the effects of the so-called Era of Reconstruction made themselves felt in many evil ways for half a century.[16]

III

Roosevelt's stays in Warm Springs exerted an enduring effect on his attitude toward public policy, for they brought him face to face with the "blasted-looking landscape" of southern poverty: a mean black slum in the town, a countryside scarred by unpainted sidings, rusting corrugated metal, glassless, screenless windows, and sagging roofs. Farmers had no tractors to work the fields, and often even the sorry mules had to be rented. When, some years after FDR arrived, Henry Wallace, as secretary of agriculture, saw the area for the first time, he expressed shock: "I was utterly amazed and appalled at the red-gashed hillsides, at the unkempt cabins. . . . What a God-forsaken region it appeared to be."[17]

One conversation between FDR and a black Georgia sharecropper has been reconstructed:

> ROOSEVELT: Who is your landlord? Where does he live?
> SHARECROPPER: De landlord is. . . . He lives in town.
> ROOSEVELT: What is his occupation?
> SHARECROPPER: He has a store in Manchester.

ROOSEVELT: How many cows do you have? How many chickens? How many hogs?

SHARECROPPER: No, sir; we don't keep er cow. We jus have one hog. De possums and de weasels and de foxes eats up de chickens so bad dat we just don't bother with 'em.

ROOSEVELT: What do you raise on your farm?

SHARECROPPER: We jus raise cotton and corn on de farm.

ROOSEVELT: How much cotton did you gather last year?

SHARECROPPER: We raise two bales er cotton dis year. De boll weevil wuz might bad dis time. . . .

ROOSEVELT: Do you have a garden?

SHARECROPPER: De cotton keeps us so busy we don't have time to bother with a garden. We just have a little patch of collard greens.

ROOSEVELT: How many children do you have?

SHARECROPPER: We has six children.

ROOSEVELT: Do your children go to school?

SHARECROPPER: No, sir; none of de children go ter school. Dey don't have no shoes and purty clothes to wear, so dey just stay home and helps me and der mama.

ROOSEVELT: Why don't you put a new roof on your house?

SHARECROPPER: I tol de landlord if he buy de tin I put it on. He say de land don't pay nuff so he afford to buy de tin. We just move de table and de beds round when it rains to dry spots.[18]

In extemporaneous remarks on dedicating a schoolhouse in 1937, Roosevelt gave another version of how "I began to learn economics at Warm Springs." He told of one day in 1924 when, while sitting on the porch of his cottage, he was approached by a very young man who requested him to take part in the commencement exercises at a school in a nearby town. Asked if he was the president of the graduating class, his caller replied, "No, I am principal of the school." The nineteen-year-old principal, with one year at the University of Georgia, said the school was very generous; he was making $300 a year. "Well, that started me to thinking," Roosevelt remembered. If the principal was making $300 a year, the three women teaching at the school must be making less. "Why do they have to pay that low scale of wages?" he wanted to know.

The answer came quickly: the community simply did not have much purchasing power. "Here was a very large part of the Nation that was completely at the mercy of people outside of the South, who were dependent on national conditions and on world conditions over which they had absolutely no control," the president explained. "The South was starving on five and six and seven cent cotton. It could not build schools and could not pay teachers; and the younger generation was growing up without an adequate education." During the following year, Roosevelt recalled, he learned still more. When he let a contract to build a golf course, he found that the contractor, an honest enough fellow, paid his help, white and black, only seventy or eighty cents a day. "We began to realize that here in this wonderful Southland there was a great opportunity," if only wages and crop prices could be elevated to those of other parts of the country, he declared. "I would like to see the pay of the teachers in the whole State of Georgia approximate more nearly the pay of the teachers in the State of New York in the country districts where I live."[19]

IV

Both before and after he reached the White House, Franklin Roosevelt acquired a considerable political following below the Mason-Dixon line. In 1920, a group of southern delegates took it upon themselves to call on the Tammany boss, Charles Murphy, to urge that FDR be nominated as the Democratic vice presidential candidate, and at the Madison Square Garden convention in 1924, both the Florida and the North Carolina delegations contemplated switching their votes to Roosevelt for the presidential nomination. As early as 1926, the Virginia senator Carter Glass was promoting him for the presidency.

Glass's initiative suggests that to at least some southerners this Episcopalian worthy from the Hudson Valley was acceptable in a way that his fellow New Yorker, the Catholic from Fulton Fish Market, Al Smith, was not. The South Carolina gentry believed, as one historian has noted, that Roosevelt "would bring to the job of addressing economic problems the same sense of noblesse oblige and paternalistic instinct that typified Southern elitist approaches." The conservative agribusinessman David R. Coker regarded FDR as "a gentleman in every sense of the word . . . allied with the best and soundest men in the party." A student of southern politics later wrote: "While Roosevelt came from the industrial East, his whole personality was appealing to the South. His rural and somewhat patrician background fitted the traditional pattern of squirearchy so much admired in the South. His frequent periods of residence in Georgia filled in the attractive picture and made him enough of a 'gentleman' to be forgiven many of the ideas which he shared with Alfred E. Smith, such as his opposition to prohibition."[20]

Roosevelt, for his part, as a number of commentators have pointed out, felt altogether comfortable with southern politicians and got on famously with them. Frank Freidel subsequently observed: "Roosevelt, during his seven years as assistant secretary of the navy in the Wilson administration, served under that ardent southern progressive, Josephus Daniels, and came to know most of the southern Democrats, both young and old. By 1920, when he ran for vice president, he had absorbed almost all of their ideology. . . . Certainly more than any other northern Democratic leader, he understood and empathized with the southerners and their problems." Similarly, the historian Jordan Schwarz remarked, "Roosevelt genuinely liked Southern party war-horses. He . . . admired their bucolic sociability, their elliptical storytelling and unhurried gossiping— so different from the intensity of braintrusters or certain urban politicians."[21]

Georgians early adopted their sometime resident as their choice for president of the United States. At the 1930 possum hunt dinner, which drew so many prominent Democrats that it had to be held at a large hotel, the toastmaster read a message from Clark Howell, editor of the *Atlanta Constitution,* which said, "Unless I am greatly mistaken, you are entertaining the next president of the United States." The *Constitution* claimed it was the first newspaper "of any importance" to propose FDR for the 1932 nomination. Roosevelt heard Governor-elect Richard B. Russell tell the 1500-member-strong Warm Springs and Meriwether County Roosevelt-for-President Club, "Georgia is happy to have a favorite son to present to the next Democratic National Convention." At the 1932 convention Russell and other Georgians made the rounds to reassure delegates from other states that Roosevelt was physically fit, and Georgia publicists showed FDR fishing, hunting, even riding horseback. Those who had hunted possum with him in the back country around Warm Springs, one newspaperman affirmed, had no doubt of his vigor.[22]

As the 1932 election approached, sectional enthusiasm for FDR intensified. By March 1931 an *Atlanta Journal* editor was reporting, "Roosevelt sentiment is growing on every hand, particularly in the South." After a reception in Raleigh given by Josephus Daniels before his former assistant spoke at the North Carolina state fair, the wife of the governor noted in her diary that the New Yorker was "a fascinating, charming and brilliant man despite his physical handicap of being cripple[d]." Three months later, she jotted down: "Now is the time for a Democratic President to win! Gov. Franklin D. Roosevelt of N.Y. our best bet." That fall, a well-connected editor informed Colonel House, "Governor Roosevelt is . . . whittling away whatever prejudice there may be in the South against the Democratic party on account of the 1928 campaign." The *Tallahassee Democrat* gauged "an almost universal demand for Franklin Roosevelt," as FDR swept the Florida primary by better than 8–1 over his nearest rival. In South Carolina Senator James F. Byrnes told a party convention, "If Roosevelt is elected, I give you my word that South Carolina will be recognized as she has never been recognized by any Democratic President before." The Memphis boss, Ed Crump, asked whom he would favor if FDR did not get the nod, replied, "I never make a second choice. I am for Franklin D. Roosevelt."[23]

Some of FDR's most ardent backing derived from sources liberals would later regard as suspect. One of the Alabamans who called on Governor Roosevelt in Albany in 1931 was George Wallace's father, and in the ensuing campaign his son helped collect signatures and raise money for FDR. Years afterward, the younger Wallace reminisced, "In school—right there in the middle of the Old South—we all learned to sing 'The Sidewalks of New York.'" In Edgefield, South Carolina, a rally for FDR, including hundreds of parading school pupils, was organized by a precocious politician, Strom Thurmond. At Mississippi's state Democratic convention, the racist congressman John Rankin assured delegates that if they were instructed for FDR, "all Hades can't stop us," and decades later Herman Talmadge told an interviewer, "I don't imagine you could have found a white man in Georgia that would have admitted publicly in '32 that he was against Roosevelt."[24]

At the 1932 Democratic convention, where Roosevelt came within an eyelash of being denied the nomination because he did not appear to have enough momentum to reach the required two-thirds of the ballots, he could thank steadfast southerners for pulling him through. Louisiana's Huey Long, in particular, played a critical role not only in delivering his own state but also in holding neighboring Mississippi, which was threatening to break away. As they rode back to their hotel at the end of the fourth ballot, Mississippi's Pat Harrison informed FDR's campaign manager, Jim Farley, that the time had come to approach one of Roosevelt's main rivals, John Nance Garner of Texas. When Senator William McAdoo, a Garner lieutenant, announced a decisive shift of votes from Garner to Roosevelt, it slowly dawned on delegates that the contest was over and FDR was going to be the nominee. "Suddenly a rebel yell split the air," reported the *New York Times*, "and the delegates from Texas . . . were out of their seats waving the standard of their State and above it their Lone Star flag." Though Roosevelt has come to be associated with the metropolitan Northeast, he was the candidate in 1932 not of that section, which was the stronghold of

Al Smith, but of the South and West. Walter Lippmann had thought that FDR, who was "being used by the seasoned politicians of the South," would never win the nomination because he had little backing north of the Ohio and the Potomac. Southern liberals admired the governor's performance in Albany, and southern traditionalists, who might in other circumstances have rejected him, clung to him as the best hope of taking the party away from the wet, Catholic element. "In a quite literal sense," concluded one historical account, "the South . . . nominated Roosevelt in 1932."[25]

After FDR became his party's choice, the South responded with enthusiasm, no state, though, matching Georgia in zeal. When in the closing days of the campaign the Democratic nominee headed toward his southern retreat, the *Atlanta Constitution* ran the headline: "Franklin Roosevelt Comes Back Home This Morning!" As he toured the Georgia capital in an open car, a "vast throng," the *Constitution* reported, crowded the sidewalks of Peachtree Street. Another newspaper commented: "The entire trip of Gov. Roosevelt from Atlanta to Warm Springs was an ovation." Georgians adorned farmhouses along the route with flags and placards, some of them cut from cardboard boxes on which messages had been printed with shoe polish. In Palmetto, he was greeted by a "Welcome Roosevelt" sign made of flowers, and he left town to the pealing of church bells.[26]

In routing Hoover in November, Roosevelt swept all of the South. In 1932 every one of the former Confederate states that had gone to Hoover in 1928, in the first significant defection since the Solid South emerged in 1880, rejoined the fold. Under the headline "Solid South Reborn," the *Atlanta Constitution* announced: "Republicans Hurled Back by Better Than 'Old-Time' Margins as Dixieland Marches Joyously Back Into Phalanx." A fierce critic of FDR's later acknowledged, "The South was particularly proud to see the return of the old Democratic Party to power in the Nation under the leadership of a friend of the South who called the State of Georgia his second home."[27]

A historian has noted the reaction of Tennesseans to his victory: "Many stayed up all night weeping tears of joy, hugging and shaking hands at party gatherings. Pistols cracked and dynamite boomed until after dawn, and in small towns across the state blacksmiths shot off anvils by jamming the swage holes with black powder and firing them with fuses. In Memphis, calliopes and trucks loaded with bells and bands raised a din, while shotguns and cannons fired over the city." Roosevelt ran so well in Tennessee, which had gone to Harding in 1920, that he came within a few votes of taking even the traditionally Republican eastern part of the state.[28]

Impressive though that showing was, he did far better in South Carolina, which gave FDR 102,347, Hoover only 1,978; in the town of Ninety-Six, the incumbent president did not get a single vote. In the Palmetto State, New York's governor was likened to Wade Hampton, whose Red Shirts had carried through the "Redeemer" movement after Reconstruction. At a rally in Camden in October, modern-era Red Shirts marched for FDR, and as late as 1938, a leading South Carolina newspaper was still saying that "Wade Hampton was of his day [the] Franklin D. Roosevelt of today."[29]

Roosevelt could take special satisfaction from the jubilation in Georgia. Stone Mountain celebrated the triumph with a bonfire of ten cords of wood, a thousand tires, two of Henry Ford's model "T's," and two barrels of oil—a blaze, it was claimed, that could be seen from atop the Washington Monument. So elated was the *Atlanta Constitution* at FDR's victory, a writer has noted, that its staff "rolled Henry Grady's miniature brass cannon onto the street and fired a salvo that set off railroad and factory whistles all over town." Though in his campaigns for the presidency FDR never carried his ancestral turf, New York's Dutchess County, he swept Meriwether County all four times—by proportions ranging from 12–1 to 50–1. "You know, Hen," he said to Secretary Morgenthau one night at dinner, "I like those people of the South for the manner they react in their voting better than I do those of Dutchess County. . . . Your neighbors and mine up there will listen to you and then go to the polls and vote the way their grandfathers did regardless of the merits of your case."[30]

Georgians exulted at FDR's inauguration on March 4, 1933, because it meant that one of their own had made it to the top. So many of the state's citizens wanted to attend the swearing-in that the Southern Railway put together two all-Pullman specials of fifteen cars each, leaving Atlanta's Terminal Station for the nation's capital. "Georgia's joy of anticipation became joy of realization today when the state's adopted son, Franklin D. Roosevelt, became president of the United States," reported the *Constitution*, "and the true sons and daughters of the Empire State of the South were on hand to cheer their foster brother on his way." At the inauguration ceremonies, a sheriff, clapping Judge Revill on the back, said gleefully, "They're taking Gawgia back into the Union." Two years later, the former state Democratic Party chairman, in seeking "a ringing acclamation" for "our fellow Georgian," remarked that in 1932, "we Georgians said: 'Our choice is our friend and neighbor, who has moved into the borders of our own state, where its waters and its atmosphere and the hospitality of its people have literally loved him from a state of physical infirmity into health and vigor.'" He concluded: "How Georgians should swell with pride that *we* furnished *him* to the Nation!"[31]

V

When Roosevelt followed up his 1932 victory with the electrifying First Hundred Days of 1933, he aroused passionate devotion in the South. In Tennessee, FDR's inaugural address found young Albert Gore, who would one day represent his state in the U.S. Senate and whose son would become the Democratic nominee for president of the United States, gathered with his friends about a radio in a Carthage barber shop. "The strength of that matchless voice and the confidence and determination in his words seemed to reach to every part of our community and to awaken hope where none had been," Gore remembered. On Roosevelt's birthday in January 1934, a Raleigh devotee walked 280 miles through wintry North Carolina and Virginia to congratulate him, and forty thousand Alabama admirers sent a wire thanking him for leading them out of the darkness. It required two days to transmit.[32]

Unsurprisingly, FDR and his program found particular favor in his "adopted" state. In June 1933 the Georgia Press Association, at its annual convention, resolved to "send its greeting and its affections to President Franklin Delano Roosevelt, and . . . hail him as a fellow Georgian and wish him Godspeed." When the president announced that he was returning to Georgia in the fall of 1935, the press billed "Roosevelt Day" as a "Home-Coming Celebration," and the Atlanta Board of Education declared a school holiday as an "expression of gratitude and honor to our beloved President." Former Senator Sam Nunn has said: "In the Georgia of my early childhood, I can remember seeing tattered magazine photographs of FDR hung in an honored spot in the backwoods tarpaper shacks of the poorest dirt farmers. Georgians considered themselves especially blessed that the president chose our own Warm Springs as his holiday retreat, and thousands lined the railroad tracks and roads each time he made the trek south." To one Georgia woman, he was "God's half-brother."[33]

The Georgia writer Ferrol Sams Jr., in relaying a popular anecdote, has recalled:

> The Reign of Roosevelt was met with rejoicing. . . . The attitude of Georgia was encapsulated in the joke about a rural teacher leading her students through morning exercises.
>
> "Children, who paved the road in front of your house?"

In response, the chorus, "Roosevelt!"

"Who put electricity into your house for you?"

"Roosevelt!"

"Who gave your uncle a job in the WPA?"

"Roosevelt!"

"Who got your granddaddy an old age pension?"

"Roosevelt!"

"All right, children. Now. Who made you?"

After a moment of silence one little boy asserted stoutly, "God."

Whereupon a gallused, barefoot towhead leaped up in the back row and yelled, "Throw that sorry Republican out of here."

Sams added, "The rural South was led into the religious enlightenment of the twentieth century under a banner peppered with popular initials: . . . NRA, CCC, WPA, TVA, NYA and others; but the most significant of them was FDR."[34]

Roosevelt proved nearly as popular in Mississippi. His inauguration on March 4, 1933, marked the climax of a three-day "Carnival of Confidence" in Jackson at which "Old Man Old Deal" was hanged on a scaffold in the Old Capitol grounds and burned. At a gathering of thousands, "The New Deal" was crowned, and the acting governor of the state cried, "Thank God today for Franklin D. Roosevelt!" Times were hard, a Mississippi woman said in the summer of 1933, but in light of a speech she had heard from FDR, "although it's pouring down rain outside, there's 'Sunshine in Our Hearts.'" The editor of the *Clarion-Ledger* likened the president's inaugural address to the Sermon on the Mount, and that fall, the rambunctious editor of the *Jackson Daily News* said of Roosevelt: "We must stick to him . . . until hell freezes over, and then skate around with him on the ice." When FDR visited the TVA facilities in the Tupelo area in 1934, the Jackson paper wrote fawningly, "The most powerful and best-beloved man in the world slept quietly on Mississippi soil last night." A year later, Theodore Bilbo summed up much of the sentiment in the state. "Just remember," he told an FDR critic in 1935, "that the one man who has contributed more to the relief of the American people than any other man living or dead is Franklin Delano Roosevelt."[35]

The president won a conspicuously strong following among the down-and-out. "Roosevelt is as good a man as ever lived," said a tenant farmer. "He's shore for the common class o' folks." A Texan who recalled that in the depth of the

Depression under Hoover "we lived in an abandoned goat shed with caliche for a floor" with an "entire side . . . open" rejoiced when he got a job in "Big D" with a wholesale jobber. "Hope and patriotism rose in me when I arrived in Dallas to find Butler Bros. flying an NRA banner," he said. "I blessed President Roosevelt." The next time FDR came to Dallas, another man wrote him, "I will fix you a real dinner of hot biscuits, fried potatoes, chicken, chicken gravy, and butterscotch pie," adding "We have a comfortable home, something that a working man could not have prior to your Presidency."[36]

"I do think that Roosevelt is the biggest-hearted man we ever had in the White House," a southern millhand said. The man continued: "He undoubtedly is the most foresighted and can speak his thoughts the plainest of any man I ever heard speak. He's spoke very few words over the radio that I haven't listened to. It's the first time in my ricollection that a president ever got up and said, 'I'm interested in and aim to do somethin' for the workin' man.' Just knowin' that for once in the time of the country they was a man to stand up and speak for him, a man that culd make what he felt so plain nobody could doubt he meant it, has made a lot of us feel a sight better even when they wasn't much to eat in our homes." Another mill worker put it more tersely: "Mr. Roosevelt is the only man we ever had in the White House who would understand that my boss is a sonofabitch."[37]

Farmers and workers openly expressed their gratitude. In the spring of 1933, the southern reformer Will Alexander picked up a Georgia tenant farmer who was hard up against it. When he left him off at the Decatur courthouse, Alexander told him, "Things are mighty bad. I'm sorry you're having it so tough." The man replied, "Yes, they're mighty bad. But ain't we got a great President?" It seemed a long way from the executive mansion in Washington to a shack outside Winder, Georgia, Alexander reflected, but "that strange man in Washington had reached across everything that divided them and had done something for that fellow. . . . A feeling of expectancy had reached into the smallest communities in the South." Two years later, a newspaperman had a similar experience on a road in eastern Kentucky where he came upon a miner, his face begrimed with coal dust. "His sudden smile of high enthusiasm and the delight which spread over his face at the mention of President Roosevelt's New Deal was almost comical," he related.[38]

Unhesitatingly, southern victims of the Great Depression credited FDR with rescuing them. In the 1930s, an Alabaman who was called "the Andrew Jackson of Southern Labor" told an interviewer that Roosevelt was "the first high-up that has ever showed any sympathy for our lot." It was Franklin Delano Roosevelt, a Hispanic social worker has said, who "threw open the doors of the warehouses and fed the people of San Antonio." Mississippi's Adams County, the *Natchez Democrat* reported, awaited the enactment of the WPA legislation the way little boys looked forward to Christmas morning. "In Mississippi," a historian has concluded, "the 'W P and A' was the best thing many people had known." The country singer Loretta Lynn, recalling that her father "would work a few days on the roads" for the WPA and come home "with a few dollars . . . proud as could be," affirmed that it was because of this program that "you'll see pictures of FDR on the wall" of any cottage in the Kentucky mountains. Four decades after the publication of *Let Us Now Praise Famous Men,* Emma McCloud, who, as a fetching young woman had so beguiled its author, James Agee, lauded FDR as "the only President I ever knew that done anything."[39]

A southern writer, thinking back to early summers on a Shelby County, Alabama, farm in the late 1940s, remembered that when his grandparents "mentioned Roosevelt's name, they'd bow their heads just a little and hood their eyes, and now and then their voices would break slightly as they called his name; they still had the feeling that he had died yesterday." One day his grandfather told him how he had acquired "the finest clock in the whole wide world," which sat in a place of honor on the living room mantel. He had been an itinerant worker in the Great Depression, with nothing but a tent to shelter him and his family, as he drifted from state to state until, thanks to Roosevelt, he landed a job with the TVA. On drawing his first paycheck he joined his union buddies in toasting the president with a slug of whiskey straight. Then, on his way home, he spotted in a drugstore window an elaborate clock featuring Roosevelt at the helm of a ship, his eyes looking confidently toward the future, with, at its base, the inscription: FDR: THE MAN OF THE HOUR. His voice nearly cracking, he recalled, "I don't think I even looked to see how much the price was. I went inside and bought it. . . . I told 'em we'd have to keep that clock forever. It was a sign that everything would be all right." A fall of more than 200 feet on the Wheeler Dam project had left him a cripple, but he thought that never again would there be a president to match Roosevelt.[40]

People elsewhere in America also expressed gratitude to FDR, but his residence in the South established a unique relationship. After a tour of the region in 1934, the *New Republic* editor Bruce Bliven reported: "Throughout the South I found that President Roosevelt's amazing personal popularity continues virtually unabated. . . . Most of the reasons for his hold on the affection of the common man are the same as in other parts of the country. . . . There is, however, one special reason, which seems to me peculiarly Southern and illuminating. The President is liked, in that area, largely because he has spent so much time in the South where . . . at Warm Springs, Georgia, . . . he still maintains a home. . . . The South feels therefore that he knows at first hand about its problems; that he is not just one more cold No'thener from the cold No'th. A little personal contact goes a long way below the Mason Dixon line."[41]

VI

Since southerners had all too much experience with defeat, they had a large stake in FDR's continued success, for Roosevelt had made the Democrats, with whom almost all the South identified, the country's new majority party. Conversely, rejection of FDR would mean relegating the South to minority status again. As W. J. Cash explained: "Roosevelt was hope and confidence after long despair. And more than that, he was hope and confidence riding under the banner of the Democratic Party, over what appeared then to be the emaciated corpse of the Republican Party, under whose rule catastrophe had arrived. For the South, in truth, it was almost as though the bones of Pickett and his brigade had suddenly sprung alive to go galloping up that slope of Gettysburg again and snatch victory from the Yankee's hand after all. And many and many a man felt in his inmost soul that it was really worth having endured the unfortunate Mr. Hoover for four years to have achieved at last the satisfaction of seeing the old Black Radical enemy and oppressor brought to complete rout and ignominy. I have myself heard the sentiment pointedly expressed."[42]

After twelve years in the Republican wilderness, southern politicians had reason to be grateful to a man who, after leading their party back into power, was granting them "recognition." Now there was a southern vice president, John Nance Garner of Texas, and Roosevelt had named three southerners to his cabinet: Cordell Hull of Tennessee as secretary of state, an accolade regarded as acknowledging the most important man in the party save for the president and vice president; Daniel Roper of South Carolina as secretary of commerce; and Claude Swanson of Virginia as secretary of the navy. The heads of the new emergency agencies included men such as the director of the Civilian Conservation Corps (CCC), Robert Fechner, a Tennessean. The White House, too, had a Dixie cast, with a distant relative of Jubal Early as his press secretary and Marvin McIntyre of Kentucky in the strategically situated post of appointments secretary; when McIntyre fell ill, "another southern Bourbon," General Edwin M. "Pa" Watson of Alabama, took over some of his assignments.[43]

Under FDR's leadership, the Democrats controlled both houses of Congress by substantial margins, a situation especially advantageous to southerners who, as a consequence of seniority, held a hugely disproportionate number of leadership and committee posts. Texas alone boasted nine committee chairmanships. At one high-level White House conference on legislative strategy, Secretary of the Treasury Henry Morgenthau Jr. noted, "In looking around the room I found that Congressman Taylor of Colorado was the only Democratic leader present who did not come from south of the Mason-Dixon line. Every other man was a southerner."[44]

Roosevelt relied upon southerners such as Pat Harrison of Mississippi in the Senate and Sam Rayburn of Texas in the House to carry through his program. "Rarely in all political history has a group of so-called conservatives and reactionaries so consistently voted for radical and reform measures over as long a period of years as did these southerners," the historian George Mowry later wrote. Alabama's John Sparkman added, "You'll find that practically every New Deal measure that was enacted into law under President Roosevelt was sponsored by a Southerner, and never could have passed without the support of Southerners." Well aware of his dependence on indispensable legislators such as the Majority Leader Joseph T. Robinson of Arkansas, Roosevelt showered patronage on them. When Robinson complained to Carter Glass, "Oh, you can't imagine the hell I have to go through," Glass allegedly retorted, "In your case, Joe, the road to hell seems to be lined with post offices."[45]

A freelance journalist from the South Carolina upcountry reflected: "In the midst of the depression we began really again to hope. We could hardly believe our eyes when we heard that President Roosevelt had appointed a Carolinian to his Cabinet. Of course, it was only Uncle Dan Roper, but just the same he was a Carolinian, and there had not been a South Carolinian in a President's Cabinet since the time of John C. Calhoun, when of course we in Carolina had run cabinets. Again we were startled when we read in the papers that Professor James Harvey Rogers, a native of Society Hill, South Carolina, had been called to the White House for a conference; a member of the Calhoun family had said that no one born at Society Hill had sense enough to advise the President of the United States. . . . Finally, the President appointed a Carolinian to the United States Supreme Court. At last, for us, things truly were picking up."[46]

Though Roosevelt was a New Yorker, the South viewed him as their commander in a warfare of sections. "Whatever their ideological inclinations," Dewey
Grantham has written, "most southerners were disposed to regard Roosevelt
and the New Deal as allies in the struggle to curb the economic imperialism of
the Northeast." The president, who accepted the southern view that history had
unfairly burdened the section, sought to diminish the disadvantages under
which it labored. No sectional grievance agitated the South more than the discriminatory freight rate structure, which FDR's appointee Harry Hopkins,
speaking from Memphis on a national radio network, asserted "was planned to
clinch the industrial supremacy of the North and East." The president demonstrated his sympathy by giving a friendly hearing to southern governors
campaigning for a change, and in 1942 he transmitted to Congress the TVA's
important study, "Regionalized Freight Rates: Barrier to National Productive-
ness."[47]

As someone who lived part of each year in the South, but also had indis-
putable credentials as a northerner, Roosevelt served as an intermediary who
could explain, and defend, southern mores to the rest of the nation. When a
New York woman, who had traveled to Philadelphia in 1936 to hear his acceptance address, wrote him, "I confess that I would be thrilled if a firmer hand
were taken with the hardhearted South in regard to the Negro, the sharecroppers and its general habit of mob violence," Roosevelt replied: "You are in the
ultimate objectives right in what you say of the South. We must, however, remember that for at least three generations the South was almost wholly lacking in property values and consequently in taxes, and, therefore, in the opportunity of having improved schools and roads and all the things that raised the
economic level. That improvement cannot come in a day but if you know the
South as I know it, you will realize that in three years they have made enormous
strides and I am confident will continue if they are given the chance for a few
years more." When the Socialist Norman Thomas, after having been driven off
a platform in Arkansas because he sought to organize sharecroppers, called at
the White House, Roosevelt told him, "I know the South, and there is arising
a new generation of leaders in the South and we've got to be patient."[48]

Roosevelt made it his business to learn all he could about the South, and
those who thought of him as an ill-informed, though well-intentioned, late-
comer were sometimes surprised by the range of his information. When Will
Alexander, author of *The Collapse of Cotton Tenancy*, was invited to Warm

Springs, the philanthropist George Foster Peabody warned him that the president did not know much about the South. Alexander later recalled: "I sat down and discovered, as most people discovered, that you never told FDR anything. . . . He knew more than Mr. Peabody thought about the South. . . . He talked about . . . the country around Warm Springs, southern leadership . . . , the importance of forests. . . . Before I left, I put a copy of the little book down on the table, and never said a word."[49]

The president believed that the "human stock" in the South matched that of any other region, but the grinding poverty sapped resources for schooling. "We have got to raise the standards of education; they are perfectly terrible," he told reporters in 1934. Ignorance, he believed, also had a political cost. "The South, because it is still educationally behind the rest of the nation, is peculiarly susceptible to the demagogue," he remarked to a group of editors four years later. In 1939 he told reporters: "New York, Massachusetts and Illinois ought not to have any aid from the federal government for schools. But Georgia and Mississippi and Alabama, South Carolina and Arkansas, I think they need aid because they have not got the values down there to build schools and run them. You take the state of Georgia. Some of you were down there with me this year. You remember the Atlanta papers? There were great headlines every morning: 'State Schools Will Probably Close Down the First of January.'"[50]

In a talk in Alabama in 1939, he recollected that on the first nights he spent at his cottage in Warm Springs he was awakened from a sound sleep by the rumble of a freight train carrying milk to south Florida, and that when he asked about it, he was appalled to learn that the milk came not from Georgia or Alabama but from the upper Midwest. The thought of that train moving through all the intervening southern states to Florida, he said, gave him "a feeling that something was wrong with the agricultural economy of these States of the lower South, because you and I know . . . that these States can produce perfectly good milk and cream." A short time later, he went into the village to buy apples, and, though "no apples in the world were better" than those grown in the southern Appalachians, he could not find any in Meriwether County, save those from Oregon and Washington. "I went to buy meat—and I know that we can make pastures in these States—and the only meat that I could buy came via Omaha and Kansas City and Chicago," he added. In the time that he had been president, he had been working, with great success he claimed, to get "the South 'out of hock' to the North." He now wanted to see an end to soil erosion in the South and he looked forward to the time when southern factories could supply local needs. "I hope to be able to come back to this State and to the State of Georgia before I die," he said, "and see at least a part of that ideal come true."[51]

Southern politicians spoke frankly among themselves, out of the hearing of northerners, about how the Roosevelt administration was mulcting other sections to distribute largesse to the South. In a 1940 interview in Jackson, the Mississippi senator Theodore Bilbo pointed out that his state had received over $900 million "in good old Yankee money" since Roosevelt had been in the White House, and had paid out only $30 million. Hence, "any Mississippian not for Roosevelt and the New Deal ought to be ashamed of himself." Similarly, in Texas, according to one account, whenever the contractor Herman Brown yelped about lavish New Deal spending, Congressman Lyndon B. Johnson would respond, "What are you worried about? It's not coming out of *your* pocket. Any money that's spent down here on New Deal projects, the East is paying for. We don't pay any taxes in Texas. . . . They're paying for our projects." In like manner, Brown's brother, after visiting Johnson in Washington, reported: "Lyndon would take me to these meetings of the Southern Congressmen, and that's the way they'd be talking. That the South would get these dams and these other projects, and it would come out of the other fellow's pocket. The Presidents before Roosevelt—Coolidge, Hoover—they never gave the South anything. Roosevelt was the first one who gave the South a break."[52]

Scholars have warned that the contributions of the New Deal to regional well-being have been exaggerated. "The areas with the lowest income and the greatest need received the least in per capita work relief funds," one survey found. "This relationship was particularly pronounced in the Southeast." The state at the bottom with respect to New Deal benefits was North Carolina; its $143 per capita contrasted with Nevada's $1130. More disturbingly, the smaller the percentage of blacks in a state, the greater the likelihood was of substantial federal spending per person. The Roosevelt government disbursed less for agriculture per capita in Mississippi than it did in an industrialized state such as Rhode Island. The most recent study, however, concludes that, though per capita federal spending under FDR was lower in the South than in other regions, New Deal programs gave the South "the highest lasting economic return" and put "the South . . . in a better position to compete with the North in the postwar economy."[53]

Many southern politicians and businessmen joined workers and farmers in expressing gratitude for nearly $2 billion in relief spending in the South and pleasure over the economic gains registered under Roosevelt, as their section began to climb out of the trough more rapidly than the rest of the nation. In the fall of 1934, Senator Josiah Bailey, not one of the New Deal's more ardent admirers, informed the White House: "Eastern North Carolina . . . has been prostrated for five years. This year the people are really prosperous. With one accord they give the credit to the President." Similarly, a small-town banker told his fellow Mississippian Turner Catledge, "I can show you papers in our current portfolios that had been cancelled out as uncollectible years ago. People come in here and ask to pay back interest on notes we literally have to fish out of the waste basket." When Catledge, Washington correspondent of the *New York Times,* asked him what he thought of FDR's approach, the banker replied, "Why I'd fight anyone who said we had not prospered under it."[54]

In a large portion of the South, in towns such as Tupelo, Mississippi, Decatur, Alabama, and Paducah, Kentucky, but especially in the headquarters state of Tennessee, FDR's popularity owed much to the cheap electric power generated by the TVA. The TVA, George McJimsey has written, "represented more clearly than any other New Deal measure Franklin Roosevelt's vision of American society. Roosevelt pictured Americans identified by some specific and distinctive characteristic—in this instance, place." In Knoxville, fifty thousand East Tennesseans, in a procession 3 miles long, paraded through the streets to celebrate approval of the Cove Creek Dam bill, and in Chattanooga, the *News* lauded FDR for his vision of the valley. "Only one major objective remains in the path of the TVA—the reelection of President Franklin D. Roosevelt," wrote a Knoxville newspaper in 1936. "Upon the approaching presidential election depends the future of the TVA."[55]

<h2 style="text-align:center">VIII</h2>

When in 1936 Roosevelt made his bid for a second term, approval for him approached zealotry—to such an extent in South Carolina as to be nearly unanimous. Early in 1934, in a New Year's editorial entitled "Thank God for Roosevelt," the newspaper of South Carolina's state capital called the president a "Providential Leader," and in 1935 a state legislator favored endorsing "the only president that ever recognized South Carolina." A South Carolina textile hand wrote the president: "You are our Moses. Leading us out of the Egypt of depression to the promised land of prosperity." For a national magazine at the beginning of the 1936 campaign year, a Jackson editor summed up the situation in his state: "Small is the growling and few are the murmurs of discontent in Mississippi concerning the New Deal."[56]

In September 1936, tens of thousands of southern Democrats from seven states gathered at a giant Green Pastures Rally in Charlotte's Memorial Stadium to pay tribute to FDR. These "southernmocrats" included the governors of North Carolina and South Carolina and the governor and both senators from Florida. A drenching rain did not deter thousands more from lining the highway to cheer the president's motorcade. It seemed to his admirers altogether fitting that by the time Roosevelt began to speak, the downpour had given way to a spectacular rainbow. "My friends," the president told the exuberant crowd, "it is because I have spent so much of these latter years in this Southland, and because I have come to know its fine people, its brave history, its many problems, that I speak not as a stranger." As "he touched these peculiarly southern subjects," a Charlotte newspaper reported, "applause born of mutual understanding roared through the stadium."[57]

As conservative a senator as Josiah Bailey wrote FDR's secretary that the president's visit to North Carolina had "added tremendous volume to the existing enthusiasm for him." Riding behind Roosevelt's car, Bailey could observe "the crowd . . . greet the President with cheers and . . . could see the broad smiles on their faces." People, he went on, "have great expectations of him and he always adds to them." He wanted Roosevelt told "that his visit to Western North Carolina was the best thing that has happened to that section of our State in a hundred years."[58]

Returning from the rally in Charlotte, a Florida legislator picked up a frail, elderly man on the road who said: "I remember back, during the Hoover Administration—when the Seaboard, Coast Line and Southern passenger and freight trains went through here almost empty. Now, take a look at them—they are loaded down. I remember, just a few years back when all these cotton mills, and factories, were shut down and only a few people around here could get work; but now look at them—they are all open and everybody is working and happy. Do you know, I would like to beat the stuffin out of these people who are criticizing our President. . . . If it had not been for President Roosevelt, thousands of poor people like myself and my family, would not be here today. We would be in insane asylums or in graves. . . . How grateful all Americans should be to have a President like Mr. Roosevelt."[59]

Texas more than matched the ardor of North Carolina. In Austin, the state Senate hung FDR's portrait in its chamber, and the House endorsed his policies unanimously. When the president attended the Texas Centennial in Dallas in June 1936, half a million people turned out to greet him. "The streets . . . were solid with masses of humanity," reported the *Dallas Morning News*. "Applause followed the President's car like waves rolling." Similar tidings came from the San Antonio congressman Maury Maverick. "The great majority of the Southern people realize that Roosevelt is the only President who has given the South full support, full recognition, since the Civil War," he wrote. "Roosevelt, heart, liver, and lights, is our man."[60]

During the campaign, Roosevelt heard murmurs of criticism from southern conservatives such as Carter Glass and Eugene Talmadge, but he easily subdued them. In a letter to the president, Glass grudgingly acknowledged, "Many Virginians . . . seemed eager to 'go all the way' with you, whether their senior Senator was so minded or not." Despite misgivings, Glass announced he would vote for FDR, though the Virginia senator implied he was doing so only because, as a good Democrat, he would naturally go down the line for the whole ticket. In Georgia, a straw poll in Harris County, regarded as strong Talmadge country, gave FDR a 17–1 advantage over "Our Gene," and in Whitfield County, the governor got a minuscule .02 percent of the vote as a presidential contender. "In Georgia in 1936," Talmadge's son later wrote, "it probably would have been easier to run against Jesus Christ than against Franklin D. Roosevelt." On Election Day, the Wild Man from Sugar Creek wound up backing FDR.[61]

The election returns, with their fantastic numbers, confirmed expectations. When the governor of Mississippi wagered the governor of South Carolina on which state would roll up a larger proportion for FDR, he had reason to crow when Mississippi gave Roosevelt better than 97 percent. But he lost the bet. South Carolina's returns showed an astonishing 98.57 percent. Numbers of localities reported staggering margins. In North Carolina, Roosevelt got 90 percent or more of the ballots in no fewer than twenty-eight counties. In Tennessee's Shelby County (Memphis), FDR ran up a 30–1 advantage over Landon, and in Mississippi both Leflore and Sunflower counties gave him 99 percent.

Adulation pursued FDR in the South in his second term too. In 1937 the governor of Alabama, Bibb Graves, calling on the president at Warm Springs, announced, "Every enemy of Roosevelt's is an enemy of mine" and in 1939 the Birmingham editor John Temple Graves, after beginning an article by citing a young southern corporation lawyer who "hates the President with a hate that passes Roosevelt-hating in the North, East, or West," concluded: "The South . . . is looking right, left, up, down, and over—but it still loves Roosevelt." In 1940 Roosevelt once again attracted 90 percent of the vote in South Carolina as well as in Mississippi where Bilbo had pleaded for an overwhelming display of gratitude to "Franklin D. Roosevelt, the best friend the South ever had in the White House." Ed Crump told the *Commercial Appeal* that he was backing the president because "he gave us [the] Tennessee Valley Authority," while if the Republican nominee, Wendell Willkie, the leading foe of TVA, "should accidentally stumble into the Presidency, in a very short time every interest in this Southern area . . . would set up a groan of despair that would be heard from Dan to Beersheba." Republicans that year accused Roosevelt, in seeking a third term, of violating a taboo established by George Washington, but the governor of Virginia, James H. Price, said, "As for me, I am willing to vote for the President for a fourth, fifth or sixth term if it is necessary."[62]

TWO

THE FDR COALITION

I

Some of FDR's liberal and radical critics charged that his great popularity in the South came at an exorbitant cost: submission to the section's racial mores. They pointed out that when he ran for president in 1932, Roosevelt, who had never shown a whit of interest in the ordeal of African Americans, had been regarded as the candidate of the white South. That year, the National Association for the Advancement of Colored People's (NAACP) organ, *The Crisis*, wrote sourly: "FDR has spent six months out of every twelve as Governor of New York and the rest swimming in a Georgia mudhole. If he is elected president, we shall have to move the White House to Warm Springs and use Washington for his occasional vacations." Furthermore, as president, he customarily deferred to the southern congressional leadership on racial matters. Not once in his long tenure did he mount a campaign on behalf of civil rights legislation. His accusers also allege that he permitted federal administrators to discriminate against blacks, and even to extend the kingdom of Jim Crow. All too true.[1]

Yet it is also true that FDR and the New Dealers initiated changes that shook established racial patterns, stirred up a resistance to the old order that would reverberate for decades to come, and, by listening to, and sometimes heeding, demands for greater equality, deeply angered the guardians of white supremacy. The age of Roosevelt also ignited small revolutions in class relations—in factory towns and on remote farms, among whites as well as blacks. These transformations had an important political dimension too. "The FDR coalition," grounded in class and ethnicity, brought about the only thoroughgoing political realignment of the twentieth century, a break with the past that seriously undermined the rationale of the "Solid South."

Both contemporaries and historians have charged that Roosevelt, in the words of the longtime head of the TVA, David Lilienthal, was "a prisoner of the Southern wing of the Democratic party." The president, Lilienthal reflected, "stayed . . . far away from the problem of the South in its most critical and important area—that is, the waste of human resources in our black population." He found it easy to adapt to southern racial mores for he did not have strong instincts about racial injustice. Still worse, though he had no peculiar hang-ups about race, he was capable when a Harvard undergraduate of descending to characterizing the Negro as "a semi-beast," and, in later years, of alluding to "darkies" and even "niggers." "I have always felt that F.D.R. was overrated as a champion of the Negro," Roy Wilkins later reflected. "He was a New York patrician, distant, aloof, with no natural feel for the sensibility of black people, no compelling inner commitment to their cause." For the president, Joseph Lash concluded, "political realities arrested an enthusiasm for equal rights that Roosevelt, a Georgian by adoption, did not feel."[2]

Under FDR, the national government had a distinct sectional tilt. Less than four weeks after Roosevelt's inauguration in March 1933, the *Washington Evening Star* recorded, "Dixie is in the saddle on Capitol Hill, all right." Nor could African Americans find any empathy in the White House staff. Reflecting on the racial views of McIntyre, Early, and Watson and his own attitude, Jonathan Daniels later said, "I don't know anybody around the President who was a strong Negrophile; I don't know *anybody*." In a subsequent summation, one historian wrote of Roosevelt: "For fifteen years, from 1930 to the end of his life, he appeased the South. He appointed its sons to the cabinet and the Court. He ignored civil rights. He vacationed in Warm Springs, Georgia, a place he loved. He would never drive the South from his party."[3]

Roosevelt infuriated black leaders by tolerating blatant discrimination by New Deal agencies, especially during his first term. The president did nothing to counteract outrageous racism by the director of the CCC, and in the Tennessee Valley NAACP investigators found not one black foreman, not one black clerk, on the rolls of the TVA. Moreover, no black was permitted to live in Norris, the Authority's showplace town. Roosevelt also sanctioned regional wage differences that resulted in southern blacks under NRA codes being paid less. "It is not the purpose of this administration to impair Southern industry by refusing to recognize traditional differentials," he stated. NRA, said black leaders, stood for "Negro Run Around," "Negro Rarely Allowed," or "Negro Robbed

Again." In one city 15 percent of whites on the Civil Works Administration (CWA) rolls were paid at skilled rates, but not one black. Often, too, landlords pocketed the AAA checks of black tenants. A columnist in a black newspaper charged: "The South is running the government, it dominates the White House, it controls the Army and Navy, all because President Roosevelt is too weak and probably feeble to do anything to stop them. He has failed to defend his wife or his close friends and party associates from the calumny of southern race hatred."[4]

With no restraining hand from the president, southern lawmakers not only insisted on strict adherence to the imperatives of white supremacy in administering New Deal programs in their own section, but also imposed their prejudices on Capitol Hill. Senator Byrnes of South Carolina objected to the requirement that there be at least one black on the advisory committee of the Farm Security Administration (FSA) in every southern state. "I venture to say that you have not had any demand from any leader of the negro race in this State that a negro be appointed to your Advisory Committee," he wrote the head of the FSA, Will Alexander, then added menacingly: "If you have, I would like to know the name of the individual." When the restaurant of the U.S. House of Representatives, a national institution, denied access to two blacks in January 1934, Congressman Lindsay Warren of North Carolina said bluntly— and with outrageous insolence—that the manager had done so on his orders. "The restaurant," he declared, "has never served negro employees or visitors, nor will it so long as I have anything to do with it."[5]

Numbers of Americans, white and black, thought that the least Roosevelt could have done was to throw his immense prestige behind legislation against the heinous crime of lynching, which had claimed so many black victims, but he never did anything effective. The black scholar Horace Cayton charged that "Roosevelt has been and is as silent about the ever mounting number of Negro lynchings as an Indian statue at the door of a cigar emporium." The president and his circle, Cayton said, regarded catering to the South "more greatly desired than justice for the masses, hence 'mum is the word.'" In the spring of 1934, Eleanor Roosevelt wrote the top NAACP official, Walter White: "The President talked to me rather at length today about the lynching bill. As I do not think you will either like or agree with everything that he thinks, I would like an opportunity of telling you about it, and would also like you to talk to the President if you feel you want to. Therefore, will you let me know if you are going to be in Washington before long?"[6]

At his wife's behest, the president gave White an extraordinary amount of time—nearly an hour and a half—to press his argument for antilynching legislation, and at the end he promised he would meet with the Senate sponsors. He kept his word, and he let them use his authority to tell Majority Leader Robinson of Arkansas "that the President will be glad to see the bill pass and wishes it passed." The next day, he made a mealy-mouthed statement at his press conference: "I frankly haven't got sufficient clarity in my own mind as to whether that particular method will work and also as to the constitutionality of it, I think there is a question." He did say, "I am absolutely for the objective," and he wanted the sponsors of the measure "to go ahead and try to get a vote on it in the Senate." More than that, though, he would not do, and Robinson understood that the president would not insist. When in 1935 Roosevelt again refused to put his prestige on the line for what he knew would be a hopeless and divisive fight against a southern filibuster on an antilynching bill, the NAACP's Charles Houston chided Walter White, "All along I've been telling you that your President had no real courage and that he would chisel in a pinch."[7]

Roosevelt responded to criticism of his behavior by citing the political constraints under which he labored. "I did not choose the tools with which I must work," Roosevelt told White. "Had I been permitted to choose them I would have selected quite different ones. But I've got to get legislation passed by Congress to save America. The Southerners by reason of the seniority rule in Congress are chairmen or occupy strategic places on most of the Senate and House committees. If I come out for the anti-lynching bill now, they will block every bill I ask Congress to pass to keep America from collapsing. I just can't take that risk."[8]

Not every southerner accepted FDR's claim that if he took firm steps against racial discrimination, "the South would rise up in protest." To that excuse, Will Alexander would reply, "'What South are you talking about, Mr. President? The South of Bilbo and Cotton Ed Smith, or the South of Frank Graham and Mark Ethridge?' . . . I assured the President that apparently I had more faith in the inherent decency of southern white people than he did in that I was certain that at least on an issue like this far more southerners would approve his taking an unequivocal stand than would disapprove."[9]

In truth, though, Roosevelt had good reason to suppose that if he insisted on civil rights legislation, he not only would fail to get it, but also would imperil hopes for other measures, many of which benefited blacks. To be sure, there is little evidence that Roosevelt had ever thought through the kinds of changes he would have liked to have achieved if the political situation had permitted them. Mary McLeod Bethune, president of the National Council of Negro Women, later recalled that on several occasions she had "proposed pretty drastic steps to end the hideous discrimination and second-class citizenship which made the South a blot upon our democracy. But FDR usually demurred, pointing out that a New Reconstruction in the South would have to keep pace with democratic progress on a national scale." Yet he was surely right in thinking that a direct challenge to the white supremacists on the Hill was foredoomed. Furthermore, he recognized that the country regarded his main tasks as achieving recovery and mitigating the suffering caused by the Great Depression, and he knew that, to accomplish either goal, he required the support of the powerful southern barons.[10]

If the president assaulted the barriers of Jim Crow, neither southern blacks, few of whom could even go to the polls, nor white liberals in the South, who were in a decided minority on racial issues, could have given him the backing he would have needed. Furthermore, contrary to Will Alexander's claim, most of the liberals shared the dominant racial presumptions. Barry Bingham of the liberal *Louisville Courier Journal* expressed dismay that "many Southerners and others will gather the impression that all of us are against segregation of the races under all circumstances, which of course is not in the least true," and as advanced a southern liberal as Claude Pepper said during the debate on anti-lynching legislation: "Whatever may be written into the Constitution, whatever may be placed upon the statute books of this Nation, however many soldiers may be stationed about the ballot boxes of the Southland, the colored race will not vote, because in doing so . . . they endanger the supremacy of a race to which God has committed the destiny of a continent, perhaps of a world." In his campaign against Governor Talmadge, Ellis Arnall, regarded as an archetypal southern liberal, assured Georgia voters that "if a nigger ever tried to get into a white school in my part of the state, the sun would never set on his head." Alexander chided the president for not relying on the South of Mark Ethridge, but as late as 1943 Ethridge was warning, "There is no power in the world—not even in all the mechanized armies of the earth, Allied and Axis—which could now force the southern white people to the abandonment of the principle of segregation." In 1944 another forward-looking editor, Ralph McGill of the *Atlanta Constitution*, declared, "Anyone with an ounce of common sense must see . . . that separation of the two races must be maintained in the South." Bearing these considerations in mind, the leading authority on blacks and the New

Deal, Harvard Sitkoff, often highly critical of FDR, has concluded, "Roosevelt had no alternative but to cooperate with the Southerners who ran Congress."[11]

III

Though evidence of the persistence of discrimination and segregation during his White House years is unmistakable, Roosevelt also presided over some important changes. As Frank Freidel observed: "While he held the South, his adopted section, in genuine affection, his attitude toward inviolable Southern institutions was intellectual rather than emotional, pragmatic rather than dogmatic. To him the greatest challenge facing the South was the alleviation of poverty, not the maintenance (or, for that matter, the elimination) of white supremacy." With that disposition in Washington, quite unlike the racist mindset that marred the reign of the last Democratic president, Woodrow Wilson, space opened up for all kinds of subtle transformations. As one scholar has pointed out, though Roosevelt took no direct action on behalf of blacks in the South, "he did not respect the color line in marshaling his attack upon poverty," and since his program was essentially national rather than sectional, southern leaders who "wanted federal assistance in bringing recovery without the concomitant alteration of existing social and economic institutions" learned that "the combination was impossible."[12]

Black leaders found FDR's appointees uncommonly accessible. Walter White, who had not voted for Roosevelt in 1932 because he promised to be no better than Hoover, quickly learned that New Deal cabinet officers lent him their ears, that the president was naming advisors on "Negro affairs" to emergency agencies, and that Eleanor Roosevelt was willing to give him the private phone number of her Manhattan flat. In its issue on the eve of the 1940 election, when FDR sought a third term, *The Crisis* stated: "It cannot be denied that colored people . . . have penetrated nearer to policy-making desks than ever before. . . . [The] most important contribution of the Roosevelt administration to the age-old color line problem in America has been its doctrine that Negroes are a part of the country as a whole. The inevitable discriminations notwithstanding, this thought has been driven home in thousands of communities by a thousand specific acts. For the first time in their lives, government has taken on meaning and substance for the Negro masses." Similarly, the biographer of the esteemed black scholar Charles S. Johnson has noted that "from the first emergency relief efforts, to the construction of the earliest public housing projects, to the enrollment of people of all races in the work projects . . . , Negroes could sense that *their* government, however careful it might be in confronting southern political sensibilities, sought to be inclusive, not racially exclusive, in seeing that African Americans received a fairer share of New Deal economic and social assistance."[13]

The Roosevelt administration, for all its grievous shortcomings, brought numerous benefits to African Americans in the region. During the fall of 1933, federal relief programs supported more than one-quarter of the black citizens of South Carolina, and in North Carolina towns with populations above 25,000, African Americans filled nearly two-thirds of the relief rolls. By the end of the decade, the WPA, which Robert Weaver called a "godsend," was the chief source of income for a million black families, many of them in the South. At a time when white state legislators were trimming budgets at the expense of African Americans, New Deal spending saved black schools in the South. Half of the housing built by the federal government in the South went to African Americans. "The response of the Black Belt employer to the NRA was better than might have been expected," concluded the sociologist Arthur Raper, in part because hostility to paying black workers the same minimum wage as whites was offset by the consideration that the employer "was personally enthusiastic about the president, who in neighborly fashion calls Georgia his southern home."[14]

Historians fully aware of the contribution of the Roosevelt administration to the perpetuation of racism, and dismayed by it, have nonetheless pointed out that the New Deal made a big difference for African Americans in the section. Anthony Badger has observed: "While New Deal agencies may have discriminated against blacks in the South, they provided blacks with greater assistance than they had ever received before. . . . State and local welfare agencies had essentially ignored black needs before 1933. . . . The Public Works Administration [PWA] spent proportionately more on projects for southern whites than for southern blacks, yet it spent four times as much on building black schools and hospitals between 1933 and 1936 as had been spent by governments in the previous 30 years." Similarly, a historian assessing the impact of the New Deal on blacks in Texas acknowledged that discrimination persisted, but declared, "The amazing factor, and the more significant one, was the degree to which Negroes were able to obtain benefits provided through federal legislation." Blacks had good reason to resent the pattern of segregation set by the CCC with Roosevelt's connivance. But such behavior was familiar. What was new was the recruitment of nearly 200,000 black youths in the tree army.[15]

During the Roosevelt era the national government initiated a number of efforts to eliminate racial bias from government programs. In 1933 the president set up an interdepartmental committee on Negro affairs, and that same year Congress, in enacting a federal unemployment relief program, forbade discrimination by "race, color, or creed." Again in 1935 Roosevelt issued an order stipulating that those qualified for the WPA rolls were not to be "discriminated against on any grounds whatsoever." That same year, the Division of Subsistence Homesteads made it known that "no new projects for whites would be constructed until a substantial beginning had been made on communities for Negroes." In 1940 the Civil Service stopped requiring application photographs, sometimes the only way of determining whether an applicant with a name such as "Thomas Johnson" was white or black. The edicts against discrimination in employment were only minimally enforced, but they gave the white South an indication of a new attitude in Washington.[16]

Certain agencies and individual New Dealers made a point of battling discrimination. The PWA under Harold Ickes, who had headed the Chicago NAACP, slowed the pace of discrimination against black construction workers in the South. Compliance from contractors there was better than in the North. In Georgia, where the National Youth Administration (NYA) was headed by two fair-minded administrators, blacks in some counties got more aid per capita than whites, and even Governor Talmadge found it necessary to be obliging when federal officials, including Frances Perkins, brought pressure on him to open CCC opportunities to African Americans. "The National Youth Administration has been as nearly color-blind as a public service agency in the South can be," wrote two leading authorities in 1940. "The Farm Security Administration has also generally worked out its benefits on an equitable racial basis, though in some communities—particularly where there are big plantations—the national policy is not too obvious." Georgia legislators were shocked that whites in New Deal agencies in Atlanta were being "instructed to address negro employees as 'Mr., Miss or Mrs.,'" and the American Legion charged that the "white" and "colored" signs over drinking fountains had been taken down.[17]

The president chose so many blacks for significant administrative posts that even one of his severest critics on racial policy, Ralph Bunche, conceded that the FDR era "represented a radical break with the past," and the prominent black activist W. E. B. Du Bois said that Roosevelt "gave the American Negro a kind of recognition in political life which the Negro had never before received." In eight years the number of African Americans in the federal civil service more than tripled—not to a token amount but to over 150,000—and the president appointed enough blacks to high-ranking positions, creating what one writer has called "the first visible and sizable set of African American bureaucrats," that he gave occasion for talk of a "Black Cabinet." He broke ground by selecting the first black ever chosen for a federal judgeship, William Hastie; picked another black, the father of an NAACP lawyer, to be assistant attorney general; and solicited advice from Mary McLeod Bethune. Early in 1939, Judge Hastie wrote jubilantly to Walter White, "The worst fears of the unregenerate south are being realized."[18]

Roosevelt also named to high office whites who were conspicuously unsympathetic to the reign of Jim Crow, though there is no reason to suppose he chose them on that account. (Nor, on the other hand, did Roosevelt do anything to discourage them in new departures.) Soon after entering the White House, FDR's choice for secretary of the interior, Harold Ickes, upset the white South by desegregating the department's restrooms and cafeterias. Aubrey Williams, a native of Alabama who headed the NYA, showed marked sensitivity to the rights of blacks, as did the FSA administrator Will Alexander. When Roosevelt appointed Frank Murphy attorney general, one of the first things the former mayor of Detroit did was to establish a Civil Rights Section in the Justice Department that subsequently petitioned the Supreme Court to invalidate white primary laws.

The Roosevelt years saw a transformation in the attitudes of a number of whites in the South. Morton Sosna has observed: "The precise relationship between the New Deal and Southern liberals was complex, but one factor stands out. The more white Southerners were attracted to the New Deal, the more liberal they tended to become on the race issue. In general, New Dealers at the national level believed that the powers of government should be expanded in order to promote the general welfare, with special attention given to those citizens who were worst off. A logical extension of this philosophy was support for federal efforts to assist Southern blacks. Although Southern liberals traditionally had been wary of federal intervention in racial matters—memories of Reconstruction lingered—those who became committed New Dealers were an exception." Sosna concluded: "Despite discrimination, the New Deal did set in motion forces that had an unsettling effect upon traditional Southern racial practices."[19]

Above all, Eleanor Roosevelt aroused the wrath of the white South by the example she set of defying the rituals of white supremacy. She was not yet the foe of Jim Crow that she would become. As late as 1944, accused by a southern white of sponsoring racial mixing, she replied that she had "never advocated any social equality whatsoever and I do not know of any Negro leaders who advocate it. In this country we are completely free to choose our companions and no one has any right to interfere." But in the 1930s the First Lady spoke out for an antilynching law and against the poll tax, appeared before groups such as the National Negro Congress, and helped raise funds for *The Crisis*. When in 1939 the snotty Daughters of the American Revolution (DAR) announced it would not permit Marian Anderson or any other black to perform at its Constitution Hall, the principal concert arena in Washington, Eleanor Roosevelt resigned from the DAR in protest. Secretary of the Interior Ickes then invited the renowned contralto to sing at the Lincoln Memorial on Easter Sunday, a historic performance witnessed by tens of thousands in the capital and heard by millions more on network radio. Ickes acted with the full support of the president. "I don't care if she sings from the top of Washington Monument as long as she sings," Roosevelt said.[20]

Though Eleanor Roosevelt was far in advance of her husband, who had different responsibilities, the president, too, gave voice to sentiments on race that displeased much of the white South. "Lynch law is murder," he told a national radio audience. "We do not excuse those in high places or low who condone lynch law." In *The Crisis*, Du Bois said that in spite of FDR's "dependence upon the bourbon and reactionary South for his political salvation," he had borne witness as his predecessors had not. "It took war, riot and upheaval to make Wilson say one small word about lynching," Du Bois observed. "Nothing ever induced Herbert Hoover to say anything on the subject worth saying." Franklin Roosevelt, though, "has declared frankly that lynching is murder. We all knew it, but it is unusual to have a President of the United States admit it. These things give us hope." Walter White, too, praised Roosevelt's "magnificent and uncompromising denunciation of lynching," and noted that the president had also heeded a request that he incorporate a condemnation of lynching in his message to Congress in January 1934. That behavior carried into his second term. "Whatever romantic notion southern senators held that an antilynching bill would be a hot potato for Roosevelt disappeared in January, 1938, when he gave it his firm support," Freidel has written. Even after a filibuster killed the measure, Roosevelt informed the press that he had been telling senators that the least they should do would be to empower the attorney general or create a standing committee to investigate mob violence.[21]

Roosevelt spoke out vigorously on behalf of voting rights as well. In 1937 the president backed Claude Pepper's campaign to get rid of the poll tax in Florida, and the next year he wrote an open letter in support of Brooks Hays's drive in Arkansas against poll taxes which, he said, were "inevitably contrary to fundamental democracy and its representative form of government in which we believe." In a statement clearly directed at the South, he declared: "The right to vote must be open to all our citizens irrespective of race, color, or creed—without tax or artificial restriction of any kind. The sooner we get to that basis of political equality, the better it will be for the country as a whole."[22]

World War II revealed the limitations of FDR's attitude. In October 1940 Roosevelt issued a statement: "The policy of the War Department is not to intermingle colored and white enlisted personnel in the same regimental organizations. This policy has been proven satisfactory over a long period of years and to make changes would produce situations destructive to morale and detrimental to the preparation for national defense." When the North Carolinian Jonathan Daniels urged him to denounce the Detroit race riots of 1943 that had taken so many lives, the president would say nothing. A generation later, Justice Thurgood Marshall, reflecting on the years when he was attorney for the NAACP, said that "Roosevelt didn't have a fucking clue as to the explosive tensions that were building up."[23]

The outbreak of war in 1939, though, also prodded Roosevelt to move in other directions. In 1940, in a special message to Congress, he called attention to a directive of the National Defense Advisory Commission banning racial discrimination in defense industries. That same year, he instructed the War Department to issue a statement insisting on equal opportunity for blacks in the armed services, though, in truth, World War II was largely fought with a Jim Crow army. In 1941, under pressure from A. Philip Randolph and the threat of a march on Washington, Roosevelt issued Executive Order 8802 requiring "full and equitable participation of all workers in defense agencies, without discrimination because of race, creed, color, or national origin," and, to carry out this directive, he created a Fair Employment Practices Committee (FEPC). Not since Reconstruction days had there been such an edict. Only reluctantly, tardily, inadequately, and under coercion did Roosevelt take these steps. "But the fact remained," a historian has pointed out, "that for thirteen million Negroes . . . FDR did respond. And perhaps in no other act of Roosevelt's four administrations was the president so politically in advance of the majority of his own party as in his creation of the FEPC." In 1943 Roosevelt strengthened the FEPC by extending its scope and authorizing funds for opening fifteen field offices. Though the agency was limited in what it could achieve, it aroused intense sectional animosity when in June 1942 it dared to invade the Deep South by holding hearings in Birmingham, and when, despite a race riot set off by white workers, the FEPC and other federal agencies insisted that black artisans be employed in skilled positions. Roosevelt never gave the committee the kind of support it required to be truly effective. One scholar has written about "the crippling debilities for which Roosevelt was ultimately accountable." Yet a powerful northern congressman later remembered that FDR's last request to him came on the morning of his death when Jonathan Daniels called on him to say that Roosevelt wanted him to do his utmost to get legislation for a permanent FEPC through the Rules Committee.[24]

In her 1939 study of "Cottonville," the cultural anthropologist Hortense Powdermaker concluded:

> Because of its more active part in their lives, many Negroes have come more and more to direct toward the government their hopes for the future. Roosevelt has become the representative and symbol of these hopes. When he first spoke of the forgotten man, most of the colored people in the community thought he meant the Negro. Some still think so, and feel that with crop diversification and Federal relief, the forgotten man has begun to be remembered. Although they have no voice in the government, and find no security through its legal institutions, government activities arouse their lively interest and something close to confidence.
>
> For these Negroes, the Federal administration has combined the rather incongruous elements of paternal benevolence and revolutionary change. In striking at the deep-rooted tradition of the one-crop system and the already weakening habit of Negro dependence upon beneficent white individuals, it has introduced the most drastic changes that have appeared in the economic situation during the past ten years.[25]

A generation later, Walter Lord, after noting all the ways that the NRA, the AAA, the TVA, and the Federal Housing Administration (FHA) discriminated, wrote that, nonetheless, African Americans understood that Roosevelt left the impression of a "new atmosphere. At last somebody really seemed to care." He went on:

On February 19, 1934, a Mississippi Negro farmer named Sylvester Harris, facing a mortgage foreclosure, knew just what to do. Taking his last $10, he put through a call to the White House. He did not even consider it unusual when he was ultimately plugged through to the President himself. "A man is getting ready to take my land," he explained. "I want to know what to do and the papers say call you. . . ."

"Sylvester," Roosevelt quietly replied, "I'll investigate and you'll hear from me." A flurry of White House calls followed, and in due course Harris' farm was saved.[26]

The episode, though freighted with paternalism, quickly became legend. The blues guitarist "Memphis Minnie" recorded a ballad, "Sylvester and His Mule Blues," and a black preacher delivered a sermon on the tale that included the passage:

I wanna talk about our President Roosevelt,
And when I said that, I'm speakin' free.
I'm a man who is now a half a century of age.
And never have I witnessed,
Never have I read, in history,
Of a man greater than our President Roosevelt.
When I say that, I mean he's a friend to everybody,
Both white and black, both brown, everybody.

The president himself was delighted when on Thanksgiving Day in 1934 in Warm Springs he received a plump turkey from Sylvester Harris, a gift that arrived faithfully each year until FDR's death. Nearly a quarter of a century later, Harris told an interviewer that he would always hold on to his farm. "I'll never let it go," he said, "because President Roosevelt wanted me to have it."[27]

Scholars who have scrutinized the flawed Roosevelt performance have underscored the "new atmosphere" highlighted by Walter Lord. Before Roosevelt, David Goldfield has noted, African Americans in the South were virtually wholly at the mercy of the white power structure, but "when [the black sharecropper] Ned Cobb looked in his mailbox for a check from the federal government to cover costs for fertilizer and seed, one strand of that web of dependence began to disintegrate." Acknowledging that the Roosevelt era brought only "limited substantive benefits," Doug McAdam has written that "the symbolic importance . . . would be hard to overstate. It was responsible for nothing less than a cognitive revolution within the black population regarding the prospects for changes in this country's racial status quo." He explained:

> It is simply impossible for us to comprehend the depths of official racism that prevailed prior to 1930. Accordingly, there is a tendency to disparage the federal actions of the New Deal era as so much tokenism and empty rhetoric. There is much truth in this criticism. What such characterizations miss is the dramatic *symbolic* contrast between these actions and those of earlier administrations. . . . To observers of the day the shift was nothing short of extraordinary, signifying the first real prospects for change on racial issues since Reconstruction. In writing of his return to America in 1939, Paul Robeson describes the change in "climate" he sensed upon his arrival. "Conditions were far from ideal," he writes, "they were not even so much changed in fact as they appeared to be, in the hopefulness of liberals and Negro leaders. But change was in the air, and that was the best sign of all."[28]

On a tour of the South a year after Robeson came back, a probing African-American investigator, J. Saunders Redding, got an earful from a black official with the TVA about the blatantly racist hiring policies of that presumably model agency, but when Redding inspected a TVA town in western Kentucky, he found: "Nothing at Gilbertsville looked as if it were going to hell. The houses, the school, the recreation building, the hospital, all of which I was told were temporary, looked stronger and were far better equipped than similar facilities for Negroes elsewhere. The children I saw in the school looked brighter, healthier than other children, and the housewives I saw sweeping the fronts, hanging clothes, or simply talking across their yards looked happy; and perhaps . . . this was because their poor little was the greatest plenty they had ever known."[29]

Though Roosevelt invited well-merited criticism for doing too little, too late, the New Deal, concluded Gunnar Myrdal, "changed the whole configuration of the Negro problem. For almost the first time in the history of the nation the state has done something substantial in a social way without excluding the Negro." He was not alone in that view. "At no time since the curtain had dropped on the Reconstruction drama had government focused as much attention upon the Negro's basic needs as did the New Deal," Henry Lee Moon concluded. Under "the charismatic Franklin Delano Roosevelt and the New Deal," another African-American commentator, Alex Haley, wrote, "a black population impoverished by the century's greatest depression was swept from their traditional political loyalties" because "the alphabetical array of NRA, WPA, CCC and FHA represented not only new governmental presences but new hopes. . . . For the first time, the first time *ever*, really, the black masses were being dealt with more as human beings, as Americans with the same needs and rights as white people."[30]

IV

Many southern blacks offered enthusiastic testimony to the truth of that statement. Even before FDR took office, a Jackson, Mississippi, man who described himself as "one of your old darkies" wrote the president-elect: "I did everything to help you get this office that a Negro could do. I am so glad until I don't know what I do. I am an ex-soldier and I am wounded and I can't get anyone to fix me up. . . . Mr. Roosevelt, I am naked and have been hungary for three days. Send me overalls and underwear and send and get me out of Miss. because it is the worst place that I ever been in all my life." Another Mississippi black wrote Roosevelt in 1934: "You must be a god Sent man. You have made a great change since you have ben President. . . . you ben Bread for the hungry and clothes for the naked."[31]

These sentiments touched off one of the most momentous transfers of party identification in the country's history. An elderly black sharecropper from Yadkinville, North Carolina, told an interviewer: "Ever since the war, the colored folks has looked on the elephant as the animal that helps 'em. But I'm coming to believe that the elephant may be all right in Africa but the American niggers had better stay close to the American mule. I honors Lincoln for freein' us. But the Republic party has changed. The GOP stands for the rich man. They jist counted on the colored man voting right and didn't do nothing for us. Roosevelt is for all the poor folks, white and black. You know, as well as I do, that they ain't one rich nigger in a thousand. If the Democrats keep bein' friendly to the poor, there soon won't be one Republican in a thousand colored people." In much the same spirit, a Georgia sharecropper, who had been raised in the party of the Great Emancipator, said he had stayed loyal to the Republicans until "President Roosevelt brought . . . the Negro out in the world. I figured I should be what my daddy was. [But] President Roosevelt did a miracle, put bread in our mouths."[32]

Throughout his years in the White House, countless impoverished African Americans in the South made Roosevelt the receptacle of their aspirations even if they could do nothing to support him because they were denied the suffrage. "They's talked more politics since Mistuh Roosevelt been in than ever befo,'" a black worker reported. "I been here 20 years, but since WPA, the Negro sho' has started talkin' 'bout politics." A Mississippi memoirist recalled: "In the 1940s neighbors would talk across the fences in black neighborhoods such as Balance Due about President Franklin Delano Roosevelt and how someday he would make it possible for blacks to vote freely. . . . Neighbors also talked about possible jobs for young black folks with the CCC and WPA and about FDR's Black Cabinet." In rural Alabama some years earlier, an elderly black man had told an interviewer: "President Roosevelt, he's a fine man, he believes in giving a man a chance. . . . Yas sir, de President he wants us ter even be able ter read, us old folks. Way back yonder in slavery de paderole would git a nigger fer tryin' ter learn ter read." Ruminating on these days, Ned Cobb remarked, "President Roosevelt, that was one President I liked—of course, I didn't vote, never voted in my life. But I felt that President Roosevelt, he was different to a heap of Presidents that I have watched along through life." This was a common view. "F.D.R. has helped us in so many ways that we no longer feel forgotten," said a black woman called "the central character in the community" in that same cotton county. "If I did vote I surely would vote for Roosevelt to be president another term."[33]

The small numbers of African Americans in the South who were able to cast ballots left no doubt about what FDR meant to them by abandoning the party of Lincoln in droves. In 1936 a ninety-year-old black woman in South Carolina walked two miles to contribute her last quarter to FDR's campaign. "I just got to give 25 cents to elect Mr. Roosevelt," she explained, "because if them Republicans get in agin, I don't expect ever to have this much money." A South Carolina election official reported: "Every Negro I have registered so far has said he would vote for President Roosevelt. They say Roosevelt saved them from starvation, gave them aid when they were all in distress." Eight years later, when the president was a candidate for what would turn out to be his final term, South Carolina blacks offered even more vivid evidence. They organized a contesting delegation to the regular white delegation to the Democratic national convention committed, "if these be necessary to continue truly democratic government," to as many as ten terms for Franklin D. Roosevelt.[34]

v

Scholars have also questioned the perception that Roosevelt was a benefactor of disadvantaged southerners, white as well as black—the jobless, the farmers, and the workers. They note that AAA benefits went chiefly to big landowners, and the program contributed to large-scale displacement of sharecroppers from the cotton fields; one historian, Pete Daniel, has grouped the AAA in its impact on southern agriculture with flood, drought, and the boll weevil. As the photos of Dorothea Lange starkly reveal, the New Deal left many impoverished rural folk untouched. Early in 1934, an Alabaman reported: "Homes without a match or a cake of soap, men too weak from hunger to work, naked children, people taking their meals from blackberry bushes and plum thickets, tattered cotton rags for winter clothing." The FSA sought to bail out tenant farmers, but Congress kept it so poorly funded that in all of Virginia only forty-six tenants got FSA loans. "At this miserly rate of support," the historian Jack Temple Kirby has remarked, "the elimination of tenancy and the achievement of the Jeffersonian dream of an America of stable freeholders would have required about four hundred years."[35]

Industrial workers, too, critics have maintained, failed in their effort to unionize southern factories because the Roosevelt administration gave them too little support. Certainly the mill workers who went down to defeat in their courageous efforts to build a union in 1934 had nothing to thank the president for. One historian has written, "The New Deal did not provide a model for all seasons, and the failure of cotton textile unionism marked one of the important limits of reform that bounded the possibilities of change that could be achieved through the New Deal," while another has stated: "The Depression era was . . . a lost decade for the Southern industrial worker. He secured no advance in organization, wages or fringe benefits, although hours were reduced and child labor abated. Not until 1939 would the number of Southern factory jobs return to the level of 1929, and even then wages still fell short of pre-Depression figures."[36]

Other writers, though, have countered that FDR's policies bettered the lives of the impoverished. Arthur Raper, in his careful contemporary study of two Alabama Black Belt counties, commented that, despite the shortcomings of the Roosevelt programs, the rural South had "reaped real benefits from the New Deal," in particular because it had lifted this chronically low-income region close to national standards. Subsequently, Rexford Tugwell observed: "West Georgia's farm people got less help from the New Deal than Franklin had hoped. But they did share in emergency expenditures, and whatever additional federal help Franklin could give them, he did. Erosion was checked and the price of cotton rose; the boll weevil was ultimately checked. One of the WPA community projects was set up nearby." From 1933 to 1935, the U.S. government accounted for 90 percent of relief spending by federal, state, and local agencies in the South, only 60 percent in the Northeast. "Relief literally kept the social fabric of Birmingham stitched together during the 1930s," one historian has written. "For chronically poor whites fortunate enough to get on relief," another historian has noted, "life was better than ever before." In one Georgia county white employers complained that the WPA provided better wages and hours than traditional farm labor. Such considerations led Anthony Badger to conclude: "Because of the South's poverty and the matching requirements of so many New Deal programmes, the South did not fare so well on a per capita basis. But as a percentage of the spending on relief and welfare in the southern states, the federal government's contribution was far greater than in any other region and the farm programme undoubtedly rescued the rural South from disaster."[37]

Southerners who gave high scores to FDR's agricultural policies did so because they were a marked change from what they had known before. A Georgia farmer who reported that he was faring well under the AAA recalled that when "Herbert Hoover turned me loose and Franklin Roosevelt picked me up, I was hunting cottontail rabbits . . . with a borrowed bitch." An Alabama tenant farmer who was also a country parson wrote Roosevelt: "We are just a crowd of old hard working farmers who could hardly live until . . . the last few years. But I wish to extend to you my sincere thanks Honorable sir for these great things your noble brain being guided by unseen power has done and if I possibly can get my 14 years back poll tax paid up you will certainly get my vote and influence in the next election." Acknowledging that "agricultural conditions failed to improve significantly," one scholar has noted that "southern farmers recognized that without the New Deal they were potentially in even worse trouble." To sustain the farmer, the federal government subsidized the growers of cotton, tobacco, peanuts, sugar, and rice, all of them southern staples, while the Rural Electrification Administration (REA), by bringing electricity to the countryside for the first time, decidedly improved the quality of rural living. Wealthy growers fared a great deal better than their tenants, but David Goldfield has seen in the decline of sharecropping in the age of Roosevelt nothing less than "a second emancipation edict."[38]

Roosevelt was not shy about presenting himself as the savior of the cotton grower. In late November 1933 from Warm Springs, he wrote Colonel House: "This Southland has a smile on its face. Ten cent cotton has stopped foreclosures, saved banks and started people definitely on the upgrade. That means all the way from Virginia to Texas. Sears-Roebuck sales in Georgia are 110 percent above 1932." Two years later, in an address in Atlanta, he bragged that cotton prices had risen since 1932 from 4 1/2 cents to 12 cents, adding, "I wonder what cotton would be selling at today if during these past three years we had continued to produce fifteen or sixteen or seventeen million bales each year, adding to our own surplus, adding to the world surplus, and driving the cotton farmers of the Southland into bankruptcy and starvation."[39]

Though FDR's policies undeniably worked out far better for big planters than for small growers, he did put considerable effort into helping farmers who were less well off, especially in the South. At Warm Springs in December 1935, a delegation of Georgia farmers called on Roosevelt and, as they departed, told the press that the president was in favor of farm tenancy legislation. Early in 1936 Gardner Jackson reported that FDR wanted the measure "hurried through" because of "the need for it in the South, politically as well as socially." Roosevelt ordered Secretary Wallace to create a Committee on Farm Tenancy and put liberals in dominant positions in the group. When the House Agriculture Committee scaled back the plan drastically, Roosevelt badgered Congress for a stronger law. In the end, he had to be content with a badly eviscerated bill, but to achieve even that much for the southern tenant farmer he exercised pressure that, one conservative Republican congressman complained, "surpassed anything he had ever known in his public life." Under the resultant legislation, more southerners were able to buy farms than residents of any other section.[40]

In part as a result of FDR's lively interest in soil conservation, but more because of technological forces and of the unanticipated consequences of New Deal policies, southern agriculture changed markedly. "Erosion control, terracing, and contour-plowing came into vogue in the hills and slopes of Dixie as never before," a liberal commentator noted a decade after FDR came to power. "The New Deal . . . has brought about an unprecedented soil saving in the South, where more land has been wasted by man than in all the rest of the country." Nearly two decades later, Thomas D. Clark wrote: "Never again after 1933 was southern cotton farming to assume its historic role of enslaving so vast an army of southerners. Fields which had grown cotton for a century now burgeoned with grass and white-faced cattle. . . . New soil conservation practices created a fantastic modern design of terrace whorls on red hills. Lands that were worn to bed clay for so many years that no one recalled their virgin state now turned green."[41]

Some industrial workers, too, saw a change in their lot. The Fair Labor Standards Act affected many times more workers in the South than in other regions, and the National Industrial Recovery Act sparked what one writer called "the

greatest movement of organized labor ever south of the Mason-Dixon line."
Though FDR's reputation as a champion of unionism was inflated, his manner
and his rhetoric gave credence to the claim that he wanted workers to join
unions and that he would back them if they did. "If I had got up before you ten
years ago as I do now and attempted to organize you, mill owners would have
taken steps to get rid of me," said a union leader at a large Labor Day rally in
Macon, Georgia, in 1934. "Now, thank God, we have the support of Franklin D.
Roosevelt, who sympathizes with us, and recognizes our right to organize and
who, I believe, is the agent of God." Despite the disappointing way Roosevelt
responded to the great textile strike of 1934, one historian has asserted that "the
New Deal was certainly the savior of the South Carolina textile worker. Under
the NRA, his wages increased, his hours decreased, he no longer had to compete with child labor, and he could join a union for collective bargaining." So
effective was the NRA in narrowing the gap between the wage scale in the
South and that in the rest of the country that Rupert Vance referred to the ma-
lign pre-Roosevelt era as "B.C.—Before Codes."[42]

Writers have especially remarked on the stark difference before and after
Roosevelt in particular communities. John Havener has noted that in Kentucky's "bloody Harlan," because of the New Deal, "union men, who in the
spring of 1937 could not safely travel the county or occupy a hotel room in the
county seat, by 1938 roamed the county soliciting union membership at will."
When in 1939 miners walked out, the WPA distributed surplus food, including
a two-week ration of thirty pounds of grapefruit. "The Roosevelt administration's support of the Harlan strike," he concludes, "accounted in large part for
the difference between union defeat in 1931 and union victory in 1939."[43]

Similarly, Charles Martin has written of one open shop Alabama town:
"Had Gadsden somehow been left to itself, the city and its major industries
probably could have destroyed all incipient union movements. Three successive
waves of unionization swept over Gadsden, the first spawned by Section 7a, the
second by the Wagner Act and the CIO, and the third by the wartime labor
policies of the federal government. . . . Within a few years union membership
at Gadsden's three major industrial plants included over 90 percent of eligible
workers. . . . By 1950 Gadsden had developed into a community about which
its boosters had never dreamed, a solid union town in the most antiunion section of the nation." Asked to explain how Georgia mill hands got the courage
to build a union at grave risk, one of them expressed a common sentiment:
"Roosevelt, he told 'em to organize." Douglas Flamming, while pointing out

that "Roosevelt did no such thing," has concluded in writing of the inspiration of FDR's leadership: "The demise of child labor and the advent of free high school education; Social Security and unemployment compensation; laws ordaining minimum wages, eight-hour work days, and overtime pay; federally sanctioned unions and political labor—all of these . . . dealt mill-village paternalism a mortal blow."[44]

VI

Roosevelt created growing disquietude in the southern political establishment by indications that, in catering to blacks and other ethnic groups, he was building so strong a base in the industrial North he could dispense with the South altogether. Southerners had long assumed that they had a larger claim than any other section on the Democratic Party. In Grover Cleveland's two victories and in Woodrow Wilson's 1916 campaign, the South had contributed the huge chunk of at least 40 percent of the winning totals. But all four times Roosevelt ran, he could have lost the entire South and still won. By the 1930s, the electoral votes of only four northern states, each with large concentrations of blacks—New York, Pennsylvania, Illinois, and Ohio—outnumbered those of all the former Confederacy. "The South," Dewey Grantham has written, "was suddenly changed by the partisan realignment of the 1930s from a majority faction in a minority party to a minority faction in a majority party."[45]

For a century, the South had taken comfort in the protection provided by the requirement that to become the Democratic presidential nominee a candidate needed two-thirds of the votes of delegates to the national convention, not just a simple majority, but in the age of Roosevelt that stipulation came into jeopardy. Many southern politicians viewed this development with consternation because they cherished the two-thirds rule for permitting them to say "no" to a candidate who might trample upon the interests of the white South. On one occasion, at a meeting of the Democratic National Committee, a southern governor explained, "We have always felt that since we never have a candidate from the South, we should at least have the right to veto a fellow whom we do not like." Hence, they were angered when at the 1932 convention FDR's managers sought to repeal the rule peremptorily. The *Memphis Press-Scimitar* pictured Governor Roosevelt as, in the words of one writer, "a calloused trickster." Confronted by a southern rebellion led by Pat Harrison of Mississippi, the governor was compelled to back down, only to return to the fray in 1936 much better organized.[46]

This time, Roosevelt had the ideal leader to head an all-out assault on the two-thirds rule. FDR's forces placed in the strategic spot of chairman of the 1936 convention rules committee Senator Bennett Champ Clark of Missouri who had seen the 1912 Baltimore convention employ the rule to deny his father the presidential nomination, though he had a majority of the votes for eight ballots. Champ Clark's son had been nursing this grievance for nearly a quarter of a century because he knew that, with the Republicans split, nomination would have put his father in the White House. Save for the two-thirds rule, "my father would have been elected in 1912," he said. "This country would not have gone into the World War." Senator Clark took on his assignment in 1936 with the zeal of a man bent on a family mission of redemption. One newspaper referred to "young Clark, cast for the moment as a modern Hamlet . . . avenging his father's political death."[47]

Four southern states—Alabama, Georgia, South Carolina, and Texas—led the defense of the two-thirds rule. The campaign for recision, they charged, was a sinister plot by FDR and his henchmen to punish the South, which had been loyal to the party, by turning over control to populous northern states that often went Republican. Congressman E. E. Cox of Georgia warned that repealing the rule would be the first step toward "a proposal to outlaw the suffrage laws of the South," and some southerners circulated the rumor that Roosevelt wanted to get rid of the provision in order to manipulate the 1940 convention, perhaps even to seek a third term.[48]

Other southerners, though, in surprising numbers, favored abrogation. At hearings during the Democratic convention, the foremost advocate of abolishing the provision was a southerner: Congressman Robert L. Doughton of North Carolina, chairman of the House Ways and Means Committee. When the roll was called, states voting to rescind included Arkansas, Kentucky, Louisiana, and North Carolina. A former Louisiana senator who had witnessed the 1912 nominating process later said that he "always thought that very unfair to Mr. Clark," and believed that ending that anomaly "certainly seems common sense and fairness." The Tennessee editor George Fort Milton went still further in calling the two-thirds rule "that Child of Hate" because, though regarded as a shield of the South, it had served at the protracted Madison Square Garden convention in 1924 to permit the followers of the New Yorker, Al Smith, to block the nomination of the favorite of the South and West, William Gibbs McAdoo. (It had also failed to prevent the choice of Smith in 1928.)[49]

The South did not put up much of a struggle against repeal for more than one reason. Some found it hard to work up concern about the nominating process in a year when Roosevelt was certain to be named again. Others, such as the administration wheel horse Joe Robinson, did not want to put themselves at odds with the leader of their highly successful party. Southern liberals, unsurprisingly, welcomed the reform. Consequently, when the resolution reached the floor, administration Democrats in the South coalesced with northerners and westerners to overwhelm the opposition. There was not even a debate on this momentous departure. From Mexico City, FDR's ambassador, the veteran Tar Heel editor Josephus Daniels, wrote the president: "I am glad to be living and in fine fettle to see this anachronism ended."[50]

A sizeable segment of the southern political elite, though, never reconciled itself to the change. Even before the convention met, Colonel Henry Breckinridge protested, "The South has been bought, paid for, and sold down the river. . . . The scrapping of the two-thirds rule means the future impotence of the South in the councils of the party." Afterward, the Democratic Party chairman in Florida lamented "crippling the South in the Convention," and Senator Bailey declared: "The abolition of the two-thirds rule will enable the Northern and Western Democrats to control the party, nominate its candidates and write its platforms. All of this will come out in 1940. Meantime, we cannot help ourselves." Less than two years after the convention, Bailey said of his party: "Since the abolition of the Two-Thirds Rule, there is grave danger that it will fall into the hands of very objectionable men whose politics are entirely distasteful to the Southern Democracy. They get elected by the negro vote in New York, Pennsylvania, Boston, Chicago, and the cities of the Middle West. They are common fellows of the baser sort."[51]

Quadrennially over the next generation, southerners were to make futile attempts to reinstate the requirement. As late as 1960, the governor of Texas set as the price for supporting Lyndon Johnson for the White House that the majority leader go on record for restoring the two-thirds rule. Throughout this period, brooding white supremacists sought explanations for why the alteration had been put through so easily. The abandonment of the two-thirds rule "was adopted without a fight by the delegates from the South," a racist Alabama lawyer alleged. "What went on behind the scenes to obtain this act of self abnegation?" he asked darkly.[52]

The results of the 1936 election alarmed some southern politicos even more than abolition of the two-thirds rule. To be sure, most southerners expressed delight in FDR's landslide. A few, though, were disturbed by the implications of so great a victory. If the popular vote in the South had been subtracted from Roosevelt's total, he would still have had a margin of more than six million, and he would, having carried all but two of the states in the Union, have prevailed overwhelmingly in the Electoral College.

In years to come, southern publicists would point to the emergence of "the FDR coalition" in 1936 as the critical moment when Democrats in the North and West first recognized that there was more to be gained from attracting African-American precincts in big bloc industrial states than in relying on their longtime allies in Dixie. In 1943 John Temple Graves alluded to "the cold arithmetic which makes the Northern Negro a more profitable object of political cajolery than the South," and in 1949, after the party splintered over civil rights, he wrote: "A break in the Solid South became inevitable with Franklin Roosevelt's capture of the Northern Negro vote for the national Democratic party. Once won, that vote was sure to be sought in elections thereafter with concessions . . . the South would not endure. No longer could the South look to the Democratic party to protect or wink at its point of view on the Negro question."[53]

The 1936 election revealed "the cold arithmetic" starkly. The South contributed nearly 93 percent of the Democratic Party's electoral total in 1924, less than 24 percent in 1936. The situation in Congress was no less striking. In 1918 the South had accounted for twenty-six of the thirty-seven seats held by Democrats in the U.S. Senate; in 1936, their identical contribution of twenty-six made up a far smaller proportion of seventy-five. In 1920 nearly every Democrat in the House of Representatives hailed from the former Confederacy (107 of 131). In the 1920s, "with the exception of the congressmen from New York City and Boston, the Democratic party in the House was a southern party," Jimmy Byrnes remembered. When the 1936 ballots were counted, southerners had been reduced to a minority—with 116 out of 333. As one historian has put it, the 1936 FDR coalition "marked . . . the beginning of the political emancipation of the national Democratic party from the grip of southerners." These figures (and their import) would, before long, turn millions of southern whites away from the party of their ancestors.[54]

THREE

LIBERALIZING DIXIE

I

Secure in the knowledge of his landslide triumph in 1936, Roosevelt set out in his second term toward a goal that had not been fully apparent in his first four years: to liberalize the South, especially the Democratic Party leadership in the region. In September 1936, commenting on a conference of progressives in Chicago organized by Senator Robert M. La Follette Jr. of Wisconsin that endorsed him for reelection, the president told David Lilienthal: "When Bob talked to me about the conference, I urged him to include [Hugo] Black [of Alabama] and [Maury] Maverick [of Texas]. They say that the Democratic Party can't be liberal because of the South, but things are moving toward progression in the South. One of the things that I am proud of is that I made men like Joe Robinson and Pat Harrison swallow me hook, line, and sinker. But the young people in the South, and the women, they are thinking about economic problems and will be part of a liberal group in the South."[1]

II

Roosevelt sought to put the future of the South in the hands of liberals, even if it meant breaching custom by infringing upon the prerogative of Senate Democrats to choose their own leaders. When in July 1937 Joe Robinson had a fatal heart attack, he not only doomed FDR's campaign to pack the Supreme Court, but also precipitated a fight over who would succeed him as Senate majority leader, a contest that pitted Pat Harrison of Mississippi against Alben Barkley of Kentucky. The majority leader had always been regarded as an officer of the Senate, not as the president's liege. Nelson Aldrich had been his party's leader in the upper house, not Theodore Roosevelt's vassal. The prideful legislators did not imagine that any president would have the temerity to meddle in their internal affairs. But in this contest between two southern senators, FDR determined that so much was at stake, for the South as well as for the New Deal, that he had to intrude.

With oddsmakers forecasting a Harrison victory by a tiny margin, the Democratic Party chairman Jim Farley thought Roosevelt would be well advised to let the Mississippian prevail—and for more than one reason. To begin with, the president owed his nomination in 1932 in no small part to Harrison, who, at a moment when the Mississippi delegation was cracking, had gotten out of bed and, not yet fully dressed, caught a taxi to the Chicago arena and cast the decisive vote that saved FDR. Furthermore, as chairman of the Senate Finance Committee, he had skillfully shepherded through both the National Industrial Recovery Act and the Social Security Act. Harrison had been faithful enough in Roosevelt's first term to be denounced by *Business Week* as the president's "mouthpiece," and as recently as May 1937, Harry Hopkins had told a Mississippi audience that, save for Joe Robinson, "no man in Washington . . . has done more for the New Deal than Pat Harrison."[2]

Suave, shrewd, the "Grey Fox of the Delta" could be counted on to cadge votes from conservatives for controversial Roosevelt measures that the Kentuckian would not get. Harrison, wrote a correspondent from the Deep South, "was a crony type, and . . . a great favorite in the Senate club rooms and cloak rooms." For much longer than Barkley, he had been taken into the senior councils of the party. While twelve senators outranked Barkley, who had not come to the Senate until 1927, Harrison had been there since 1919. Six-feet three, round-shouldered, high-domed, pot-bellied, and with a receding chin, he shuffled about the Senate floor slovenly dressed, chewing an unlit cigar, like a horse trader at a county fairgrounds. Yet Harrison was regarded as so trustworthy that on occasions when Republicans were in the majority he was permitted to vote absent Democrats. Harrison, said one Republican admirer, "always gave the country an even break when he could possibly afford to."[3]

To the New Dealers the most important distinction between the men lay in outlook. Each, to be sure, had an all but impeccable record of support for Roosevelt measures. Barkley's votes, however, seemed to come from conviction, Harrison's from considerations of party loyalty and expediency. Harrison had been visibly unhappy about FDR's "soak the rich" tax message in 1935, and in 1937 he had kicked over the traces to impose restrictions on the president's relief program. His wit had a sarcasm, even cynicism, that chilled some of the more ardent liberals. Though few could quarrel with his voting performance up to then, it seemed only a matter of time before he would wander into the conservative corral. "A man's man," he was an expert card player and won large sums at golf, sometimes perhaps because those who sought his influence deliberately lost to him. Harold Ickes caught the suspicion of many of his fellow New Dealers neatly in saying that "Senator Harrison is one of the Baruch collection of southern 'old masters,'" that is, senators the Wall Street financier Bernard Baruch, who boasted a "barony" in South Carolina, had put in obligation to him.[4]

Liberals had far more faith in the staying power of Alben Barkley, who was in nobody's pocket. In the land of bonded bourbon, he was an ardent dry; in the country of burley, he did not smoke; and in the turf of the Kentucky Derby, he had campaigned for governor as a foe of legalized betting on race horses. "Alben golfs a little, but not enough to corrupt his morals," a columnist noted. A spokesman for rural interests who had emerged as a tribune of urban liberalism, he had reason enough to feel sympathy for the impoverished. Born in a log house in backwoods Kentucky, he had worked as a boy in the dark fired tobacco rows and wheat fields and had put himself through obscure Marvin College by laboring as a janitor. (BARKLEY SWEPT HERE reads a sign commemorating the site.) When Harrison deserted Roosevelt in the struggle for relief legislation in 1937, Barkley rallied support for the jobless. It may also have been relevant that Barkley, who came from an Ohio River town in the northwestern corner of a border state, did not have the Deep South Harrison's hang-ups on race. Barkley, perhaps correctly, believed that the president was distressed that Harrison, who sat at the desk that had once been Jefferson Davis's, did not share his concern about poll taxes and lynchings.[5]

Barkley drew virtually all of his support from FDR enthusiasts. One Washington correspondent noted, "Senator Barkley might receive a vote or two from the anti-administration bloc, but to all indications his prospect lies entirely with the administration strength." Heading Barkley's campaign were outspoken advocates of change, notably Hugo Black. Harrison was the candidate of the party veterans; Barkley, the favorite of the younger Democrats. These men, who had come to national prominence in the Great Depression, were often more committed to the New Deal than the old-timers, and they were certainly more conscious of how much they owed their political success to Roosevelt.[6]

Both wings of the party recognized that a great deal was at stake. Victory for Harrison, warned the Washington correspondent of the *Louisville Courier-Journal*, "would be rated as a triumph for the conservative movement to wrest party control from the President," and, declared the progressive columnist Heywood Broun, would cause "a 99.78 percent sabotaging" of all of FDR's plans. A labor leader and former Colorado congressman noted in his diary that the Mississippi senator was "much more reactionary than Barkley. Huey Long once described Harrison as 'a timid thief.'" The character of the Grey Fox's backers also disturbed New Dealers. A conspicuously liberal newspaper said of Harrison: "Vigorously campaigning for him behind the scenes were Bernard M. Baruch, New York financier, and representatives of the National Manufacturers' Association and power interests." From the other side, Woodrow Wilson's secretary, Joseph Tumulty, who had moved considerably to the right since his New Freedom days, wrote Harrison, "It seems to me that we are at the cross-roads and that you may be the instrumentality to point the way to saving and conserving the very precious processes of free Government." Afterward, Senator Bankhead wrote Jimmy Byrnes: "I voted for Pat, largely to stay with my crowd. A radical group of new Senators are trying to take charge of the Senate."[7]

While assuring Harrison that he would be scrupulously neutral, Roosevelt devised a clever way to let his preference be known. In a two-and-a-half-page single-spaced open letter bearing the intimate salutation "Dear Alben," the president, saying, with regard to Robinson's death, that his opponents, instead of manifesting "a decent respect for his memory," were taking "advantage . . . of what, in all decency, should be a period of mourning," asked Barkley to exert his influence for the administration's program. He did so, he said, because the Kentuckian was "acting majority leader," a title Harrison's forces denied that Barkley held. There could be no mistaking that the document, which infuriated FDR's critics, constituted a laying on of hands that was intended to affect the outcome of the rivalry between the two southerners. An hour after it appeared in print, one Harrison man, Morris Sheppard of Texas, told the Mississippi senator that he was switching to Barkley. "I am sorry, Pat, but the President's wishes come first with me," he explained.[8]

Not content with this oblique maneuver, Roosevelt moved directly to line up votes for Barkley, though he did so covertly. The "Dear Alben" letter had eliminated Harrison's advantage but without giving an edge to Barkley. The opposing managers counted thirty-one for Harrison, thirty-one for Barkley, with six senators claimed by both sides and four unknown. To get Barkley what could turn out to be the one more ballot he required, the president decided to concentrate on legislators thought to be under the thumb of city machines that, in return for favors, would do his bidding.

Roosevelt had one particular quarry in mind: Big Bill Dieterich, even though the senator from Illinois was publicly pledged to Harrison and had even promised to make a seconding speech for him. Dieterich, however, needed the support of the Chicago machine headed by Edward Kelly if he expected to be renominated in 1938, and when Mayor Kelly ordered him to switch to Barkley, Dieterich caved in. No one supposed that Windy City politicos would be concerning themselves with a quarrel on Capitol Hill unless they had been egged on by the White House circle, and, in fact, one of FDR's aides—either Harry Hopkins, who controlled WPA funds, or Tommy Corcoran—had phoned Kelly at his Eagle River retreat in Wisconsin to instruct him. On the day before the vote was scheduled, Dieterich had conferred with Harrison on how to muster votes for him, but on the morning of the balloting he regretfully informed the Mississippian that he would be voting for Barkley. Jim Farley, who encountered Dieterich on his way to see Harrison, later recalled, "I never saw a more crestfallen man in my life."[9]

The Democratic caucus proved to be even more spine-tingling than had been anticipated. After over three score senators had filed by in alphabetical order to cast their marked white cards into Carter Glass's crumpled Panama, the two tellers read out the ballots, with the secretary of the conference, Hugo Black, keeping a running tally. The race could not have been closer, as first one, then the other, forged ahead, only to drop back. With every vote but one recorded, the count stood 37–37. The room tensed as the final tiny white card was pulled out. To Barkley, smoking his ever-present pipe, it looked "as big as a bedquilt." As it was unfolded, each senator, he thought, was eyeing him silently. "Barkley!" the teller cried. Barkley bit his pipestem in two. "WON BY ONE," the new majority leader wired his wife. "It took all my will power," he later wrote, "to resist the temptation to sign it, 'DEAR ALBEN'"[10]

Embittered Deep South senators recognized that a number of elements had contributed to the result, but they knew, too, that they would have prevailed if it had not been for the determination of Franklin Roosevelt to give a more liberal cast to Capitol Hill and to the South. Two headlines summed up concisely what had occurred. One read:

VICTORY FOR BARKLEY
IS TRIUMPH FOR F.D.

while the other said:

BARKLEY VOTE
PROVES "MAGIC"
OF ROOSEVELT.[11]

III

Scarcely more than three weeks after meddling in the leadership contest, Roosevelt gave southern conservatives another shock when he named to the first vacancy that opened up on the U.S. Supreme Court during his presidency not a distinguished, uncontroversial jurist but the most liberal southerner in the U.S. Senate, Hugo Lafayette Black of Alabama. "Black," Tommy Corcoran later observed, "was the first of a new breed in Dixie: a prophet of the New South." For some years, he had antagonized the Old Guard by his assaults on corporate interests, and at that very moment he was leading a battle in the Senate for a wages and hours bill that southern industrialists loathed. "His choice," wrote Turner Catledge of the *New York Times*, "presented an opportunity to Roosevelt to put on a 'thumping' New Dealer and to throw him right in the face of certain Southern Democrats who had fought him and were then fighting him on the wages and hours bill."[12]

FDR's effort to pack the Supreme Court, and the ensuing "Constitutional Revolution of 1937," had alarmed the southern elite earlier that year. After the Court gave a broad reading to the commerce power in validating the Wagner Act (the National Labor Relations Act), a Washington correspondent wrote: "The Wagner decision particularly has confronted the Democratic South with the possibility that Congress will enact laws fixing minimum wages and working conditions applicable to . . . cheap Negro labor. . . . To say that this prospect has brought home to the South the ultimate possibilities of the New Deal is picturing the situation mildly. Certainly no development in recent years has so much disturbed the southern representation in Congress as this one." An even more unsettling conclusion had been foreshadowed by an entry in the diary of a grimly anti-FDR Charleston editor on the day the rulings were reported in the press: "Will the U.S. Supreme Court's decision as to the Wagner 'labor relations' law lead to an effort to abolish separation of the races in the textile and some other Southern industries? The Southern followers of Mr. Roosevelt are digging pits into which they will fall—fools and knaves, fools *or* knaves, that they are."[13]

The selection of Black brought these anxieties to a peak. Though in designating an Alabaman—and, as it happened, a former Klansman—for elevation to the highest court, Roosevelt was giving the section "recognition," his action incensed rightwing southerners. Senator Ellison "Cotton Ed" Smith, noted Harold Ickes in his diary, "'God-damned' the nomination all over the place," and another South Carolinian wrote Senator Russell of Georgia: "Today, more so than ever, we need fearless men; no spineless political puppets, appointed by a madman, crazy from greed for power. Black's nomination is more than an insult to Americans." A prominent labor leader, after hailing Black as "the foremost Progressive from the South," noted in his diary, "If he had picked the devil himself he would not have aroused nearly so much resentment in the reactionary camp." The southern establishment understood that in his choice of the Alabama hotspur Roosevelt was deliberately giving preference to a younger generation of southern liberals bent on overturning the old order. In the midst of the controversy, the Tar Heel progressive Josephus Daniels, who hailed the appointment because Black's views revealed "an emancipation from the hardworn creeds which dominate the minds of our Southern public men," wired Black, "The stars cannot fall in Alabama as long as you hold high the liberal spirit of an awakened South." A year later, the much more conservative North Carolinian Josiah Bailey confided to his Senate colleague, Jimmy Byrnes, "When he appointed Black, he finished himself up with me."[14]

Roosevelt also permitted liberal office-seekers to use his name against their conservative opponents in southern races, notably in a critical Alabama contest. After he had created a vacancy in the Senate by choosing Black for the Supreme Court, word reached the governor of Alabama that "the Boss" wanted the liberal congressman Lister Hill appointed to succeed Black. Instead, the governor named his wife and called a special primary. For a time, it seemed that the winner would be Tom Heflin, bankrolled, it was said, by "the Southern pine barons, the owners of the turpentine camps, the managers of the steel and rubber mills, and the local Liberty Leaguers." A notorious demagogue, he not only was a race baiter but also sought "to flush Jesuits from the foliage." Hill asked the White House for help, and Roosevelt complied by inviting him to ride on the presidential train. In January 1938, after a campaign in which pictures of Hill and FDR blanketed the state, Hill finished first, an outcome the *Birmingham News* called a victory "for the New Deal, Rooseveltism, Democracy, and the WPA."[15]

The president intervened on behalf of liberals in Texas too. At Wichita Falls in 1938, he began remarks at trackside with the code words, "My old friend, Congressman McFarlane." That same year, Maury Maverick, fighting desperately for survival, urged Tommy Corcoran to persuade the president to identify himself with the San Antonio congressman, the only southerner in the House to vote for the antilynching bill. "He also promised to write me a letter extolling my many virtues, my pious character—and also how much dough I got for San Antonio," the irrepressible Maverick reported. Roosevelt came through by goading the Budget Bureau to approve an appropriation of more than $2 million to build Kelly Field in San Antonio, and, on arriving in Amarillo, he invited Maverick, whom he introduced as "my friend, Congressman Maury Maverick," to hop aboard his train. Shortly thereafter, Washington announced a slum clearance project valued at $3.5 million for Maverick's district. Three years later, the president permitted another southern liberal, Lyndon B. Johnson, to announce his candidacy for the U.S. Senate from the steps of the White House, and as he toured the Lone Star State, the congressman featured the slogan FRANKLIN D AND LYNDON B![16]

IV

Two months after Lister Hill's gratifying victory, Roosevelt articulated for the first time his vision of the South. He had offered any number of brief comments in the past. He had also taken a great many significant actions—from asking Congress to establish the TVA to appointing liberal southerners such as Aubrey Williams and Hugo Black to intervening in the Barkley-Harrison contest. He had, in addition, made a good many symbolic gestures like welcoming Lister Hill aboard his train. But not until he stopped off in a sleepy north Georgia community on his way to Warm Springs in March 1938 did he attempt to spell out what he thought about the southern past, present, and future. He did so, appropriately enough, in Gainesville's Roosevelt Square, recently renamed in his honor. The city had been all but leveled by a tornado in 1936, but had been rebuilt thanks to large-scale aid from three New Deal agencies.[17]

After some opening banter about how Gainesville's citizens (with conspicuous support from Washington, he did not neglect to say) had triumphed over disaster, he jolted his audience by abruptly switching mood. "Today, national progress and national prosperity are being held back chiefly because of selfishness on the part of a few," he declared. Speaking of "conditions in this, my other State," he asserted: "Georgia and the lower South may just as well face facts—simple facts presented in the lower South by the President of the United States. The purchasing power of the millions of Americans in this whole area is far too low. Most men and women who work for wages in this whole area get wages which are far too low." Improved buying power, he pointed out, "means many other kinds of better things—better schools, better health, better hospitals, better highways. These things will not come to us in the South if we oppose progress—if we believe in our hearts that the feudal system is still the best system." Not content with these strong words, he then let loose a salvo that he must have anticipated would shake the walls of every boardroom and editorial office in the region: "When you come down to it, there is little difference between the feudal system and the Fascist system. If you believe in the one, you lean to the other." Any employer who paid low wages and any editor who condoned such policies, he implied, was a fascist.[18]

The festive Georgians who turned out to greet FDR numbered twice the population of the town, but when they heard these words, their demeanor rapidly changed. "It was a warm day," the White House physician Admiral Ross McIntire later remembered, "but you could feel the ice forming as the people sat in angry silence." Afterward, *Time* reported, "Reaction to the President's curt speech by a tobacco-chewing crowd which had expected a few congratulatory truisms was one of silent, hurt amazement." *Time*'s assessment was disputed, but without question the address infuriated many southerners. "It has frequently been said that one cannot indict a nation, but Mr. Roosevelt came very close yesterday to an indictment of a large section of the republic," commented a North Carolina newspaper. A prominent Georgia businessman said, "If I expressed my opinion of his speech, no self-respecting newspaper would print it," while another southerner wrote Roosevelt, "If you lack the private morality (character) and intelligence to appreciate the culture of the people of the South, surely you knew of the discriminatory freight rates, tariffs, etc. which affect the South adversely. . . . You cannot impose a complex of inferiority upon us." A Nashville, Tennessee woman, outraged by this "slanderous indictment of the South," instructed the president, "For heaven's sake please cease stirring up class hatred."[19]

"Roosevelt," asserted the *Atlanta Constitution*, had "declared open war on the conservative wing of the Democratic party." Years later, Jim Farley reflected: "The words the President spoke were not many but they were as heavy with ominous portent as the chains that Marley's ghost dragged to the bedside of Ebenezer Scrooge. . . . What was . . . galling to southern members of Congress was the inference that those who had opposed him had been purchased by the vested interests. I found members of Congress seething. Garner told me that the speech had made a solid bloc that would vote against almost anything the President might propose."[20]

Editorial writers in the region had a stock response to the president's address. Yes, wages were lower in the South, but then the cost of living was much cheaper, so less pay was justifiable. Besides, it was not the South that was to blame but the North, which had imposed high tariffs and unfair freight rates. "Give us a break, Mr. President, at least the break of a kindly word instead of a scolding for economic conditions which the South has had no responsibility in creating and imposing upon itself, and which so far it has had no luck in escaping," the *Charlotte Observer* protested. A modest wage scale was the only way the South could compete with other sections. Come to think of it, though, thanks to the genius of business leaders below the Mason-Dixon line, wages were not low. In fact, they were just as high as in most other sections. And if Washington would stop meddling, wages would climb even higher. Southern industrialists were quick to endorse these views. "In my contacts with other manufacturers in this area," a prominent Georgia businessman reported, "I have learned there are no 'low wages' in Chattanooga."[21]

Roosevelt's admirers presented a very different explanation of the unusual quiet in the Georgia square as the president spoke. A Gainesville lawyer wrote FDR's secretary that "after the ceremony, any number of people came to me and told me that they were too full of sentiment and happiness to yell or applaud much." In support of this view of the crowd's response, he enclosed a letter from a worker in a local ice cream plant who had written him:

> No living man loves Franklin D. Roosevelt more than I do. I sat thru-
> out that long night back in 1932 pulling for that Chicago Convention to
> nominate Mr. Roosevelt. . . . I believed then that he was a God-sent man
> to lead us out of that wilderness. . . . I never dreamed that some day he
> would ride down the same streets of Gainesville that I played on as a kid.
>
> Wednesday I stood on the west side of the public square with thou-
> sands of others, a most solemn crowd. Suddenly the President's car ap-
> peared in front of me—there he was. I tried to shout. Ed, I swear to you
> I couldn't say a word. The tears just gushed out. At first I felt terribly em-
> barrassed, but looking around me I saw lots of others actually sobbing. . . .
>
> When the President appeared on the platform my emotions gave way
> again, again, and again. Everybody around me had tears in their eyes.[22]

FDR's followers also discounted his critics. After all, the *Augusta Herald* pointed out, "there was a time not so long ago that our trade bodies in southern cities held out cheap labor as an inducement for industries to move southward" and "the South is yet looked upon as a favored section for sweat shops." It asked: "What would the president's opponents have him do? Would they respect him if he abandoned, in any degree, his fight for the nation's under-privileged? Is it not a fact that most of the opposition to his policies yet comes from those who are specially favored?" The Georgia newspaper maintained, "If Georgia and the Southland are to ever correct labor abuses it has got to come through a frank recognition of the fact that evils of this nature actually exist. Bring them out in the open." True, "the president, we dare say, had in mind giving the people of the South a shock." But "little is accomplished these days without there being a certain degree of drama involved."[23]

Response to the Gainesville talk broke sharply on class lines, with numbers of southerners sharing the sentiments of a Birmingham railroad engineer who expressed gratitude to the president for "that fine speech you made . . . in behalf of the low paid workers of the South" and of a Jacksonville, Florida, man who told him, "Your inspiring frank address at Gainesville yesterday gives the working classes of the South new hope and inspiration." From Columbus, Georgia, a worker wrote: "I wish to thank you for the straght from the sholder speech you made in gansvell and to let you know I wosent suprised for I knew you wosent a quiter and I wish to let you know I am hartly in favor of your brave fight for the wage and houir bill for we working people know who it is that is fighting you and why." He ended: "I wonto tell you I faver every peace of laslatin you have askfor exsept the antilinchen bil."[24]

Class distrust of the southern establishment came through clearly in numbers of letters. A North Carolina government employee wrote the White House to say "how thoroughly some of us Southerners appreciated the President's speech. . . . It is time to tell some of our so-called . . . leaders here below the Line that any pull away from economic humanitarianism as preached by Mr. Roosevelt and other liberals in the party is not going to be unanimous. Not by a jugful it isn't!" And a Tennessee factory worker who sent the president a clipping from a newspaper hostile to the address did so, he explained, "so you could see what the big man is saying about your speach," adding "I am for you 100 per cent." He concluded, "Mr. Roosevelt I sure do hope you get this letter. Withhold my name from any papers."[25]

V

FDR's Gainesville address suggested that by 1938 the president was ready to take the offensive to revamp southern politics, and nothing demonstrated that so well as his bold intervention in Democratic primaries to assure the victory of liberal incumbents and, more controversially, to oust conservatives. The prospect that Roosevelt might oppose them gave officeholders no little concern. "The big boy has scared the lard out of them," said the governor of North Carolina. Borrowing from contemporary European developments, the press labeled the effort "the purge." The campaign, which included a move against a reactionary Tammany congressman in New York, was ostensibly national in scope, yet only in three southern or border states—Georgia, South Carolina, and Maryland—did Roosevelt seriously seek to drive a U.S. senator from office. Hence, the purge was universally recognized as yet another attempt by FDR to liberalize the South.[26]

Any hesitation about risking the president's prestige in party contests ended with the 1938 Florida primary where Senator Claude Pepper faced challenges from two strong opponents. The only member of Florida's congressional delegation to stand by FDR on the wages and hours bill, Pepper had begun one letter to the president, "Your whole record emphasizes your interest in the problems of the South and your earnest desire to be helpful to us." Years later, Pepper wrote, "If I knew anything, I knew the South needed help, and Roosevelt was our only chance to get it. He inspired me, and I wanted to be identified with him." The president, in turn, regarded Pepper, in Ickes's paraphrase, as "one of the best men who have come out of the South for a long time." On the other hand, Pepper's main opponent, James Mark Wilcox, "the Congressional mouthpiece of the lush interests residing in his West Palm Beach constituency," one historian has written, was "no friend of the President in any sense, and was as conspicuous in opposition to the President's program as Pepper was conspicuous in its support." When the wages and hours bill reached its moment of decision in committee, Wilcox flew up to Washington to vote against it, "after which he promptly returned to sunny Palm Beach."[27]

The victory of Lister Hill in Alabama in January encouraged a White House cadre to help Pepper. In early February in Palm Beach, the president's son Jimmy told reporters: "Of course, the Administration does not want to dictate to voters, but Senator Pepper has been loyal to the Administration and has worked hard for his state, and it is our hope that he will be returned to the Senate." His use of the word *our* was understood to imply that he was speaking for his father too, something the president would neither confirm nor deny. Wilcox, in a fit of temper at this intrusion, said, "Now that Jimmy has announced his personal preference, I am sure that thousands of Florida voters are waiting with bated breath for the announcement of the views of Sistie and Buzzie." FDR's young grandchildren did not intervene, but the president did. As early as December Pepper had recorded in his diary a White House gathering of Senate liberals with FDR: "Discussed whether the President should enter the primaries and try to defeat the reactionary Democrats. Consensus: he should and would. . . . He said my case was clear—he would simply say I had the record—Wilcox did not. What a real God-made man!" Roosevelt raised money for Pepper and bolstered the senator's reputation by adding five thousand WPA workers in Florida.[28]

On May 3, Pepper won convincingly, with a better than 2–1 showing over his most dangerous rival. "The true principles of democracy as exemplified by your leadership have just received a striking vote of confidence and approval in Florida," Pepper wired Roosevelt. FDR and his circle were delighted by the evidence of a liberal sentiment in the electorate not reflected in the behavior of many of the southern legislators. Pepper noted in his diary a rendezvous at the White House after his victory: "When I walked in, the President said, 'Claude if you were a woman I'd kiss you.' I told him I regretted missing the thrill."[29]

VI

After Pepper's triumph, the president's liberal advisors urged him to mount a campaign to evict the powerful Georgia senator Walter George, regarded as a prototypical southern conservative much too closely linked to the utility combine, as well as to Atlanta corporations such as Coca-Cola. "The Georgia fight," Tommy Corcoran later reflected, "was fundamentally a fight over the cheap electricity of the TVA with George tied up in the power companies." George had fought against both old age insurance and FDR's wages and hours bill. So incensed was he by the Court-packing plan that in the first draft of a speech denouncing it he had called the president a "traitor." Yet he had voted for most of FDR's measures, and in March he had called the president "the greatest leader among English speaking people in the world today." Roosevelt may have given close attention to his counselors' recommendations less because he thought George was hopelessly reactionary than because he was convinced that as an adopted son he was so popular in Georgia that he could easily put across a candidate more in harmony with his outlook.[30]

The president made no declaration of intent to take part in the Georgia primary, but by late June the senator was so perturbed by the prospect that FDR might oppose his reelection that he wrote him a note in longhand, which he asked the president's secretary Marvin McIntyre, as a personal favor, to hand deliver. In it, George said: "I have learned indirectly that you felt that I had in public address and on some occasion spoken in offensive terms regarding your good self. If my information is correct, I hasten to assure you that I have never meant to be offensive to you. . . . I may have, and regret it, too little self-control at times but I am unwilling to have you think I have . . . at any time felt anything but deep affection for you."[31]

"Mac has given me that mighty nice note of yours and I want you to know that I appreciate it," Roosevelt responded disarmingly. "I had never even suggested that you had spoken in offensive terms about me." So far, so good, George must have thought on reading it. But the president added, "though I did feel at the time of the Court fight you were a bit emphatic in suggestions that I had horrid designs on the Judiciary," and "then, of course, there was the usual crop of cloak room rumors about things said in conversation." He paid no heed to such gossip, he claimed, and he continued to hold George in "high respect and affection." Given that "mutual regard," it was possible for them to "disagree with each other heartily and deeply" in regard to policy. There was no ethical reason why George should not try to lead the Democratic Party in a conservative direction. "I take the other point of view," Roosevelt wrote, "because I honestly believe that such an attitude on the part of the Party will, first of all, destroy the Party in a few years, and, second, jeopardize the Nation and its government." If George lived in the North, the odds were ten to one that he would have been a Republican senator, and if that had happened, "you would have been an old and close friend of mine just as Bert Snell and Jimmy Wadsworth and Fred Hale [are]." Never had a Democratic stalwart been read out of his party more deftly.[32]

For a while, despite this private exchange, Roosevelt and George continued to maintain formal good relations, but under trying circumstances, for the president was determined to find a candidate capable of ousting the senator. "I am going to endorse someone, if I have to pick my tenant farmer, Moore," he confided. In the end, the best he could come up with was the former chairman of the Democratic Party and attorney general in Georgia Lawrence Camp, who had been an effective prosecutor but lacked a strong statewide following. Furthermore, the contest was muddled by the entry into the race of Eugene Talmadge. While FDR's agents rounded up support for Camp, the president himself still said nothing, and George called Roosevelt "a great and good man." The White House did, however, announce that the president planned to deliver an address shortly in Barnesville, Georgia, in the course of another of his journeys to Warm Springs. On accepting his invitation to attend the event in Barnesville in August, Senator George said, "I am happy to know the President . . . is coming. He will be welcomed then, and he will always be welcomed in Georgia." Roosevelt, though, stole a march on him. At a homecoming luncheon for patients at Warm Springs, he caught reporters by surprise, and bemused the assembled children, by introducing a man "I hope will be the next Senator from this state, Lawrence Camp." His impromptu announcement, the *Atlanta Constitution* reported, "literally stunned the state."[33]

VII

On his way to Barnesville for his confrontation with Walter George, Roosevelt stopped off at Athens, Georgia, where, in an address on the University of Georgia campus, he offered the most contemplative summary of his ambitions for the South. "Many years have gone by since I first came to Warm Springs and got to know and to love the State and its people," he said. "I wonder if you, who live here in the State all the time, can realize as well as I, who have been coming here once or twice a year, the amazing progress that has been made here in a short decade and a half—and especially in the past five years. If you see a person intimately morning, noon and night, you do not note the changes of growth or of health of that friend as readily as if you see him only at intervals; and that is why I feel that I can speak of Georgia with true perspective." In his first years in Warm Springs, he had observed "a South in the larger sense forgotten," and then had come "the tragic years of the depression . . . —a picture of despair— I knew Georgia of those days, too."

Having positioned himself as someone both in and outside the South, Roosevelt continued soberly:

> Yet, through all those years the South was building a new school of thought—a group principally recruited from younger men and women who understood that the economy of the South was vitally and inexorably linked with that of the Nation, and that the national good was equally dependent on the improvement of the welfare of the South. They began asking searching questions: Why is our . . . earning capacity so low? Why are our roads so bad? Why are our sanitation and our medical care so neglected? Why are our teachers so inadequately paid? Why are our local school buildings and equipment so antiquated?
>
> I do not mince words because, first of all, I have a right, a Nation-

wide right, a State right and withal a sympathetic and understanding right, to speak them, and, secondly, because you as well as I know them to be true.

Soon after arriving in Georgia, he went on, he learned that, contrary to what he had been told, in district after district, schools were open only four or five months a year, or they were too small to accommodate all who wanted to go, or there were not enough teachers, and parents could with impunity take their children out of school and put them to work. He asked himself why, and he concluded that it was not from lack of interest but because there was not enough money. "That analysis of mine—made even before I was elected Governor of New York—led my mind to many other questions," he continued, especially an overriding one: Why were the land values so low? And that query led him to study a whole host of things—from soil erosion to crop prices to low wages. "So you will see that my thoughts for the South are no new thing," he said. "Long before I had any idea of reentering public life I was planning for better life for the people of Georgia. In these later years I have had some opportunity to prac-tice what I have long preached." The president concluded: "At heart Georgia shows devotion to the principles of democracy. Georgia, like other states, has occasional lapses; but it really does not believe either in demagoguery or feu-dalism, even though they are dressed up in democratic clothes." In that com-ment, he was suggesting obliquely that the people of the state would reject both Talmadge and George.[34]

The Athens address elaborated on thoughts he had expressed earlier that year at a special press conference with members of the American Society of Newspaper Editors. Asked whether he sensed any growth of racial intolerance in the country, he answered: "Less than there was ten or twenty years ago." He explained, "We are wiser and there is less sectionalism," an obvious allusion to the South that led to the next question: "Do you think the South—what we call the solid South—will stay Democratic very long?" The president repeated the question, as though turning it over in his mind, then remarked, "The South is a funny place. I have lived there a long time." When his interrogator persisted, Roosevelt replied:

You and I remember things that have happened in the South in our life-time, before you and I went down there. We remember the days of Tom Watson in Georgia. That was an appeal to prejudice. It was an appeal addressed to a very, very ignorant vote. We have to recognize that fact, because the average boy or girl in my State of Georgia—I am talking about the average in the days of Tom Watson—had had no high school and, as far as the grade school was concerned, had had an average school year of three or four months. . . . They did not read the daily paper, they did not read a magazine. They were getting the lowest form of pay in the entire Nation, and they were therefore completely susceptible to the demagogue. And, in Georgia, we have had our demagogues, as we all know. You can still have demagogues in Georgia.

After this remark, which his listeners must have taken as an allusion to Gene Talmadge, Roosevelt declared: "I think the South is going to remain Democratic, but I think it is going to be a more intelligent form of democracy than has kept the South, for other reasons, in the Democratic column all these years. . . . Because the South is learning, it is going to be a liberal democracy. The South cannot be fooled any more by the kind of things that were published in southern magazines this past winter."

That last sentence referred to a full-page ad by the Southern Pine Association under the banner, "Farmers! To Arms!" in opposition to the wages and hours bill. "That was a definite, deliberate inciting of the farmers of the South to take up arms," the president told the assembled editors. "It was wholly indefensible; it was an unpatriotic act for any newspaper to publish that headline. Now you are getting it straight from the shoulder. 'Farmers! To Arms!' How did you dare publish an advertisement of that kind in your paper? How did you dare to do it?" Furthermore, he stated, in an uncharacteristic display of rancor at the press, the ad "went on to tell lie after lie . . . and every editor who ran that ad knew it was a lie."[35]

VIII

Barnesville, bedecked in red, white, and blue bunting, regarded the arrival of Franklin Roosevelt as the greatest day in its history, for FDR was both an eminence and a native son. Though the town boasted a population of only three thousand, an overflow crowd of 25,000 to 30,000 crammed the Gordon Military Institute stadium and the grassy slopes above the amphitheater to hear what Roosevelt had to say. The master of ceremonies, Senator Richard Russell, resplendent in an ice cream white suit, declared, "The warm and responsive heart of Georgia responds today to the presence of him who is most beloved by Georgians of any man in the life of our state." This effusion was matched by

Governor Eurith Rivers, who rejoiced that for the first time ever Georgia had one of its "very own" in the White House. These words stirred applause from the enthusiastic spectators—women hoisting parasols, men respectfully outfitted in shirts and ties despite the intense rays of the sun. In the throng, wrote Ralph McGill, on this "terribly hot" afternoon with "a smell of pine and of peaches riding the small wind that blew vagrantly through the stadium," were "many of the colored population of the county . . . , excited as on circus day."[36]

Roosevelt, hailed by Governor Rivers as "our fellow-Georgian," made the most of that conception from his opening salutation, "My Neighbors of Georgia." In a resonant voice familiar to millions of Americans grouped around radios to hear his fireside chats, the president said: "Fourteen years ago a democratic Yankee, a comparatively young man, came to a neighboring county in the State of Georgia, in search of a pool of warm water wherein he might swim his way back to health; and he found it. . . . His new neighbors . . . extended to him the hand of genuine hospitality, welcomed him to their firesides and made him feel so much at home that he built himself a house, bought himself a farm and has been coming back ever since. Yes, he proposes to keep to that good custom. I intend coming back very often."

After these pleasantries, Roosevelt adopted a more serious tone. Improving economic conditions in their section, he continued, could not be done by state governments alone, but required national action by the federal government. Warning against the "type of dangerous leadership . . . represented by the man who says that he is in favor of progress but whose record shows that he hinders or hampers or tries to kill new measures of progress," his first unmistakable allusion to Senator George, he asserted that if the people of Georgia wanted a vigorous response to their problems, they needed to send to Congress men "who are willing to stand up and fight night and day for Federal statutes . . . with teeth in them."

That thought brought him to the main subject of his talk: the forthcoming Georgia primary. Roosevelt declared: "Because Georgia has been good enough to call me her adopted son and because for many long years I have regarded Georgia as my 'other state,' I feel no hesitation in telling you what I would do if I could vote here next month. I am strengthened in that decision to give you my personal opinion of the coming Senatorial primary by the fact that during the past few weeks I have had many requests from distinguished citizens of Georgia—from people high and low—from the Chief Justice of the highest court of Georgia and many others." Senator Walter George, he went on, was a good friend, "a gentleman and a scholar," but "on many public questions he and

I do not speak the same language." George, he maintained, had failed to demonstrate "a constant active fighting attitude in favor of the broad objectives of the party and of the Government," nor "deep down in his heart," did he "believe in those objectives." Some of these remarks evoked cries of "Hurrah for George!" but twice as frequent were shouts of "Hurrah for Camp!" or "Goodbye George!" One of George's opponents, former Governor Talmadge, the president added, "would contribute very little to practical progress in government. That is all I can say about him." This jab at "Gene of the red suspenders and the cornfield wisecrack," in the words of a columnist, drew loud cheers and laughs. So, "if I were able to vote in the September primaries in this State, I most assuredly should cast my ballot for Lawrence Camp."[37]

The president, wrote *Time*, had "proceeded to excommunicate Conservative George . . . about as completely as any Pope ever cut off from grace an unrepentant sinner," but the senator, carefully coached, turned aside the rebuff nimbly. When Roosevelt finished, George, who, as one observer noted, was "sitting on the platform, so close that he could have been touched," grasped FDR's hand and said, "Mr. President, I regret that you have taken this occasion to question my democracy and to attack my public record. I want you to know that I accept the challenge." Flustered by this unexpected response, Roosevelt murmured, "God bless you, Walter," and left, forgetting the ostensible purpose of his visit—to throw the switch that was to give REA power to the region. He was not the only one discombobulated by the day's events. The mayor of Barnesville was so furious at FDR's remarks that he drove off "like a wild man," and the mayor's wife deserted the White House passengers assigned to her. Newspapers in small Georgia towns printed not one word of what Roosevelt said in Barnesville, only editorials denouncing it.[38]

In the ensuing campaign, called by McGill "the greatest and most thrilling political spectacle in Georgia's history," Camp's theme was "If he is good enough for Franklin D. Roosevelt, he's good enough for me," but Camp was seeking to unseat a senator who had become a totemic figure in Georgia. Walter George, Talmadge's son later remarked, "was a distinguished gentleman who looked like he had reached full maturity back when God was still a boy." A stiffish man, who on the steamiest days wore dark double-breasted suits with a white handkerchief folded in the left front pocket, he was so austere that even his wife called him "Mr. George." Hardly a crowd pleaser, he nonetheless could rise to an occasion "with a voice," one journalist later wrote, "like Lauritz Melchior singing Wagner in an elevator." Moreover, many Georgians took pride in his growing stature in Washington. On his death nearly two decades later, the *New York Times* characterized him as "the greatest Senator—Southern style—of this century, to say the least."[39]

In his very first address after the Barnesville encounter, George lashed back at the president by treating him not as a neighbor but as a northern intruder whom he even likened to General Sherman. Calling Roosevelt's intrusion "a second march through Georgia," the senator asserted: "We answered this question before when federal bayonets stood guard over our ballot boxes and when honest men walked down under the shadow of bayonets in alien, carpetbagging hands and cast honest ballots for the redemption of this state," a remark that drew rebel yells from the "white Democrats" to whom he appealed. "I'm a Georgian bred and born, a *full-time* Georgian, too!" he said pointedly. "For the first time in more years than I can remember, there's a real issue in Georgia politics, and a bitter issue," Margaret Mitchell, author of *Gone with the Wind*, wrote some northern friends. "People who were for Roosevelt before go around muttering 'I'm damned if any Yankee is going to tell me how to mark my ballot!'" Camp, jeering at George's "waving the bloody shirt," said that "if a hungry man asked Senator George for bread he might feel constrained to refuse, but at the drop of a hat or a standard of living he will sing Dixie." These taunts got him nowhere, for he was regarded as FDR's puppet. An *Atlanta Constitution* survey found that 85 percent of those polled resented FDR's intervention. When the votes were counted in September, Georgians demonstrated that however much they loved their adopted son, they would not permit him to dictate their political choices. Notwithstanding all of FDR's exertions, Walter George prevailed, and, though Lawrence Camp carried Warm Springs handsomely, he finished third and last.[40]

IX

No sooner had Roosevelt initiated his campaign against George than he took off after the "grumpy," "walrusy" senator from South Carolina Cotton Ed Smith, who was called "the Senate's No. 1 mossback," "the last of the spittoon Senators," and a "conscientious objector to the twentieth century." He has also been said to have been "unmatched as an exponent of white supremacy, and without peer as a defender of southern womanhood," but, in truth, his two opponents in 1938 were just as noxiously racist. His chief rival, Governor Olin Johnston, charged, "Why, Ed Smith voted for a bill that would permit a big buck nigger to sit by your wife or sister on a railroad train," while a third contestant, Edgar Brown, declared, "We are all anti-nigger in the black belt." Brown was fond of telling crowds: "Let me tell you what Ed Smith voted for—he voted for the World Court. You know who is on the World Court? A nigger is on the World Court." Unlike Smith, though, Johnston, the mill workers' champion, announced that he was "100 percent for the humanitarian policies of Franklin Roosevelt." Indeed, he added, "I would be a traitor to my people if I wasn't with Roosevelt in his great program." The *New York Times* reported that FDR was being pressed to "play possum" and say no more than "Howdy-do" when he reached South Carolina on his way north. But, as luck would have it, the engineer of the president's private train was Olin Johnston's brother, who obligingly made an unscheduled stop just over the Georgia border and when on August 11 the president traveled through the South Carolina piedmont, Governor Johnston was riding with him.[41]

Not until late that night did the train chug into Greenville, South Carolina, where Roosevelt found a crowd, mostly composed of mill hands, who hoisted placards reading, "Our Friends Olin D. and Franklin D.: A Vote for Olin D. is a Vote for Franklin D.—We Need Them Both." Under a full moon, as his northbound train began to leave the station yard in Greenville, where it had tarried to change engines, the president, speaking for only two minutes, appeared content with a few obligatory remarks to the crowd of many thousands who had been waiting for hours in the hope of catching a glimpse of him. But as the locomotive was pulling out of the depot, he could not resist a provocative impromptu comment: "I don't believe any family or any man can live on fifty cents a day." That observation was understood to be a gibe at Cotton Ed, and though the senator's backers were able to document that the president had misquoted him, the New Deal faction in the state, with FDR's implied blessing, massed behind Johnston.[42]

From the moment that he announced his entry into the race from the venue of the White House, Johnston, whom Smith dismissed as a "linthead," had a single focus for his campaign: his "record of constant, unshakable loyalty to . . . President Roosevelt." He claimed, "Roosevelt is my friend and I'm his friend; I'm proud of him," and declared, "The main issue is this: 'Shall the people of South Carolina elect a man antagonistic to the peerless leader, Franklin D. Roosevelt, or one who is willing and able to cooperate?'" Brown, too, identified himself as "a Roosevelt New Dealer" and viewed the president as "a big-hearted Christian man." His opponents, Smith sneered, were trying to ride in on FDR's coattails. "I wonder what in the name of merciful God would happen if Franklin

Roosevelt pulled his coat off." A vote against him, Cotton Ed said, would be "a vote for the Yankee-nigger-loving gang."[43]

In a radio address on August 22, Johnston maintained, "For the first time since the War Between the States the Sons of the South are in the saddle in Washington. Our great President is a part-time Southerner. . . . The outstanding heads of the legislative branches are Southerners." It was the "mighty responsibility" of the people of South Carolina to decide whether they wanted to send to the Senate a man "who will cooperate wholeheartedly with these Great Southerners." He added: "Newspapers and my opponents have said with a sniff and a sneer that I am for Roosevelt and that I am a New Dealer. I certainly am. That bitter experience gained yonder while working between the looms gives me a deep appreciation for the glorious humanitarianism of President Roosevelt. . . . I am anxious to walk shoulder to shoulder with him and the other loyal Southern leaders."[44]

Two days before the primary, Brown pulled out of the race, leaving Roosevelt too little time to redress the balance by going to South Carolina to campaign for Johnston, as he had implied he might. Instead, he issued a statement from Hyde Park: "The voters of the state now have their choice between two candidates representing entirely different political schools of thought. One of these candidates thinks in terms of the past and governs accordingly. The other thinks in terms of 1938, and 1948 and 1958 as well." Cotton Ed responded: "I do think 'in terms of the past,' because I cannot forget when Federal powers extended into South Carolina and all but destroyed our Commonwealth."

When Johnston, in a monumental act of stupidity, sent Brown a willfully insulting wire demanding that he fall in line with the president's endorsement and thereby affirm that he had not been "only a stalking horse . . . for . . . Roosevelt-haters," Brown rejoined: "I have been a New Dealer for twenty years and when you were fighting the resolution endorsing Roosevelt in the 1932 state Democratic convention I was for Roosevelt. When you brought Huey Long to South Carolina to vilify and abuse the Administration I was for Roosevelt. . . . When you were lying in the political bed and were a disciple of Talmadge of Georgia, the bitterest enemy that Roosevelt has in the South, I was . . . for Roosevelt. The fact that you, after observing Roosevelt's personal popularity, swung on to the Administration and now want to be the torch of Roosevelt . . . does not change your true character. The choice now is strictly a matter for the people of South Carolina. I would not presume to dictate to them."[45]

The president's intervention in South Carolina failed miserably. Once again, Roosevelt found himself characterized as a carpetbagger. On the day before the primary, the editor of the *Charleston News and Courier* ran a front-page editorial in which, after noting a statement the president had made in Hyde Park on the South Carolina contest, pointedly referred to him as "a New York voter" and "the gentleman from New York." In part because of resentment at an interloper, Cotton Ed survived FDR's attempt to eliminate him. He would, in fact, go on to set a record by serving six consecutive terms in the Senate, "yielding his seat only to a summons from his maker."[46]

Southerners had divergent responses to the outcome. A South Carolina professor wrote a colleague sardonically that he knew he must be "rejoicing that States' rights, white supremacy, Bourbonism, low wages, long hours, and the right to ignorance, prejudice and superstition are no longer in jeopardy in S.C." A South Carolina newspaper, though, said, "This is the worst slap Mr. Roosevelt has ever received by the people of the South, but he deserved it," and a North Carolina doctor informed the president: "I have seldom experienced such a profound thrill or felt such keen joy as last night and today as returns from the South Carolina senatorial primary indicated that Senator E. D. Smith is going to be returned to the United States Senate. I have been joyful mainly because this election indicates to me that the tide is turning and that the BLIGHT of your influence in this country seems at last, at long last, to be lifting. There is a God in this nation, for he has answered my prayers for your political undoing. Your grip is breaking! and the joyful tidings should ring through the land." Cotton Ed, unrepentant about his obsession with the past, celebrated his victory by putting on the red shirt of the Redeemers and addressing a gathering of similarly attired supporters at Wade Hampton's statue. As he stood by the foot of Hampton's steed under Chinaberry trees, Smith told his Orangeburg followers, "No man dares to come into South Carolina and try to dictate to the sons of those who held high the hands of Lee and Hampton. We conquered in '76 and we conquered in '38."[47]

Observers differed, too, about the effect of FDR's remark. Edgar Brown said: "Either Olin or I could have handled Ed on the race issue, but we were both licked the day Roosevelt came out against him. The most powerful force you can turn loose in a political campaign is the voter's feeling that some outsider is trying to tell him what to do." Jimmy Byrnes, however, wrote his patron, Bernard Baruch, "Had the President remained out of South Carolina, Smith would undoubtedly have been elected." FDR's comment, he said, had put the outcome in question.[48]

Whatever the impact of Roosevelt's intervention in southern primaries, it had not been adequate. Only in the border state of Kentucky, where he endorsed Alben Barkley, did the president prevail, and he did so there less because of his influence, though it was helpful, than because the majority leader had so great a following. "What Roosevelt said that day" in Barnesville, James Cobb has concluded, "ruined Talmadge's chances," but that was an incidental, though welcome, outcome, since George had been his main target. In no state did FDR succeed in ousting an incumbent senator. Sadly, Roosevelt concluded when the South Carolina returns were in, "It takes a long, long time to build the past up to the present."[49]

X

Though the purge came to nothing in the Deep South, it had an important unanticipated by-product. In the spring of 1938, Roosevelt had met with Clark Howell Foreman, grandson of the founder of the *Atlanta Constitution* and a protégé of Will Alexander, guiding spirit of the Commission on Interracial Cooperation. As a young man of seventeen, Foreman had witnessed a lynching, and, a friend said, the sight had "burned a hole in his head." The president wanted to find out whether Foreman, "a sort of roving adviser to the executive branch on southern affairs," knew of a liberal who might oppose Senator George in that year's primary. He did not, but he seized upon the opportunity of the meeting to raise an idea he had picked up at a Washington gathering of the Southern Policy Committee, an informal organization of liberal southern congressmen, notably Lister Hill and John Sparkman of Alabama, and federal officials of southern origins such as Abe Fortas and Brooks Hays. Occasionally, the young Texan, Lyndon Johnson, turned up. They had been meeting at a seafood restaurant on the Potomac waterfront where, one participant later said, "conversation . . . about the Southern agrarian crisis, Negroes, rural education, the sharecropper system, natural resources, Huey Long, and TVA competed for attention in a rising clatter of glasses, dishes, and Southern accents." Foreman himself had joined the New Deal as special advisor to Harold Ickes on the economic status of the Negro. He had told the secretary that he would resign whenever the government thought it could put an African American in the position. Meantime, he had chosen Robert Weaver as his assistant and hired a black secretary. By 1938, Foreman had moved on to become director of another Ickes organization, the PWA's Power Division.[50]

At one of the Southern Policy Committee dinners, he had heard the counsel of the Power Division, Jerome Frank, recommend putting together a pamphlet calling the attention of the nation to the economic problems of the South. Such a publication, Foreman pointed out to Roosevelt, could be used in the southern primaries to demonstrate the benefits the New Deal had brought the region. It would be better, the president responded, simply to offer the bare facts of the economic difficulties confronting the South. "If the people understand the facts," he said, "they will find their own remedies." But he liked the notion and requested Lowell Mellett to supervise the project. An ardently liberal editor in the very influential Scripps-Howard chain of newspapers, Mellett had gotten into hot water with his publisher by refusing to oppose FDR's Court-packing plan. So well-tuned were FDR's information antennae that on the very day in 1937 Mellett resigned he got a call from the White House, though the news of his breach with the chain was supposed to be a secret. In his characteristically chummy way, the president greeted him with a "Hello, Lowell" (he did not actually know him) and asked him if he would like to work for the government. That invitation was premature, but in April 1938, Roosevelt named him director of the National Emergency Council, an umbrella agency for the New Deal recovery program that had fallen into disuse until Mellett gave it a spark.[51]

In carrying out Roosevelt's assignment, the National Emergency Council (NEC) made a point of recruiting southerners in federal agencies. Mellett and Foreman set New Deal officials such as Hugo Black's brother-in-law, Clifford Durr, Tex Goldschmidt of the Bituminous Coal Commission, and another Texan, Jack Fischer (later editor of *Harper's*), to work on assembling data, and they created an advisory committee of prominent southerners, including Frank Porter Graham, who as president of the University of North Carolina had made his institution a beacon of liberalism in the South, and Lucy Randolph Mason, a descendant of the author of the Virginia Declaration of Rights who was southern director of public relations for the Congress of Industrial Organizations (CIO). The ensuing report, the *Kiplinger Washington Letter* later said sniffily, "was drafted largely within gov't, but with a front of southern citizens, hand-picked by New Deal." Before they had written a word, a North Carolina editor who would subsequently become chairman of the Democratic Party in his state was already calling the members of the committee "macabre leaders of the dying south."[52]

To the Conference on Economic Conditions of the South that met in Washington on the Fourth of July, Roosevelt said: "My intimate interest in all that concerns the South is, I believe, known to all of you, but this interest is far more than a sentimental attachment born of a considerable residence in your section and of close personal friendship with so many of your people. It proceeds even more from my feeling of responsibility toward the whole Nation." The president's next sentence went on to place sectional concerns in a national context, but some arresting words in that sentence grabbed the attention of the southern elite. "It is my conviction," Roosevelt continued, "that the South presents right now the *nation's No. 1 economic problem*—the nation's problem, not merely the South['s]. For we have an economic unbalance in the Nation as a whole, due to this very condition of the South." In the rest of the message, the president, perhaps sensing that southerners might be affronted by the rubric of "the nation's No. 1 economic problem," went out of his way to be deferential. He called the South "this truly American section of the country's population . . . still holding the great heritages of King's Mountain and Shiloh." The document that would come out of these deliberations, he declared, should be "representative of the South's own best thought."[53]

The mischievous "No. 1 economic problem" phrase, though, raised a ruckus. One critic has seen Roosevelt's designation of the South as "the nation's No. 1 economic problem" as the counterpart to *Absalom, Absalom!* in that both FDR and Faulkner rejected the myth of Dixie as the land of a benign plantation culture. Another commentator has called FDR's expression "inept," for "while everybody enjoys hugging the notion that his own problems are peculiar and most difficult, nobody likes to be considered a problem to his family and neighbors." After the conferees took off for lunch, a *New York Times* reporter stole into the meeting room and swiped a copy of the draft. The next morning, the *Times* printed the text of FDR's letter, including his reference to the South as a "drag on the Nation," under the provocative headline, "South Is Declared 'No. 1' by President in Economic Need."[54]

That dispatch triggered a heated response before Mellett and his aides had a chance to revise their preliminary findings. The textile industry's weekly bulletin, under the title, "Roosevelt Appoints a Slumming Commission," expressed resentment that the president, "a man who lives just north of . . . the densely crowded slum districts of New York City," was "singling out the South." A *Miami Herald* writer protested:

> Another group will set out to investigate the South and find out what is wrong with it. The South was not aware that it was in serious shape.

Thought it was doing nicely. That is compared to most of the country. But President Roosevelt thinks differently. Declared it was the "Number 1 economic problem." That it unbalanced the Nation. Not the budget.

So the Southerners will be investigated; their doors opened, inquiries made on grits and grunts and pay. The truth is that the North is jealous of the South, of its conservative independence, its rising economic status. The North is a bit afraid. It wants to see what can be done. Not to save the South. But the North. From Southern competition.[55]

So swiftly did the NEC team work that by early August Mellett was able to transmit to the president the final document, *Report on the Economic Conditions of the South,* and Roosevelt, a master of timing, ordered it released so that it would have the maximum impact on the talks he was scheduled to give in Athens and Barnesville. The sixty-four-page inventory offered a bleak reckoning. "The low income belt of the South," it stated bluntly, "is a belt of sickness, misery, and unnecessary death." By "the most conservative estimates," it asserted, half of the families in the South needed to be rehoused, for more than half of Southern farmhouses "are unpainted and more than a third do not have screens to keep out mosquitoes and flies." A fifth did "not even have privies." In the South, "many thousands" of tenant farmers were "living in poverty comparable to that of the poorest peasants in Europe," while sharecroppers averaged an income of only ten cents a day. It was "hardly surprising," then, "that such ordinary items as automobiles, radios, and books are relatively rare in many southern country areas." The *Report,* in the words of *The Nation,* exposed "the crowding of [the South's] rural slums, the draining of its youngest blood and best talent, its ramshackle housing, its starvation wages, its monopoly of pellagra and its subjection to syphilis and malaria, its sparse schooling, its exploitation of the labor and women and children, its dependent farm tenantry and brutalized and impoverished landowners."[56]

The situation in the South contrasted markedly with that in other sections. "The richest State in the South ranks lower in per capita income than the poorest State outside the region," the *Report* noted. "Even in 'prosperous' 1929 southern farm people received an average gross income of only $186 a year as compared with $528 for farmers elsewhere." The consequences for education were dramatic. New York spent more than five times as much per pupil as did Mississippi. A school teacher in New York state averaged $2361 a year; in

Arkansas, $465. The endowments of all the southern colleges and universities put together, the *Report* pointed out, did not amount to as much as those of Harvard and Yale combined.

It put a great deal of the blame, however, not on the South but on the nation, more particularly on northern corporations that had exploited the section. "Much of the profit from southern industries goes to outside financiers," the *Report* declared. Northerners possessed the railroads, the public utilities, and the rich resources of iron ore, coal, bauxite, and zinc, and this "large absentee ownership of the South's natural resources and the South's industry makes it possible for residents elsewhere to influence greatly the manner in which the South is developed and to subordinate that development to other interests outside the South." More particularly, the "efforts of southern communities to increase their revenues and to spread the tax burden more fairly have been impeded by the vigorous opposition of interests outside the region which control much of the South's wealth," for "these people do not pay their share of the cost of southern schools and other institutions." The *Report* asserted: "The paradox of the South is that while it is blessed by Nature with immense wealth, its people as a whole are the poorest in the country. Lacking industries of its own, the South has been forced to trade the richness of its soil, its minerals and forests, and the labor of its people for goods manufactured elsewhere."[57]

In highlighting such disparities, the *Report* reflected the contentions of writers such as Walter Prescott Webb in his polemic, *Divided We Stand,* that the troubles of the South derived from outside the region with the main obloquy falling on the imposition by the North of high tariffs, discriminatory freight rates, and other hegemonic policies that had reduced the South to colonial status. "The idea that the South was in economic thralldom to the capitalistic North was a staple of southern social thought and southern political rhetoric during the 1930s," Edward Shapiro has written. The Northeast, with its urge to "devour," was able to "walk in silk and satin," the Nashville agrarians were convinced, while the South, reduced to sucking at the "hind tit," had to make do with "shoddy." Not long after the *Report* appeared, Maury Maverick, in an article with the suggestive title, "Let's Join the United States," elaborated this thesis: "The South actually works for the North: mortgage, insurance, industrial, and finance corporations pump the money northward like African ivory out of the Congo. . . . The South, as much as any British colony of old or today, is a colony, with headquarters in New York. There live the Privy Lords of Trade and Plantations, who . . . govern the South by remote control." As George Tindall has noted, "Publication of the report placed the Roosevelt administration squarely behind the sectional rebellion against colonial bondage."[58]

Neither at the time nor subsequently did everyone find the colonial metaphor satisfactory. In *Forty Acres and Steel Mules* (1938), H. C. Nixon acknowledged that the South had been exploited by outsiders, but pointed out that "many Southerners had participated in the winnings." It was important to recognize, wrote C. Vann Woodward in a favorable review of Nixon's book, that the South had been "an agent as well as victim of economic exploitation," and instead of indulging in Yankee-baiting the section would be well-advised to look at internal class and racial divisions. Though Rupert Vance believed that "the South remains largely a colonial economy," he refused to blame that situation on the North. (Consequently, the Nashville agrarians accused him of having "produced a *Hamlet* without an evil uncle.") A 1941 study published by the University of North Carolina Press asserted that the South had been "handicapped . . . less by outside opposition than by inside complacency." A generation later, Clarence H. Danhof concluded: "The colonial-imperialistic thesis of conspiracy must be considered an unfortunate episode—a resurgence of a crude sectionalism—that diverted the attention of some of the South's ablest men from constructive approaches to the region's problems." He contended that phenomena such as freight rate schedules had no effect, that the South was to blame for its difficulties, and that only if the South made a stronger effort to enhance its "human capital" by improving areas such as education and research would it better its economic record.[59]

The *Report* drew heavily on the work of the Chapel Hill regionalists, especially Howard Odum, who had been the first choice to chair the sponsoring committee for the *Report*. Only when he turned them down did Mellett and Foreman go to Graham. A recent critic has said of "Odum's opus," *Southern Regions of the United States* (1936), that "even his greatest admirers had to turn often to caffeine to stay awake reading it," but so highly was it regarded by his liberal contemporaries that Gerald Johnson advocated "capital punishment" for every southern journalist "who could not prove within a specified time" that he had perused it as well as the writings of Odum's Chapel Hill colleagues. Not long after the North Carolina sociologist died, the *Washington Post* wrote: "Howard W. Odum was the Eli Whitney of the modern South. He inspired a revolution. Certainly there was no one—unless it was Franklin Roosevelt—whose influence was greater than Odum's on the development of the region below the Potomac." As David Carlton and Peter Coclanis have pointed out, the regionalists, notably Odum, "replaced the South of Confederate glory, the South of traditional culture, with a South whose very definition was 'that part of the United States whose people are most deprived.'"[60]

Roosevelt could readily identify with Odum's crucial distinction between sectionalism, which was divisive, and regionalism, which gave preeminence to the nation. Odum's "fondest dream," one of his colleagues said, was "that the South would rejoin the Union, discarding . . . its pathologies of ideological separatism." In contrast to sectionalism, the concept of regionalism, Odum maintained, would "point toward a continuously more effective reintegration of the southern regions into the national picture. Thus, regionalism envisages the nation first, making the national culture and welfare the final arbiter." Moreover, though some conservative theorists thought of regionalism as a form of devolution that moved counter to the centralizing tendencies of the New Deal, Odum said, "As is everywhere agreed, the old American unlimited free competition must now be replaced by something better." Richard Maxwell Brown has written: "Paradoxically, regionalism in the 1930s and 1940s drew much of its impetus from the center—that is, the federal government in Washington, D.C. Regionalism flourished in some great United States governmental action programs carried out as an integral part of the New Deal. President Franklin D. Roosevelt was, in effect, one of the great regionalists of the age."[61]

The reliance on regionalism, however, had one baneful consequence: the *Report* conspicuously failed to acknowledge racial antagonisms in the South. As Carlton and Coclanis have perceptively noted, regionalism rested on the premise that whites and blacks were united by their confrontation with problems that were "essentially *common* and *geographically based.*" Hence, "what was good for *southerners* was . . . good for both blacks and whites."[62]

Roosevelt and those who undertook the study saw it as a way to call attention to northern avarice, and one of the leading organs of northern liberalism, *The Nation,* which found the *Report* "almost terrifying in the simplicity with which it exposes the poverty and economic brutality of the South," counseled: "Northerners need not feel condescending about it, nor need Southerners feel singled out for censure. Northerners have tended to regard the South as a cultured European might feel about some primitive and backward people; but here is proof that the South is what it is largely because of the financial imperialism of Northern big business. . . . The roots of what is wrong with the South are not sectional but national. The South is tributary to the utilities and banks and lumber companies and textile companies and big industries of the North."[63]

The *Report*, though, wounded the self-esteem of chambers of commerce from Newport News to El Paso. At a time when New York theatergoers were being confirmed in their prejudices by the image of southern degradation conveyed by Erskine Caldwell's *Tobacco Road*, the document, one scholar has noted, disturbed "the sectional *amour propre* of the South and bade fare to lay before the world's gaze certain aspects of southern life which its governing class preferred to be settled locally." To be sure, by not rejecting "the ancient vision of an opulent South," the *Report*'s "exposition of Southern possibilities sounded like a paraphrase of Henry W. Grady's rhetoric." Nonetheless, it was perceived as challenging what Paul Gaston has called "the enduring myth"—that the South was a land "of abundance and opportunity," a "New South Creed" that constituted "a bulwark against change."[64]

Politicians and publicists in the South responded indignantly. "It is bitter to be discovered as a national liability, a kind of regional slum," remarked one journalist, and Pat Harrison said, "No one can tell me that the South is the most ignorant and poorest section in the country." North Carolina's Senator Bailey stated: "With the national policy against us, our population has multiplied by 3, our wealth by 14. And now they tell us we are the Nation's problem child. Bankrupted by war, razed to the earth by Reconstruction, and throttled ever since by an adverse national policy, the progress of the South under the circumstances proclaims its advantages and the capacity of the southern people." Moreover, as a historian has noted, southerners who objected to the *Report* "sensed that even though President Roosevelt chose not to create problems for himself by directly challenging the southern tradition of white supremacy, his New Deal did imply equality for *all*."[65]

Southerners resented the *Report* as an intrusion by a meddlesome national government and a thrust by envious northerners in a war of sections. "I regard my State as a stalwart, supporting member of the family rather than a problem child," declared the governor of North Carolina, while Senator John E. Miller of Arkansas commented, "To put it bluntly, the South needs letting alone worse than anything." In Charleston, W. W. Ball asserted: "The Roosevelt administration is not bent on assisting the South. It is bent on assisting the East and the Middle West against the South. . . . The federal government still looks upon the Southern states as tributary provinces." Even southern liberals, a political scientist noted, "felt that the President's *Report* was in rather bad political taste, officially sanctioning the morbid interest in the South that had become the literary and academic fashion in the thirties."[66]

Reaction to the *Report* did not always hew to class and ideological lines. A North Carolina tobacco farmer declared: "I'm a Democrat; I stand for the New Deal and Roosevelt. I am for the WPA, the NYA, the NRA, the AAA, the FHA, and crop control. I'm going to vote for control in December. We've got mighty little of the government money but I'm still saying that the WPA, CCC, and all the rest is shore doing a big part for North Carolina." He added, however: "I'm proud of North Carolina, too, and I don't like for our President to call it no problem 'cause it ain't as much a problem as some of the other states what air running over with foreigner gangsters."[67]

Long after it was written, the Roosevelt-sponsored *Report* continued to rankle. During World War II, the general manager of the Beaumont Chamber of Commerce told the conservative governor of Louisiana: "I didn't like that booklet 'The South, the Nation's Number One Problem.' The only reason we are a problem is because we are making such great progress under such difficult circumstances that it is annoying to some of our neighbors to the North and East." More than a decade after the *Report* appeared, William T. Polk commented:

> The period from 1930 to the present may be described as the Golden Age of the Gadflies. Great swarms of them hovered all over the region from Virginia to Texas; the South, like the white heifer, Io, who in human form incurred Hera's wrath as Zeus' mistress, bounded wildly before their stings, but mainly along the road to progress. . . .
>
> The report, which stressed Southern defects and needs, hit the South in the face as squarely as H. L. Mencken's "Sahara of the Bozart" did some twenty years before, and it did for the South in the economic field what Mencken's article did in the cultural field; it waked the South up and set it to work to disprove what had been alleged against it.

As late as 1950, John Temple Graves observed that the revolutions that were making "political theater of the South" could be traced to a reaction against FDR's saying that the section was the "nation's Number One Problem," and a generation after it first appeared, a Texas congressman was still bristling.[68]

Though conservatives often sounded shrill and even irrational, they did not raise objections without reason. Bruce Schulman has pointed out:

> The *Report on Economic Conditions of the South* was not the straightforward presentation of facts it purported to be. It embodied the diagnosis of the southern liberals. . . . The pamphlet . . . recommended the liber-

als' preferred treatment for the South, national action that would . . . eliminate barriers to southern participation in the national economy, and restructure the region along the lines of the rest of the nation.

The NEC report signaled a shift in the direction of federal policy toward the South. It marked the onset of a concerted effort to restructure the regional economy, and the end to the national administration's conciliation of southern interests. . . . Disguised as an objective analysis of the regional economy, the *Report on Economic Conditions of the South* was a manifesto for the southern liberal program for regional development.

In Chapel Hill the following year, Frank Porter Graham stated flatly, "The Federal Government is the only agency which can redress this economic and educational imbalance." Furthermore, the *Report* reflected the attitudes of New Deal economists, who, blaming the Great Depression on underconsumption, believed that "the southern economy's tangled pathology . . . seemed a weight pulling the nation down as well," Carlton and Coclanis have noted. The South, in this view, not only was incapable of buying the goods of northern factories but was impoverishing other sections by seducing runaway shops to move to its nonunion, low-wage mill towns. Hence, "to many nonsoutherners, the South was an enemy within, a parasitic region whose employers were benefiting from the degradation of their own labor and that of others."[69]

Predictably, southern liberals found the premises of the *Report* decidedly more acceptable than did conservatives. The *Chattanooga News* reprinted the document in its entirety and its editor, George Fort Milton, in praising it, warned that if nothing was done to raise the standard of living in the South, the section, undeniably "the poorest," would continue to dwell "on the fringes of hunger and heartbreak." In the *Baltimore Sun*, Gerald Johnson, a North Carolina native, expressed dismay at southern politicians who had "snorted and brayed and pawed the earth, denouncing the President as if he had attacked the South instead of coming to its aid." Much of the responsibility for maladies in the region was not the fault of southerners, he continued, but of "the bland indifference of the rest of the country to what was going on below the Potomac. . . . The rest of the country didn't care; and it didn't care because it was not informed of the truth." Then a president came along who not only did alert the rest of the country, but even went "so far as to say that those problems take precedence"; yet southern politicians reacted not with gratitude but with "surliness," "boorishness," and an "utter absence of any evidence of breeding." That behavior could be expected, though, for "its predilection for putting jackasses in high office has damaged the prestige of the South as much as erosion has damaged the land," and all too many of them "wear the collars of rich owners."[70]

Jonathan Daniels, Josephus's son and his heir as editor of the *Raleigh News and Observer,* thought that FDR's characterization was "one calculated to stir the South out of its lethargy and the Nation to an awareness of its own obligation in . . . Southern problems." Not unmindful of how arrogant northern intruders could be, Daniels remarked in a book published that year: "Cato did not ride through Carthage on the train and blame its conditions on the Carthaginians. That much only I ask of the Yankees." But he counseled Mellett that Roosevelt should ignore critics of the *Report* who were the "same old Daughters of the Confederacy—though some in pants—who in all the long years have been a more destructive crop than cotton. They are not talking for the thoughtful men and women in every class in the South. . . . We know we are in a hell of a fix even when we sit in the shade and we are grateful for his help out of our hole."[71]

XI

The purge and the *Report on Economic Conditions of the South* also led to the founding of the most important organization of southern liberals that had ever been created. The critical encounter that launched the group took place at Hyde Park where the president and Mrs. Roosevelt gave encouragement to two callers, Lucy Randolph Mason ("Miss Lucy of the CIO") and Joseph Gelders, a Birmingham man who had given up his post as assistant professor and chief of the physics laboratory at the University of Alabama to unionize workers. "A lanky, soft-voiced, academic-looking man" with an "odd, dancing gait," Gelders had become southern secretary of a communist front and was a secret member of the Communist Party. During attempts to organize the Tennessee Coal and Iron Company, he had been kidnapped and so badly mauled and trampled by corporation goons that he never fully recovered. "They not only beat him, but they jumped him, if you know what I mean, up and down," the Alabama progressive Virginia Durr later explained. "When he died at a rather young age, his whole chest was just a mass of broken, splintered bone." Gelders had been planning for two years a regional conference on civil liberties, but the Roosevelts persuaded him to broaden the notion to embrace all of the South's problems.[72]

After Gelders returned home with word of the Roosevelts' approval of a gathering of southern New Dealers, William Terry Couch, the innovative director of the University of North Carolina Press, raised funds to send the political scientist H. C. Nixon, who resigned his position at Tulane, on an organizing tour through the region. Nixon, his biographer has written, was an Alabama "hillbilly . . . born the year that Henry W. Grady announced his New South creed to the New England Society at fashionable Delmonico's Restaurant in New York." Nixon took pride in being "a product of the folkways of the hills . . . born in a house that burned, by the side of a dirt road that was changed, and across the road from a post office that was discontinued." A contributor to the 1930 manifesto of the Nashville agrarians, *I'll Take My Stand*, he did not share their political outlook. Nixon later wrote, "I cannot go with them in their unwillingness, as I understand them, to give the Negro a square deal. . . . This is no day for Tories." He believed that "the South will never itself escape exploitation until an end is put to the exploitation of farmers, laborers, and Negroes."[73]

Essential though the activities of Gelders, Couch, and Nixon were, it was the experience of drafting the NEC *Report*, which brought together people who had worked in isolation before, that was the rite of passage for southern liberals. "The stimulus for the meeting," Couch explained, "was the . . . *Report to the President on the Economic Condition of the South*." As a result of the president's mission statement to the committee, Hosea Hudson, an outspoken black Communist in Alabama, later said: "All these leaders, particularly the whites, but many of the blacks . . . in the South, from Washington all the way down, they became very indignant. Professors, big professors, some of the congressmen, and doctors, cause Roosevelt said the South was the number-one problem of the nation. They said, 'Look, we got to do something about it.' So they called this Southern Conference for Human Welfare [SCHW] in Birmingham."[74]

Two days after FDR's Barnesville challenge to Walter George, conference organizers mailed off invitations to a meeting over the Thanksgiving weekend, a date chosen because Mrs. Roosevelt said she could drive there from Warm Springs then. In November 1938, three months after the president had alluded to a new generation of southerners in his Athens talk, the first meeting of the SCHW took place in Birmingham's municipal auditorium. It also came three months after the publication of the *Report*, and Nixon shrewdly made the document the text of the meeting. He tied the new group even closer to the Roosevelt administration by his roster of speakers, which included Eleanor Roosevelt, Aubrey Williams, and Justice Hugo Black. Those who had arranged the gathering, Nixon explained, aimed "to make it much easier for Southern politicians to be progressive and harder for them to be tory than has ever been the case." Never before, Couch told the *New Republic,* had anything of this magnitude happened in the South. "For the first time in the history of the region," Gunnar Myrdal later said, "the lonely Southern liberals . . . experienced a foretaste of the freedom and power which large-scale political organization and concerted action give."[75]

Of the more than a thousand people who turned up in Birmingham, blacks made up about a fifth. On the first day, blacks and whites met together without incident, but on the second day Birmingham police insisted that the local segregation ordinances be obeyed. "The whole place was surrounded by Black Marias," Virginia Durr later recalled, "surrounded on all four sides." Directing the police raid was the commissioner of public safety, Eugene "Bull" Connor, "a stout, jug-eared man with a mean squint" and a "bullfrog voice." With creatively mangled phrasing, Connor announced, "I ain't gonna let no darkies and white folk segregate together in this town." Though the delegates bent to the necessities of the moment, they adopted a resolution vowing that no future meeting would be segregated. That straightforward declaration led southern newspapers that had been well disposed toward the new organization to turn against it, and prominent backers departed. Jonathan Daniels regretted that the SCHW "began in tragic mistake when action was taken which resulted in placing emphasis upon the one thing certain angrily to divide the South."[76]

In what has been celebrated as an imaginative bit of political theater, Mrs. Roosevelt, refusing to be jim crowed, got a folding chair and plunked it down in the middle of the aisle. For the rest of the meeting, it has been said, she carried that little camp chair with her wherever she went. The accuracy of that oft told tale has been questioned, and, in fact, it is not altogether clear that Mrs. Roosevelt intended to upset Jim Crow customs. Certainly, her comments in Birmingham on segregation were not defiant. Contemporary evidence, though, supports the main elements of the legend. An Atlanta paper reported that Mrs. Roosevelt, detained by a lengthy luncheon discussion, arrived late at the hall and found that the only seats were in "the front row of the corral which the police were maintaining . . . for the negroes." She sat down there, only to be told by the police that she could not remain in the colored section. After awkward milling around, "some chairs were brought out, and Mrs. Roosevelt and her escorts moved—to a spot between the two sections."[77]

There can also be no doubt that the First Lady was an inspiriting presence.

Virginia Durr later reflected: "Something that young people in the civil rights movement never had as strong as we had in the 1930s was a feeling of support. We knew Eleanor just had to pick up the telephone and call Franklin. We had the feeling of having the power of the government on our side. Bull Connor, in spite of all the police and black marias, just made us nervous. We never were afraid of him, because we knew he was not going to arrest the wife of the president of the United States and he was not going to arrest a Supreme Court justice."[78]

The southern establishment viewed the organization, which was to have a stormy history, with great suspicion,[79] and it flourished as long as it did in no small part because of its association with FDR. Openly identifying himself with the cause of southern liberalism, and with a pointed allusion to the *Report on Economic Conditions of the South,* the president sent a message to the founding convention of the SCHW:

> The long struggle by liberal leaders of the South for human welfare in your region has been implemented on an unprecedented scale these past five and one-half years by Federal help. Yet we have recognized publicly this year that what has been done is only a beginning, and that the South's unbalance is a major concern not merely of the South, but of the whole Nation. It is heartening, therefore, to see the strength of Southern social leadership mustered to face these human problems . . . in a united front from Fort Raleigh to the Alamo.
>
> If you steer a true course and keep everlastingly at it, the South will long be thankful for this day.[80]

In 1940 Roosevelt once again sent greetings to the SCHW, a gesture indicating he was standing by his friends, the southern liberals. Furthermore, he made a point of reminding the South of the "especial benefits" it had received from the New Deal. "The Wage and Hour Law, the AAA program, the Farm Security Administration, the National Labor Relations Board Act, the Work Projects Administration, Public Works Administration, Civilian Conservation Corps, National Youth Administration and the Reciprocal Trade Agreements have all brought to the South means and resources of a helpful character," he claimed.

Yet he couched his remarks in a way that suggested he was seeking to appease critics of his earlier statements about the section. "While we have at times spoken of the South's problems, we have never forgotten its great wealth of human and natural resources," he pointed out. He recognized, too, that the South had "not always been paid a fair return" for the products it had sent north. Nor, he stressed, was he "unmindful of the efforts which the southern people have made and are making toward the solution of their problems. I am aware of the sacrifices they have made to provide schools for their children. I know of the large financial burdens they have borne in behalf of public health. The South can well be proud of what it has been able to accomplish from its available means." But, he concluded, "we must find a way to increase its means."[81]

XII

Southern liberals never doubted their great debt to FDR. "I really rather worship that man," Aubrey Williams later confided. "He was just about what I wished I was. . . . What a truly great and good man he was." In 1944, at a time when the president was preoccupied with the battle zones of World War II, he asked the secretary of state to think of Williams for a high government post. When that did not work out, he nominated Williams, over strenuous objections from his secretary of agriculture, to head the REA, only to have the Senate turn him down when southern senators, unable to stomach an Alabaman who opposed racial segregation, broke with the leader of their party. (Of the nineteen Democrats who rejected Williams, all but two came from the South.) As a college student in 1934, Carl Elliott had met "the man who was and who remains a political God to me—Franklin D. Roosevelt," and, as Dan Carter has noted, "from the time of his election to Congress in 1948, Elliott never wavered in his support for a national government that reached down to help the poor people of Alabama." A few weeks after FDR died, Lister Hill said: "Twice the people of Alabama elected me to the Senate as a Franklin Roosevelt Senator. In the past twelve years I have not made a single speech of any consequence in Alabama that I did not pay tribute to him and his leadership. In the days to come I shall again and again proclaim him in Askalon and tell of him on the streets of Gath." He served under five presidents, but, one of his colleagues in Congress from Alabama recalled, in the words of his biographer, "even years after Roosevelt's death, Hill would shed a tear when he talked about his Chief."[82]

If Roosevelt sometimes tempered his words and deeds, he nonetheless had a very considerable effect on liberalism in the South. "The New Deal clearly changed the frame of reference for nearly all southerners who considered themselves liberals," John M. Matthews has observed. "Onto older positions of dissent from cultural norms and commitment to individual rights now was fastened the realization that social reform on a grand scale was at last possible and that the federal government, which had never really entered into their calculations, was the agent of change." Asked in 1974 how he had come to be a liberal, Claude Pepper replied, "I guess that I came probably under the spell of Roosevelt more than anything else."[83]

Morton Sosna has observed that "a new breed . . . came to the fore during the Roosevelt years: dedicated Southern liberals who in their own states would never have achieved the prominence they found in New Deal administrative positions." He added, "In this period, Washington became a congenial center for white Southern liberals, one which allowed them to bypass the closed political systems that they found back home." Aubrey Williams, he noted, "was precisely the kind of Southern liberal who would not have achieved prominence were it not for the New Deal," and in federal agencies, Will Alexander and Clark Foreman "had authority and influence that they would not have had in the South. In Washington their perspectives broadened, and both men left the Roosevelt Administration with decidedly more radical outlooks on the race question than when they entered. . . . Little wonder so many Southern liberals looked upon the New Deal as their patron." Still, he concluded, "the New Deal took Southern liberals only halfway."[84]

FOUR

INTIMATIONS OF A COMING STORM

I

FDR's partiality toward southern liberals in his second term led conservatives in the region to give voice to a displeasure with the president that had been building for a long time. The initial delight of southern politicians at the prospect of another Wilson in the executive office soon faded when they realized that, unlike the Colonel House era, "there was no eminence grise in the White House who hailed from Dixie," and his advisors from Yankee metropolises did not regard states' rights or racial rituals as hallowed. Indeed, W. J. Cash went so far as to say: "The basic Rooseveltian ideas, with their emphasis on the social values as against the individual, and on the necessity of revising all values in the light of the conditions created by the machine and the disappearance of the frontier, ran directly contrary to the basic Southern attitudes."[1]

II

From the earliest days of FDR's presidency, certain southerners found fault with his programs, especially the centralization of authority in the national government. Even at the outset, in the banking crisis that opened Roosevelt's tenure, Carter Glass said, "The President of the United States had no more valid authority to close or open a bank in the United States than has my stable boy." A Kentucky congressman called the TVA "a stench in the nostrils of those who cherish the ideals of Thomas Jefferson," and the Fugitive Donald Davidson noted that some people thought "that the TVA is virtually a foreign experiment conducted on southern soil" or "another Yankee raid into southern territory." Davidson, who regarded Roosevelt's appointment of Will Alexander to head the FSA as an action that Charles Sumner would have approved, warned a fellow agrarian that FDR might turn out to be a Kerensky paving the way for a regime in which his plantation would be expropriated for black tenants and he would be reduced to teaching "a class where kinky-heads and blond tresses mix . . . and do not even nod politely." A Mississippian protested that the battle of Chancellorsville could not have been waged under FDR because the South would have had "to secure from Washington thirty days' rations and a permit to fight," and a country gentleman in Georgia, according to one report, "said he was going to stay drunk until Franklin D. Roosevelt left the White House, and eventually had to go away for treatment."[2]

Southern businessmen viewed the wage provisions of NRA codes, despite the incorporation of sectional differentials, as a Yankee conspiracy against their region. In the spring of 1934, a meeting of the Southern States Industrial Council cheered when a Birmingham manufacturer said, "Sherman's march to the sea was no more destructive than the NRA is going to be to the South. Before it is over, we may have secession." In FDR's second term, the fiercely antiunion Birmingham coal baron Charles De Bardeleben, who, an interviewer said, "spits his words out of bitter lips," declared: "The South is worse off as a result of the Roosevelt Administration than it was as a result of the Civil War. This infernal administration is sending the country to hell as straight as the martin to its gourd."[3]

Opposition to the New Deal centered in what one political scientist called the "banker-merchant-farmer-lawyer-doctor-governing class," personified by, in Ralph McGill's words, "a certain type, small-town rich man." This character, McGill explained,

> owned, according to his geographic location, the gin, the turpentine works, the cotton warehouses, the tobacco warehouses. He was a director in the bank.
>
> He was the owner of all, or part of, the biggest store. . . .
>
> At least one of the popular automobile agencies was in his name, or owned by a brother, uncle, or son.
>
> He controlled credit. . . .
>
> He was, more often than not, a deacon in his church. If not a deacon, he was a "pillar," in that he gave liberally. . . .
>
> He usually owned and operated a few farms, taken in on foreclosures. . . .
>
> [He] hated Roosevelt, the New Deal, the triple A, and the Federal Land Bank, which took mortgages and farm loans out of his hands.
>
> He damned the WPA because it took away farm labor.

He hated all union labor. . . . He did not want new industries in "his" town. They competed for "his" labor.

He fondly regarded himself as the bulwark of all that was "best" of the Southern "traditions."[4]

Though critics on the left reproved Roosevelt for cooperating with the ruling class in the South, and even enhancing its authority, many of those who regarded themselves as the section's elite viewed matters differently. As Dewey Grantham has pointed out:

> If the New Deal did not dislodge those who dominated the power structure in the South, it threatened them as they had never been threatened before—and in this respect it was unlike the New Freedom of Woodrow Wilson, which the conservative South made peace with. . . . The New Deal was different. Try as politicians might—by joining it for a time, by endeavoring to water down its program, by resorting to subterfuge, ingenious arguments, and clever appeals to old-time shibboleths—the threat remained, and it promised to grow larger in the future. Not only did it seem more and more unlikely that the South could ever dominate the Democratic party again, but it was also increasingly apparent that the national policies adopted during the thirties would ultimately strengthen organized labor, farmers, Negroes, and middle-class people sufficiently to force concessions from those who had long had the upper hand in the region. This was the real measure of the New Deal's challenge to southern conservatives.[5]

This disapproval of FDR's policies came at the very time when millions of southerners were displaying enthusiasm for Roosevelt that approached adoration, a phenomenon that led more than one commentator to remark on how sharply southern society fractured with regard to how the president was perceived. As John Temple Graves put it: "For the masses Roosevelt was the Democratic Party, the rebel yell, Woodrow Wilson, and Robert E. Lee rolled into one present help in trouble. For the classes he came to be Satan, maker of class hates, destroyer of the Southern system, gathering place of crackpots, enemy of God and advance agent of communism. Or, as they put it more compactly, 'that man.'"[6]

III

Southern whites particularly resented New Deal programs that treated blacks equally, or that markedly raised black incomes. "Programs such as the WPA,"

Richard Current has noted, "had the odor of abolitionism about them, since they tended to emancipate blacks from low-paid domestic service by offering alternative sources of income." The acronym NRA, said southern white critics, stood for "Negro Relief Act," or, they hoped, for "No Roosevelt Again." A Selma, Alabama, manufacturer mailed thousands of leaflets to southern lawmakers urging them to persuade the government to designate the Negro as a "subnormal" worker who should be paid a subnormal wage. Money from a number of federal projects bypassed the traditional wielders of power in the South and went directly to blacks and poor whites. From New Orleans in 1934, a New Deal field investigator reported, "A lot of these people who used to look up . . . to their paternalistic landlords and their employers have now switched to the President and Mrs. Roosevelt!" A North Carolina landlord protested to an agency official: "I don't like this welfare business. I can't do a thing with my niggers. They aren't beholden to me anymore. They know you won't let them perish."[7]

Disgruntled whites blamed both the president and the First Lady for the erosion of the caste system. A suburban Virginia newspaper noted with alarm that in a single speech to an African-American group in 1936, Mrs. Roosevelt had used the words *equality* or *equal* eighteen times, and that a photograph showed her seated next to a black woman "so close their bodies touched." The conspicuous meetings of Walter White with the Roosevelts led one southern paper to intimate that the NAACP leader must have a secret tunnel from his hotel room across Lafayette Park to the White House. When Senate Majority Leader Alben Barkley refused to reconfigure the Senate calendar without White's consent, because he had pledged that an antilynching measure would be taken up, Jimmy Byrnes ranted, "Barkley can't do anything without talking to that nigger first." In the *Georgia Woman's World*, the president of the Woman's National Association for the Preservation of the White Race, who knew for certain that Lincoln had been murdered by international Jewry, complained that the white women of the South did not have as much access to the "august presence" of "Madam Roosevelt" as did African Americans. She added: "Negro newspapers are full of Mrs. Roosevelt's pictures . . . coupled with such statements as 'She waited to hear the address of the Hon. Walter White'—the same little negro who, like thousands of others, ran the streets of Atlanta a very short time ago."[8]

Black voters distressed southern whites by their massive move to FDR in 1936. That year South Carolina racists circulated a postcard stating: "A vote for Roosevelt and Byrnes means the day is coming closer when dirty, evil smelling negroes will be going to church with you, your sister, your wife, or your mother. Busses, trains, hotels, picture shows, bathing beaches will all see the ne-groes rubbing shoulders with your loved ones. From this it will only be a step when negroes will be allowed to propose wedlock to white girls. All under Roo-sevelt laws." In Georgia, a Democratic Party official said, "You ask any nigger on the street who's the greatest man in the world. Nine out of ten will tell you Franklin D. Roosevelt. . . . That's why I think he is so dangerous."[9]

At the 1936 Democratic national convention in Philadelphia, Cotton Ed Smith found a dramatic way to demonstrate southern animosity toward FDR's racial policies. When a black minister was invited to give the invocation, Smith stalked out of the hall in protest. The black pastor remarked that if Senator Smith was "looking for a party without Negroes it looks like he will have to form his own little party right here in South Carolina." The senator re-sponded: "I don't have to form my own party. The party already exists. It was born in the red-shirt days of the Reconstruction period when the gentlemen of South Carolina donned red shirts to rid our State of carpetbaggers, scalawags and Negroes." Cotton Ed returned to the convention the next day only to find on the platform the sole black member of Congress. Once again he left in a huff, this time announcing he was going "to stay gone."[10]

His walkout made him a local hero. The Richmond editor Virginius Dab-ney wrote: "The Senator was sometimes interrupted when discussing his New Deal record or the price of cotton with some such ejaculation from the audi-ence as: 'Come on, Ed, tell us about Philadelphy!' It is said that he never failed to respond. Hill-billies spat tobacco juice and leered, as 'Cotton Ed' described, in well-embroidered detail, his refusal to be prayed over by a 'nigger.'" Smith's recounting of his experience has become a staple of virtually every chronicle of southern politics in this period:

> When I came out on the floor of that great hall, bless God, it looked like a checkerboard—a spot of white here, and a spot of black there. But I kept going, down that long aisle, and finally I found the great standard of South Carolina—and, praise God, it was a spot of white!
>
> I had no sooner than taken my seat when a newspaperman came down the aisle and squatted by me and said, "Senator, do you know a nigger is going to come out up yonder in a minute and offer the invoca-tion?" I told him, I said, "Now don't be joking me, I'm upset enough the way it is." But then, bless God, out on the platform walked a slew-footed, blue-gummed, kinky-headed Senegambian!

And he started praying and I started walking. And as I pushed through those great doors, and walked across that vast rotunda, it seemed to me that old John Calhoun leaned down from his mansion in the sky and whispered in my ear, "You did right, Ed."[11]

Well before the end of Roosevelt's first term, southern senators who merged racial antipathy with solicitude for business interests had become caustic opponents of FDR and his programs, nowhere more conspicuously than in Virginia. When invited to a Patrick Henry bicentennial commemoration, Carter Glass wrote his Senate colleague Harry Byrd, "I almost feel as if old Patrick had lived in vain, since the liberty that he preferred above his life has largely been sacrificed by this so-called democratic administration at Washington," while, as the historian Richard Polenberg has remarked drolly, "one could always be certain that when Harry Byrd talked about an 'orgy,' he was alluding to federal spending." In a memoir, the foremost liberal in Virginia wrote sadly: "The tragedy of Virginia, and even of the South, during 1940–60, resulted from the fact that shortly after the inauguration of Franklin Roosevelt in 1933, Harry Byrd, . . . who had originally supported Mr. Roosevelt for the nomination, turned against the president and over the years since had become more and more intransigent and vindictive." A month before the 1936 election was to decide whether FDR would be returned to office, Glass told Byrd, "I hate the New Deal just as much as I ever did and have not the remotest idea of making any speeches for it."[12]

IV

Southern politicians as disparate as Georgia's rightwinger Eugene Talmadge and Louisiana's Share-the-Wealth advocate Huey Long held one common sentiment: hostility to Roosevelt, though for diametrically opposite reasons. As Talmadge's biographer has observed, "Long wanted FDR out of office because he didn't think he was doing enough for the people, and Gene wanted him out because he felt he had done too much." Asked what he and Long had talked about when they met, Talmadge would only reply, "We cussed Roosevelt."[13]

Governor Talmadge felt altogether alienated from Roosevelt and his circle. On the campaign trail in the 1920s, Talmadge had cried, "People of Georgia, you've got only three friends: The Lord God Almighty, Sears Roebuck and Gene Talmadge. And people of Georgia, you've got only three enemies: Nigger, nigger, nigger!" Ol' Gene, who said, "We in the South love the Negro in his place—but his place is at the back door with his hat in his hand," lauded chain

gangs that "kept men out of doors in God's open country where they could enjoy the singing of the birds and the beautiful sunrises and sunsets." John Gunther later wrote: "This man is darkness. All you have to do is look at him. Lank
hair flapping sideways on the forehead; cold malicious eyes full of hate; the
strained pouting lips of a Torquemada; a bitter closed tightness of expression
and narrowness—above all narrowness." Following a brief period in which Talmadge was willing to attribute the "failure" of the president, "a great and admired man," to "ill advice from high-powered professors and cracked stenographers," he launched an all-out assault on him as a Bolshevik. The NRA, TVA,
and AAA, he charged, were "all in the Russian primer and the President has
made the statement that he has read it twelve times."[14]

On each return to Warm Springs, Roosevelt knew he was entering a state
in which he was pitted against a governor who sought to depose him. As one
historian has written: "The state of Georgia thus became a battleground on
which met two opposing wings of the Democratic party. One was for economy, the other for spending; one for rugged individualism, the other for a service state; one concerned chiefly for the farmer, the other for the farmer and labor; one for state rights, the other for centralization; one for Georgia, the other
for the nation; one led by Eugene Talmadge, the other by Franklin D. Roosevelt." In 1935 Talmadge, who boasted to his drinking buddies, "I'm just as
mean as cat shit," even stooped to referring to FDR's physical handicap, saying:
"The greatest calamity in this country is that President Roosevelt can't walk
around and hunt up people to talk to. He can only talk to those his secretaries
and assistants allow to come and see him, and 99 percent . . . is the 'gimme'
crowd. The next President who goes to the White House will be a man who
knows what it is to work in the sun fourteen hours a day. That man will be able
to walk a two-by-four plank too."[15]

Talmadge came out of one session with the president at the White House
denouncing him to reporters as a "damned communist," and his commissioner
of agriculture declared, "If the yoke of Rooseveltism cannot be thrown off any
other way, Georgia can secede from the union." Much of the rest of the country viewed such comments as batty, but in Georgia Talmadge commanded a following that was as uncritical as it was rabid. Backwoods balladeers warmed up
his rallies by singing:

I've gotta Eugene dog, I gotta Eugene cat
I'm a Talmadge man from ma shoes to ma hat.

To the true believers at the forks of the creek, Talmadge's attacks on FDR offered proof that their hero was a man of national stature, a fighter who was not afraid to take on even the most powerful man in the country. "Tell 'em about Ruuzevelt," one of his fans would yell. "I'm a-comin' to that," Talmadge would shout back.[16]

Early in 1936, Talmadge convened an assembly of "Jeffersonian Democrats," including executives of Coca-Cola, the Central of Georgia Railroad, and a large textile mill, to "save the Nation and the Democratic party by blocking Mr. Roosevelt's renomination." One bewhiskered codger volunteered that his pappy had "killed a sight of damn Yankees" and he "wished he'd killed some more." A main instigator of this "Grassroots Convention" was Thomas L. Dixon, author of *The Clansman*. On arriving in Macon, delegates found a huge Confederate flag dominating the stage and on each seat a copy of *Georgia Woman's World* with a photo of Eleanor Roosevelt flanked by two blacks, or in the words of the man responsible for the material, a "picture of Mrs. Roosevelt going to some nigger meeting, with two escorts, niggers, on each arm." The publication, which contended that the purpose of the antilynching bill was "permissive ravishment," denounced the president for permitting "negroes to come to the White House banquets and sleep in the White House beds." When the convention of the Southern Committee to Uphold the Constitution got underway, orators castigated FDR as a "Red Rasputin" surrounded by "dadgummed foreigners" whose "names you can't pronounce and you can't sneeze."[17]

In Roosevelt's second term, criticism of him intensified—over issues such as his Court-packing scheme, his tolerance of sit-down strikes, and his interventions in party affairs. A Tennessee woman recently returned from Europe found that everywhere she traveled she encountered denunciations of the president for what "he's doing to the South," and a country editor who claimed that he was the "first in Mississippi to plug in print for the nomination and election of F. D. Roosevelt" wrote, "I split with the administration long before the alphabet was exhausted with economic abracadabra." Southern politicians deplored the rise of strange sorts of Democrats "with pigmented skin, thick accents, the smell of mine and factory about them, or the cultured pallor of the college classroom; new leaders with ideas as alien to southern traditionalists as if they were from another planet." In Alabama, a Republican publicity agent paid youngsters a dollar apiece to go to newsreel theaters and hiss every time the president's face was shown. The disappointed governor of North Carolina,

O. Max Gardner, told a columnist, "The Roosevelt of 1938 does not appear to be related by blood or marriage to the Roosevelt of 1933."[18]

Southern publicists and politicians threatened more and more loudly to break away from the party headed by FDR, even though they had ancestral ties to it. In the fall of 1937, a Mississippi newspaper editorialized: "The thirteen Southern states which for so long have given absolute loyalty to the national Democratic party . . . have been actuated by one prime consideration—the preservation of white supremacy in the south. . . .The 1936 Democratic Convention at Philadelphia seated 22 negro delegates. A negro clergyman delivered the invocation. . . . The only negro congressman is a Chicago Democrat. The New Deal has . . . absolved southerners from any further obligation of loyalty to a party that has betrayed its most loyal adherents." Early in 1938, Carter Glass wrote, "The South would better begin thinking whether it will continue to cast its 152 electoral votes according to the memories of the Reconstruction era of 1865 and thereafter, or will have spirit and courage enough to face the new Reconstruction era that northern so-called Democrats are menacing us with." When South Carolina Democrats convened in 1938, one delegate said: "I saw a jackass being led around by a negro boy and that is symbolical of our party today. Our national party is being led around by the negroism of the North. I am mortally afraid of the negro in our national party."[19]

Josiah Bailey, no longer disguising his dismay at the transformation of his party, became a magnet for malcontents. In the late winter of 1938, Bailey, in promoting a whites-only primary in North Carolina, declared: "The catering by our National Party to the negro vote in Philadelphia, Chicago, New York, Boston and St. Louis is not only extremely distasteful to me, but very alarming indeed. . . . You would have to be in Washington only about three weeks to realize what it is meaning to our Party in the Northern States. It is bringing it down to the lowest depths of degradation." In the summer of 1939, he wrote another U.S. senator about FDR: "He figures on hard times and does not wish for recovery. He would perish like a rattlesnake in the sun under conditions of prosperity. . . . Perhaps you know the rattlesnake must stay in the swamp for the reason that he does not have any means of sweating or panting. His heat accumulates. Mr. Roosevelt belongs to that type of man who lives on hard times and discontent." A year earlier, a prominent Texas Baptist had written the North Carolina senator: "I have long thought that Roosevelt was insane, but it's an uncanny quality of insanity that he has. He may be no crazier than the devil is. At any rate, he is destroying our United States Government just as rapidly as the wheels of time can roll around," and the "ghastly tragedy" was that the president was doing so "in the name of the grand old Democratic Party" in which he and Bailey were reared.[20]

With reports circulating of a vendetta against conservative senators, Bailey told a confidant: "Our Party is being taken away from us by John Lewis, Harold Ickes, Robert Vann, White of the Society for the Advancement of the Negroes, Madam Perkins, Harry Hopkins, Cothran and Cohen. . . . It is a singular thing that we have permitted men who were not Democrats to take our Party captive and that we have so many Democrats in the South who seem to be willing for those men to put men like Senator George, Senator Smith, Carter Glass, Harry Byrd and myself out." When in the following month Roosevelt delivered his purge address, Bailey wrote Senator Byrd, "The President's message was a plain declaration of war, and whether we wish to or not, we must fight now."[21]

The South found it particularly hard to understand how the Squire of Warm Springs could advocate anything so nefarious as wages and hours legislation, which threatened to deprive the section of a competitive advantage in attracting cheap-labor industry. "If a minimum wage scale should be set," said the mayor of an Alabama town, "the Yankees would again whip us worse than in '61–'65." Furthermore, opponents charged, the bill jeopardized racial hegemony. "There is a racial question involved here," Martin Dies of Texas cried on the floor of the House. "And you cannot prescribe the same wage for the black man as for the white man." These remarks were acclaimed by his colleagues with a round of rebel yells. "Mr. President," a Mississippi editor warned, "your political nose will be out of joint . . . in Dixie just so long as you advocate that wage-hour bill and the anti-lynching measure." On the eve of the Senate debate on wages and hours legislation, shortly after the divisive Barkley-Harrison leadership fight, Pat Harrison, as he prepared to deliver his first speech against the New Deal, confided angrily to a friend, "I'm going to give Franklin Roosevelt a licking tomorrow. . . . I just can't take any more." When the House approved the wages and hours bill, fifty-two of the fifty-six negative votes came from the South. Despite ferocious southern opposition, Roosevelt pushed through the Fair Labor Standards Act in 1938, and southern manufacturers had a new source of grievance in federal administrators snooping about their factories to see if they were adhering to the law.[22]

FDR's decision, reached in the same season the wages and hours law was enacted, to enter Democratic primaries with the aim of ending the careers of prominent southern senators left even deeper wounds. Shortly after the campaign fizzled, Cotton Ed Smith, in a moment of exasperation in the Senate cloakroom, said to Walter George, "You know, Roosevelt is his own worst enemy." To which George replied, "Not as long as I am alive." The president sensed this. At one point, in pressing Senator George to support a particular piece of legislation, Roosevelt began, "Walter, if I know anything at all about Georgia politics . . . ," then catching George's expression, broke off with a laugh, saying "and certainly I don't." During World War II, a Washington correspondent noted, "More than once in the last year, George's powerful speeches have turned the tide against Roosevelt in the Senate," while Cotton Ed even referred to the president as "that thing."[23]

In 1940 a number of southerners, including the former governor of Alabama, Frank M. Dixon, nephew of the author of *The Clansman,* opposed FDR's bid for a third term, with anti-Roosevelt sentiment clustering around the southerners Cordell Hull and John Nance Garner as alternatives. In Virginia, a movement by liberal Democrats to instruct the state delegation for FDR failed even to get to the convention floor. So divided were the Texas delegates in their sentiments toward FDR in 1940 that in the Democratic convention city of Chicago, John Connally recalled a half-century later, "it was not possible to conduct a meeting, or finish a breakfast prayer, without the most bitter feelings and denunciations erupting." At one point, he had to step in to separate the pro-Roosevelt Lyndon Johnson from a conservative newspaperman as they were about to engage in a fist fight. "In truth," Connally concluded, "the feuds of 1940 were the foundation for the emergence of the Republican Party as we know it in Texas today."[24]

After Roosevelt beat down this opposition to his renomination, he gave the South additional cause to be miffed. Instead of seeking to placate Dixie malcontents, he ditched the southerner Vice President Garner as his running mate and replaced him with the Iowan Henry Wallace, a renegade Republican, when he might have turned to Jimmy Byrnes of South Carolina or Sam Rayburn of Texas. At the convention, the southern favorite, Speaker William B. Bankhead of Alabama, outpolled Wallace in Deep South delegations by well over 4–1, but fell short when the president insisted on having his way. Roosevelt in 1940 was courting the farmer of the corn-hog and wheat states, not the cotton or tobacco grower whom he knew he could take for granted. As a result, several southern party leaders sat out the ensuing campaign, in the spirit of the nineteenth-century New York senator who said, "I am a Democrat still—very still."

After Lee County, South Carolina, instructed its delegate to the Democratic national convention to cast his ballot for a third term for FDR, Senator Smith refused to go to Chicago. "I don't approve of him and I couldn't vote for him," Cotton Ed said of the president. "It is impossible for me to consider voting anything but the Democratic ticket and there is no Democrat to vote for."[25]

v

In World War II, southern conservatives castigated Roosevelt for economic policies they claimed discriminated against their section. Southern legislators backed an amendment sponsored by Alabama Senator John Bankhead to free farm commodity prices from government controls and vociferously supported an antiunion measure bearing the names of two other southerners, Howard W. Smith of Virginia and Tom Connally of Texas. Flouting the imperative for unity in wartime, southern leaders freely criticized the president. Roosevelt, grumbled the governor of Louisiana, Sam H. Jones, in 1943, was "magnificently ignorant of the South" and the progenitor of policies that "continued to kick an already prostrate South in the face." In the summer of the following year, a Washington correspondent noted, "Since the convening of the 78th Congress in January 1943, the Southerners have chosen *not* to follow the White House on practically any major domestic issue."[26]

Much of the unhappiness with FDR during the war arose from the conviction that he was still intent on upsetting racial mores. The FSA, complained a Mississippi planter, was refurbishing the pledge of "40 acres and a mule, the same promise the other Yankees made to the negroes during the other Civil War." In his 1942 presidential address to the Southern Historical Association, a scholar saw the age of Roosevelt as perpetuating the unfair treatment of the South during Reconstruction when "Negroes had been so pampered." The problem with northerners, he said, was that they "either could not or would not understand the necessity of race segregation." That same year, the chairman of the Alabama State Democratic Executive Committee wrote an open letter in which he declared: "President Roosevelt and his wife have done more toward . . . disturbing the friendly relations heretofore existing between white people and the colored people of the South than all of the other Presidents and their wives who have occupied the White House during the time I have been old enough to take notice of such matters." A Mississippi editor found "the Roosevelts . . . as repugnant to Southerners as the worst carpetbaggers of reconstruction days." She was especially incensed at the thought of mixing blood donated by blacks in a blood bank with that of whites.[27]

When in the following year the Supreme Court invalidated the white primary, Roosevelt got the blame. Since all but one of the justices who handed down the ruling had been named by FDR, "it was not remarkable," a racist theoretician later observed, "that many regarded the decision as practically the act of President Roosevelt himself. (In the subsequent Presidential campaign, negro orators urged their fellow negroes to vote for President Roosevelt on precisely this ground.) And it was natural that in the South the decision was received as the latest treacherous blow from the national Democratic party." So irate was the Democratic leadership of Arkansas at this ruling, and at other racial changes it attributed to Roosevelt, that it amended its rules to liberate the party from the obligation to support the national ticket in 1944. "This decision by a modernized court, picked by a Democratic President," said an Arkansas congressman, "threatens to revolutionize the existing social set up and bring back the Reconstruction days."[28]

That same year, Senator Russell of Georgia denounced Roosevelt for countermanding an order by the comptroller general gutting the powers of the FEPC, which he called a "greater threat to victory than 50 fresh divisions enrolled beneath Hitler's swastika or the setting sun of Japan." Even more aggressively, Mississippi's James Eastland declared on the Senate floor: "I am of the opinion that we should have segregation in all the States of the United States by law. What the people of this country must realize is that the white race is a superior race, and the Negro race is an inferior race. Social equality is growing in this country, and in addition to teaching the white race the importance of racial purity, we must prevent racial intermingling by law."[29]

In expressing their wrath at the changes wrought, or threatened, by the national government during the war, critics once again lumped the president with his wife. Less than three months after Pearl Harbor, Ed Crump was griping, "Mrs. Roosevelt has done this country more harm than any other individual, and the people are doing a lot of wondering about her husband." At a time when Herbert Hoover was the only surviving former chief executive, a Mississippi publicist turned out a pamphlet with the pointed headline: "What This Country Needs Most Is TWO Living Ex-Presidents," warning that "the re-election of Mr. and Mrs. Roosevelt, et al, means the ultimate destruction of the American way of life." Planters in the Mississippi delta groused about Eleanor Roosevelt's "association with the darkies," and a Charleston businessman wrote

Senator Maybank of the need to "put a stop to our negro-loving Mrs. Eleanor Roosevelt and her speeches over the country. . . . I move that we place a demur on her and keep her in her place at home." When a Florida congressman learned that the Army had purchased 55,000 copies of Ruth Benedict's *The Races of Mankind* to use in officer candidate schools, a Fort Myers paper responded, "Of course it may not be possible to get President Roosevelt to sue for divorce, but if he is going to let people like his wife take a hand in running the Army there are plenty of things Congress can do to deter him."[30]

Rumors swept the South that black domestics had conspired to found "Eleanor Clubs." In the summer of 1942, the *Richmond Times-Dispatch* reported: "All over Virginia, the rumor that Negro domestic workers are forming 'Eleanor Clubs,' and preparing for a wholesale evacuation of the kitchens, has been going the rounds." These cabals, it was said, committed black maids to resign on the spot if anyone belittled either the president or his wife. (In another version, servants grilled prospective employers to ascertain their views of the First Lady; if dislike was scented, they informed the heads of households that, as members of the Eleanor Clubs, they would not work for them.) In keeping with the presumed doctrines of these clubs, black women allegedly insisted on coming through the front door and on being addressed as "Miss" or "Mrs." Eleanor Clubs, it was believed, mushroomed immediately after the First Lady appeared in a community. "Wherever she has spoken," it was reported, "the Negroes always act like they are white folks."

Southerners in a position to have known better gave credence to these rumors. After South Carolina's Law Enforcement Division authorized a statewide investigation, a constable dutifully reported a meeting in Cheraw at 8:00 p.m. on September 3 at 311 Church Street where Eleanor Society members plotted to demand six-dollar weekly wages for cooks and nurses. An attorney teaching at a North Carolina college in Asheville informed Howard Odum, the main student of the phenomenon, of an Eleanor Club "made up of young Negroes who want certain social privileges, such as the right to go to drug stores and be served as others." Furthermore, friends told him that, as a consequence of Eleanor Clubs, "their colored cooks come to work on Mondays sullen." None other than the publisher of the *Raleigh News and Observer* Frank Daniels, brother of FDR's advisor, Jonathan Daniels, aired the widely believed charge that the Eleanor Clubs aimed at "putting every white woman in her own kitchen by Christmas." If blacks "keep on insisting for more privileges," he warned, all blacks "that can read and write are going to be eliminated in the Hitler style."[31]

The Federal Bureau of Investigation (FBI) took the rumors seriously enough to launch an investigation. Its Houston division accumulated various reports of organizations of female black servants called the Eleanor Club, the Daughters of Eleanor, or the Eleanor Roosevelt Club, but "in no instance" unearthed any evidence that such groups existed there or anywhere else, as J. Edgar Hoover troubled to inform the First Lady. Odum pointed out, "Since there were no Eleanor Clubs in reality . . . , it was clear that the basic complaint was [that] the main mode of domestic southern folkways of servant and mistress was being violated, both in the actual scarcity of help [as black women moved to assembly lines] and in the revolutionary change in attitudes and status."[32]

Even men regarded as moderates on race viewed Eleanor Roosevelt as a troublemaker. "My considered judgment," wrote Virginius Dabney, "is that Mrs. Roosevelt . . . and a few others are doing tremendous harm. In fact, I believe they have had as much to do with stirring up the Negroes in this period as anybody." His counterpart on the other Richmond daily, Douglass Southall Freeman, chimed in: "There were two abolitionist movements, the Civil War and Mrs. Roosevelt's movement to abolish segregation. The South is too much influenced in its treatment of the individual Negro by the ignorance of the mass. But the North is too much misled by the ability of a few conspicuous Negroes. Mrs. Roosevelt has been misled because she has seen only the best. The South is going to keep the line drawn between civil rights and social privileges. Civil rights should be recognized; social privilege is a matter of individuals. The South is going to keep that line drawn and that's all there is to it."[33]

Others in the South showed considerably less restraint than the Virginia journalists. A Democratic county chairman in Mississippi told the national party chairman, "Our people resent the attitude of Mrs. Roosevelt in regard to social equality of the colored race, and in our section she is the most unpopular lady in the country," while an Arkansas county leader reported, "We are sick and tired of . . . Eleanor. . . . We have no patience with the President's wife being pictured and radioed in every radical, long-haired, black and tan, Communist, 'do gooder' group." Her presence at a nonsegregated dance for servicemen at a Washington, D.C. canteen at which both white and black women served as hostesses infuriated white southerners. "How can anyone be party to encourage white girls into the arms of Negro soldiers at a canteen dance while singing 'Let Me Call You Sweetheart'?" asked a Louisiana congressman.[34]

Some of her critics got altogether carried away. In a June 1943 editorial that an Alabama congressman placed in the *Congressional Record,* the *Jackson Daily*

News declared: "There is blood on your hands, Mrs. Eleanor Roosevelt. More than any other person, you are morally responsible for those race riots in Detroit where two dozen were killed and fully 500 injured in nearly a solid day of street fighting. You have been personally proclaiming and practicing social equality in the White House and wherever you go, Mrs. Roosevelt. In Detroit, a city noted for the growing impudence and insolence of the Negro population, an attempt was made to put your preachments into practice." In Texas a leaflet jeering at the First Lady's globetrotting to engage in activities such as rubbing noses with "some wild Zulu king" and watching natives engage in tree planting ended:

> The happy thought occurred to me
> As homeward bound she sped;
> Why couldn't they have shipped the tree
> And planted her instead?

At a Georgia club when discussion got around to Mrs. Roosevelt's trip to England, one society matron interposed, "I wish she'd drown on the way back!" So high did the pitch of animosity ascend that by 1944 a southern writer concluded: "Mrs. Franklin D. Roosevelt has become the most hated woman in the South since Harriet Beecher Stowe."[35]

VI

Across the South in 1944, in considerably stronger array than four years earlier, foes of the Roosevelts mobilized to block the president's nomination for another term. Even some of his longtime supporters nursed grievances. From Memphis, Ed Crump wrote Senator McKellar: "The negro question is looming big in this part of the country—in fact, all over the South. . . . The Roosevelts dug up the negro question. . . . There was a big dinner, social equality, negroes and whites—at the Roosevelt Hotel in New York last Thursday, honoring Walter White, a negro leader. Mrs. Roosevelt and Wendell Willkie spoke, as well as two or three negroes. If they load down the Chicago platform with repeal of Poll Tax, Anti-Lynching and endeavoring to erase Jim Crow—that will certainly be something for us to think about. . . . We may have to be for Roosevelt whether we like it or not, but I would hate to think it wise to be placed in that position." A South Carolina legislator agreed. "If it is necessary to be crucified politically," he said, "I am willing to be crucified provided it is on an anti-Roosevelt cross."[36]

In Louisiana early in 1944, the chairman of the Democratic Party urged voters even to "go far enough to follow the example of secession furnished by the states of the South at the cost of a war," and in June anti-fourth-term Democrats from six states met in Shreveport "determined to whip the New Deal and all that it stands for." The choice of Shreveport was understandable, for Louisiana was a stronghold of anti-FDR sentiment in 1944. A Baton Rouge man wired Sam Jones that in his stand against Roosevelt the governor was true to the vital traditions of Louisiana and the South, and several Democratic electors resigned rather than commit themselves to cast Louisiana's ballots for the ticket headed by the president.[37]

Roosevelt's opponents rallied around the senator from Virginia, Harry Byrd, the "apple-cheeked apple-grower from the Shenandoah," who had long been anathema to the president. In FDR's first term, the president had complained to Carter Glass that his fellow Virginia senator had never publicly disavowed sympathy with a third-party movement to advance a rightwing candidate in the next election, and Byrd worked so strenuously against the president's reorganization plan that it was said he had "impregnated Mr. Roosevelt with such a feeling that today he cannot hear the Senator's name without exhibiting temper." After the 1944 election, Byrd's son, who would succeed his father in the Senate, claimed: "Father has been continually embarrassed by the use of his name in connection with the presidency. I was with him when he got news that the Mississippi delegation had instructed for him and he was visibly disappointed and displeased, and after we returned home from the convention I heard him talk in definite, blunt and undiplomatic tone to political leaders and personal friends who sought to use his name as presidential candidate . . . especially . . . in Texas, Miss. and Louisiana." During the campaign, however, Senator Byrd issued no Shermanesque renunciation, and he was widely perceived to be a feasible option. In the Florida primary, almost as many votes were cast for Byrd as for FDR, and at the 1944 convention, Louisiana, Mississippi, Virginia, and a Texas faction gave all their votes to Byrd, who also picked up scattered support in South Carolina and Alabama.[38]

Not even FDR's decisive victory over Byrd at the national convention quieted the rebellion, though Roosevelt got well over a thousand delegate votes to less than one hundred for the Virginian. In Florida in late August, anti-Roosevelt Democrats launched an "Independent Party" that fielded a slate of electors including such prominent state figures as the mayor of St. Petersburg, the editor of the *Fort Myers News Press,* and the owner of the *Winter Park Her-*

ald. In Alabama that same month, a Mobile lawyer resigned as candidate for presidential elector because the Democratic Party headed by Roosevelt was "like some mythical and fantastic beast, . . . devouring with a carnivorous appetite its own flesh and blood, its mother whose body gave it birth and at whose breasts it was nurtured for more than a century—the Southland." Though he could only write this "with sadness," he now hoped that the party of his fathers would go down to defeat so that the national administration would be forestalled from violating the "sacred traditions of our Southern life, indispensable to order and good feeling among our races." During FDR's reign, he charged, "the Democratic national administration was ingratiating to the South, then it became condescending; and now it is insulting."[39]

South Carolina Democrats, already upset at FDR's racial policies, found added reason for grievance when the president bypassed their favorite, James Byrnes, for the vice presidential nomination in 1944. Roosevelt agreed that Byrnes was the ablest man but ruled that no southerner could go on the ticket, particularly one who had been so vocal about his anti-Negro views. After FDR "pitched Jimmy Byrnes in the creek," the editor of the leading paper in the state capital wrote, "Speaking of minorities, do you know of any that is more neglected than the Democratic Party in the South?" The foremost newspaper in Charleston declared that Roosevelt's "Reconstruction" program created, in some respects, a "peril . . . much greater than . . . in 1867," for his FEPC edict implied that "*The News and Courier* will be ordered to employ colored printers, pressmen, reporters, desk men. When that order shall be issued, *The News and Courier* will disobey it or go out of business."[40]

Mississippi, too, smoldered with anti-FDR sentiment. "There was scarcely a man in the area who had not received a federal handout or benefited in one way or another from handouts received by others," observed the Mississippi writer David L. Cohn. "But once the Delta had been restored to prosperity, many of its leading citizens sat in their new houses amid their paid-up furniture and denounced Roosevelt as though he were the Antichrist." At the 1944 convention, Mississippi had voted 22–2 for Byrd over FDR. Little more than a week before the November election, three of the nine designated electors in Mississippi announced that no matter what the voters did they would not mark their ballots in the Electoral College for FDR because to do so would be "against the best interests of the Southland." Two of them had written Senator Eastland to explore impeachment of the president. Four of the six remaining electors indicated they might join them. Since the ballots had already been printed, the renegades assumed it was too late for anyone to foil their scheme, but their action aroused Roosevelt loyalists. Thoroughly alarmed, the governor called the legislature into extraordinary session to provide for a supplemental slate of electors pledged to FDR. The measure carried overwhelmingly (126–2 in the House, 45–1 in the Senate), and highway patrol cars racing around the state distributed copies of these pink ballots to the polling places in the nick of time.[41]

The steamiest cauldron of the anti-FDR movement in the South proved to be Texas, where Senator "Pappy" Lee O'Daniel, who had once composed a stirring march, "On to Victory, Mr. Roosevelt," called the president a greater menace than Hitler. In 1944, Texas bankers, publishers, lobbyists, and other large business interests joined with oil men, including representatives of Humble, Sinclair, Socony-Vacuum, and Sun Oil, to reject Roosevelt. A short while later, after touring the entire country for his book *Inside U.S.A.,* John Gunther reported: "Nowhere in the United States, not even on Wall Street or the Republican epicenters in Michigan and Pennsylvania, did I find such perfervid hatred for Mr. Roosevelt as in Texas. . . . I met lifelong Democrats . . . who had been unfalteringly convinced that if FDR won again, 'it would mean that the Mexicans and niggers will take us over.'"[42]

At the state Democratic convention, anti-administration delegates resoundingly defeated a motion to bind Texas electors to voting for the winner of the popular tally and rejected a resolution to include the commander-in-chief in a resolution praising members of the armed services. When the pro-Roosevelt faction bolted, the organist played "God Be With You Till We Meet Again," but the delegates remaining in the hall showed no interest in reunion. They instructed their delegation to the Democratic national convention, headed by former Governor Dan Moody, to "demand restoration of the two-thirds rule and to revolt if Franklin D. Roosevelt were the nominee of the Democratic Party." They further enjoined the electors that, should the president somehow manage to carry Texas, they were not to give him their ballots in the Electoral College. They also required "restoration of the supremacy of the white race, which has been destroyed by the Communist-controlled New Deal," and ran full-page ads exhorting, "Let's Keep the White in Old Glory," though they appeared to be motivated less by racism than by hostility to FDR's economic policies.[43]

In the ensuing campaign, Texas voters faced three choices. Democrats loyal to Roosevelt, who had walked out of the hostile state convention carrying a portrait of FDR with them, saw to it that their favorite's name appeared on the ballot. (At a rump session, the mayor of Austin called the anti–New Deal leaders "those evil men who would destroy the President, our Commander-in-Chief," and when O'Daniel appeared at Houston's civic auditorium to denounce Roosevelt, FDR's admirers pelted him with eggs, tomatoes, and other overly ripe missiles, a demonstration he maintained was organized "by the gang of Communists close to the throne of Franklin the Fourth in Washington.") The conservative faction entered a separate anti-Roosevelt slate of electors. Though it constituted, in essence, a third party, it claimed for itself the name of "Regulars." Voters in the Lone Star State also had the opportunity to cast their ballots for the Republicans. That was not usually an option seriously considered in the South, but in 1944, both the *Houston Post* and the *Beaumont Enterprise* backed the GOP nominee, Thomas E. Dewey, the first time in its history that the Beaumont paper had endorsed a Republican presidential candidate. The Texas situation, Roosevelt told Houston's Jesse Jones, was like the split of the Democrats in 1860 that had permitted a Republican to gain the White House for the first time.[44]

The president, however, continued to hold the loyalty of an overwhelming proportion of voters and politicians in the South. Despite misgivings, Ed Crump said, "It is beyond me to understand how any Southerner who has any memory at all could vote against President Roosevelt." The Memphis mayor added, "There are three great days—birth of Jesus Christ, birth of our Republic, and the years of Roosevelt's work since Pearl Harbor." His biographer has written: "The election of 1944 was the last great fight Crump made for the Presidential nominee of the Democratic party. He had fought for them all—from Wilson through Roosevelt, but it was Roosevelt who laid the greatest claim on his allegiance. It was not only that Roosevelt and the New Deal had given Memphis TVA; it was that Roosevelt spoke powerfully for the common man and spoke with certainty; it was that Roosevelt, dragging his withered limbs in steel braces, moved so positively and confidently through the history of that troubled era that one seldom thought of him as afflicted. Crump admired the President and stood by him through his last campaign." Toward the end of September, a Washington journalist entered in his diary: "The last feeble embers of the Great Southern Revolt flicker and die on the Hill these days. Josiah Bailey, last to capitulate, has issued an apologia. . . . Others have been equally circumspect. The dinner bell is ringing and the wayward youths are returning home. All the furious indignations, the violent damnations, the dark, desperate threats—all, all are forgotten, swallowed with an obvious effort and a great, convulsive gasp." In South Carolina that year, a leading politician asked, "What President has ever meant so much to the South as Roosevelt?" If a Republican administration came to power, he warned, there would no longer be a "Southern accent in the voice of government in Washington."[45]

On Election Day, Roosevelt refused to oblige his enemies by fading away. For the fourth straight time, he swept every state of the former Confederacy. He received 69 percent of southern ballots whereas in the Midwest he fell short of a majority. Mississippi went to him, 14–1, and Texas, which had appeared to be in open insurrection, gave Roosevelt 822,000, Dewey 191,000, the Regulars only 135,000. The South recognized the palpable benefits the New Deal had brought, and, more attuned to the military than any other section, it rallied behind the commander-in-chief. Moreover, the uprising against Roosevelt in 1944 was tempered, as Robert Garson has pointed out, because "he had not instigated any single overt act to which southern voters could point as being directly contrary to their regional interests. Dixie's rebellion was directed at tendencies and not at particulars."[46]

No one personified that perception better than the unabashedly racist senator from Mississippi, Theodore G. Bilbo. In 1944 Bilbo declared, "If I can succeed in resettling the great majority of Negroes in West Africa—and I propose to do it—I might entertain the proposition of crowning Eleanor Roosevelt queen of Greater Liberia." Yet Bilbo was so staunch an FDR man that even the Supreme Court's white primary decision did not faze him. He told one correspondent, "This Court may lean too far on the liberal side but the Courts we have had most certainly leaned too far to the right." He reassured another, "The present court is bad but the courts heretofore appointed by the Republican Administration were worse; and if you put a 'pee-wee' like Dewey or a 'blow-hard' like Bricker in the President's chair, God save the country."[47]

On closer scrutiny, FDR's victory in 1944 did not seem so impressive. Though "President Roosevelt carried all the Dixie States," a Hearst columnist noted, "there are danger signals flying for him all over the old Confederacy." Dissident Democrats not yet ready to vote Republican stayed home. In Louisiana, support for the Democratic Party fell to the lowest point since 1928, and even in Mississippi his margin was little more than half that of 1940. Noting that the failure of nearly three-quarters of a million normally Democratic southerners to vote for FDR in 1944 had no impact on the Electoral College, the British embassy in Washington informed Whitehall that "it does indicate that a New Deal candidate not endowed with the singular attributes of a Roosevelt can, in a foreseeable, if not near, future lose these States." The South was "Solid" for the Democrats in yet another election, but, though no one could know this at the time, 1944 was the last year it would be. Nor did anyone know that never again would the South, or the nation, have the opportunity to vote for (or for that matter against) Franklin Delano Roosevelt.[48]

VII

On March 30, 1945, the train from Washington took Franklin Roosevelt to Warm Springs for the thirty-ninth time. He looked ashen, and his hands shook. After a few days of being driven through the greening Georgia countryside, though, he seemed a new man. He found, his adoring companion Daisy Suckley recorded in her diary, "lots of azaleas in bloom & some dogwood trees, the country . . . beautiful in its new spring dress." Once again, a Georgia springtime, fragrant with honeysuckle and wisteria, vivid with wild violets, was proving a tonic for his spirits. He acquired a healthy tan and put back eight of the pounds he had lost in the North. "Beautiful weather," Suckley noted on April 9. "F. looks splendidly." When on April 12, Elizabeth Shoumatoff got ready to paint his portrait, she later recalled, "he looked cheerful and full of pep. As I started mixing my paint, I was struck by his exceptionally good color." But that afternoon, in the little southern village he had come to know so well, the president died. That evening his secretary, William Hassett, wrote in his diary: "Today the great and final change. In the quiet beauty of the Georgia spring, like a thief in the night, came the day of the Lord. The immortal spirit no longer supported the failing flesh, and at 3:35 p.m. the President gave up the ghost."[49]

News of FDR's death plunged Warm Springs into grief. "In the manner of religious testimony," a writer observed, villagers who congregated in the Community Building "one by one arose to tell a memory of their departed neighbor." When the cortege, making its way slowly down the hill from the Little White House, halted briefly at the polio facility, the patients sobbed as a black accordionist, Chief Petty Officer Graham Jackson, tears rolling down cheeks crumpled with despair, played a haunting refrain with the resonance of a Negro spiritual. Jackson later remembered:

> I saw everything and I heard every sound and what I heard seemed to mean even more than what I saw.
>
> I heard the sighing of the pines and the singing of a mockingbird; the throbbing of airplanes and the whistling of a train down the mountain. Regiments of soldiers had come in during the night. I heard the scraping of their leather boots and the noise of thousands of shifting ri-

fles; the sound of wheels on the gravel and the click of camera shutters.

The hearse came around the small flower-bed in front of Georgia Hall and stopped there a minute, just like he used to pause and wave to the patients as he drove along. . . . So I lifted my accordion and sounded the opening chords of the Largo of the New World Symphony, and I played "Going Home."[50]

As the funeral train with its black-flagged engine slipped out of the Warm Springs depot, the engineer touched the throttle very gently so that no noise broke the stillness until the cars had cleared the village on their way north through the piedmont. "The ride back to Washington was sad and slow," the United Press White House correspondent A. Merriman Smith recalled. "At every stop, from Atlanta to Alexandria, people thronged the railroad stations large and small. Men stood with their arms around the shoulders of their wives and mothers. Men and women wept openly. Church choirs gathered at the trackside and sang 'Rock of Ages' and 'Abide with Me.'" Each time the train halted, local leaders would board with "sprays of beautiful southern spring blossoms," and as it crawled through one small Carolina town with only a few lights blinking, Smith, looking out from an open door, saw mourners clustered blocks deep, their voices raised in a chorus of "Onward Christian Soldiers."[51]

Fifty years later, the syndicated columnist Sandy Grady remembered:

In my Southern boyhood town, time stopped. . . . Cool April evening, dogwoods budding in Charlotte, N.C. I was sitting on the porch . . . gabbing lazily of the future. . . . Then there was a melancholy whistle, floating across the pines. Tommy and I looked at each other wide-eyed. Somebody said, "The Roosevelt train!" Wordlessly, the two of us began running non-stop the mile and a half up the Trade Street hill. Chests heaving, we stopped at the Southern depot tracks. The train had pulled into the station, lights of every car but one dimmed. The last car was illuminated like the stage in a darkened theater. You could see the raised bronze casket holding Roosevelt's body. . . . Every eye was riveted on that floodlit casket. People huddled in the dark, a silent choir. Every hair on my body was standing up, like an awestruck animal.[52]

VIII

Roosevelt's final months opened the curtain to the postwar political scene. A year before the end of the war, a young southern newspaperman, Allen Drury, entered in his diary: "We seem to be perched on a cliff, in Washington, above a vast and tumbled plain that stretches far away below us: the South, unhappy, restless, confused, embittered, torn by pressures steadily mounting. As far as the eye can see there is discontent and bitterness, faint intimations of a coming storm like a rising wind moving through tall grass."[53]

The bulletin from Warm Springs on April 12, 1945, dismayed many southerners. "The sense of deep personal loss, as well as sadness, resulting from Roosevelt's death . . . was genuine in the South," Albert Gore Sr. has reflected. "For though many Southern political leaders . . . had grown hostile, the mass of the people never wavered in their affection. Roosevelt—glamorous, charming, inspiring and dedicated—remained the people's hero." More than thirty-five years later, Robert McElvaine pointed out, "*Southern Exposure* . . . published a recent photograph of a Kentucky coal mining family in their home. On the wall above the family members is a wall hanging showing Jesus tending His flock. Above that hangs a picture of FDR."[54]

Conservatives, however, soon revealed that they viewed FDR's demise as a deliverance. "Not until the prosperity of World War II and the postwar reaction of 1946 did the name of Franklin D. Roosevelt fail to provoke ringing applause in a Mississippi audience," Frank Smith observed. "But as the years went by and Mississippi became more and more anti-government (while the state's economy benefitted more and more from government funds), it became popular to picture Roosevelt as the sinister conspirator who had laid the foundation for all of the South's woes." In the late 1950s in Virginia, one account has noted, "mention of Franklin D. Roosevelt was enough to turn most members of the General Assembly pale; hearing Mrs. Roosevelt's name . . . was very likely to induce apoplexy." When a bill was introduced to observe "First Lady's Day" in the commonwealth, it was enacted only when a diversion was created to eliminate Eleanor Roosevelt from the observance. By 1960 the racist Louisiana boss Leander Perez was ordering any book that mentioned Franklin or Eleanor Roosevelt removed from the Plaquemines Parish Library. Fifteen years earlier, a prominent FDR loyalist had foreseen this happening. "Now the sons of bitches will start trying to dance all over his grave," Sam Rayburn muttered. "Well, by God, let them try."[55]

FDR's departure set his successors a difficult assignment. As Samuel Lubell observed: "Roosevelt's death . . . removed another restraint against open political rebellion in the South. Many Southern voters felt a deep personal gratitude to 'that man in the White House' who had saved their homes or farms from foreclosure, had raised their wages, and had introduced social security and other benefits. With his death these ties of loyalty were snapped. The battle for dominance in the Democratic party between the white Southerners and the Northern liberals could at last be fully joined."[56] Roosevelt bequeathed Harry Truman a legacy of achievements on which he could build, but also this fiercely contested theater of war.

HARRY S. TRUMAN

FIVE

BORDER-STATE DEMOCRAT

I

Harry Truman approached national politics with divided memories and divergent loyalties. He was reared in a border-state county as southern in its sympathies as any Mississippi delta town and by a family who shared Mississippi's racial outlook and paid homage to the Stars and Bars. Yet Truman also harbored a very strong nationalist strain. He took pride in his service in the U.S. Army, did not regret that the Civil War had ended in a Union victory, and came to view Lincoln as a man of heroic stature. Nothing revealed so well the conflicting tugs upon him as a letter to his daughter he wrote in 1941, when he was a U.S. senator from Missouri: "Yesterday I drove over the route that the last of the Confederate Army followed before the surrender. I thought of the heartache of one of the world's great men on the occasion of that surrender. I am not sorry he did surrender but I feel as your old country grandmother has expressed it— 'What a pity a *white* man like Lee had to surrender to old Grant.'"[1]

II

When an inquisitive interviewer once asked Truman whether his ancestors were slaveholders, he answered: "Oh, yes. They all had slaves. They brought them out here with them from Kentucky. Most of the slaves were wedding presents." All four of his grandparents were born in Kentucky, and, his cousin later remarked about her great-grandmother, "As usual in Virginia and Kentucky families, she and her husband were given enough darkies to establish a new home in the Southern manner." On moving to Missouri by river packet in the 1840s, they took their slaves with them into a state that, as a consequence of the Compromise of 1820, had entered the Union as a slave commonwealth. When Truman's grandparents were married, they did, indeed, receive slaves as a wedding gift, and in Missouri one of his grandfathers owned some two dozen slaves on his 5,000-acre plantation.[2]

Truman's direct ancestors and their neighbors identified strongly with the slave South. One of Truman's forebears lived in Platte County, Missouri, where in 1855 abolitionists were attacked, and Harry himself was to be born in irreconcilably southern Jackson County. His parents, Truman recalled, were "Lincoln haters." His mother, who had once flung Harriet Beecher Stowe's *Uncle Tom's Cabin* on the floor and kicked it around, was an ardent admirer of William Quantrill, scourge of the abolitionists. As a boy, Harry listened with rapt attention when his favorite teacher, who taught him Latin, told of how her father, thrice wounded in Pickett's charge, refused to swear allegiance to the United States and hence spent the rest of the war in prison. She had no difficulty in understanding why "William Quantrill is a hero to many people in this part of the country."[3]

Not everyone in Missouri in the Civil War era admired Quantrill, the Confederate guerrilla leader, who, in pillaging Lawrence, Kansas, in 1863, slew at least 150 of its citizens. The historian Albert Castel, calling him "the bloodiest man in American history," has placed him "in the company of Simon Girty and John Wilkes Booth as one of the great national villains," but in Truman's Jackson County he was revered because he had his counterpart in James Lane, "the Grim Chieftain" of the pro-Union Jayhawkers who rained fire on Confederate sympathizers. "We like to think of the Civil War as the last romantic war—as a sort of gallant duel between gentlemen," Castel wrote. "There was a certain aura of 'swords and roses' in the East, but . . . in the bloody war-within-a-war that raged along the Kansas-Missouri border, . . . a border strip forty miles wide was a no man's land of desolate farmhouses, brush-grown fields, and prowling gangs of marauders." It was said that "the Devil came to the border, liked it, and decided to stay awhile."[4]

Truman's grandmother never wearied of telling of the morning in 1861 when, with her husband away, Jim Lane, at the head of a scruffy band of horsemen flaunting red sheepskin leggings, rode into her farmyard; ordered her to hop to it and cook for him and his men; then killed the hens, slaughtered all the livestock (including more than four hundred hogs), toted off the still-bloody hams, pocketed the family silver, and set the barns afire. Years later, Truman remembered when Grandmother Young "had to cook all those biscuits for Jim Lane's Red Legs," while Truman's mother, his daughter has recalled, "always talked as if the Yankee guerrillas from Kansas Territory . . . had appeared at the Young farm only a few weeks ago to slaughter the pigs and cattle, kill the chickens, and steal the family silver and featherbeds. . . . As for Republicans, Mamma Truman always talked about them as if, at that very moment, somewhere in Kansas they were all collectively dining off her mother's silver."[5]

His family rehearsed, too, the awful time in the late summer of 1863 when a Union commander, retaliating for Quantrill's sack of Lane's hometown of Lawrence, issued the notorious General Order No. 11 which routed all the people of Jackson County, the den of Quantrill's bushwhackers, and some other Missouri counties and herded them to a U.S. Army post where for months, stripped of nearly every possession, they were compelled to live on handouts. ("They called them posts," Truman once told an interviewer, "but what they were, they were concentration camps.") As a girl of eleven, Truman's mother, Martha, trudged through the dust with her mother and five other children behind an ox cart carrying all that was left of a once-proud holding. After the Trumans and their neighbors were evicted, Union forces set the countryside ablaze for miles by torching farmhouses, barns, and hay fields. In later years, Martha would have no compunction about saying, "I thought it was a good thing that Lincoln was shot."[6]

The family also told and retold the story of Uncle Harrison, a lad of thirteen whose head was put in a noose by Union raiders bent on getting him to acknowledge that his father (who was at the time freighting goods across the Western plains) was a Confederate soldier, while the nine-year-old girl who was to be Harry's mother hid in terror. Truman remembered: "They tried to make my Uncle Harrison into an informer, but he wouldn't do it. . . . They tried to hang him, time and again they tried it, . . . but he didn't say anything. . . . He's the one I'm named after, and I'm happy to say that there were people . . . around at the time who said I took after him."[7]

Truman grew up steeped in the lore of these Civil War experiences. Margaret Truman recalled hearing from her father, and at her father's prompting her grandmother, tales of the days when guerrillas ravaged Missouri, and Truman knew well that his uncle, who had served in the Confederate army, had named his daughter after Jefferson Davis's daughter. Boy and man, Truman could see the bullet holes from a Civil War encounter that were plainly visible on the exterior of a bank in Independence. Hence, it is not surprising that in 1951 Lyndon Johnson told Truman that a Kentucky senator, after an evening with the president, had said "that he had now met somebody that knew as much about the Civil War as he did."[8]

The women in Truman's life imbued Truman with, in Alonzo Hamby's words, an "intense distaste for New England and the Northeast that was the obverse side of the family's Southern sympathies." The atmosphere in which he was raised is suggested by a remark of his great-aunt who, as a young woman, wrote a friend while on a visit to Missouri, "I have been having a real pleasant time, but haven't seen any cute boys yet; the boys and girls are pretty fast here and are so yankeefied." When in 1905 twenty-one-year-old Harry Truman, proud of his spiffy new uniform in the National Guard, visited his grandmother, she gave him a once-over, then told him sternly, "Harry, this is the first time since 1863 that a blue uniform has been in this house. Don't bring it here again."[9]

More than four decades later, when the president's mother visited him in Washington, her son teased her by saying, "Tonight, Mother, we are going to give you a special treat, a chance to sleep in the most famous room in the White House, the Lincoln Room, and in the very bed in which Abraham Lincoln slept." After a moment's pregnant silence, she turned to her daughter-in-law and said, "Bess, if you'll get my bags packed, I'll be going home this evening." When at a White House dinner with a former ambassador someone mentioned a name, Mother Truman interjected, "Isn't he a Yankee?" The president's sister responded, "Now, Mother—" but Mrs. Truman would not be quieted. "Well, isn't he?" she persisted. "Yes, Mother," her son responded, "but you know there are good Yankees as well as bad and good Rebels." Mother Truman shot back, "Well, if there are any good Yankees, I haven't seen one yet." At ninety-two, she broke her hip and shoulder, and, before her son could express a word of concern, she glowered at him and said, "I don't want any smart cracks out of you. I saw your picture in the paper last week putting a wreath at the Lincoln Memorial."[10]

Truman literally learned at his mother's knee to share the South's view of the War Between the States. He detested the insolent abolitionists; was sure the slave masters were benevolent; decried the racial experimentation of Reconstruction; and sneered at Thaddeus Stevens, that "crippled moron." In 1948, on his whistle-stop campaign, he carried his denunciation of the "do-nothing, good-for-nothing 80th Congress" to the point of saying, at a meeting with reporters in Spokane, that the 80th was the "worst" Congress in history. Later that day, two newspapermen tracked him down to ask whether he really did think it was the worst ever. He paused, then rejoined, "Well no, not the worst. The worst Congress was the Thaddeus Stevens Congress." Asked to account for why Andrew Johnson had been impeached, Truman replied: "Johnson tried to carry on Lincoln's policy. Lincoln was going to treat the South not as a conquered nation but as a sinful child. Johnson tried that, and what happened was a case of the power of Congress ruining a President of the United States. Old Thad Stevens was the cause of that. He just wasn't any damn good. Period."[11]

"I was raised amidst some violently prejudiced Southerners," Truman once acknowledged. His brother informed an inquirer that the family Bible was burned when "a nigger wench was filling a lamp," and his sister told an interviewer, "Harry isn't any more in favor of nigger equality than I am." Not one black lived in Grandview, she added, and none was wanted. The childhood sweetheart he married apparently shared this outlook. When in 1952 Francis Biddle said proudly that Groton was integrated, Bess responded that blacks "should have their schools and we should have ours." Jim Crow Chiles, Mother Truman's brother, added a special viciousness to his sobriquet. He got the same pleasure from killing as his superiors, Quantrill and Bloody Bill Anderson, "always," as a Kansas City newspaper said in his obituary, "exhibiting the traits of the most inhuman savage." On one occasion, he took part in hacking to death a Union captain and his men. "To black people he was a living terror," David McCullough has written. "On drinking sprees, he would mount a horse and hunt them down with his whip. It is recorded that he killed two black men in cold blood on two different occasions in Independence, shot them 'to see them jump.'"[12]

Truman acquired from his family and the Jim Crow school he attended an abiding belief in white supremacy. He thought nothing of using words like "darkies" or of referring to a black man as "Rastus." In 1911, when he was twenty-seven, in a proposal of marriage to Bess Wallace, he wrote: "I think one man is just as good as another so long as he's honest and decent and not a nigger or a Chinaman. Uncle Will says that the Lord made a white man from dust[,] a nigger from mud, then He threw up what was left and it came down a China man. He does hate Chinese and Japs. So do I. It is race prejudice I guess. But I am strongly of the opinion that negros ought to be in Africa, yellow men in Asia[,] and white men in Europe and America." That same year, on the eve of a business trip to South Dakota, he told Bess: "I'll bet there'll be more bohunks and 'Rooshans' up there than white men. I think it is a disgrace to the country for these felows to be in it." More than a quarter of a century later, in a letter home to his daughter about dining at the White House when he was a U.S. senator, he described the waiters, "evidently the top of the black social set in Washington," as "an army of coons," and in a letter to his wife in 1939, he referred to "nigger picnic day." He was even capable of writing, "Just killed a cockroach. He walked right out on the armrest . . . as impudently as a sassy nigger." Over high-balls with other senators, primarily from the South, he relished stories that, it has been said, "were grossly racist, featuring 'nigga preachers,' or Stepin-Fetchit-like buffoons, or hypersexual blacks."[13]

Truman made no effort to conceal his racist convictions. He did not desire to mingle with blacks, and he resented efforts to compel integration. Nor did he see any reason to apologize for his views. When Kansas City blacks faulted him for not committing himself to the goal of social equality, he replied that he alone would decide who would come into his home and dine at his table. He told one of the country's foremost black newspapers, the *Pittsburgh Courier,* that he would not permit his daughter to ride on Washington streetcars because he accepted as true the baseless rumor that every Thursday blacks conspired to push whites off the vehicles. If African Americans staged a sit-down at a lunch counter in Missouri, he said in 1944, "they would be booted out," and rightly so, for owners had the prerogative to decide whom they would serve.[14]

Not even his elevation to the presidency in 1945 led him to cleanse his tongue. When Representative Adam Clayton Powell criticized Bess Truman's presence at a DAR tea, despite its refusal to permit Powell's wife, the pianist Hazel Scott, to perform at its Constitution Hall, President Truman said, a diarist recorded, that he wanted one of his aides to "look up that 'damn nigger preacher' and kick him around." Never again would Congressman Powell be allowed to set foot in the White House on a social occasion. In his Merry-Go-Round column in 1948, Drew Pearson wrote: "Ordinarily, Negro voters would be out shouting and drumming up votes for Truman as a result of his civil rights message. But too many times the President has talked to intimates about 'the ——— niggers' in exactly the same way he talked about 'the ——— New York Jews.' These conversations leaked out." Pearson's allegation is, un-happily, credible, for when Truman, on his way overseas in World War I, first set eyes on New York City, he sent home his verdict: too many "wops" and too many of "Israelitist extraction" in "Kike town."[15]

III

Yet if Truman absorbed his family's and his county's southern heritage almost by osmosis, other legacies drew him in a different direction—toward identification not with a section but with the nation.

Early in 1860, one of Truman's great-uncles in Kentucky wrote his brother

(Harry's grandfather) in Missouri: "Andy, times are very tight and money quite scarce caused by the blamed secessionists. I am in hopes that you are not a seceder. I am for the union now and forever & so is old Ky." In the following year, he wrote again: "It is a shame to think that Ky. has voted three times for the union by an overwhelming majority and still Jeff Davis & Co. want to force her into the southern confederacy. But I think they will have a good time before they do it. Ky. is not willing to turn traitor yet awhile. God forbid that she ever should. You see I am a union man yet and expect to live and die one. . . . Are you still in . . . the union, or have you seceded? Oh I hope not. I hope you have not turned against this glorious union to follow Jeff Davis and Co."[16]

Truman's forebear's passionate loyalty to the Union, though, did not carry with it admiration for Abraham Lincoln, which was not at all a feature of the family tradition. "My old woman is distant relation of old Abe Lincoln," he commented in 1864, "but we are not Lincolnites." On the contrary, he ardently backed McClellan in the election that year. Another of Truman's great-uncles reported in 1860 the vote tally in his Kentucky precinct: Bell, 95; Douglas, 59; Breckinridge, 18; Lincoln, zero. "I am for Bell & Everett—first, last and all the time," he declared. "I fear your state will go for Lincoln."[17] The comment is suggestive. Harry Truman's ties to the Confederacy would be tempered, but not by empathy for Lincoln and emancipation, though he did come to appreciate Honest Abe. Rather, Truman should be thought of as pursuing his political career as a Bell-Everett man: moderate, conciliatory, steadfast for the Union, but responsive to southern sensibility.

Even when in later years he took a bold stand on behalf of the constitutional rights of blacks that led some to liken him to the Great Emancipator, he did so with discomfort and felt called upon to justify this apparent breach with the past to his family. In 1947 he wrote his sister: "I've got to make a speech to the Society for the Advancement of Colored People tomorrow and I wish I didn't have to make it. . . . Mamma won't like what I have to say because I wind up by quoting Old Abe. But I believe what I say and I am hopeful we may implement it."[18]

His capacity for perceiving a national interest transcending his family's devotion to the Lost Cause owed a great deal to the fact that the community in which he was raised, instinctively southern though it was, turned its face, in a highly self-conscious way, toward the West. "The new town of Independence, but twelve miles from the Indian border," reported Josiah Gregg, a Jackson County man, in his nineteenth-century classic, *Commerce of the Prairies*, had become "the general 'port of embarkation' for every part of the great western and northern 'prairie ocean.' Besides the Santa Fé caravans, most of the Rocky Mountain traders and trappers, as well as emigrants to Oregon, take this town in their route." Missouri, called "Mother of the West," was the home of such legendary frontiersmen as Kit Carson and Jim Bridger, and it was a Missourian, "Broken Hand" Fitzpatrick, who led the party that discovered South Pass. More than half a century later, Independence still registered that early experience. As Alonzo Hamby has pointed out, "In the 1890s, when Harry was a child there, Independence had emerged from a Wild West stage to the point where they had built the schools and the churches, but it still had a lot of the elements of a frontier town. The biggest businesses were several saloons on various sides of the courthouse, the streets were all dirt and became muddy when it rained, and men frequently carried knives and sidearms."[19]

Truman had a keen awareness of Independence as the entrepot to the Santa Fe, the Mormon, and the Oregon trails. As a boy he played on the tracks of the first railroad that ran west of the Mississippi, and in the 1920s he became president of the National Old Trails Association, which required him to travel about the country to promote using the historic routes to the West for interstate highways. On one of his trips he visited Boot Hill in Dodge City and encountered a gunslinger who had confronted Bat Masterson. Truman was happy, he said on one occasion, to be "back home—once more a free and independent citizen of the gateway city of the old Great West." After winning election to the U.S. Senate in 1934, he continued at times to think of himself as a westerner. "It is rather lonesome here in Washington, when you don't know anybody, and I'd like very much to see a lot of people with a western viewpoint," Truman wrote an army buddy. "Most of the people in this town think the western boundary of the United States is the Allegheny Mountains."[20]

While often conjuring up his Confederate heritage, Truman's family also relayed to him vivid recollections of his ancestors' experiences on the frontier. His great-grandfather, the son of an adventurer allied with Daniel Boone, is said to have been the first white child born in Kentucky, at the primitive settlement in Boonesborough, and his great-grandmother, according to legend, wore a lace cap to conceal a scar from being scalped in a Shawnee raid in 1788. As a boy Harry heard these tales countless times, and an uncle regaled him with yarns of the Old West.[21]

But it was the saga of his grandfather, Solomon Young, a huge, full-bearded man who took young Harry on buggy rides and on trips to local fairs, that made the most lasting impression. A Conestoga wagon master who drove huge herds

of cattle across the plains, he had first headed west in the "year of decision," 1846, the same year as Francis Parkman's journey on the Oregon Trail.
Solomon Young would leave in the spring and not get home until the following spring. He was once away so long that when he returned his young daughter did not know him. He set out one year from Westport and Independence
with no fewer than fifteen hundred head of cattle, and in the summer of 1860
he reached Salt Lake City with forty wagons and 130 yoke of oxen. During the
Civil War he lived on his ranch of nine Spanish leagues (some 40,000 acres)
near Sacramento. Truman even maintained that his grandfather owned the land
on which Sacramento was built, though, in fact, Sacramento had been founded
before Solomon Young's first visit there.[22]

Truman reaped full political advantage of this frontier past. As he barn-
stormed the West in 1948, he claimed so many places were spots at which
Solomon Young had stopped that reporters wondered how the man had ever
made it to Sacramento. In that campaign, Richard L. Strout, the veteran correspondent of the *Christian Science Monitor* and the *New Republic,* recalled, "the
further west he got the more his western vernacular increased. . . . All the way
across the West as his vernacular got thicker he told about Grandpa's covered
wagon trip to Oregon and produced an historical relative or two in virtually
every area where he spoke." When Truman appeared at the Mormon Tabernacle in Salt Lake City, he pleased the audience by telling of how when Grandfather Young had come there as a trader, none other than Brigham Young had
gotten him out of trouble. Some years later Truman recounted how his grandfather on one of his trips had "made a deal to sell some goods to Brigham
Young," then added, "That was in Utah, and you can bet I made some use of
that incident when I was campaigning in that state."[23]

His behavior in that campaign left observers at the time, and commentators
since, bewildered as to just where he located himself. If in talking to western
gatherings he exploited his grandfather's feats on the Great Plains, he reminded
southern audiences of his Kentucky ancestry and his fondness for Stonewall
Jackson. To add to the confusion, some perceived him to be neither western nor
southern. When Truman became president, Jonathan Daniels has said, conservatives believed he was going to be "a good old middle westerner," and David
Lilienthal thought that Truman "came out of the Middle West kind of progressivism." One of his biographers, too, has asserted that "Harry Truman was
a thorough midwestern creation." A journalist analyzing "the revolt of the south
and the west" alluded to him as "Truman, the Southwesterner," while another

writer called him at different places in the same book a man "from a midcontinental state," "a Midwesterner," and "coming from a border state, . . . neither a Northerner nor a Southerner."[24]

The last comment hits closest to the mark. Truman was a border-stater, a man from Missouri, "a representative," as John Blum has said, "of its partly Southern, partly Midwestern culture." Hamby has described Truman's voice as "a blend of upper South and heartland Midwest." It was a Missouri Supreme Court that ruled against the quest for freedom of a slave, Dred Scott, and as late as 1922 a Truman follower observed, "Missouri is far enough south to adopt the plan of white votes only in a Democratic primary." A poet wrote of one section of the state:

> It's the heart of Missouri, blooded of three, Virginia, Kentucky,
>   and Tennessee,
> It's a tall spare man on a blue-grass hoss.
> It's sugar-cured ham without raisin sauce.
> It's son or brother named Robert E. Lee. . . .
> It's a bluebird singing in a hawthorn thicket.
> It's vote to a man the Democratic ticket. . . .
> It's sorghum sweetenin' and belly-warming corn.
> It's old Jeff Davis a-blowin' on his horn.

Missouri, though, also embraced other outlooks. Its northern reaches touched the Iowa corn belt, and as recently as the 1980s a historian wrote, "Kansas City looks westward, and it has the feel of a western city." Missouri, it has been noted, "is a microcosm of the nation: it borders eight other states, straddles the North and South as well as the East and West, and contributed troops to both sides during the Civil War."[25]

IV

Despite Truman's southern affinity, blacks in Jackson County came to regard him as a just man. In 1924 the NAACP opposed Truman because it was displeased with his careless response to a questionnaire on civil rights, but when in 1928, as state commissioner of the Federal Reemployment Board, he expanded job opportunities for African Americans, attitudes changed. In his first race for the U.S. Senate in 1934, he received 88 percent of black ballots in Kansas City. After Truman became president, the national NAACP leader Roy Wilkins wrote: "When Truman took office, there had been a raft of worries among

Negroes—he was an untested haberdasher from Klan country. But I had known him when he was a judge back in Kansas City, and one of the things he had done back then was to save a home for Negro boys that the white folks thought was too good for colored children. . . . Anyone who mistook Harry Truman for a pint-sized Bilbo was making a big mistake."[26]

Truman's conduct appears to have derived both from conviction and from self-interest. One writer has pointed out, "His business partner after the war was Jewish, his political mentor was Catholic, and his record as presiding judge demonstrated a remarkable empathy for the twenty thousand Jackson County African Americans." Wilkins noted that Truman was "politically astute on the race question before he ever came to Washington, because the Pendergast machine was politically astute on the race question. They . . . didn't necessarily love the Negro, but they believed in . . . marshalling whatever votes it took to keep the machine in power." Truman always had to bear in mind that there were a great many African-American voters in Missouri.[27]

As a U.S. senator, Truman built a staunch pro–civil rights record. According to an account that has frequently been cited, Senator Truman, confronted by an antilynching bill in 1938, told a southern colleague: "You know I'm against this bill, but if it comes to a vote I'll have to be for it." After relating his Confederate family background, he added, "All my sympathies are with you, but the Negro vote in Kansas City and St. Louis is too important." As he started to walk away, he said, "Maybe the thing for me to be doing is to be playing poker this afternoon. Perhaps you fellows can call a no quorum." Maybe that conversation took place, but, even if it did, Truman may simply have been cozening a fellow legislator. All we can say for sure is that when Senator Wagner circulated a petition to close down the filibuster on the antilynching measure, Truman was one of only sixteen Democrats to put his name on it. A year earlier, he had voted against tabling an antilynching bill, and, as temporary presiding officer of the Senate, ruled against the dilatory tactics of the southern bloc. In 1940 he supported an amendment to the Selective Service Act banning discrimination against minorities volunteering for the armed services. Once again in 1944 he signed a petition to cut off a filibuster, this time in order to expedite outlawing the poll tax as a suffrage requirement, despite his doubts about its constitutionality. Walter White declared in 1948: "Few men in public life have ever had so consistent a record as has been that of President Truman. As a member of the Senate, long before he or anyone else ever dreamed that he would sit in the White House he voted consistently for anti-lynching legislation and other measures. . . . He did this in a quiet, diffident way without fanfare or publicity or boasting."[28]

Truman articulated his commitment to equal rights for African Americans most forcefully in 1940 when he sought a second term in the Senate. In the opening speech of his campaign in Sedalia, Missouri, before, it has been said, "an audience mostly of farmers, many of them ex-Ku Kluxers, and not a black face anywhere," he declared: "I believe in the brotherhood of man; not merely the brotherhood of white men, but the brotherhood of all men before law. . . . If any class or race can be permanently set apart from, or pushed down below, the rest in political and civil rights, so may any other class or race when it shall incur the displeasure of its more powerful associates, and we may say farewell to the principles on which we count our safety. . . . The majority of our Negro people find but cold comfort in shanties and tenements. Surely, as freemen, they are entitled to something better than this." At the Democratic national convention in Chicago that same year, he declared, "Every community owes the Negro a fair deal in regard to public utilities, lights, sewers, street improvement, and water mains. We owe the Negro legal equality . . . because he is a human being and a natural born American."

Yet in both addresses, he made no pretense of favoring desegregation. In his first remarks, he said, "Their social life, will, naturally, remain their own," and he alluded, patronizingly, to the exploitation of blacks by "the vendors of vice." To a black assembly in Chicago he said bluntly: "I wish to make clear that I am not appealing for social equality of the Negro. The Negro himself knows better than that, and the highest types of Negro leaders say quite frankly that they prefer the society of their own people."[29]

V

Even while voting for civil rights measures, Truman never ceased catering to the South. On entering the Senate in 1935, he gravitated toward southerners such as Pat Harrison. In later years he was to share a desk with another Mississippian, James Eastland. He felt comfortable with them as he did not with New Deal enthusiasts from the Northeast. Southerners in turn accepted him as one of their own, a man with ancestral ties to their section which he told them about. They even tolerated his desertion on civil rights legislation because they assumed that, since he came from a state with 130,000 black voters, he had to make a show of going along with proposals that were doomed to defeat.[30]

Months before the 1944 campaign, some southerners had come to view Truman as a feasible vice presidential nominee. A Missouri woman reported to him cheerily in the spring of 1943 that her nephew, who was with the *Hereford Journal*, "has just returned from a trip through Alabama & Mississippi and he tells me that the Southern folks say Harry Truman is the biggest man in our country. You remember I told you sometime ago we want you for our President." The following year, the head of a Norfolk firm touted Truman to be FDR's running mate, and a Tampa official wrote him that "everyone . . . I came in contact with after you left was very much impressed with you and nearly everyone I talked with would like to see you Vice President." (Truman responded: "I have no desire to be Vice President, as I told you when I was in Florida, but I will try my best to keep a straight face until that hurdle is passed.")[31]

When at the 1944 Democratic national convention southerners gradually realized that no one from a former Confederate state was likely to win the vice presidential nomination, they flocked to Truman as the most acceptable candidate. "I have never seen such cold-blooded speculation as there was among the Democrats, particularly those from the deep South, as to how many years of a fourth term President Roosevelt could last," Walter White later reflected. Southern politicians wanted to dump Vice President Henry Wallace, regarded as altogether unreliable on racial issues, and were prepared to deliver their votes to the Missouri senator in his place. "Truman, as a county seat Missourian, and former county judge, and the greatly advertised rebel views of his aged mother suited the county seat elite [in the South] much better than the Iowa Robespierre," said one writer. "Hell's fire," a southerner cried, "the man nominated as Vice President at this convention may be President one day. The South knows that. President Roosevelt may not serve out this term. And we won't have Henry Wallace. It's up to you, Harry, you or nobody." Truman, though, had promised to support Jimmy Byrnes, and, for a time, he could not be budged.[32]

Neither the South nor, after he had heard from his political advisors, Franklin D. Roosevelt would take no for an answer, and southerners mobilized their forces to substitute Truman for Wallace. The decisive shift came on the second ballot when Senator John Bankhead gave up on his own candidacy. Congressman Frank Boykin of Alabama, who managed Bankhead's campaign, said that he switched his state's votes to the Missouri senator to prevent the choice of Wallace, "who we thought would be against the South and our great traditions that are priceless to us," understood to be code words for racial mores. Boykin claimed, "We had practically every Southern state except Georgia for us and we threw them to Harry Truman." From Louisiana the sullenly anti–

New Deal Sam Jones congratulated Truman on his nomination, adding, "Louisiana is proud to have played a part in your behalf."[33]

In the South, a few doubts about Truman remained, for he was, after all, committed to antilynching and anti–poll tax legislation, not to mention that unspeakable measure, a permanent FEPC,[34] but a number of commentators rushed in to quiet them. In North Carolina, Josephus Daniels pointed out that the vice presidential nomination had gone to a "Southern Senator whose father was a Confederate soldier" (a common misapprehension), and a Missouri attorney assured a group of prominent southern lawyers: "The people of the South need never have any fear of Truman, as his people were in the Civil War on the Southern side, and his grandparents driven from Missouri by Order Number Eleven, which depopulated western Missouri. When they returned, they found their property destroyed."[35]

Southern politicos understood the significance of the choice of Truman. North Carolina's senator-elect, Clyde R. Hoey, expressed pleasure that the convention had ditched Wallace and had chosen instead "a very much safer and wiser man, from the Southern standpoint." Truman, for his part, issued a statement placating southerners by expressing solicitude for their section and admiration for the two senators from Georgia, Walter George and Richard Russell. "The South," Governor Chauncey Sparks of Alabama said, "has won a substantial victory. I find him safe on states rights and the right of the state to control qualifications of its electors. In the matter of race relations Senator Truman told me he is the son of an unreconstructed rebel mother."[36]

Conversely, the selection of Truman dismayed some liberals and black publicists. A New York college student who was a Wallace follower regretted that her hero had been replaced by "a Southerner, whose life-long environment has steeped him in narrowness and prejudice and sectional ethnocentricity." And a black newspaper denounced the nomination of Truman as an "appeasement of the South which must rank in cowardice and shortsightedness with the ineptitude shown by Chamberlain at Munich."[37]

So closely was Truman identified with the South in 1944 that FDR's opponents sought to exploit this affinity to disrupt the Roosevelt coalition. In the closing days of the campaign, Hearst's *Chicago Herald American* featured a front-page story with a crimson headline: CHARGE TRUMAN JOINED KLAN. It published a series of affidavits alleging that Truman had not only been a member of the KKK in 1922 and 1923 but the principal speaker "with the fiery cross blazing at one great nocturnal countryside rally." Truman, though, denied he had ever been a member of the KKK, and the account did not gain credibility.[38]

In the course of the campaign, a reporter for a black newspaper interviewed Truman. He found it "easy to see why he was at once acceptable to the southern bourbons and the northern progressives and union leaders as well." When at the outset the journalist challenged the nominee by asserting that in its platform the Democrats "had gone some lengths to conciliate the South," Truman responded, "Why shouldn't we conciliate the South? Why shouldn't we conciliate the colored voter as well? Both are parts of the party." That answer fudged the question, but the senator went on to say that "the only solution lies in equality of opportunity for all people. . . . There must be no regard for race or color." As he listened to Truman's replies, the writer perceived "some non-verbal quality about him that makes it possible for him to be at home on a cotton planter's verandah where the colored people are all 'boys' or 'gals' and bow and scrape. He is also at ease with educated colored people and sincere progressive democrats." In the end, despite Truman's "Southern accent and vague ties with ardent race haters," the correspondent concluded that when the senator spoke on behalf of "complete freedom in employment" for all races, he was believable.[39]

The outcome of the 1944 election suggested that, though the choice of a vice presidential candidate is never decisive, Roosevelt and the southerners knew what they were doing in picking Truman. He had selected the Missouri senator, the president confided to a caller, because the other prospects had too many liabilities—Bankhead was "too Southern"—and "the one fellow that Southerners liked, and the one fellow that labor could accept, was Truman." The Missourian's place on the ticket helped sweep every state of the former Confederacy. By rejecting Wallace for Truman, who was thought by the southern elite to share its outlook on civil rights, the Democrats eased sectional doubts and scored a fourth successive triumph. In sum, this border-state Democrat proved to be, in the words of the *New York Times*, "the second Missouri Compromise."[40]

VI

When Franklin Roosevelt's death in Warm Springs on April 12, 1945, catapulted Harry Truman into the presidency, the white South felt confident that Truman, grandson of a slaveholder, would be sympathetic to its racial code. The Speaker of the Mississippi House of Representatives, Walter Sillers Jr., who was a vocal white supremacist, wrote Senator Eastland: "We are deeply grieved at this hour, yet there is no reason to fear for the future with the reins of government in the hands of President Truman. I have sought all the information available about him since he was nominated vice president by the convention last summer and I am convinced that we made no mistake in switching our vote from Senator Bankhead to Senator Truman. . . . He is friendly to the South, respects its traditions, and appreciates the support we gave him. . . . Jim, that is my opinion of our president and I am glad I was given the opportunity to play a small part in the events which contributed to his elevation to the presidency." On the funeral train carrying FDR's body, the Democratic senator from South Carolina Burnet Maybank assured a southern friend, "Everything's going to be all right—the new President knows how to handle the niggers."[41]

Publicists confirmed this impression. In a pictorial spread on "Harry Truman's Missouri," *Life* called Jackson County "the last frontier of the Old South" and told its readers that "the Southern-style pillars" of the courthouse in Independence were "appropriate," for "Independence is still a Southern stronghold." Roy Roberts, the managing editor of the *Kansas City Star*, wrote: "The country thinks of Truman as a Kansas Cityian. He isn't. He's a rural Jackson Countyite—down where they really fought the Civil War. The offspring of a Confederate veteran, he is really more Southern in viewpoint than Midwestern. . . . In the Senate Truman's closest friendships were with the Old South." The *Richmond Times-Dispatch* considered the new president's first radio address "especially pleasing to Southern ears" because of Truman's unmistakable regional twang. "Indeed," it went on, "when he pronounces such words as 'all' and 'pass' he sounds practically like a Virginian. Perhaps the fact that he is the son of a Confederate soldier accounts for this."[42]

African Americans, on the other hand, found Truman's succession unsettling. A black woman wrote FDR's former press secretary: "you know what Mr. Rosevelt ment to Negroes. the thing I am riting you for, is will you try to make clear to Mr. Trueman what the Negroes want. and that is first class citicinship. we know Mr. Rosevelt would have give us that. . . . Most Negroes believe Mr. Trueman is a Negro Hater, the town he came frome is very unfair to Negroes. I feail you can explain to him that God crated all men Equal." All black leaders could do was to make the best of it. W. E. B. Du Bois said of Truman: "He . . . was born in a former slave state," but "he may do far better than his antecedents indicate," and the *Chicago Defender* wrote, "Doubtlessly many Negroes will find the man from the Jim Crow state of Missouri suspect." But remembering his support of an FEPC, "they solemnly hope that Truman can prove himself another Justice Hugo Black."[43]

Truman's first appointments, while delighting white southerners, heightened the concern of blacks. When he named Tom Clark of Texas attorney general and James K. Vardaman Jr. of Mississippi to his White House staff, these anxieties grew. But it was his choice of James Byrnes of South Carolina as secretary of state that rang the fire alarms, for Truman, as a Missourian, appeared to be signaling his inclination to elevate fellow southerners to the highest offices. By selecting this "white supremacist of the first rank," in the words of the *Pittsburgh Courier,* Truman had not only given Byrnes the most prestigious place in the cabinet, but also had placed him, under the provisions of the Constitution in 1945, next in line of succession to the presidency. The *Afro-American* concluded, "It is plainly the policy of Mr. Truman to make the executive department as full of southern ideas as is Congress."[44]

But less than two months after he took over, Truman surprised blacks and shocked southern politicians by writing a public letter to the Illinois congressman Adolph J. Sabath asking him, as chairman of the House Rules Committee, to restore funds to the FEPC. He added: "To abandon at this time the fundamental principle upon which the Fair Employment Practice Committee was established is unthinkable. . . . Discrimination in the matter of employment against properly qualified persons because of their race, creed, or color is . . . un-American. . . . The principle . . . of fair employment practice should be established permanently as a part of our national law." A leftwing New York newspaper announced, "*PM* takes off its hat to Truman for the bold stand in behalf of FEPC," and a black weekly rejoiced in Truman's initiative. On the very next day, a Maryland congressman expressed to the president his sentiments on the temporary wartime FEPC: "Right at the present time they are trying to force the C & P Telephone Company of Maryland to employ colored girls as telephone operators to work along side of our white girls. The white people of Maryland are not going to stand for this." The president responded: "I am sorry that you feel as you do. . . . Some such program is necessary." It was beginning to look, wrote a columnist, "as though the orange blossoms and magnolias which symbolized the honeymoon of the new President and his Southern political leaders are about to wither."[45]

However much southern legislators might grumble, Truman would give them no satisfaction. *Time's* White House correspondent informed his editors that the president's letter to Sabath "served only to make southern Democrats mad, but they can't say anything publicly. They'd like to get up and tell Truman off, but he's a new president, serving under difficult conditions, and they can't very well do that." Both parties in Congress, he added, were "weaseling" on FEPC, and "Truman sent his forthright letter to Sabath against the advice of Congressional leaders." Toward the end of June, an Alabama congressman wrote the president that several days earlier 103 Democratic members of Congress had caucused, and since then seventy-five more had joined them in opposition to FEPC. Before any additional action was taken on behalf of such legislation, he continued, the whole group wanted to descend on the White House to give him their "view of this terrible thing that is not only tearing *our Party* to pieces, but the *entire Nation*." On the bottom of this letter, Truman scrawled terse instructions to an aide: "Matt: The answer is not enough time to get [them] in."[46]

In the ensuing months, the breach widened. When in his twenty-one-point "bombshell" message to Congress of September 6, 1945, Truman included a recommendation for enactment of a permanent FEPC, the southern press insisted that the proposal be rejected even at the cost of defeating all the rest of his program. The message, one historian has noted, "confirmed that the south was definitely no longer the main bulwark of the Democratic Party, the edifice around which major policies had to be constructed. Roosevelt's influence had permanently altered the nature of the Party's constituency." Truman, for his part, was losing patience with his southern critics. In November, Harold Ickes noted in his diary that Truman, irritated by reactionary southern congressmen, had said "he wished that there might be organized a liberal party in this country so that the Southern Democrats could go where they belonged into the conservative Republican party."[47]

Early in 1946 the anger of southern Democrats flared up again after Truman, in a radio address, attacked the "small handful of Congressmen" who were forestalling a vote on a permanent FEPC, which Texas Senator Pappy Lee O'Daniel called "this nefarious, communistic brain abscess No. 101." Truman also followed up his earlier appointment of a prominent black, Ralph Bunche, to the Anglo-American Caribbean Commission by naming William Hastie governor of the Virgin Islands, the first of his race to hold that post. In the course of a filibuster on the FEPC bill that tied up the Senate for days, Walter George protested: "If the President of the U.S. has nothing more important to submit to the American people in a time of industrial crisis, when the very life of the nation is at stake, then I must say to the President that I will follow the best course that my judgment leads me to follow. If this is all that Harry Truman has to offer, God help the Democratic party in 1946 and 1948."[48]

After the FEPC bill was smothered, though, Truman took a more conciliatory attitude toward the southern legislators. Even before the filibuster began, Walter White had wired him that he was unhappy at the president's decision to set up the FEPC only as a fact-finding agency, and when the bill came to the Senate floor, Truman did nothing to expedite it. Nor was he willing to do anything to advance poll tax repeal legislation. He may well have reckoned that, with his price control program disintegrating, he could not afford a costly battle over civil rights, especially since he depended on southern congressmen to support him in pursuing the Cold War. The staggering losses the Democrats sustained in the November 1946 midterm elections further undercut his authority. After the returns were counted, the Memphis boss E. H. Crump declared, "It will be foolish for Truman to offer himself for reelection in the 1948 Presidential campaign," while Senator J. William Fulbright of Arkansas instructed the president to resign on the spot. As 1946 was drawing to a close, southern politicians had good reason to conclude that, with Truman now so docile and with his prestige apparently shattered beyond repair by the election debacle, he would not disturb them about civil rights ever again.[49]

VII

On December 5, 1946, Truman demolished these comfortable assumptions by making a dramatic announcement: he was creating a President's Committee on Civil Rights (PCCR). He directed the committee "to make a very broad inquiry" with the aim of answering a pressing question, "How can State, Federal and local governments implement the guarantees of personal freedoms embodied in the Constitution?" In launching this inquiry, Truman dwelled on problems in the South, but he named only two southerners to the committee and both were renowned liberals.[50]

Truman had been moved to act after a delegation from the National Emergency Committee Against Mob Violence called on him in September to tell him of outrages against blacks. He was appalled especially by an incident in South Carolina where, only three hours after Isaac Woodard, a black sergeant who had earned a battle star in the Pacific fighting, received his separation papers from the U.S. Army, he was arrested following a minor fracas with a white bus driver and hauled off to jail. There the police blackjacked his eyes so severely that he was blinded. Sergeant Woodard was within sixty miles of home and seeing his wife and child again. In Georgia, the president also was made aware, the only black to have voted in his area was murdered by four whites in his front yard. Near Monroe in another Georgia county, Truman was reminded, two black men, one of them a Bronze Star veteran of the North African and Australian campaigns who had served five years in the Army Air Corps, had been dragged from a car and gunned down by a white mob. When one of their wives recognized one of the assailants, a white man had ordered, "Go back and get those bitches," and both women had been murdered too. On hearing of the blinding of the black sergeant, the president, hands clenched, his face "pale with horror," rose and said in a trembling voice, "My God! I had no idea it was as terrible as that! We've got to do something!"[51]

The very next day the president wrote his attorney general that the time had come to set up a national commission on civil rights, adding, "I know you have been looking into the Tennessee and Georgia lynchings, and also been investigating the one in Louisiana, but I think it is going to take something more than the handling of each individual case after it happens—it is going to require the inauguration of some sort of policy to prevent such happenings." Exactly one week after the meeting, Attorney General Tom Clark announced that, under authority of a federal civil rights statute, criminal charges had been filed against the chief of police in Batesburg, South Carolina, for depriving Isaac Woodard of his constitutional rights by beating and torturing him, an intervention that proved futile when an all-white jury deliberated only thirty minutes before acquitting him.[52]

Warned by Walter White that if he approached Congress to get authorization for a blue ribbon probe racists in both houses would obstruct him, Truman responded, "I'll create it by executive order and pay for it out of the President's contingent fund." Over the next weeks, the administration put together the structure of a national investigation. "I am very much in earnest on this thing," he informed his minority affairs assistant David Niles, "and I'd like very much to have you push it with everything you have." When on December 5 Truman signed the order creating the PCCR, he charged it with looking into not merely racial violence but the entire universe of civil rights. A historian of the NAACP later said of Truman's order that NAACP founders "Moorfield Storey, James Weldon Johnson, Joel Spingarn, and Louis Marshall, cold in their graves, might have written the draft."[53]

After the process of recruitment had been completed, Truman instructed the assembled members of his committee:

I want our Bill of Rights implemented in fact as well as on paper. . . . This country could very easily be faced with another situation . . . similar to the one with which it was faced in 1922 [when] I was running for my first elective office . . . —County Judge of Jackson County—and there was an organization in that county that met on hills and burned crosses and worked behind sheets. There is a tendency in this country for that situation to develop again, unless we do something tangible to prevent it.

I don't want to see any race discrimination. I don't want to see any religious bigotry break out in this country as it did then.

He informed the men and women in the room, "I have been very much alarmed at certain . . . happenings around the country that . . . show that there is a latent spirit in some of us that isn't what it ought to be." In some places jury trials had become "travesties." He believed in local sovereignty. "But there are certain rights under the Constitution of the United States which I think the Federal Government has a right to protect, and I want to find out just how far we can go." It was a big job, he told the committee. "Go to it."[54]

Truman had a powerful influence on the nature of the report that emerged from his committee. The venture might well have been of little consequence. He could have named a committee evenly balanced between supporters and critics of traditional mores; he could have intimated to the committee subtly not to do anything that would be politically injurious to him; and he could have asked it to tone down its findings. His own attorney general warned the committee that "you can't legislate morals," and one of the country's most highly regarded scholars urged the members to stress the "constitutional limits upon the federal government" in order to forestall the "steady stream of demands that Congress do things which it quite obviously does not have the constitutional authority to do" and to eschew the "politically impossible." But the president named a committee without a single representative of conventional racial attitudes; he gave his appointees carte blanche; he expressed strong encouragement for a forthright stand; and he did nothing to temper the recommendations, though he knew they would be explosive. Truman had acted as Roosevelt, confronted by the dreadful race riots in World War II, had not.[55]

The white South struggled to understand why Truman had become so much more committed to civil rights than had been expected. According to one theory of social change, elites act only when the masses compel them to, but that conception falls short in this instance. True, black veterans had returned from the war in a more militant mood. "Throughout the Pacific," Walter White warned a U.S. Senate committee, "I was told with grim pessimism by Negro troops that 'we know that our fight for democracy will really begin when we reach San Francisco on our way home.'" Yet in the 1940s the civil rights movement was not nearly as well mobilized as it later would become, and Truman felt no coercion from mass demonstrations or ghetto rioting.[56]

There is more substance to the allegation that he modified his attitude for political reasons. In World War II, over a million African Americans had migrated to northern and western states such as Michigan and California with big blocs of electoral votes. During the 1940s, the black population of Detroit grew 40 percent, of San Francisco 227 percent, of Portland-Vancouver 437 percent. In the 1946 elections, dismayed by southern racist demagogues, blacks had drifted away from the Democrats, conspicuously in New York where Governor Thomas E. Dewey was the likely Republican nominee in 1948.

It was not at all clear, however, that a strong stand for civil rights was a vote-getter. Political considerations might have inclined Truman to hunker down after the staggering losses his party had suffered in the November midterm elections. Pundits interpreted the returns as a rebuke delivered by the American people to the president for failing to curb rising prices. The country was far more interested in having Truman do something about inflation than in seeing him engender new controversies on civil rights. Moreover, his action might lead southern states to break away, and he could lose the ballots of racists in the North. "It is this observer's measured opinion," wrote Walter White, "that if the President wanted to play politics he would have followed the course of his predecessors of evading or postponing action on this most explosive of American issues." One civil rights activist concluded: "Mr. Truman had faults, but his presidency was ennobled because of his stubborn conviction that a problem was something to be faced and a President's job was to make decisions. Here was a Democratic President from a border state, with many personal and political attachments to Southern politicians, facing an election which appeared likely to go against him, harassed by labor problems at home and the most desperate sorts of problems abroad, yet nevertheless deliberately choosing a position bound to antagonize his party's traditional bastion of strength."[57]

When, in the course of an interview, the historian George Tindall asked Jonathan Daniels to what extent Truman's interest in civil rights was politically motivated, Daniels replied, "Oh, I don't have any doubt that he considered the political implications, . . . and yet I'm sure he also felt it was the right thing to do. And I don't think it was a pure political motivation, because I never saw any instance in which he grinned about it behind the back of the public." Still, Daniels expressed puzzlement. He ruminated: "I don't think anybody could go inside Truman's soul and determine. He came out of a family— . . . his sister was a conventional Eastern Star Southerner with the same attitudes toward the blacks that you would find in the Lodge in Greenville or anywhere else. I don't know of any place where Truman saw the Burning Bush, the blinding light on the road to Damascus. . . . I don't think anyone can go and strip Truman down and find where is principle, where politics."[58]

Foreign policy concerns unquestionably prompted Truman. Discrimination against people of color put the U.S. government at a disadvantage as it vied with the Soviet Union for the allegiance of the third world. The Russian periodical *Trud* called the awful incident in Monroe, Georgia, to the attention of the world; *Al Yaqdha* in Baghdad denounced the American version of apartheid; and the Fiji *Times and Herald* featured an article saying that blacks in America suffered more than under slavery, for they were subjected to "the most terrible forms of racial persecution." The NAACP embarrassed the administration by petitioning the UN Committee on Human Rights to get "the nations of the world to persuade this nation to be just to its own people" by ending "barbaric" treatment. In *An Appeal to the World,* the NAACP declared, "It is not Russia that threatens the United States so much as Mississippi, not Stalin and Molotov but Bilbo and Rankin: internal injustice done to one's brothers is far more dangerous than the aggression of strangers from abroad." Henry Lee Moon of the NAACP noted that the South Carolinian James F. Byrnes, as secretary of state, was demanding "free and unfettered elections" for Rumanians, Bulgars, and Poles when millions of southern blacks were denied the right to vote. Cold War concerns, however, also hurt the civil rights cause, for opponents argued either that activists were agents of the Kremlin or that, at a time when it was imperative that the nation be unified against the Soviet menace, no one should be agitating the very divisive issue of race. These arguments cut no ice with Truman. "The top dog in a world which is over half colored ought to clean his own house," he believed.[59]

Probably most important in accounting for the White House initiative, though, was Truman's indignation at the denial to blacks of their fundamental rights as American citizens. He later said: "There was a Georgia sheriff who took four niggers in a car, two men and two women, ordered them out of the car and shot them down, and nothing was done about it. It's true. Nothing was done about it. . . . That I don't like." Southern politicians found it hard to grasp that, as president, Harry Truman was growing into the job and, with respect to race, was expanding his horizons, even to the point of embracing integration as public policy. What they thought could be explained only as political expedience actually represented maturing convictions.[60]

He found it especially intolerable that these outrages were being inflicted upon men in uniform, with whom he readily identified. As one commentator has written: "The future world figure liked soldiering. As a 'teen-ager' during the Spanish-American War, he and his friends had regular drill periods." He had "thirsted for a West Point education," Robert Ferrell has pointed out, and after passing every exam for entrance into the United States Military Academy save for the physical requirement, he was crushed that poor eyesight denied him a place. Decades later, when he was commander-in-chief of the armed forces, he told the Corps of Cadets at West Point: "In my youth, many, many years ago, I had hopes of being a member of this Corps. I didn't make it. I am sure— morally certain—that if I had made it, I think I would have made a good officer. At least I would have tried." When he came of age, he signed up for the National Guard, and when America entered World War I, Truman, too old for the draft and with weak vision but feeling "all patriotic," organized an artillery battery. As he bustled about Kansas City in uniform recruiting men for his unit, he gained a sense of personal worth that he had never known before. Captain Harry, who served as battery commander in a field artillery regiment on the Western Front, opened his first campaign for public office as the American Legion candidate at a rally of war veterans where the doughboys of Battery D turned out in force. Having seen men's lives cut short in the trenches, he had a keen sense of how much men in uniform were called upon to sacrifice, and he demanded that they be shown respect. In deciding to set up the civil rights committee, Truman was especially affected by the South Carolina bludgeoning because Isaac Woodard was a soldier. In his letter to Tom Clark proposing a civil rights investigation, he emphasized his revulsion on hearing that a "Negro Sergeant" had "his eyes deliberately put out, and . . . the Mayor of the town . . . bragged about committing this outrage," and in his executive order creating the committee he made a point of noting that "ex-servicemen, even women, have been killed, maimed or intimidated."[61]

Truman also came to office with vivid memories that affected him the way book learning might have influenced another man. One of his appointees to the PCCR, the civil liberties attorney Morris Ernst, later told an interviewer: "I asked him how come he was doing more on this anti-lynching business than FDR had, and the President said, 'Well, when I came back from the Army after the First World War and went back to my hometown, there were regular meetings of the KKK going on—and it scared the shit out of me. And I'm still scared!' I think that was typical of the man: a single event might have a shaping effect on his pragmatic outlook on life and politics. To show the priority he meant the Civil Rights committee to have, he said to me, 'And you'll hold your meetings in the Cabinet Room.'"[62]

On June 29, 1947, Truman delivered an address to an NAACP rally at the Lincoln Memorial and to a worldwide audience by radio that Walter White called "the hardest hitting and most uncompromising speech on the subject of race which any American President has ever delivered." Niles had advised him to limit his comments on civil rights to one paragraph, but Truman had a larger view. He solicited White for suggestions, and he asked two members of the staff of the PCCR to draft his remarks. In his address to the NAACP gathering, Truman advanced an idea that sent chills through the white South: "The extension of civil rights today means, not protection of the people *against* the Government, but protection of the people *by* the Government. We must make the Federal Government a friendly, vigilant defender of the rights and equalities of all Americans. And . . . I mean *all* Americans." After pointing out that "many of our people still suffer the indignity of insult, the narrowing fear of intimidation, and, I regret to say, the threat of physical injury and mob violence," he declared, "We cannot wait another decade or another generation to remedy these evils. We must work, as never before, to cure them now." One of his listeners, who would later become a prominent African-American officeholder, has recalled, "All around me, blacks in the audience were reacting with *uh huhs* and *God bless yous* as President Truman repeated his words pledging civil rights equality for all Americans."[63]

When Truman concluded, he turned to White and said, "I mean every word of it—and I am going to prove that I do mean it." As a not uncritical historian has observed, "For the first time in the twentieth century, an American president publicly discussed the problem of racial discrimination with frankness and humanity." Truman's address to the NAACP, Garth Pauley has pointed out, was "not merely a symbolic gesture but rather a complex statement of civil rights.

He calls for a change in the very concept of rights and is the first president to define civil rights as a crisis." Instead of merely responding to pressure, as a number of writers insist he did, "Truman rhetorically constructs an urgency."[64]

The NAACP organ, *The Crisis,* called Truman's speech "the most comprehensive . . . statement on the rights of minorities in a democracy, and on the duty of the government to secure and safeguard them, that has ever been made by a President of the United States," and the black press agreed. "We cannot recall when the gentleman who now sleeps at Hyde Park made such a forthright statement against racial discrimination," said the *Pittsburgh Courier.* So aroused were African-American troops stationed on a tiny Pacific island by Truman's words that they passed the hat and mailed a contribution to the NAACP.[65]

Truman's talk to the NAACP, the first ever by a president, had one notable consequence. It came just a day before a critical meeting of his civil rights committee. As the session began, a historian has pointed out, "PCCR members, many of whom had listened to the speech on the radio, were buzzing with excitement about Truman's remarks," and, as they began to discuss what to propose, they realized that they could hardly "recommend less than the President's own rhetoric anticipated."[66]

In its historic 178-page report, *To Secure These Rights,* the committee found a gaping disparity between the country's ideal of equality and its behavior, especially toward blacks. This grievous shortcoming, it asserted, had resulted in "a kind of moral dry rot which eats away at the emotional and rational bases of democratic beliefs." Furthermore, it said, with an eye toward the Cold War, the United States "is not so strong, the final triumph of the democratic ideal is not so inevitable, that we can ignore what the world thinks of us or our record." The committee's recommendations included expanding the civil rights section of the Justice Department; creating a permanent Commission on Civil Rights; enacting an antilynching statute and a law punishing police brutality; expanding the suffrage by banning the poll tax and safeguarding the right to cast ballots; and outlawing discrimination in private employment. It also favored "renewed court attack, with intervention by the Department of Justice," on restrictive covenants in housing and ending "immediately" discrimination in the armed services and in federal agencies. Most controversially, it opposed not only racial discrimination but segregation. In particular, it advocated denying federal money to any public or private program that persisted in Jim Crow practices and making the District of Columbia a model for the nation by integrating all of its facilities, including its school system. "I do not believe," said the one southern white woman on the committee, Dorothy Tilly, "that there is anyone in the United States, who, had he been with us and seen the things we did, would have signed his name to any less strong a report."[67]

When the committee members arrived at the White House on October 29, 1947, carrying with them nearly three dozen far-reaching proposals, Truman greeted them by saying, "I have stolen a march on you. I have already read the report and I want you to know that not only have you done a good job but you have done what I wanted you to." That same day, he asked all citizens to read the report, "an American charter of human freedom in our time," that he expected would be "a guide for action." He was "confident," he told the president of Dartmouth, "that it will take its place among the great papers on Freedom." The Man of Independence had come a country mile from the world of William Quantrill and Jim Crow Chiles.[68]

SIX

SCOURGING THE SCALAWAG

I

The report of the PCCR reached the white South at a time of rising resentment of black assertiveness in the aftermath of World War II. Three months earlier, a South Carolinian had written Senator Maybank:

> I want you to know I really and truly appreciate your stand on the nigger question. They are getting completely out of hand . . . now and we must have leaders with nerve enough and love enough for our white womanhood of the South to let them know that we don't want their society nor their vote.
>
> A plan I am pushing is one of not hiring them to do anything at all, not talking with them at any time and not buying anything from them. If we could put this plan across, we could freeze them out of the South.

The letter was written on the stationery of the school board in the village.[1]

White elites saw no need to dissemble their determination to reduce African Americans to a subservient caste. In response to an inquiry from an Ohio man about company policy, Thomas R. Waring Jr., managing editor of the *Charleston News and Courier*, wrote:

> Since most of our subscribers are white people, we do not go after news of negroes. Should they crop up in the news, we designate them as negroes if our reporters have seen them or have implicit faith in the accuracy of an informant. To call a white person a negro is libel per se in South Carolina and we cannot afford to make an error. . . .
>
> We do not call negroes Mr., Mrs., or Miss and sometimes it is awkward in designating women but we manage somehow.[2]

Southern liberals confided to one another their dismay at the sectional mood. In 1946, Mark Ethridge, publisher of the *Louisville Courier-Journal,* had written Jonathan Daniels of the *Raleigh News and Observer,* "I don't think the South was ever any more reactionary than it is at this moment," and Daniels himself, in a 1947 memo, expressed despair. The few "rebels" against folkways in the South, he observed, "seem to be working in the dark. And they need all the help they can get anywhere." But after the conservative triumphs in recent elections, "some Southern liberals are hedging on their hospitality to itinerant and articulate visiting liberals from the North." The "peculiarly brutal and irrational lynching" near Monroe, which had taken place in the state of "the region's most enlightened governor," Ellis Arnall, remained unsolved, with the chief of Arnall's state police force reporting, "The best people won't talk." Daniels concluded: "The darkness which seemed to become darker around the mass lynching spread like a fog across the South. . . . 'Leave us alone,' the South seemed to say."[3]

No better evidence of that sentiment could be found than in Columbia, Tennessee, where, after a racial affray in 1946, scores of blacks were arrested, a black district was looted, and two black prisoners were killed in their cells. The district attorney general secured indictments against thirty-one blacks (twenty-eight for attempted murder or incitement to murder) but against only four whites. Outraged by the injustice, the NAACP created a national coalition to defend the accused blacks, which Eleanor Roosevelt agreed to co-chair. In his closing argument to the jury, the district attorney general flailed critics of southern racial mores as "filthy, loathsome birds of prey, . . . lousy pinks and pimps and punks . . . male and female who need to learn to stay at home, and quit gallivanting over the country spraying discord and racial hatred like a pole-cat." He would liken them to "dogs in sticking their infernal, snooping, sniffing noses in everybody else's business," save that to say so would be to insult the canine kingdom. "To these long-nosed men and short-chinned women—who have attained as near to perfect depravity as the infirmities of human nature will permit," he went on, "the South replies: 'Take thy beaks from out our heart and take thy forms from off our door.'"[4]

A direct challenge to this spirit of truculence, the committee's findings, *Time* wrote, "dropped a match into the dry and prickly underbrush of Southern pride and fear." Though the response was not as intense as might have been anticipated, southern whites blamed Truman for a document widely regarded as "anti-South," in the words of the Democratic state chairman in Alabama.

"These recommendations, aimed directly at the South," a North Carolinian protested, "even exceed in fervor the preachings of the murder-minded old John Brown . . . who, for his butcherings of southern sympathizers, and other outrages, was justly hanged." A Memphis man wrote the president, "Your civil rights body is fixing to stir up more Hell and Damnation than Carter has oats," and a Missourian urged Bess Truman, "There is a lot of Southern Blood in your veins. Am sure you are bitterly opposed to . . . [the report], so please bear down on Harry and persuade him to drop this Tolerance Question."[5]

A number of his correspondents warned the president of the political consequence. The Democratic chairman in Danville, Virginia, wired Truman, "I really believe that you have ruined the Democratic Party in the South," and a Baptist minister in Jacksonville, Florida, informed him: "The report of your civil liberty committee today put you in bad south of the Mason and Dixon line. If that report is carried out, you won't be elected dogcatcher in 1948. The South today is the South of 1861." From Southside Virginia, a woman wrote: "If you do away with segregation, allow negro children in white schools, churches, etc. you might as well drop a few bombs on us and not prolong the agony."[6]

In the following month, one of the president's top aides, Clark Clifford, sent him a lengthy memorandum counseling him not to worry about all this clamor. Widely referred to subsequently as "the Clifford memo," it was actually prepared by James H. Rowe Jr., though after a young administration aide, Richard Neustadt, took Rowe's thirty-three-page, 16,000-word statement to him, Clifford altered it slightly and added ten pages. In his forty-three-page communication to Truman, Clifford recommended a concerted appeal to labor and to northern blacks. "This course of action would obviously cause difficulty with our Southern friends, but that is the lesser of the two evils," he maintained. "It is inconceivable that any policies initiated by the Truman Administration, no matter how 'liberal,' could so alienate the South in the next year that it could revolt. As always the South can be considered safely Democratic. And in formulating national policy, it can be safely ignored."[7]

Developments in the first month of the new year suggested that Clifford was being too sanguine. Though Truman had not asked for any action on the report, but had merely released its contents, resentment against him, and even defiance, built ominously. In Alabama, the State Democratic Executive Committee resolved "That the Democrats of Alabama would be most deeply hurt, shocked and disillusioned should any attack upon racial segregation be adopted as a plank in the 1948 party platform or directly or indirectly as an expression of party policy. . . . Such an action by the National leadership of the Democratic party could but force every Southerner into the undesired position of determining which is the greater loyalty, that to the South, or that to the party."[8]

II

Truman, though he was told a civil rights message "would cause a terrific explosion in Congress," resolved, after a bit of hesitation, to go ahead anyway. On February 2, 1948, the president, undaunted by the many threats, dispatched a special message up to the Hill asking for enactment of a number of the committee's recommendations. "I sent the Congress a Civil Rights message," Truman entered in his diary on February 2. "They no doubt will receive it as coldly as they did my State of the Union message. But it needs to be said." He called for an anti–poll tax statute, an FEPC, an antilynching law, and a Commission on Civil Rights. To end intimidation at the polls, he asked for legislation banning interference by either public officials or private citizens with the free exercise of the suffrage. Democrats seeking to placate the South pointed out that Truman had not embraced all of the committee's proposals, notably those attacking segregation. Yet his message did strike at Jim Crow in two respects— by asking Congress to outlaw segregation in interstate travel and by promising executive action to desegregate the armed forces. "As a presidential paper," one historian has written, "it was remarkable for its scope and audacity."[9]

Harry Truman, "having been partially southern himself," one of his aides has said, knew that the South would be displeased, but neither he nor his aides anticipated the full fury of the storm his words unleashed. "Two lines in the President's message touched the south to the quick," *Time*'s White House correspondent observed. "Those were the lines in which the President advocated ending segregation on trains, buses, trolleys etc." A Louisiana congressman asserted that war had "been openly declared by the chieftain of the National Democratic party against the traditions and Caucasianism of the South"; the *Nashville Banner* attacked Truman's proposals as "vicious"; and in Florida, the State Association of County Commissioners declared that "all true Democrats" found his program "obnoxious, repugnant, odious, detestable, loathsome, repulsive, revolting and humiliating." Within a few days after Truman acted, southern Democrats canceled close to half a million dollars in contributions to the party. A South Carolinian informed Jimmy Byrnes that in "small towns it's fever hot. People are scared. One man told me that he was much more afraid of Truman than of Russia."[10]

White southerners could not fathom how anybody with Truman's background could foster civil rights. "Be a Southernor," a disgruntled citizen wrote him. "You are one. Stick to your colors. You are a white man. Be one." A South Carolina man told Truman: "It may be all right for your set to love up the negro in the North for the sake of his vote, but you have no right to . . . demand that we take him into our crowded textile plants and try to fix it so he can be elevated to 'Boss' over our wifes and daughters as they work day after day. . . . You of all people coming from a border State, one that half of it stood by the South in its struggle during the 1860's and yet you ask the Congress to pass such nefarious acts." In like manner, an irate Texan wrote a southern moderate: "You say Truman is a son of a Confederate veteran? What would that father think of his son's selling out what the South fought for and suffered the Reconstruction for to get the negro vote?"[11]

North Carolina had drawn praise as a model of civility in race relations, but the mayor of one North Carolina town wrote a Tar Heel congressman, John H. Kerr: "Down here, the civilization works through the idea of white supremacy. . . . This is as it should be and I just can not believe that the *very* small *little* man in the White House is going to get his wishes. . . . I am for anybody other than Truman and that is the general feeling around here." Kerr replied that Truman's "outrageous message" was "the biggest fool thing I have ever known a politician or public official to do." One of North Carolina's U.S. senators got an earful. A Winston-Salem man warned him that Truman's stance meant that the "National Dem. Party will go up Salt Creek without a paddle," while a Raleigh constituent fulminated that since the president had "adopted the philosophy of the carpetbaggers and therefore hurled the superlative of insult to the South, I find it impossible to continue loyalty to such an embezzler faith." A North Carolina woman was even more emphatic. "Mr. Truman and his civil-rights program," she asserted, "is just about as dangerous as the atomic bomb."[12]

From the capital of Georgia, which thought of itself as leading the state toward modernity, the two southern members of the president's committee received an anonymous communication saying: "By your actions you have precipitated and agitated more assault, more rape and more bloodshed than the South has ever seen. You have prepared more hangman's nooses than have ever been prepared. . . . You are not worthy to live in the South. The Southern public knows that you are not Southerners." A journalist wrote of one of the two, Dorothy Tilly, "Born in Hampton, Georgia, raised on a plantation, sweet-voiced and with a fondness for roses in her hats, she is the perfect prototype of the Southern lady," but she received a phone call warning her that the Klan was planning to blow up her home.[13]

Atlanta's Ralph McGill, probably the best-known editor in the South, reported that southern Democrats were "of a temper to offer to lick any Truman man in the house, in the manner of the late John L. Sullivan, even though they don't have his punch." He declared: "In the first white heat of the boiling anger felt generally by the average Southerners . . . the most fabulous rumors ran like fevers through rural communities and towns: Truman had come out for intermarriage; Truman was for compulsory mixing of the races at dances, dinners and swimming pools. Knots of men on courthouse lawns, before country hardware and drug stores, discussed the rumors as Truman's words." In fact, Truman had "touched off the loudest political pyrotechnics since 1860." McGill himself, editor of the *Atlanta Constitution*, which did not have a single black journalist until the 1960s, thought most of Truman's program "mild stuff," but deplored the FEPC proposal as "new evidence of a national sickness," nothing less than a "Boris Karloff creation" that would destroy the civil rights of whites and their employers.[14]

The bitterness in Georgia manifested itself in more than one way. "The immediate and instinctive reaction of some southerners was to parade in percale," one historian has noted. "The day after the President's message nearly 200 hooded klansmen of Swainsboro, Georgia marched to the courthouse, ignited the cross, and sang 'America.'" The turnout, though, was disappointing, one KKK leader explaining, "There would have been more Klansmen present but others were unable to obtain sheets." From Atlanta, *Newsweek*'s correspondent wired: "The Klan is making hay while the Truman sun sinks low in the South."[15]

On the eve of the Democratic primary in Johnson County, Georgia, where four hundred African Americans had registered to vote, seven hundred citizens of the small town of Wrightsville (pop. 1760) gathered early in March to applaud a procession of nearly 250 white-robed Klansmen and Klanswomen. By the light of a fiery cross, Georgia's Grand Dragon took advantage of the occasion to denounce Harry Truman. "Again you will see Yankee bayonets trying to force social and racial equality between the black and white races," he warned. "If that happens, there are those among you who will see blood flow in these streets." Next day, not a single black went to the polls. In the race for the U.S. Senate, Herman Talmadge, seeking to complete the final two years of his father's term, exploited resentment at Truman's civil rights message. Flaunting Ole Gene's red suspenders and long black stogies, Herman drummed upon a single theme: "Let's keep the nigger in his place."[16]

No state, though, matched Mississippi in the intemperance of its rhetoric. In a front-page editorial under the banner MISSISSIPPI IS THROUGH WITH TRUMAN, the *Jackson Daily News* expostulated:

> We cannot maintain our self-respect if we blindly follow President Truman. . . .
>
> He is a renegade from his own race.
>
> He has quit the white folks and gone over to the negroes.
>
> He has declared himself an enemy of the South and the Southern people. . . .
>
> Insofar as Mississippi is concerned, Truman is through, finished, washed up, blotted out.
>
> And we don't mean maybe either.

Frederick Sullens, editor of the paper, summed up his feelings about Truman by saying, "Mississippi has about as much use for him as a bull has for a blue brassiere."[17]

Mississippi's delegation in Congress echoed the Jackson paper. "Not since the first gun was fired on Fort Sumter, resulting as it did in the greatest fratricidal strife in the history of the world, has any message of any President of these glorious United States . . . resulted in the driving of a schism in the ranks of our people as did President Truman's so-called civil rights message," asserted Representative William M. Colmer, who has been called "Mississippi's most consistent supporter of the . . . New Deal" in the House of Representatives. "No President, either Democrat or Republican, has ever seen fit heretofore to make such recommendations." People recognized however, said Mississippi Congressman John Rankin, the evil spirit behind the president's "stupid message": Eleanor Roosevelt.[18]

Still another Mississippi congressman, John Bell Williams, who turned one of the portraits of Truman in his office to the wall and draped the other in black, accused the president of lending "aid and comfort to . . . radical . . . organizations which, conceived in hate, whelped in treason and deceit, and nurtured on the breast of communism, are attempting to bring about in this great country moral disintegration and mongrelization through a forced amalgamation of the races" while "hiding the rotten stench of their insidious aims." Williams continued: "The people of the South are directly responsible for Mr. Truman's ascendancy to the Presidency; yet, despite this, he has seen fit to run a political dagger into our backs and now he is trying to drink our blood." Conditions in 1948, Senator James O. Eastland of Mississippi agreed, were "similar to those that existed in the 1850s." Indeed, he said, at the end of a long harangue on the Senate floor: "This much is certain. If the present Democratic leadership is right, then Calhoun and Jefferson Davis were wrong. If the present Democratic leadership is right, then Thaddeus Stevens and Charles Sumner were right, and Lee, Forrest, and Wade Hampton were wrong. If the President's civil-rights program is right, then reconstruction was right. If this program is right, the carpetbaggers were right."[19]

Mississippi's fire-eating governor, Fielding Wright, carried Eastland's analogy a step further by calling for secession from the Democratic Party if its leaders persisted in advocating laws "aimed to wreck the South and our institutions." Under his guidance, Mississippi Democrats chose, of all days, Lincoln's birthday for a grassroots meeting in Jackson to protest "anti-Southern legislation." Less than two weeks after the president fired his message, the Mississippi legislature adjourned for the day, then assembled en masse in Jackson's city auditorium where, the *New York Times* reported, four thousand "wildly cheering and stomping Mississippians" approved a resolution calling for "all true white Jeffersonian Democrats" in America to fight the president's civil rights proposals and "three times lustily booed the name of Mr. Truman."[20]

Wright, "as smooth and cold as a hardboiled egg," headed off for a Southern Governors' Conference in Wakulla Springs, Florida, as the leader of a burgeoning band of mutineers. John U. Barr of New Orleans saw the outcry against Truman as an opportunity for frustrated southerners to fulfill the aspirations of the aborted dump-Roosevelt campaign. He leafleted the South with the message: "In 1944 genuine Democrats made the first serious move to eliminate from the real Democratic Party the alleged Negro-LOVING, pink and red MONGRELS who FALSELY called themselves Democrats. True, we were whipped and humiliated and on election day 1944 real Democrats found themselves with no place to go. BUT, THE SEED OF OUR STRENGTH HAD BEEN PLANTED." Wright, however, met stiff resistance. Though the governors of both Georgia and Alabama thought Truman's civil rights program "unwise," they also opposed bolting the party. "Well, I see you are against me," Wright said frostily on the eve of the Wakulla Springs gathering. "Yes," Governor M. E. Thompson of Georgia responded, "and we're going to beat you."[21]

At Wakulla Springs, Wright could claim only partial success. Jonathan Daniels, who attended the meeting, reported to the president: "My judgment . . . is that it is the same old phony Claghorn movement which usually gets started this time every election year. I know that North Carolina is not interested in joining up with any bush league secessionists of 1948." The governor of Texas urged his peers to unite "so that we may regain important privileges that have been lost, such as the two-thirds rule," but the governors were not ready to consent to Wright's proposal for a section-wide political gathering to organize a rebellion against Truman. The motion to consider seceding from the party could not even get a second. Instead, the governors adopted a more moderate procedure—a forty-day cooling-off period, but with one proviso: that Strom Thurmond head a committee in defense of white supremacy that would call upon the national chairman of the Democratic Party to turn away from Truman's policies. In addition, the conferees warned: "The President must cease attacks on white supremacy or face full-fledged revolt in the South."[22]

Southern congressmen showed no disposition toward "cooling off." The president's message, Robert J. Donovan has noted, "touched off such an outburst of comment on Capitol Hill from members from Mississippi, Alabama, Louisiana, South Carolina, and Georgia as often exceeded the standards of what was printable in the newspapers." The attitude of the southern officeholders reminded some of the days after Sumter. "Fetch me out my gray store suit, Scipio, roust my sword with the yellow tassels, and hand me my horse," wrote one columnist mockingly. "Today I am a Southern Democrat and I aim to se-cede." Those in the Truman circle, though, took matters more seriously. "Things certainly are popping on the Civil Rights front," the former director of research for the president's committee wrote his superior. "I hope we have not cost the man his election!"[23]

At the Jefferson-Jackson Day dinners in mid-February, Truman got rude reminders of southern hostility to his civil rights program. Asked whether he would attend the annual party celebration, Congressman L. Mendel Rivers of South Carolina exploded: "Hell no, I'm not going. I wouldn't think of sitting down at the table with those people." Rivers warned, "One of these days the so-called leaders are going to find out that the so-called Solid South is not as solid as some of the heads of our so-called leaders." In Washington at the most important dinner, a table at the Mayflower Hotel reserved and paid for by Senator Olin Johnston of South Carolina was deliberately left vacant in a conspicuous spot near the dais. Though nearly three thousand people showed up at the event, the press focused on the empty table—with *Time* even troubling to send a photographer to the Johnstons to catch the senator and his wife fixing supper alone at home. The senator, who *Time* called "a coon-shouting white-supremacy man," not only allowed a thousand dollars in tickets go to waste, but also employed a former heavyweight boxer to see to it that no one filled the empty seats. Mrs. Johnston, a vice chair of the dinner committee, decided not to turn up, she explained, "because I might be seated next to a nigra." (One of Johnston's constituents later told him happily that, in the wake of the May-flower incident, "applications for Ku Klux Klan membership are booming and there's a healthy increase in the manufacture of Red Shirts in South Car-olina.")[24]

Democrats in other southern cities delivered additional rebuffs that night. When the toastmaster at the assemblage in Little Rock announced that Tru-man's broadcast would be piped in shortly, more than half of the nine hundred diners noisily shoved back their chairs and filed out of the banquet hall, some shouting, "He has said enough already." In Mississippi, John Bell Wil-liams stated, "You will find most of us having our own Jefferson-Jackson Day dinners in gatherings in which white supremacy is the order and segregation is the rule." At the affair in Richmond, Senator Byrd asserted that Thomas Jeffer-son "would be shocked and alarmed" to learn that a Democratic president had advocated "a mass invasion of states rights never before even suggested . . . by any previous President of any party affiliation in the nation's history," and in Raleigh, Senator Tom Connally of Texas, calling Truman's message "a lynching of the Constitution," assured his North Carolina audience, "We will not take it lying down."[25]

When the delegation of southern governors deputized by the Wakulla Springs conference met with J. Howard McGrath four days after the Jefferson-Jackson Day dinners, Governor Thurmond asked, "Will you now, at a time when national unity is so vital to the solution of the problem of peace in the world, use your influence, as Chairman of the Democratic National Commit-tee, to have the highly controversial Civil Rights legislation . . . withdrawn from consideration by the Congress?" Senator McGrath replied bluntly, "No." In-deed, *Newsweek* reported, the chairman, "puffing a huge Ulysses S. Grant–like cigar," said "No" so many times, at first soothingly then more gruffly, that the petitioners "got no further than Gen. George E. Pickett did at Gettysburg." Grim-faced, Thurmond refused to sit down and instead paced the floor hurl-ing questions at McGrath as though he were a county prosecutor. McGrath, seeking to be ingratiating, would not be drawn into speculation about matters such as school integration that went beyond Truman's recommendations, and he was not one, he told his visitors, who took the attitude that the southern states "are with us anyway so the 'H' with them." But he would not back away from anything the president had already proposed, including the FEPC. Would he be willing to support return to the two-thirds rule? That, McGrath answered, would be "a backward step." Still more menacingly, he had made a point of saying at the outset that "the President has called attention of the Congress to the fact that segregation has been declared to be unconstitutional." Governor Ben Laney of Arkansas wanted to be sure he was referring only to Jim Crow in interstate commerce. "There conceivably could be other fields," McGrath replied. After the session, Governor R. Gregg Cherry of North Carolina said: "There was just a lot of talk, talk, talk. McGrath handled himself pretty well." Governors who came "with blood in their eyes didn't get exactly what they were after." But on leaving the meeting, the governors issued a joint statement: "The Southern states are aroused and the Democratic Party will soon realize that the South is no longer 'in the bag.'"[26]

III

The failure of the southern governors to make headway with McGrath gave added impetus to a fast-growing movement to deny Truman nomination for another term. On the very next day in South Carolina, half of Jasper County's four thousand whites turned out for a rally at which a longtime Democratic chairman urged his neighbors to "strike the match tonight that will set the South aflame." A resolution to secede from the Democratic Party drew a resounding chorus of "ayes," one defector from the party of Blease and Tillman raising a banner with the legend: "You can have her, we don't want her, she's too black for me." In both South Carolina and Mississippi, state Democratic organizations began to collect and sequester funds for a possible southern third-party candidacy. Clark County, Alabama, Democrats declared that any communication they received from national party headquarters would be returned unopened. Fifty-two southern congressmen had already announced that they would not back the president for reelection. "Red-hot, they raced up one side of Truman's frame, and down the other," a journalist reported. In Arkansas, Governor Laney pledged to combat Truman's "distasteful, unthinkable, and ridiculous" proposals—"even to extreme measures."[27]

Four days after the abortive meeting with McGrath, Governor William M.

Tuck asked the Virginia legislature to alter the state's election law so that electors could run independently of the party's presidential nominee, a maneuver patently aimed at denying citizens of the Commonwealth the right to vote for President Truman by keeping his name off the ballot in November. *Time*'s White House correspondent informed his head office in Manhattan: "The Southerners—men like Byrd (who probably wrote Tuck's message, since Tuck is one of the prize fatheads among governors)—say privately that they haven't got a ghost of a chance of winning with Truman, anyway; that it's time to shake the party down, tear it all to hell if necessary, and start building from the ground up. Truman's fraternizing with colored Judge William Hastie of the Virgin Islands has only served to nettle the Southerners more. . . . This time the Old South isn't revolting against [the] Union, just against Harry Truman, grandson of Confederate[s]." Tuck encountered fierce criticism, but he insisted that he would not be deterred by "New Deal flugelmen and political thimbleriggers," nor by "lickspits and apostates." The governor had to modify this "anti-Truman" law, as it was labeled, but even in amended form it empowered the Democratic state convention to place on the ballot a candidate for president other than the one chosen by the national convention.[28]

In little more than a month, Truman's situation had taken a dramatic turn for the worse. In January, despite the release of the report of the president's committee, the Alabama party chairman Gessner T. McCorvey had said that his state would "not . . . talk of seceding" and that the quarrel over civil rights should be fought out "within our party," words that he underscored. Even after Truman sent his controversial message, the *Montgomery Advertiser* had counseled its readers not to be too disturbed, since the president was only offering a meaningless gesture of the sort any chief executive would have to make in response to strong pressure. One should bear in mind that Truman was a "descendant of Confederate soldiers and from a border state." In a confidential memo, *Time*'s White House correspondent had written: "[Secretary of the Senate] Les Biffle said (NOT for attribution) that the Southern Democrats are really boiling, both in cloakrooms and in private conversation. But he knows Senators pretty well, and he doesn't believe the South will muster a real revolt." By late February, though, he was reporting, "Wherever two Southerners get together, it is an indignation meeting." On the last day of the month, Senator Fulbright told a constituent: "You are quite right about the effect of the President's message. Everyone is . . . mad about the whole thing." McCorvey, so moderate a few weeks earlier, had reached the point of saying that the South must deny its electoral votes to a civil rights candidate even if it meant a Republican victory. Summing up this rapid turn of events, *Newsweek* reported, "Even Democrats agree that Mr. Truman's chances of election, which seemed fair two months ago, are moving close to the vanishing point."[29]

Over the month of March the breakaway from Truman turned into a stampede. Pollsters found that Truman would lose in November to any of four Republican contenders, including Harold Stassen. At the beginning of the month a racist publicist in Mississippi wrote, "The ingratitude, treachery and sanguiness of President Truman and the Left Wing Northern Democrats would make Geronimo and Yellowhand blush with shame," and Ed Crump told newspapermen: "The South has had enough of Mrs. Eleanor Roosevelt. . . . Mrs. Roosevelt frogging around with her Communist associates in America has practically been Truman's mentor. The time has come for a showdown in the South."[30]

On March 13, after Thurmond reported on his lack of success with McGrath, six southern governors, including the moderate-to-liberal Jim Folsom of Alabama and M. E. Thompson of Georgia, approved a document calling for a "fight to the last ditch" against the nomination of any candidate for president who favored a national civil rights program. (Governor Tuck was not present, but so readily did he do Harry Byrd's bidding that the senator added the Virginia governor's name to the statement.) Though the manifesto did not mention Truman, everyone understood that he was the target. In South Carolina, Governor Thurmond had said on October 2, 1947, only days before the president's committee issued its report, "We who believe in a liberal political philosophy . . . will vote for the election of Harry Truman." But he now delivered a special message to a joint session of the legislature advocating changing the method of choosing presidential electors to deny Truman that state's votes in the Electoral College.[31]

Before March was out, Truman had suffered two especially grievous losses. His main hope in the South lay in holding on to liberal senators such as John Sparkman and Lister Hill of Alabama, both of whom had been his friends when he was senator and had publicly endorsed him for reelection. But feeling against the president had become frenzied. A rural Alabamian wrote his congressman that the struggle against Truman's civil rights program was more important than World War II. Admonishing Sparkman to "carry the flag of white supremacy," the former Klansman Horace Wilkinson, outraged by "President Truman's villainous program," told him, "You mark my words, if Truman is re-elected, we will have black supremacy." On March 18, Sparkman announced, "I shall certainly not run as a Truman Democrat," and two days later he expressed the hope that the president would withdraw. At a University of Chicago Round Table that spring, Senator Sparkman said: "I have just been down in my state, and I know that the people have been terribly stirred by this thing. They fear that the President of the United States—a son of a Confederate veteran and a man in whom they had implicit confidence—has gone back on them in recommending a program that would destroy the traditions of the past and would take away the thing which has made the South the solid South throughout the years."[32]

Sparkman's defection left Hill isolated, and his advisors warned him he would be in trouble if he remained loyal to the president. "I have talked with people from all groups and I have found not one who will say he is for Truman," a supporter confided, while another Alabamian reported, "People . . . are mad as the very devil with Truman." Before long, Hill was writing of "how impossible Truman is and just how necessary it is to get rid of him." His switch came just in time. "Had you followed Mr. Truman," a voter informed him, "I could not have followed you."[33]

The rebellion in Alabama peaked when each of its presidential electors signed a pledge stating: "We will not cast our electoral votes for Harry S. Truman for President. If the Philadelphia convention adopts a program hostile to the fundamental principles on which our civilization is based, or nominates a candidate who advocates such hostile principles, we will not cast our votes for the nominee of that convention, but will cast our electoral votes for some other Democrat who understands and sympathizes with the peculiar racial problems of the South. . . . If, under the leadership of Truman, the national party attempts to . . . crucify the South, the Democratic party of Alabama owes it no allegiance." A jubilant Senator Byrd wrote Governor Tuck: "The action taken by the Alabama candidates for electors is conclusive in that it shows Mr. Truman cannot possibly be elected. In my opinion, he will seek an opportunity to withdraw between now and the Convention." To one of his closest associates Senator Byrd confided, "Lister Hill told me . . . that he did not think Truman would carry more than one State, should he be a candidate, and that was Rhode Island."[34]

Alabama had more in mind than denying the president its electoral votes. Colonel Marion Rushton declared: "We are going to fight the Truman civil rights program . . . in the Democratic convention, in the platform committee, in the nomination of the candidate. We are going to fight it in Congress and if

defeated there we shall fight it in the Supreme Court and if defeated there—
well, I hesitate to say what we would do then. Jefferson, you recall, said that the
tree of liberty must be refreshed from time to time with the blood of patriots
and tyrants. At least, you may rest assured that no Southern jury would convict
an employer for refusing to take a Negro into his white office force."[35]

Through the spring of 1948, the mood of insurrection intensified. In the
South that season, one journalist found, "the voice of reaction was loud at every
filling station: people were humming like wasps over President Truman's Civil
Rights message." At the biennial convention of the Democratic Party of South
Carolina in May, the delegates, singing "Let's Send Harry Back to the Farm" (a
ditty composed by Strom Thurmond's executive secretary), resolved that presidential electors should be Democrats who "are now and will continue to be opposed to the nomination of and election of Harry S. Truman as President of the
United States." As one historian has said, "The state had not spoken so sharply
since 1860; it would bolt rather than accept Truman." An Alabama Democrat,
Bull Connor, assured a party leader, "I am against Truman, and will do everything in the world I can to eliminate him—in other words, put the extermina-
tor to him."[36]

On the eve of a rally of defectors scheduled for May 10 in Jackson, Governor Fielding Wright set the tone for the forthcoming gathering by delivering a
crass address to the black citizens of his state: "I must tell you that regardless of
any recommendation of President Truman, despite any law passed by Congress,
and no matter what is said to you by the many associations claiming to represent you, there will continue to be segregation in Mississippi. . . . If any of you
have become so deluded as to want to enter our hotels and cafes, enjoy social
equality with whites, then kindness and true sympathy requires me to advise
you to make your home in some state other than Mississippi."[37]

A thousand fractious Democrats descended on Jackson in chartered buses
from Birmingham, Fort Worth, Little Rock, and other southern towns over
highways festooned with the Stars and Bars. Crowded into the stifling civic auditorium, they cheered exuberantly when Governor Thurmond said, "Harry
Truman never has been elected President of the United States and never will
be," and again when he declared: "We are going to preserve our civilization in
the South. Not all the laws of Washington, or all the bayonets of the Army, can
force the Negro into our homes, our churches, and our schools, or into our
places of recreation and amusement." The delegates voted unanimously that if
the Democratic national convention persisted in nominating Truman and ap-

proving his civil rights policies, they would hold a rump convention. *Newsweek* commented: "That happened once before—in 1860, when the South bolted Stephen A. Douglas. The result was the election of Abraham Lincoln. But the Dixiecrats asserted they didn't care if they again helped to elect a Republican, as long as they helped to defeat Mr. Truman." The president "was the target of virtually every speaker," the *New York Times* reported. A Texan accused him of "selling the South down the river for a shirttail of Northern votes," adding, "Even Judas made a better bargain."[38]

Truman's opponents often did not disguise their racist assumptions. On the same day that the Jackson rally took place, Ed Crump wrote Senator McKellar: "It is going out, 'We must love the world—love America.' Why not love the South? I love the South better than any political party. The white people in Memphis and Shelby County will vote 95% against Truman's Civil Rights." "I wish that you had to spend the next four years in Harlem," where Margaret could marry a Negro "as you seem to desire," a North Carolinian wrote the president, and from Asheville, Governor Cherry, a racial moderate, heard from another Tar Heel: "You are letting us down by not fighting the Civil Rights Bill. The Nigger is write where we want him and thats where he stays."[39]

Truman, shocked by the ferocity of the assault on him and recognizing that his reelection was in jeopardy, attempted, in a number of ways, to placate his southern critics. He sought to forestall a bolt of southern states from the Democratic Party and to retain the backing of southern legislators for the Marshall Plan. "We badly underestimated the reaction of the South to the civil rights message," Clark Clifford later confessed. "We began to realize that we were facing a nastier time with the South than we had expected—but how much nastier we still could not imagine." The president tabled executive orders to curb discriminatory practices in the federal government and to desegregate the armed forces and would not send Congress a civil rights bill that had been drafted. Furthermore, he said little about the race question. In seventy-three speeches in June, he mentioned civil rights only once. As the Democratic convention approached, he sponsored a moderate civil rights plank rather than the more advanced one favored by northern liberals. "The strategy," one of Truman's aides later said, "was to start with a bold measure and then temporize to pick up the right-wing forces. Simply stated, backtrack after the bang."[40]

He would not, though, appease the South by acknowledging his civil rights program was mistaken or by abandoning fundamental principles. When southern politicians reacted angrily to his message of February 2, the president told his staff the next day that it might be a good thing if this issue split the party in the South. After all, Senator Byrd was no different from the Republican Robert Taft, and another Democrat, Pappy Lee O'Daniel, was never right about anything. On March 8, Truman deliberately bracketed an announcement that he would run for another term with a defiant statement that he would not yield on his civil rights message. As the *Washington Post* stated, "By refusing to retreat on his civil rights program, the President in effect challenged Dixie to do its worst if it wanted to smash the party in November."[41]

With Truman unrepentant, the South wrote him off as, in the words of the Grand Dragon of the Ku Klux Klan, a "gone goslin," or, in the phrase of an Alabama legislator, "a lost ball in the high grass of discord and unrest." A Gallup poll found that only 6 percent of Americans supported the civil rights program; even among nonsouthern whites, it was favored by a mere 21 percent. When Truman announced formally that he would stand for reelection, John Bell Williams told his congressional colleagues that the president should "quit now while he is still just 20 million votes behind." The governor of Arkansas agreed. "The Democratic Party," he asserted, "doesn't want to run the race with a politically dead Missouri mule."[42]

His critics could speak with such conviction because, with Henry Wallace and the Progressives eroding Truman's strength in the North, the president had no likely hope of victory without the South, and the South was rising against him. A Gallup poll of southern voters found that disapproval of Truman had jumped from only 18 percent in October 1947 to 57 percent in April 1948. The South and the border states were going to cast 147 electoral votes in November, said Senator Olin Johnston, "and they won't be for Truman. They'll be for somebody else. He ain't going to be re-elected. He ain't going to be renominated." On the floor of the House, another South Carolinian, L. Mendel Rivers, shaking his finger, his voice trembling, cried, "Harry Truman is already a dead bird. We in the South are going to see to that."[43]

Southern politicians would have been furious at any president who delivered the first significant civil rights message of the twentieth century, but they were especially incensed at Truman because they regarded him as an ingrate. In 1948 one journalist wrote: "What rankles in the minds of Southern party chiefs today . . . is that they thought Harry Truman was 'in the bag' for counseling and manipulation by Southern Democrats. After all, he owed his job to them. . . . It has astounded the Southern party leadership to find Truman giving segregation the unambiguous White House condemnation which they have managed to forestall since the time of Andrew Johnson." Democrats from Louisiana and Arkansas, who remembered that their delegations had voted solidly for Truman in the vice presidential contest in 1944, could not comprehend his subsequent behavior. Nor could those from Mississippi who recalled that they had been so eager to switch to Truman that year that they had attempted to vote out of turn. "If it were not for Southern Democrats, Henry Wallace would be in the White House today instead of Harry Truman," John Bell Williams remonstrated. "Southern Democrats have always been the best friends that President Truman . . . ever had. May I say, Mr. Speaker, that this is a mighty poor way for him to evince his gratitude."[44]

Still worse, they viewed him as a turncoat. When Truman presented his civil rights program, one writer has said, "Southerners felt as if they had lost one of their own." The last thing they expected was that a man with such strong ties to the Confederacy would go over to the enemy. When it became clear that Truman was serious about civil rights, the county seat elite in the South, a political scientist has noted, felt "betrayed in their own household by one of their own kind." Jimmy Byrnes's South Carolina confidant later explained: "The South was shocked in part because Truman had always been considered friendly to the region. His hometown, Independence, Missouri, was in many ways typical of towns throughout the South and Truman's philosophy on civil rights was thought to be closer to that of the Democratic Party below the Mason-Dixon line. In fact, many believed the President's views were similar to those of his mother."[45]

Governor Jester summed up these sentiments at a Texas Democratic barbecue where he employed imagery that had become common that spring. Charging that "President Truman's anti-Southern proposals" constituted "a campaign of aggression upon the sovereignty and Civil Rights of the Southern States," he regretted that "the most unexpected and cruelest wound has come from the dagger blow of a trusted friend," a man guilty of "back-stabbing morality." Truman, the governor concluded, was "a betrayer of the South."[46]

IV

Everyone understood that much was at stake at the 1948 Democratic convention in Philadelphia, the first national conclave of the party since the death of FDR. As John Frederick Martin has written, "If Truman was nominated and his programs endorsed, the party was certain to continue in a direction inimical to the South. If Truman could be ousted, however, perhaps the South and its conservative economic and racial ideology could dominate the party for the foreseeable future." In particular, with the Democrats having their first opportunity to choose a presidential nominee other than FDR since the two-thirds rule was abolished, white southerners would learn whether they were still powerful enough to block the choice of someone of whom they strongly disapproved.[47]

No one caught so vividly as H. L. Mencken the sectional animosity that enveloped the 1948 convention. His dispatch of July 9 began, "With the advancing Confederate Army still below the Potomac, Philadelphia was steeped tonight in the nervous calm that fell upon it in the days before Gettysburg." On the following day, he started out, "Save for some cavalry patrols and a few spies who arrived by air, the Confederate Army, sworn to knock off President Truman, had not yet got to Philadelphia tonight, and as a result there was an air of confidence among the Yankee hordes already assembled . . . that the rebels would begin falling to fragments before they crossed the Chickahominy."

Though Mencken had no sympathy for Truman or his civil rights notions, his story a day later indicated that Yankee swagger was justified. When the southerners caucused in Philadelphia, they revealed that they had little strength outside a few Gulf states, he said, adding: "After the count of bayonets . . . [Governor] Laney [of Arkansas] asked if there were any copperheads present. . . . A lone Trumanocide from Indiana then made himself known, and was politely applauded. But there were no others, and the gathering broke up in depressed spirits."[48]

Southern Democrats continued to send off salvos against the president, but it did not take long for them to learn that their threat to deny him renomination was an empty one. At the southern caucus, Thurmond declared that Truman has "stabbed us in the back with his damnable program. . . . We have been betrayed and the guilty shall not go unpunished." When the roll was called, however, Truman defeated the southern favorite, Senator Russell, handily, 947½ to 263. In seconding Russell's nomination, an obscure Alabama legislator, George Wallace, had declared that the Georgia senator would "see that the South is not crucified on the cross of the so-called civil rights program." Russell did sweep almost every southern delegation, but that is about all he got. So mutinous was the South, however, that the convention chairman did not dare attempt to make Truman's nomination unanimous, as was traditionally done to signify party harmony.[49]

Truman's opponents sustained an even greater setback on the platform. Unlike the president, who was willing to make concessions to the southerners for the sake of party unity, a determined group of liberals mobilized by Americans for Democratic Action insisted upon a very strong civil rights plank sponsored by Hubert Humphrey, the mayor of Minneapolis, and Andrew Biemiller, a former Wisconsin congressman. Not a single southern vote was cast for the Humphrey-Biemiller resolution, but after a rousing appeal by the Minneapolis mayor, enough northern states fell in line to carry the day. One northern big city boss who agreed on the need for a strong civil rights plank if the Democrats hoped to win added, "And besides, I'd also like to kick those southern bastards in the teeth for what they did to Al Smith in 1928."[50]

Humphrey sought to convey the impression that there was no breach between the liberal upstarts and the administration, but Truman and his aides were not taken in. Humphrey insisted that a statement be added to the substitute plank commending Truman for "his courageous stand on the issue of civil rights," and he drew delegates to their feet cheering when he said, "I ask this Convention to say in unmistakable terms that we proudly hail and we courageously support our President and leader, Harry Truman, in his great fight for civil rights." Nonetheless, Clark Clifford, who thought the Humphrey-Biemiller effort "was the wrong time, the wrong place, and the wrong way to further the civil rights case," later characterized the convention's adoption of the plank as "a stunning rebuke to the President." Truman, hoping to hold his fragile party together, was incensed. On July 14 he recorded in his diary: "Platform fight in dead earnest. Crackpot Biemiller from Wisconsin offers a minority report on civil rights. . . . The Convention . . . votes for the crackpot amendment to the Civil Rights Plank. The crackpots hope the South will bolt."[51]

The white South felt a great deal more discomfited. One Alabama delegate, noted a Montgomery paper, "sat suffering . . . because a colored woman was allowed to sing the national anthem and Negro congressmen [to] address the convention." Left at the end of the proceedings with Truman at the head of the ticket and an emphatic civil rights plank, southerners were irate. Jim Loeb, ADA's executive director, later recalled, "As I walked with the young mayor of Minneapolis out of that hall, I actually thought he was going to be shot. . . . It was very tense, very tense."[52]

Embittered southern delegates acknowledged that, as *Time* commented, "The South had been kicked in the pants, turned around and kicked in the stomach." Southern Democrats, said *Newsweek*, had been "defeated at Philadelphia as disastrously as their forefathers had been at Gettysburg," and a Richmond newspaper, too, described the convention as "A Gettysburg for Dixie," while a South Carolina paper declared grimly, "The President won at the cost of a 1948 version of the Confederate war." Senator George, in what a writer has called "a splendid Catherine wheel of mixed metaphors," expostulated: "The South is not only over a barrel—it is pilloried! We are in the stocks!" Having sustained severe losses, "the defeated army," Mencken concluded, "retired . . . to a prepared position on the swamps bordering the Swanee River."[53]

At the end of a day in Philadelphia "so long, so gruelling and turbulent," wrote the editor of the *Montgomery Advertiser*, "one thing stands out like a jagged iron pike—the South asked this Democratic convention for under-standing and forbearance, and received a savage blow on its face in return." He continued: "It is clear that we of the South are alone, quite alone with our op-pressive and gathering problem. We stand alone somewhat as England did in 1940. The attitude of this convention towards Alabama and the South this af-ternoon was cold, forbidding and contemptuous." Whereas in the past the West had been the ally of the South, in Philadelphia "the three corners of our coun-try pressed down upon us with cold savagery."[54]

After the civil rights plank was adopted, the chairman of the Alabama del-egation rose to say, "We will never vote Republican, never vote for Truman, and never accept the civil-rights program. We therefore bid you good-bye." He and twelve other Alabama delegates, Bull Connor carrying the standard, and all of the Mississippi delegation then stalked out of the hall into a drenching rain to catcalls and booing. As they departed, the band struck up taunting traveling music; gallery observers waved white handkerchiefs; and a Wisconsin man shouted at them, "We'll win in November without you." The leader of the Al-abama rebels yelled back, "The hell you will. Harry Truman won't get $5.50 from the white people in Georgia to help his campaign." Florida's Claude Pepper rendered the verdict: "We are witnessing the complete break-up of the Demo-cratic party. This might be Charleston, South Carolina in 1860."[55]

V

The bolters resolved to reconvene in Birmingham to organize a third party. A Mississippi editor who had been a convention delegate headlined his account: "It's On to B'Ham! Mississippi and Alabama Take a Walk as Truman Is Nom-inated, Harsh Civil Rights Anti-South Program Is Adopted." Other Missis-sippi editors viewed Truman's nomination as the culmination of "the infiltra-tion of aliens, scum, slum renegades and 'South baiters' into Democrat ranks," and warned, "Those who manipulated the rape of the South at Philadelphia will live to rue the day." Yet another Mississippi editor summed up white sentiment in his state by asserting: "We met the enemy last night but we still ain't his. We are Alabama bound today on the Southern railroad."[56]

The founders of the States' Rights Party sought to strangle Truman's program by winning enough electoral votes to throw the presidential contest into the House of Representatives where the South would have strong bargaining power. As Albert Gore Sr. later pointed out: "The immediate objective was not to defeat Truman—an event which they, along with most political observers, assumed would occur anyway—but to force the decision into an electoral college box while they sat on the lid. This short-term objective was not beyond possibility, nor was it foreordained to failure. . . . The prospects of a Dixiecrat attack from the right looked pretty good—if they could carry the 'Solid South.'" If Dewey did not get a majority in the Electoral College, "these Republicans, not realizing the bitterness of our people towards Truman, would be scared to death that the South might throw its electoral vote to Truman," the Democratic chairman in Alabama wrote Herman Talmadge. "For that reason, I think we can get all kinds of assurance from the Republican Party, agreeing to stay off any of this Civil Rights Legislation if we will just promise *not to vote for Mr. Truman.*"[57]

On a sweltering day in mid-July, Birmingham drew to its red-brick municipal auditorium six thousand ecstatically anti-Truman enthusiasts, among them, one paper reported, "scowling, cigar-waving men" in seersucker suits, looking "like a Yankee thinks Southerners ought to look." The roster of racists at the jam-packed auditorium included the rabble-rousing anti-Semite Gerald L. K. Smith; the erratic former governor of Oklahoma Alfalfa Bill Murray, accompanied by his male nurse who had written *The Jews Have Got the Atomic Bomb*; and the notorious Chattanooga anti-Semite J. B. Stoner, who had petitioned Congress to make adherence to Judaism punishable by death. Stoner had the distinction of having been expelled from the Klan because his racism was so extreme. In its report on the convention, a leading Alabama newspaper expressed disgust at the "ugly carnival scene" where delegates "shouted 'nigger.'"[58]

Though most of those in attendance were more moderate, their devotion to the Lost Cause could not be mistaken. "The magic names were Robert E. Lee and Jefferson Davis," noted a local paper. "They never failed to bring swelling roars from the audience." When students from the University of Mississippi and from Birmingham Southern marched into the auditorium bearing Confederate battle flags, the audience rose reverently, hats over hearts. Then, as the "Texas Beauties" warbled "Dixie," the demonstrators held high photographs of General Lee.[59]

In his keynote address to the "Dixiecrats," as the new party was familiarly called, former Alabama governor Frank M. Dixon, who had been educated at Phillips Exeter, Columbia, and the University of Virginia Law School, charged that Truman's civil rights program was an attempt "to reduce us to the status of a mongrel, inferior race, mixed in blood, our Anglo-Saxon heritage a mockery." The Birmingham assembly adopted a "declaration of principles" which, after denouncing the government for promoting totalitarianism by such actions as intruding upon white primaries, concluded: "We call upon all Democrats and upon all other loyal Americans who are opposed to totalitarianism at home and abroad to unite with us in ignominiously defeating Harry S. Truman," as well as Tom Dewey and all other advocates of a police state.[60]

To lead them in the forthcoming campaign, the Dixiecrats chose Strom Thurmond as their presidential candidate and Fielding Wright as his running mate. When the nominees were introduced to the cheering throng, the band played "Dixie" and demonstrators let out rebel yells. Governor Thurmond, escorted to the platform under Confederate and American flags, declared: "If the South should vote for Truman this year, we might as well petition the Government for colonial status." When Thurmond said that "Truman has forced himself upon the Democratic Party, but he can't force himself on the people of this country," the mutineers bounded up applauding until their palms ached. "The name of Harry Truman," noted the *Birmingham News-Age-Herald*, "drew the convention's loudest boos."[61]

The delegates displayed brutal contempt for the man who held the highest office in the land. From a balcony of the Tutwiler Hotel, demonstrators hanged the president in effigy, the chest of the dummy bearing a sign: "Truman killed by civil rights." On the convention floor fifty-five "leather-lunged" students from Ole Miss milled before the speaker's stand chanting noisily, "To hell with Truman!" One speaker drew gales of laughter when he derided the president as "the little man with the sickening smile." Thurmond himself sneered at the "accidental President." The South, he said, could not "tuck its tail and vote for Truman. If we did, we would be nothing worse than cowards." A former judge who was one of the organizers of the Birmingham meeting explained: "I'm against Truman for the same reason I was against Al Smith. He thinks too damn' much of the nigger."[62]

In addition to appealing to virulent racists, the Dixiecrats attracted southerners who disliked the New Deal and its progeny. The columnist Stewart Alsop remarked that "almost every States' Rights politician speaks as bitter[ly] of Franklin Roosevelt, who never really pressed the racial issue, as of Harry Truman, who did." They resented the way the Democratic Party, once the home of states' rights, had become, in the words of a Dixiecrat, the abode of "radicals of as many hues as Joseph's coat." The Dixiecrats, reported one journalist, were "supported by all the investing and managing communities, from the Southern industrial metropolis to Old Man Johnson's 'furnish' store at the unnamed crossroads." One account pointed out that "Smell of Crude Oil Mingles with Magnolia in that Southern Revolt," and the anti-Truman elements led by Sam Jones and Leander Perez in Louisiana have been characterized as "representing the new economic forces of oil and gas interests (rather than the old cotton-rice-sugar complex.)" A leading Mississippi Dixiecrat acknowledged that "the states' rights campaign of 1948 can be seen as an outgrowth of the thinking of the rednecks, the coonasses, and the hillbillies. But it was acceptable to the political elite as well."[63]

The rogue Democrats found their main sources of strength, though, in Black Belt counties where politicians were obsessed with race. The rebellious chairman of the Democratic Party in Alabama wrote a loyal Democrat a fortnight before the election: "Here in my office we have eight fine young ladies as secretaries, typists, stenographers, clerks, etc. Mobile's population is about forty percent negro. According to Truman's program, I would be required . . . to employ at least three negro girls in my office so that . . . there would be no discrimination on account of race or color. How can you support a man who advocates any such diabolical plan? Your letter really shocks me." Another leader of the Alabama Dixiecrats, Horace Wilkinson, protested: "President Truman . . . is now training federal police . . . to go in each hamlet of the country and impose the will of a strong federal government upon the people. Federal police! What could be more un-American? We must face the race question frankly and fairly as we have learned to face . . . venereal disease." Whereas the opposition to FDR in Texas had come largely from conservative precincts that took exception to his economic policies, support for the Dixiecrats against Truman centered in East Texas where racism was most pronounced. The motivation of the Dixiecrats, Jonathan Daniels later remarked, was "race, pure and simple race."[64]

Numbers of radio listeners in rural areas of another Southern state heard a paid political announcement that said:

Farmers of North Carolina. . . . Do you want your wives, daughters, sisters and mothers to have to share rest rooms, cafes, beauty shops and picture shows with Negroes? Of course, you don't. . . . You are a Southerner, a red-blooded Southerner. . . . But, remember, that is just what President Truman has said he is going to make you do. . . . He brags he is now having trained a federal police force to make you do just that thing. Demonstrate your independence . . . on November 2nd by voting for Thurmond and Wright, . . . States' Rights candidates pledged to keep North Carolina just as Southern as your fathers made it.[65]

In Thurmond and Wright, the Dixiecrats had the governors of the two states with the largest proportion of African Americans, and their determination to maintain white dominance fixed the character of the party. The Dixiecrat governors, V. O. Key later observed, "spoke fundamentally for the whites of the black belt and little more, at least if one disregards their entourage of professional Ku Kluxers, antediluvian reactionaries, and malodorous opportunists." Mencken, who thought Thurmond "the best of all the candidates," admitted that "all the worst morons in the South are for him." A correspondent for the *Louisville Courier-Journal* concluded: "On the platform Mr. Thurmond and his fellow travelers shout of Americanism, our way of life, the right to choose one's associates, Communism, Reds. But they mean Nigger."[66]

Though Thurmond said that the theme of his campaign was not animus toward Negroes but states' rights, his own behavior belied that claim. When a friendly editor of the *Shreveport Times* who met with him for two hours tried to talk to him about a range of questions, Thurmond kept bringing the interview back to a single topic: race. A gaffe late in the campaign revealed nakedly Thurmond's racial attitudes. When Thurmond sent a form letter to all governors inviting them to stay with him at his South Carolina mansion, the missile unintentionally reached the black governor of the Virgin Islands, William H. Hastie. A week before the election, Thurmond felt compelled to issue a statement: "Governor Hastie knows that neither he nor any other Negro will ever be a guest at the Governor's house in Columbia as long as I am governor."[67]

The Dixiecrats drew extra energy from their conviction that Harry Truman was faithless. They sought to block his civil rights legislation, Zachary Karabell has pointed out, "and if Truman could be humiliated, all the better, because the fight wasn't just political—it was also personal. Truman was a son of the South—from Missouri, but a southerner nonetheless." A Mississippian said, "If we do nothing but beat Truman, I'll be satisfied. We are going to have the pleasure of beating a Southern renegade. Any man whose grandfather was a member of the Confederate Army and who would recommend such laws as Truman has is a renegade Southerner. I'd rather have an enemy than a renegade as president."[68]

In the Deep South, the Dixiecrats constituted a serious threat to Truman's bid for reelection. In Mississippi and South Carolina, state Democratic committees chose Thurmond as their presidential nominee, and in Louisiana Democratic Party officials replaced Truman's name on the ballot with Thurmond's. It required strenuous efforts to restore Truman's name, and he still could not run under the traditional Democratic symbol, the rooster, which the Dixiecrats appropriated. Voters in his state, a Louisiana congressman later explained to Sam Rayburn, adhered to their longtime custom of being guided by the rooster without realizing that they were choosing a third-party candidate. Alabama went still further in keeping the name of the president of the United States off the ballot altogether. No citizen of the state, no matter how enthusiastic about his policies, could vote for the man one Alabama leader denounced as "that quondam Democrat, Truman." Straw polls indicated how badly Truman was trailing. In Spartanburg, Thurmond ran well ahead (not surprising in his home state); in Tuscaloosa, he outdrew the president 210–43; and in Macon, the Dixiecrats trounced the Democrats, 1699–180.[69]

Elsewhere in the South, too, Truman came under siege. In Tennessee, Boss Crump bolted to the Dixiecrats, and in Virginia, Congressman Howard Smith, who for a generation would plague liberals from his berth on the House Rules Committee, identified not with Truman, the head of his own party, but with Thurmond. "If Chincoteague Island was to vote tomorrow," a Virginian wrote Senator Byrd's secretary after an eight-day inspection tour, "it would pass a strictly Republican vote, based on the civil rights proposition and all that it conveys." The Democratic Party chairman in North Carolina heard from his predecessor that he could not "possibly hope" to carry the state for the president because "people around me in Durham say that they'll never vote again for that civil rights S.O.B.," while the veteran congressman "Muley" Doughton warned, "Mr. Chairman, you can't help Harry Truman. If you try, you're going to get us all whipped. He's through and if you try to do anything about him, you'll get the whole ticket defeated."[70]

Truman appeared to be faring no better in the Lone Star State. One Texas woman wrote, "I tell you the good women, the best women and the wash women are up in arms and could be fired to frenzied wrath against Truman." When Thurmond came to Texas in August, the political editor of the *Houston Press* declared: "Just as it was given to Hood's First Texas Brigade to try Cemetery Ridge and just miss winning the Civil War at Gettysburg in 1863, so today the hopes of the rebel South again will ride with the Dixiecrats of Texas," the state with the biggest electoral bloc in the South. Thurmond himself, in an interview at the Rice Hotel, adorned in bunting to welcome him, said, "We believe we will carry more states than Truman."[71]

If Thurmond's expectation proved out, and many thought it would, Truman would be returning home in January. At the close of the Birmingham convention, one cocky Dixiecrat had said, "Harry Truman won't be able to carry Independence, Missouri." Even some of the southerners who remained loyal to the Democratic ticket did so with extreme reluctance. One of the most prominent Texas Democrats said that his state was obliged to stay with the convention's choices though "there is no man or woman . . . who despises the idea of voting for Truman any more than I do." Summing up the situation in the aftermath of the Philadelphia convention, the *Chattanooga Free Press* concluded, "This should be a day of mourning for Southern Democrats. Their only consolation is the grim satisfaction that President Truman and his unfaithful cohorts are going down in ignominious defeat."[72]

SEVEN

THE LIBERAL NATIONALIST

I

In the course of the 1948 campaign, Truman encountered repeated evidence of the wrath of the white South against him. One political correspondent recalled, "They hated Truman more than they hated Dewey in Mississippi and places like that. My God, I went to a picnic in the heat of the campaign near Jackson, Mississippi and I almost got lynched." At the beginning of July, a Meridian editor wrote, "Truman has already defeated his own self," and a McComb editor called Truman "a disease." Later that month, a third Mississippi editor placed the president on a dishonor roll of those "unfaithful to the cause of America including FDR, Henry Wallace and Benedict Arnold." Sometimes the expressions of dislike for Truman took petty forms. When Mississippi considered a measure compelling every radio station within its borders to conclude its broadcast day by playing "Dixie," one legislator offered an amendment banning the playing of "The Missouri Waltz."[1]

On the eve of the election, a writer in a national periodical reported the response on the courthouse lawn when "Cracker Boy" declared that he was going to vote the Democratic ticket because "Me and my folks has been Democrats plum back to the Confederate War":

> The politicians in the courthouse yard almost screamed with pain at the Boy's announcement. They said to him, "Po' White Boy, you don't know what you are sayin'. All of us been votin' the Democratic ticket ever since the First Battle of Bull Run, except a few people in 1928 that went runnin' after Hoover, and they ain't never been received back into good society since. But this year ain't none of us votin' the Democratic ticket."
> "How come?" asked the Boy.
> "On account of Truman."[2]

Southerners did not hesitate to chew the president out in order to set him straight. "I like you, Harry S. Truman," a Texas woman told him. "There's something so calm and straightforward about you. I wanted to support you, . . . but why, oh why, did you bring up Civil Rights? Didn't you know that for us Southerners the Civil War is not over? It has not ended. Probably it shall never end." In like manner, a Georgia woman wrote him: "We Southerners can't understand—even though you liked President Roosevelt and his wife still seems to want you to sell your soul for a 'mess of pottage'—how you can and did try to carry out their wishes to equalize the Southerner and the negro."[3]

On the last day of September an outraged southerner wired Truman aboard his campaign train:

YOU AND YOUR CIVIL RIGHTS HAS COST YOU THE ELECTION. I HAVE ALWAYS VOTED FOR A DEMOCRAT NOW I AM VOTING FOR THURMAN [sic]. WHY DON'T YOU KNOW THAT THE SOUTHERN MAN WILL NOT TOLERATE A NEGRO LOVER? HARRY YOUR THROUGH. YOU'VE DONE NOTHING SINCE YOU'VE BEEN IN THERE BUT TRY TO PUT MY DAUGHTER IN THE SAME CATEGORY AS A SOUTHERN NEGRO. I'LL BE GLAD WHEN NOVEMBER FOURTH COMES SO I CAN PROTEST YOU OUT OF THE WHITEHOUSE. YOU'LL NEVER NEVER AGAIN BE RESPECTED IN THE SOUTH. . . . WE SOUTHERN MEN DON'T LIKE YOUR CIVIL RIGHTS. PERSONALLY I AM VERY BROADMINDED BUT I HAVE SOME DECENCY.[4]

Truman initially absorbed these attacks with considerable equanimity and avoided roiling the waters unnecessarily by harping on the question of race. After listening to the president, Secretary of Defense James Forrestal recorded in his diary: "He made the observation that he had not, himself, wanted to go as far as the Democratic platform went on the Civil Rights issue. He said he had no animus toward the delegates from the Southern states who had voted against the Civil Rights plank and against his nomination. 'I would have done the same thing myself if I were in their place and came from their states.'" In his whistle-stop campaign denouncing the 80th Congress, he referred to civil rights legislation only twice, though he did turn up for a rally at Rebel Stadium in Dallas which he insisted be integrated, and in Waco he drew boos when he shook hands with a black woman.[5]

At the same time, he had a firm commitment to upholding the constitutional rights of blacks, and no amount of verbal abuse could shake it, as he revealed in a response to an old army buddy. In a crudely typed "Saturday Nite" letter from a Salt Lake City hotel on Mormon Temple Square, a former corporal in Battery C, addressing him as "Dear friend Harry" and calling himself "your silent pardner," wrote:

> Oh Harry, you are a fine man but you are a poor salesman so listen to me. You can win the South with*out* the "Equal Rights Bill," but you cannot win the South *with* it. Just why? Well you, Bess and Margaret, and shall I say myself, are all Southerners and we have been raised with the Negros and we know the term "Equal Rights." Harry, let us let the South take care of the Niggers, which they have done, and if the Niggers do not like the Southern treatment, let them come to Mrs. Roosevelt.
>
> Harry, you are a Southerner and a D—— good one so listen to me. I can see you do not talk domestic problems over with Bess. ????? You put equal rights in Independence and Bess will not live with you, will you Bess.

The president replied: "I am going to send you a copy of the report of my Commission on Civil Rights and then if you still have that antebellum proslavery outlook, I'll be thoroughly disappointed in you."[6]

Truman, who had written his sister that summer of "the cockeyed Southerners," went on to say: "When the mob gangs can take four people out and shoot them in the back, and everybody in the county is acquainted with who did the shooting and nothing is done about it, that county is in a pretty bad fix from a law enforcement standpoint. When a Mayor and a City Marshal can take a negro Sergeant off a bus in South Carolina, beat him up and put out one of his eyes, and nothing is done about it by the State Authorities, something is radically wrong with the system." On the Louisiana and Arkansas Railway, he went on, "it became customary for people to take shots at the negro firemen and a number were murdered" on the grounds that such choice jobs belonged only to whites. "I can't approve of such goings on," he concluded, "and . . . I am going to try to remedy it and if that ends up in my failure to be reelected, that failure will be in a good cause."[7]

At the finale to the Democratic convention and in the days following it, Truman showed he meant what he said. When in his electrifying speech to the Democratic convention on July 15 the president announced he was calling Congress back, one of the "vitally needed measures" he said he would ask it to enact was civil rights legislation. At a session in the White House, he told Senator Russell that a more moderate civil rights program was unacceptable, and, though he quieted his rhetoric, he took forceful action. On July 26 he surprised the country by issuing two executive orders. One, drawing upon his authority as commander-in-chief, declared that it was "the policy of the President that there shall be equality of treatment and opportunity for all persons in the armed services, without regard to race, color, religion, or national origin," the first step in the eventual desegregation of the armed forces. The other directive forbade racial and ethnic discrimination in the federal civil service and established a Fair Employment Board to monitor hiring. A Natchez editor denounced Truman's ukase on the armed services as "another foolhardy fling into the sordid world of racial equality," and Congressman John Bell Williams, who had imbibed too much elixir of alliteration, said of Truman's edicts that "they reeked of Putre-facient Politics, Pendergast Pusillanimity, and Paranoidal Pomposity." Though his orders dealt not with segregation but with discrimination, Truman made clear that he had more in mind when he publicly reprimanded the army chief of staff, the revered war hero Omar Bradley, for defending Jim Crow in the military, and in September he named a conspicuously liberal seven-member committee to wipe out racial distinctions in the armed services. The secretary of the army insisted that no men be put on the committee who "have publicly expressed their opinion in favor of abolishing segregation in the Armed Services." In particular, he wanted to be sure that the Urban League's Lester Granger was not appointed. Truman responded by selecting Granger and the outspoken editor of the *Chicago Defender,* one of the leading black newspapers.[8]

Despite such efforts, Truman could not be sure he could count on solid support in black precincts. Republicans sought to turn African-American voters away from the president by calling him "the son of a Confederate," though, as one writer noted, "his father could not even have qualified as a drummer boy in the War Between the States." Both of Virginia's black papers endorsed Dewey. The *Richmond Afro-American* conceded that Truman "always believed that colored people should vote and get a square deal in the courts," but added, "If colored people sit down . . . at a counter in a downtown drugstore in Independence, Missouri they will be booted out." In endorsing Henry Wallace in 1948, W. E. B. Du Bois dismissed Truman as a "border state politician of apparent good will but narrow training and small vision."[9]

These proved to be decidedly aberrant views, however. As Harry Ashmore later reflected: "Truman, as far as Blacks were concerned, . . . had been certified. I mean this Civil Rights Commission . . . was a very powerful thing. . . . And then . . . Thurmond had walked out on the Democratic Party on the issue. . . .

I think any sensible Black of the time would think he had nowhere else to go but Truman." After the president issued his executive orders, *The Crisis* responded on its editorial page:

> Mr. Truman's opponents are crying that his moves in the civil rights field are purely political. . . . But no one has explained just how a man fighting to win the greatest prize, the highest office in America, can be insincere when he stubbornly and stoutly insists on a civil rights program that everyone knows is dynamite—and death—to political ambitions in this country.
>
> Mr. Truman has not retreated one inch from the declarations in his Lincoln Memorial speech of June, 1947. His new orders represent a spirit and a courage on these issues as refreshing as they are rare.

In August the leading black politician in South Carolina stated in a memo to co-workers of the Re-elect Truman Committee: "No American citizen has gone farther nor stood his grounds firmer in behalf of Civil and other rights for Negroes than President Truman. And because he has taken his stand for us, no American is being persecuted as is President Truman today. We must show President Truman and his supporters that we will . . . give back to them ten times anything they lost fighting for us. . . . If President Truman loses we can kiss ourselves goodbye, and also kiss Civil Rights goodbye." But in the Deep South in 1948, black suffrage was so restricted that Truman realized that he was inviting retribution from the white electorate that would determine the outcome in each state.[10]

When the president's initiatives drew further recriminations from below the Mason-Dixon line, his aides stepped up their counsel to write off the South. In late June Truman had received a memo from the Research Division of the party reprising the spirit of the 1947 Rowe-Clifford document by stating, "The South cannot win or lose the election for the Democratic Party." Not even the walkout and the Birmingham convention caused reconsideration. Sam Rosenman, who served both FDR and Truman as speech writer and advisor, later remembered, "I had no apprehension about Senator Thurmond's organizing the Dixiecrat Party. I thought it would be a very good thing for the Democratic Party for the Dixiecrats . . . to leave the Party. I felt certain that if Truman was going to be elected, he would be elected by the Midwest." Liberals reasoned that Roosevelt had won all four times without needing the South, and that the section was not as essential to a Truman victory as some supposed. In August,

William Batt sent Clifford a six-page memorandum on campaign strategy that Clifford, after modest revisions, passed on to Truman. The memo indicated that the president could bypass the South in his campaign, except for one brief trip in which he reminded its citizens of the benefits they had derived under Roosevelt.[11]

Truman heeded this advice. Save for his whistle-stop tour across Texas and an address to an American Legion convention in Miami, he spoke in only one city in the South in the entire 1948 campaign, Raleigh. There he took part in the dedication of a monument to three former presidents from the upper South—Jackson, Polk, and Andrew Johnson, with all of whom he identified. Each of the three, he said, "did his duty as President of the whole Nation against the forces of pressure and persuasion which sought to make him act as a representative of a part of the Nation only." In a shaft aimed at the Dixiecrat bolters, Truman remarked that "Jackson also knew that the way to correct injustice in a democracy is by reason and debate, never by walking out in a huff."

At the same time that he struck this nationalist note, Truman took pains to appeal to southern sensibilities. In his formal oration at the North Carolina state capitol, he asserted: "In 1865 passions were as furious as the war had been long and bloody. There were men in and out of Congress who lost their heads completely. In their madness they were determined that the blood-letting should not stop. They would have sent scores of brave and honorable men to the gallows and stripped thousands more of all they possessed. They wanted to keep a whole region in chains." He followed up this recital of the Old South's view of Reconstruction later that day in a partisan speech to a Democratic rally at the fairgrounds in Raleigh by saying that southerners faced an easy choice in this election because Republicanism meant "the rule of the carpetbaggers," another evocation of sectional feeling bound to please his listeners. "It had been said that Truman couldn't come South at all because he'd be hooted as the feeling was so strong against him," Jonathan Daniels later observed. But in Raleigh Truman was "heartily received, and I think that had much to do with his carrying the state and showing that he could come into the South and not be spit upon."[12]

Daniels personified the support Truman received in 1948 from southern whites, though he did so within a particular context. In a featured piece in the *Raleigh News and Observer* on the eve of the election, Daniels wrote, "I do not think there has ever been a President who more deserved the support and confidence of the South." He went on to affirm that "Harry Truman in the pattern of his mind and the purposes of his heart is more the best type of Southerner than almost anything else. His heritage is Confederate from a region where the conflicts of the War Between the States were most bloody and most bitter." The Tar Heel editor assured his readers that the president was one "who would have little sympathy with any headlong proposals to alter the customs of any people." The charge that Truman favored "mixing of the races" was "a lie." Indeed, "nobody has given him any credit for courage" in his rejection of the "radical racial proposals made by the Civil Rights Committee" to end segregation. Given that performance, Truman was "a man the South does not need to fear." He was, in fact, "the one man in whom the South could with good sense put its hopes."[13]

The president, who in the final month of the campaign was still being described as "Harry Truman, son of a Confederate father," continued to mollify southern moderates by saying almost nothing about race, but on the eve of the election, on the first anniversary of the report of his civil rights committee, he ended that self-restraint in dramatic fashion. On October 29, Truman became the first president ever to solicit votes in Harlem. There, in the country's largest black community, he promised an enthusiastic crowd of 65,000 to fight for his civil rights program "with every ounce of strength and determination" in him. "Thus," noted the New York Times, "the Chief Executive lifted the controversial issue that has split the Democratic party out of the limbo in which it has lain since the Democratic National Convention last July," and his words "appeared to foreclose any possibility of compromise between Mr. Truman and the States' Rights Democrats." Southern whites were shocked that he would ignore major cities like Atlanta but bid for the favor of blacks in a Manhattan ghetto.[14]

Well before the Harlem speech, forecasters gave Truman little chance of carrying the former Confederacy. "Not since the South rebelled against Stephen Douglas in 1860," Time declared, "has the party seemed so hopelessly torn and divided." Even states that were not, like Mississippi, in outright rebellion appeared to be implacably hostile. In mid-September, a poll of Florida legislators found Truman running third to Dewey and Thurmond. Save for Claude Pepper, not a single Florida politician of any prominence backed the president. Pepper himself, as he noted in his diary, was advised by party leaders "not to mention Truman's name." In Virginia the Democratic organization refused to chip in a dime for the campaign, and, by remaining silent, Senator Byrd signaled his followers that it was acceptable to abandon Truman. Furthermore, his wife made her sentiments public by turning up at a banquet for Thurmond, and Governor Tuck gave the Dixiecrat candidate a heartfelt introduction at the Richmond fairgrounds. Few doubted what the consequences of the southern defection would be. The revolt of the South, declared *Newsweek* shortly before the election, "all but dooms the candidacy of President Truman." In assuming that the South would do no more than bluster, as it had in protesting against FDR's policies, Truman, it said, "had made the most substantial miscalculation of his political career."[15]

II

To no one's surprise, Truman lost four Deep South states to Strom Thurmond in November, the four with the highest proportion of African Americans. Whites in the Black Belt who had been the mainstays of the Democrats, who had even gone along with Al Smith in 1928, found Truman too much to take. Louisiana gave Thurmond over 49 percent of its votes, Truman less than 33 percent. In some northern parishes, the president ran third—behind both Thurmond and Dewey. He fared still worse in other Deep South states. In South Carolina, Thurmond got 72 percent, Truman 24 percent, marking the first time that South Carolina had failed to support a Democratic presidential nominee since the Reconstruction year of 1876, when it went to Rutherford B. Hayes. In Mississippi, where the president's campaign was chaired by a black editor, Thurmond received 87 percent to Truman's pitiful 10 percent. There, it was said, "the Truman branch of the Democratic Party is a negro party." In Alabama, as a result of the Dixiecrat coup, no votes at all were recorded for the president because his name did not appear on the ballot.[16]

Thurmond, though, gained no states beyond these four. At a rally in Shreveport on election eve, he claimed that he would poll 142 electoral votes, but he wound up with just thirty-nine. Thurmond won only those states where he pirated the Democratic label; he got nothing as a States' Rights candidate. (In that regard the South remained "Solid" in 1948, for in every state voters chose the presidential candidate running under the Democratic symbol.) If, however, the Dixiecrats had managed to take Texas and two other southern states, their scheme of throwing the race into the House would have succeeded. "The real reasons for the failure of the Dixiecrats, then," one analyst has written, "lay in their inability to produce the votes in their own backyard."[17]

Truman astonished prognosticators by sweeping all the rest of the South. He received 50 percent of the popular vote in the section, with Dewey and Thurmond left to divide the other half between them. In Virginia, Truman upset the Byrd machine by defeating Dewey handily and getting nearly five times as many votes as Thurmond. The attorney general (and future governor) of Virginia expressed his loyalty to the Truman ticket by saying, "The only sane and constructive course to follow is to remain in the house of our fathers—even if the roof leaks and there may be bats in the belfry, rats in the pantry, a cockroach waltz in the kitchen and skunks in the parlor. . . . We cannot take our inheritance and depart into a far country." Despite all the fulminations against Truman in Texas, Thurmond failed to carry a single county, and the president came close to doubling the combined Dewey-Thurmond vote. "Those Dixiecrats," said Sam Rayburn, "are as welcome around here as a bastard at a family reunion."[18]

The president also scored well elsewhere in the South. The Democratic leadership in North Carolina had no trouble holding the Tar Heel state for him. A former North Carolina governor, Cameron Morrison, wanted no part of "this revolting business" against Truman. Instead, he said, "let's step under the Democratic flag and help elect him. Then, we'll let our Congressmen and Senators beat him down when he needs beating." In Raleigh, after Truman phoned him to say, "Jonathan, we're in," Editor Daniels jubilantly ran off one hundred thousand copies of the *News and Observer* with, on the front page, the vivid red rooster that had been the signal of Democratic victory in every election in this century. Not even Senator Kenneth McKellar would follow Boss Crump into opposition in Tennessee. In Arkansas, where Governor Ben Laney had toyed with the notion of secession, a columnist predicted, "The Dixiecrats will not get any further than you kick an anvil barefooted," and he proved to be right when Truman doubled Thurmond's vote. Liberals beat back conservative challenges in Florida, where Democrats refused to abandon the New Deal tradition because of a dispute over race, and in Kentucky, the president outpolled Thurmond by nearly 45–1. Truman pulled the biggest surprise in Georgia, where few had given him a chance, especially after Hummon Talmadge, who was Thurmond's cousin, scored a big victory in September by stressing white supremacy. On Election Day Truman shocked the Dixiecrats by trouncing Thurmond, 3–1, and rolling up a landslide 61 percent over both his Dixiecrat rival and Dewey.[19]

His unexpected success in the South has several explanations. A small minority of white southerners strongly favored his civil rights recommendations. "Let me assure you," a Tennessee man wrote the Democratic national chairman, "that there is an ever growing group of us who have had quite enough of

Bilboism and cries of 'White Supremacy.'" When in early August a convention of Mississippi Democrats embraced the Dixiecrats, students from Millsaps College in Jackson dissented, and the head of a Vanderbilt delegation declared, "You cannot force the Democratic national party to go backwards. . . . The trend is toward civil rights, and you are only setting the South back." Others, even when they could not shake off all of the inherited attitudes, drew back from repeating the errors of the past. The Norfolk editor Louis Jaffé dismissed the Dixiecrat insurgency as "an ill-considered sortie up a magnolia-scented blind alley." The Thurmond hotspurs, said another southern journalist, Gerald Johnson, brought to mind the disunionists who had flocked to Breckinridge in 1860, and "their ruin was so complete that the South has never really recovered." The Dixiecrats, observed Virginius Dabney, had climbed into "the same political bed with an evil-smelling lot of Ku-Kluxers, Negro-haters and exploiters," and in the *Raleigh News and Observer* Jonathan Daniels lashed out at racist fireaters who "have a positive addiction for making the South a dark and bloody ground, a region of hate and hotheadedness, a land where children are bred on bitterness and old men die as Calhoun did, with less hope than despair ('The South! The poor South!')."[20]

More representative were southern Democrats who could not bring themselves to bolt the party of their fathers or jeopardize the perquisites accrued over many years. Neither Richard Russell nor Harry Byrd had attended the founding meeting of the States' Rights Party, while Governor Laney had made it as far as a hotel room in Birmingham, where he hunkered down throughout the convention. Allen Ellender refused to defect to the Dixiecrats, despite the taunt of a Louisiana congressman who said, "I am ashamed of the sorry spectacle of a Senator from my state. I suppose Senator Ellender would have dined with Sherman as he marched through Georgia." Not even such arch-white supremacists as Herman Talmadge and Olin Johnston would go over to the Dixiecrats. Still others did not yet feel comfortable with switching to the party of Thad Stevens. In 1948 GOP voters remained curiosities in many parts of the South. Once, in introducing an associate from Mississippi to his wife, Truman pointed out that the man had not seen his first Republican until he was twelve. Bess replied, "He didn't miss much."[21]

III

His altogether unexpected victory put Truman in a feisty mood with regard to the South. Asked at a news conference a month after the election how Dixiecrat electors should cast their ballots, he replied, "I don't want the Dixiecrat vote. We won without New York and without the Solid South, and I am proud of that." A while later, the president told the Democratic National Committee that the Democrats had triumphed in 1948 without the South (or the industrial East). "The Democratic Party is a national party, and not a sectional party anymore," he said, in what was clearly a gibe at the South. "The tail no longer wags the dog. And I am prouder of that than anything that has ever happened to me." He neither acknowledged, nor expressed gratitude for, the reality that he had received the electoral votes of most of the states of the former Confederacy.[22]

Ralph McGill became so exercised about this misperception that he wired fifteen prominent publicists: "I am disturbed . . . by the tenor of some of the current comment which generally takes the position that President Truman won without the South. It is very important from the viewpoint of those who . . . successfully . . . fought the fraudulent and hypocritical Dixiecrat movement that the rest of the nation understand the revolt in the South was confined to four states. It is also my opinion that, had the people in those states been given a free opportunity to vote without fear and intimidation, these also would have gone Democratic. . . . It . . . would be enormously helpful if it could be pointed out that Mr. Truman would not have won without Georgia, Florida, Tennessee, Virginia, North Carolina and other Southern states which voted for him."[23] (Technically, Truman was right. Since he had a 114-vote margin in the Electoral College, he did not require the eighty-eight electoral votes he received from states of the former Confederacy. If, however, a substantial portion of those votes had shifted to another candidate, which was presumably what McGill hypothesized, Truman would have lost.)

The president showed his disdain for his southern foes in January 1949 at the inauguration ceremonies, the first desegregated event in the nation's history. When a band marched by playing "I'm Just Wild About Harry," Truman, on the reviewing stand, danced a little jig, but on seeing Governor Thurmond approach on the South Carolina float, he turned aside. Vice President Barkley raised his hand in greeting, but the president pushed it down, and then, in a calculated snub, looked right through the Dixiecrat defector. A hostile columnist later reported: "Thurmond arose in his car and honored the presidential office with a polite bow and Mrs. Thurmond threw the gloating victor a nod and a smile. . . . Thousands of witnesses saw Truman stare with cold malice at the Thurmonds with never a twitch of recognition." One of the president's guests, Tallulah Bankhead, "let out a foghorn of boos." Truman's circle scoffed, too, at the "Wednesday morning Democrats" who suddenly perceived virtues in the president on the day after the surprise win that they had not noticed before.[24]

Subsequently, Truman inflicted punishment on southern malcontents, though not as much as northern liberals would have liked. For a considerable period after the 1948 election, he denied patronage to those in the South who had defected or had sat out the campaign. In particular, he retaliated against Senator Byrd by freezing all appointments in Virginia. In August 1949 the Democratic National Committee removed five Dixiecrats, including the national committeeman from Louisiana who was boisterously defended by his attorney, Leander Perez. Louisiana's Democrats ratified the ouster, despite Perez's insistence that Truman should be "impeached rather than appeased." Asked by a reporter, "Do you imply that the people you refer to as Dixiecrats you do not regard as good Democrats?" Truman answered testily, "Of course they are not. Of course they are not good Democrats." When Congressman John Rankin of Mississippi sought to win Truman's support for a project to link the Tennessee River with the Gulf of Mexico, the president replied: "I've been interested in the Tombigbee Canal for a long time but the economy bloc, made up principally of Dixiecrats and Southerners who have been against my program, have rather cooled me off on this subject. They are extremely on the economy side when Social Legislation is up but when it comes to 'pork barrel,' and this is a 'pork barrel' project, they are right in the front line with hats off and their hands out."[25]

The president also pushed ahead on civil rights. Shortly after the 1948 election, an Alabama congressman told Mobile Rotarians that they had nothing to fear, for Truman had said to him, "Frank, I don't believe in this civil rights program any more than you do." But in the month after the election, the Civil Aeronautics Administration, acting on Truman's instructions, ordered the desegregation of National Airport in Washington, and in 1949 the president named the former dean of Howard University Law School, William Hastie, to the U.S. Circuit Court of Appeals, the most elevated position in the federal judiciary ever held by an African American. Furthermore, at the very beginning of his new term, Truman, reported the *Washington Post*, "flung down the gauntlet to Southern Democratic Congressmen" by reiterating his demand for the full panoply of legislation to achieve greater equality for blacks. "The civil rights proposals I made in the 80th Congress, I now repeat to the 81st Congress," Truman said in the first week of his new term. "I stand squarely behind these proposals." When his brother advised him to abandon the FEPC measure, Truman retorted that he was going "to put the whole program over before I leave this office because it is right."[26]

By proving himself resolute on civil rights, Truman won a very positive response from blacks. When the Arkansas moderate Brooks Hays called on the president in 1949 to see if he could reconcile differences with southern Democrats, Truman, Hays later noted, "conceded nothing." On leaving the White House, Hays told reporters he had gotten nowhere in trying to persuade the president to be less resolute. That same year, the *Pittsburgh Courier* asserted that "Negro Americans feel that the man in the White House is their special champion and their patron saint," and Henry Lee Moon, noting all that Truman had done, concluded, "He has risen above the provincialism of his origins."[27]

In taking this course, Truman could count on a certain amount of support in the South. The leading authority on the Southern Conference Educational Fund (SCEF) has written: "As individuals in the Educational Fund saw it, President Truman's victory in 1948, despite his civil rights proposals, changed the climate of the South. . . . [Truman's triumph] made it possible for SCEF to be more outspoken on the issue of racial equality. . . . SCEF recognized that the administration's commitment to ending discrimination, . . . augmented by its determination to establish the United States as the moral leader of the world, . . . would make it all the more difficult for southerners to continue to demand racial discrimination in contradiction to the ideals of American democracy." During Truman's second term, a Virginia woman urged him: "Now, please, Sir, do something about Civil Rights! Being a white Southerner, I can only be an onlooker to the Negroes' miseries, but what I see is enough to make my heart sick to realize that every day persons masquerading as loyal United States Citizens repeatedly disregard our Constitution. Don't, please, tend to be gradual! Cut out this destroying tumor immediately, drastically." Truman received a letter from another woman saying, "I am happy to tell you that I am ardently supporting your Civil Rights program as a matter of common justice to our Negro Americans." The writer of this letter? The widow of Confederate General Longstreet.[28]

But the president continued to find decidedly more resistance. "What are you trying to do, turn traitor like Horseshit Truman?" an Alabaman asked the moderate, Jim Folsom. "Hurrah for the K.K.K." A constituent identifying himself as "A Rail Road Man" from Bastrop, Texas, indignant at "Truman's negro proposal," wrote his senator menacingly, "The agitators of this negro question are the ones that are going to be sorry." As moderate a congressman on racial matters as Albert Gore gibed in a tribute to Truman on his sixty-fifth birthday in 1949: "It is said that the President's mother made one short spontaneous remark upon learning that her son had become president. She said, 'Tell Harry to behave himself.' As a Democrat from south of the Mason and Dixon, I have upon a few occasions thought this a particularly fitting admonition." Indignant at Truman's ban on federal funds for segregated housing projects, the speaker of the Mississippi House of Representatives stated, "How any loyal Southern white man can support any phase of the Truman administration in its purpose to destroy the South, trample under foot its traditions and force social equality and mongrelization on its people, I cannot understand, except that he be disloyal to his people and his race." From the president's own state of Missouri, Truman heard from a St. Joseph man: "I am not prejudiced against the Negro. But God Almighty is. It was God who gave them the black skin and the lower-than-the-whites character. God is WHITE. Jesus Christ is WHITE. Moses is WHITE. There were no BLACK APOSTLES FOR JESUS CHRIST. THERE NEVER WILL BE! The negro question, God alone will settle, and He will do nothing about it until the RESURRECTION."[29]

Many southerners still found it incomprehensible that a man with Truman's background could be advocating civil rights laws. In the summer of 1949 a Tennessee physician wrote the White House that he and his family had been enjoying a delightful trip to Quebec, in the course of which they dropped off a son who was entering the University of Virginia Medical School and a daughter at the New England Conservatory, until in Connecticut they saw two black men and two white women in the same car, a sight that produced "feelings of disgust and outrage" at this "mingling of races." He asked: "Do you, Mr. President, with your southern ancestry and traditions, not realize that your Civil Rights program, which seeks to destroy segregation and bring about social equality, will eventually lead to miscegenation to mongrelization of this great nation of ours?"[30]

With the avid support of such constituents, southern legislators mounted stiff resistance to Truman's program from the outset of his second term. Roy Wilkins later reflected on the aftermath of the 1948 election: "Anyone who expected Harry Truman to take us by the hand and lead us right into Canaan was mistaken. The inauguration passed, winter turned into spring, and the heart of Congress remained as cold as ever to the cause of civil rights." In 1949 the House passed FEPC and anti–poll tax legislation, but both died in the Senate. In March of that year the *New York Times* reported that, thanks to an alliance of southern Democrats and Republicans, "the Senate was giving funeral honors to the President's civil rights program." The Dixiecrats had polled less than 3 percent of the vote in the recent election, it observed. Nonetheless, "in the matter of federal action on civil rights we will continue to be ruled from Birmingham." At a University of Chicago Round Table, Senator Ellender of Louisiana said that without white leadership, "the Negro race . . . will invariably go back to barbaric lunacy." Indeed, the Negro was so close to savagery "that he almost has his foot in Africa."[31]

His opponents stifled all of Truman's civil rights efforts on Capitol Hill, and they threatened to bolt the party if Truman persisted. In the spring of 1950, a writer remarked sadly, "Not one of the recommendations to Congress of the President's Committee on Civil Rights has found its way into law." Langston Hughes's Simple observed that, though the government had no trouble enacting loyalty legislation, it "cannot and will not and won't pass no bill to keep me from getting lynched if I ever look cross-eyed at a white man when I go down south. That is one reason I am not going down south no more." Early in 1949 a Floridian claimed that 90 percent of people in the state opposed Truman's civil rights measure, "that slave bill." Over a bottle of Jack Daniels Green Label in Lexington, Virginia, that same year, Sam Rayburn sought to dissuade Jimmy Byrnes from leading a southern rebellion against the president, but at the end of their liquid encounter, Byrnes, though mellowed and "woozy," remained certain that the Democratic Party was not big enough to contain both him and Harry Truman.[32]

The president found the midterm campaign even rougher. In 1950 the leader of the Alabama States' Righters said that their forefathers "were men who marched with Lee and Jackson and not with the likes of President Harry Truman," while a Mississippi newspaper, under the headline "We Must Beat Harry Truman," urged a bipartisan coalition to subdue the president, for it was "well-known . . . that Mr. Truman has no love for us down here below the Mason & Dixon line." In Louisiana, Leander Perez made his usual contribution to public enlightenment by saying, "Now a Trumancrat is a . . . cross between a Jeffersonian Democrat and a Socialist or Communist or a homo, of whom there have been thousands exposed in Washington lately, which can only produce an illegitimate offspring called a Bastocrat."[33]

In the 1950 senatorial race in South Carolina, the two rivals for the Democratic nomination, Olin Johnston and Strom Thurmond, instead of accusing one another of being pro-Communist or pro-black, noted the *New York Times,* "gave the impression that their chances for election . . . rested upon the vehemence with which they could denounce President Truman and his civil rights program." A Sumter, South Carolina newspaper trumpeted: "Who Dislikes Truman Most? It's the Burning Question in South Carolina's Race for Senate." Thurmond accused Johnston of being "a Trumanite, . . . a man who wants to break down all separation of the races," and the Sumter paper alleged that Johnston was "tainted with Trumanism." To exculpate himself, Johnston called Truman "a blabbermouth" and "a political mishap." In an encounter that nearly resulted in fisticuffs, Johnston, accused by Thurmond of the unforgivable lapse of being "silent as a tomb" as Truman desegregated the armed forces, screamed at his rival, "That's a lie! That's a lie! That's a lie!" One Thurmond poster showed "Southern voter at blackboard," with the names of the defeated liberals Claude Pepper of Florida and Frank Porter Graham of North Carolina crossed out, running his chalk through the name of Olin Johnston. The placard bore the caption, "Two Down—One to Go!" and the admonition, "Attention Harry Truman." Peter Molyneaux's *Southern Weekly*, which carried a quotation from John C. Calhoun on its masthead, rejoiced that the rejection of Graham and Pepper signaled "the growing Southern revolt against Trumanism." Two weeks before Election Day, Samuel Lubell began an article in a national magazine with the sentence: "President Truman and his Fair Deal are on the run in the South today."[34]

Southern coastal states, conspicuously Texas, also disliked Truman's stand on questions other than civil rights, especially the conundrum of who owned the oil-rich "tidelands." Here, too, they felt betrayed, for Texans believed that from the back of his 1948 campaign train in Austin Truman had used code language to signal that, if reelected, he would not dispute the state's sovereignty over oil resources. But not long after he was returned to office, Truman, once again putting national interest above a sectional claim, ordered U.S. Attorney General Tom Clark to bring suit against Clark's native state. Price Daniel, the attorney general (and later governor) of Texas, was informed of the action by telephone from Washington. "Those who were in the room," he later recalled, "told me that tears rolled down my cheeks when I was getting the message that we had been sued by the same attorney general who had only such a short time before recognized the validity of our claim." Daniel would become the first Democratic official in the country to announce that under no circumstances would he support the president for another term.[35]

When Congress voted in 1950 to give Texas title to lands 10½ miles off its shores, Truman vetoed the legislation as "robbery in broad daylight," thereby exasperating the Democratic establishment in Texas. Before giving up its right to the tidelands, the state land commissioner declared, Texas should secede from the Union. So distressed was Congressman Lloyd Bentsen Jr. about the assertion of federal jurisdiction over far offshore lands that he proposed that the former Lone Star Republic exercise its unusual prerogative to divide into five states, thereby assuring ten senators who would defend its oil claims. When in the spring of 1952 Truman accused entrepreneurs who wanted to drill in the Gulf of Mexico of "stealing from the people," Senator Lyndon B. Johnson of Texas denounced his statements as "reckless" and "intemperate."[36]

At odds with Truman not only over civil rights and tidelands, but also over the tilt of the Fair Deal away from the southern tradition of states' rights, and fortified by the gains made by conservatives in the 1950 elections, southern congressmen fought relentlessly to deny Truman any legislative success in his final two years in office. In 1951, Georgia's governor, Herman Talmadge, responded to a plea for party unity by saying, "The way to avoid a split is to restore the two-thirds rule, knock out the FEPC and not nominate Harry Truman," and Senator Byrd declared that "the Democrats of the South" should no longer "permit the Trumanites to press down on America the undemocratic crown of waste, of Socialism, and of dictation from Washington." When the president failed to get much of his program through in his second term, he knew where to place the blame. There were, he said, "too many Byrds in the Congress."[37]

The adamant southern opposition and the distraction of the Korean War cooled some of Truman's ardor for civil rights, but neither the president nor his lieutenants ever abandoned the field. Balked in Congress, they turned to the courts. When a ruling by the Interstate Commerce Commission (ICC) upholding segregated dining cars on the southern railroad was challenged, the Justice Department was expected to back the ICC, since it was a government agency; instead, Truman's appointees pleaded error and asked the Court to go all the way and overturn *Plessy v. Ferguson,* the 1896 decision validating segregation. They followed this up by filing briefs in support of African-American students in two important higher education cases—*Sweatt* and *McLaurin*—that stripped the separate-but-equal doctrine to the buff. "Together," one scholar has written, these three intercessions "constituted the most formidable legal assault ever made on Jim Crow." The administration also intervened in *Brown v. Board* with a thirty-two-page brief that Richard Kluger has called "a good deal more useful to the Justices than all ten briefs filed . . . by the litigants." Racial segregation, said the government attorney, was especially noxious in Washington, D.C., "the window through which the world looks into our house." The president even encouraged Attorney General Clark to use Reconstruction-era statutes to prosecute southern officials accused of crimes against blacks, though the laws were of doubtful validity. Truman was not always forthright; in particular, he moved slowly on establishing an FEPC during the Korean War. But he did resist the efforts of racists to impose their will. When Congress passed a bill validating segregation in southern schools in federal areas such as Oak Ridge, Tennessee, Truman pocket-vetoed it.[38]

As the 1952 campaign got underway, the very word *Truman* had become a catch-term for everything that conservative southerners detested. "By early 1952," one historian has written, "the South's hatred of Truman bordered on the fanatical." In Virginia "Trumanism" had become "almost a curse word and a 'Trumanite' was little different from a Socialist or Communist," another historian has noted. "I've been asked what kind of a Democrat I am," said Senator Byrd. "Well . . . I'm a Virginia Democrat, a true Democrat, and if any further definition is needed, I am not a Truman Democrat." In 1952, in an address in which he called Trumanism "the dominant issue" of the presidential election, Byrd, a Virginia newspaper reported, "riddled the Truman administration. He took it apart, exposed it to the gaze of all and threw its pieces in the garbage can." So venomous had disapproval of Truman become by 1952 that when the president walked into a room at the national Democratic convention, the governor of Virginia slipped out by a side door to avoid any contact with him.[39]

Democrats in the other southern states more than matched the Virginians in vitriol. He would "rather die fighting for states' rights than live on Truman Boulevard in a Nigger heaven," Horace Wilkinson told a Dixiecrat gathering. "We'll be in there slugging, kicking shins and skinning heads until the last communist, left-winger and Trumanite knows there is no place for him in the Democratic party." A Dixiecrat elector in Alabama, Kari Frederickson has noted, "even swore under oath that he would be willing to steal votes to prevent Truman's nomination." South Carolina precinct and county meetings adopted resolutions denouncing Truman, and in Texas it was said that the only bad mark against Governor Allan Shivers, who as early as 1951 had launched a movement to deny the president renomination, was that he had attended Truman's inauguration. In sum, wrote the *Augusta Chronicle,* "Southerners are tired of being the slaves of the left wing, socialistic, anti-Southern wing of the Democratic party. Many Southerners still prefer a Democrat for President, but not one of the Truman stripe."[40]

When in February 1952 Senator Russell announced his candidacy for the presidency, publicists construed his action as a warning to Truman not to seek another term. One newspaper thought it would "galvanize anti-Truman sentiment in the South," while another called it "the real thing, the main event, the long-heralded attempt of Southern Democracy, perhaps with some help from north of Mason-Dixon, to rid itself and the Republic of Trumanism." The *Louisville Courier-Journal* even saw the Georgian's declaration as "the makings of another SUMTER." On March 29, at a time when polls showed him faring badly and his wife wanted to go home to Missouri, Truman revealed that he would not stand for reelection. (His decision was not at all the result of Russell's announcement for he knew that the Democratic convention would never choose a man with the racist convictions of the Georgia senator, even though Russell was a man of "ability and brains.")[41]

After the Russell boom fizzled, a number of southerners carried their abhorrence of Truman over to the Democratic nominee Adlai Stevenson, though Stevenson was no firebrand on civil rights and had chosen as his running mate a Deep South senator, Alabama's John Sparkman.[42] In a speech in Charleston in late October, Jimmy Byrnes, whom John Egerton has called "a chronic, absolute, unquestioning believer in the natural inferiority of the African stock" and "an unreconstructed closet Rebel in his heart of hearts," said: "Four years ago the people of South Carolina at long last realized that the Democratic Party had deserted the principles upon which it was founded. There is no reason why a man who voted against Truman four years ago should not now vote against Truman's candidate, Adlai Stevenson." Instead of bolting the party, the governors of Louisiana and Texas headed a "Democrats for Eisenhower" movement, an action that Vice President Barkley likened to the behavior of "the woman who keeps her husband's name . . . but bestows her favors [on] the man across the street." Unchastened, Truman gave his critics no quarter. Once again, he campaigned in Harlem, where he pledged that the fight against racial injustice "will never cease with me as long as I live." He took special pride in being able to say that the navy and the air force had ended discrimination and that all the troops in Korea were integrated.[43]

Three years earlier, at a gathering of Dixiecrats, John Temple Graves had said, "Gentlemen, let us not wince anymore when we hear the word Republican," and in the following year Samuel Lubell had written that "the anti-Truman tide may even rise by 1952 to the point where the GOP will have the first real chance to split the Solid South since 1928." In fact, Dwight Eisenhower, in handing the Democrats their first defeat in a quarter of a century, captured 50 percent of the ballots marked by whites in the South and four southern states—Tennessee, Florida, Texas, and Byrd's Virginia. Place of origin continued to be pertinent. Byrnes, in supporting the Republican ticket, pointed out that Eisenhower was "a son of the South, born in Texas." After the 1952 debacle, Clyde Hoey of North Carolina wrote a constituent, "I think the country was tired of Truman and his candidates. We lost several of the Southern States this year on that basis and if it continues, we will lose other Southern States in the years to come." Senator Hoey's presumption turned out to be on the mark. The 1948 election foretold the end of the Solid South, at least of a South solid for the Democrats. As one historian has observed, "If Thurmond in 1948 did not lead many Southerners directly into the Republican party, he at least led them in a significant way out of the Democratic party." To be sure, not until the 1960s, when Lyndon Johnson pushed through far-reaching civil rights legislation would the most serious cleavage occur, but Truman was the one who opened the fissure that has never been mended.[44]

IV

In one respect, his enemies misperceived him, for Truman never wholly forsook the racist attitudes he had absorbed from his family or his sympathy for the southern tradition of localism. At the 1956 convention Truman made so strong a plea for a mild civil rights plank, one that George Wallace characterized as "palatable," that he received a standing ovation from southern delegates. Congratulations to Truman came from Lyndon Johnson, who wrote him, "You took the heart out of the extremists." In 1958, at a time when southern racists were plotting to evade the *Brown* decision, Truman came out in support of their favorite schemes: local option and freedom of choice. Even after blacks hailed him as the champion of their cause, he continued to sprinkle his private conversation with racist jargon. Asked how, as a southerner, he had become an advocate of civil rights, Truman gave a ringing endorsement of fundamental liberties, then added, "But personally I don't care to associate with niggers."[45]

On several occasions Truman expressed outrage at the civil rights movement. He not only opposed the 1960 sit-ins, but thought they might well be communist-inspired, a notion he later said he got from J. Edgar Hoover. "If anybody came to my store and tried to stop business," asserted the former haberdasher, "I'd throw him out." He added, "The Negro should behave himself and show he's a good citizen." (Ralph Bunche remarked, "I would have been happier if Mr. Truman had said, as I believe would have been the case, that the problem wouldn't have arisen because he wouldn't have had segregation in his store.") He used the same rationale to denounce the Freedom Rides.[46]

Truman's statements triggered exchanges with his former secretary of state, Dean Acheson, who was a great admirer. "What is all this anti-sit-down attitude of yours?" Acheson asked him in April 1960. Could the explanation be that "Missourians are Confederates at heart?" Truman responded: "I sometimes become so upset by these yellow halfbreeds from New York and Chicago that I almost go segregationist. If they'd stay up no'th and let those of us who know the problem settle it, we could and will do it." Two months later, Acheson sent Truman a stern warning against making stupid statements to the press about sit-ins: "Do not say they are communist inspired. The evidence is all the other way, despite alleged views of J. Edgar Hoover, whom you should trust as much as you would a rattlesnake with a silencer on its rattle." He added: "Do not say that you disapprove of them. Whatever you think you are under no compulsion to broadcast it. Free speech is a restraint on government; not an incitement to the citizen."[47]

In September 1963, as reporters struggled to keep pace with the aging former president on his morning walk along Madison and Park avenues in Manhattan, one of them asked him whether integration would lead to intermarriage. "I hope not," Truman retorted. "I don't believe in it. What's that word about four feet long? Miscegenation? The Lord created it that way. You read your Bible, and you'll find out." Pressed further, he asked whether a newspaperman would want his daughter to marry a Negro. "If she loved him," the man answered. "She won't love somebody that's not her color," Truman responded.[48]

That same month, he called the march on Washington "silly," and at a banquet in Cleveland to honor an Ohio legislator, Truman declared: "If the Northern busybodies would stay at home and clean up their own backyards, the rest of the country will obey its laws. The argument on civil rights has been stirred up by Boston and New England demagogues just as the War Between the States was brought about by old Harriet Beecher Stowe and William Lloyd Garrison. Those Southerners are anxious to do what the law required them to do. They want to give equal rights to Negroes. . . . You can be sure of that." Bewilderingly, he added, "They showed that in 1861," then continued: "These youngsters who are running around the country trying to institute mob rule were raised under the nutty theory of let the child grow like a weed with no home discipline. It is a lazy way to raise a family. These young rioters were not spanked enough as they grew up. The police should be furnished with nice old-fashioned butter paddles and be authorized to use them in the place intended for spanking." When the former president was introduced, he had received a standing ovation from the crowd of more than a thousand guests, but these words were heard in stony silence.[49]

In 1965 Truman once again used the word *silly,* this time to characterize the Selma-to-Montgomery march, which, he judged, had "not accomplished anything." Reminded that Martin Luther King had received the Nobel Peace Prize, he snapped, "I didn't give it to him." Told his statements were likely to provoke controversy, he spat out, "What the hell do I care?" These comments drew a telegram of gratitude from Alabama's brutal Dallas County sheriff, Jim Clark, who reported "unbelievable" scenes in Selma that had not been witnessed "even in the worst days of the world. The sex orgies in the streets and the churches were worse than in the days of ancient Rome." Truman's remarks would "do more than any statement that has been made by anyone up to this time," Sheriff Clark said. "We here in this great beloved Southland want to thank you for the sensible, splendid statement you made about Luther King who has caused so much trouble down here."[50]

Truman's comments also elicited some savage criticism. "Why don't you drop dead, you old haberdasher?" a Los Angeles man wrote him. "Every time you open your mouth you do nothing but spew . . . poison around. Drop dead! So that the country will have cleaner air." He ended cruelly, "Soon old boy!" A Greenwich Village resident troubled to send him a registered letter: "Dear Harry: Pathetic senility has turned you into a damned fool. Do yourself a favor and keep your big mouth shut when in N.Y." More unexpectedly, a southern newspaper, calling Truman irresponsible for giving comfort to King's violent opponents, likened the black minister to "a great Trouble Maker of a couple of thousand years ago" who was being honored that week in the Easter season. King, the editor said, was "trying to get the South to save itself."[51]

The former president, though, sometimes expressed quite different views on race, as he did in an interview a few years after he left office. True, he said, "You cannot force social equality on people," and he remarked, "You know my mother died an unreconstructed Southerner—and you couldn't blame her. Missouri was the scene of bitter clashes in the Civil War." He quickly added, however, "But we must set an example to the rest of the world," and, despite his sentiments about coercion, insisted that "FEPC is only fair and just" and boasted, "I forced integration in the Army and Navy, and particularly in the Marine

Corps." He concluded: "I don't think God cares anything about the color of a man's skin. The same melting pot that worked up North will solve this problem. Men who associate together in the Army and Navy and work together and learn together will find out that, under the skin, there is no difference between people."[52]

African-American leaders did not permit Truman's contemptible statements in his final years to distract them from recognition of the breakthrough he had made. Carl Rowan, who had written a highly favorable article on Truman's civil rights record not long before, said, "I have no explanation except to conclude sadly that Mr. Truman must be feeling the effects of senility." But Rowan went on, "I do not think this diminishes in any measure the important actions that he took during his years in the presidency—actions that . . . called for a great measure of political courage—certainly a measure of courage not being exhibited in Washington today." Clarence Mitchell, director of the NAACP's Washington bureau, concluded that Truman's "forthright declaration on civil rights made it possible to talk about the evil of segregation openly"; no longer did people "regard it as a subject that was taboo in polite society."[53]

Truman left the White House in January 1953, having moved the quiet insurrections started by FDR considerably farther along. To be sure, the Supreme Court's decision in *Brown v. Board*, in which the Truman administration had intervened, was still a year away. Another year would go by before Rosa Parks refused to budge on a Montgomery bus. Not until 1957, thanks in good part to the leadership of a Texan first elected to the U.S. Senate in the Truman era, would Congress enact a civil rights law. Yet when Truman returned to Independence, the town of his boyhood, he had the satisfaction of knowing that he had placed civil rights irrevocably on the national agenda, had reconfigured America's election maps, and had set in motion a chain of events that made the greater achievements of the 1960s possible.

LYNDON B. JOHNSON

EIGHT

THE LONE COWPOKE FROM DIXIE

I

Neither Lyndon B. Johnson nor the country could ever get quite straight where he came from. Much of the time he saw himself, and was seen by others, as a southerner. He was reared in a state that had left the Union for the Confederacy, and when he took aim on the White House he was tagged as the candidate from Dixie. Early in LBJ's career, a cabinet officer reported, Franklin Roosevelt had said, "This boy could well be the first Southern president." On other occasions, though, Johnson presented himself as a western rancher. One commentator referred to him as a "cowboy President," while a foreign correspondent called him "the first uninhibited product of the American frontier to take over since Andrew Jackson came out of Tennessee with his long white hair and sparky talk to beat the British at the Battle of New Orleans."[1]

A number of Johnson-watchers gave up on trying to categorize him and were content to observe that he incorporated more than one section in his makeup. "In his name, Lyndon Baines Johnson, he carried forward the two families that converged in his birth," Ronnie Dugger noted. "The Baineses were southern slave-owners, the Johnsons western cattle-drivers." Jonathan Daniels made a related point: When Lyndon served in the House, he "represented a Texas district which straddled, like a Congressman on horseback, the West and the South." To some historians that district offered another clue. Johnson, they declared, was neither southern nor western but a man of Texas, the onetime Lone Star Republic that continued to behave like a separate country. Still others chimed in that he came from none of these places but was a figure of the national scene whose only real abode was Washington, D.C.[2]

Johnson eventually offered his own view, but even it was inconclusive. In his memoirs, he wrote, "There were no 'darkies' or plantations in the arid hill country where I grew up. I never sat on my parents' or grandparents' knees listening to nostalgic tales of the ante-bellum South. In Stonewall and Johnson City I never was a part of the Old Confederacy." Yet he added: "That Southern heritage meant a great deal to me. It gave me a feeling of belonging and a sense of continuity. But it also created—sadly, but perhaps inevitably—certain parochial feelings that flared up defensively whenever Northerners described the South as 'a blot on our national conscience' or 'a stain on our country's democracy.'"[3]

II

Lyndon Baines Johnson claimed kin in almost every southern state. He could trace the Baines line to his great-great-great-grandfather in North Carolina whose son served as a Baptist minister in Georgia, Alabama, and Mississippi. The minister's son, in turn, after winning election to the Arkansas legislature, migrated to Louisiana where he became the most renowned preacher in the area. On the Johnson side, Lyndon could fairly assert in the 1964 campaign, "My roots are deep in Georgia." His great-great-grandfather had left England in the eighteenth century for the Oglethorpe colony. The president's great-grandfather, the son of a Revolutionary War veteran, had served as sheriff of one Georgia county and as justice of the inferior court in another, and it was from Georgia that the original Samuel Ealy Johnson, the namesake of Lyndon's father, migrated to Texas. Hence, it seemed natural to Lyndon Johnson when talking to the Texas Congressman Wright Patman, whose ancestors also came from Oglethorpe County, Georgia, to speak of *our* farms."[4]

He took pride, too, in one forebear who was governor of Kentucky and another who was a congressman from Tennessee. "So many of my ancestors come from Kentucky," Johnson told a crowd at the Louisville courthouse in the 1964 campaign, "that I can sing 'My Old Kentucky Home' with almost as much feeling as you." His grandmother was born on the dark and bloody ground; his great-great-grandmother was the sister of prominent state officials in the land of bluegrass and burgoo; and his great-great-grandfather, who "was the first man to breed shorthorn cattle in Texas," had "introduced the Sir Archer breed of horses to . . . Kentucky."[5]

Some of Johnson's ancestors immersed themselves in the plantation-and-slavery culture of the antebellum era. The president's great-great-grandfather bequeathed each of his daughters a slave girl, and his great-grandfather owned no fewer than seventeen slaves in Georgia. When Lyndon's great-grandfather led his family in covered wagons on a trek of nearly nine hundred miles across

Alabama, Mississippi, and Louisiana into East Texas, he carried a number of slaves with him. After arriving in Texas, one of his forebears, his biographer Robert Dallek has pointed out, "built a traditional Old South mansion—a two-story house with white verandas attended by slaves and surrounded by cotton fields and pastures."[6]

When Johnson campaigned in the South in 1964, he identified himself as "the grandson of two Confederate veterans." As he often did, he fibbed, but, in truth, a number of his ancestors did take part in the Civil War in a uniform of gray. One of them enlisted in the Confederate cavalry, and in one engagement had his horse shot out from under him. When Lyndon's father courted the young woman who would be Lyndon's mother, he took her to a Confederate Reunion, and as a legislator he sponsored a bill to construct a home for Confederate widows and to provide pensions for Confederate veterans. Lyndon's mother remembered her grandfather's "sorrow over the losing cause." In college Lyndon wrote an editorial for the school newspaper lauding Jefferson Davis.[7]

Lyndon's wife, Lady Bird, nee Claudia Alta Taylor, had even stronger ties to the South. She recalled: "Our house was in very deep East Texas, about fifteen miles from the Louisiana border, which is totally part of the Old South in . . . the look of the land . . . and the economy, which was cotton, principally. And . . . many, many blacks." Lady Bird was raised, one of her admirers bragged, in "an ante-bellum manor house . . . whose bricks had been hand-baked by slaves on the site." Her grandfather had fought at Shiloh, and her father, the imperious monarch of 15,000 acres of cotton, two general stores, and two cotton gins, lived, in Lady Bird's words, "a whole feudal way of life." Whites called him "Cap'n" and blacks called him "Mister Boss." Asked in the 1960s how Lady Bird could be so serene in the midst of turmoil, her press secretary, Elizabeth Carpenter, replied: "She has a certain quality . . . that I would call a remnant of the managerial plantation. The aristocratic class of Southern woman was the manager of the homestead. She had many things to care for. She had the mind of Scarlett and the magnetism of Melanie. . . . Mrs. Johnson inherited the strain. Unless you learn it under a magnolia tree or at your mother's knee, you don't have it." Lady Bird also referred to Alabama as "the state I think of as my second home," and with reason. Each summer of her girlhood, one writer noted, she visited her Alabama relatives "rather like a small princess making her annual chevauchee."[8]

With these antecedents and associations, Lyndon Johnson understandably viewed himself, at least a good deal of the time, as a southerner. In one of the editorials he wrote for his college paper he boasted of "my heritage of Southern blood," and in 1937, he sent his mother a photograph taken at the White House of "a group of us Southern Congressmen." In a 1949 address on behalf of a filibuster, he spoke of "we of the South." His close advisor, Jim Rowe, recalled, "He always had this complex that the South was discriminated against, the southerners and the Texans, whether it was by the intellectuals or by the rest of the country."[9]

Many of his colleagues and associates, too, regarded him as a southerner. A Louisiana senator remembered him as someone who so "truly liked Southern cooking" that he was forever asking when he was next going to be invited for gumbo and pralines, and a congressman from the Pacific Northwest recalled that Johnson could get around the chairman of the Naval Affairs Committee, a Georgian, better than he could because LBJ "had the southern syrup." Johnson's stories, wrote James Reston, were "vivid with the memory of the South. He would talk about a man who was 'as wise as a tree full of owls' or 'as busy as a man with one hoe and two rattlesnakes.'" Similarly, the dean of White House correspondents, Merriman Smith, stated: "By breeding, rearing, and taste, he was a Southerner. There was nothing phony about his drawl and sometimes, in private and when speaking excitedly, his speech could become . . . grammatically shuddering."[10]

As a southerner, Johnson absorbed the assumptions about segregation pervasive in his section. He has been said to have gotten liberal views on race from his father who opposed the KKK of the 1920s, but, in fact, when a newspaperman interviewed the Texas legislator, he made a point of saying, "I am for the old Ku Klux Klan." In the 1930s, when Lyndon Johnson was state director of a New Deal agency, he responded to a proposal to integrate its advisory board by stating: "The racial question during the last one hundred years in Texas . . . has resolved itself into a definite system of mores and customs which cannot be upset overnight. So long as these are observed there is harmony and peace between the races in Texas. But it is exceedingly difficult to step over lines so long established and to upset customs so deep-rooted, by any act which is so shockingly against precedent as the attempt to mix negroes and whites on a common board."[11]

Yet, as one historian has noted, unlike many other southern politicians, "he could take white supremacy or leave it. Race was never an issue that deeply stirred his soul." In the 1920 census, compiled when Johnson was a boy of twelve, Blanco County numbered 4063 inhabitants, of whom only 350 were black, with none at all in Johnson City. "There were no blacks in the county, I guess, except at a little segment some eight or nine miles from Blanco," one of Johnson's schoolmates recalled. "Not being visible, blacks were not an issue in his life," a scholar has remarked. Johnson grew up with no particular animus toward blacks, nor with any revulsion at Jim Crow. The NYA in Texas under Johnson enrolled 14 percent of eligible white college students, but 24 percent of eligible African-American college students. When he had an assignment in Houston, he would spend the night in the dorms of black students. As NYA director, he won a national reputation among black leaders for his fairness. He went to Washington to urge an extra appropriation solely for black college students; he saw to it that a dormitory was built at the black institution, Prairie View A & M; and he persevered until he obtained funds to make it possible for black women to enroll in courses there. The courses, however, were aimed at training them to be servants in the homes of whites. Moreover, he refused to hire a black assistant, though NYA directors in eight other southern states did. A decade later, it seemed natural to him to become a member of the anti–civil rights bloc in the U.S. Senate. Nonetheless, the assistant administrator of the FSA, Milo Perkins, called him "the first man in Congress from the South ever to go to bat for the Negro farmer." And Johnson did not indulge in race baiting. When he wanted to pay Huey Long and his brother one of the highest compliments, he would say, "Don't forget, the Longs never niggered it."[12]

III

Not a few of his contemporaries scoffed at the notion that Johnson was from Dixie. Though his press office informed the world that the president favored "bourbon and branch water," journalists knew "that LBJ drank bourbon only if the Scotch ran out." The South "was an important base," Hubert Humphrey acknowledged, but "Johnson did not consider himself a Southerner. . . . He was a Democrat and a Texan, enjoying the benefits of southern hospitality, southern power, southern support, but who carefully avoided the liabilities of being clearly labeled a Southerner." The reporter William S. White said of him in 1958: "In the twenty-five years that I have known him, I have never heard Johnson speak nostalgically of 'the old South.' I have never known him—even in the most unguarded of moments, even, let us say, over a glass or two of whiskey in a midnight hour of reminiscence and remembrance—to identify himself with emphasis as a Southerner or to speak of a way of life now long gone." Similarly, in a manual published in 1960 to assess the prospective candidates, a political correspondent said of Johnson: "His is no nostalgic yearning for the South of Jefferson Davis. For all that members of his family fought under the Confederate flag, his imagination doesn't go back to darkies singing in cotton fields around the old family mansion. In fact, his people had no connection with that South. They were relatively poor pioneers scrabbling a living out of the ranch country of West Texas and the only Negroes in Johnson's community are those employed by him."[13]

Lyndon's hometown, Johnson City, and its environs seemed only marginally southern. "His part of Texas is not the 'magnolia honey child,' and 'God bless Marse Lee,'" observed his press secretary, George Reedy. In 1861, Gillespie County, where Johnson was born, voted against secession, 398–16. Those who settled in the hill country dwelt not in the South of the Black Belt but in scrub pine hills and woodlands. Their new land appeared to be a continent away from the Mississippi delta, even though the school year was set so that it came "between the end of cotton picking and the beginning of cotton chopping" and "Johnson City," one of the future president's schoolgirl companions recalled, "ginned five hundred to six hundred bales of cotton per year." As one historian has observed: "Born in Blanco County, just west of the 98th meridian, on the very edge of the Great Plains, Johnson came of age in a South that would pay about as much homage to Big Gas and Big Oil as to King Cotton."[14]

The line between South and West in Texas is abrupt. One popular writer, noting that Fort Worth's slogan is "Where the West Begins," added, "Men wearing cowboy boots and big white hats are a common sight in Fort Worth; in Dallas, thirty miles to the east, such sights, though not unknown, are relatively rare." Johnson grew up almost precisely on the division line—the Balcones Fault. "East of this fault line are the flatlands, given over to agriculture for the most part (the Southern touch); to the west is the broken country, the grassy lands, the long stretches of nothingness," the same writer observed. A more scholarly study pointed out: "The Blanco-Pedernales region of the Hill Country lies just west of the 98° meridian, labeled by Walter P. Webb . . . 'an institutional fault' (compared to a geological fault). . . . At this *fault* the ways of life and living changed. Practically every institution that was carried across it was either broken and remade or else greatly altered.'" West of the Balcones Escarpment, Frank Vandiver has noted, travelers found "brownish hills where trees grew short and scrubby, where animals shrank into tough customers who shunned water."[15]

Johnson City on the Pedernales is, by some miles, farther west than Omaha or Fargo, and Lyndon was raised in a land not of tidewater gardens and Carolina wrens but of prickly pear, rattlesnakes, and the nine-banded armadillo, "arid country," in Maury Maverick's words, where "gnarled oaks fight their way toward a boiling sun." When Lyndon was a boy, mountain lions, ocelots, and red wolves, even a stray jaguar, still roamed the hill country. Walter Prescott Webb wrote that "the battle of the Pedernales [in 1844] has good claims to being the first battle in which the six-shooter was used on mounted Indians." A nineteenth-century Blanco merchant recalled the garb of those times: "The men . . . did not put on much style—hickory shirts with woolen skin leggings, a six-shooter and a butcher knife, hung by a broad belt around the waist and with large, jingling spurs. . . . All carried six-shooters, from the cowboy to the minister."[16]

Consequently, a good many regarded LBJ as a westerner. Hubert Humphrey, who thought Johnson "a westerner at heart," once said of him: "When he went home it was to the ranch, not to the plantation. He was a cattleman, he identified with the economy of the West." After noting that "Lyndon Johnson understood Washington with a Westerner's disdain for status symbols," Liz Carpenter, Lady Bird's effervescent and partisan secretary, added: "Both the Johnsons reflected the land that nurtured them. She had been reared in the rich plantation country of deep East Texas, and she was gentle and serene as the cypress trees there—quiet, deep-rooted, protected. The President was as strong and open as the weather-worn hills of West Texas. His was the land of wide skies and white caliche, limestone clay soil and men of uncomplaining determination." A journalist described the big man as a "Western movie barging into the room," and when in the 1960s a British journalist sought to resolve the many paradoxes about Johnson, one of LBJ's longtime friends counseled him, "Go west. The further west you go the nearer you get to Lyndon Johnson."[17]

Publicists and politicians confirmed this perception. "Two weeks' exposure to Mr. Johnson on his own stomping ground along the Pedernales River," wrote Tom Wicker early in 1964, left little doubt that the new president was a westerner, not a southerner, "a big, breezy, rough-cut man of the plains and of the dust." Lyndon Johnson, he later insisted, "was very western indeed." Johnson "had a touch of the High Plains rather than the Deep South," Senator Paul Douglas agreed. "We thought of Lyndon Johnson more or less as a westerner," a former governor of Mississippi recalled. "He was not considered a southerner at all," save only in the sense that he came from a state that had been in the Confederacy. In 1960 a journalist discussing that year's presidential aspirants observed: "Even though Johnson cannot escape the label of 'southerner,' and would not try to do so, his part of Texas bears little resemblance to the Deep South, the Old Cotton South of Mississippi, Georgia, and Alabama. His thinking is more nearly that of an Oklahoma senator or one from Montana, Idaho, or New Mexico." Jim Rowe of Montana remembered, "Quite early he pointed out . . . that there is not a hell of a lot of difference between Texans and Montanans."[18]

Johnson liked to appear in the guise of an old cowpoke. He once described his father as a "rough mountain man" even though the low Texas hills bore little resemblance to the rugged Rockies, and he would toss off references to "one of our old cow-puncher friends." In 1946 he campaigned with a western band that strummed "Home on the Range" and "Sioux City Sue." Later the caravan was joined by another Texan, Gene Autry, who helped out "that old vote-wrangler from Johnson City" by crooning lyrics such as "Just a ridin',' rockin',' ropin,' / Poundin' leather all day long." At an Oklahoma State Fair, Johnson surprised his entourage by leaping on a palomino and parading it in front of the stands, one hand on the reins like a young buckaroo, the other waving his Stetson to the crowd in the manner of Buffalo Bill. On recovering from a serious heart attack in the 1950s, he returned to the political arena to the tune of "Back in the Saddle Again," struck up by a Texas band. When in the 1960s he met Wernher von Braun, director of the Space Flight Center, he handed him a Stetson and told him to "put it on the moon by 1970," and when during the Vietnam War he was asked to negotiate with Hanoi, Johnson responded, "I am a reasonably good cowboy and I can't even rope anybody and bring him in that is willing to talk reason."[19]

The LBJ Ranch, Hal Rothman has observed, "allowed Johnson to remake himself from Southerner to Westerner, from a man of the old and, by the middle of the 1950s, seemingly decadent and atavistic South to a representative of the West, a region aglow with new development in the post–World War II era. . . . The West held the future, the South the past, and Johnson sought a future in national politics. The LBJ Ranch became a symbol as well as a home, transforming Johnson from someone tied to the Old South into an individual affiliated with the mythic West and with all the promise contained in that concept" in an era when "on television and on the movie screen, the West became the crucible of American values, the ranch the setting in which these values were forged and honed."[20]

Johnson flaunted the garb not of a southern planter but of a western rancher.

Lady Bird recalled that in LBJ's very first campaign in 1937, the governor, taking one look at the young man's narrow-brimmed fedora, said, "You will never win in Texas with that kind of hat. I'm going to give you one." For the rest of the campaign Johnson sported a Stetson. When a generation later the Washington press corps went to Texas, one correspondent reported, "a Johnson we had never seen emerged. . . . Gone were the low shoes, conservative necktie and tailored dark suit. In their stead were tooled leather boots, open-neck khaki shirt and matching Western pants, and a light-colored five-gallon hat set at a rakish angle." John F. Kennedy had a similar experience. On a trip to the LBJ Ranch, he and his party encountered their host "in an open-throated cream-colored leather jacket, ranch pants, cowboy boots, and ten-gallon hat loping toward them."[21]

At his Texas spread, Johnson as westerner came into his own. He particularly enjoyed showing off to visitors the fort with extra-thick stone walls and rifle slits built by his grandfather as a neighborhood shelter against Comanche marauders a century before, a vivid reminder of a living past. In 1959 the columnist Stewart Alsop wrote: "Much of the LBJ Ranch could be rented out as the background for a Wild West movie, and the ranch house itself is most decidedly a Western ranch house—it has nothing at all in common with the pillared and magnolia-draped Southern plantation house of tradition. By the same token, there is a great deal of the West of the longhorn days in Lyndon Johnson, and very little indeed of the Deep South. . . . He is a frontiersman by instinct, with the roughness and restlessness of the frontier; . . . he is a Westerner at heart rather than a Southerner."[22]

A radio personality with the appropriately regional sobriquet of Cactus Pryor recalled: "Mostly at his parties the president liked a western atmosphere. Round tables with checkered tablecloths and coal oil lanterns. All of his help dressed in western attire. He had big old washpots full of melted butter in which you would dip your corn on the cob. It had all the look and feel of the 'chuck wagon' dinner. And we would depict in pageant form the settling of Texas, and of course, we were settled at first by the Spaniards. We actually had the early Spaniards in costume coming down the Pedernales River and the friars and the Indians meeting them. Then we had the settlers coming, and they came roaring down on horseback, shouting, the stagecoach coming full speed, the buckboards; and the settlers in their old costumes sang songs of windmills and cattle drives." Pryor added, "They actually staked out the cows on the other side of the river for atmosphere."[23]

Not everyone, though, swallowed Johnson's projection of himself as the old cowhand. "His self-painted portrait of a cattleman tending his herds," Reedy has said, "was difficult to accept with a straight face. He *did* know something about cattle but he 'tended' them from a Lincoln Continental with a chest full of ice and a case of Scotch and soda in the back seat." Similarly, the columnist Joseph Kraft has written of the LBJ Ranch: "The basic elements are the authentic stuff of Western life: hardscrabble soil and a scraggly river; sunsets and sage; boots, saddles, and guns; horses and cattle; foreman and hands; Howdies and Hi Podners; towns marked only by a widening of the road and a post office. But the President wears his Western shirts monogrammed. . . . The barbecues are catered by a firm from Fort Worth. Muzak pipes 'The Yellow Rose of Texas' into his living room." Johnson later told Doris Kearns of how he manipulated Washington correspondents. With Stewart Alsop, who fancied himself a historian, you "emphasize . . . your roots in Texas, so much so that even when it doesn't fit the conversation you make sure to bring in maxims from your father and stories from the Old West," he explained.[24]

Johnson's vision of himself as a westerner may have owed as much to Lady Bird's favorite television program, *Gunsmoke,* as it did to the derring-do of his ancestors. At one point, looking at a small house across the valley from the ranch, Lady Bird said, "I can just picture Marshal Dillon riding up to that place." Johnson, for his part, suggested to Kennedy's press chief, Pierre Salinger (whom he called "Peer"), during the 1960 campaign that he be presented "like Marshal Matt Dillon . . . big, six-feet-three, good-looking—a tall, tough Texan coming down the street."[25]

On the question of whether Johnson was primarily western or southern, one of LBJ's favorite anecdotes is suggestive. In a tale he loved to tell, an applicant for a teaching job is asked by the school board whether the world is round or flat; the man replies, "I can teach it either way." In like manner, Johnson could, and did, tell it either way with respect to his sectional locus. Occasionally, he sought fusion. In paying tribute to an Arizona senator in 1952, Johnson said, "We of the Southwest," and in a 1957 interview, he insisted that he was not a southern senator but came from the Southwest. Those moments, though, were rare. As Paul Conkin has observed, "Born at the unclear boundaries of South and West, he never fully identified with either and, as political need dictated, alternatively claimed one or the other."[26]

But Johnson was far from being at liberty to make that choice, for, no matter how many times he donned cowboy boots, most of the country would always view him as a man from the Southland. The Washington correspondent William S. White, who was an admirer, wrote in 1958: "Senator Johnson, a tall, rangy man with a ranch background, is far more Western than Southern. Nevertheless, Texas is historically a Confederate State. This fact powerfully works against the possibility that the Democratic convention of 1960 would ever give him what he insists—sometimes with loud, unprintable Texanisms—he doesn't want anyhow. The presidential nomination."[27]

IV

Whatever else Johnson might be, everyone acknowledged that he was a Texan—which might make him southern or western or both or neither. Texas, one scholar has written, "was the end of the South, not quite the beginning of the West, but its threshold. It was . . . a place secreted within the ambiguity of . . . regions; it bore a different character from either South or West." A Texan politician once boasted, "I am a Southerner before I am an American, and a Texan before I am a Southerner." The most important definer of regionalism, Howard Odum, excluded Texas, alone of the former Confederate states, from his conception of the South. "The votes of hordes of Mexicans," he wrote, indicate "a different South from the Virginia of Carter Glass or from a black belt in Alabama, Georgia, or Mississippi." As recently as 1999, an official of the Texas Historical Association said, "I don't think people do think of moonlight and magnolias when they think of Texas. They think of cactus and mustangs." Similarly, a Texan who was the travel editor of *Southern Living* contended that there was "a definite place where The South ends," and that place was the Brazos, which divides eastern fauna and flora from those to the west. On the other hand, Eugene Genovese has remarked that "even the vulgar parvenu of the Southwest embraced the plantation myth," and Walter Buenger at Texas A & M has chided historians for not recognizing that in the western reaches of the state as much as on the Louisiana border the essential fact about Texas is that it was "a southern, slave holding place."[28]

Johnson's connections to Texas have impressed numbers of observers. In a 1959 article titled "Lyndon Johnson—Tall Texas Marshal," Mary McGrory wrote, "During debates, he ranges around the floor like a nervous marshal on the lookout for cattle rustlers," and when Johnson sought the presidential nomination in 1960, *Time* said: "He still has an ineradicable touch of Texas backlands about him. . . . A hint of the carnival snake-oil seller shows in his voice." On the outgoing president's last days in office, an incoming Virginia congressman was still observing, "Lyndon Johnson . . . has Texas written all over him." Conkin has commented: "The live past for a youthful LBJ was entirely a Texas past and, more recently, a past limited to the hill country of Texas. . . . Despite his Confederate progenitors, one suspects that he simply did not feel very southern. He transferred his regional loyalties to his home state. To him, Texas was his section and region and, in many ways, even his nation. As much as any Texan he identified with the state's unique history—its period of nationhood and its uniquely voluntary allegiance to the Union."[29]

On a BBC panel in 1965, one correspondent led off by saying, "The first thing about Johnson is that he's a Texan," and another chimed in: "And he thinks that people look down on him because he hasn't had a proper, Eastern-type of education. This is the reason why he goes back to Texas as often as he can— that's the place he feels at home. He knows that he has succeeded in Texas. Everywhere he looks around him on his ranch, with his LBJ stamp on the gatepost, his own LBJ brand on his heifers, the Lyndon B. Johnson Lake, . . . everywhere he looks down there he knows that he has been a success." A year later, a writer, noting the "mythogenic" aspects of LBJ's persona, pointed out the perils of the Texas image. "His future gaucheries will be attributed to his provincial origins," she foresaw. "If his actions result in mistakes, he will characterize the impulsive two-gun Texan; any . . . shady compromises effected will be considered Texas wheeling and dealing."[30]

Johnson knew that the lives of his ancestors were tightly woven into the history of Texas. His great-great-uncle fought under Sam Houston at the decisive battle of San Jacinto; was said to have led the party that captured Santa Anna; was a signer of the Texas Declaration of Independence; and, as a member of the First Congress of the Lone Star Republic, drafted the legislation creating the Texas Rangers. His maternal great-grandfather edited the first Baptist newspaper in Texas, drew Sam Houston to the Baptist faith in the church at which he preached, and was president of Baylor during the first two years of the Civil War. Johnson's father served five terms in the Texas legislature, to which his maternal grandfather, at one time secretary of state in Austin, had also been elected.

In his schoolboy years, "the early history of the Lone Star State . . . constituted a religious experience for Lyndon," one of his biographers has contended.

He pored over the details of the attack by Ol' Ben Milam in December 1835 on the Mexicans holding San Antonio; yelled the patriotic war whoop "Who'll go into Bexar with Ol' Ben Milam?"; and cried because Ben Milam had died leading the successful attack. He felt utter despair in the telling of the massacre of Colonel Jim Fannin and his three hundred and ninety men by the treacherous Santa Anna after Fannin had been assured fair treatment when he surrendered at Goliad on March 25, 1836.

But worst of all and also the most glorious event in Texas history was the tragedy of the Alamo.[31]

In the very air he breathed Johnson inhaled his state's obsession with the Alamo legendry. The novelist William Humphrey, recalling his boyhood in the Texas centennial year of 1936 when Johnson was twenty-eight, has recounted: "With school out, on Saturdays, in vacant lots all over town, the Battle of the Alamo was refought weekly, and the following day, in Sunday school, there was a deliberate confounding of that exodus led by Moses of Egypt with the one of Moses Austin, and of Sam Houston at San Jacinto with Joshua at Jericho. In every home, whatnot shelves accumulated commemorative plates and miniature plaster busts of Texas revolutionary heroes. The winds of bombast, seldom still, blew over the land as incessantly as dust storms."[32]

LBJ's fascination with the tale of the Alamo became almost compulsive. When Lyndon was six, his mother taught him a poem on the massacre, and he grew up hearing of how his father had drafted the Alamo Purchase Bill to restore the mission—with the stipulation that it be administered by the Daughters of the Republic of Texas. When the Alamo purchase bill was enacted, a committee from the Texas Senate fetched Sam Johnson from the House so that he could be honored by the Senate as "the savior of the Alamo." One newspaper wrote: "Santa Anna took the Alamo—that was 1836. Sam Johnson saved the Alamo—that was 1905." His son often reminded visitors proudly that his father's portrait hung inside the mission. In Korea in 1966 Lyndon got so carried away that he said his great-great-grandfather had died at the Alamo. As Hugh Sidey has written, "Lyndon Johnson longed for some blood connection to those dead heroes. . . . It was something that should have been, at least in Johnson's mind, and so he just said it was so."[33]

When Doris Kearns, while helping Lyndon Johnson put together his memoirs, started to recount Sidey's story, the former president erupted: "God damn it, why must all those journalists be such sticklers for detail? Why, they'd hold you to an accurate description of the first time you ever made love, expecting you to remember the color of the room and the shape of the windows. That's exactly what happened here. The fact is that my great-great-grandfather died at the Battle of San Jacinto, not the Alamo. When I said the Alamo, it was just a slip of the tongue. Anyway, the point is that the Battle of San Jacinto was far more important to Texas history than the Alamo. Why, the men who fought there were as brave as any men who have walked the face of the earth." By the time he had finished his harangue, a quarter of an hour later, his illustrious ancestor wound up as the hero of that historic engagement. Only afterward did his listener find out "that Johnson's great-great-grandfather had not died at San Jacinto, or even been there, just as he had not been at the Alamo. He was a real estate trader and he died at home, in bed."[34]

Throughout his public career, memory of the Alamo and of other moments of valor in the struggle of the Texans against Mexico loomed large. In 1941, in his first important speech in Congress, an address delivered four days before the vote on extending selective service, Johnson said: "Texas boys come from a race of men who fought for their freedom at the Alamo and Goliad and San Jacinto. . . . Texas boys prefer service now to slavery later." During World War II, Johnson boasted of "our gallant Texans, under command of our Texas admiral, Chester Nimitz," and said that the Allied fighting forces, who "all had love of country in their souls, but only murder in their hearts for the enemy," were "imbued with the spirit of Bowie and Crockett and Houston." Eventually, these recollections of brave men who did not know the meaning of surrender would affect the course of his policies in Vietnam.[35]

Though his forebear at the Alamo was a figment of his imagination, Johnson could make legitimate claims to heroic ancestry on the Texas frontier. His great-great-uncle's reputation as an Indian fighter, an admirer said, made his name "a household word in all the scattered log cabins that dotted the woods and prairies of Texas." When Johnson's grandfather moved into the buffalo grass hills, it was still the domain of Indians, some of whom were said to be "ritualistic cannibals," and Lyndon told and retold the story of his grandmother's courage and guile in escaping a Comanche raid in 1869. When an Indian party killed and scalped two of the Johnson neighbors, Lyndon's grandfather joined a posse that pursued the raiders into the hills, leaving his wife and child alone. As she was drawing water from a spring, Eliza spotted a Comanche party and, undetected, raced back to her cabin. She grabbed her infant and dropped down into a root cellar, cleverly manipulated a stick to pull a braided rug over a trap door, and, with the babe in her arms hushed by a diaper tied over her mouth, hid for hours in the darkness until it was safe to emerge. The highest compliment Lyndon Johnson could pay someone was to say that he was "a good man to go to the well with." He explained, "When the Indians were in these hills, raidin' and scalpin,' during my granddaddy's time, you had to have somebody you could depend on go with you when you had to draw water from the well."

The Johnson family saga marched chapter by chapter through the history of Texas. Lyndon's grandfather regaled him with tales of the great cattle drives north to Abilene. He and his brother were the biggest trail drivers in a six-county area. In 1870 they drove seven thousand longhorns up the Chisholm trail, and when Lyndon's great-uncle returned from the last drive he set his Colt revolver on a table alongside his saddlebags from which he counted out $100,000 in gold coin.[36]

Johnson calculatedly cultivated the image of himself as a longtime Texan. In 1940, in a letter to Henry Wallace, he described himself as "a successor of some of those squirrel-shooters" from the Texas hill country who wanted to sign up with Sam Houston's army, and when he became Democratic leader in the Senate, he sported jumbo-sized solid-gold cuff links in the configuration of the Lone Star State with a diamond to pinpoint Austin. In 1959 he told a gathering in Odessa that "sometimes Bird bakes a buncha little cookies in the shape of the State of Texas to go with the coffee," and that same year he served guests at the ranch hamburgers molded to the silhouette of Texas. Concerned that the hamburger looked so lopsided that it was gauche, he instructed guests, "Eat the panhandle first." After becoming president, he said one day at the White House: "All my life I have drawn strength, and something more, from those Texas hills. Sometimes, in the highest councils of the nation, in this house, I sit back and I can almost feel that rough, unyielding, sticky clay soil between my toes, and it stirs memories that often give me comfort and sometimes give me a pretty firm purpose." Late in 1968, as his reign drew to a close, Johnson told a Houston crowd, "In all my years in Washington, I have never ceased to be a Texan."[37]

"During his days in power, he had made the Texas hill country part of the national scene," Harry Middleton has written, reflecting on Johnson's presidency, adding: "During those years, he had proudly demonstrated his deep affection for that land and its resources. Presidents, chancellors, and prime ministers had dined in the ranch house where his forebears had gathered for family festivities; had been treated to the sectional epicurean pleasures of cabrito and pinto beans; had been entertained by high school choirs and country dancers. The places of interest they were taken to see were the coliseums, the Place d'Etoiles and the Versailles of the hill country—the German houses of

Fredericksburg, the forts at Johnson City, and always the pastures, where deer leaped at dusk and where the land projected in the day's last glimmering light an endless promise of serenity."[38]

Johnson's association with Texas provided him with an identity that was, to a degree, independent of South or West but tilted toward the West. To be sure, when his mother taught him the poem on the Alamo, she was tutoring him to recite it at a Confederate reunion, and Johnson could always remind southerners that from 1861 to 1865 Texas was aligned with the Rebels. More common, though, was the perception that Johnson, as a Texan, represented not the Old South but the new Southwest of oil derricks and aerospace. In his classic 1948 study, V. O. Key Jr. wrote: "The changes of nine decades since 1860 when a substantial proportion of its population consisted of Negro slaves have weakened the heritage of southern traditionalism, revolutionized the economy, and made Texas more western than southern. . . . In 1940 only one Texan in seven was a Negro. White Texans, unlike white Mississippians, have little cause to be obsessed about the Negro. The Lone Star State is concerned about money and how to make it, about oil and sulfur and gas, about cattle and dust storms and irrigation, about cotton and banking and Mexicans." As the 1960 convention approached, Thurgood Marshall told Averell Harriman he saw "no problem at all" in nominating Lyndon Johnson "because in my book Texas is not South; it's Southwest."[39]

So much did Johnson seem a southwesterner of Houston skyscrapers that doubt was raised even about how much he really knew or cared about Texas's past. George Reedy has recalled: "Once I wrote a speech for him to deliver at some historical society. He read it and called me immediately to give him an explanation of what had happened at Goliad and Washington-on-the-Brazos. I had not known myself until I looked up some dates prior to writing the speech, but I was not a Texan. I had the same reaction as though an Irish nationalist had asked me what happened at the Boyne and Drogheda. This does not mean there was nothing of Texas in him. He was shaped by Texas and the hill country. But it was modern Texas and he had to be briefed with care before talking to an interviewer or an audience of Texas buffs on the days of the pioneers."[40] Unlikely. Since his great-grand-uncle was one of the fifty-nine who signed the Texas Declaration of Independence in the blacksmith's shop in Washington-on-the-Brazos, it seems highly improbable that Lyndon Johnson did not know well the circumstances of this cherished bit of family lore.

Quite a few observers concluded that the key to understanding Johnson was recognizing that he belonged to no section—to the Southwest no more than to the South or West, for, ever since coming to Washington, he had developed a national, not a sectional, identity. In 1931 Johnson took a "temporary" leave of absence from his teaching job at Sam Houston High School in Houston, where he was debate coach, to run the office of a Texas congressman, and he remained in Washington for the next thirty-eight years. After so long a stay, a writer has said, he had become "a Washington provincial, an avatar of the capital's peculiar brand of insularity." In the many decades following his first election to Congress in 1937, he "would return to Texas only to convalesce or campaign for office," one historian has noted, while another has written that Johnson "loved his home state and did what he needed to build and maintain support in Texas, but he never held a state office and, as the years passed, he slowly emancipated himself from its distinctive political culture." A columnist maintained: "Mr. Johnson is not intrinsically a Texas rancher, either in outlook or behavior. . . . He is seen in his real self in the midst of political strife and controversy in Washington. . . . He is like the ancient Romans. The historian Will Durant says they could not wait to get their country seats, but, once there, paced the atrium until they could leap into their chariots to return to Rome."[41]

Some of those who had served under him, and knew him intimately, agreed. Lyndon Johnson, Reedy observed, was "a politician who was *from* Texas but not truly *in* Texas. His political career had been spent on the national scene, and while at one time he had built a powerful organization within the state, its sole purpose was to sustain him in Washington." Similarly, another of his aides, Harry McPherson, pointed out that Johnson's "true province was not the South. It was Washington. He had been there almost constantly since 1932, and even his years away from it had been spent in working for a federal program . . . or in campaigning to return. . . . He believed that what Washington did—what the Congress passed, what the President executed—counted for more than all other cities and institutions in the land." The American correspondent for the *Times* of London agreed. "As president," wrote Henry Brandon, Johnson "was too much a provincial. I do not mean a Texas provincial, as so many assumed . . . , but a Washington provincial. The world that mattered to him was the world between the two ends of Pennsylvania Avenue, the world between the White House and Capitol Hill."[42]

V

A national identity Johnson may have had, but for two decades no one could differentiate his behavior from that of any other southern congressman who dutifully followed the lead of ardent white supremacists such as Tom Connally, the senior senator from Texas. Not long after Johnson first came to the House, Connally is said to have told him, "Lyndon, you're here as a Texan. And don't ever forget that as a Texan, you're a Southerner. If you throw down the South and forget your origins, you're going to foreclose your progress. Because the only people that will stand with you are the people from the South. The people from the North are never going to have any respect for you." Senator A. Willis Robertson of Virginia, like Connally a foe of civil rights statutes though a more moderate one, later said of Johnson: "He was a Southern man. . . . They called him Western, but we called him Southern, and Texas was in the Confederacy." From the other side, one of the leaders of the civil rights bloc, Congressman Richard Bolling, thought of Johnson, quite simply, as a "Southern politician."[43]

From 1937 on, Johnson consistently opposed civil rights measures that came before Congress. One tabulation found that between 1940 and 1960, Johnson "voted as a Southerner, with the other Southerners, no less than thirty-nine times on matters of civil rights: six times against proposals to abolish the poll tax, six times against proposals to eliminate discrimination in Federal programs, twice against legislation to prohibit and punish lynching, twice to support segregation in the Armed Forces, once against a Federal Fair Employment Practices Commission, once to maintain segregation in the District of Columbia." He gave new meaning to the gibe "as thin as the liberalism of a Texas congressman."[44]

In the 1948 senatorial race in Texas, Johnson made his attitude explicit. His narrow defeat in a bid for the U.S. Senate in 1941 owed not a little to his poor showing in racist areas of East Texas, and that experience inclined him to be more forthright about avowing his commitment to white supremacy. "For the past eleven years," Johnson boasted, "I voted against all the civil rights bills in Congress." In 1948 pollsters found that only 14 percent of white Texans approved of Truman's civil rights policies, and that year, in speeches from Texarkana to Waco to San Antonio, Johnson attacked the president's proposals. "Harry Truman knows I am against him on this program," he told Texas voters. "I just don't think Congress should try to cram his program down the throats of southern states." He added: "This civil rights program, about which you have heard so much, is a farce and a sham—an effort to set up a police state in the guise of liberty. I am opposed to that program. I fought it in Congress. It is the province of the state to run its own elections. I am opposed to the anti-lynching bill because the federal government has no more business enacting a law against one kind of murder than another. I am against the FEPC because if a man can tell you whom you must hire, he can tell you whom you cannot employ."[45]

After winning election to the Senate by the infinitesimal, and hotly disputed, margin of eighty-seven votes, "Landslide Lyndon," in his maiden speech early in 1949, joined a southern filibuster against a civil rights initiative by giving an address free of the racist excesses of a Bilbo but suffused with cant. To be sure, he asserted, "When we of the South rise here to speak against . . . civil-rights proposals, we are not speaking against the Negro race. We are not attempting to keep alive the old flames of hate and bigotry." He also said that he favored getting rid of the poll tax as a prerequisite for suffrage. When he denounced prejudice, which "inflames, excites, exaggerates," however, he was not deploring vicious discrimination against black citizens but criticism of the southern bloc in the Senate. "Prejudice is most wicked and most harmful as a majority ailment, directed against minority groups," he stated, and by "minority groups" he meant white Southerners. Defending the filibuster, he declared that "it seems almost criminal . . . for us to spend our time whittling away at the few remaining safeguards against unchecked and uncontrolled majority rule." Drawing on rhetoric of the ranch, he warned that if a "gag rule" curbed filibusters, "the bridle will be upon the tongues of all minorities, and no mount is free, once the bit is in its mouth." In his worst descent into sophistry, he maintained that if an FEPC act "can compel me to employ a Negro, it can compel that Negro to work for me. . . . Such a law would do nothing more than enslave a minority." After he finished, his southern colleagues queued up at his desk to offer congratulations. Though, as one commentary observed, Johnson had "avoided a church wedding" with southern racists, he did "slip easily into a common law union" with them.[46]

Johnson took such pride in this first effort, which, despite its moderation, placed him squarely in the Dixie camp, that he mailed off thousands of copies, only to encounter reproof from civil rights advocates. A Texarkana man wrote him, "You have greatly betrayed all trust that we the Negro Citizens of Texas had placed in you," and the executive secretary of the Houston branch of the NAACP wired him: "The Negroes who sent you to Congress are ashamed to know that you have stood on the floor against them today. Do not forget that you went to Washington by a small majority vote and that was because of the Negro vote. There will be another election and we will be remembering what you had to say today." Unfazed by these rebukes, Johnson wrote one constituent about the filibuster, "It would be particularly foolish . . . to take away this freedom of debate merely to permit the enactment of the so-called Civil Rights legislation, most of which is probably unconstitutional as well as unsound and unnecessary," and assured another, "When I sought the office of Senator from Texas last summer, . . . I pledged my opposition to the current Civil Rights proposals. I intend to live up to *my* pledge."[47]

White liberals, in his own state and elsewhere, kept hammering away at him. One man sent back a copy of the talk with an arrow drawn on it to the "B." in "Lyndon B. Johnson" and a scrawled message: "Does the 'B' stand for 'Bilbo'? Really, now—we Texans aren't as ignorant (or as proud of our traditions) as you give us credit for being. Have the courage to defend your own convictions, Mr. Johnson, and you'll gather more votes than you will by aligning yourself with the old die-hards of the South." Another of his white constituents in Texas wrote him: "You aren't living in the days of John C. Calhoun, even if . . . you seem to think so. When Lee surrendered at Appomattox, Calhoun's ideas—and his methods—surrendered along with him. Come out of the brush—the Civil War's over. Haven't you heard?"[48]

Johnson shunted aside all the reprimands self-righteously. When FDR's former assistant Jim Rowe, who was one of LBJ's closest advisors, chided him on his performance, he replied:

> When you and Humphrey—and others before you—reach the point of translating your humanitarian spirit into law you seem always to lose any sense of charity, faith in your fellow man, or reasonableness. The civil rights legislation brought to Congress is not benevolent; it is, if I may say so, almost sadistic. . . . At Philadelphia you saw two blind unreasoning minorities collide. Both of them, judging from what I know of their character, are cruel, ruthless, and vicious. Justice, to their way of thinking, carries a cat-o'-nine-tails in one hand and salt in the other.
>
> You may think that characterization applies only to my Dixiecrat friends; I believe it applies to both sides equally.

Lyndon Johnson in these years could discern no difference between fanatical racists and people who sought recognition of the constitutional rights of black citizens.[49]

On Capitol Hill, Johnson gave the country good reason to think that he was just another member of the Dixie bloc. When as senator-elect he first encountered the young Senate official Bobby Baker, he said: "I gotta tell you, Mr. Baker, that my state is much more conservative than the national Democratic party. I got elected by just eighty-seven votes and I ran against a caveman. . . . I've got a Southern constituency and so I'm going to be more conservative than you would like me to be or than President Truman would like me to be. President Truman's about as popular as measles in Texas, and you'll waste your time trying to talk to me when I know it would cut my own throat to help him. . . . If I go to voting for the Fair Employment Practices Commission and so on, they've got a good start toward forming a lynch mob." In 1949 he voted to make Jim Crow mandatory in the District of Columbia, and in 1950 he went along with his southern colleagues in supporting an amendment to the selective service law to sanction racially segregated military units and in beating down an attempt to establish a permanent FEPC.[50]

Civil rights advocates regarded Johnson as a menace. Walter White wrote Adlai Stevenson in 1953 that he was "stunned" by words of praise from him for Lyndon Johnson. In 1948, when Johnson was elected to the Senate by such a tiny margin, more than 100,000 blacks in Texas had voted for him as preferable to his more racist opponent, White pointed out. "But despite the fact that Senator Johnson owes his election . . . to the support of Negro Texans, he has voted without exception against every civil rights measure which has come before the Senate. As a result he has earned the disfavor of every thinking Negro of Texas." When Johnson connived to kill a civil rights bill in 1956, the national chairman of Americans for Democratic Action, Joseph Rauh, charged that Johnson had "brought the Democratic party to its lowest point in twenty-five years" and was "running the Democratic party for the benefit of the southern conservative viewpoint." Roy Wilkins, asked years later whether in the 1950s, "as the NAACP man," he regarded LBJ as "friend, foe, neutral?" replied bluntly, "We didn't consider him a friend."[51]

In the self-pitying manner he would sometimes adopt, Johnson saw himself as the victim of circumstances. When the Supreme Court handed down its landmark ruling in *Brown v. Board of Education,* he ranted: "I'm damned if I do and damned if I don't. The Dixiecrats, and a lot of my people at home, will be on me like stink on shit if I don't stand up and bray against the Supreme Court's decision. If I do bray like a jackass, the red hots and senators with big minority blocs in the East and the North will gut shoot me." In the spring of 1957, he complained to Arthur Schlesinger Jr., who was critical of his leadership, that, despite the burden of having to cope with "the Confederates," he had a more progressive voting record than senators whom liberals admired, "yet they look on me as some kind of southern bigot."[52]

Johnson also exasperated liberals by the way he snuggled up to the Senate leader of the anti–civil rights battalion, Richard B. Russell. "I am young and impressionable," he wrote Russell shamelessly in the fall of 1949, the year he arrived in the Senate, "so I just try to do what that Old Master, the junior senator from Georgia, taught me how to do." To woo Russell, he enlisted Lady Bird, who later recalled: "I'd always try to have things that I thought he liked— Southern type food, which was very natural in our household, . . . cornbread, black-eyed peas, and turnip greens, and broiled ham, and fried chicken and . . . peach ice cream." So much a member of the family did Russell become that Lynda Bird called him "Uncle Dick." Johnson not only cultivated Russell, but in 1952, despite Russell's racist record, worked indefatigably to make the Georgia senator his party's choice for president of the United States. "I have a very vivid recollection," said Russell's secretary, "of Senator Johnson's operating on the floor of the convention at Chicago and . . . buttonholing people in Senator Russell's behalf."[53]

According to one account, the attempt to curry favor with Russell took a nasty turn. A black chauffeur, who had reason to be grateful to Johnson, his benefactor, nonetheless remembered: "Whenever I was late, no matter what the reason, Johnson called me a lazy, good-for-nothing nigger. He especially liked to call me nigger in front of southerners and racists like Richard Russell. It was, I soon learned, LBJ's way of being one of the boys." On one occasion, when Johnson laced into him mercilessly and unfairly and employed a racial epithet, he justified himself by saying, "I can't be too easy with you. I don't want to be called a nigger-lover."[54]

Harry McPherson, who served on LBJ's staff in the 1950s, has enhanced the credibility of this story by pointing out that, though Johnson, as a senator from a southern state, operated under inescapable constraints with respect to civil rights, "this is not to suggest that he was then totally committed to desegregation and was prevented from saying so only by the realities of Texas politics." McPherson added: "Johnson was much closer to country-born Southern politicians than to those from Northern cities. . . . He could be amused by stories in which Negroes seemed fearful, or lazy, or raffishly cunning—Stepin Fetchit or Sportin' Life stories. The growing militancy of Negro spokesmen disturbed him."[55]

Johnson's assiduous courtship of Russell paid off when at the beginning of 1953, at the highly respected Georgian's behest, Senate Democrats chose Johnson minority leader, the first step toward his elevation to majority leader after the party won back control the following year. Some weeks before the 1953 caucus, Russell had scribbled on his desk calendar, "Buttoned up leadership for him." The Georgian saw Johnson as a useful go-between among the sections. As Russell's biographer has observed, "Johnson had been raised in a segregated society and had voted with Southerners on civil rights bills, but he was not identified so clearly with white supremacy and segregation that he could not work with northern liberal and moderate Democrats."[56]

Yet if Johnson was a conciliator, his inclinations had a decidedly southward bend. A contemporary writer observed that, though LBJ's admirers were claiming that he was a centrist, equidistant from Strom Thurmond on the right and Paul Douglas on the left, "Johnson never strays far from his real power base in the Senate—his fellow-Southerners." Subsequently, the senator from New Mexico Clinton P. Anderson wrote in his memoirs: "I don't know precisely what understanding was reached between Russell and Lyndon Johnson. But I do know that throughout the years that Johnson was leader, Russell's power remained intact. Johnson, whose aspirations were national rather than simply senatorial, liked to call himself a 'western' senator. . . . But, in his conduct, he followed Russell down the line, at least on the issues that were important to the South. . . . While he was Democratic leader, Lyndon Johnson was as southern as hominy grits."[57]

Johnson left the impression that he was no sectionalist when he did not put his name on the Southern Manifesto against the *Brown* decision. That document exalted Jim Crow as "a part of the life of the people of many of the states" and praised "the motives of those states which have declared the intention to resist forced integration by any lawful means." The manifesto accused the U.S. Supreme Court of substituting "naked judicial power . . . for the established law of the land" and denounced inflammatory "outside meddlers" for "destroying the amicable relations between the white and Negro races" that had been built up over ninety years before the justices had created "chaos." It was not drafted on impulse but came nearly two years after *Brown,* and hence was, as John Egerton has written, "a calculated declaration of defiance by one hundred men in the houses of national political power." After listening to the document read, Wayne Morse responded, "One would think that Calhoun was walking across the floor of the Senate today." As a consequence of the absence of Johnson's signature, night riders burned a cross on the LBJ Ranch, and the director of the Washington Bureau of the NAACP told a conference of Texas branches of the organization, "Texans will note with pride that Senator Lyndon Johnson did not sign the so-called Southern Manifesto which was a bugle call to defiance of the U.S. Supreme Court."[58]

Johnson's reputation as a lonely dissident had little basis. Only five of the twenty-two members of Congress from Texas signed the Southern Manifesto. When Strom Thurmond came to the desk of Albert Gore Sr. on the Senate floor to ask him to add his signature, the Tennessee senator, who later said that he thought it was "the most spurious, inane, insulting document of a political nature claiming to be legally founded that I had ever read," barked, "Hell no," but Johnson did not have to reject it outright because he was never asked to sign. "On a personal basis and just Senator to Senator, of course we wanted him to sign it," John Stennis later explained, "but at the same time we recognized that he wasn't just a Senator from Texas, he was a leader and he had a different responsibility in that degree. It wasn't held against him, I'll put it that way, by the Southerners that he didn't sign it. . . . There might have been some word of disappointment spoken, but nothing held against him." Senator Russell, as his biographer has written, "knew that no one who signed such a document could ever become president of the United States. Russell was much more interested in pushing Johnson for president . . . than in having another name on the manifesto." Furthermore, Johnson, when asked why his name was missing, insisted that he was "not a civil rights advocate." His stand was connected both to his Senate role and to his long-term political ambitions. "I'm not gonna sign that Southern manifesto," he declared. "I'm the leader, and I can't lead Democrats over a cliff. It would preclude me being thought of as anything more than just another Southern mushmouth."[59]

His behavior understandably led many champions of civil rights to conclude that he was simply another sectional legislator who "smelled of magnolias." Though he tried to position himself to modify that perception, he thought it more important to keep in the good graces of his southern colleagues. Johnson was viewed, a Georgia governor later said, "as a Deep South southerner who had pretty much the same political philosophy that the solid southern bloc in Congress represented." As late as 1956, Johnson told Adlai Stevenson he should ease up on civil rights in order to increase the former Illinois governor's appeal to the South. That same year, he informed a group of Texans, "I didn't think my friends needed to be told again that I don't favor integration since I have said so time and again through the years."[60]

Johnson got his reward for fidelity to his section in 1956 when he became the South's favorite son for the Democratic presidential nomination. When

Texas advanced Johnson's name, southern legislators shook his hand on the Senate floor, for, as the *Washington Star* observed, his candidacy was "an answer to a prayer, so far as Southern Democrats are concerned." After not only Russell, but also Sam Rayburn and both of Virginia's senators endorsed LBJ for president, one Washington correspondent wrote that it was "expected that Johnson will be the man around whom almost all the Dixie delegations will rally at the Chicago convention." As another correspondent later remarked, "Some of the older southern senators were pretty proud of him. They thought he was their boy even though they didn't always like what he did."[61]

His willingness to run is odd, for it had long been regarded as axiomatic that no southerner could be nominated, and the majority leader knew perfectly well that, in the words of a British correspondent, "the curse of the South" was upon him. The inscription on a plaque presented to the Speaker of the House in 1946 read: "To Our Beloved Sam Rayburn—Who would have been President if he had come from any place but the South." In 1953, not long after being chosen Senate minority leader, Johnson told a reporter that he had no presidential aspirations, since, he said, "I come from the wrong part of the country," and when Helen Gahagan Douglas asked the majority leader, "Lyndon, are you thinking about offering yourself as a possible candidate for Presidency?" he replied, as she said he always did to this question, "I was born at the wrong place at the wrong time." He could never be elected president, he wrote Joseph P. Kennedy, "because it was too close to Appomattox."[62]

He did not always send out the same signal, though. Asked years later whether in the 1950s Johnson had ambitions that went beyond the majority leadership, Jim Rowe replied: "I think he always had ambitions. But I think he was ambivalent. I remember once, I think it was 1956, he just made a flat statement that he had better recognize that Texans and also the South, their base for power was in the Senate. That was all they were going to have. . . . He'd believe that one day and want to be president the next." Johnson's pious disavowals sometimes left his field agents exasperated. One of them expostulated: "You're out there bustin' your ass and eatin' sorry food and stayin' in third-rate motels while you kiss the butts of some of the most boring bastards in America. About the time you've half-convinced somebody LBJ is a viable candidate, you pick up the newspaper or turn on television and there's Johnson saying 'Ah jes' wanna be the very best Senate majority leader and Texas senator that God ever allowed to draw air.' It pulls the rug out from under you."[63]

The notion of Johnson as *vice* presidential candidate in 1956 seemed more promising. Early in the summer of 1955 Jim Rowe wrote the majority leader: "Although it is no longer a startling idea that Lyndon Johnson might become President of the United States, I can think of nothing more remote at present. All the old shibboleths of American politics are against it," since the Democratic Party would not accept a southerner at the head of the ticket. Why then, one might ask, even "bother to talk about Lyndon Johnson?" Rowe responded: "There is a very simple answer. The compelling necessity for Lyndon Johnson is . . . that he begin to move from his present geographical position to a national position." There was "only *one* way in the foreseeable future to achieve this wider canvas which is required if you are to go any farther. That is to get the nomination for Vice President in 1956." To Johnson that might sound "like rather small potatoes when what one really wants is the Big One," but if he got to campaign as the Democratic vice presidential nominee, attitudes would change. "The people in the party will think of you as a national figure rather than a regional one."[64]

Johnson in 1956 had even higher ambitions, for he entertained the notion that he might be his party's presidential candidate. Both Russell and Ellender announced that they were behind Johnson's bid "one hundred percent," a commitment not nearly strong enough for Florida's Senator Smathers who said, "I'm for him not one hundred percent but one thousand percent." Johnson also gathered some supporters outside his own section, Joe Kennedy for one, but he was still seen as a man of the South and hence unacceptable. John Steele, *Time-Life*'s White House correspondent, thought "it would be hard for Lyndon Johnson to . . . emerge as a truly national figure. He has consistently refused to show himself in the northern baronies of his party's strength." Johnson, wrote Stewart Alsop, could "have virtually the entire Southern delegate vote without lifting a finger," but "Johnson is no ardent advocate of Negro equality, and as a Southerner he would probably alienate a big slice of the Negro vote, increasingly vital in the Northern industrial states." Calling the Chicago convention site a "fantasy" stage where "normally serious, intelligent, experienced men, sweating under the Presidential fever . . . can convince themselves of anything," James Reston of the *New York Times* wrote that one example of this malady was that "Lyndon can persuade himself that he is really a national and not a regional figure." As it turned out, Johnson fell far short, winding up with no state beyond his own Texas save for incorrigibly Jim Crow Mississippi. At every Democratic convention where there was a contested nomination, Theodore White later pointed out, there had always been a southern candidate who would fight "the good, if hopeless, fight." Lyndon Johnson was "the traditional hopeless Southern candidate in 1956."[65]

VI

Yet if most of the country in 1956 still saw Johnson as a sectional figure, he had, from the very beginning of his tenure in the Senate, been distancing himself from his comrades in the former Confederate states. When southern senators caucused to plan strategy on protecting the right to filibuster in January 1949, Johnson, who was just starting his six-year term, was conspicuously absent. "I think that I can be more effective by not putting any regional label on myself," he said. He and Estes Kefauver were the only newly elected senators to shun the group. "Lyndon . . . never did join what they call the Southern bloc," the head of the Washington bureau of the *Dallas News* later pointed out. "Now, that's another indication to me that Lyndon was looking ahead to being a national figure. He didn't want to be branded as [a southerner]." When he sought leadership posts in the Senate, he wanted northerners to understand that he was not the Dixie candidate, and he hinted that, if his southern colleagues had asked him to sign the manifesto, he would have turned them down.[66]

Both southern and northern politicians grasped that he was not body and soul in the bosom of the South. Johnson, Senator Russell's secretary later said, "was just not a person who was identified as in the 'Amen Corner' of the caucuses on civil rights." From the opposing camp, Hubert Humphrey reminisced: "My first impression of the Senate was that the people who ran it were the southerners or their allies. . . . Lyndon Johnson had a kind of—I sensed that he had a different relationship; this was the one thing that intrigued me about him. He was a close friend of Dick Russell's; a close associate of Walter George, who was a powerful senator from Georgia; he was on good working relationships with every southerner, but he wasn't quite southern. . . . Johnson never was a captive of the southern bloc. He was trying to be a captain of them, rather than a captive."[67]

No journalist knew Johnson more intimately than William S. White, who in 1958 wrote of him: "Geographically, he is a Southerner—and it is entirely fair to say that to some of his critics this is his true, his infamous, his inexpiable and unremittable sin. . . . He is wholly acceptable there, yes. He knows his way around there, yes. He has a stentorian voice there, yes. But he is not, in a certain deep and intimate way, totally and instinctively at home there. For in . . . his blood and his bones and his inherited memories and attitudes, he is hardly a Southerner at all in any common meaning of the term." Years later, White observed, "Because he had reached the Senate majority leadership with heavy and critical Southern sponsorship, most notably that of Senator Russell of Georgia, it was widely supposed that he was essentially a Southern agent there. No estimate could have been more wrong. For Johnson was always in but never of the Southern world of the Senate."[68]

When Douglass Cater, managing editor of the national magazine, *The Reporter*, visited Johnson after the senator's heart attack in 1955, he found that, contrary to the implications of a story in the *New York Times*, the majority leader had no intention of following "the traditional route of the southern senator, but . . . really did have a national vision." Cater later reflected: "I was all the more impressed with this because at the time he could have no intimation that he would physically ever be able to run for President." Cater added: "Coming from Alabama, I watched many outstanding members of Congress reach a certain height and then level off because of the limitations of their regional commitment. This is true of Lister Hill and John Sparkman and others. I had always regarded it as a tragedy because some of the Southern politicians were among the nation's best. What seemed hopeful and optimistic to me was that Johnson could break through this barrier."[69]

Despite his record of consistently voting against civil rights measures, Johnson diverged from the extreme views of some of his colleagues. His aide Horace Busby remembered that during his 1948 campaign for the Senate Johnson would not speak until blacks in a small Texas town were permitted to stand on the same side of the railroad tracks as whites. "Buzz, Buzz," he asked afterward, "how many votes you think I'll get here?" Ten, Busby reckoned, holding up both hands. "Oh, no," Johnson answered, and raised two fingers. Another assistant, Harry McPherson, told an interviewer later: "I had the feeling, and I can't give you specifics about this, that Lyndon Johnson had a kind of contempt for the intellectual and political laziness of a racist position. That the combination of racism and reaction was so familiar in the South and so antipathetic to Franklin Roosevelt and to the sense that Johnson had of what the government ought to be in business to do, that he was contemptuous of it almost on a level of aesthetics as much as ethics." In his memoir, McPherson observed: "Johnson was not a thoroughgoing Southern apologist. He did not pretend, as many Southerners did, that Negroes 'really enjoyed' the Southern way of life. He did not romanticize the fifth-class schools, the bad housing, the menial jobs, the political powerlessness. He did not expect white Southerners to make early and significant changes in their political and social system without pressure from Washington. He did not attribute Negro living conditions solely to white neglect and discrimination; but he did not deny their central role."[70]

Furthermore, he believed a solution to the race question imperative for the nation. On his first day at work in the late 1940s, Busby got an unexpected lecture from Johnson: "The Negro fought in the war, and now that he's back here with his family he's not gonna keep taking the shit we're dishing out. We're in a race with time. If we don't act, we're gonna have blood in the streets." Another of his former aides, Bill Moyers, has recalled: "Our faith was in integration. . . . Lyndon Johnson . . . championed that faith. He thought the opposite of integration was not just segregation but disintegration—a nation unraveling." Unlike many other senators from the South, too, Johnson recognized that with the country stirred by Truman's edicts, the *Brown* ruling, and the Montgomery bus boycott, Congress could not put off acting much longer. As Congressman Richard Bolling expressed it, "While he might have hoped that the civil rights problem would go away, he knew it would not."[71]

The 1956 election brought home the political penalties of temporizing. That year Republicans enlarged their share of the African-American vote in every city; in Harlem, they doubled their numbers of four years earlier. "Of all the groups in the nation's population," the poll taker George Gallup found, "the one that shifted most to the Eisenhower-Nixon ticket was the Negro voter." If southerners continued to dominate the Democratic Party, the departure of blacks would go on, warned the *Washington Post*. "Sometime soon the Democrats will have to choose between white supremacy and civil rights." Black support for the Democratic national ticket in 1956 plummeted to 61 percent, and Johnson feared that, if the GOP entered the 1958 midterm elections espousing civil rights legislation Democrats opposed, the precipitous drop could not be halted.[72]

As early as 1956, at a time when the southern political establishment viewed Johnson as its champion, some southerners had sniffed out enough of his attitude to find him objectionable. When he fought Governor Allan Shivers for control of the Democratic Party in Texas, twenty-three prominent Houston men wired him to ask, since he had come out against "forced" integration, "Does this mean you are in favor of integration so long as it is not forced?" These "hotheads," as well as the anonymous telephone caller who had threatened his life, the majority leader told a reporter, were the kinds of extremists, left and right, who had brought on the Civil War in 1861 and were seeking to instigate blood-letting now. Shivers himself found Johnson much too moderate, for he had not demanded restoration of the two-thirds rule or backed interposition to uphold Jim Crow schools. The following year, one Texan wrote of Johnson: "The senator's tenuous leadership of Texas Democrats is something of a paradox. It is an article of faith among both liberals and conservatives that no good can come of his leadership. Each side feels that the senator will bear watching, much as a chained mastiff keeps an eye on a postman who enters the yard."[73]

VII

LBJ's performance on 1957 civil rights legislation added to the uneasiness. According to one account, when in 1957 Senator Humphrey urged him to push a civil rights measure, Johnson replied, "Goddamn it, Hubert, I'd get strung up by my balls in Texas if I'd get behind this bill." When he did move gingerly toward it, the Texas Citizens Council wired him from Houston: WE ARE TOLD YOU ARE READY TO SELL OUT THE SOUTH STOP IS THIS TRUE? Johnson cleverly replied, "I do not know where you could have gotten the idea that I am supporting the 'so-called bill for civil rights legislation now before Congress.'" In reality, he did not favor that particular proposal, but his response failed to acknowledge that he was actively seeking an alternative civil rights law.[74]

Early in February the *Augusta Courier* ran a headline, two rows deep, across its entire front page: PEOPLE OF SOUTH DOUBLECROSSED AGAIN / BY U.S. SENATE FLOOR LEADER JOHNSON. The subhead in the Georgia paper read: "'Gentlemen's' Club Life and Political Ambition Saps One's Manhood." The accompanying article charged that "this so-called Southerner, the Senator from a great Southern state," was a "traitor to his own people," for he was conspiring with northerners to set up a "Gestapo" to impose "race mixing," a course that might gain him the backing of northern liberals but was sure to cost him "the support of the decent white people of the South." Though a Yankee senator "could be honest in his opinion," it said, "a Southerner such as Johnson can never be honest in his change of position because if he were right in his lifelong position, he is certainly wrong now." The Georgia paper concluded that "whether his stab in the back becomes fatal depends upon the courage of the other members of the United States Senate from the South." The South would give close scrutiny to whether they would "stand up and fight the efforts of Lyndon Johnson, the renegade from Texas."[75]

At the same time, Johnson felt powerful pressure to recognize that the movement for a civil rights statute was irresistible and that he should be at the head of the forces of change, particularly because of his southern origins. In December 1956 Phil Graham, publisher of the *Washington Post,* who concluded that racial tensions were rising to a dangerous pitch and that only a southerner with the capacity to "go national" could cope with them, wrote Johnson: "It is believed that LBJ (through fortunate eugenics, broad experience, lucky marriage, and other fortuities) has arrived at a place in personal development and political career where he may just have a chance to play a major national role. This may well be wrong. Fate's decree may be that LBJ is destined only to be a Jimmy Byrnes or a more energetic Dick Russell. On the other hand, he may be permitted to play a truly consequential role in the mainstream of history." Graham even tried to recruit a former Luce editor, Emmet Hughes, to teach the Texan how to talk like a northerner.[76]

Everything depended, Johnson heard, on whether he had the courage and foresight to break away from the Dixie bloc on civil rights. Johnson listened especially attentively to Jim Rowe, for, said George Reedy, he had "an almost mystical belief in Jim's powers. He thought Jim might make him Pope or God knows what." In a strongly worded memo, Rowe reminded him: "Both your friends and your enemies are saying that this is Lyndon Johnson's Waterloo. They are saying that you are trapped between your Southern background and your desire to be a national leader and that you cannot escape." In truth, this was "Armageddon for Lyndon Johnson. To put it bluntly, if you vote against a civil rights bill, you can forget your presidential ambitions in 1960." He urged that Johnson, instead, take on Henry Clay's role of The Great Compromiser, "as a man with the confidence of the South" and "as a Southerner and a national leader speaking to the North" to put through a reasonable measure that would get rid of the issue for a few years and let time and the courts take over while a Republican attorney general was stuck with the unenviable task of enforcing the new law. "The wave of the future is with the civil rights advocates, with the North this time because the whole world today stands behind the North," Rowe pointed out, and "I do not think it is essential . . . that Lyndon Johnson get in the way of that wave." Rowe told his longtime friend: "I know that the Stars and Bars are flying and that the Alamo is still in San Antonio. I know also that Lyndon Johnson is emotionally a Southerner and that the friends who see him on the Pedernales River are even more so. But I know also that Lyndon Johnson is intellectually not a Southerner but a national leader."[77]

Johnson, hearing this counsel from several quarters in 1957, quickly saw the wisdom of it. Early in the year, he confided that he had "come to the conclusion that we are going to have the civil rights controversy with us for many years. However it may have started, it has now gone beyond the point where it can be called off." Johnson, David Halberstam has noted, "legitimately feared the risk of trying for a position as a national liberal only to find himself rejected by the liberals and cut off from his southern base." Nonetheless, Johnson, always a political animal, could not help but sense the consequences for his career of going national. The Tar Heel–born writer Tom Wicker later recalled thinking in 1957 that if Johnson could carry through the civil rights bill, he would get "the racial stain of the South off of him" and could become a presidential contender. "Lyndon Baines Johnson, the old Br'er Fox of the Senate," Roy Wilkins wrote later, "dreamed of becoming President . . . and knew that so long as he had Jim Crow wrapped around him, the rest of the country would see him only as a Southerner, a corn-pone Southerner at that, rather than a man of national stature. So around 1957 he began to change his course on civil rights." Still, "with Johnson, you never quite knew if he was out to lift your heart or your wallet."[78]

VIII

The majority leader approached the 1957 legislation focused less on how it might help African Americans than on what it could do to safeguard his party, the nation, and his career. "LBJ, the centrist, the compromiser, was the Crittenden or Bell of this new crisis," Paul Conkin has written. "He was determined to hold his party together. . . . Such a concern was more important than the content of the bill. He understood that the Democrats, to survive as a competitive party outside the South, had to join Republicans in passing a Civil Rights bill, one with some bite although he hoped not enough to alienate all southern congressmen." Munching venison sausage and holding forth "in a salty, Mark Twain way," Johnson told a reporter, "A civil rights bill is going to be passed by this Congress. There's no getting around it." But he added, "I'd like to see a bill the country can live with and not be torn apart."[79]

He recognized that his main obstacle was the threat of a southern filibuster, which had proven deadly effective in the past, and that to get around it he needed to appease the Dixie bloc by watering down the bill. Richard Russell railed that "neither Sumner nor Stevens, in the persecution of the South in the twelve tragic years of Reconstruction, ever cooked up any such devil's broth as is proposed in this misnamed civil rights bill," and even Lister Hill wanted to "send the measure down to the tongueless silence of dreamless dust." One indication of the viciousness of resistance was the declaration by South Carolina's

Olin Johnston that he was introducing an amendment to fund "shipping home the bodies of civil rights investigators who might die in the line of duty." In mid-June 1957 Johnson camouflaged his intentions by reporting to his constituents: "A strong group of Senators is doing everything possible to defeat the so-called Civil Rights bill. I will help them in any way I can." A month later, he informed Texans that he was endeavoring "to prevent the passage of legislation that would allow the Attorney General to haul our people into a Federal Court and prosecute them without a jury trial and that would make it possible for the Army and Navy to be sent into the South to enforce this statute." But by late July, Johnson was confiding to his mother, "We are having great victories in amending the Civil Rights Bill so far, and if the situation doesn't change, I believe we can get it down to just a 'right to vote' bill that won't be too hard to live with."[80]

Johnson weakened the measure not because he was a racist but because he believed that if he did not do so he had no chance of success. George Reedy has commented: "LBJ didn't give a good whatever we want to use about how the southerners felt about civil rights, except to the extent that it set certain limits on what could be done with a bill. LBJ had no sympathy whatsoever for the anti–civil rights movement. If he had had the votes to do it, the legislation that would have passed would have been far more extreme than what was passed. . . . LBJ was not a southerner in that sense. It was rather unfortunate that the poor devil came from a Confederate state, which . . . historically was not very Confederate." Reedy added on another occasion: "His Dixie colleagues had no illusions as to where he stood on civil rights. He was determined to get the strongest possible bill that he could. But they also knew that he would give them some 'face savers' and that he had sufficient understanding of their plight to do things in such a way that they would not be isolated from the legislative process. What was much more important, however, is that the most important Southern leader [Russell] (and I suspect several others) thought of LBJ as the only Southerner who could become President . . . and were aware of the fact that he could not become President if he shared their unyielding opposition to civil rights."[81]

In return for Johnson's moderation the southern contingent agreed not to filibuster, though a defiant Strom Thurmond broke ranks to set an all-time record by orating for twenty-four hours and eighteen minutes. Abandoning their ancient weapon did not mean that the southerners were being accommodating; rather, they calculated that they would gain more by not antagonizing their colleagues. As the former Mississippi congressman Frank Smith pointed out, "When Lyndon Johnson promoted the strategy that changed the 1957 bill to a voting rights measure, the southern senators did not resist to the point of cloture because they realized that the right to vote was the one issue on which not enough northern and western senators would help them." Even Florida's Senator George Smathers, who had denounced the *Brown* decision and signed the Southern Manifesto, thought that voting was unequivocally a constitutional right. Johnson maintained contacts in both camps by goading the liberal Paul Douglas to mount an offensive to "make sure this long-overdue bill for the benefit of Negro Americans will pass," then alerting Sam Ervin that an objectionable section of "the nigger bill" was approaching but telling John Stennis, "Our ass is in a crack—we're gonna have to let this nigger bill pass."[82]

When the moment arrived to call the roll on the 1957 bill, Johnson felt the need to offer an explanation of how he was going to vote. It was "national—rather than sectional—legislation," he declared. He catalogued the numbers of ways that the measure advanced civil rights, but he also took care to point out, for the benefit of his southern constituents, that it repealed "a bayonet-like Reconstruction Statute whose very existence inflames passions." The majority leader concluded: "I am aware of the implications of my vote. It will be treated cynically in some quarters and misunderstood in others. No Texas Senator has cast a vote for a civil rights bill since 1875. But . . . this is legislation which is good for every State of the Union, and as far as I am concerned, Texas has been a part of the Union since Appomattox. I could not have voted for the bill that came to the Senate. But the measure now before us seeks to solve the problems of 1957—and not to reopen the wounds of 1865."[83]

Johnson's success, however, came only as a result of surrendering a good deal to his southern colleagues. His mentor Dick Russell had warned him that if he did not strike a provision authorizing the attorney general to employ, in the Georgia senator's words, "the whole might of the federal government . . . to force a commingling of white and Negro children in the state-supported schools of the South," Russell would lead a filibuster and Johnson would be in deep trouble in his home state. Russell later called his managing "to confine the Federal invasion of the South to the field of voting and keep the withering hand of the Federal Government out of our schools and social order" his "sweetest victory" in a quarter of a century as senator. Johnson himself assured his Texas constituents not only that he had forestalled "a punitive sectional monstrosity," but also that it would be "a serious mistake to regard this legislation as a civil rights bill."[84]

In truth, the law did not amount to much. When the bill emerged from the Senate, one scholar has concluded, it "was largely a victory for the forces of segregation." The statute was "a modest forward step" only because it was altered in the House. THE CIVIL RIGHTS BILL IS STRIPPED TO ITS CORE, one periodical reported. Though "the consummately skillful Dixie Senators" had eschewed the traditional tactic of a filibuster, they had cleverly accomplished a "remarkable shrinkage in the scope of the bill." By yielding on the schools, Johnson, the civil rights attorney Joe Rauh charged, "set back integration in the South for seven years." The pitiful shard that remained, wrote a well-regarded national columnist, was just what might be expected of Senator Russell's "errand boy." Eleanor Roosevelt, who called Johnson's agreeing to subject the rights of blacks to southern white juries an effort "to fool the people," told Johnson in a biting letter: "I can't say that I really believe the Democrats have intended to do much . . . , particularly those of you who come from Southern states or borderline states as Texas is."[85]

Prominent blacks bombarded Eisenhower with messages expressing their dismay. Ralph Bunche called the bill "disappointingly weak"; the publisher of the *Pittsburgh Courier* denounced it as "lifeless"; and the publisher of the *Chicago Defender* urged the president to veto the measure. So, too, did A. Philip Randolph, saying "It is worse than no bill at all." Another well-known African American shared this view. "Have been in touch with a number of my friends," Jackie Robinson wired the White House. "We disagree that half loaf better than none. Have waited this long for bill with meaning—can wait a little longer."[86]

Still, Johnson could reasonably claim that he had won concessions too, and that as a consequence he had achieved the first civil rights law of the twentieth century. The majority leader had persuaded Russell and his allies that if they insisted on obstructing this moderate measure, they would soon get a much more punitive one. He thereby blunted southern resistance and created a precedent on which he and others could build. "Once you break the virginity," Johnson said, "it'll be easier next time." To northern Democrats, he pointed out that whereas "the ultra-liberal position would have left eleven states solid," he had driven a wedge into the southern phalanx and five states of the former Confederacy had broken away. As a consequence, "we . . . have bought ourselves needed time—time to reconcile the North and the South so we can present a united front in 1960." Even after the bill had been diluted, a Georgia congressman called the measure, which established a permanent Civil Rights Commission and expanded the authority of the Justice Department, "the most vicious piece of anti-South legislation since Reconstruction Days" and deplored the failure of his southern colleagues in the Senate to employ the filibuster. "If this is not the time to use it, when the very foundations of our way of life are being attacked, . . . what are they saving the filibuster for?" Reedy later observed: "It's difficult in the present age to realize just how much crockery was being smashed with the passage of that bill. After all, since 1875 they hadn't been able to even get a simple resolution through the Senate saying civil rights was nice. . . . and yet finally, my God, they got a bill through. The bill was not everything the civil rights people wanted by a hell of a long shot, but it had meaning to it."[87]

Though a number of civil rights groups contemplated rejecting the bill in its final version, the director of the Washington office of the NAACP reasoned that enacting a civil rights measure after eighty-two years of frustration constituted an accomplishment, no matter how anemic the legislation was. For the first time, disfranchised blacks had a national agency, a Commission on Civil Rights, to which they could complain, thereby accumulating a corpus of evidence to demonstrate the need for national voting rights legislation. Wilkins, though disappointed, commented, "If you are digging a ditch with a teaspoon and a man comes along and offers you a spade, there is something wrong with your head if you don't take it because he didn't offer you a bulldozer." Eugene McCarthy, not LBJ's most ardent admirer, later said of Johnson's leadership in brokering the 1957 bill, "Truly it was a masterful piece of legislative work, for the pro–civil rights strength in the Senate was marginal."[88]

A remarkable number of observers abandoned all restraint in maintaining that the 1957 act Johnson had shepherded was a landmark. Dean Acheson categorized the law as "among the greatest achievements since the war," and the *New York Times* deemed it "incomparably the most significant domestic action of any Congress in this century." A woman prominent in Democratic Party affairs recalled: "I sat in the Gallery the night of the vote. You held your breath as to whether they would make it or not, the Majority Leader and his people. It was a tremendous emotional purging for the American people to find out that . . . the . . . agreement between the Republicans and the Democrats in the South and the Southwest that nothing could be done about human rights, . . . which existed tacitly for eighty years from Reconstruction on, was finally broken." Hubert Humphrey, with characteristic exuberance, even claimed that southerners "took a licking the likes of which they have never taken before in their lives."[89]

Johnson's bill survived southern fractiousness not only because it was so modest, but also because many in the South wished to boost one of their own for national office. As William S. White explained, "The southern elders had no intention of allowing Johnson to fail as majority leader not even if they had to take some considerable risk back home in supporting him." Even a senator from Mississippi was willing to bend his views toward that end. "We knew that he had presidential ambitions," John Stennis recalled, "and most of us wanted to see him become president."[90]

Not all of LBJ's southern colleagues were as flexible as Stennis, though. Mississippi Congressman William Colmer subsequently pointed out that Johnson had always opposed civil rights measures, but "after he really got the presidential bug he changed over." An interviewer inquired: Was the switch the result of conviction or political ambition? "Let me answer it this way," Colmer responded. "Ninety percent of his colleagues in the House thought it was political." "Did his part in the '57 civil rights bill cause much resentment among Southern Senators like yourself?" Allen Ellender was later asked. "Yes, it did," Ellender answered. "We just thought that he—well, some of them accused him of being a traitor to the South by making an about-face." "Did you have any idea that Mr. Johnson, because of his Southern background, might not push so hard in things like civil rights?" the questioner persisted. "I surely did," the Louisiana senator replied. "All of us were disappointed. . . . All of us, all members of the Senate who worked with him when he was part of us in the fight against civil rights, why this sudden change was quite a hard blow to us."[91]

A good number of LBJ's Texas constituents had a considerably sterner attitude. From one, he received a two-word wire: NIGGER LOVER. A Mt. Pleasant, Texas couple, who had been his supporters, told him, "You're a dead pigeon now"; a woman wrote a Fort Worth paper that Johnson and Rayburn had "betrayed the South"; and another constituent scolded Johnson, "Remember there is someone in Texas beside the niggers who are due some consideration." A district attorney thought he had an explanation for his fellow Texan's aberrant behavior, one heard with increasing frequency as the decade wore down. "Could it be," he asked Johnson, "that your aspirations for national office have led you to 'sell your people down the river' in exchange for the Negro vote?"[92]

NINE

SOUTHERNER WITH
A NATIONAL FACE

I

Johnson's commitment to the civil rights legislation, however modest, constituted a decisive departure. By 1957, Theodore White later wrote, the majority
leader "had been swept far from his Southern anchorages to a sense of the
broader flow of the country's politics. Pressed by these national forces, enticed
by the Presidential campaign of 1960, in which he hoped to be a candidate, he
followed a new direction in his voting. He broke more and more consistently
with his old friends, until in 1960, he defied them on eight identifiable roll calls
to vote *for* civil rights."[1]

Washington correspondents drew from the episode precisely the conclusion
that LBJ's sponsors had hoped they would. In the course of the struggle the
columnist Roscoe Drummond wrote, "The senior senator from Texas is at one
stroke removing from his path the single barrier which . . . has made it imprac-
ticable for the Democratic Party to select a Southerner for its presidential nominee—the barrier of opposition to civil rights legislation." As the "architect" of
the 1957 breakthrough, "he is the first Southern Democratic leader since the
Civil War to be a serious candidate for the presidential nomination." After the
bill had been enacted, William S. White commented in the *New York Times* that
up until 1957, Johnson, for all of his achievements as majority leader, had not escaped the verdict that he was "at bottom only a Southern as distinguished from
a national politician," but his success in steering through the civil rights measure had, in the words of the headline on White's story, signaled LBJ's "Arrival
as National Political Figure." He was fast becoming, in the phrase of one historian, "a southerner with a national face."[2]

As Johnson increasingly took a national rather than sectional perspective, criticism of him in the South mounted. Southern legislators opposed his effort to make it easier to cut off filibusters, and they took even stronger exception to his action in blocking attempts to curb the Supreme Court, which was seen as the source of much of the region's troubles. Johnson in 1958 separated himself from almost every southern senator in bringing about the defeat by one vote of a bill to narrow the jurisdiction of the Supreme Court. Though the main target of conservatives was "Red Monday," when the Court had safeguarded the liberties of alleged subversives, civil rights leaders believed that enactment of the measure would also severely hamper them. In his syndicated column, David Lawrence asserted that rejection of legislation checking the Court was accomplished by "a Democratic Senator who comes from the South but who, through his position of leadership, was able to thwart the will of his fellow Southerners." Capitol Hill was asking, he wrote, "Did Senator Lyndon Johnson . . . betray the South . . . in order to curry favor with Northern 'liberals' who might help him get the Democratic presidential nomination in 1960?" In 1959, as he surveyed prospective presidential candidates, Roy V. Harris, the racist former Speaker of the Georgia House, said: "Johnson is as sad as any of them." One journalist wrote, "From Nashville to Charleston there were cries that never, never would this traitor to his section be Dixie's candidate for the presidential nomination."[3]

In September 1959 Johnson aggravated this simmering resentment when, in response to the entreaties of liberals, he served notice that in February 1960 another civil rights measure would come to the floor. His announcement signaled a serious breach in his relations with Dick Russell, for in contrast to 1957, he was acting without prior consultation with his southern colleagues. He may have done so because he sensed that inaction was imprudent. That fall, Virginia Durr wrote a friend:

> There is a curious lull in the South right now. The Negroes have realized that unless the rest of the country helps them they simply cannot win this battle alone. Five years after the Decision and 76 Negro children in all schools! That is fantastic as you will admit. If nothing happens in February at the Special session of Congress, then I think we will begin to see some sort of violence erupting, especially from the soldiers who are the bitterest of us all. I see them every day getting off the bus

and wearing the same uniform and yet the Negroes have to go to the "COLORED" waiting room to wait for their connections. It makes them simply furious and I don't blame them. Often they have never been South before and this is where I look to see the real violence break out as it is really intolerable for them.

Early in 1960 Senator Johnson told a group of black leaders that he would put through a civil rights bill that year, adding, "You know I'm going to have to go against the South to do it." Floyd McKissick later remembered that many blacks responded, "You know he ain't going to do that. I been knowin' white folks a long time and he's a Southerner."[4]

Johnson, however, proved true to his word. When southerners denied him the opportunity to redeem his promise by bottling civil rights legislation in committee, he outfoxed them. On February 15, 1960, he caught them by surprise by calling up an obscure bill that the House had already passed to lease Army land to a Missouri country school, a measure that had nothing at all to do with civil rights, so that civil rights amendments could be tacked onto it.

The majority leader's ruse ignited a brush fire that raged across the South, which oscillated between viewing Johnson as a renegade southerner and no southerner at all. For the first time ever, Russell broke openly with Johnson. "You have just heard a motion that I thought would never be made in the Senate by the leader of my party," the Georgian told his colleagues. Pounding his desk, Russell denounced the maneuver as a "lynching of ordinary procedure" and an attempt to "hell-hack the Southern people." (Off the record, Johnson said this was the only time Russell had ever deplored lynching.) The *Jackson Daily News* excoriated "Lyndon Johnson, the traitor"; the *Shreveport Journal* said he was "despised by the people he has betrayed"; and a Florida newspaper called him both a "Fifth Columnist" and a "Southern Benedict Arnold."[5]

Only crass political ambition, his critics charged, could account for such chicanery by a southerner. A member of the Citizens Council of Ouachita Parish, Louisiana, wrote him: "To great masses of the voters of the South it was a supreme act of perfidy. . . . You would not only place your own flesh and blood on the altars of a political Baal, in order to secure personal political gain, but you would place the South and the entire nation in the fiery embrace of the political god you worship. . . . The legislative strategy . . . is a means to sell the SOUTH AND NATION down the river in order to . . . secure for yourself . . . election to a great national office for which you are not fitted morally, spiritually or politically." Simply for reasons of expediency, Lester Maddox later said, had Johnson "deserted his friends of old" to cater to "the bums and the beatniks and the parasites and the Socialists—and to totally ignore the achievers and the conservatives in this country."[6]

After Johnson announced on February 29 that to break a filibuster he would keep the Senate in continuous session, his southern opponents counted on his old mentor, Dick Russell, to outduel him. Enclosing an editorial from the *Mobile Press* entitled "Senator Johnson Betrays South in Unbecoming, Sneaky Fashion," an Alabamian wrote Russell, "The Senator from the great State of Texas, which furnished so many gallant soldiers on the Confederate side during the Civil War, has betrayed his own state." From Atlanta, Russell heard: "I know the odds are against you and your little band of patriots in this fight but some how some way you will defeat Judas Johnson and his mongrel Senators. When you win this fight please make it your business to see that Judas does not get any Southern delegates to the Democratic convention in Los Angeles."[7]

His rupture with Russell, who called Johnson's insistence on around-the-clock sessions a "kind of legislative torture," left Johnson isolated and vulnerable in a way he had not been before in the Senate. "I never had a parliamentary fight that I didn't hope Senator Russell was on my side," Johnson told Walter Cronkite years later. "You never have a man oppose you . . . like Senator Russell opposes you without your feeling it and without it wounding you . . . and perhaps wounding him." When he told Russell he had given notice, the senator, "rather cool, aloof," rejoined, "Yes, I understand that you let them jockey you into that position. I understand." After a long fight, Congress enacted the civil rights law of 1960, "but not," Johnson recalled, "with Senator Russell's vote . . . and not without what you said, Walter—both of us feeling it."[8]

Johnson had taken another step toward winning acceptance as a statesman of national rank, but at considerable cost. He had to settle for legislation so weak that the liberal Democratic Senator Joseph Clark of Pennsylvania called it a "sham" perpetrated by "implacable defenders of the way of life of the Old South." Clark added: "Those of us who supported a meaningful civil rights bill have suffered a crushing defeat. . . . Surely in this battle on the Senate floor the roles of Grant and Lee at Appomattox have been reversed." Even more bruised were Johnson's hopes of uniting the South behind his aspirations for the 1960 Democratic presidential nomination. Louisiana Congressman F. Edward Hebert recalled, "I could never forget on one of these television or radio shows when he first indicated that he would run for the presidency and he switched on civil rights. I remember I said, 'I'm sorry, I have to leave my dear old friend, Lyndon.'" More biting still was the conclusion of Mississippi's John Bell Williams: "I think more Southern people would vote for Adam Clayton Powell [the black congressman from Harlem] than for Lyndon Johnson. The people have more respect for a carpetbagger than they do for a scalawag."[9]

III

Southerners who believed that Johnson's sudden enthusiasm for civil rights laws derived from political ambition discounted too easily other motives, but they were surely right in thinking that the Texas senator recognized that he had to rid himself of the stigma of section if he hoped to reach the White House. In the summer of 1959 the *Wall Street Journal,* in an article with the subhead, "Sectional Tag Hurts Lyndon Johnson in Massachusetts," reported: "Stop random citizens on the street in Boston, or in the industrial center of Lynn, or in the little western Massachusetts town of Lee and like as not the name draws a blank stare. To those voters who do identify the Senator, he is seldom looked on as a figure of national stature. He is often regarded as almost a curiosity—a Southerner trying to get to the White House at a time when the South's political stock has seldom been lower."[10]

The majority leader had continued to maintain that he had no national ambitions, largely because the odds against gaining acceptance for someone from the South were too long. When in 1958 a Richmond editor expressed the hope that he would offer himself in 1960, Johnson retorted, "I won't do it." Quite apart from the fact that he had suffered a severe heart attack, "I couldn't get the nomination, because no Southerner can get it under existing conditions. The northern and western liberals in the Democratic party hate us; they simply hate us, there is no other word for it. They will never allow a Southerner to be nominated." He made a similar remark in 1959 to a reporter in a Washington hotel lobby who asked why, when in New Deal days he was thought of as a liberal, people now called him a reactionary. "Because," Johnson answered, "I'm from below the Mason-Dixon line and you think we all have tobacco juice on our shirts." He thought big-city power brokers were conspiring against him because he was "a Texan rather than a Harvard." In 1960 he requested that an unauthorized Washington headquarters to boost him for president be shut down because "a Southerner could not, and probably should not, be elected."[11]

Johnson's intimates, however, had learned better than to take all of his disavowals literally, and by 1960 he was, in fact, a serious contender determined to show that his appeal was not confined to one section. After his ambitions were dashed in 1956, Johnson, one caustic critic has written, "got the message: . . . he who gets the South gets naught. . . . LBJ saw that he had to get that magnolia blossom out of his lapel, and he coolly set about it." Not only Johnson but also his backers deliberately downplayed his sectional allegiances. When in the fall of 1959 the governor of Texas Price Daniel stressed the need to mass southern support behind Johnson, Senator Russell replied, "I must say that if there is public knowledge of any concerted action that would stamp Lyndon as the 'Southern' candidate, I do not think it would contribute anything to his nomination."[12]

In 1957 one of Senator Johnson's aides suggested a different strategy in a memo to him that began: "Western Films and Stars are very popular right now as you know. And I can't think of a more perfect *Western Star* than the tall, dark and handsome, horse-riding, gun-toting-shootin' 'n huntin' Lyndon Johnson of the Hill Country of Texas." She thought an episode in which LBJ would be the lead rider "in a cloud of dust . . . coming over the rise from . . . in back of the ranch house" would be a natural for Ralph Edwards's popular television program, *This Is Your Life.* "This kind of appearance," she emphasized, "would . . . discredit those who write of you as a *Southerner.*"[13]

With his image of himself as a descendant of frontiersmen, Johnson took naturally to this notion. He shucked off his southern identity and began to attend the caucus of western Democrats. In August 1959 *Congressional Quarterly* reported: "Sen. Lyndon B. Johnson (D Texas) is voting more like a Westerner and less like a Southerner this year than at any other time since the 1956 election." It found that in 1957 Johnson had sided slightly more with his native section than with the Pacific and Mountain states, but that in 1959 "his pro-Western leaning has become unmistakable"; that year, he gravitated to the West on twenty-five roll calls, to the South on only fifteen. "The increasing Western accent in the Majority Leader's voting record," it added, "seems certain to feed the speculation about his possible Presidential ambitions." In Santa Fe, the publisher of *The New Mexican,* noting "the voluntary accession" of Texas to the Democratic western caucus, stated that "Lyndon is the only serious possibility from our own part of the country."[14]

Johnson's backers strenuously wooed Democratic movers and shakers in Zane Grey country. "By God, we've just got to bring out the fact that this man is Western rather than Southern," cried Indiana Senator Vance Hartke. "All through the fall and winter of 1959 and 1960," Theodore White wrote later, "the 'noisemakers' of the Johnson campaign—local Texas politicians seeking to test their skills on a national level, supported by fuglemen of the Texas little-rich ... chanted 'All The Way With LBJ.' ... Instantly identifiable by their Texan garb, their yellow rose insignia, their ten-gallon hats (and, said their enemies, by the cowflap on their boots), they came and went in waves of frolic and fun, making tumult at every Democratic gathering between the Missouri and the Pacific."[15]

At the Western States Democratic Conference early in 1960, "at least 75 Texas supporters—tall, virile men in string ties and high-heeled boots"—told everyone in sight that "that great Westerner" Lyndon B. Johnson was, in the words of *Newsweek,* "a true son of the purple sage." The magazine reported: "In all the spacious precincts of Albuquerque's Western Skies Hotel there was hardly a place for a Western Democrat to hide. If he lounged against the huge, fieldstone fireplace of the lobby, a Texan was at his side, hands reaching for his lapels, or pressing on him an 'LBJ' button. In the dimly lit dining room, a Texan was always at the next table, nodding and smiling. And in the swank bar, a Texan was sure to want to buy him a drink. Johnson himself posed for photographers with a burro."

The "great Texan invasion" had mixed results. The governor of Colorado allowed as how Johnson looked like a down-home westerner to him, and a Democratic committeewoman remarked that Montanans and Texans, who came from the same kind of big-skied cattle country, were "quite a lot alike." Yet despite the antics of the Texans who cried "Howdy" at every opportunity, California's Pat Brown said that it "would be an impediment" for a Democratic presidential nominee to come from the South, and that though "Johnson is a strong man, I hadn't thought of Texas as part of the West," while the Democratic national chairman went out of his way to insist that Texas was "one of the states of the Union not in the Western region."[16]

George Reedy has noted how difficult it was for Johnson to shake off the burden of section. He realized that his candidate was not going to pick up many votes in the West, but any show of support would deflect the impression that LBJ was Dixie's chosen one. "Coming from a Confederate state was not a very good platform as a spring toward the presidency, and, God, it kept bobbing up all over the place," Reedy later recalled. He went on: "I'll never forget ... he decided to land at Las Vegas to spend an evening. That was very popular with the press; they wanted to see Las Vegas. And, damn, we walked into the hotel and they had a review, 'Save Your Confederate Money: The South Will Rise Again.'

And that stupid bastard of a publicity man for the hotel kept trying to point out to me what a great picture it would make of Johnson alongside of this Confederate general. You know, with ten newspapermen standing there! I could have broken his neck. I would have if the newspapermen hadn't been there. It was just something hard to shake."[17]

These efforts exasperated southern lawmakers. Dick Russell's chief aide later remarked: "You know Senator Johnson came here as a Southern Senator, but then all of a sudden he began to claim he was a Western Senator. Texas was no longer a 'Southern' state, it was a 'Western' state." A Mississippi congressman reflected bitterly: "Johnson even tried to take Texas out of the Southern orbit by asserting that it was a Western state, which was an attempt on his part to divorce himself from his background and raising." Herman Talmadge, too, later groused, "Johnson had disavowed his southern heritage."[18]

No politician, though, matched the venom of the press. The editor of the *Richmond News Leader* James Jackson Kilpatrick wrote during the 1960 campaign: "Before a cock could crow thrice, this son of Confederate Texas was denying every identification with his Dixie brothers. A Southerner? Not he. He was a one-hundred-percent American, and if some regional label were required, why, he was a Westerner, podner. Look at the chaps and cowboy boots. . . . His campaign literature had a fine mesquite flavor."[19]

The *Shreveport Journal*, which viewed Johnson as "a political renegade," relished quoting the judgment of the *Jackson Daily News:*

As in a dream, many keen political observers are rubbing their eyes for they have seen Sen. Lyndon Johnson of Texas, in the dead of the night, steal quietly like a gopher inching his way from his native heath toward the New Mexico border.

Suddenly, there he is in broad daylight, across the border, acting like New Mexico's "third Senator" or a synthetic Westerner or some other geographical prairie mongrel pup.

Surely, it comes as a ghastly shock to the average Texans to see their stalwart Lone Star hero . . . posing across the border, but a handful of kingmakers know that Lanky Lyndon must not . . . be caught with bluebonnet blossoms on his campaign boots.

The Madison Avenue boys singing in the same choir with the vote snatching, South-hating politicians don't want any Texas clover odor bothering Sir Lyndon in his pursuit of White House happiness. . . .

Now that he is safely across the border, we hope he finds comfort in the cactus bed he has made for himself, sleeping snugly alongside the NAACP, AFL-CIO, the Civil Rights Selfish Committee and a host of other Texas-hating left-wing punks who delight in slaughtering the South in the pious name of tolerance.[20]

He also aroused the anger of southerners when he used his legislative skills in 1960 to defeat H.R. 3, a bill sponsored by Howard Smith of Virginia that aimed to restrict the Supreme Court's power to integrate public schools. "I was surprised and disappointed at the attitude of Lyndon Johnson," Jimmy Byrnes wrote a constituent. He particularly took exception to "a boastful statement of the cloakroom maneuverings by which at the last moment a majority in favor of the bill was converted to a majority of one against its passage" in the Senate, after it had been approved overwhelmingly in the House. "Johnson had been quoted several times as claiming to be a Westerner instead of a Southerner," Governor Byrnes noted. "It hurts to be punished by a Senator from a State whose soldiers fought with South Carolinians in the War Between the States and whose people, until now, have elected to represent them in Congress, men who were proud to call themselves Southerners."[21]

Johnson himself knew that while offering himself as a westerner, he could not sever his ties to the South. Early in 1960 a Tennessee correspondent said:

Senator Johnson is the only contender the South unquestionably can defeat at the Democratic Convention at Los Angeles. He and he alone is the only hopeful who clearly cannot win the presidential nomination without Southern support.

His convention strategy obviously is based upon solid Southern and border state support, strong Western backing, and enough votes from other areas to put him over. If the South should desert him, he's had it.

And already there are signs of stress upon his ties with the South. The 1957 civil rights act did not set too well in all parts of Dixie. And the current insistence that the Senate must pass another one isn't helping his Southern position.[22]

The two civil rights laws, and especially his trickery in 1960, did dampen enthusiasm in the South for LBJ. "Like many other southern white politicians of his generation, Jimmy Byrnes loathed Lyndon Johnson with an intensity that was almost familial," Byrnes's biographer has written. "Johnson was perceived by Byrnes and other southern politicians not only as a political traitor but also as a regional one, who had renounced the principles of the southerners 'fathers' house' for personal advancement." Under the headline "Southern Democrats Face a Bleak Future," the *New York Times* reported in February 1960 that sectional leaders were despondent because they no longer expected Johnson, "though he also represents a former Confederate state," to block civil rights legislation. Squeezed between the need to hold on to the South while having "some civil rights credentials in order to be acceptable to a large part of the North," Johnson, his sagacious aide Harry McPherson later recalled, "was as restive and as full of asperity and hot temper as he could be, and the whole thing was irritating the hell out of him. He'd made the southerners mad. Here he was going to Los Angeles as . . . the South's candidate. He couldn't abandon the South. And I think he thought that he had overstepped the line, and the South thought that he had abandoned them."[23]

Though some of Johnson's support in the South slipped away because of anger at his advocacy of civil rights legislation, most southern politicians continued to regard him as the section's only prospect. In the fall of 1959 the governor of Texas gave Senator Byrd a frank accounting. Lyndon Johnson, he said, was the "best candidate available for us on whom we can get a sizable bloc of votes with whom to have some final say in who the nominee shall be. . . . He might even win the nomination." At about the same time, Virginia Senator A. Willis Robertson wrote the state's governor that "we in the South hope that as a Southern Senator, Lyndon Johnson will not support drastic Civil Rights legislation," and hence he was prepared to tell questioners that Johnson was the best choice for 1960. He added: "Unless the fact that Woodrow Wilson was born in Virginia would enable us to call him a Southern Democrat, to which Northern Democrats have never agreed, there has not been a Southern Democrat elected to the Presidency since Zachary Taylor of Louisiana. The prejudice against a Southern man for the Presidency is still so deep seated that the nomination of Lyndon Johnson next year would be little short of a political miracle." In 1960 a state Democratic convention in Virginia, while voicing "unalterable opposition" to compulsory integration of the schools, bound all of its delegation to LBJ. That action so delighted Senator Byrd, a reporter later recalled, that "he sat on the press table under the speakers' stand and kicked his heels and laughed like a boy sitting on a plank bridge over a river on a Saturday morning."[24]

Kennedy's pollster, Louis Harris, reported that, save for the benefit Johnson derived from his experience, the main reason North Carolina voters gave for positive feelings toward him was "He's a Southerner," a sentiment that combined recognition that he spoke out for the section and "a belief that he can handle the race problem in the way the South wants." Harris added that "the only sizable negative" was that "he's not strong enough for segregation." The pollster further found that "more South Carolinians would cast their votes for Senator Lyndon Johnson of Texas, were he the Democratic nominee, than for any other Democrat." Johnson's supporters claimed that since he was the only Democrat who could capture the South, he was the only one who could defeat Nixon.[25]

North Carolina governor Terry Sanford later recalled that in 1960 "it was almost disloyal to the South not to be for Johnson." Sanford explained his own support for the Texan by saying: "I thought we ought to have a Southerner for president. This has been something on my mind for thirty years or so, and it's time for the South to get back in the union. I would like to have voted for Richard Russell earlier, but Richard Russell never had a chance because of the stance he had to take on the race issue. You know how every real leader in the South was held back. All of a sudden, really all of a sudden, we'd reached a point in history where that wasn't so. Lyndon's record on the race issue was all right, partially because he wasn't from the South."[26]

In a review of presidential prospects in 1960, suggestively entitled "The South *Could* Rise Again," one correspondent wrote:

For the first time in a century, the South is sending to a Democratic national convention a candidate who is justified in hoping he can win the presidential nomination.

Because of his political skills, his talent for persuading people, his adroitness as a leader of Democrats from every section, Lyndon B. Johnson has a chance to erase the ban that has been imposed upon the states of the Confederacy ever since they bolted the Charleston convention in 1860.

In the hundred years since the political skirmishing which preceded the firing of the guns at Fort Sumter, many a son of Dixie has desired the nomination as fiercely as does the Texan. . . . But not since the Civil War has any man from the South had so much reason as Johnson to believe he might win the prize.[27]

Johnson, however, still had to reach out beyond his southern base, and, in good part for that reason, confusion about his sectional identity persisted. In

1959 a journalist reported that a southern senator had recently told him that Johnson had said to him, "I don't know why they're jumping me for being a Westerner. Why, I'm a goldurned Southerner," and that subsequently Johnson had complained to a western senator, "I don't know why they're jumping me for being a Southerner. Why, I'm a goldurned Westerner." The historian Joe B. Frantz has written:

> As the 1960s approached, nationally syndicated cartoonists had their usual field day with unannounced presidential candidate Lyndon B. Johnson. . . . They depicted him, stretching his long frame over at least nine feet of height, looking still taller in a high-crowned, wide-brimmed Stetson and high-heeled, hand-tooled cowboy boots. He was typical Texan, whatever that image conveys, and the words that issued from his ample mouth were pure Texanese, as western as John Wayne, except that each sentence invariably ended with the phrase "you all," a concession to his southernism. Sometimes one boot would be planted firmly in West Texas, the other in the spongy soil of the Deep South. All that was lacking were the Sons of the Pioneers singing "Cool Water" in one corner and blacks strumming mandolins as darkness gathered on the delta— any delta—in the opposite corner.
>
> The cartoons showed Johnson's dilemma. Was he a western candidate or was he a southern one? Or was he, as most cartoonists hinted, trying to straddle both sections, utilizing his Texas background to illustrate his transitional position? Never mind. You could accept him as belonging to one section or the other, or to both; but you never suggested that he represented the nation.[28]

IV

In trying to bracket sections in 1960, Johnson ran the risk of pleasing none and alienating all. As far back as when he was minority leader, Johnson, one of his biographers has noted, "at times commented wryly on the circumstance that too many people in Texas considered him little better than a Communist and too many people in Washington were firmly convinced that he was a Dixiecrat." He knew that unless he could demonstrate that he favored meaningful civil rights legislation, he could abandon any hope of significant support in the North. On the other hand, he dared not advance so far that he cut himself off from his base in the South, which was what made him a credible candidate in the first place.

"For the anti-Southerners," one critic has asserted, Johnson in 1960 "was still a Southerner in spite of all he had done to deny it; with the Southerners he was a . . . traitor."[29]

While Johnson, by his exertions on behalf of civil rights laws, antagonized some southern politicians, he failed to win over most northerners. His voice registering bewilderment, the longtime Pittsburgh boss David Lawrence asked, "Now, how can I ask Pennsylvania Democrats to vote for Lyndon Johnson?" Liberals still did not forgive him for eviscerating the 1957 bill. As Reedy later said, "They suspected him of seeking to patch up the racial sores in the body politic with a meaningless cosmetic." The editor of a black newspaper in Houston said, "Johnson is no better than the other Southern bigots." As Herbert Parmet has written, "The Southern label was lethal. If Kennedy had his religion, Johnson had the burden of regionalism."[30]

In 1960, pundits declared, the Democrats could win only if they captured the big electoral bloc industrial states with large proportions of black voters; hence, "to put Lyndon Johnson, 'Mr. Compromise' himself, on the national ticket would probably be fatal." One observer remembered: "On the first day of the convention in the basement of the Conrad Hilton Hotel, Johnson called a press conference and announced that he was a candidate for president of the United States. We were all flabbergasted. This Texan, this southerner. Outside of the Senate, who was he?" The majority leader's decision not to enter primary races constituted a fatal blunder, Jack Kennedy believed, for "Johnson had to prove that a Southerner could win in the North, just as I had to prove a Catholic could win in heavily Protestant states."[31]

Americans for Democratic Action, the leading organization of northern liberals, troubled to put out a pamphlet, *Lyndon Johnson Is Unqualified*, which concluded, "Senator Lyndon Johnson's record in the Senate is one of service . . . *not* . . . to the national welfare, . . . but . . . to Southern and Texas special interests." It also sent a letter to every delegate to the national convention charging that Johnson was "a conservative, anti–civil rights, gas-and-oil Senator" supported by Dixiecrats in segregationist states, and it enclosed a memorandum asserting that "Johnson more often than not votes with the Southern minority of his Party rather than with the Northern majority."[32]

Cosmopolitan liberals found it hard to imagine, too, this man from the provinces conducting foreign affairs. They recalled occasions such as the one in 1958 when the United Nations lounge reeled in shock after "that incredible American, Mr. Johnson," who introduced himself as "a country boy from Texas," paid a call. What, the diplomatic correspondent of an Amsterdam newspaper wanted to know, did he mean when he said he had "come to howdy and shake," and why had he forsaken discussion of foreign affairs to relate anecdotes that began, "I said to Lady Bird—that's my wife, Lady Bird—Lady Bird, I said to her, hon. . . ."?[33]

Northerners took neither to his manner nor to his style. "Southern political personalities, like sweet corn, travel badly," wrote A. J. Liebling. "They lose flavor with every hundred yards away from the patch. By the time they reach New York they are like golden bantam that has been trucked up from Texas—stale and unprofitable." Theodore White, in highlighting the handicaps Johnson had as a presidential aspirant in 1960, commented: "When Lyndon B. Johnson is in good form and seen in the proper setting—say, at a small-town Masonic temple at a dinner for small-town Southern Democrats where the hot food is being served by the good Ladies of the Eastern Star—one can observe a master performance of native American political art. Yet when the same performance is transferred to a dinner of Brooklyn Democrats, . . . it has no smack of Presidential quality about it. It is, sadly, . . . as remote from the dignity of the Presidency as was Alfred Smith's bad grammar, East-side enunciation and New York provincialism."[34]

Johnson never succeeded in shaking off the onus of the section of his birth. Early in 1960 J. W. Fulbright informed the master of his Oxford college, "Senator Johnson, the Majority Leader, is probably the best qualified man—by experience and temperament—to make a forceful President but unfortunately he comes from the wrong part of the country and necessarily has been identified with certain issues lacking in national appeal." In a letter to his pal, Jack Kennedy, Ben Bradlee of *Newsweek* dismissed Johnson as a potential rival for the presidential nomination by saying, "He's somebody's gabby Texas cousin from Fort Worth." When a prominent New York woman sought to assure Mrs. Roosevelt that Johnson was for civil rights and hence a viable presidential candidate, the former First Lady replied, "He's from the South, and it's impossible." Roy Wilkins declared: "Unfair though it may seem to be, the Majority Leader, although not a Deep South man in residence or in personal attitude, of necessity must bear (in the minds of the Negro voters) the cross made up of the sins of unreconstructed Mississippi, Alabama, South Carolina, and most of Georgia and Louisiana."[35]

The majority leader, understandably, resented that presumption. Evelyn

Lincoln, who served as secretary to President Kennedy and to Johnson, has written: "Mr. Johnson, like Mr. Kennedy, was championing a minority cause. Mr. Johnson felt that if he couldn't get the nomination with his great record it would be only because he was from a minority, a Southerner, and it would be a long time before another Southerner would have a crack at the White House." In January 1960 Johnson told reporters: "I don't want anyone to vote for me because I am a Southerner. But I don't want anyone to vote against me because I am a Southerner, either." Yet for all of his efforts to establish himself as a national candidate in 1960, the core of his strength remained in the South. Of the somewhat more than five hundred votes his forces claimed on the eve of the convention, 385 came from southern and border states, only eighty from the West (some thought he had far fewer), and less than forty from the rest of the country. When at the 1960 convention Johnson was nominated, the band struck up "Dixie." After the roll was tallied, Jack Kennedy's strategy of depicting Johnson as a sectional, not a national, figure prevailed. The idea of choosing a southerner in 1960 was, in Jonathan Daniels's words, "just out of the ball park." The outcome led Johnson to a mournful conclusion—that he had been denied a chance at the White House in 1960 only because sectional bigotry against a southerner was stronger than religious bigotry against a Catholic.[36]

V

Johnson's defeat in his bid for the presidential nomination, far from being a finale, turned out to be only a prelude, for, to the astonishment and even dismay of his advisors, John F. Kennedy offered Johnson the vice presidential slot on the Democratic ticket. Kennedy took this controversial step not because he thought of Johnson as a man of national stature, certainly not because he regarded him as a representative westerner, but quite simply because the majority leader was a southerner who might be able to hold his section for the party in November. A Virginia governor later recalled that he had told Kennedy, "You have got to carry Texas in my judgment and you will be enabled with Lyndon Johnson on that ticket to carry maybe one or more Southern states that you otherwise wouldn't have carried." The governor added: "Now I honestly felt that way. And there was right much agreement with that approach." Similarly, Governor Ernest F. Hollings lectured the young Massachusetts senator, "Let's face facts, Jack. As things stand this morning, you would lose South Carolina. . . . Lyndon Johnson is your best bet for the support of the South." Kennedy realized he had gotten only 9½ southern votes at the convention, and putting Johnson on the slate, he is said to have reasoned, "could certainly attract vitally needed electoral votes in the cotton and molasses country."[37]

Kennedy's invitation presented Johnson with a difficult decision. When news of it got out, southern colleagues besieged him to turn it down. They could not imagine that Johnson would agree to run on a platform that endorsed civil rights with a man who was both a Catholic and a Yankee. Price Daniel said of Kennedy, "We in the South just can't carry this boy." For Johnson to accept would be "a betrayal of the South." A Texas congressman recalled: "He caught the dickens! Some of Lyndon's strongest supporters in Texas gave him unshirted hell." On the other hand, on the eve of the 1960 convention a Texas patriarch, former Vice President John Nance Garner, had sent word to Sam Rayburn: "If this boy is smart enough to go this far and get nominated, . . . he is smart enough right now to know he couldn't possibly be elected president without our Lyndon being on the ticket with him . . . and he will, as sure as a gun's iron, come to Lyndon with this suggestion, and he won't wait long. I urge you to play your cards close to your chest and wait for the boy to make the approach—which I'm sure he will—and Lyndon must be ready to accept." Another influential figure, Phil Graham, is said to have told Johnson, "By God, you ought to be vice-president. You don't want to be a southern senator all your life."[38]

In the end, Johnson yielded, much to the displeasure of a number of his closest associates. When Bobby Baker told Senator Robert Kerr of Oklahoma that Johnson, who had always insisted on being treated as numero uno, had settled for second place, Kerr slapped Baker's face. Another follower, however, two columnists wrote afterward, "immediately supported Johnson for he knew what Johnson knew; he had emancipated himself from Texas." As a southerner, Johnson had no hope of vaulting to the White House. But "as Vice-President he could cast off the Southern regionalism that had plagued him all those years in the Senate and become a *national* politician."[39]

Johnson quickly found, however, that, though he was a national nominee, most Americans still thought of him as a senator from Dixie. Many in the seaboard elite, a Texan has written, "regarded Johnson as a hard-shell Southern conservative, a native racist, a drawling, backslapping political whore with no guiding lights other than the oil-depletion allowance. They despised Johnson in the East because he represented the insurgent Southwest." Kennedy's decision especially outraged civil rights activists. "I was not only surprised," the NAACP's Washington lobbyist later said. "I was pained." When in 1969 an interviewer inquired whether there was "a certain amount of dismay among civil rights advocates at Mr. Johnson being on the ticket," Roy Wilkins quickly retorted, "Oh, yes. Oh, yes." James Farmer recalled that he regarded the selection of Johnson as "most unfortunate, probably . . . a disaster, because of his Southern background and his voting record on civil rights," and Bayard Rustin remembered, "I was very distressed when Mr. Johnson was picked because I felt that—well, I suppose in part it was prejudice. I was fearful of a Southerner." Lillian Smith worried that Johnson would cost Kennedy the black vote in the South, "because no matter what he says he is a symbol to the Negroes *of what has not been done for them.*" Though Johnson later changed his mind, he initially said he would not campaign in Chicago, California, or New York City because "I'm not going to let the liberals cut me up and embarrass Jack Kennedy. And they will, just because I'm a Texan and a southerner." When a Democratic Party speech writer turned in a draft of an address for Johnson, he explained that it was "designed primarily to reassure the Yankees along the Northeastern seaboard that our candidate for Vice President is no land-locked Texan but a world-minded statesman." Northerners, however, were unimpressed. When Johnson took to the campaign trail, a Brooklyn man said of his Texas accent, "It makes your throat hurt to hear him."[40]

His "Boston-to-Austin" trek produced some daft incongruities. When he flew into the Massachusetts capital, Elizabeth Rowe later reported, "Lined up at the Boston Airport were a dozen and more little dumpy women, all with great big cowboy hats on. They were all the Italian population of Boston, all good Democrats, and all absolutely overpowered by these great big hats." As he rode through the crowded downtown streets in the lunch hour, Johnson, in the land of the shamrock, tossed out green passes to the Senate gallery. At Copley Plaza, he persuaded a mounted policeman who was directing traffic to get off his horse, and in the saddle LBJ dumbfounded onlookers by galloping about the busy square.[41]

In late August, Jim Rowe admonished his friend to regard himself less as a regional candidate, whose job was to bolster the Kennedy ticket in the South, and more as a national candidate, willing to reach out to those in other sections "who regard Johnson, for very *understandable* reasons, with suspicion." If the ticket lost in November, and it very well might, that would finish Kennedy politically, but it would not be "the end of Lyndon Johnson. Therefore this campaign should be used to make Lyndon Johnson the 'national man' he says he is."[42]

Johnson, however, concentrated on his main assignment: holding the South, which could no longer be counted on to be "Solid" for the Democrats. "We've lost Louisiana, I tell you," one Democratic delegate said. To save the state, Lyndon Johnson was going to have to "come across the border now and talk 'magnolia' to them." In August, Nixon, campaigning in Georgia, received, in Teddy White's words, an "unbelievable welcome," with cheering crowds "gathered in ranks five deep, six deep, eight deep that blotted the sidewalks and then . . . choked the streets," while "from the windows above a storm of confetti, of paper streamers, of torn scrap, of red, blue, gold spangles rained down, thickening to a blizzard." Ralph McGill called it "the greatest thing in Atlanta since the premiere of *Gone with the Wind*." During the closing weeks of the campaign Kennedy appeared to be fading in the South. Especially alarming was the prospect that he might lose Texas, which, for the first time ever, had gone Republican in the last two presidential elections. Former Governor Allan Shivers was spearheading Texans-for-Nixon there, and Kennedy knew that LBJ was his best bet to keep the state in the Democratic column.[43]

Some of Kennedy's staff told the majority leader bluntly that he had been placed on the slate with the expectation that he would not let that happen. On this point, no one was more brutally frank than Robert Kennedy, who loathed Johnson. To appease Texas oil and gas interests, the head of the Democratic campaign in Houston drafted a statement that he wanted Jack Kennedy to make avowing that on such issues he would consult with Rayburn and Lyndon Johnson. On arriving in Texas as his brother's advance man, Robert Kennedy read the document, shredded it to bits, and retorted, "We're not going to say anything like that. We put that son of a bitch on the ticket to carry Texas." If they could not do that, the oil depletion allowance was their headache.[44]

At a gathering in Tennessee Governor Buford Ellington's home, a well-connected southern politician found Johnson distraught. He later recalled: "Lyndon Johnson spent a half hour telling me—and it got to where tears were in his eyes and . . . it wasn't any phony histrionic thing; . . . he was a very emotional man at times—that he wanted me to go to Senator Russell and he wanted me to go to Senator Talmadge and tell them that . . . they were almost obligated to come out publicly for him . . . because he had to have the support of Southern leaders, that he had been put on the ticket with the expectation that he would be able to accomplish the votes of the South for the Democratic ticket. . . . This was a man who was very depressed . . . that Southern leaders who were sort of old-line politicians . . . were not coming out and were not showing enthusiasm for him."[45]

In October, Johnson, accompanied by his wife, set out in an eleven-car "whistle-stop special" that, in the words of one observer, "rambled along through the cotton fields, tobacco farms, peaches and peanuts, to the very heart of darkest Southland." In the course of this 3,500-mile "Campaign in Dixie" through eight southern states, Johnson frequently abandoned all pretense of being a westerner or anything save a good ole boy. "I want to be remembered by how I live, not where I live," he told a Salisbury, North Carolina, crowd, "but the longer I stay in North Carolina, the more sectional I'm likely to become." One southern writer rejoiced that when Johnson spoke, there was "none of that Baa'ston Broad A" of Jack Kennedy and Henry Cabot Lodge or of "that almost regionless accent" of Richard Nixon. After what the press called the "Cornball Express" pulled into a depot, Confederate flags fluttering in the waiting crowd, the local brass band playing "Dixie" or "The Yellow Rose of Texas," Johnson would say, "This grandson of a 'federate soldier feels lahk I'm in may-ty tall cotton, let me tell you," a sentiment that would trigger a round of rebel yells. He was sure to talk, too, of "mah grandpappy" and "mah greatgrandpappy." (It appeared, a writer has reported, that "one or the other had lived in that particular community, or had passed through it, or had a brother there, or something.") As the train left the station, he would call out, "God bless yuh, Rocky Bottom. Ah wish ah could stay an' do a little sippin' an' whittlin' with yuh." A while later, it would be "God bless yuh, Gaffney." One campaign correspondent, listening to Johnson speak from the "Cornpone Special," said, "Lyndon ought to serve dish gravy with this," while another wired the *Chicago Tribune*, "The son of a bitch will carry the South."[46]

Lady Bird, who was to remember the journey as a time of "cold hotcakes and early sunrises," made just as big a hit. "Lady Bird's Southern accent is very much in evidence when she speaks because she uses 'y'all' very frequently," noted one writer. Lady Bird, reported a North Carolina paper, "never misses a chance to say 'thank yuh,' and 'We sho do appreciate it.'" She revealed her roots in remarking that a child was as "noisy as a mule in a tin barn," and that she would give "a pretty" to see Lyndon win. A writer has said: "Lady Bird found that she enjoyed talking, and her Southern accent, so much thicker than Lyndon's, made crowds respond enthusiastically when she spoke. She had a gracious thing or two to say about each locality where the train stopped, and when townspeople gave her a present, she knew how to say breathlessly, 'Ah can tell you ah'm powerful proud.'" In Chattanooga, Lady Bird expressed "fondness and kinship with the state of Tennessee," adding, "There might not have been a

Texas if it had not been for Sam Houston." Alabama, one reporter has commented, "was 'kissin' kin' territory, and as the train pulled into Montgomery, she dashed onto the rear platform to greet her blood kin who had come to welcome her. At almost every whistle stop thereafter, Bird found long-lost 'cousins' in the milling crowds." At one Alabama depot twenty-five of her cousins turned out. That was only a tiny portion of her relations, one of them explained. "Afta aw-awl, Lady Bird's daddy's Mama had thirteen chillen in the fo' times she was married."[47]

Despite these way-down-South-in-Swanee melodies, though, Lyndon Johnson frequently found himself regarded more as a cowpoke from the Lone Star State than a true son of Robert E. Lee. At some stops, string bands played "Home on the Range." One North Carolina paper commented, "The big, smiling Texan brings his bid for the Vice Presidency out on the train's back platform in a Stetson hat at each whistle stop," while another wrote: "It's roundup time in the Carolinas for Texan Lyndon Johnson, who comes riding on an iron horse onto the Carolina range Monday. The vice presidential nominee and a lot of top Democratic cowboys are struggling to get a rope on a kicking and bucking maverick—the South with its 85 electoral votes."[48]

Furthermore, Johnson sometimes presented himself not as a southerner but as a national statesman. At the end of the first day of his whistle-stop tour, he declared, "The South, like every other section of the nation, realizes that its best interests lie in the election of a truly national ticket—not a ticket which seeks to play different sections of the country against each other." At Kennedy's request, a leading Georgia Democrat set up a gathering in Nashville so that Johnson could demonstrate that "though he was a Southerner . . . he had to be more an American than a Southerner," and in Nashville, Johnson emphasized that he would "never speak as a Southerner to Southerners," but would campaign "as an American to Americans—whatever their region, religion or race." The *Charlotte Observer,* noting that Johnson had been put on the ticket "to appease the South and the border states," expressed pleasure that the vice presidential nominee, instead of singing "the moonlight and magnolia song," was shunning "rampant sectionalism."[49]

The whistle-stop campaign, however, dealt circumspectly with the touchy issue of civil rights, save in the upper South. In Richmond, Johnson made an exception in saying forthrightly: "I did not come down here to promise Virginia exemptions from the obligation to carry out the decision of the Supreme Court. . . . A hundred years of debate among ourselves is enough, I think. Don't you?" Both in Greensboro and in Charlotte, he said, "All Americans are equal under the law and we have to prove that not only to our own satisfaction but to the rest of the world." Senator James Eastland, though, informed the voters of Mississippi: "Lyndon Johnson took everything relating to integration out of those civil rights bills. He has always opposed Congress' implementation of the segregation decisions of the Supreme Court." That statement, which Johnson did not challenge, improved Democratic prospects in Mississippi, but reinforced doubts in the North about whether LBJ was anything but a sectionalist.[50]

In touring the South, Johnson found it more productive to stress how much stake his listeners had in restoring the Democrats to power. For eight years under Eisenhower, he told his audiences, the Republicans had treated the South as a golf course. "Don't desert the party of your fathers," he would implore a gathering at a train station. "Don't throw away your preferred status in Congress." On discerning that a Texas crowd disapproved of his decision to go on a ticket with Kennedy, he pointed out that the vice presidency would put him in an excellent position to preserve the oil depletion allowance and fend off integration.[51]

Johnson especially knew how to work over the Democratic officeholders he encountered along the route. With his obsession with counting, he tallied 1,247 southern politicians who boarded the train and heard his spiel on behalf of the ticket. According to one reconstruction of a typical message, Johnson, after empathizing with southern leaders about having to put up with a Catholic running on a civil rights platform, would go on: "Senator Buford and Senator Baxby, I just don't see how, if your defection is the cause of our defeat, you're ever going to get one little old bill through that Senate. Governor Beauregard, you say you have to have that new airport and you want to keep the Army base down here. How do you think you're going to get such bills through the Senate if Mr. Kennedy and I are sitting there solely because you didn't produce the vote that would have elected us?"[52]

During the campaign, a number of southern politicians, including not a few who had little in common with him, rallied to Johnson, often on the grounds that he shared their antipathy to civil rights agitation. In Macon, Georgia, Herman Talmadge, likening Johnson to Henry Clay, said that Johnson, by "thwart[ing] extreme legislation," had "kept our region from dividing," and under the headline "Lyndon Johnson's leadership saved the day!" a South Carolina campaign publication, *Dixie News,* claimed that in 1957 "Lyndon Johnson led the band of heroic Southern Senators" who staved off the attempt to amend the rules to make it easier to break a filibuster. "Under Lyndon Johnson as vice president, . . . it would be almost impossible to kill the filibuster, the South's most potent weapon." The governor of South Carolina, Fritz Hollings, told a Democratic gathering that the choice of Lyndon Johnson for the vice presidential nomination was "an historic victory for the South," for those who knew him best knew "that he had a Southern heart." Hollings confessed, "Now I myself had questioned his bringing up the Civil Rights Bill last February." But, he went on, "our own Senators said that he had only hastened the inevitable by a matter of days, that he had fought for the South. . . . The expression was that if we did not vote for those who . . . had helped us in Washington then how could we ever expect to get any . . . protection ever again for the South."[53]

Some southerners, though, rejected Johnson's message contemptuously. "The band broke into 'Dixie,' the night they nominated Lyndon out in L.A., but there wasn't much singing back home in the South," commented James Jackson Kilpatrick. "Love that Lyndon? Not down South. And it was down South that the Senator was expected to charm the Byrds from the trees." The initials "LBJ," his critics said, stood for "Let's Beat Judas," and he sometimes confronted placards reading "The *Yellow* Rose of Texas."[54]

Critics alternated between lambasting the national Democratic ticket and bawling out Johnson. Southern editorial writers asked for the defeat of "the Yankee from Boston and the turncoat from Austin." After Governor Hollings, reckoning that 95 percent of the newspapers in the state were backing Nixon, said that the "morning newspapers are making me sick at breakfast," the editor of the *Charleston News and Courier* inquired how, "with such a squeamish digestion," Hollings could "stomach the Kennedy and Johnson combination." An elderly South Carolina physician wrote his senator, "As to . . . Lyndon B. Johnson, he is only a first class traitor to the Southern States . . . [who] makes Benedict Arnold appear as a SMALL FRY. He . . . as you know now brands himself as a WESTERNER and NOT A SOUTHERNER. However, he now has the affront to ask the Southern people to support him." In Mississippi, Willie Morris was "struck by the raw, unyielding hatred expressed for Johnson."[55]

Again and again, Texans disowned the Democratic vice presidential nominee. "The Los Angeles Convention finally settled forever the question of whether Johnson is . . . Southern," a Texas couple told their senator. "No man could be Southern and swallow the civil rights plank." The very next day a Texas woman said, "Lyndon B. Johnson may be a Texan to the rest of the U.S., but to us in Texas he just lost his citizenship." A week after Kennedy picked LBJ as his running mate, newspaper editors received a form letter from a Houston man proposing the creation of cells of thirty people, each of whom would put a nickel in a box bearing the label "Late Blooming Judas" and containing a message to the vice presidential candidate: "Judas had his 30 pieces of silver. Here are yours." Many Texans detested Johnson for running on a ticket with Kennedy, a man, who, as the department store mogul Stanley Marcus said, "worse than being a papist," was "suspected of being against the oil depletion allowance." A racist publication in Texas said of him: "The Senator is so intent upon wooing the votes of the Northern and Western radicals that he does not wish to be identified as a Southerner—to the extent, even, that he refuses to stand when 'Dixie' is played."[56]

When the Johnsons arrived in Dallas, they encountered an ugly crowd outside a downtown hotel hoisting placards with legends such as I DREAMED I WENT TO WASHINGTON IN MY TURNCOAT. The most conspicuous figure in the raucous mob was the tall congressman from Dallas, Bruce Alger, so hardbitten a rightwinger that he took pride in the distinction of being the only member of Congress to vote against free milk for schoolchildren. (Sam Rayburn thought him a "shitass.") Alger frenetically pumped up and down a sign depicting the Senate majority leader lugging a carpetbag and the words LBJ SOLD OUT TO YAN-KEE SOCIALISTS. Stylish young women, a number of them Junior Leaguers, attired in snazzy red, white, and blue outfits with gold watch chains and red coif bonnets and toting models' handbags thick with Republican literature, screamed catcalls at the Johnsons and raised placards urging LYNDON GO HOME. No longer, they implied, was Johnson's home in the South. Lady Bird blanched when one of the demonstrators tore her gloves from her and flung them into the gutter.

As the Johnsons inched their way through the engulfing mob across the jam-packed street and into the lobby of a second hotel, some in the expensively coutured "Mink Coat Mob" spat at them. (A few of the young women claimed they were not spitting; they were frothing.) One reached out and mussed Mrs. Johnson's hair. Scared, white-faced, Lady Bird appeared to be on the verge of tears. It has been said that "for years afterward when she thought about returning to Dallas, Mrs. Johnson's hands made nervous fists." Lady Bird herself remembered that she felt "quite steely; that I just had to keep on walking and suppress all emotions and be just like Marie Antoinette in the tumbrel. But I must say that Lyndon was nine times steelier than I was. I think once he was in it he was determined to make the most of it." Johnson later recounted: "We went to the hotel to wash up before we went to a luncheon meeting, but the entrance was blocked and the hecklers were there, and they harassed us and they hounded us and they knocked my wife's hat off, and they spit on us and they called us traitors and they called us treason artists. . . . It took us more than an hour to walk across the block because of the chants and the saliva that was running out of their mouths and, really, some of them were diseased."[57]

Johnson may well have fabricated some of the details, and he certainly knew how to exploit the situation to his advantage. As they made their way past the taunting, jostling gauntlet, Johnson, as one writer has said, "moved with excruciating slowness through the chanting mob and the rain of spit," taking half an hour to complete what should have been a five-minute walk. Well aware that television cameras were filming every minute of their ordeal, Johnson recognized that, when seen on the evening news, the melee would prove to the rest of the country that he was not an agent of the South but was reviled in his own state because of his national vision. Evans and Novak later wrote of the episode:

> The incident was unique in American political history. In one sudden revelation, it portrayed Johnson to the critical North in a wholly new light. The stereotyped Johnson was a Texas rancher with cowboy boots and Stetson, owned by oil and gas, possessed of a Deep South racial prejudice, arrogant toward the labor unions, moved only by the pretensions of great wealth. Now, that stereotype, for years the target of ridicule and suspicion by Northern intellectuals and liberals, was *himself* under attack, and in his own state and by the very crowd that was supposed to own him! Suddenly, a "new Johnson" appeared to those who always thought they had his number.
>
> But beyond that, the ugly incident . . . outraged thousands of Texans and many more thousands of Southerners in other states.[58]

George Reedy regarded the affair as a turning point. "The South Carolina politicians have told me they think that that's what converted South Carolina to Kennedy," he said. "And you know it brought Russell out. Russell up until that point had just sat down in Winder [Georgia] and sulked, but he was very fond of Lady Bird and, boy, he came roaring out of his home." Reedy continued: "That night it was on NBC, and Mr. Nixon was the ex-next president of the United States. Because really, it looked awful, and it was awful. There was no actual physical assault or anything like that, but you just saw those ugly, distorted, hateful faces. You know, you wanted to push those noses in of these hideous, spiteful women."[59]

When Kennedy won narrowly in November, many analysts credited Johnson with the slim margin of victory in the Electoral College. Contrary to expectations, the Kennedy-Johnson ticket triumphed in seven of the former Confederate states; three went Republican, while Mississippi wound up with an independent segregationist alignment. In a postmortem, "Why It Wasn't Nixon," *U.S. News and World Report,* saying its answers reflected Nixon's own conclusions, answered the question "What states in the South would Nixon have carried if Johnson had not been on the ticket?" with the response: "Obviously, Texas. And there's no question about the Carolinas." Some went further. Senator Eastland thought that if Johnson had not been on the ballot, Kennedy would not have taken any southern state and would have gone down to defeat, and Allan Shivers later remarked, "There's no question in my mind but what Johnson on the ticket was responsible for the Kennedy-Johnson election. You'll get lots of agreement on that." Hence, it was Johnson's lingering sectional identity that kept Richard Nixon from the White House in 1961.[60]

For all of Johnson's attempts to establish himself as a national figure, the southern connection proved to be the critical consideration. "Johnson helped the ticket that go-round in Alabama because at that time Johnson was still looked at as a Southerner," recalled an Alabama congressman some years later. "He was considered to be a Texan and a fellow traveller, you see." An interviewer suggested, "Could be trusted?" The congressman replied, "Yes. We knew that Lyndon Johnson, well, after all, Lady Bird owned some property around Prattville, you know." Despite their serious misgivings about Kennedy and civil rights, almost every southern senator fell in line for the majority leader. "I am afraid that I go too much on personalities," Dick Russell said, "for when my friend Lyndon Johnson called me the third time and said that he was really in trouble and I could help, I stopped weighing issues and went out."[61]

Johnson's main contribution came in Texas, where the presidential contest in 1960 was the closest in history. At a barbecue in the hill country, the mayor of the town called the Kennedy-Johnson slate "a kangaroo ticket, one with all its strength in the hind legs," but the governor of the state, though agreeing that "we have a good ticket—in reverse," declared, "If I had no other reason to support it than that a Texan was on it, why I'd be workin' for it all the way." In 1960, one writer has said, Lady Bird "was the brightest spot in the campaign. She breezed across Texas like a prairie fire—a petite, vibrant figure always dressed in red. She stood on tiptoe to reach the microphones, set up on hurriedly erected platforms in parking lots at shopping centers, to beg Texas voters to support a native son—her husband—for Vice-President." On Election Day, the Kennedy ticket carried Texas—by fewer than fifty thousand votes. A Texas congressman later said, "Kennedy would never have been President, never made it, if it hadn't been for Lyndon Johnson. He helped him carry Texas, carried Texas for him, *did* it—there's no way it could have been done!—and helped in the South and helped all over, and it was *so* close."[62]

VI

On the afternoon after the 1960 victory, Willie Morris asked, "Liberated now from his Texas constituency, will he have the vision to rise above the provincial interests which have so often seemed to enclose him and become . . . a genuine national leader?" It was not clear that the country was willing to give him that opportunity. Even as vice president of the United States, a correspondent wrote, Johnson continued to be thought of as "an insular Southerner." T. Harry Williams noted that "Johnson, who knew about power and had exulted in its use, now had none and could only watch others use it, most of them younger men, the courtiers of Camelot who ignored or patronized him and out of his hearing called him Uncle Cornpone." Some of "Kennedy's people," recalled William S. White, believed "that Johnson was bad for Kennedy, that he was associated with the South and oil and what not." From a different quarter, Dick Russell had phoned the vice president–elect on successive days to remind him that the South had elected him and expected him to safeguard its interests— code language for the imperative to preserve white supremacy. When Johnson, as presiding officer of the U.S. Senate, ruled that a filibuster could not be ended by a majority vote, Joe Rauh said that he had "shown that his first loyalty is to the Southern racists."[63]

President Kennedy, treating Johnson as his sales agent for the South, called upon him to keep his fellow southerners in the Senate in line, notably on the highly controversial nomination of his young brother to be attorney general, though he had no conspicuous qualifications for the post. "Jack's asked me to tone down the Dixiecrats," Johnson informed his Capitol Hill aide, Bobby Baker. "I want you to lead all our Southern friends in here by their ying-yangs, and let me work on 'em. We've got to smooth Dick Russell's feathers, and kiss ol' Jim Eastland's ass, and mute Strom Thurmond's brayin'." Grabbing the southern legislators by the lapels to confront them nose-to-nose, Johnson, according to Baker, said, "Now, look, Jack Kennedy's put this thing square on my head. It's the first . . . test he's put me to, and if I have to go back and say 'Mr. President, I'm sorry, but I can't persuade my friends to confirm your brother,' why shit, I'm ruined before I get started. You think he's gonna trust me with anything else, huh?" And if he did not, how was Johnson supposed to get them the dams or the judgeships they wanted?[64]

Kennedy, though, also assigned Johnson a number of other tasks, such as banning racial discrimination in government contracts, that offered him the chance, in the words of another writer, to "defuse his image as a southerner." A series of confrontations from Oxford, Mississippi, through Birmingham and Tuscaloosa opened up new vistas for him. As Taylor Branch has written: "The racial crisis . . . helped lift Lyndon Johnson from the torpor of the vice presidency. . . . Johnson, who had felt so superfluous and insecure among the fast-track Kennedy globalists, responded as though to a shot of adrenaline [to] the chance to slough off his past as a regional politician. . . . In private White House meetings, the Vice President changed from a sullen lump of self-pity into the gleefully rapacious arm-twister of the Johnson legend. . . . When Kennedy suggested that it might be unwise to force showdowns with entire Southern states, Johnson said, 'Yeah, but I want the governor of Texas and the governor of Arkansas and the governor of Georgia . . . to know that when they stand up there and come out for segregation, it may cost them the economy of that state.'" Johnson's stance became evident enough for George Wallace to call him "a low-down, carpetbaggin,' scalawaggin,' race-mixin' liar."[65]

More than one observer has seen Johnson's tenure as head of the President's Committee on Equal Employment Opportunity (PCEEO) as the time when his views on civil rights underwent a sea change. "It seems, although no one can be completely sure, that finally the issue of black equality touched the inner recesses of his character, if he had such inner recesses," Paul Conkin has written. "He was now exposed, almost daily, to the injustices confronted by blacks, and he experienced—really felt—the injustice of it all. He now not only had a national perspective on the issue, but his extensive world travels persuaded him that the United States, even to protect its reputation abroad, had to undo the whole system of exclusion in the South. From this point on he added moral fervor to his advocacy of civil rights legislation." Johnson scolded a group of Texas editors, "You sons-of-bitches have got to find out that the world doesn't belong to all one group of people, that this is a black man's world as well as the white man's world," and he told a delegation of Southern liberals to the PCEEO, "If any of these contractors think they can get around this order, they're gonna find out we've got 'em right here," grasping his crotch.[66]

By 1963 Johnson had come to think of himself as a man not of a section but of the nation and to speak out on behalf of civil rights in a way that would have been inconceivable only a short time before. Early in 1963, on the centennial of the Emancipation Proclamation, Johnson, noting that the government was being advised to be cautious in pursuing the goal of equality, declared: "The counsel of delay is not the counsel of courage. A government conceived and dedicated to the purpose that all men are born free and equal cannot pervert its mission by rephrasing the purpose to suggest that men shall be free today—but shall be equal a little later."[67] He even began to foreshadow what would be known as affirmative action. "To strike the chains of a slave is noble," he said in January. "To leave him the captive of the color of his skin is hypocrisy."

Commentators remarked upon a new note of urgency in his voice. In a Memorial Day address in Gettysburg in 1963, Johnson said:

> One hundred years ago the slave was freed. One hundred years later the Negro remains in bondage to the color of his skin. The Negro today asks, "Justice." We do not answer him—we do not answer those who lie beneath this soil—when we reply to the Negro by asking, "Patience." . . .
>
> To ask for patience from the Negro is to ask him to give more of what he has already given enough. . . .
>
> The Negro says, "Now." Others say, "Never." The voice of responsible Americans—the voice of those who died here and the great man who spoke here—their voices say, "Together." There is no other way.[68]

Early in June, in a telephone conversation with Kennedy's special counsel, Ted Sorensen, he urged the president to make a strong commitment to civil rights in a speech in the South. "I know these risks are great and it might cost us the South, but those sorts of states may be lost anyway," Johnson said. He continued: "But if he goes down there and looks them in the eye and states the moral issue and the Christian issue, and does it face to face, these Southerners at least respect his courage. . . . When he does, the decent people and the preachers, they'll support him. I've been to North Carolina this year. I've been to Florida. Neither place would they allow Negroes to come. I said, 'I'm going to come and I'm going to talk about their constitutional rights and I want them on the platform with me, and if you don't let them I'm not coming, period.' By God, they put them on both places, right on the platform and right eating with us, the first time George Smathers ever had dinner with them in St. Augustine. . . . They'll probably boo me off the platform, but I'll be right there with him." In the late summer of 1963 a nationally syndicated column reported: "Vice President Johnson is deliberately cutting his ties to the Old South and is trying to forge a new alliance with the big-city North in pursuit of his ambition to run for President in 1968. Odds on his success: far less than 50–50. Because, try as he will, he will always have trouble in the North, and yet he is already losing the South. Talk to Southern Senators, tried-and-true Johnson men until recently, and the full measure of his descent from Southern grace is inescapable." One southern senator confided: "Lyndon never had a more devoted admirer than myself. Now, I wouldn't give 2 cents for his winning an election in my state. In fact, I wouldn't vote for him myself."[69]

Despite his alienation from southern lawmakers, Johnson, in his vice presidential years, could not fully escape the impression that he was a sectionalist. Certainly the Kennedys—especially Robert, who despised him—never thought of him as a man of national stature. When Johnson, fearing that Bobby Kennedy was trying to paint him into a corner on civil rights, sought to duck the PCEEO assignment, Jack Kennedy told him, "You've got to do it. . . . you're from the South, and if you don't take it, you'll be deemed to have evaded your responsibility." (Johnson's instincts were right, for Bobby Kennedy savagely criticized his performance.) To be sure, the president scoffed at rumors that he planned to choose a new running mate in 1964, as his brother wanted him to. He drolly informed a political banquet, "The merger of Boston and Austin was one of the last that the Attorney General allowed, but it has been one of the most successful." He refused to dump Johnson primarily because of LBJ's sectional ties. "We've got to carry Texas in '64 and maybe Georgia," he revealed to an intimate, and, given Johnson's southern connections, the vice president was indispensable.[70]

The president especially concentrated on Johnson's Texas, with its big bloc of electoral votes and its well-oiled campaign contributors. So John F. Kennedy took off for Dallas in the fall of 1963, despite a number of warnings to the White House that rightwing animosity there was so rabid that it was unsafe to go. A month earlier, protesters had stormed the podium at which Adlai Stevenson was speaking and spat on him, and a woman had bashed the UN ambassador on the head with a "Down with U.N." placard. One demonstrator kept yelling maniacally, "Kennedy will get his reward in Hell. Stevenson is going to die. His heart will stop, stop, stop. And he will burn, burn, burn." Lavishly sheathed young socialites jangled their bracelets to drown out Stevenson, and in the lobby men garbed in the uniforms of Hitler's storm troopers goose-stepped. Dallas was becoming, in the words of one Texas liberal, a "deranging city." The Secret Service had recorded thirty-four threats on the president's life in Texas during 1961 and 1962. On the eve of Kennedy's scheduled departure, a Dallas woman wrote his press secretary: "Don't let the President come down here. I'm worried about him. I think something terrible will happen to him." After leaving the White House for what turned out to be a final time, Kennedy told his wife, "We're heading into nut country today."[71]

In the mournful days following the assassination, numbers of commentators blamed Johnson for Kennedy's decision to take the fateful journey. The president had been compelled to go to the Lone Star State, it was said, in order to effect a truce between feuding Democrats who "were stalking one another with shivs." Kennedy thought, one reporter wrote, that "Johnson ought to be able to resolve this petty dispute himself; the trip seemed to be an imposition." In fact, Kennedy went to Texas, not at Johnson's behest, but because he wanted to line up votes and cash for 1964. "Nobody had to force President Kennedy to go to Texas, least of all Lyndon Johnson," two of his aides have stated; "he could not have been held back from going there." Untrue and unfair, the allegation, nonetheless, was believed. Furthermore, it could not be denied that Jack Kennedy had been murdered in LBJ's state—predictably in the Big D, which Sarah Hughes, the Dallas judge who administered the oath of office to Johnson on Air Force One, was to call "a city of hate, the only city in which the President could have been shot." Once again, Lyndon Johnson, who muttered so often about the burden of "geography," had that perception painfully confirmed.[72]

TEN

NIGRA, NIGRA, NIGRA

I

From the moment Johnson entered the White House, commentators stressed that he was the first resident of a southern state in a century to get there—the first since another southerner named Johnson had taken power, also as the result of an assassination. Lyndon Johnson himself, when he met with a group of intellectuals on a notable occasion at the White House, was to refer to himself as a "Southern President."[1]

Not a few white southerners rejoiced that the country at last had a president who spoke with a familiar accent. A limousine driver in Greensboro, North Carolina, said, "He sounds like one of us!" At first, despite his moving address to Congress on behalf of civil rights legislation, "most Southerners," Samuel Lubell wrote, "dismissed the pledge as 'something Johnson had to say' and felt certain 'he's bound to go slower' on civil rights." A Birmingham factory foreman remarked, "That was a rotten way for Kennedy to go, but I'll be frank with you, I think Johnson will be a big improvement. He understands the South."[2]

Civil rights advocates, especially blacks, on the other hand, expressed dismay. A leading African-American journalist later recalled, "When President Kennedy was killed and Johnson assumed the awesome duties of the presidency, millions of blacks figured that their fate would be similar to that of the Jews in Germany. Gloom and fear were rampant when the Dixie Chief Executive was sworn in." The *Mississippi Newsletter* of the Council of Federated Organizations (COFO) foresaw the "probability of a major setback," with "a Southern President controlling the country," and at Student Nonviolent Coordinating Committee (SNCC) headquarters, Mary King prepared a memo warning that if they thought Kennedy was bad, Johnson was going to be twice as bad. "I resented Johnson," an African-American leader said. "He was a Texan, and to me Texas was South, and he sounded South, and that's where my enemies were, more than in the Soviet Union, more than in North Korea." Johnson himself subsequently acknowledged, "Just when the blacks had had their hopes for equality and justice raised, after centuries of misery and despair, they awoke one morning to discover that their future was in the hands of a President born in the South." He told Doris Kearns: "For millions of Americans I was still illegitimate, a naked man with no presidential covering, a pretender to the throne, an illegal usurper. And then there was Texas, my home, the home of both the murder and the murder of the murderer."[3]

Some even intimated that Johnson had conspired to kill Kennedy. Nearly two decades later, one critic wrote: "No doubt the truth about the assassination of Jack Kennedy will be a long time coming, if ever, but there is an old legal principle that can stand us in temporary stead in the meantime: *cui bono*—to whose advantage?—the idea that probable responsibility for an act lies with those with something to gain. *Cui bono* Dallas? A confluence of forces including organized crime (especially its Southern branch), the defense industry (especially its Texas components), the oil industry (especially by the newer and Texas-based elements), the Far Right (especially the Texas and Floridian branches), and beyond doubt Lyndon Johnson, thirty-sixth President of the United States. Or, to put it in three words, the Southern Rim." In November 2003, on the fortieth anniversary of the slaying, nearly one in five Americans still thought Johnson was implicated, a higher proportion than suspected Castro or the Kremlin. "Vice President Johnson," it was said, "grew tired as the No. 2 man and devised a scheme on his home turf to kill Kennedy, enlisting loyal Texas oilmen and warmongers who wanted to profit from Vietnam." As recently as 2004, the History Channel saw fit to run a documentary presenting Johnson, in the words of one critic, as "Hill Country Claudius, conspiring to bait the dueling rapier, poison the wine, and do away with America's sweet, brainy prince."[4]

When Johnson addressed Congress for the first time as president in November 1963, he spoke, as Taylor Branch has noted, with "slow Texas twang and Southernisms (' . . . as I did in 19 and 57 and again in 19 and 60')," and a black writer, Louis Lomax, remarked afterward: "We watched our new President on television and remembered that he comes from a state that has had 47 lynchings since 1920. We could not recall a single time when he had spoken out against these murders of our brothers. As we listened to him talk, the cracker twang in this voice chilled our hearts. For we know that twang, that drawl. We

have heard it in the night, threatening; in the day, abusing; from the pulpit, sanc-
tifying segregation; in the market place, denying us opportunity; everywhere,
abrogating our human dignity. Yes, we know that twang."[5]

In the pages of *Ebony,* Lerone Bennett reflected the ambivalent black response to Johnson's abrupt accession to power: "Ninety eight years ago, the new
President was Andrew Johnson, a Southerner who began, Frederick Douglass
said, by 'playing the role of Moses and ended playing that of Pharaoh.' Today,
incredibly, the new President is another man named Johnson . . . who is also the
first Southern-based President since Andrew Johnson. But the second Johnson
is an abler and more imaginative man than his predecessor." It was also true,
though, that "Johnson, on his record, is more of a compromiser than Kennedy"
and that he "will probably select different personal advisors—some of them
Southerners." In sum, "the cord between black America and the White House
has been severed and will have to be re-established."[6]

Lyndon Johnson, declared Malcolm X, was "a Southern cracker—that's all
he is," and in a no-holds-barred attack Jackie Robinson said of Johnson that it
took more than "big gestures to wipe out the bad taste, the poison, of a three-
year record of adamant opposition to the cause of civil rights." It was a matter
of record, Robinson alleged, that when Johnson arrived in Washington in November 1963 from Dallas, his first words were "Where's Dick?" Suddenly Dick
Russell "and the rest of the segregation gang" have become strangely quiet,
Robinson continued. "Could it be that they have been assured that a civil rights
bill administered by one of their own would be a fraud and a farce which still
enables the South to maintain its recalcitrant refusal to give the Negro his place
in the sun?" Even after Johnson gave a Lincoln's birthday address calling for
"full human rights" irrespective of color, James Farmer told a national television
audience that most blacks distrusted him. After all, he was a southerner, and he
spoke with a southern accent.[7]

Both white supremacists and civil rights activists misread Johnson. Bill
Moyers has recorded what Johnson communicated to him, when he was a young
aide to the senator in 1960: "He said if he could talk to just one man who
had passed through the Senate before him, it wouldn't be Daniel Webster or
Henry Clay or any of the other great figures other men might summon. The
senator with whom he would have conversed was Pitchfork Ben Tillman of
South Carolina. 'Here,' said LBJ, 'was a fella who stood up for the farmers and
sent the bankers and the lawyers packing. Here was a fella who took on the railroads, started colleges, and invited women to get a first class education and per-

suaded the legislature to jack up money for schools. And yet,' said Lyndon Johnson that night, 'here was a fella who wanted to repeal the fifteenth amendment, who took the vote away from the colored folks, who got so passionate about these things that he almost got kicked out of the United States Senate.' Except for the poison of race, . . . 'he might have been president of the United States. I'd like to sit with him and ask how it was to throw it away for the sake of hating.'" On another occasion, Moyers reports, Johnson, after he had become president, remarked on Senator Russell who had just been in to see him: "God damn it. Jim Crow put a collar on more smart men as sure as if they were sentenced to a chain gang in Georgia. If Dick Russell hadn't had to wear Jim Crow's collar, Dick Russell would be sitting here now instead of me."[8]

Johnson had long since ceased to condone racism, and he was determined to be a change-maker. "I'm not going to bend an inch," he told Dick Goodwin. "Those civil rightsers are going to have to wear sneakers to keep up with me." He explained: "Those Harvards think that a politician from Texas doesn't care about Negroes. In the Senate I did the best I could. But I had to be careful. I couldn't get too far ahead of my voters. Now I represent the whole country, and I have the power. I always vowed that if I ever had the power I'd make sure every Negro had the same chance as every white man. Now I have it. And I'm going to use it." He assured a member of the White House staff: "I'm going to be the best friend the Negro ever had. I've lived in the South a long time, and I know what hatred does to a man." Three years earlier, Johnson had called the 1960 act a "vindication of the old ideal that this is one nation and not two."[9]

This quest for unity sometimes served to constrain Johnson. In a talk to the National Association of Broadcasters in the spring of 1968, the president noted that he had often been criticized as "a seeker of 'consensus.'" He responded: "I have never denied it. Because to heal and to build support, to hold people together, is something I . . . believe is a noble task. . . . In my region of the country where I have spent my life, where brother was once divided against brother, my heritage has burned this lesson . . . deep in my memory." Lyndon Johnson, Nicholas Lemann has observed, "had come of age hearing all the standard Southern stories about the humiliations of the post–Civil War years, and he used to tell his aides that if he overplayed the power of the federal government even a little, the result could be a permanent occupation of the South, or, in the event of a counterrevolution, the restoration of segregation." When he met resistance from Governor Wallace in 1965, he told his staff, "If I just send in federal troops with their big black boots and rifles, it'll look like Reconstruction all over again."[10]

Yet, when it proved necessary, Johnson did not balk at employing the full power of the national government on behalf of the constitutional rights of blacks, even if it meant resorting to force against his own section. When news reached him in 1964 that three civil rights workers were missing, and then that their burned-out station wagon had been found, the president, knowing that his mettle as a southerner was being tested, ordered J. Edgar Hoover to go to Jackson to set up an FBI office there to investigate, a move that told state officials they could not be trusted. (Hoover reported that his investigations of violations of civil rights in Mississippi were impeded by "water moccasins, rattlesnakes, and red-necked sheriffs, and they are all in the same category as far as I am concerned.") Johnson also sent military helicopters, two hundred sailors, and the director of the CIA to help in the search. Mississippi expressed more resentment at this intervention than grief over the slain young men. Burke Marshall, who had headed President Kennedy's civil rights operation, later reflected that, in contrast to Kennedy, who tried to avoid even symbolic displays of force, Johnson "didn't have any real feeling against using troops in the civil rights areas in the South."[11]

In a short while, black leaders formed a decidedly more favorable perception of Johnson. The Leadership Conference on Civil Rights, one participant recalled, "approached his first public appearance with dread." But when, seated in the office conference room around a portable TV, they heard Johnson, "in his flat-tone Texas drawl," call for enactment of civil rights legislation as a memorial to President Kennedy, they "whooped with surprised delight." After meeting with Johnson, Dr. Martin Luther King Jr. declared, "As a Southerner, I am happy to know that a fellow Southerner is in the White House who is concerned about civil rights," and the head of the National Urban League, Whitney M. Young Jr., told reporters: "Ten years ago, if we had heard a new President speaking in a deep southern drawl, there might have been so much fear among Negro leaders that some of us might have gotten on the next boat for Ghana. But we know where Lyndon Johnson stands and we realize that he is a sincere and dedicated supporter of civil rights. A magnolia accent does not mean bigotry." James Farmer, too, later said, "I had the . . . very distinct feeling that," though Johnson was a "Southern President, . . . he wanted to go down in history as a person who really accomplished something in civil rights for blacks, and that would secure his place in history." Ramsey Clark, who served as LBJ's attorney general, has concluded: "By and large, . . . the civil rights leadership loved President Johnson. His being a Southerner was really a tremendous asset rather than a handicap—to have a man with a Southern accent really concerned about civil rights meant a lot because black Americans have heard Southern accents all through their history."[12]

The new president's place of origin also put on him political obligations from which his predecessor had been exempt. "Now fully emancipated from his Southern base," remarked two columnists, "there was no need to trim his civil rights position to please Dixie. . . . On this issue, Johnson's political imperatives as a *Southern* President foreclosed compromise, whereas Kennedy's would not have." Johnson later remarked on his liberal critics: "I knew that if I didn't get out in front on this issue they would get me. They'd throw up my background against me. They'd use it to prove I was incapable of bringing unity to the land. . . . I had to produce a civil rights bill even stronger than the one they'd have gotten if Kennedy had lived. Without this, I'd be dead before I could even begin." *Newsweek* commented: "The Texan in the White House has reason to go all-out for a strong bill. He already projects all the 'Southern image' he needs. . . . Now Mr. Johnson wants to embellish his national image with a meaningful bill." James Forman of SNCC was more blunt: "Kennedy could get by on words, Johnson has to deliver."[13]

His longtime southern colleagues sensed immediately how the situation had changed. On a November afternoon driving through the Shenandoah Valley en route to Mississippi, Senator Eastland, noticing flags at half-staff, turned on the radio and learned of the murder of John F. Kennedy. "Good God, Lyndon's President," he said to his wife. "He's gonna pass a lot of this damn fool stuff." At the beginning of 1964 Senator Russell said: "We would have beaten President Kennedy, but now I won't predict. It will be three times harder." Kennedy, he explained, "didn't have to pass a strong bill to prove anything on civil rights. President Johnson does." If Kennedy had caved in, the country would have reasoned that token legislation was all he could get. But Johnson did not dare agree to a compromise because, if he did, he would be accused of succumbing to his southern origins. He would be called "a slicker from Texas." Russell confided: "We're going to have some head-on collisions, because he feels he's got to go one way and I've got to go another. It's too late in life for me to change." Johnson's intentions, a national column reported, "terrified" the southern delegations on Capitol Hill. "Lyndon," a powerful "Southern grandee" grumbled, "is talking about passing the whole damn bill, FEPC and all, and I think he really means it."[14]

Only grudgingly, however, did this southern president win regard from civil rights advocates. Though the action agency of the Union of American Hebrew Congregations acknowledged early in 1964 that "so far, he has given every evidence of exerting a maximum effort in behalf of civil rights legislation," it nonetheless doubted "whether . . . President Johnson will . . . practice what he has preached." Louis Lomax observed: "The affair between Johnson and the American Negro is an uneven experience. For Johnson, it has been an almost pushy effort to convince us that his is the desegregated heart. For the Negro, the affair has been an exercise in polite suspicion." But, he added, when, in his first address to Congress, Johnson called for enactment of civil rights legislation, Dick Gregory jested, "Twenty million of us unpacked."[15]

II

Johnson sealed this impression by the vigor with which he pushed the civil rights bill Kennedy had recommended. At the time Kennedy was assassinated, southern legislators had sidetracked the measure, some thought permanently, but Johnson strove mightily to overcome southern obstruction and achieve a significant civil rights law. On a Sunday morning early in December, he invited Dick Russell to the White House for coffee. After giving him a bear hug, and telling him that he would never have reached the White House without the senator's sponsorship, Johnson said softly: "So I love you, and I owe you. Which is why I want to tell you, please don't get in my way on this civil rights bill, which has been blocked so long, because if you do, I'll run over you. I don't want to hurt you. But don't stand in my way." (Without raising his voice, Russell responded, "Well, suh, you may very well do that, but if you do, . . . you will lose the South forever.") When Joe Rauh, one of LBJ's most vociferous critics, returned from a meeting with the president and the NAACP's lobbyist Clarence Mitchell in January 1964, he recorded: "The President said he wanted the bill passed by the House without a word or a comma changed," and he also made "it perfectly clear that he wouldn't care if the Senate didn't do another thing for two or three months until the civil rights bill was enacted." A Kennedy intimate recalled Johnson's haranguing his former associates in the Senate from the South: "You've got a southern president and if you want to blow him out of the water, go right ahead and do it, but you boys will never see another one again. We're friends on the q.t. Would you rather have me administering the civil rights bill, or do you want to have Nixon or Scranton? You have to make up your minds." Again and again, he rehearsed the tale of his employee, Zephyr Wright, a black woman who was a college graduate. When she and her husband drove the vice president's government car from Washington to Texas, she could not find a filling station that would let her use its rest room. They had to "pull off on a side road," he told Senator Stennis, "and Zephyr Wright, the cook of the Vice President of the United States, would squat in the road to pee."[16]

He demanded that, unlike the 1957 and 1960 laws, the 1964 legislation be far-reaching. In his State of the Union message in January 1964, he declared, "Let this session be known as the session which did more for civil rights than the last hundred sessions combined. . . . As far as the writ of Federal law will run, we must abolish not some, but all racial discrimination." When the Senate Republican leader Everett Dirksen held out against provisions desegregating restaurants and other public places and creating an FEPC, the president said, "Without those sections there's no damn civil rights bill worth a fart in a hailstorm." Johnson distanced himself from some of the legislative maneuvering because he was afraid that if the bill was too closely associated with the White House, "they'll say that it's a plot of the cotton South." But he kept a weather eye on the progress of the measure and warned that he would call Congress back into special session if it was not enacted before the party conventions. "We'll debate civil rights . . . around the clock," he told Walter Reuther just before Christmas. "That's the only thing that's ever going to beat Dick Russell." He lectured his agent on the Hill, Larry O'Brien: "I'm for civil rights—period. Just as it passed the House—period. And that means all night, every night. I'll stay here all night, every night to do it myself." He had no patience with "any 9-to-4 business." Johnson, recalled James Farmer, "indicated that he'd have an easy time getting it through if he would give up the public accommodations section, but he felt that was the guts of the matter. . . . So he fought for it, . . . was on the phone, . . . was cracking the whip, . . . was cajoling, . . . was threatening, everything else—whatever tactic was required." At a conference with Senator Humphrey, Johnson said: "Hubert, the country can't go on like this. Little girls are getting their heads busted open 'cause they wanta drink a Coca-Cola at the soda fountain at Rich's Department Store in Atlanta." Earlier, he had informed his African-American appointee Carl Rowan: "Old Dick Russell is against me, and he's the one I worry about. I told your friend Hubert that if you damned liberals don't get off your asses and do something, Russell is gonna wind up with your peckers in his pocket."[17]

Neither then nor later could his colleagues from the South dope out what had come over their good friend Lyndon. The *Dallas Morning News,* noting that Johnson had once said about FEPC, "I can only hope sincerely that the Senate will never be called upon to entertain seriously any such proposal again," found it "ironic that the man who hoped the Senate would never have to consider FEPC again is today urging the Senate to approve it." In the spring of 1964 Willis Robertson expressed displeasure that "the President is putting all of the power of his office behind a most iniquitous civil rights bill which undoubtedly will change our form of government." Years afterward, the Virginia senator, asked why LBJ as president went so far beyond his earlier record on civil rights, replied, "He probably realized that the nation was demanding a broader coverage . . . and that he owed it to the nation to give them leadership on it." But a moment later, he suggested a different explanation: "Or else, it may have been that when we thought he was a kind of moderate in the Senate, he was a liberal all the time but just conceding to the sentiment in Texas. And that this was his real sentiment all the time. I just don't know."[18]

Johnson's Texas associate Wright Patman, who got more exercised over economic exploitation than about race, eventually came to a simple situational construction of LBJ's transformation. "While he was a congressman from a district in Texas, he voted against every civil rights bill because it was known that the people he represented were against civil rights and he was a true representative in voting against every bill," Congressman Patman reflected. "But when he became President of the United States it was obviously a civil rights country and he felt in honor bound to go the limits of civil rights, and he went further on civil rights than any other President."[19]

In an interview after his death, Lady Bird offered a similar explanation: "He changed with the years. Don't think he was a red-hot civil rights man back in '37. But always, *when* he could, he did *what* he could." She emphasized: "When he finally got up to the presidency, there's something about that job that's a cold and shivery feeling, but you've got the responsibility—if it exists anywhere, and leadership *must* exist there where you can't take refuge in being one of 100 like you in the Senate or one of 435 like you when you were in the House. When you become President and you believe in something, that's your time to strike, especially during the short period of time when you are fresh with victory. . . . So by that time in his life he knew that he just had to do those things that he and many others had talked about."[20]

Johnson himself acknowledged a seismic shift. Not long after he entered the

White House, he called Rauh into his office and said, "If I've done anything wrong in the past, anything that offended you, I'm sorry." In 1964 he told Richard Goodwin: "I know a lot of people around those Georgetown parties are saying that I wasn't much of a crusader for civil rights when I was in the Senate. Hell, I got through the only civil rights bill since Reconstruction. . . . But on balance they're right about me. I wasn't a crusader. I represented a southern state, and if I got out too far ahead of my voters they'd have sent me right back to Johnson City where I couldn't have done anything for anybody, white or Negro. Now I represent the whole country, and I can do what the whole country thinks is right. Or ought to. We've kept the Negro down for a hundred years, and it's time we let him up." Years later, he explained to Doris Kearns: "I'm not prejudiced nor ever was, but I will say that civil rights was not one of my priorities in those days. . . . Nor did I have the power to do anything about them but to stand up and sputter out. That'd be nonsense, like . . . going to Dallas with one-half a tank of gas left, so you'd be left . . . stranded on the road. But all that changed when I became President. Then I had the power and the obligation to do something. Then it did become my personal priority. Then something could happen."[21]

Dick Russell found it hard to be detached about Johnson's apostasy. When, in his first address to Congress, the new president called for early enactment of a civil rights law, his declaration drew a burst of applause, but Russell sat with hands on his lap. One historian has written: "Initially, Russell believed that Johnson had turned his back on his southern heritage, including segregation, for political expediency. This saddened and disappointed Russell. His friend, it seemed, had a serious character flaw. Later Russell came to believe that Johnson had been brainwashed on civil rights and could not be reeducated." Yet Russell hesitated about terminating their relationship. He did not want to be cut off from the main source of political power, and he was reluctant to disown a man who had adopted him as a surrogate father.[22]

A seasoned politician, Russell recognized, at least some of the time, that Johnson could not be expected to behave as chief executive the way he had as a legislator from Texas. "Many Southern Senators felt a resentment against Lyndon Johnson when he became president" because "he deserted his role as a member of the Southern bloc," but not Russell, one commentator recalled. Russell thought "forces were too strong," and Johnson had to respond to them if he hoped to succeed. Similarly, Senator Stennis later reflected: "A man becomes president as President Johnson did—quick succession, has to make adjustments. I can see that. I think Russell saw it, realized it. I am sure he did."[23]

Russell, however, found that shock of recognition burdensome. Theodore White concluded: "Russell was caught emotionally. He was devoted to . . . Lyndon B. Johnson, whom he had tutored and shaped in the President's early Senate career. Yet Russell, leader of the South, could see the problem of this man, the first Southern President since Reconstruction. Lyndon Johnson was now President of all the people, forced to act for the will of the majority. Russell could not attack Johnson personally, so he must fight against the President's bill—which crippled him." The Georgia senator continued to oppose the civil rights measure, but he did so wearily. He was increasingly aware that, with his former ally committed to wielding all of the authority of the White House against him, resistance was futile. Bill Moyers has recalled, "Dick Russell would say to me, 'Now you tell Lyndon . . . I've been expecting the rod for a long time, and I'm sorry that it's from his hand the rod must be wielded, but I'd rather it be his hand than anybody else's I know. Tell him to cry a little when he uses it.'" Russell, though, did not conceal his dismay. In his very last address on the legislation, he said, "The moving finger is writing the final act of . . . the greatest tragedy ever played out in the Senate of the United States."[24]

As the struggle over the civil rights bill dragged on month after month in the most prolonged filibuster in history, southern disaffection with Johnson mounted once again. Johnson had been in office only a few weeks when Senator Stennis reported to his constituents: "We in Mississippi, of course, are deeply interested in his position on those domestic issues of most vital concern to us. . . . Unfortunately, it is already abundantly clear that his position on civil rights is extreme." A North Carolina man told his congressman that "President Johnson has disappointed a great majority of the people in our Southern States and is rapidly losing their support," and from Daytona Beach, the acting chairman of the Southern Democrats for State Rights wrote a Democratic senator from New England: "Please be advised that we southern democrats consider that voting for Lyndon Johnson would be treason to the cause of States Rights." To many in the South who had once admired him, he had become "a turncoat son-of-a-bitch." In sum, a southern Republican strategist has concluded, "LBJ was perceived by Southerners as being anti-South . . . even more so than . . . President . . . Truman."[25]

The new president kindled an especially caustic response from a number of citizens in his own state. Only ten days after Kennedy was assassinated, a Texan, infuriated by the "vicious civil rights bill," wrote his congressman that Kennedy was not martyred, he was "executed." He added, "As for Lyndon Johnson, you had best put your high powered rifle where it will be handy." A San Angelo, Texas, woman told her congressman, "Johnson is a way off his course and maby should see a doctor along with any other brainwashed government official that would vote for the inslavement of white people."[26]

Undeterred by such abuse, Johnson drove his southern foes into submission. When one of Ross Barnett's sidekicks asked Senator Eastland about the civil rights bill, he shook his head forlornly and replied, "We had Kennedy stopped. But I'm afraid we can't stop Johnson." The opponents had even less strength in the House. "Now it was southerner against southerner—President Johnson against Howard Smith," Joe Rauh later recalled. It did not take long for Smith to run up a white flag. "I know the facts of life around here," the reactionary Rules Committee chairman said. When the House passed the bill, Rauh thought he was entitled to rest for a few minutes to relish the victory, only to have Johnson track him down and demand, "What have you done to get the bill on the floor of the Senate?" In early February an outraged Texas congressman informed a constituent, "It begins to look like we are going to lose about a half-dozen Texans on this issue. In fact, there were eleven in our delegation who signed the discharge petition!" In late May, after being beaten down again and again on attempts to add crippling amendments, Senator Sam Ervin said, "I don't think I could even get a denunciation of the Crucifixion in the bill." For many weeks, besieged southern senators resisted, but on June 11 McClellan regretfully informed a constituent that a cloture resolution would pass. "There were only 19 of us fighting it and we held out . . . for 75 days," but the power of the proponents was too great.[27]

For the first time ever, following eleven successive setbacks for the civil rights forces, Johnson broke the southern filibuster. With his characteristic flair for ceremony, he signed the landmark Civil Rights Act of 1964 in the rotunda of the Capitol. "Through a deep Texas twang he made the strongest civil rights speech ever given by an American president," Andrew Young has written. "It was a powerful symbol . . . that a president born and raised in a Confederate state was the one to sign the Civil Rights Act into law."[28]

Some who had followed his career from the beginning found his activity difficult to comprehend. Virginia Durr, the sister-in-law of Hugo Black, wrote:

"Here was my sister married to a man who was a member of the KKK and he becomes one of the chief legal bulwarks of integration as a Supreme Court Justice. Here was Bird whose husband took part in every filibuster there was— went through the same old procedure of orating nonsense every time, and he turns out as President of the United States and gets the Civil Rights Bill through."[29]

Johnson's triumph at the end of such a nasty and protracted battle meant a great deal to him. "For LBJ," one writer has said, enactment of the 1964 civil rights measure "was a tremendous boost to his emerging image as a powerful President. In one swift stroke, he had proved that he could pass major legislation that JFK could not, and that he could no longer be tied to the racist Southern past." But victory exacted a high toll. A decade later, Johnson reflected: "The decision to press for the civil rights bill was not without penalties for me. It was destined to set me apart forever from the South."[30]

III

In the 1964 campaign, Johnson's foes launched a two-pronged attack on him. Groups such as the "Southern Committee to Help Elect the Next President of the United States" raised money for the governor of Alabama, George Wallace. A more serious threat to Johnson's following in the former Confederate states came from the Republican Party, which also fielded a presidential candidate whose views pleased white supremacists, Barry Goldwater. In *The Conscience of a Conservative*, published in 1960, the Arizona senator had not only written that "the federal Constitution does *not* require the States to maintain racially mixed schools," but also questioned the validity of *Brown*. Calling the Court's decisions "jackassian," Goldwater later remarked, "I don't necessarily buy the idea that what the Supreme Court says is the law of the land." He said of the racist governor of Mississippi: "Barnett had every right to do what he did in the case of James Meredith, and President Kennedy should not have used troops to force the Negro's admission to the University of Mississippi." Goldwater claimed to have been at the forefront of efforts to desegregate Phoenix as well as the Arizona Air National Guard that he organized, and when he entered the Senate he was a contributor to both the NAACP and the National Urban League. He believed, however, that discriminating against blacks in stores was "morally wrong but not legally wrong," and he even analogized the right to reject customers to the right to throw a drunk out of the Goldwater department store in

Phoenix. "Property rights are our most basic rights," he insisted. When Wallace dropped out of the race, his avid supporter Lester Maddox renamed his organization Democrats for Goldwater.[31]

Goldwater fully understood the political payoff from his attitude. At a regional conference of southern Republicans in Atlanta in the fall of 1961, he had said bluntly, "We're not going to get the Negro vote as a bloc in 1964 or 1968, so we ought to go hunting where the ducks are." His state of Arizona, he assured Georgians, was "Confederate territory." As early as the summer of 1963, when it was assumed that Kennedy would be the Democratic nominee in 1964, Stewart Alsop wrote in the *Saturday Evening Post* that "Goldwater is regarded as a sort of honorary Southerner where the racial issue is concerned." A month before Kennedy's assassination, the correspondent Robert MacNeil reported: "Goldwater and his advisers now believe that the civil rights controversy can put him in the White House. They are reluctant to talk about it; Goldwater himself seems a little conscience-stricken by it." The election, Goldwater said, "frankly . . . all depends on civil rights repercussions. . . . We can't use it. It's too dangerous. All we can do is watch."[32]

He did more than watch. In 1964 he cast one of the few votes by a senator from outside the South against breaking the southern filibuster on the civil rights bill, then voted against the legislation on the critical roll call. Goldwater, reported *Newsweek,* "astonished nearly everybody by the depth and harshness of his position." Key features of the legislation, Goldwater said, were "the hallmarks of the police state." (He had nothing at all to say about the brutal behavior of the police in Mississippi and South Carolina.) Goldwater was strengthened in his conviction that the act was unconstitutional by memos from two of his advisors: William Rehnquist and Robert Bork. His behavior made him Dixie's favorite son at the Republican national convention in San Francisco. South Carolina's state GOP chairman later remembered that "on the night of his nomination when our South Carolina vote put him over the top, I got so excited that I waved the South Carolina standard so vigorously that it broke in two and cut my hand, hit our state party treasurer on the head, so I tied it together with my necktie and got into the demonstration." Of the 279 votes cast by southern delegates, all but eight went to Goldwater. "There's an insanity in the air around here," said a Rockefeller backer, with "unmistakable signs that party leaders from outside the industrialized states of the eastern seaboard were seriously contemplating transforming the Republican Party into the White Man's Party." That was the judgment, too, of America's foremost columnist. "It is impossible to doubt," Walter Lippmann concluded, "that Senator Goldwater intends to make his candidacy the rallying point of white resistance."[33]

That record, however, did not dissuade the GOP state chairman in Maryland from making a brazen appeal to blacks to support the Republican ticket because President Johnson was a "Southern segregationist," or Goldwater from calling LBJ "the biggest faker in the United States." The president, he charged, "opposed civil rights until this year. . . . He's the phoniest individual who ever came around." In San Francisco, the Goldwater campaign set up a front organization of ministers that prepared a leaflet claiming, on distorted evidence, that Goldwater had a better civil rights record than Johnson. Its memo stipulated, "Distribute to Negro homes only!" Goldwater also exploited the issue of sectional ambiguity. "Well, now, I don't know how much of a Southerner he is," the Arizonan said of Johnson. "When he's down in my country he talks like a Westerner and when he's in Alabama he says 'you all.'"[34]

Though Goldwater never indulged in blatant racist rhetoric, and sternly rejected the use of film footage of black riots to inflame voters, his campaign had decidedly racist implications. At the San Francisco convention, the delegation from Michigan, a state with a large concentration of black citizens, was as white as Ivory Snow. Clarence Mitchell, Washington director of the NAACP, called Goldwater's defense of his vote against the civil rights bill before the Platform Committee at the convention "an invitation to defiant elements in the South to rally around him." In March 1964 Goldwater declared that he could "not condone or support" civil rights demonstrations and in October he asserted that "forced integration is just as wrong as forced segregation." The *New Yorker* correspondent, Richard Rovere, concluded: "The Goldwater movement . . . appears to be a race movement and almost nothing else. Goldwater seemed fully aware of this and not visibly distressed by it. He did not, to be sure, make any direct racist appeals. . . . The fact that the words did not cross his lips does not mean that he ignored the realities. . . . He talked about them all the time in an underground, or Aesopian, language—a kind of code that few in his audiences had any trouble deciphering. In the code, 'bullies and marauders' means 'Negroes,' 'criminal defendants' means 'Negroes,' . . . 'women' means 'white women.'"[35]

Other commentators confirmed the perception that Goldwater's behavior and lingo had racist connotations. One analysis noted: "The Arizonan's failure ever to attack the perpetrators of violence against Southern Negroes or civil rights workers or to lecture his Confederate flag-draped, all-white Southern audiences on the need for compassion for the Negro and for compliance with the law of the land seemed to many clear evidence of his unconcern for the plight of the American Negro." Roy Wilkins later observed: "Goldwater . . . said over and over that he believed in leaving civil rights issues to the states; to the same states . . . that had violated civil rights every time they had the chance. No matter how . . . decent a man he might have been, he was still offering a grant of immunity to the South for its cattle prods and shotguns, for the armored tanks and police dogs of Birmingham, the bomb murders of little children in Alabama churches, and the death of Medgar Evers. Goldwater was playing a cynical game of politics with an issue in which the life and death of 20 million black Americans were involved."[36]

Southern Republicans might claim that they were conservatives, not racists, but they gave themselves away. "There was only one nigger in the crowd," a GOP leader said of a party rally in Augusta. "If Johnson comes in here it'll look like a checkerboard out there." The Republicans chose as regional chairman of their Operation Dixie a man who had demanded that Kennedy be impeached for sending troops in support of a federal court order to desegregate Ole Miss, and a party telecast in Arkansas featured a justice of the state's Supreme Court who backed Goldwater because he had voted against the "damnable" 1964 civil rights bill. Goldwater's campaign organizer in Georgia, the vocal segregationist Roy V. Harris, later acknowledged that the Republican candidate was simply an instrument for southerners to lash out at the national Democratic Party. "They weren't voting for Goldwater," he said. "We didn't even like him."[37]

Goldwater's swing through the South, observed Rovere, "made it possible for great numbers of unapologetic white supremacists to hold great carnivals of white supremacy." At Cramton Bowl near Montgomery, Republicans planted a huge field of white lilies and spotlighted seven hundred Alabama girls adorned in full-length white gowns to leave no one in doubt that the GOP was exclusively the party of the white race. Rovere wrote: "I don't suppose . . . that anyone before us ever logged several thousand miles in the South and visited a dozen or so of its great centers of population without seeing any more Negroes than one might expect to encounter on, say, an average winter afternoon in Spitzbergen. In a Negroless Memphis or Atlanta or New Orleans, some of us had the feeling of having lost our bearings, of being not where we were but on some immense stage set; we would peer out beyond the edges of the crowds and down side streets as we passed them in the buses, trying to see if we could find a single Negro and, whenever we saw one, advising one another of our rare discovery." Similarly, the *New Republic*'s Richard L. Strout reported: "A foreigner traveling with Barry Goldwater in the South wouldn't know there were any Negroes in it. They seem to have withdrawn from the main streets; they don't appear at his political gatherings; they aren't asked to sit on the speakers' platform."[38]

Senator Goldwater's candidacy, in presenting the electorate with such a stark choice, offered white southern Democrats an opportunity to demonstrate their outrage at LBJ's racial policies by crossing over to the Republicans. No Democrat did so more conspicuously than Strom Thurmond. In mid-September, Senator Thurmond, saying that the Civil Rights Act was "another Reconstruction," announced he was bidding farewell to the party of his ancestors and joining the once-despised party of Lincoln. The next day, as he welcomed Goldwater to South Carolina, he sported the GOP symbol: a gold elephant tie clip. LBJ's opponents justified their defection by denying that Johnson was a true son of Dixie. At a Fourth of July rally in Georgia, Ross Barnett called him a "counterfeit Confederate . . . who [might] someday resign from the white race." Goldwater's southern regional director ridiculed the president as "a sometime Southern Democrat" and "a sometimes Western Democrat," and Goldwater himself did not hesitate to tell a "wildly cheering throng" in Greensboro, North Carolina, that Johnson "is not a Southerner."[39]

That year, Hale Boggs later recalled, "an irrational type of dislike" for President Johnson swept the South. A BBC correspondent who toured the section early in the spring of 1964 reported: "The bitterness . . . about Johnson personally that the ordinary Southerners expressed really startled me and . . . I'll be surprised if the very fact that he's a semi-Southerner from Texas would . . . lead to his being able to carry the whole South against Goldwater." Rovere wrote: "It has been my lot to attend political gatherings of many sorts for many years, but never until I went south with Goldwater have I heard any large number of Americans boo and hoot at the mention of the name of the President of the United States. In Alabama and New Orleans, there were thunderous, stadium-filling boos, all of them cued by a United States Senator." In 1964, noted another writer, small town white southerners "spoke of Johnson with real loathing" in "the whined or outraged or anguished cry that he had betrayed the South, had been a traitor." Less than a month before the election, Virginia Durr reported sardonically on the sentiment in her own state: "Lyndon is guilty of everything but child rape; he is a murderer, liar, thief, communist, liberal,

nigger lover, drunkard, adulterer, prepared to sell out the USA and so on endlessly."[40]

Feeling against the president ran particularly high across the Deep South.
In Plains in the heart of Georgia, Jimmy Carter's mother bravely volunteered
to run Johnson's campaign office. "Almost every day, when she returned to her
car," Carter has recalled, "she found it covered with graffiti, the windows soaped
over, or the radio antenna tied in a knot." An Alabama congressman reflected
on Johnson's approval of the 1964 civil rights bill: "People were infuriated. Johnson was a bad word. You couldn't stomach Johnson in the South. He was really
despised." Louisiana, it has been said, "seemed engulfed by a wave of pro-
segregation and anti-Johnson feelings." If LBJ was reelected, Leander Perez
warned, "race riots will break out to such an extent that our civilization will be
pushed back into the jungle age." Perez sought to "force Mr. Lyndon B. Johnson to come to Louisiana and tell the voters what he has been doing to them—
and then the voters will give him a kick in the pants."[41]

In Mississippi, where not one Democratic politician of any importance
spoke out in support of the head of their party, Goldwater buttons outnumbered LBJ's 25–1. A GOP operative reported: "The oddest political experience
in Mississippi is to see a battered pickup truck with a typical 'Red Neck'... behind the wheel puttering up the highway bearing a Goldwater sticker. There
are thousands of old timers who never dreamed of voting Republican before
who have unabashedly come out for Goldwater. (One 84-year-old farmer in . . .
Lamar County rubbed his leathery chin and spit, and said, 'The Democratic
Party just doesn't mean what it used to mean.')" When the three civil rights
workers disappeared in the vicinity of Philadelphia, Mississippi, a woman wrote
the Meridian newspaper: "So the big Philadelphia show goes on—people and
news printing trash about our nice Americans in the Philadelphia area and the
state of Mississippi. All of it for one purpose and one only—Lyndon Johnson
wants to be re-elected President of the United States. When and if he thinks
he has the Negro vote he will stop all this useless searching."[42]

So palpable was southern hostility that when Aaron Henry, Fannie Lou
Hamer, and other disfranchised Mississippi blacks created consternation at the
Democratic national convention by demanding to be seated as representatives
of the Mississippi Freedom Democratic Party (MFDP) in place of the regularly
elected white delegation, Johnson feared he would lose the entire section. "You
let those bugaboos march in," John Connally warned him, "and the whole South
will march out." Even as moderate a governor as Carl Sanders of Georgia

threatened to bolt. "It looks like we're turning the Democratic Party over to the nigras," Sanders told Johnson. "Alabama's done gone and they tell me that Louisiana and Arkansas are going with them," Johnson informed Hubert Humphrey. "And I'm afraid it's going to spread to eight or ten." He gave an even gloomier reckoning to Connally: "Now my judgment is we're gonna lose every Southern State, including Kentucky and Oklahoma and Missouri. . . . I just don't think they can take this nigra stuff. . . . We're not going to carry any Southern states, John." The consequences he foresaw were devastating. "I am going to lose the election because of the fact that I'm going to lose the South," he told Walter Reuther.[43]

Johnson appeared to have reason to worry. Rick Perlstein has written of his opponent's triumphal tour through the South: "In Charlotte, where ten thousand supporters had to be turned away, the *Observer* reported teenagers 'near emotional collapse,' when Goldwater walked past. Sobbing, tears running down their faces, several girls moaned 'Barry, Barry.' His motorcade down Peachtree Street was showered with so much confetti that it felt like Atlanta had suffered its first blizzard. . . . 'Thank God he's safe,' the Memphis Chief of Police could only sigh after Goldwater escaped mauling from a throng of 100,000." In mid-August a veteran *Newsweek* columnist wrote: "The pollsters, the political experts, and the politicians were all saying the same thing about Dixie. If the election were held today, they tell us, Barry Goldwater would top Lyndon Johnson in popular vote and walk off with the larger share of the electoral vote of the Old South. At this point not a single state once part of the Confederacy is completely safe for the South's first President since Andrew Johnson."[44]

Morose over antipathy to him in the North as well as in the South, convinced that he had no authentic sectional identity, Johnson contemplated withdrawing from the presidential race at the Atlantic City convention. "By God, I'm gonna go up there and quit," he cried. "Fuck 'em all!" He just did not think, he confided, that "a white Southerner is the man to unite this nation in this hour." He doubted "whether a man born where I was born, raised like I was raised, could ever satisfy the Northern Jews and Catholics and union people." He drafted a statement in his own hand declaring that he would not run for re-election. "The times require leadership about which there is no doubt and a voice that men of all parties, sections, and color can follow," it read. "I have learned after trying very hard that I am not that voice or that leader." He told his chief aide, "I do not believe I can physically and mentally carry the responsibilities of the bomb and the world and the nigras and the South and so forth."

The president soon thought better of stepping down (no one ever knew how seriously to take him) and prepared for the forthcoming contest, but with continuing anxiety about his sectional vulnerability.[45]

IV

With the convention melodrama behind him, Johnson resolved not only to defeat Goldwater, but also to hold the South for the Democratic Party. "*As a Southerner*," Tom Wicker later wrote, "Johnson desperately wanted to carry the South. No triumph is as sweet as those scored among the home folks." Similarly, Theodore White observed, "Lyndon Johnson wanted his Southland with him as much as Kennedy had wanted his New England." To achieve his goal, he adopted two different personae, at times reminding southerners that he was one of them, at other times presenting himself as the leader of a nation in which the South was an integral component.[46]

The president made his boldest move when he sent his wife on an eight-state tour of the South, a trip she was eager to take. "We must let them know that we love the South," she said. "We have not turned our backs on them. I don't think there's much chance of carrying it for Lyndon, judging by the letters I get from my Alabama cousins. But at least we won't lose by default." The First Lady elaborated: "I know the Civil Rights Act was right, and I don't mind saying so. But I'm tired of people making the South the whipping boy of the Democratic Party. There are plenty of people who make snide jokes about the corn-pone and red-neck. . . . What I want to say to those people is that I love the South. . . . And I want them to know that as far as *this* President and his wife are concerned, the South belongs to the United States."[47]

Despite her benign words, however, she knew that she was on a political assignment, and she had no illusions about what might await her. One aim of the enterprise, the pro-LBJ governor of Georgia later explained, was "bringing some of the, you might say reluctant, so-called Democratic leaders out in the open or finding out just how cowardly or weak they felt about getting involved in behalf of a candidate who represented their party." To be certain that the trip had an impact, Mrs. Johnson insisted that nothing be made easy for her. "Don't give me the Atlantas," she instructed her aide. "Give me the Savannahs."[48]

On October 6 the dazzling red, white, and blue nineteen-car Lady Bird Special took off from Washington's Union Station for a 1682-mile jaunt aimed at persuading the South to stay with Johnson. After forty-seven stops and four "slowdowns," the eight-state pilgrimage was to end in Louisiana three days later. The First Lady's large entourage featured a bevy of attractive young women wearing blue shirtwaists and skimmers bearing the LBJ monogram. All of them knew how to accentuate the president's southern origins. As Liz Carpenter remarked, the Lady Bird Special was politics "with the flavor of fried chicken and mustard greens and cornbread." From the back platform of the train, Mrs. Johnson would wave to the waiting crowd and tell them in a fetching southern drawl, "I'm mighty glad to be here and see all you folks. You-all may not agree with what I say, but you sure can understand the way I say it."[49]

At her first whistle stop in Alexandria, Mrs. Johnson revealed the motif of the journey: "I wanted to make this trip because I am proud of the South, and I am proud that I am part of the South. I'm fond of the old customs—of keeping up with your kinfolks, of long Sunday dinners after church, of a special brand of gentility and courtesy. I'm even more proud of the new South, the spirit of growth, advances in economy and progress in education, and I share the irritation when unthinking people make snide jokes about me." After these disarming words, she struck the national chord her husband had been pounding. Robert E. Lee, she reminded her listeners, had advised his fellow southerners: "Abandon all these local animosities and raise your sons to be Americans!" The Civil Rights Act of 1964, she asserted, had "been received by the South for the most part in a way that is a great credit to local leadership. . . . This convinces me of something I have always believed—that there is, in this Southland, more love than hate." And she instructed her audience that the "hard duty of assuring equal and Constitutional rights to all Americans falls not only on the President but upon all who love their land."[50]

The First Lady encountered responses ranging from warmly welcoming to implacably antagonistic. In the upper South, gatherings were friendly, save for one minor dust-up at Virginia's capital. At Broad Street station a huge banner with red letters against a white background read "Fly Away Lady Bird. Here in Richmond, Barry Is the Cat's Meow," but no one was disruptive. In Raleigh the president, who flew in for a night rally of close to thirty thousand Tar Heels, was so cheered by the enthusiasm that he would not stop talking until his wife passed him a note telling him to shut up. As the Lady Bird Special got deeper into the South, however, crowds at some stations were so ill-natured that the Secret Service had to move in to rescue the women and convey them back to the train. Placards read, "You've Got the Feathers, We've Got the Tar." Asked later how the Johnson party was received in Georgia, Herman Talmadge replied, "Oh, they were booed from one end of the state to the other."[51]

LBJ's political missionaries ran into their ugliest ordeals in South Carolina. In Columbia, Lady Bird appealed to tradition in saying, "I am here on behalf of the Democratic party—the party of your ancestors and mine," but she had to shout over booing Goldwater supporters to be heard. She recalled: "I . . . felt intensely the hostility which certainly did exist, particularly in South Carolina—more in South Carolina than anywhere else by a long shot. There would be banners with unpleasant things like, Go Home, or Fly Home, Lady Bird, something like that. And then if you got up and started to make a speech, some people would begin to make so much noise that you couldn't be heard. It was not frightening. It was not bad, really, but it was enough hostility so that you could feel it, palpably, in the air."[52]

Charleston alternated between shunning Mrs. Johnson and drowning her out when she tried to speak. She later wrote:

> The silent town was one of the loveliest towns I know—Charleston, South Carolina. The train stopped for several hours there. Part of the day was planned as a sort of sight-seeing trip through the Battery area— lovely old houses along the waterfront where there were magnificent live oaks and stately white houses. As I went down the street in this open carriage with a liveried black driver, I kept noticing that all the houses were shuttered. All the shutters were closed tight. It looked like everybody had left town.
>
> Then I began to see signs in windows that said, This House Sold on Goldwater. Very occasionally I would see a face peering out from behind the curtains, but the only people I saw were a few small children in the yards accompanied by their black nurses.
>
> That's all I saw in that hour or two in that lovely area.

When the time came for her to talk, hecklers were so boisterous that the ailing, aged wife of South Carolina's Senator Olin Johnston, no friend of civil rights, seized the microphone and, lacing into the disturbers as "white trash," cried, "Shut your mouths and listen to a First Lady."[53]

Though she knew that her message would not be welcome, she did not retreat. After introducing herself as a "Southern girl who grew up loving Southern ways," she told the Charleston crowd, "My husband and I have always felt that the South has had a little corner on life that people elsewhere are missing," and it was this "quite special" sense of individual and family that inspired "such a fierce loyalty that no Southerner ever loses. I will never lose it, and I know

Lyndon will never lose it." She went on, however, to say bluntly: "Today, the South like the rest of the nation is at a crossroads . . . between a glory that can be—and a glory that was. A choice has been forced upon us. It is the choice between a new progress—and a new nullification. Here in Charleston, once the hub of the Old South, you have to make that choice."[54]

Mrs. Johnson felt infinitely more at home in Alabama. "Until I was about twenty," she told audiences there, "summertime always meant Alabama to me. With Aunt Effie, we would board the train at Marshall and ride to the part of the world that meant . . . picnics at the creek and a lot of company every Sunday." At stops along the route Lady Bird encountered kissing cousins from Alabama towns—Atmore, Billingsley, Prattville—that were, she said, "filled with memories of watermelon cuttin's and pallets on the floor." She later recalled: "In Alabama I always saw relatives. The newspaper people got to asking, 'Is this a one-cousin town or a two-cousin town?' Sort of joking, you know. They were very loyal and dear about showing up everywhere that they possibly could." On one occasion, no fewer than fifty-nine of her Alabama relatives showed up, outdoing the big turnout of kin in 1960. Even in Alabama, though, not all was tranquil. Virginia Durr reported: "Bird made a huge hit in Mobile, in spite of the heckling. It was all done by these poor, pitiful, nasty little pimply-faced teenagers." (Far worse awaited the First Lady in Mississippi, where the Ku Klux Klan had laid plans to blow up the railway bridge outside of Biloxi. But the plot was thwarted, and the governor of Mississippi and his wife made a point of boarding the Special in Biloxi to pay their respects.)[55]

At each stop before Lady Bird spoke, the train commander, the faithful Louisiana Congressman Hale Boggs, in what one reporter called "a suspender-snapping, tie-stripping performance," would warm up the crowd by asking, "How many of you-all know what red-eye gravy is?" After getting the expected hand waves of assent, he would respond, "Well, so do I. And so does Lyndon Johnson!" He would promise, "When Lyndon Johnson is reelected we're gonna have ham in every pot. We're gonna have ham and grits on every plate. We're gonna have ham with plenty of good ole red-eye gravy." Having made this profound campaign pledge, he would continue, "You know what we had on this train this morning? Hominy grits. About noontime we're gonna start servin' turnip greens and black-eyed peas. Later on, farther South, we're gonna have some crawfish bisque, some red beans and rice, and some creole gumbo." His face lit by "a hush-puppy grin," Boggs would conclude, "Now about this race. You're not gonna turn your back on the first Southern-born President in a hundred years?" The crowd, laughing and smiling, would answer with a shout: "All the way with LBJ!"[56]

When the train pulled into Union Station in New Orleans in Boggs's home state on the night of October 9, Lady Bird found the president there to greet her and their daughters. With his flair for political theater, he walked half a mile down the track to meet his family. In informal remarks, he said, "I want all of you to know that I think so much of the South that gave me birth that I have given the South the best I had for the last four days." Later that night he claimed that for four days he had "followed that train trip through every yard of the South" and had phoned three or four times a day. "I don't need to tell you what great pride I have had in my wife and in my daughters," he added. William S. White, a correspondent especially partial to Johnson, has offered a different impression: "The president was both very pleased with her success and, I thought, in a slight way somewhat jealous of it. I think he didn't particularly like it when people suggested that she'd made a major contribution to the campaign."[57]

Johnson had come to New Orleans with more in mind than being a dutiful husband and father. He knew he was being hard-pressed in the Deep South by Goldwater. A correspondent covering a rally wrote, "New Orleans had the Beatles, but Memphis had Barry Goldwater, and it's doubtful that the hairy lads from Liverpool would have gotten a better reception than the Republican candidate for president in the Bluff City." In late September, a high-ranking campaign official reported to him, "The election in the South hangs in the balance more than in any other region." Pollsters found that, of the gains Goldwater had made since the campaign began, three-quarters could be attributed to a vicious white backlash. Hence, it was advisable for him to soft-pedal the race issue. On the very day Johnson arrived, Bill Moyers wired that "several people in New Orleans, including our advance men, feel the President should not refer to 'civil rights.'" If he felt compelled to deal with this risky matter, he should allude to "constitutional rights." But Johnson brushed this counsel aside and decided to make a major declaration on behalf of the rights of African Americans, "not in New York or Chicago or Los Angeles," he later noted, "but in New Orleans— near home, in my own backyard."[58]

That evening, Johnson appeared at a banquet of more than two thousand in the grand ballroom of a New Orleans hotel. As toastmaster, Hale Boggs, seeking to present the Johnsons to the audience as fellow southerners, said of Lady Bird that she "knows the sound of the wind in the pines and the song of the mockingbird in the morning." The president, though, chose a national rather than a sectional emphasis. "Our cause is no longer the cause of a party alone," he told the Louisiana Democrats. "Our cause is the cause of a great Nation. Our cause is the cause of a country that you love." He then went on to assert: "If we are to heal our history and make this Nation whole, prosperity must know no Mason-Dixon line and opportunity must know no color line."[59]

After a time, Johnson put aside his prepared speech and spoke from the heart, without text or notes. He told his Louisiana audience: "Whatever your views are, we have a Constitution and we have a Bill of Rights, and we have the law of the land, and two thirds of the Democrats in the Senate voted for it [the Civil Rights bill of 1964] and three fourths of the Republicans. I signed it, and I am going to enforce it, . . . and I think any man that is worthy of the high office of President is going to do the same thing. . . . I am not going to let them build up the hate and try to buy my people by appealing to their prejudice." The applause, Johnson observed dryly some years later, "was less than overwhelming."[60]

Undismayed, he plunged ahead to tell the story of a great southern senator, near the end of his days, who had once spoken eloquently to young Sam Rayburn, recently come to the House, about the critical economic needs of their section, then added: "Sammy, I wish I felt a little better. . . . I would like to go back down there and make them one more Democratic speech. I just feel like I have one in me. The poor old State, they haven't heard a Democratic speech in thirty years." Bellowing, arms outstretched, Johnson gave his New Orleans listeners the ancient senator's final words: "All they ever hear at election time is 'Nigra, Nigra, Nigra!'"[61]

The audience let out a gasp. "This took the breath away from most of us," a Washington correspondent has written. "The crowded ballroom became strangely silent." Jack Valenti remembered: "Over that audience there flowed a consternation that could be felt everywhere in the auditorium. It was a physical thing, surprise, awe; ears heard what they plainly could not hear, a cataclysmic wave hit everyone there with a stunning and irreversible force." Then, led by blacks in the room, the audience rose to its feet and the hall was "rocked by a thunderous cheer" that lasted fully five minutes. The Washington correspondent concluded, "I am not certain that all who joined in the applause approved of what LBJ had said, but they surely had to admire his courage in saying it."[62]

Many of his most acerbic critics have affirmed that this was Johnson's finest hour. There was no way a northerner could have delivered that speech and have had it carry the same meaning. He spoke, in the words of Theodore White, "in the presence of other Southerners as a Southerner who had come to wisdom." When Johnson "publicly chided Southerners for their treatment of blacks," George Reedy has written, he "drew applause that is still ringing in my ears. He could be superb!" The Texas progressive Bill Brammer has said, "The highlight of the 1964 campaign, a highlight any way you look at it, was the speech in New Orleans, what people call the 'nigra, nigra, nigra' speech. It galvanized me. I was ready to go out and kill. That's how great he was."[63]

V

The New Orleans crowd rewarded Johnson with a mighty ovation, but a month later Louisiana denied him its electoral votes—by registering a thumping 57 percent for Goldwater. So, too, did four other Deep South states, none of which had gone Republican in any national election since Reconstruction. "In his guaranty of racial justice, he especially needs the South's help," the Atlanta columnist Gene Patterson had written in May. "I think the Southern president can count on this Southern state not to fail him." But, despite appeals from Lady Bird, whom he adored, and ardent Democrats, including the young legislator Jimmy Carter, Dick Russell refused to endorse the ticket headed by his protégé. In November Georgia, the only state in the Union never to have voted Republican, ended that skein because Goldwater's stand against the civil rights bill made race the critical issue in a national election in the state for the first time in the twentieth century, and hence, as an Atlanta liberal Congressman told a Yale University audience, "disaffection for Mr. Johnson . . . carried the day." Afterward, Ralph McGill wrote Johnson, "I am embarrassed and ashamed about what Georgia did." Goldwater also walloped LBJ in Strom Thurmond's South Carolina (59 percent), and in George Wallace's Alabama, where the president was not permitted any votes.[64]

No state, though, recorded such stunning results as Mississippi, where Republicans had long been anathema. In the Magnolia State Goldwater rolled over Johnson with an incredible 87 percent. As one commentary put it, "Given a choice between Democrat Lyndon B. Johnson—the first southerner to become president in modern times—and Barry Goldwater, the voters in the most 'southern' state in the country chose the Republican candidate." Walker Percy explained: "The Roosevelt farm program succeeded too well. Planters who were going broke on ten cent cotton voted for Roosevelt, took federal money, got rich, lived to hate Kennedy and Johnson and vote for Goldwater—while still

taking money." The "bizarre seven-to-one margin in favor of Senator Goldwater," he added, "attests to the undiminished obsession with race. It would not
have mattered if Senator Goldwater had advocated the collectivization of the
plantations and open saloons in Jackson; he voted against the Civil Rights Bill
and that was that."[65]

To be sure, Johnson had much to rejoice about. He was the first resident of
a former Confederate state ever to be chosen for the White House—and in a
landslide. Save for the five Deep South states, Goldwater won nothing but his
home state of Arizona. A New Orleans radio and television editorial, while re-
gretting that five states "were seduced by Senator Goldwater's siren song,"
pointed out that "Tuesday's outcome showed that the Democrats can win the
national election without the deep South." One analyst has characterized Goldwater's showing in the South as "rather pathetic," for he did not do as well as
either Eisenhower or Nixon had despite the sharp line he had drawn on civil
rights. Goldwater's success in capturing five southern states sometimes led observers to overlook Johnson's better showing in winning six southern states, as
well as all the border states. In fact, despite his advocacy of civil rights legislation, Johnson won back three former Confederate states that had gone Republican in 1960—Virginia, Florida, and Tennessee—and also restored the border
state of Kentucky to the Democratic column. By taking Virginia, he broke a
string of three straight GOP victories there.[66]

A number of southerners preferred Johnson to Goldwater because they continued to regard him as one of their own while respecting his obligations as head
of government for the entire country. "Now is not the time for this region or
the nation to turn back," a Georgia paper said during the campaign. "The 'good
old days' were in truth grim and even desperate. Dixie was the nation's No. 1
economic problem. Lyndon B. Johnson is the kind of president who, though
loving his native South and feeling a close kinship with its people, will be the
leader of all Americans. In truth, isn't that the way it should be and must be?"
Johnson showed to particular advantage when compared to his rival. In the
summer of 1964 Hale Boggs wrote a friend: "Some time ago I listened to one of
our strong-minded friends who inveighed at some lengths against the Negroes
and others. I said to him, with Goldwater in the White House you might not
have to worry about that problem; as a matter of fact you probably won't have
to worry about anything. For the first time there is a real threat of a man who
would actually push the button." After Harry Byrd sent out word that there was
to be "no endorsement" of the Johnson ticket, Virginia insurgents handed the

Byrd machine the worst defeat it had ever suffered when the state Democratic convention voted to endorse LBJ. A Virginia congressman reasoned, "Nothing has happened to cause us to turn our backs on Lyndon B. Johnson."[67]

The raw totals indicating LBJ's electoral predominance in the South are deceptive, though, for they conceal evidence of dramatic slippage. Goldwater carried 507 southern counties, 233 of which had never voted for a Republican. Johnson's percentage in the South fell more than ten points short of what he received elsewhere in the country. Save for Texas, those southern states that gave the president a majority in 1964 did so barely. For the first time since Reconstruction, the South provided the smallest proportion of the vote for a Democratic presidential candidate. Johnson ran better in snowy Maine and Vermont than in any state of the former Confederacy.[68]

In at least four states where Goldwater won a majority of white votes, Johnson prevailed only because he received an estimated 96 percent of votes cast by southern blacks, who fully comprehended what the Goldwater movement represented. Balloting broke sharply on race and class lines. In a black working-class precinct in Richmond, Johnson triumphed 1770 to 6, but in a posh white precinct in the Virginia capital, Goldwater outpolled the president 1066–173. Even the embattled cadre of the Mississippi Freedom Democrats rallied to LBJ. "I took off the whole month of October of 1964 to travel this nation in support of Lyndon Johnson and Hubert Humphrey," recalled Aaron Henry. "Fannie Hamer campaigned for him." In Florida, where Johnson had only a 37,800-vote edge, 211,000 African Americans marked almost every one of their ballots for him. A Republican politician in North Carolina, stunned by a tally sheet from a black precinct showing Goldwater with no votes at all (to LBJ's more than 1300), cried, "Surely to God, at least one would have made a mistake!"[69]

Goldwater mobilized the southern white electorate at a phenomenal rate. In northern states, turnout in 1964 fell off slightly from 1960, but in Arkansas and Louisiana it increased 40 percent, in Georgia 55 percent, and in Mississippi a staggering 125 percent, as whites swarmed to the polls to repudiate Johnson. Goldwater captured a majority of the ballots cast by whites in every state of the former Confederacy except Texas. Jimmy Carter later reflected: "In 1964, Johnson . . . had to show the rest of the country that he wasn't just a Southern politician. . . . But . . . there was a deep wound inflicted on the Southern people, who were kind of like a scorned bride who had been loyal to her fiancé for twenty years or a hundred years, and then at the time of the wedding, you know, the bridegroom ran off with other females." In Mississippi, where Goldwater got something close to 95 percent of the white electorate, his appeal, in the words of one analyst, "supersaturated" white voters. In cities such as Birmingham, Mobile, and Shreveport, Goldwater won not only the middle and upper classes as Eisenhower and Nixon had done, but also blue-collar whites who had been the mainstays of the Democrats. The president drew only 29 percent of white ballots in the Deep South, and in Charleston, where Lady Bird Johnson had been sent to Coventry, Goldwater chalked up considerably over 80 percent in white precincts. Though most observers saw the Goldwater debacle as a total disaster for the Republicans, Richard Strout, who thought the Arizonan was "an amiable no-think, a man who shouldn't have been named by either political party," nonetheless sagely observed: "Senator Goldwater is going to leave his impress on America. His nomination and campaign in the South come at a moment of historic party fluidity and realignment. The GOP will never be the same again. What he is achieving is a lily-white southern Republican Party that isn't likely to be effaced easily."[70]

No one agreed more strongly with that judgment than Lyndon Johnson. Far from luxuriating in his landslide victory, he warned his aides sternly that within a few months much of his advantage would evaporate. Not even his success in putting through the landmark civil rights legislation earlier that year gave him comfort. Hours after Johnson signed the bill into law, Bill Moyers walked into the president's bedroom, expecting to find him jubilant. Instead, Johnson was steeped in gloom. As he lay in bed reading the first edition of the next morning's *Washington Post* recounting his great triumph, Johnson told Moyers, "I think we just delivered the South to the Republican party for a long time to come."[71]

ELEVEN

THE AGONY OF VICTORY

I

In his second term, Johnson chalked up further gains for civil rights, but his actions often earned him disdain, both from southern racists and from black nationalists. Only in retrospect were his attainments acknowledged. Each group, in contrasting ways, found fault with his sectional identity. "In Louisiana," Congressman Hebert has recalled, "he was absolutely hated because they considered him a turncoat. They considered Lyndon Johnson the most horrible man that ever lived." From the opposite end of the spectrum, he received no less abuse. "Lyndon B. Johnson," declared Malcolm X, "is the head of the Cracker Party." In spite of all that the president had achieved, noted Dick Goodwin, "he was still . . . the honkie intruder on black ground. What would it take, I thought, how many years of struggle and purgation before they could fully trust a white leader? Johnson sensed it too, must have sensed it—an awareness bred of the experience of a southern lifetime." One commentator, reflecting on LBJ's final lacerating year in office, has written of "Lyndon Johnson, the man chased out of the White House like a wounded bear fleeing hounds." A distinguished African-American novelist, though, reached a different judgment. "When all of the returns are in," Ralph Ellison concluded, "perhaps President Johnson will have to settle for being recognized as the greatest American President for the poor and the Negroes, but that, as I see it, is a very great honor indeed."[1]

II

Lyndon Johnson learned how far the white South had departed from him when in 1965, in a stirring address to Congress, he demanded legislation to enfranchise black citizens. "Johnson knew that to secure passage of the Voting Rights Act he had to raise the matter to the level of a national imperative," Carl Rowan has written. "And there was no better way to do that than to have a president from Jim Crow Texas go before a joint session of the Congress and exhort the nation to heed his cry for political justice." As "a man whose roots go deeply into Southern soil," Johnson said, "I know how agonizing racial feelings are. I know how difficult it is to reshape the attitudes and the structure of our society. But a century has passed, more than a hundred years, since the Negro was freed. And he is not fully free tonight."

Speaking as only someone who bridged different parts of the country could, he declared: "There is no Southern problem. There is no Northern problem. There is only an American problem." He took care not to offend southern sensibilities by saying: "Now let none of us in any sections look with prideful righteousness on the troubles in another section, or on the problems of our neighbors. There is really no part of America where the promise of equality has been fully kept. In Buffalo as well as in Birmingham, in Philadelphia as well as in Selma, Americans are struggling for the fruits of freedom."

Yet he left no doubt of his resolute determination. Drawing upon his experience as a young teacher of Mexican Americans in Cotulla, Texas, he told the joint session:

> My students were poor, and they often came to class without breakfast, hungry. They knew even in their youth the pain of prejudice. They never seemed to know why people disliked them. But they knew it was so, because I saw it in their eyes. I often walked home late in the afternoon, after the classes were finished, wishing there was more that I could do. . . .
>
> I never thought then, in 1928, that I would be standing here in 1965. It never occurred to me in my fondest dreams that I might have the chance to help the sons and daughters of those students and to help people like them all over the country.

Pointing his finger at the assembled members of Congress, he said, "But now I do have that chance—and I'll let you in on a secret—I mean to use it. And I hope that you will use it with me."

The most dramatic moment in his address came when, arms raised, he stunned the audience by declaring, "And we *shall* overcome." He thereby identified himself directly with the cause of African Americans by, in John Lewis's words, "citing our favorite freedom song, the anthem, the very heart and soul of the civil rights movement." Lewis, one of the president's sternest critics, has written: "I was deeply moved. Lyndon Johnson was no politician that night. He was a man who spoke from his heart. His were the words of a statesman and more; they were the words of a poet." Out of the corner of his eye, Dean Rusk said, he could see the Supreme Court justices, expected to be reserved, get so carried away by Johnson's words that they clapped.[2]

Observers, both at the time and subsequently, have recognized that this was a pivotal event in which "the big man from Texas with a Southern drawl gave the ultimate commitment of federal power and moral leadership to the Negro's cause." Johnson, "the first Southern president in a century," *Newsweek* emphasized, had "ranked the bloodied ground of Selma . . . with Lexington and Concord and Appomattox among the great landmarks of the American quest for freedom." The president's "official declaration that the government is an ally of the Negro struggle, even when that struggle assumes unconventional or extralegal forms," noted two civil rights activists approvingly, was the most radical pronouncement by a president since Jefferson's justification of the right of revolution. Elated by what was described as the "joyous pandemonium" in the Rotunda, Johnson instructed his aides to launch a no-holds-barred attack on poll taxes and literacy tests right away.[3]

As the president ruminated with the draftsman of the address, Richard Goodwin, about the day's events in a White House sitting room, the phone rang. "That was King," Johnson reported when he hung up. "He said it was ironic that after a century, a southern white president would help lead the way toward the salvation of the Negro." He paused, both gratified and affected by what he had just heard, then went on: "You know, Dick, I understand why he's surprised, why a lot of folks are surprised, but I'm going to do it. . . . Hell, we're just halfway up the mountain. Not even half." One of the Southern Christian Leadership Conference leaders has recalled: "When we heard LBJ give that famous speech, we were all sitting around together. Martin was sitting in a chair looking toward the TV set, and when LBJ said, 'And we shall overcome,' we all cheered. I looked over toward Martin and Martin was very quietly sitting in the chair, and a tear ran down his cheek. It was a victory like none other, it was an affirmation of the movement, it guaranteed us . . . that millions of people in the South would have a chance to be involved in their own destiny."[4]

The president's words, though, infuriated southern senators. At breakfast the following morning, Spessard Holland of Florida asked angrily, "Did you hear ol' Lyndon say 'We Shall Overcome'?" Strom Thurmond replied that "the president betrayed the southern cause," and the moderate Lister Hill, turning to Richard Russell, asked, "Dick, tell me something. You trained that boy. . . . What happened to that boy?" The Georgia senator, who had hoped that Johnson would change in his second term, responded, "I just don't know, Lister. . . . He's a turncoat if there ever was one." These exchanges were overheard by the black headwaiter in the Senate Dining Room, who later wrote: "To me, the week after Johnson's voting rights speech was the darkest I had ever seen in Washington. I could feel the hurt, anger, and hatred of the southern bloc in every corner of the Senate Dining Room. It was hatred born of humiliation. Lyndon Johnson of Texas had challenged and insulted the sovereignty of the southern states." Herman Talmadge subsequently grumbled: "It's splendid now, you know, they're demanding that churches pay reparations and Black Panthers are making a business of trying to assassinate policemen. . . . It's all part of the same pattern. . . . The President was encouraging it and addressed a joint session of Congress and shouted, 'We shall overcome.' When they hear the President shout, 'We shall overcome,' they think they can take over the town square with impunity if they want to." Years later, when Robert Caro asked him how he felt when Johnson said, "We shall overcome," Talmadge twice answered, "Sick."[5]

Johnson's address antagonized a broad spectrum of southern politicians and publicists who were offended both by the "And we *shall* overcome" remark and by the thought of federal registrars snooping about their states. "If the President's law is passed," said one right-wing organization, "the South will disappear from the civilized world." It was hardly surprising that one of those who heard that speech, Senator Thurmond, reported, "I did not clap one time, even though Lady Bird was looking right at me." Thurmond deeply resented the legislation, which he viewed as targeted at Goldwater states in the South. "Deep down in his heart," his lieutenant reported, Thurmond "felt Lyndon Johnson was getting even." Not long after, Thurmond was to denounce the president as "a traitor to the nation as well as to the South." More unexpected was the vehement reaction of Virginius Dabney. Regarded as one of the more liberal southern editors, Dabney sent "fervent congratulations" to Senator Byrd on his statement denouncing the voting rights bill "in which you practically blew LBJ out of the water, and left him hanging in the top of the tree."[6]

LBJ's voting rights message came in the context of a confrontation with Alabama's governor in the Oval Office where the president made clear that he was not going to back down:

JOHNSON: George, you see all those demonstrators there in front of the White House?

WALLACE: Yes, Mr. President, I saw them.

JOHNSON: Those goddam niggers have kept my daughters awake every night with their screaming and hollering. . . . Wouldn't it be just wonderful if we could put an end to all those demonstrations?

WALLACE: Oh, yes, Mr. President, that would be wonderful.

JOHNSON: Then why don't you let the niggers vote? . . .

WALLACE: I don't have that power, Mr. President. Under Alabama law, that belongs to the county registrars.

JOHNSON: George, don't you shit me. Who runs Alabama? . . . I had on the TV this morning and I saw you and . . . you was attacking me, George.

WALLACE: Not you, Mr. President. I was speaking against federal intervention.

JOHNSON: You was attacking me, George. . . . George, you and I shouldn't be thinking about 1968. We should be thinking about 1988. We'll both be dead and gone then. What do you want left behind? You want a great, big marble monument that says, "George Wallace: He Built"? Or do you want a little piece of scrawny pine laying there that says, "George Wallace: He Hated"?

Johnson then herded Wallace into an "ambush" in the Rose Garden where, with the Alabama governor his captive, the president declared: "What happened in Selma was an American tragedy. . . . It is wrong to do violence to peaceful citizens in the streets of their town. It is wrong to deny Americans the right to vote. It is wrong to deny any person full equality because of the color of his skin." Hence, he was sending a bill up to the Hill that would put an end to this discrimination. When, some time later, Johnson signed the Voting Rights Act into law, he did so at a desk in the Capitol said to have been the one used by Lincoln to emancipate slaves drafted into the Confederate army.[7]

For many black leaders, Johnson's behavior demonstrated once again that this white southerner could be counted on. After enactment of the bill in 1965, Roy Wilkins, who later called LBJ's address "the goddamnedest commitment to the civil-rights cause I had ever heard," put his arm around Jack Valenti, and said (or at least this is what Valenti says he said), "You know, Jack, God does move in strange and wondrous ways. It is a fact and a truth that the bravest, most compassionate, and most effective friend the Negro in America has ever had is a southern president." Years later, Louis Martin, an African American who had been editor of the *Chicago Defender* and then a prominent national Democratic Party official, reflected: "Now my feeling about Johnson, and this is what I used to tell many Negroes in the newspaper business and others—is that since Johnson was a southerner, he would normally, being a good politician, lean over backwards to prove that he was not a racist. Further, there's something in the folklore of Negro life that a reconstructed southerner is really far more liberal than a liberal Yankee."[8]

III

Yet despite all of the evidence that Johnson had become a man with strong national priorities, he could never altogether overcome his reputation as a sectionalist. At New York parties, he was "a cracker liar," and a Herblock cartoon depicted Johnson, bullwhip in hand, striding past craven White House aides, with the caption, "Happy Days on the Old Plantation." In 1965, at a time of national outrage at violence against civil rights protesters in the South, demonstrators outside the White House carried placards reading "LBJ, open your eyes, see the sickness of the South, see the horrors of your homeland." In his memoir, Johnson comments: "Once again my Southern heritage was thrown in my face. I was hurt, deeply hurt." When the three civil rights activists were reported missing in Mississippi, and at the time of the Selma demonstrations, pickets near the White House toted signs saying, "LBJ, just you wait . . . see what happens in '68," and demonstrators in front of the U.S. Court House in Manhattan's Foley Square hoisted placards reading, "L.B.J. Must Go—to Mississippi." Subsequently, Johnson's many achievements notwithstanding, critics dwelt upon "the bruised and gloomy low of 1968, when he . . . shelved the report of his own riot commission without so much as a word of praise." In fact, Johnson, though exasperated at the Kerner Commission's refusal to explain where the money was supposed to come from for its proposed multibillion-dollar program for black ghettos, called its report "very thorough," "very comprehensive," with "many good recommendations." John Hersey, however, wrote of LBJ's response: "The spectacle of this man running for cover from the conclusions of the Commission which he created . . . was not only disgusting; it was positively inflammatory. . . . The Texan seemed to want to deny the charge of white racism."[9]

Some black leaders, too, continued to believe that he bore the stigma of his origins. H. Rap Brown called Johnson a "white honky cracker, an outlaw from Texas," and a correspondent alluded to "the scorn heaped on Mr. Johnson from time to time by some Negro speakers for his Southern background and accent." James Farmer later observed, "My impression of Johnson was that with all of the goodwill that he had . . . he did not have an in-depth understanding of the mood of black America. . . . Part of it is that . . . coming from the South as he did, there was still an element of paternalism which he had not been able to get over." Not even the president's voting rights message in which he cited "We Shall Overcome" impressed Jim Forman. "Johnson," he said, "spoiled a good song that day." Johnson especially resented the attacks on his foreign policy by Martin Luther King: "Calling me a murderer—me, the Texas motherfucker who went against every goddam white adviser I ever had to stand up and say black people in America must be equal."[10]

Though his critics were unfair, they had a point, for Johnson never did fully free himself of prejudice. At the beginning of 1964, he informed a Texan, "I'm gonna try to teach these nigras that don't know anything how to work for themselves instead of just breedin,'" and at the same moment that he was driving the civil rights bill through Congress, he was haranguing his deputy budget director: "Bob Byrd's just raising hell about us putting in this money . . . in the D.C. budget for all these illegitimate kids. I told you to take that out. . . . They want to just stay up there and breed and won't work and we have to feed them. . . . I don't want to be taking any taxpayers' money and paying it to people just to breed." Roger Wilkins has asserted that, as troops were being readied to intervene in the 1967 Detroit riots, Johnson stated, "I don't want it said that one of my soldiers shot a pregnant ni——," then "looked at me and his face went red and then he finished his sentence without finishing that word." Even in his final years, he was capable of speaking of "the Negroes in Reconstruction who got elected to Congress and then ran into the chamber with bare feet and white women."[11]

Too often, critics have been tendentious in their accounts of the dispute over seating the MFDP delegation in 1964, but as a Wisconsin congressman observed, Johnson's comportment during the episode "was not one of the high moments in his record as a civil rights president." Too few historians bear in mind the reality of the situation. Aaron Henry later conceded: "As for the president, he knew that the MFDP could not muster enough votes to carry Mississippi, and, if we were seated, it could not gain him any states. It could only anger other southern states and harm his chances of taking them." Much of the commentary is manifestly unfair. Though John Lewis acknowledges that Martin Luther King, Andrew Young, and Bayard Rustin all favored accepting the compromise on MFDP, he has written nonetheless that, as a consequence of his action, Johnson "lost the faith of the people." He has even maintained that "the spirit of cynicism and suspicion and mistrust" that subsequently infected the attitude of citizens toward their government began with LBJ's actions in Atlantic City, an allegation difficult to sustain. Scholars who present the settlement as a blatant sellout to southern whites do not take note that a Virginia congressman denounced it as "an obvious surrender to the Far Left." Never again would white supremacists have their way at Democratic national conventions as they had in the past; compromise opened the path for a marked increase in black representation beginning at the very next convention. Yet it is also true that Johnson imposed an arrangement that was nakedly paternalistic and that he turned a hard heart to the searing outcry of Fannie Lee Hamer. Indeed, he saw "no justification for messin' with the Freedom Party at all" and viewed the MFDP delegation as nine or ten "emotionally unstable" radical "Nigras."[12]

These deplorable lapses should not obscure how steadfast Johnson was in fighting southern racists or how much empathy he felt toward the plight of impoverished blacks. Not content simply with nominating an African American, Carl Rowan, to head the U.S. Information Agency, Johnson phoned the racist Arkansas senator John McClellan to make sure that, as chairman of the Government Operations Committee, he would not strike back by slashing Rowan's budget. "I didn't want you to . . . [leave] him one day without his peter," the president explained. After the 1964 civil rights bill was enacted, he phoned Mississippi Senator James Eastland to say: "Now we got to appoint a conciliator under this law, Jim. I've got to have some Southerner that knows something about the South and that the Negroes will have confidence in and won't say that I've fixed 'em. If you've got any ideas, anybody that's worth a damn, I wish you'd let me know. . . . One of 'em suggested I get Le Roy Collins." The former Florida governor, Eastland responded, was "a damned cheap double-crosser, . . . a goddamned, lying son of a bitch." Johnson went ahead to name the liberal Collins. Though the MFDP exasperated Johnson, he expressed sympathy for the movement even when warned by a southern moderate that there would be "a wholesale walkout from the South" if any of its members were seated. The president retorted hotly that blacks ought to be in the Mississippi delegation.

"Pistols kept 'em out," he said. "These goddamn fellas down there . . . have got to quit that. And they got to let 'em vote, and let 'em shave, and let 'em eat, and things like that. And they don't do it."[13]

In 1965 Johnson stepped up the pace. He instructed Attorney General Katzenbach, "I want you to write the goddamnedest toughest voting rights act that you can devise." Two months after delivering his voting rights address, Johnson told Dick Goodwin: "Now, voting rights are important. But it's only the tail on the pig, when we ought to be going for the whole hog. During the depression I ran an NYA project in Texas. All the boys, white and Negroes, were poor. But the poor Negroes were kept separate over in Prairie View, and always got the short end. They didn't even have a decent place to sleep. Now, the whole country's like one big Prairie View. Not everywhere, but most places. The problem's not just civil rights. Hell, what good are rights if you don't have a decent home or someone to take care of you when you're sick? Now we've got to find a way to let Negroes get what most white folks already have. At least the chance to get it."[14]

Instead of resting on his laurels as the leader chiefly responsible for the only civil rights legislation in the twentieth century, Johnson, at a Howard University commencement in June 1965, dismissed these laws as merely, borrowing a phrase from Winston Churchill, "the end of the beginning" and heralded the "next and the more profound stage of the battle for civil rights" to "move beyond opportunity to achievement." The gap between black and white incomes and the reality that "Negroes are trapped . . . in inherited, gateless poverty" he characterized as "this American failure." For his part, he aimed to "shatter forever not only the barriers of law and public practice but the walls which bound the condition of many by the color of his skin." Before the Howard speech, most presidential actions had been responses to initiatives of the civil rights movement—from A. Philip Randolph's threatened March on Washington to the Selma demonstration—but Johnson, in this address, managed to "leap frog the movement." The president, Roy Wilkins felt, "was not only with us but ahead of us." The NAACP executive director, "astonished" by Johnson's "fervor and by his daring," said that the Howard address provided "the textbook for civil rights activity for the next ten or fifteen years." At Howard, Ralph Ellison declared, Johnson "spelled out the meaning of full integration for Negroes in a way that no one, no president, not Lincoln nor Roosevelt, no matter how much we love[d] and respected them, has ever done before. There was no hedging in it, no escape clauses."[15]

The Watts riots irked and depressed him, but did not deter him from pushing ahead on civil rights. "Negroes will end up pissing in the aisles of the Senate" as they had during Reconstruction, he fumed. That nasty remark represented not a rejection of the black cause but an expression of dismay that rioters were hurting themselves by buttressing the racists and making it all the harder for him to do anything effective. He still wanted the American people to understand what the residents of Watts were up against: "out of work . . . living in filth . . . homes torn up." While Watts was still smoking, he told his aides to put together a parcel of federal programs for the area, even though he feared that doing so would be interpreted as rewarding violence. The federal government delivered more than one hundred tons of food to the curfew zone and increased War on Poverty funds for poor families in the city sixfold. That same month, he ordered a strict watch kept on how rapidly school districts were desegregating. He was especially tough on Texas.[16]

When the co-chairmen of a White House conference, "To Fulfill These Rights," scheduled for June 1966, asked him what kind of session he wanted, the president replied: "In the hill country in the spring, the sun comes up earlier, and the ground gets warmer, and you can see the steam rising and the sap dripping. And in his pen, you can see my prize bull. He's the biggest, best-hung bull in the hill country. In the spring he gets a hankering for those cows, and he starts pawing the ground and getting restless. So I open the pen and he goes down the hill, looking for a cow, with his pecker hanging hard and swinging. Those cows get so Goddamn excited, they get more and more moist to receive him, and their asses just start quivering and they start quivering all over, every one of them is quivering, as that bull struts into their pasture." As his distinguished visitors gaped at him in stunned silence, Johnson smacked his hands together noisily, then continued, "Well, I want a *quivering* conference. That's the kind of conference I want. I want every damn delegate quivering with excitement and anticipation about the future of civil rights."[17]

Well aware that his policies were increasingly unpopular, Johnson continued to push for civil rights legislation. Constrained by the mounting deficits occasioned by the Vietnam War, and with support for aid to blacks eroded by ghetto violence, he did tone down his emphasis on racial issues in his second term. But in 1966, for the third consecutive year, Johnson prodded Congress to enact a civil rights law, this time a highly controversial proposal to ban discrimination in housing, a measure that, in keeping with his emphasis on nation above section, would affect the North as well as the South. He persisted in this course even when letters to Congress were running 100–1 against it. HEW Secretary Joseph Califano has written that the bill "prompted some of the most vicious mail LBJ received on any subject (and the only death threats I ever received as a White House assistant)." Three-quarters of whites polled in 1966 said that blacks were getting ahead too quickly, and British investigators discovered "in district after district, and city after city, . . . an undercurrent of resentment concerning civil order and gains made by the Negro population." Yet in 1967, the *New York Times* reported: "There is no thought that the Administration would compromise its strong civil rights stance in trying to appeal to the southern Governors. President Johnson has prohibited any attempt to talk one way in the North and another in the South." The fair housing measure also forbade discrimination in jury selection and penalized civil-rights-related crimes, and he matched this omnibus bill with a Model Cities program to eliminate urban blight. When his advisors cautioned him that the "housing proposal will be impossible to enact," Johnson demanded that backing be mobilized "for all of the package and not just for parts of it." And in 1968, in the most unpropitious circumstances, he managed to drive through the fair housing law. That same year, he issued an order requiring federal contractors to recruit minority workers. "He was relentless," Califano remembered. "I mean there was no give."[18]

Johnson, though, had to absorb ongoing pitiless criticism from black leaders and organizations who distrusted this southerner. Some members of SNCC even blamed him for the assassination of Malcolm X. Andrew Young, well aware that the Voting Rights Act of 1965 had doubled black registration in Alabama in just one year and had led to thousands of African-American officeholders, nonetheless accused Johnson of having gotten the law through by promising enforcement would be weak. In 1966 Stokely Carmichael called the fair housing bill "a sham," and Martin Luther King's organization, the Southern Christian Leadership Conference, accusing Johnson of having "retreated before the bigot's onslaught," declared, "The bitter, rancid taste left by this sordid performance in the year 1966 will not leave us." Fannie Lou Hamer wired Johnson to take the troops out of Vietnam "where they have no business anyhow, and bring them to Mississippi and Louisiana because if this is a Great Society, I'd hate to see a bad one," and James Forman reviled "Lyndon Bloodbath Johnson," who "sent napalm to burn our sisters and brothers in Vietnam." In 1967 Rap Brown, denouncing "America's Gestapo tactics to . . . commit genocide against black people," declared, "We blame Lyndon Johnson." In his 1968 book, *Look Out, Whitey! Black Power's Gon' Get Your Mama!* Julius Lester, jeering at "President Lyndon Cracker Baines Johnson," wrote: "Johnson's civil rights speeches were the best the black community had ever heard from an American President. But blacks weren't fooled. Typing paper is cheap, and so are speech writers. . . . They know what White Power is and that LBJ is simply its spokesman."[19]

IV

Not only black militants harbored suspicion of LBJ's background. Throughout his tenure, the Texan in the Oval Office encountered leeriness and disfavor from men and women who might have been expected to be friendly allies in a common cause. The chasm between Johnson City and the Northeast even contributed to his venomous feud with Bobby Kennedy. "No affection contaminated the relationship between the Vice President and the Attorney General," Arthur Schlesinger has written. "Johnson was seventeen years older, six inches taller, expansive in manner, coarse in language, emotions near the surface. It was southwestern exaggeration against Yankee understatement; frontier tall tales, marvelously but lengthily told, against laconic irony."[20]

Within a short time after Johnson became president in his own right, observers were sneering at a novel phenomenon: "The Texanization of Washington." Thousands from the Lone Star State massed for his inauguration in 1965, one woman with an electric hair ornament that lit up to spell T-E-X-A-S. A thoughtful Boston-bred Washington hostess had nine hundred tamales flown up from Austin to go along with her vintage champagne and paté. Kennedy clan *haute cuisine* gave way to barbecued ribs and pickled black-eyed peas; Kennedy's chief of protocol, Angier Biddle Duke (St. Paul's, Yale), to a Texas longhorn. Boutiques featured southwestern duds, and square dancing became de rigueur, though LBJ preferred moving a curvaceous young woman across the floor to the swift rhythm of a fox trot. Even when, in later years, Johnson advanced important initiatives, they were put in this provincial context. In accounting for the grandiose character of the report on the Negro family, Pat Moynihan explained that he wanted to catch the attention of those wielding power and "this was, after all, an administration of Texans who could hardly help exaggerating the importance of the dismantling of the segregationist social structure that had been the shame and the burden of the South for so long." Often, the comments were a great deal more patronizing. One journalist commented: "Washington has survived worse. The British burned down the White House in 1814, the Whiskey Ring looted the Treasury in the 1870's, and the Ohio Gang tapped the nation's oil reserves in the 1920's. But the most the Texans have done is slop chili con queso on the State Dining Room rug."[21]

Johnson had been in the White House only a month when he emphasized the imperative need to do away with this "country-hick, tobacco-chewing Southerner" impression of him, but to no avail. When the president addressed Southern Baptists in the Rose Garden, the *New York Herald Tribune,* the favorite paper of the Manhattan social set, began a caption of a photograph of the event, "In a Southern setting, Texas-born Lyndon B. Johnson . . ." and went on to state, "Any Southern politician worth the salt to go on his 'pone soon learns to deal adroitly with Baptist preachers." A writer, reporting on the Johnson presidency, noted: "Washingtonians are bored by his taste for telling long 'Ah-recall-mah-cousin-Aliza-once' type of stories. . . . When the First Lady serves raspberry icebox pie or Texas bean soup, they make clever jokes about her. . . . Ol' Lyndon . . . was the most powerful man in the world, but to Washington he still seemed very provincial." Similarly, Randy Roberts and James Olson have written: "Raised in a region where the frontier was still visible and its values still paramount, Johnson looked almost as if he had just walked barefoot out of the hill country and put on his first suit and tie. The handlebar ears, the baboon-like nose, the slicked-back, Brylcreemed hair, and the Texas twang contrasted too sharply with . . . Jack's perfectly coiffed, air-dried hair, and with Jackie's impeccable style. While Kennedy would not have been caught dead shredding a lobster in front of photographers, Johnson wore barbecue sauce on his lips as a badge of honor."[22]

Rejection came as no surprise to Johnson. He once mused to reporters, according to a paraphrase by *Washington Post* writers: "The Kennedy crowd and the intellectuals and the fancypants were never going to accept him as President of the United States. . . . They would cut him to pieces because of his speech, his mannerisms, his Southern origins. . . . He knew . . . his backwoods accent would gain him the nickname 'Cornpone' in the smart Georgetown salons." He asked a White House correspondent: "What about that Georgetown crowd? How come when I say it, it comes out 'Horse Shit,' but when they say it, it comes out 'Chanel Number Five'?" On hearing a rumor that Stokely Carmichael was mobilizing black militants to march on Georgetown, Johnson cried, "Goddamn! I've waited thirty-five years for this day!"[23]

Johnson likened his situation to that of a member of a downtrodden minority. "No colored man in Jackson, Mississippi, ever took as much abuse as a President of the United States who comes from the South," he told two of his intimates in the spring of 1964. That same season, he complained to his press secretary that publications such as the *New York Times*, the *Washington Post*, and *Newsweek* revealed "some of the same attitude toward a Southerner that Mississippi shows toward Harlem." Alluding to the well-known cartoonist of the *Washington Star*, he said: "It's kinda like Berryman's cartoons. They always put a string bow tie on me because of where I was born. I never wore one in my life." "Bigotry is born in some of *The New York Times* people," he complained. "I told Scotty Reston at a meeting two months after my election that it wouldn't be long before my geography and parentage catches up with me in the minds of these people." When not many hours before he was to deliver his acceptance address at the 1964 convention he informed George Reedy in the course of a midnight stroll on the South Lawn of the White House that he was planning to announce his withdrawal, he explained that he was doing so in part because, in Reedy's words, "liberals thought he was just a tobacco-chewing Southerner."[24]

Early in 1963, in the midst of an address in Detroit advocating racial equality, Johnson suddenly broke away to say: "In speaking today as I do, I am personally aware that I speak as a grandson of Confederates to grandsons and great-grandsons of Union soldiers. I am aware, as an heir to Appomattox, that the barriers of bias and prejudice within our society are not all barriers of race and color—or of religion and creed. In our land, as in many lands, men know discrimination for the geography of their birth as well as the genetics of their birth."[25]

Johnson encountered a particular kind of sectional difficulty in his conduct of foreign affairs. "Foreign policy was a constant irritant he could neither ignore nor relieve," Robert Dallek has observed. "It agitated his feelings of inadequacy or long-standing concern that he was not the powerful, competent, can-do person he wanted everyone to see him as but a Texas hick." To those in European chancelleries, Johnson seemed "a caricature out of an American western," one writer noted. "He was . . . Western rather than Eastern, and the world had long since grown accustomed to dealing in the international arena with Americans who were either Easterners or acted like them—with Harrimans and Roosevelts and Stevensons and Kennedys." More particularly, he appeared to be a Texan who conflated twentieth-century challenges with those on the nineteenth-century southwestern frontier. "Even more than the rest of the South, Texas has been the buckle on the U.S. Gun Belt," Kevin Phillips has written. "Texans . . . have had an extra hawkish chromosome or two." Johnson liked to ask callers what the difference was between a sheriff and a Texas Ranger. The answer: "Well, the Ranger is one that when you plug him, . . . he just keeps coming. And we must let the rest of the world know that . . . if they ever hit us it is not going to stop us—we are just going to keep coming."[26]

Early in his tenure he concluded that because of his upbringing he had the best hope for success in Latin America, where his Texas background gave him an advantage over Kennedy whose Alliance for Progress had been faltering. When a rebellious colonel led an insurrection in the Dominican Republic, the president instructed McGeorge Bundy: "Tell that son of a bitch that unlike the young man who came before me I am not afraid to use what's on my hip." Johnson confided to journalists: "I grew up with Mexicans. They'll come right into your yard and take it over if you let them. And the next day they'll be right up on your porch, barefoot and weighing one hundred and thirty pounds and they'll take that too. But if you say to 'em right at the start, 'Hold on, just wait a minute,' they'll know they're dealing with somebody who'll stand up. And after that you can get along fine." Bundy believed that LBJ's "problem in foreign affairs at the beginning was . . . 'I'm going to show these guys I'm not a Texas provincial. I'm a world statesman. I can talk to De Gaulle.'" Texas, in the words of Alistair Cooke, was LBJ's "horoscope for the world outside."[27]

Recollections of the Alamo legendry proved especially compelling. "In the scene that is central to the Alamo story," Ronnie Dugger has written, "the commander drew a line in the dust with his sword and told all the men who would stay and fight to the death with him to step across the line. The one who did not, the arch-coward of Texas history, skulked away one night before the massacre and survived in immortal disgrace, an object lesson for generations of Texas school children, including Lyndon B. Johnson." For the legatee of that legend, "the Alamo became Khe Sanh." Hence, savage irony, said another commentary, "In the very birthing moment of his state was planted the seed that would bring ruin to the presidency of Lyndon Johnson."[28]

Time-Life's White House correspondent, who had ample opportunity to observe the president, reached the same conclusion. In 1968 Hugh Sidey wrote: "The names on that famous casualty list have long been part of Johnson's vocabulary—Travis, Davy Crockett, Jim Bowie, James Bonham. He brings them up when he talks of heroes he has decorated or men under fire at the DMZ. When the Marines dug in on the hilltop at Khe Sanh, Johnson remarked one night aboard the jet, 'It's another Alamo.'" A year later, Sidey recalled that Johnson had said "he wasn't going to put his tail between his legs, insisting that he had gone into South Vietnam because, as at the Alamo, somebody had to get behind the log with those threatened people."[29]

In their study of the legendry of the Alamo, Randy Roberts and James Olson have written:

> On several occasions—sometimes with just a person or two in a room with him, other times before White House dinner guests—Johnson would without warning begin to recite a poem his mother had taught him when he was a child. With a low, solemn rumble he would intone:
>
> . . .
>
> And thirty lay sick, and so were shot through;
> For the siege had been bitter, and bloody, and long;
> "Surrender, or die!"—"Men, what will you do?"
> And Travis, great Travis, drew sword, quick and strong,
> Drew a line at his feet . . . "Will you come? Will you go?
> I die with my wounded, in the Alamo!"

"For Johnson," they conclude, "the soldiers in Vietnam were descendants of the Alamo, and, he, at least in spirit, was William Barret Travis." They add: "Eventually, as a politician, Johnson died on the walls of Vietnam."[30]

It would be reductionist to say that the legend of the Alamo compelled Johnson to expand the war in Vietnam. Despite his memory of his great-great-uncle who had bravely followed old Ben Milam at Béxar, he had opposed intervention in 1954. When other Western powers rejected a plea to bail out the French besieged at Dien Bien Phu, Johnson had cautioned against America's assuming lone responsibility by sending troops to Southeast Asia. He asked, "Would you tell us who will go in with old Ben Milam?" Yet the Alamo mythology remained important to him, and in the 1960s it was in his memory bank to prod him.[31]

Again and again, Johnson analogized the Vietnam challenge to the problem Mexico posed for the early Texas settlers. Sixty years after his father sponsored the Alamo Mission bill, Johnson told the National Security Council: "Hell, Vietnam is just like the Alamo. Hell, it's just like . . . you were surrounded, and you damn well needed somebody. Well, by God, I'm going to go—and I thank the Lord that I've got men who want to go with me, from McNamara right on down to the littlest private who's carrying a gun." When the North Vietnamese refused to respond to his bids for negotiation, Johnson said sourly, "They've given the same answer from the start. It is just like the answer that Travis gave at the Alamo when they asked if he would surrender. A cannon shot."[32]

Though a liberal critic of his Vietnam actions complained, "He's got this Texas policy of shoot first and ask questions afterward," Johnson saw himself not as an ill-tempered gunslinger but as a man caught in an Establishment trap who was being unfairly persecuted. Two days after becoming president, Johnson, having committed himself to vigorous prosecution of the Vietnam War, confided to his East Texas aide, Bill Moyers, "Right now I feel like one of those catfish down in your and Lady Bird's country—down there around the old Taylor store. . . . I feel like I just grabbed a big juicy worm with a right sharp hook in the middle of it." But in another rant he said, "If I don't go in now and they show later I should have gone, then they'll be all over me in Congress. They won't be talking about my civil rights bill, or education or beautification. No sir, they'll push Vietnam up my ass every time. Vietnam. Vietnam. Right up my ass." David Halberstam has written: "He was haunted by regional prejudice, and even the attainment of the Presidency did not temper his feelings. Later, after he had left office, he became convinced that it was his Southern origins, not the war, which had driven him out, that *they* had lain in wait for an issue, any issue, and had used the war, which was their war in the first place, to drive him from office." Early in 1968, when Eugene McCarthy was challenging Johnson for the Democratic nomination, the nationally syndicated columnist Jack Germond learned that disapproval of U.S. actions in Vietnam did not account for why so many "didn't like LBJ" in New Hampshire. "Talking to voters in Portsmouth one day," he writes, "I found several who were suspicious of the president simply because he was a Texan with a pronounced southwestern accent."[33]

V

In 1968 dissatisfaction with LBJ's feckless policies in Vietnam expelled him from office, but it was the backlash in the South against his racial program that imperiled his party's hold on the White House. "I am quite frank to say," declared John Bell Williams, "that the President has made statements which . . . can be taken as nothing less than an invitation to the Negroes to engage in insurrection." When Johnson named Thurgood Marshall to the U.S. Supreme Court, the first time an African American had ever been chosen, a man wired him: "You despicable bum. How do you have the guts to do it coming out of Texas?" In the spring of 1965, to express his rancor at federal action in Selma,

Lester Maddox picketed the U.S. courthouse in Atlanta with a sign reading, "Treason is the Reason! DOWN with Johnson, the Justice Department, Socialism and Communism—UP with Wallace, Free Enterprise, Capitalism, Liberty, Private Rights and America." By 1966, the chairman of the South Carolina Young Democrats has said, "Among normal, middle-class white people, it was about as popular to be a Democrat as it was to have bubonic plague. Lyndon Johnson was Satan incarnate. . . . In the common vernacular, he was 'doing all these things for the niggers.'"[34]

Johnson's persistence on racial issues reaped a bitter harvest in Lady Bird's East Texas. A Tyler man wrote his congressman: "If Johnson was running for president now, he wouldn't carry Texas. It's not the Viet Nam war people are mad about, but the socialistic and civil rights program he is jamming down our throats." That same year, a Sherman woman, fuming over LBJ's fair housing legislation, declared: "Believe me if Mr. Johnson thinks that this kind of thing will get him the Negro vote . . . it will lose him more white votes than he will ever be able to get from the Negroes. . . . I just can't believe that their constituents want some of the laws that have been ramroded through by Mr. Johnson."[35]

North Carolina prided itself on its progressive views on race, but Tar Heels, too, vilified him. In 1966 the head of a corporation in that state wrote his congressman: "I have never heard any man so badly hated . . . here in Statesville as President Johnson is. . . . They consider him a traitor to his Southland and the worst and most dangerous man who has been President during our lifetime." A North Carolina woman urged that same congressman: "please don't put a negro in no office for they are to[o] much like a animal. . . . If we had a president we might do something. He goes all out for the Black Race so I Consider him Black to[o]. that is a Lot to Say but I said an Mean it to[o]. I Cant Say anything Bad Enough about him."[36]

In the 1968 election, Johnson paid the price for his advocacy of civil rights when the Democratic presidential candidate Hubert Humphrey lost every southern state save LBJ's Texas and carried that only because of an increased turnout by blacks and Mexican Americans. Georgia, which had given 92 percent of its ballots to FDR in 1932, went only 27 percent Democratic in 1968. John Egerton has written: "At a time of such crucial importance in its history, when it seemed so close to escaping from 350 years of imprisonment in the master-slave mentality—whites over blacks, North over South, rich over poor—the replacement of Lyndon Johnson with Richard Nixon was a devastating blow."[37]

As his days in the White House were running out, though, Johnson may have divined that History—or at least a good number of historians—would hold a quite different view of his effect on the South. "Whatever his shortcomings, and they were many," Steven Lawson has written, "LBJ was the last president to offer committed leadership that challenged racial injustice. . . . The transformative power of the black freedom struggle converted him from a routine defender of African Americans into the most rigorous advocate of racial equality ever to occupy the office." Thanks to this "Improbable Emancipator," Lawson said, "most of the uncompleted civil rights items on the legislative agenda he had inherited upon taking office in 1963 were enacted by the time he retired to his Texas ranch in 1969." In the course of doing this, he "had started a quiet political upheaval in the South." Similarly, Carl Degler observed: "The two most significant and effective figures moving white Americans to resolve the American dilemma have been southerners. . . . These two southerners, of course, were Martin Luther King Jr., and Lyndon Baines Johnson. Without them, the history of the United States in the last half of the twentieth century would have been much different."[38]

For Johnson, as Bill Moyers has pointed out, civil rights also "offered a reprieve from the past"—an opportunity both to make up for early wrongs he had committed and to liberate himself from the burden of history. At one press conference, a newspaperman asked Johnson how he could explain an enthusiasm for civil rights that had not been evident earlier. The president bristled, then calmed down, and, Moyers writes, "said in effect: 'Most of us don't have a second chance to correct the mistakes of our youth. I do and I am.' That evening, sitting in the White House, discussing the question with friends and staff, he looked around the room, gestured broadly about the mansion where he was living, and said, 'Eisenhower used to tell me that this place was a prison. I never felt freer.'"[39]

Little more than a month before he died, Johnson, a melancholy figure who popped a nitroglycerin pill into his mouth as he shambled up onto the stage, told a civil rights gathering: "The progress has been much too small; we haven't done nearly enough. I am sort of ashamed of myself, that I had six years and couldn't do more than I did. . . . So let no one delude themselves that our work is done. By unconcern, by neglect, by complacent beliefs that our labors in the fields of human rights are completed, we of today can seed our future with storms that would rage over the lives of our children and our children's children. . . . To be black in a white society is not to stand on level and equal ground.

While the races may stand side by side, whites stand on history's mountain and blacks stand in history's hollow." Later he added, "While I can't provide much go-go at this period of my life, I can provide a lot of hope and dream and encouragement and I'll sell a few wormy cows now and then and contribute."[40]

Many, probably most, African Americans, however, thought that Johnson, far from being ashamed, should be proud. Asked to respond to the statement that Johnson had been an excellent president, two-thirds of white voters in Alabama said no, three-quarters of blacks said yes. In the spring of 1966 a black reporter for a New York paper came upon a seventy-seven-year-old African American at a polling place in Alabama who was voting for the first time in his life. "It's good," he cried. "So good. God, it's good." What had made this extraordinary change possible, he was asked. Emphatically, the man replied: "You ever hear of Mr. L.B.J. Johnson? That man's something else again. To my way, he sure is."[41]

When the time came to assess Johnson's presidency, numbers of black leaders diverged conspicuously from liberals and radicals—white and black—who were focused on the devastation wrought by the Vietnam conflict. "I couldn't understand all those kids mad at LBJ," remarked Charles Evers, brother of the martyred Medgar. "Domestically, he was the best president we ever had. So what if he had that war? All presidents have had wars." In his autobiography, Evers added: "Johnson is a favorite of mine. . . . I'm not going to let Johnson's domestic programs be overshadowed by his stand on Vietnam. . . . Black folks should be the last to knock Johnson. That goes for Stokely Carmichael and H. Rap Brown. It was Lyndon Johnson who put the Civil Rights bill through, who made it possible for us to eat in the hotels and motels and to get a drink of water out of any fountain."[42]

At a farewell party Johnson's black appointees gave him, Thurgood Marshall told the outgoing president, "You didn't wait for the times, you made them." Robert Weaver, appointed by Johnson to be secretary of HUD, the first black cabinet member in the history of the country, declared, "I don't know when he got religion or how he got it, but he really understood what was bugging poor people and black people." At Johnson's final public appearance, Julian Bond, who had been denied his seat in the Georgia legislature for opposing the Vietnam War pursued by Johnson, might have been expected to sound a different note. But Bond remembered fondly the years when a "human-hearted man had his hands on the levers of power" in the White House. "O, by God," he cried, "do I wish he was there now!"[43]

CONCLUSION:
THE WHITE HOUSE LOOKS SOUTH

In his seventeenth-century chronicle *The Generall Historie of Virginia, New England, and the Summer Isles,* John Smith observed that "as Geography without History seemeth a carkasse without motion, so History without Geography wandreth as a Vagrant without a certaine habitation." No one would think of writing a history of Europe without sensitivity to the differences between Yorkshire and Surrey, Normandy and the Dordogne, Lombardy and Calabria. To know Napoleon, it has been said, one must start by studying Corsica. Consciousness of the spatial dimension is important, too, to comprehend the experience of Americans, voyagers who peopled a continent. "The love of place," Max Lerner has remarked, "was the earliest loyalty brought to the American shores." In a pathbreaking conference paper on "Why Place Still Matters," Edward Ayers has expressed the point well: "We've let our . . . perception of the transience of place rob us of one of the historian's essential perspectives. Place is not talked about with the same gravity as race, class, or gender even though a moment's reflection will show that where we live shapes our lives just as much." History, John Lewis Gaddis has written in an imaginative metaphor, is "a kind of mapping," for "the past is a landscape and history is the way we represent it."[1]

Political analysts find awareness of place quintessential. V. O. Key maintained, as one commentary noted, "that territorial allegiances could trump class behavior in determining political behavior," and Ayers, noting that "it is one of the great truisms of the age that everything is being rendered placeless," responded: "Think about what decides the most fundamental expression of power in America: politics. Region is by far the most salient characteristic of that process. How a district votes, a state votes, a region votes determines elections far more than how a class votes, a gender votes, or even how an ethnicity votes. . . . People in a place often vote the same way despite the screaming class differences among them, with poor men voting for candidates who seem to act contrary to their interests, whether that was for Democrats in the Jim Crow South or for Republicans today. That is because people think of themselves as residents of a place as much as or more than they think of themselves as embodiments of other kinds of characteristics." The presidential election of 2000 gave some sustenance to his argument. Though voting outside the South that year broke predictably on class lines, with those less well off gravitating to the Democrats, below the Mason-Dixon line, the Republican George Bush drew 57 percent support from low-income white males.[2]

Even in a period of increased homogenization local differences persist and sectionalism remains a vital force. A 1967 study found not only that it was untrue that regional cultural diversity was rapidly vanishing, but that contrasts had actually increased. When voters in one 1976 survey were asked which region they would least like a president to come from, only 6 percent said it did not matter. In 2000, at a time when pundits were insisting that national politics had become unitary, Al Gore launched a "state-specific" campaign with messages aimed at West Virginia voters distinct from those directed to Oregon or Nevada. On observing the race that year, a demographer, noting that the statements of candidates "play quite differently in one area than in the other," foresaw that henceforth presidential candidates would jettison national appeals for a target approach "because regional differences are becoming more pronounced across the country."[3]

Franklin Roosevelt, Harry Truman, and Lyndon Johnson each had an acute sense of place, not cabined by a single section. As early as the winter of 1929, FDR wrote a Mississippian, "I have spent so much time in Georgia during the last few years as to give me, I think, a rather better understanding of the southerner's point of view than many northerners possess." Roosevelt, his secretary of agriculture, Henry Wallace, recalled, "prided himself on being from Georgia just as much as from New York." Truman, tugged south, west, and north when young, and, in later years, east to Washington, spent a lifetime sorting out his regional identity. Of Lyndon Johnson, his biographer Paul Conkin has said, "Few presidents have been more conscious of where they came from or introduced more images of place in their speeches," and Kent Germany, who has edited recordings of LBJ's telephone conversations, has reported, "He consistently invoked his sense of place, family, and culture."[4]

This consciousness of place and this capacity to bridge sections contributed mightily to the achievements of the three presidents because it sensitized them to the predicaments of the South and because it gave them entrée to southern power brokers that outlanders were denied. "The secret of Roosevelt's success," H. Brandt Ayers has said, "was that he regarded the people of the South, not as abstractions, but as friends and neighbors." Even before FDR took office, another Alabama editor wrote of him: "He comes nearer approaching the status of a Southerner than most of our late presidents. He, by adoption, chose one of the Southern states for a part-time home. . . . The South almost claims him as her own." Once he was in office, the South did lay claim to him, though sometimes in a calculating way. When in 1937 Senator Theodore Bilbo of Mississippi sought approval for a pet scheme to help southern agriculture, he wrote to Roosevelt "as one Southern cotton farmer to another."[5]

Harry Truman owed his national career to his fortuitous siting. In accounting for how Truman came to be the Democratic nominee for the vice presidency (his avenue to the White House), FDR's speech writer, Sam Rosenman, said, "Coming from the central part of the country, he was geographically very acceptable as a candidate. He was from a border state which was politically doubtful." Moreover, his Missouri locale won him indulgence from civil rights leaders. "Truman's own views on race were border state, not Deep Dixie," Roy Wilkins observed. "He didn't believe in social equality, but he did believe in fair play. No one had ever convinced him that the Bill of Rights was a document for white folks only."[6]

Perplexity about his sectional identification abetted Lyndon Johnson, but it also vexed him. His Confederate pedigree served to mitigate some of the southern hostility to his program. With a southerner in the White House, "the civil rights pill will be just as bitter, but it will go down easier," said a North Carolinian. "He's one of us." A White House aide, seeking to explain Johnson's success in getting the legislation passed, said that the president "had the benefit at least of being, if not from the South, from the Southwest. The accent helped him enormously." Many southerners, though, dismissed him as an interloper, in part because he masqueraded as a western rancher. During his presidency, a draft of a brochure on his birthplace stated: "Today the Johnson City area is thoroughly Western. But in the boyhood of Lyndon Johnson people used to say, 'Here the South ends and the West begins.' Johnson City itself was an amalgam of the two regions. Most of its residents were southern in descent and proud of it but they also wore boots and Stetsons." One southern commentator remarked, "I do not count Lyndon Johnson as a Southerner, although from time to time he pretended to be one." In sum, as Bill Moyers who knew him well concluded, Johnson was "a man of time and place" who "felt the bitter paradox of both."[7]

II

Though FDR's funeral procession is indelibly associated with the haunting strains of "Going Home," his final "home" was not to be the pastures of Georgia but the alien corn of a New York valley. In many ways in the last quarter of a century of his life, he had learned to see the world through a casement with a southern exposure, but he never truly abandoned his northern, or, more to the point, national perspective. As Theo Lippman Jr. has said, "There is no denying how much Warm Springs meant to him, in every way, but he had always been a sojourner." Still, he was a "sojourner" who became so much a part of his new land that he, and others, seemed uncertain about whether he was a southerner, a northerner, or both.[8]

At times, Roosevelt conveyed the impression that, for all of his identification with the South, he still regarded himself as a Yankee, though he usually did so in the context of instructing the North on the needs of the South. In 1934 he made reference to "some of us Northerners," but he said that to correct a misapprehension northerners held about the South and the West. Five years later, he alluded to southern states as "down there," and talked of northerners as "we rich people up here," but once more he made these comments in the course of lecturing the press on why federal aid should go to the South, not the North. Again in 1941 he spoke of the South as "down there" and of southerners as "them," but he also referred to Warm Springs as "our village."[9]

Yet if Roosevelt remained a northerner in significant respects, his adopted homeland unquestionably had a profound effect on him. As Hugh Gregory Gallagher has written: "In Warm Springs, driving his open Ford about the back roads of rural Georgia in the severe agriculture depression of the 1920s, FDR came to understand the problems and fears of the farmers, the tenants, the poor whites, and the blacks of red-clay Georgia. FDR would never have had this leavening experience had he continued the life of a New York society attorney/broker with a career in politics."[10]

In the White House, Roosevelt frequently drew upon his Warm Springs experiences. "This locality was his window to the whole of the South," the Brain Truster Rexford Tugwell once observed. The term *New Deal* had been employed by Judge Revill in an editorial the week that FDR first arrived at Warm Springs. At the time of Roosevelt's death, the judge said at a service there: "Much of his New Deal was occasioned by his observation here in Georgia, especially soil renovation and a credit system for those who needed it."[11]

FDR's strong commitment to create a national program to help the farmer puzzled Tugwell, who served as under secretary of agriculture in the New Deal. "Where had the emotional involvement come from?" he wondered. To be sure, any American leader would have recognized that the wounded farm economy required attention. "But there had been something more, some special feeling in his expressed concern," Tugwell ruminated. "About this one thing he had been endlessly inquiring, endlessly urgent." Though Roosevelt gabbed a lot about his Dutchess County "farm," Hyde Park was an estate that could not have taught him much about what dirt farmers faced. From whence then had this understanding derived? Tugwell thought he knew the answer: "West Georgia." He reflected: "Roosevelt had spent part of nearly every day, sometimes whole days, exploring the back roads, visiting with farmers—simply driving into yards, pulling up under the inevitable chinaberry tree, and hailing whomever he could see. In these casual conversations, he had learned more about farmers' grievances than he would ever have discovered in New York."[12]

The idea of electrifying the countryside first came to him, Roosevelt said, one day in Warm Springs. When a prominent South Carolina politician spoke in the village in 1931, Roosevelt told him, "If I was in position or ever had the power, I'd light up all those rural areas in America." In a talk in Georgia in 1938, Roosevelt, after speaking fondly of his first stay at Warm Springs fourteen years before, recalled that there had been "only one discordant note." When his electric light bill arrived the first of the month, he found he was paying four times as much as in Hyde Park. "That light bill started my long study of proper public utility charges for electric current, started in my mind the whole subject of getting electricity into farm homes throughout the United States," he remarked. "So, my friends, it can be said with a good deal of truth that a little cottage at Warm Springs, Georgia, was the birthplace of the Rural Electrification Administration."[13]

Roosevelt in turn, from his vantage point in Georgia, had a very considerable impact on southern society. "Franklin Roosevelt, who had witnessed the poverty of the rural South firsthand during visits to his vacation home at Warm Springs, Georgia, was the first President to take a serious interest in the economic development of the South," a political scientist has written. Numbers of southerners bore witness to that conclusion. FDR, said H. C. Nixon, "dramatized the statement of Southern problems as no one at Washington had done since the Civil War." Early in 1934 Lorena Hickok, one of Harry Hopkins's field agents, reported to FDR's relief administrator about the mayor of Charleston, Burnet Maybank: "He is almost fiercely loyal to the President and the Administration generally. You see, he and several other prominent Southerners I've met feel that Mr. Roosevelt is the first President since the 'War between the States' who has recognized the South as a part of the Union. Really, that's the way some of them feel. I've had it said to me over and over again: 'He's the first President who has even tried to help us, down here. He's the first President who has made us feel that we really are a part of the United States.'"[14]

Some years after the halcyon days of the New Deal had passed, the Richmond editor Virginius Dabney, who did not suffer northern intruders gladly, commented: "No President since the Civil War has revealed the understanding of, and the concern for, the South's problems that Franklin D. Roosevelt has evidenced. Woodrow Wilson was a Southerner by birth and upbringing, but his preoccupation with the first World War and its aftermath seems to have made him relatively unaware of regional problems, and he may well have hesitated before addressing himself too vigorously, as President, to the needs of his native section. But Mr. Roosevelt, whose part-time residence in his 'adopted state' of Georgia has given him a deep interest in Southern social and economic relationships, and whose birth and official residence in New York lends a flavor of nonpartisanship to his regional predilections, has been interested for a good many years in the well-being of the South, and more specifically in that of its underprivileged elements."[15]

Dabney might have been still more effusive had he written at the end of the FDR presidency, for Roosevelt and his appointees calculatedly exploited the war crisis to funnel federal money southward. To be sure, as George Tindall has pointed out, "throughout the war, the South remained more campground than arsenal." Nonetheless, in communities such as Mobile the war had an electrifying effect in speeding industrialization and creating new pockets of prosperity. "For the first time since the War Between the States," *Fortune* reported, "almost any native of the Deep South who wants a job can get one." Morton Sosna has even asked whether World War II did not have a greater impact on the South than the Civil War, and Numan Bartley has concluded: "While it would not be entirely appropriate to insist that nothing very important happened in the 1860s and the 1890s, those decades no longer seem . . . the great watersheds that they have often been depicted. Instead, contemporary scholarship increasingly suggests that far more fundamental changes occurred during the middle years of the twentieth century, with perhaps 1935 and 1945 best qualifying as the latest crucial decade of New South historiography. Developments set in motion during these years produced massive changes in southern life."[16]

In state after state, historians have contended, the age of Roosevelt marked a turning point. One scholar has said of Tennessee: "The New Deal wrought a revolution in the state," while another has maintained that FDR's policies "affected every segment of Texas society . . . in a manner not envisioned by the most perspicacious Texan at its start. For Texans, whether residing in Washington, the Panhandle, or the shores of the Rio Grande, life would never be the same. Conservative Texas had been introduced to the twentieth century." As late as 1983, a historian reported, "Hardly can any Texas town be visited without a traveler finding some evidence of improvement which was a direct result of some New Deal program."[17]

The biographer of Lister Hill, who entered the U.S. Senate in January 1938, has written of the Alabama voters who elected him that year:

> Behind Hill they sensed the larger shadow of Franklin Roosevelt to whom they had given 86 percent of their votes only one year earlier. Had it not been for Roosevelt, would their state have enjoyed a major share of the revitalizing Tennessee Valley Authority? Had not FDR, with his pet scheme of a Civilian Conservation Corps, put their sons to work cutting trees and clearing forests? Was it not Roosevelt who had brought electricity to their rural homes, liberated them from the tasks of cooking over wood stoves, lifting heavy "sad irons," and pumping water from wells, and even made it possible for them to enjoy the miraculous diversion of radio? Had not they and thousands like them escaped from the demeaning dole to the more respectable payrolls of his Works Progress Administration (WPA)? Were not Birmingham's miners and steelworkers strengthened in their efforts to secure higher wages and better work conditions now that the New Deal had sheltered unions under the protective eye of the National Labor Relations Board?[18]

Even historians of particular states who acknowledge the limitations of FDR's program have insisted upon its importance. Roger Tate has observed: "Because the New Deal did not end the depression, many scholars, especially those of conservative or radical views, have argued that it failed as a reform movement. A more reasonable interpretation is that the depression was so severe that no democratic government in the United States could have coped with it successfully, given the institutional restraints imposed by the federal system and the nation's traditional hostility to big government. The New Deal did not fail. In Mississippi and in the nation, it halted the downward spiral of the economy, extended relief to the needy, and had achieved a limited recovery by 1936. After 1938 it resorted to a holding action, but most of its gains were preserved." In the 1970s, a generation after the age of Roosevelt ended, the federal government was still Mississippi's main source of income.[19]

Historians of other states, too, have been impressed by the long-run consequences of the FDR years. The imprint on Georgia "should not be measured on the basis of the results visible at the end of the period," Roy Edward Fossett has written. "Instead, a true measurement must consider the later growth of the seeds which had been planted. For one thing, the Roosevelt-Rivers era brought an awakening of political consciousness on the part of the tenant farmers and the Negroes. For another, it shook the old agricultural establishment founded on the planter-tenant relationship. . . . The New Deal had created a ferment on all levels and in all shades of opinion within the state." Another commentator has written that it was the experience with federal aid in the "Little New Deal" that readied Georgia for entry into "Roosevelt's War." He adds: "Without the improvements of the late thirties, the military presence in . . . Savannah . . . might have been far less. As it turned out, . . . a city in which an airplane with two engines was a rare sight soon grew accustomed to the heavy bombers of the Eighth Air Force. . . . The war turned Savannah from a sleepy, traditional, backward-looking town on a muddy river into a full-fledged, twentieth-century American city."[20]

Eliot Wigginton, the teacher who sparked the Foxfire publications, has emphasized the enduring impact on Georgia. "The widespread perception in the mountains . . . is that Roosevelt saved America," he has said. "In Rabun County alone, there were four active CCC camps and one large Federal Emergency Relief Administration (FERA) program." The former head of the FERA operation told *Foxfire* in the 1980s, when he was a lively ninety-two-year-old, that he recalled vividly opening the first FERA office in the county seat of Clayton and finding several hundred men waiting outside, some of them so famished they could barely stand. Long after the New Deal ended, Wigginton, on his first visit to that Georgia mountain county, found that "a framed portrait of Roosevelt still hung over the cash register of Gillespie's farmers' market in downtown Clayton." Moreover, he added, "the legacy lives on. Aunt Arie's *sole* means of financial support up to the last years of her life was her Social Security check," and "buildings are still in use today in Rabun County that were erected by WPA labor."[21]

The changes wrought in the age of Roosevelt should not be exaggerated, as a number of commentators have pointed out. Tony Badger has observed that "the New Deal left the basic economic, social, racial and political structure of the region largely untouched," and neither in Dallas nor Memphis did Roger Biles find the New Deal transforming. "Despite all the enthusiasm for overhauling the Southern system," Paul Gaston concluded, "economic power, at the end of the 'thirties, continued to rest where it had been before; impoverished croppers and mill hands continued to symbolize the region's economic failures; the Negro, despite modest improvement in his status, remained ensnared by the ramifying tentacles of the Jim Crow system." Some found the southern scene painfully familiar. "If one had traveled from Raleigh, North Carolina, through neighboring South Carolina, on through Georgia, Alabama, Mississippi, Louisiana, and as far west as Dallas, Texas, in 1945, he would have observed many more similarities than differences in the rural landscape from any prewar trip," Gilbert Fite has commented. The traveler "would have passed poorly fed and poorly clothed people living in unpainted, weather-beaten shacks made worse with age, eroded fields, much idle land grown up in brush and weeds, and other signs of low productivity and poverty."[22]

Yet even those who stressed continuity acknowledged that the Roosevelt years had made a difference. Badger admired much about the FDR program, and Gaston did not doubt that "the New Deal wrought profound changes in the social, economic, and political structure of the nation" or that "programs of action jostled the established order." Seven years after FDR's death, the sociologist Arthur Raper, author of *Preface to Peasantry,* wrote: "The Roosevelt New Deal . . . helped thousands of tenant farmers to become owners and some old-line owners to get on their feet; it financed many a new school building, court house, community house, bridge and emergency airport. There was, however, no real shift in the balance of power. The people who had been running the region ran it still." Two decades, later, however, Raper had second thoughts. He said of the New Deal projects: "The South wouldn't be what it is today, if they hadn't come. A whole lot of young chaps that never would have gotten to high school or even college got there because of the NYA. There are a whole lot of buildings and a whole lot of separate campuses that never would have been built if it hadn't been for the WPA and the PWA. There's a whole lot of fellows who know what it is to get an eroded hillside farm so the soil doesn't go on down into the river, and on into the sea, because they learned through the SCS." While granting that most politicians in the South "viewed the New Deal as a way of keeping themselves in power rather than a way of liberalizing state policy," Monroe Billington has said that the Roosevelt programs nonetheless created "a new relationship between the national and state governments. Never again would state governors or legislators act on major matters without first considering the consequences of their acts in relation to the federal government—including its regulations and its largess."[23]

Though FDR was often frustrated by entrenched power groups in the 1930s, he and his lieutenants laid mine fields that would detonate a generation later. As Dewey Grantham observed: "The effect of Franklin D. Roosevelt's program on southern politics can scarcely be overestimated; in some ways it was revolutionary. Addressing itself directly to the South's problems, the New Deal precipitated an unprecedented popular agitation on social and political issues in the region below the Potomac. It frightened the conservatives, shocked the section out of its normal complacency toward national politics, promoted the growth of organized labor, and encouraged the spread of liberal ideas throughout the South. It introduced codes and standards that did much to undermine the old faith in freedom of contract and state rights."[24]

Commentators have likened Roosevelt's relation to his adopted section to that of a state-builder in a third world country. In 1930, it has been said, the South "presented an almost classic picture of an underdeveloped society," and when FDR took office in 1933, "the region," in the words of the former Mississippi Congressman Frank E. Smith in 1965, "could best be compared with the status today of some of the Latin American countries. . . . The federal programs begun under the New Deal, some directed especially at the South and some of which merely received special emphasis in the South, still rank as the best modern example of how a government can develop a backward country." The Atlanta editor Ralph McGill later wrote: "Once, on a visit to Warm Springs, I'd heard Franklin D. Roosevelt say that Georgia was an unfinished state and the South was an unfinished region. He explained, saying the development of the Southern states had been halted by the Civil War and that postwar recovery had been tortuous and slow because of the corrosive poverty and the pressures of politics, prejudice, and economic exploitation which had developed after the reconstruction years. There must be a beginning again, and perhaps, he said, it will come out of this depression." At a talk at Hyde Park in 1959, Lyndon Johnson said of Roosevelt: "One of the first tasks which he set himself was the raising up of the South, economic problem number one, still suffering from the destruction of capital in the War between the States."[25]

In this ambitious venture, many historians contend, Roosevelt could claim considerable success. "The New Deal," Jordan Schwarz found, "did work profound changes in Dixie," and Robert McElvaine has asserted, "The region's economy, its relationship with the federal government and the Democratic party, and social relations between the races were all profoundly and lastingly changed by the New Deal." The *Report on Economic Conditions of the South*, Numan Bartley has observed, "signalled a fundamental shift in national policy that was to make the federal government a major sponsor of southern economic development." Policies and trends in the Roosevelt years "encouraged urbanization, economic diversification, and social and governmental 'modernization,' and their cumulative impact contributed crucially to the evolution of a New South greatly different from the one left behind."[26]

A quarter of a century after FDR's death, Charles Roland, in an essay on the southern mystique, concluded: "The epoch of President Roosevelt's New Deal and of World War II . . . has given the South the greatest affluence of its history. Most of the implicit recommendations of the National Emergency Council have been carried out: TVA, rural electrification, soil conservation, and farmers' and home builders' credit. . . . Government price support has vastly increased the farmers' income. Discriminatory taxes on Southern cotton oil products . . . and prejudicial freight rates against Southern manufactures have long been gone. The munitions and armaments industries of World War II, and the thriving aluminum, synthetics, and petrochemical industries of the post-war years have changed the base of the Southern economy from agriculture to industry. Cotton has been dethroned and reduced to the ranks of the minor nobility."[27]

Roosevelt, for his part, had no doubt that he was a change-maker. In December 1938 he made his way north by train from Warm Springs to Sanford, North Carolina, where ten thousand Tar Heels braved a downpour to greet him, then by automobile past thousands more soggy well-wishers on the rain-soaked road to Chapel Hill. Attired in the cap and gown of an honorary Doctor of Laws, the president told a University of North Carolina audience crowded into a stifling gymnasium:

A few days ago in Georgia I talked with an old friend whom I have known for ten years. He was what might be called an old-fashioned Southern conservative. We got to "reminiscing" about the old days when I first lived in Georgia. He reminded me of the days when cotton was selling at five cents a pound, and, while he admitted that the ramifications of our federal legislation . . . were somewhat beyond him, he allowed that some principle of crop control . . . was the most democratic way to prevent the return of five-cent cotton.

He reminded me of two little banks in Warm Springs, Georgia—banks in which many thousands of dollars of local savings had been deposited—of the failure of both of these banks and the loss of the savings—and . . . today that deposits in the banks of the United States are safe, and, he remarked, "I hope that that type of liberal legislation will not be repealed."

He reminded me of the white men and Negroes who never saw, as the heads of families, $100 in cash the whole year round. . . .

And when he left he said, "Young man, I don't know the United States the way you do but I know this section of the Nation pretty well . . . and I want to tell you there is a new spirit abroad in the land. I am not talking just about the fact that there is more buying power, that houses are painted that were never painted before, that our banks are safe, that our roads and schools are better. What I am talking about is that all of our young people in my section of the country think that we are 'going places.'"[28]

We may well doubt whether the president's "old friend" actually existed, and in the second year of the "Roosevelt recession," his claims were a bit cheeky, but they connected enough with the experiences of his Chapel Hill audience to generate an enthusiastic response.

Scholars have particularly remarked on the consequences of FDR's policies for southern politics. In his magisterial study published only four years after Roosevelt's death, V. O. Key wrote: "The New Deal affected the masses of the South as had no political movement since the Populist uprising. . . . The southern voter had long been accustomed to a politics that consisted mainly of oratorical fulmination steeped with cadence and pompous promise but with little effect on the world of reality. In the New Deal, oratory came to life. . . . The New Deal aroused the political interests and the political hopes of classes of people left unmoved by traditional southern politics." That same year, a political scientist asked: "Is it going too far to attribute to the over-all influence of TVA at least in some measure the high level of Alabama's representation in the United States Senate and the currently low ebb in the political fortunes of Mr. Crump? To be sure, the Senator Claghorns are still with us; but the Ellis Arnalls and the Estes Kefauvers are becoming more numerous and more effective." In Alabama, farm families, grateful for TVA benefits, provided an electoral base for the New Deal senators Hugo Black and Lister Hill; sent moderately progressive congressmen such as John Sparkman to Washington; and continued after Roosevelt was gone to rally to Governor Jim Folsom. "From the New Deal," a study of Texas politics found, "came the origins of the state's gradual shift away from questions of race, personalities, and alcohol toward the more fundamental issue of economics."[29]

Kari Frederickson has seen the 1948 election outcome as reflecting the ongoing influence of the age of Franklin Roosevelt. "The Dixiecrats failed to capture more states because the New Deal and the war had altered the southern political landscape in new and important ways," she writes. "White southerners . . . remained overwhelmingly united in their defense of white supremacy; however, their willingness to remain wedded to the conservative economic agenda of the Black Belt elite had weakened. Workers encouraged by New Deal labor legislation and a generation of white men who served overseas began to see the South and politics in a slightly less parochial light and to view the federal government's role in the economic life of the region in less defensive ways." The Dixiecrats fell short, she added, because they "conceived of political relations in familial ways and privileged patriarchal dominance. . . . Such a message failed to resonate fully in a region . . . in which rival groups had come to see themselves as potential political actors."[30]

Though the national government under FDR often perpetuated, and even extended, the domain of Jim Crow, it also sabotaged the institutions of white supremacy. In 1949 the NAACP's Henry Lee Moon declared, "The encouragement which many Southerners now openly give to Negro suffrage stems from the New Deal policies of Franklin D. Roosevelt which created a political climate in which such ideas—long taboo—could be openly expressed," and the historian John B. Kirby has pointed out that "prior to the New Deal the 'Negro problem' was never a central consideration of white reformers or reform philosophers." Roosevelt was no crusader for racial justice, yet Garth Pauley has concluded: "FDR's particular way of managing racial issues . . . changed the relationship between the presidency and African Americans. Earlier presidents did nothing that would impinge upon how their successors would manage civil rights, but Roosevelt brought the presidency to the threshold of leadership on racial matters. Roosevelt's occasional public statements, policies, and symbolism on race led many blacks to expect more from the presidency. Roosevelt's words and actions shaped the contexts in which future presidents would be heard." In 1947 a Mississippi legislator from Yazoo, while acknowledging that blacks had been treated unfairly and that their school was a pig sty, saw a crisis impending, not because such dreadful conditions aroused justifiable resentment, but because the Roosevelts had brewed trouble among people who in the pre-FDR era had accepted their lot.[31]

These activities stirred up southerners, both black and white. "Although FDR's policies, as it turned out, often worked to the detriment of black sharecroppers," one historian has observed, "his New Deal fueled . . . new black activism in a myriad of ways." Another historian has gone so far as to call June 15, 1941, "the starting date of the modern civil rights movement," because "the FEPC's records . . . show . . . the extent to which blacks were awakened to the importance of the leadership of the President and federal agencies in ending discrimination" by FDR's order. "The New Deal marked a departure from the national complacency that characterized the 1920s," Patricia Sullivan has written. "When Franklin Roosevelt became president, said civil rights activist Modjeska Simkins, 'he took the jug by the handle. He tried to give the people who were down and had nothing a little something. He put some strength in the backbone of people. . . . It was a shot in the arm for Negroes.'" Sullivan added: "The depression and the New Deal sparked indigenous protest movements and organizing efforts throughout the South, from tenant farmers to miners to textile workers. . . . And the Roosevelt administration nurtured a new breed of southern reformers who began to view southern problems within a national context, causing them to confront their region's racial and political structure." "Beneath the surface of traditional southern politics," she concluded, "an important change was taking place."[32]

This insurrection of ideas reverberated long after Roosevelt's death. When in the troubled 1950s Le Roy Collins took over as governor of Florida, he sought to lead the state in new directions on race in part because of his memory of the 1930s. "I came along with an attitude of being a reformer," he later recalled. "The New Deal helped to stir this. I knew things needed to be changed, and the New Deal in the early days of Franklin D. Roosevelt was a symbol of progress and change." The civil rights movement of the 1960s, Robert Norrell has determined, originated in "the fundamental shift in the location of power within the American polity that took place during the 1930s," for, as a consequence of the New Deal and the Roosevelt Court's expansive reading of the Constitution, "the stage had been set for the national government to override the southern states' autonomy in . . . race relations."[33]

"What, then, must we conclude about the impact of Franklin Roosevelt and the New Deal on the politics of the South?" Alan Brinkley has asked. "Clearly the New Deal wrought no internal revolution in southern politics," he responds. "And yet little more than twenty years after Franklin Roosevelt's election to the presidency, . . . a series of profound transformations did begin to occur in southern social, economic, and political life. This Second Reconstruction, arguably the most significant period of change in the entire history of the South, was not the direct work of the New Deal. But it was to a striking degree a result of New Deal policies that, indirectly and often inadvertently, paved the way for the transformation to come."[34]

Brinkley goes on to make an important point—that while "some of those policies helped to transform the South's own social and economic structure," FDR's most consequential contribution lay in his impact *outside* the South by building a national Democratic coalition on which he imposed "a new liberal outlook," an achievement that "shattered the South's grip on the party forever." No one foresaw this so acutely as "the embittered Old Guard conservatives of the South. . . . They were often unhappy, of course, about what the New Deal was doing within the South. But what most alarmed them was what it was doing in the North. They realized that the Democratic party as they had known it was vanishing, and that a new coalition was emerging in which they could never again hope to play a decisive role."[35]

FDR's long association with Warm Springs gave him an empathy for southern problems, but it was his perspective on the region as a New Yorker that enabled him to place the South in a national context. When Roosevelt announced his intentions for Muscle Shoals in January 1933, he declared, "The development here is national and is going to be treated from a national point of view," and in his second term, he wrote Senator Hattie Caraway of Arkansas: "Frankly, what I am fearful of is that the Nation as a whole will say that Democratic Senators and Members of the House from the South in voting against *any* legislation to increase the wages of the 'lowest third' in industry or to eliminate unconscionably long hours are flying in the face of modern civilization."[36]

Roosevelt repeatedly used his lectern to preach the supremacy of nation over locality. In a 1934 address on "the doom of sectionalism," he said, "As a Virginian, President Washington had a natural pride in Virginia; but as an American, in his stately phrase, 'the name of American, which belongs to you, in your national capacity, must always exalt the just pride of patriotism, more than any appellation derived from local discrimination.'" Three years later, on the Antietam battlefield, he declared: "The past four years mark the first occasion, certainly since the War between the States, and perhaps during the whole 150 years of our government, that we are not only acting but also thinking in national terms. Deeply we appreciate that the distress . . . of any one part of the Union adversely affects each and every other part. We stand ready in all parts to lend a helping hand to those Americans who need it most."[37]

In 1946, surveying the scene in the post-FDR era, one commentator observed, with some exaggeration: "President Roosevelt was a Northerner who loved the South. By his works he proved, once and for all, that sectionalism can be killed. His aim was for one prosperous united country with equal opportunity in all its sections. He was intent, not on favoring one part of the country, but on removing restrictions from all of it. It would be good to cite a long list of Northern leaders in politics, commerce, banking, and education who are following in Roosevelt's footsteps, but he was the exception. Because of him the South has at last gotten off the ground."[38]

The age of Roosevelt went a long way toward integrating the South into the national economy. By 1940, Gavin Wright has written, "the economic underpinnings and social glue that had kept the regional economy isolated were no longer present," and in World War II Roosevelt accelerated the changes initiated in the Great Depression to foster southern economic development. From 1940 to 1945, income in the South climbed at a 145 percent rate while it was rising in the rest of the nation by 97 percent, and the biggest source of the gain was government expenditures. The dovetailed impact of the New Deal and World War II had long-lasting effects. "Once southern leaders accepted federal intervention in their region, they could not completely control the forces they had unleashed," Bruce Schulman has pointed out. "Like a virus the New Deal seeped into the region's economic body, infecting traditional political and economic arrangements and preparing the way for more extensive federal action in the future." As a consequence, Biles has asserted, "the New Deal marked the beginning of the end of southern exceptionalism."[39]

Not a few southerners regarded Roosevelt as a liberator who rescued the South from its isolation. "There seems to be a bottom-deep awakening, a breaking up of the thick shell that has for decades covered the South," said Aubrey Williams. At the start of FDR's second term, a former Virginia congressman wrote the president, "I admire the work that you are doing, because . . . the indirect effect of many of your policies is to unfetter the South and make it free," and during World War II, H. C. Nixon declared: "The South during the years of the New Deal has experienced a development that enables it and tempts it to talk the confident language of a regular child of the national household, not the subservient terms of an undernourished step-child or orphan. . . . It is more a real and integral part of the United States today than at any other time since the administrations of Polk and Taylor, the last Presidents elected from the South." From Roosevelt's "second state," another writer has said of FDR: "He made us in Georgia a part of the Nation in a way that our local politicians never did. In fact, our local politicians did just the opposite. They glorified our separateness, insisted that it would always be that way. This was most directly related to the racial issue, but in other subtle and not-so-subtle ways Georgians (and Alabamians and Mississippians) were always being reminded that we were outside the mainstream of American life. That a Georgian could ever become a national leader was not only unspoken but unthought. . . . To the extent that he was a Georgian, Roosevelt made our American-ness whole."[40]

In the 1980s, nearly a half-century after the president's appearance in Chapel Hill, a North Carolina editor, Roy Parker Jr., summed up what the intervening years had meant: "The fact is, as far as Dixie is concerned, what we are today, we owe largely to Mr. Roosevelt's beginnings. . . . More than 90 percent of the schools built between 1933 and 1940 in the 11 Confederate states were built with federal money or because of it. Industrial output tripled. When the minimum wage law was passed, not a single Southern textile worker was making the minimum! Even the neglected battlegrounds of the Southern Cause were cleaned, restored, and equipped as national monuments by the men and boys of Mr. Roosevelt's Civilian Conservation Corps. . . . If it wasn't for the attention of the federal government, a concern which began with FDR, Dixie would *still* be the nation's number one economic problem." Parker continued:

FDR . . . inspired a generation of southern writers, businessmen, teachers, editors and politicians to study, to think about, and to make over their region in an image of progress, fair play, and opportunity. . . . Local and state governments became more than the tools or playthings of the planters, mill owners, and courthouse politicians. . . .

Because the New Deal was a national scheme, because it tended to knit every region together in common purpose, and because FDR was himself the charismatic focus of so popular a cause, Dixie began to throw off her backwardness, her regional hubris, her insularity, and join the Nation in the national purpose. . . .

So, the New Deal and Mr. Roosevelt really transformed not only the southern economy and southern polity, but the southern mind as well.

The South, Parker concluded, "bears his enduring mark more than it bears the mark of even a Washington or a Lee."[41]

III

In contrast to the New York–born FDR, whose identification with the South derived from an act of free will, Harry Truman was all but preordained to acquire a sense of sectional ambiguity. Roosevelt did not develop an association with the South to accompany his northern heritage until the age of forty-two, when he first went to Warm Springs, and by then he had already served in Wilson's junior cabinet and had run for the vice presidency. Truman's experience was altogether different. From the moment that his family moved to Independence, Missouri, when Harry was six, the future president was locked into a community that, arguably, more than any other in the country, looked in antipodal directions—southeast toward the Cradle of the Confederacy and northwest to the terminus of the Oregon Trail. A boy as sensitive as Harry Truman could hardly have escaped awareness of the imperatives of place.

The town in which he grew up reinforced his family's commitment to the Southland and the Lost Cause. David McCullough has written of Independence in Truman's youth: "The atmosphere remained pervadingly southern— antebellum Old South, unreconstructed. Handkerchiefs were waved whenever the band played 'Dixie.' The United Daughters of the Confederacy thrived, and . . . formal parties attended by genteel young folk . . . were hardly different from those put on in Macon or Tuscaloosa, from the floral decorations entwining stair rails to the refreshments of chicken salad and charlotte russe. The biggest memorial in Woodland Cemetery was the Confederate monument. Portraits of Lee and Jackson were displayed prominently in many front parlors, and in summer Quantrill's 'boys'—grizzled, tobacco-chewing, Border War veterans dressed as if for church—gathered for daylong outdoor reunions, a portrait of Quantrill draped in crepe as their centerpiece. Often Jesse James's brother, Frank, appeared . . . , causing great excitement." Blacks, consigned to the "Nigger Neck" quarter, were not even permitted to use the town library. In the very year that Truman became president, Missouri engraved in its Constitution separate schools for black and white children; not until 1976 would the provision be rescinded.[42]

This background led many to take for granted that he was a true-gray southerner. A dozen years after he left the White House, Truman was still outspoken about his allegiance. When in 1964 he accompanied Lady Bird Johnson as an official U.S. representative to the funeral of the king of Greece, Prince Michael said, "I feel very close to the United States because my great-great-grandfather was aide-de-camp to General Grant." Slapping the prince on the knee, Truman retorted, "Well, son, as far as this lady and I are concerned, he was on the wrong side!" Not even his advocacy of civil rights persuaded all southerners he was an outlander. In an address in South Carolina during the 1948 campaign, Secretary of the Army Kenneth Royall, speaking as a North Carolinian, said the South was needlessly worried about Truman's racial views, for "the President was raised in an atmosphere much like ours."[43]

That perception, however, disregarded two important considerations. One is that Truman did not only look south. He once reminded Oregonians that the "Oregon Trail people used to outfit themselves out of Independence and Westport in Missouri," a circumstance Thomas Hart Benton celebrated in his mural for the Truman Library titled "Independence and the Opening of the West." Furthermore, Truman, like FDR, saw himself as a modernizer who would dispense with worn-out mores. "The main difficulty with the South," he stated in 1948, "is that they are living behind the times and the sooner they come out of it the better it will be for the country and for themselves."[44]

In particular, Truman veered away from inherited preconceptions on race, though that was difficult for him. Clark Clifford's chief aide, George Elsey, reflected: "As an individual, given his family background, and the part of the country he grew up in, and simply his generation, it was not as easy for him to deal on a face-to-face and one-to-one basis with members of other races. . . . but this didn't lessen Truman's determination as President to fight hard for civil rights. . . . As President, he saw what he thought was his duty, and he went right ahead with it." The author of the principal work on the origins of the *Brown* decision agreed. "Franklin Roosevelt may have opened the White House door wide to Negroes, but Harry S. Truman risked his future tenancy there in their behalf—and because of his conception of what America was all about," Richard Kluger wrote. "No President before or since Lincoln had put his political neck on the chopping block to help the colored people of the nation."[45]

Truman persisted right through his final year in office. In May 1952 he gave a rousing speech to a liberal rally that torpedoed the scheme of Democratic centrists to dilute the civil rights plank in the party platform. A month later, in a commencement address at Howard University, he expressed pleasure in signs of progress during his tenure such as the 177 public housing projects opened in 1950 "to families of all races and creeds." They were "the trumpet blast outside the walls of Jericho—the crumbling walls of prejudice." But, he declared, "we still have a long way to go." He took special pride in the advances made in desegregating the armed forces. Some of the country's "greatest generals" still believed that a Jim Crow army was necessary, but that was "plain nonsense," he told the Howard students. "From Tokyo to Heidelberg," the former artillery captain announced, "orders have gone out that will make our fighting forces a more perfect instrument of democratic defense." Before long, African-American GI's from Mississippi were sharing double-decker bunks with whites from South Carolina, and a white rifle platoon was taking orders from a black sergeant.[46]

Once Truman set out on this course, he would not relent. When Democratic leaders asked him to back down, he replied: "My forebears were Confederates. . . . Every factor and influence in my background—and in my wife's for that matter—would foster the personal belief that you are right. But my very stomach turned over when I learned that Negro soldiers, just back from overseas, were being dumped out of army trucks in Mississippi and beaten. Whatever my inclinations as a native of Missouri might have been, as President I know this is bad. I shall fight to end evils like this." Truman showed how resolute he could be when, at a White House banquet, Alabama's national committeewoman lectured him. "I want to take a message back to the South," she said. "Can I tell them you're not ramming miscegenation down our throats? That you're not for tearing up our social structure—that you're for all the people, not just the North?" Truman responded by reaching into his pocket, whipping out a copy of the Constitution, and reading her the Bill of Rights. "I stand on the Constitution," he replied. "I take back nothing of what I proposed and make no excuses for it." So wrought up did a black waiter at the White House become in listening to this exchange that he knocked a cup of coffee out of the president's hands.[47]

Harry Truman's attitude had formidable consequences, as the two most prominent leaders of the NAACP attested. "No occupant of the White House since the nation was born has taken so frontal or consistent a stand against racial and religious discrimination as has Mr. Truman," declared Walter White in 1952. In Truman's final week in the White House, Roy Wilkins wrote him: "Mr. President, no Chief Executive in our history has spoken so plainly on [civil rights] as yourself, or acted so forthrightly. We have had in the White House great men—great diplomats, great politicians, great scholars, great humanitarians, great administrators. Some of them have recognized inequality as undesirable, as being at variance with the democratic principles of our country; but none has had the courage . . . to speak out or act in the Truman manner. . . . As you leave the White House you carry with you the gratitude and affectionate regard of millions of your Negro fellow citizens who in less than a decade of your leadership, inspiration and determination, have seen the old order change right before their eyes." Other commentators agreed. "It was Harry Truman," C. Vann Woodward maintained, "who broke through the old bipartisan consensus on racial policy," and the civil rights leader James Farmer said, "The little haberdasher from Independence, Missouri, took charge with something approaching greatness."[48]

Truman's bold initiative in launching a national investigation of racial injustice marked a watershed. "No political act since the Compromise of 1877," Taylor Branch has asserted, "so profoundly influenced race relations; in a sense it was a repeal of 1877." In addition to causing a "fateful rupture between South and non-South" and drastically affecting the legislative agenda, it signified "a shift of emphasis from Negro 'uplift'—essentially a paternalistic approach—to civil rights, i.e., the achievement of more than nominal citizenship." Indeed, noted another writer, it was the report of the president's committee that "brought the phrase 'civil rights' into common political parlance, replacing 'the Negro question.'" Moreover, Truman's action echoed long after he had left the White House. As Steven Lawson has stressed, "His civil rights committee's program—a multifaceted one that challenged both disfranchisement and segregation—would serve as the legislative agenda during the next three administrations." Truman's civil rights effort also had the huge, though unintended, effect of ending the South's isolation from national politics as a one-party region and beginning a process of nationalization in which both parties would compete for the section's favor.[49]

Even historians who found fault with Truman's record on racial issues have acknowledged the significance of his commitment to constitutional rights in enabling him to overcome his prejudices. "Truman firmly believed that as president of the United States he was obligated to defend the Constitution not only by upholding the laws of the land but by strengthening them as well," William Berman has written. "Although he was destined to be attacked in the South and elsewhere as a dangerous innovator for his seeming disregard of local customs, Truman actually appears to be a traditionalist who decried acts of injustice because they violated what he thought constituted the American heritage of political liberty and fair play." By 1952, Barton Bernstein has remarked, Truman "had become a conscience for the Democrats. He was bolder on civil rights than his party and its presidential candidate."[50]

In *The Cold War and the Color Line*, Thomas Borstelmann observed: "People do not choose the circumstances into which they are born, but what they make of those in later life provides a measure of their character. In contrast to his siblings, Harry Truman chose to move away from the explicit racism of his childhood as his political career developed and his contacts in the world widened. . . . By the standards of later generations and of more liberated contemporaries, Truman remained a racist in his personal attitudes. . . . But for a man of his place and time, the Missourian made impressive strides on matters of race." Borstelmann, a sharp critic of American policy toward the third world, went on to say: "The obviously political timing of Truman's initiatives on race in 1948, combined with his continuing effort to keep white Southerners on board his campaign, seem less significant in retrospect than the unprecedented fashion in which he placed the authority of the White House and the Democratic Party behind the goal of racial equality. The Democrats, it must be remembered, had long been the party of the white South, of slavery and the lynching rope. It was Truman's rejection of racial discrimination that began to shatter that historic identification and started the seismic shift of a majority of white voters in Dixie to the Republican Party by the 1990s."[51]

The crumbling of Democratic strength in the South that gained momentum so rapidly under Truman proved to be long lasting. Strom Thurmond later tabbed the breakaway from Truman in 1948 as the great divide in the history of the Democratic Party. "We got the people to feel that if they didn't vote the national Democratic ticket the sky wouldn't fall," he said. More than one observer has agreed that 1948 was the pivot. The rate of defection from the Democrats in the South in these decades was highest in the years between 1949 and 1952, and the pace is best explained not by socioeconomic changes but by disaffection from Roosevelt and Truman. In 1948 four Deep South states deserted to the Dixiecrats; in 1952 four additional southern states defected to the Republicans. So in the Truman years, eight of the former Confederate states underwent the experience of abandoning the Democrats.[52]

When in the post-Truman era white supremacists looked back on how the South had changed, they had no doubt of who was the author of their misery. In 1959 a Mississippi congressman, deploring the annual flood of civil rights bills, said that his section had been plagued "ever since President Truman shocked and divided the 'solid south' in 1948 with his message to the Congress demanding so-called civil rights legislation." Truman, the biographer of Leander Perez has observed, "eventually vied with Lyndon Johnson for the top spot on the Judge's list of most hated national leaders. Years later, the Plaquemines boss pointed back to the Truman administration as the time it had all begun: 'uppity' Negroes, collusion with the Communists, federal giveaway programs, and deliberate destruction of states' rights."[53]

A decade after he left office, Truman told an interviewer who was creating an oral history: "All those Southern fellas were very much surprised by my program for civil rights in 1948. What they didn't understand was that I'd been for things like that all the time I was in politics. I believe in the Constitution, and if you do that, then everybody's got to have their rights and that means *everybody*, doesn't matter a damn who they are or what color they are. The minute you start making exceptions, you might as well not have a Constitution. So that's the reason I felt the way I did, and if a lot of folks were surprised to find out where I stood on the colored question, well, that's because they didn't know me."[54]

Though Truman had an affinity for the South, he had a much stronger attachment to the Union, which he had developed on his own when a Missouri schoolboy. He especially revered the memory of Andrew Jackson, a southerner but a nationalist. In his Raleigh address during the 1948 campaign, Truman offered a homily about Jackson that was clearly intended to point a contemporary moral: "He has always been held up as a symbol of courage, but often for reasons that are not the best. It takes courage to face a duelist with a pistol and it takes courage to face a British general with an army. But it takes still greater and far higher courage to face friends with a grievance. The bravest thing Andrew Jackson ever did was to stand up and tell his own people to their faces that they were wrong." His action "was all the braver," Truman declared, because Jackson knew that the tariff of abominations "did inflict injustice upon South Carolina and the other Southern States." He added, "Let me say how fine a thing it is that this monument was raised in the South by Southerners."[55]

His NAACP address made explicit what this nationalist vision of the intent of the Constitution signified for race relations. "We must make the Federal Government a friendly, vigilant defender of the rights and equalities of all Americans," he asserted. "And again I mean all Americans." In a sentence that appeared to be directly aimed at the South, the president declared, "We cannot, any longer, await the growth of a will to action in the slowest state or the most backward community." In his speech to the NAACP, Kansas City's black newspaper remarked, "Truman so strongly denounced race prejudice . . . that even his enemies were convinced that the Missourian in the White House had left behind him Missouri's tradition of second-class citizenship for Negroes."[56]

Truman acted as he did not because he believed in social equality of the races, not because he was "anti-South," but because his reading in history and in documents such as the Declaration of Independence and the Bill of Rights led him to question the assumptions on which he was raised, and because he took altogether solemnly the oath he had sworn to sustain the Constitution. Furthermore, Truman's personal code moved him to embrace civil rights. If something presented itself to him as involving an issue of justice, there was little doubt where he would come down. "While my ancestors may have thought that slavery was a proper thing and that the suppression of the black race was a good thing in this country," he once said, "I came to the conclusion, on my own hook, that it isn't."[57]

Despite his Confederate lineage, he was even able to bring himself to cherish Abraham Lincoln. When in 1950 Truman received a letter from Tennessee alluding to John Bell, he replied, "It was the Bell and Everett fight that gave Abraham a chance to enter the White House on a minority vote. In the long run I am satisfied it was best for the country but my mother and father never thought so." In informal reflections on his predecessors, Truman offered his assessment of the Great Emancipator:

> Old Abe Lincoln is . . . a president I admire tremendously. In a way, it's surprising that I feel the way I do about Lincoln, because I was born and raised in the South . . . and a lot of southerners still don't feel that way about him at all. And that included the Truman family, all of whom were

against him. Some of them even thought it was a fine thing that he got assassinated.

I realized even as a child that was pretty extreme thinking or worse; let's just call it dumb thinking, or no thinking at all. But it still took me a while to realize what a good man Lincoln really was, with a great brain and even greater heart, a man who really cared about people and educated himself to the point where he knew how government should work and tried his best to make ours work that way. I felt just the opposite of the rest of the Truman family after I studied the history of the country and realized what Lincoln did to save the Union. That's when I came to my present conclusion, and that was a long, long time ago. . . . Lincoln was a great and wonderful man in every way.[58]

As a border-state Democrat, Truman carried within himself the conflicts that divided not only Missouri, but the country. Like FDR, he was poised to be at the same time inside and outside the South, able to identify with its hurts and its hopes but to believe that its destiny lay not in separateness but in finding a place for itself within the nation. Tom Clark later reflected, "Mr. Truman, by the Southerners' standards, was not a Southerner,"[59] but Truman knew differently. He had been nurtured on the valor of Robert E. Lee, schooled in the iniquities of the Union raiders, and taught to share the melancholy memory of the Lost Cause. When he said, "I was born and raised in the South," Truman thought he was simply stating a truism. Only someone who understood himself to be a southerner could have felt such affection for the traditions of the South. Yet he also had a schoolboy's love of the history not of a section but of a nation, took pride in having been an artillery officer in the army of the United States of America, and viewed the Constitution as sacred text. In the end, that nationalist theme, a muted one when he was a boy, prevailed. As a consequence, Truman altered the character of southern and of national politics. He made civil rights, for the first time since Reconstruction, a proper concern for the national government, and for the first time ever the Democratic Party became the main protagonist for the rights of blacks. Without Truman, the much more far-reaching changes wrought by Lyndon Johnson would not have been possible.

IV

In January 1969, his great coalition of 1964 in shambles, his policies objects of derision, Lyndon Johnson said good-bye to the national capital that had been his main domicile for nearly four decades. On their first night at the ranch as private citizens, the Johnsons noted an eerie silence with the customary entourage gone, and Lady Bird said to the former president, "The coach has turned back into a pumpkin, and the mice have all run away." His final years he spent "down at the Pedernales where," he said, "my grandfather and grandmother and mother and father and uncles and cousins and aunts are all buried on the banks of that little river."[60] There he brooded over what his presidency signified.

Johnson questioned whether, despite the example he had set as a leader who put nation over section, the North would ever get over "a disdain for the South that seems to be woven into the fabric of Northern experience." He speculated: "Perhaps it all stems from the deep-rooted bitterness engendered by civil strife over a hundred years ago, for emotional clichés outlast all others and the Southern cliché is perhaps the most emotional of all. Perhaps someday new understanding will cause this bias to disappear from our national life. I hope so, but it is with us still." In a 1969 interview, he told Walter Cronkite: "It may be that I was a pessimist, but I have always had doubts that a man that was born where I was born—was reared up in the atmosphere where I was reared, that lived in the communities and went to the schools and the churches . . . that I went to— could over a long period of time provide the leadership that would take all of this conglomeration of people, the masses that we have in these fifty states, and keep them united . . . . I don't believe we've reached a point yet where I could do that."[61]

Furthermore, a good many southerners had made Johnson painfully aware that they rejected him too. In 1967 the *New York Times* characterized the South as the "section of the country where candidates of both parties now compete to outdo each other in condemning the President." The powerful Virginia congressman Howard Smith called Johnson a "rattlesnake" who harbored a "great hatred for the South" and was trying to "punish" his native region. In Barbara Garson's satirical drama *MacBird!* (which substitutes Johnson for Shakespeare's regicide, Macbeth) a Bobby Kennedy aide says:

The southern racists think MacBird a traitor,
And so may not impede his overthrow.

Indeed, George Wallace's chief advisor declared, "As for LBJ, he ought to be tried in the docks as a traitor." When Johnson, despite his ostensible withdrawal from the 1968 presidential race, sought covertly to be drafted by the Democratic convention, southern governors turned thumbs down. From an altogether different perspective, his longtime friend Virginia Durr, who thought Johnson had "become almost a kind of monster," wrote a friend in 1967, "Shall I simply say what I think of him now for the future historians? I really think he is off his rocker." Two years later a member of the staff of the Southern Regional Council was capable of writing, flagrantly unfairly: "It might have seemed in 1964 that Southerners, white Southern racists, would have known in their bones, just by the very sound of his nasal intonations of certain words, that Lyndon Baines Johnson was more thoroughly, more fundamentally racist than Goldwater— whose nervous-talking speeches showed unfamiliarity with the idiom of racism, with even the first subtleties of it. Indeed, it is difficult to say what Johnson was on the question, having moved in his political postures along every inch of the line from segregationist to integrationist, back and forth, or even what he was unconsciously, subconsciously, ideologically or psychedelically. But the performance of his Administration, its nearly complete failure to achieve any of the simple goals of desegregation, was racist, maybe more completely so than Goldwater's might have been."[62]

Likening LBJ to Martin Luther King, another southerner, Gene Patterson, wrote in his *Atlanta Constitution* column:

Lyndon Johnson, a Southern president, tried to turn away from the ancestral vices. . . . Yet his efforts were not credited. Southerners who believed what they liked to believe called him a turncoat. And although he may not have expected the viciousness of the assaults, Johnson was a realist who always knew he would not be appreciated in the North either.

As early as April, 1964, riding to the White House through the dark streets of Washington, he leaned his head in his hands wearily and predicted in a quiet voice that the Eastern press and intellectuals would not rest until they had ruined him. . . . I suggested he was hypersensitive and mistaken. . . . He raised his head, looked out the window of the moving car, and said thoughtfully, "No, you're wrong. Just wait until I make one mistake—or what they think is a mistake. Then you'll see how they're going to go after me."

Lyndon Johnson read the patronizers who sneered at his Southernism better than they read him. . . . Lyndon B. Johnson readily accepted his political death to emancipate his white southern kinsmen from wrongdoing their fellow Americans . . . any longer.[63]

Lyndon Johnson went to his grave knowing that, quite apart from his contribution to the agony in Vietnam, he was for millions of Americans, a pariah. In Johnson's last year in the White House, a Texas progressive wrote sardonically, "His subjects had grown . . . weary of their great, vain cowboy king," that "hog-calling arm-waver." At the 1969 inaugural, as Johnson bowed out, a team of British reporters, observing Lady Bird, thought "there was something about the way she looked at her husband that brought to mind Kent's lines at the end of King Lear: "He hates him much / That would upon the rack of this tough world / Stretch him out longer." In the 1972 campaign, a friend remarked, "Lyndon just doesn't carry any weight in the party anymore, and he knows it. It's a miserable fact for a man who only four years ago was President of the United States. But it is a fact." Many in the North still viewed his southern manner as alien. Many in the South still perceived him to be a renegade. It is hard to imagine how much more any leader could have done to reconcile section and nation. But it proved not to have been enough for what T. Harry Williams called "this tormented man from his tormented region who had such large visions of what his country might become."[64]

Johnson had often had occasion to explore with William S. White issues that affected the South because, White explained, "he regarded me as somewhat more Southern than he was." Asked what single subject dominated Johnson's thoughts, White later told an interviewer:

> I think what probably most of all concerned him—and this is what concerned him all his political life—was . . . that he wished to be an agent for healing in the country, or an agent for reunion; an agent to get rid of the divisions following the Civil War, to get rid of the dichotomy, as he saw it, of the two nations. Domestically what most concerned him was anything that he thought would reduce the abrasion, the sectional abrasion, in the country.
>
> You see, he was never a typical Southerner in the stereotyped term, primarily because he didn't think that way, and secondarily because his part of Texas was not really Southern. The war there, if anything, was the war with Mexico.[65]

White's perception is buttressed by the president's own words. In his address to Congress following Kennedy's assassination in 1963, Johnson said, in espousing civil rights legislation, "We will serve all the Nation, not one section or one sector, or one group, but all Americans. These are the *United* States—

a united people with a united purpose." The following year, in New Orleans, he declared, "When the Democrats win this election, our first work must be to bind our wounds, heal our history—and make this nation whole." During the 1964 campaign, at a breakfast of the Georgia legislature in Atlanta, Johnson stated: "I come . . . to speak to you as an American. As I am President of all the people, you are part of all that people. I speak to you not therefore, as Georgians, this morning, or as Southerners, but as Americans. Your hopes are the nation's hopes; your problems are the nation's problems. You bear the mark of a Southern heritage proudly, but that which is Southern is far less important than that which is American."[66]

Johnson repeatedly sounded this nationalist theme in 1964. In his acceptance address, he said, "Tonight we offer ourselves . . . as a party for all Americans, an all-American party for all Americans! . . . The needs of all cannot be met by . . . a Southern party or a Northern party." Often he gave a stock speech in which he asked for "a truly national party which is stranger to no region, . . . knows no North, no South, no East, no West," though he was also fond of another version which was essentially a self-parody. He would tell a crowd: "Of course, I do not want to go as far as the Georgia politician who shouted from the stump in the heat of debate, 'My fellow citizens, I know no North, I know no South, I know no East, I know no West.' A barefooted, freckle-faced boy shouted out from the audience, . . . 'Well, you better go back and study some geography!'"[67]

At an election eve rally at the Astrodome in November 1968, Johnson, noting that he had left Houston in 1931 when he was a high school debate coach, announced that he was returning "to take part in another debate, which is one of the great issues of our time: . . . 'Resolved, that union is good for Texas, for this region, and for our entire Nation.'" He asserted: "My fellow Texans, this is the same issue that confronted Texas 100 years ago when our Nation was torn apart by an awful war. It is the same issue that a great southerner, Andrew Jackson, addressed when he raised his glass and toasted: 'The Union: It shall be preserved.' . . . The issue was clear to young Sam Rayburn. Only with union—only with real union—could the South 'rise again'—as a vigorous, progressive part of America." He pledged, "As a southerner—as one who knows the bitter fruits of disunion—I shall do all I can, for as long as I can, to achieve harmony between the races based on the only foundation that can endure: Justice and tolerance among all men, for all people."[68]

Johnson sought to be the greatest president of all time, greater even than Franklin Delano Roosevelt, and, Nicholas Lemann has noted, "Johnson knew exactly what it was that Roosevelt hadn't been able to do," including: "Guarantee blacks in the South the right to vote, and the other appurtenances of full citizenship. Break the hold of the Southern segregationists on the Congress and the Democratic Party. Heal, finally, the wounds left by the Civil War and Reconstruction and bring the country together. Nobody had been able to do that—not Washington or Jefferson, not Lincoln, not Roosevelt. Johnson thought that given his skills, his historical moment, and his roots in the South, he could." Another *New York Times* correspondent, assigned to cover the movement for racial justice, wrote: "One has to believe that Johnson was sincere about civil rights. It was in domestic affairs that he intended to make his mark. And what better way than to overcome once and for all the great failure that had for so long bound the black man and blighted the soul of the white? The Johnsons of Texas knew this. . . . Hubert Humphrey, the Northern liberal, indicated along the way he did not fully *understand* what was involved. Johnson, brought up as a Southern conservative, *understood* thoroughly."[69]

To persuade southerners to share his vision, he needed to speak to them as a fellow child of the South, which he could do convincingly because most of the time that is how he saw himself. When Johnson spoke in Georgia in May 1964, Tom Wicker reported, he "identified himself wholeheartedly as a Southerner with family roots in the red earth of Georgia, where one of his forebears was sheriff of Henry County; and when his daughter, Lynda Bird, rose to speak, she said 'y'all' as naturally as she smiled." The historian Eric Goldman, who served on the White House staff, said of Johnson: "Although not a Southerner in basic ways, an important part of him belonged to Dixie. When that strain came to the fore he sounded like most members of a group who feel themselves misunderstood and abused. He became intensely introspective; he talked about the Southern mentality a great deal, poked into it, defended and attacked it, kept trying to explain it to others and perhaps to himself." Intimates from other parts of the country did not doubt where he was rooted. "I think he understood the southern party," Jim Rowe later said, "but you get him north of the Mason-Dixon line, and west, and he was gone."[70]

Johnson found it hard to understand how any of his onetime comrades on Capitol Hill could think he was an enemy of the South. No matter how much he might on occasion showcase himself as a westerner or a denizen of one end or the other of Pennsylvania Avenue, he always believed that when he recommended programs that affected the South he did so with the instincts of a native. At a rally in Augusta during the 1964 campaign, he reminded his audience that there had lived in that Georgia town the last president before him to be born and raised in the South, Woodrow Wilson, and he wished to reiterate what that boy, when grown to manhood, had once said: "The only place in the world where nothing has to be explained to me is the South." Johnson continued: "I know the burdens that the South has borne. I know the troubles that the South has seen. I know the ordeals that have tried the South through all of these years. And I want to see those burdens lifted off the South. I want the ordeals to end and the South to stand where it should stand as the full and honored part of a proud and united land."[71]

Southern particularism on race, Johnson had long ago concluded, exacted too high a cost. Quite apart from the pain it inflicted on blacks, to which he was not insensitive, racism was an indulgence southern whites could not afford if they expected to thrive in a global economy. Wicker wrote, "*As a Southerner, Lyndon Johnson was better placed than any man to recognize that full national unity and sweeping national progress, on civil rights or any other questions, was not possible until the South had somehow been brought back into the Union.*" Only by abandoning Jim Crow, Johnson deduced, could the South merge with the rest of the nation to address its economic necessities. Alabama's space program at Huntsville needed scientists, he told a writer in 1964, and no Einsteins would go to a place where they thought George Wallace ate people like them for breakfast.[72]

Johnson surmised that as a southern-born president he was destined to carry his section gracefully through this difficult transition. A month after the 1964 election, a *New York Times* correspondent reported on a conversation with Johnson about his quest for a new attorney general: "He wants someone . . . who will not be vindictive or punitive against the South. He wants to avoid rubbing the South's nose in its own troubles. In the first place, he thinks the 'good people' of the South have suffered quite a bit. Most of all he thinks there is a more effective way of bringing about acceptance of the Civil Rights Act, in spirit as well as letter, than trial and punishment." In his first address to Congress, Johnson, Wicker has written, "held out to the South . . . what no politician but a Southerner in the White House could have offered with such sincerity—the hope of reconciliation, the suggestion of a future in which Southern states and Southern men would no longer have to stand together against all the rest." Wicker added: "Now the President of the United States, a Southerner, speaking in the unmistakable accents of their own region, was saying to Southern men *that they were not outlaws.* They were not immoralists or degenerates or colonial subjects but men who had lost a struggle. He held out a promise, not a threat. . . . Magnanimity, not righteousness, was being offered at last to the South, by a man who shared its heritage of defeat, and who had suffered for it in his own way."[73]

The big difference between Kennedy and Johnson, Wicker went on, was that Johnson could appeal to blacks and to the South "*at the same time.*" He explained: "Lyndon Johnson could do it because he was a Southerner cast into the White House by accident. Southerners knew he had shared their bitter alienation; among other things, it had helped lose him the Democratic nomination they and he thought he deserved in 1960—just as it had cost the able Richard Russell his chance at the Presidency in 1952. Johnson . . . did not come to the South with vindictiveness in his heart; there might be a little Scalawag in him but a Carpetbagger he could never be. He was one of the South's own; he had a sympathy for their outlook that many Southerners could believe was genuine. He understood them, and they him." Similarly, Steven Lawson concluded: "Johnson never deviated from his ultimate goal of extending the right to vote to the mass of southern Negroes, but he was anxious to achieve his objective without stirring up the wrath of the opposition. Unlike the suffrage crusaders filled with burning rage against their racist oppressors, LBJ did not view southern white leaders as evil men whose sin must be painfully exorcised with righteous indignation. Instead, he preferred to reason, negotiate, and cajole. . . . He sought to expand first-class citizenship for southern blacks and, at the same time, convince the white South to make the required adjustments peacefully and permanently."[74]

Johnson's origins in a state below the Mason-Dixon line, William S. White has observed, not altogether accurately, "inevitably earned him the forgiveness of the Southerners in times of intraparty crisis." He added: "At such times they spoke of him with the pained and exasperated affection of some Back Bay Bostonian uncle toward a nephew who had, through the mystery of providence, chosen to transport himself to San Francisco there to become a hippie in the Haight-Ashbury. After all, Lyndon's grandfather had been a Confederate soldier, and, . . . to see the attitude of such an Old South patriarch as . . . Senator Harry Flood Byrd, Sr., to Lyndon when Lyndon, as not infrequently, was coaxing his Southern brethren into the most wildly improbable legislation from their viewpoint was to see real-life theater."[75]

When Johnson sought the Democratic presidential nomination in 1960, even ardent foes of civil rights laws gave him their blessing. At the beginning of 1959 Dick Russell had scrawled on a pad, "LBJ for president," and in 1960 the Georgia senator was still maintaining that Johnson was "in every way qualified to serve as President of the United States." Herman Talmadge, in a televised program directed to five southern states, endorsed the majority leader, and Strom Thurmond was heard to say to Johnson, "I hope you're the next president of the United States." It would be the last time that Thurmond would support a Democratic aspirant for the White House. True, the South had been critical of LBJ, but, as one Kentucky legislator put it, "Things have come to a hell of a pass if we can't cudgel our own jackass." When John Kennedy said he could not understand why Luther Hodges was backing Johnson rather than him, since the North Carolina governor had been his strong ally, Hodges replied: "Well, I'm doing this, Senator, because of prejudice. . . . The prejudice of the North against a Southern candidate because we've been written off . . . for a hundred years along these lines, and I don't like the prejudice of the North and other parts of the country against the South. This seems to be the best chance we've had in a hundred years, so I'm going to support Mr. Johnson for the nomination."[76]

More than one commentator pointed out that Johnson was able to accomplish so much precisely because he was a southerner. Ramsey Clark, a Texan, stated that enforcing civil rights statutes was "harder for a President from Massachusetts than a President from Texas," and Clark's father, Tom, later said of the southern bloc in Congress, "Lyndon was able to dissipate it, at least put some cracks in it, because he was part of it," and hence get through civil rights legislation that had been stymied before. "Civil rights legislation was all Johnson," Richard Helms told an interviewer. "I don't think Kennedy could have gotten it through Congress the way Johnson did—not even in a second term. I don't think Kennedy could have talked to Richard Russell and the other Southern senators the way Johnson did." James Farmer agreed. "It had to wait for a Southern president—Southern accent, a back-slapper and arm-twister— like LBJ to get it through," he said.[77]

"A Texan who was an expert at speaking southern," Johnson talked instinctively in cadences that invited confidence. "I want to wipe poverty off the face of the South," he told his southern audiences, but to do that the section had to abandon the old folkways on race. A *New York Times* correspondent observed: "Only a Southerner could talk that way to Southerners and make them listen. It was not only a matter of understanding or of approach. It was also a matter of style. To the Easterner, President Kennedy had style. In the South, President

Johnson has it. . . . It is part corn pone, as when, traveling in his car on the way to a meeting he grabs an electronic megaphone and calls out: 'I like to see the sunshine, I like to see these smiling faces. Come on, now, let's all go to the speakin.'" On Johnson's 1964 campaign trail in Georgia, Scotty Reston heard the president speak out uncompromisingly in favor of civil rights and express his determination to see "every section of this country . . . linked in a single purpose." Reston commented, "The South would probably hesitate to take this from anybody else, but even the most segregationist Southerner cannot wholly disown President Johnson."[78]

In the fall of 1965 Lillian Smith, who had made her home atop Georgia's Old Screamer Mountain a command post for racial integration, wrote a correspondent: "It is not easy for President Johnson; I trust this man more than many of my northern friends do. . . . I knew from things Johnson said in his southern speeches when running for vice-president that he put the state of being human above the state of being white; no white southerner can deceive me; we speak down here a cryptic language at times; we speak a form of lie that every white southerner immediately translates into the truth it is intended to convey. . . . When Johnson spoke it I knew he was OK: I knew and I got—and millions of southerners got—the message he was sending across to us. From this time on, he was saying, I am for the human being first, the American second, the southerner third; but 'whiteness' does not count any more. So—what has happened? He has done more than any President in a hundred years to see that Negroes get their rights and their privileges."[79]

Johnson's leadership had large consequences not only for the nation but also for the South, especially in carrying forward the process begun under FDR and carried on under Truman of liberating the section from its isolation. When he broke the eighty-three-day filibuster in 1964, Johnson, one historian has asserted, "removed the stigma of being a southerner," while another has said that "he helped the South to join the United States." Virginia Durr, despite her caustic antipathy to Johnson's actions in his second term in the White House, came to conclude: "Lyndon brought the South into the mainstream of the policies of the United States. That is my belief, that he really struck the shackles. I mean, Lincoln struck the shackles off the slaves, but Lyndon struck the shackles off the South. He freed us from the burden of segregation." Virginia Durr's husband, Cliff, too, was convinced, in the words of his biographer, "that Johnson, more than any other politician, 'freed the South from its generations of bondage to racism'—indeed, made it, at last, a region where he and others like him could finally live in increasing serenity." Another commentator, suggesting a different consideration, has concluded, "It does not go too far to describe the South as virtually a poor country within the confines of a rich one until the Civil Rights Act made it respectable for national corporations to locate there."[80]

It was left, appropriately enough, to an eminent historian, southern-born, to put these developments in historical perspective. C. Vann Woodward wrote:

> Lyndon Baines Johnson was as southern in origins, accent, personality, and political style as a politician with aspirations for national leadership could have been at mid-twentieth century. Here the ironies begin to multiply. Johnson was quite aware of the penalties and limitations his southern identity would entail in any circumstances but more especially given the role into which history had thrust him—to preside over and implement the Second Reconstruction. . . .
>
> The contrast between the way in which the two Presidents Johnson responded to their reconstruction assignments could hardly have been more striking. Andrew Johnson aligned himself politically with opponents of equal rights for black freedmen in the North and with white resistance in the South. . . . Lyndon Johnson a century later pursued precisely the opposite course in his reconstruction strategy. And it *was* his in the peculiar sense that it was he and not northern crusaders who proposed and railroaded through Congress the Second Reconstruction laws. . . . And for the black people he could lay claim to doing more for their civil rights than any president since Lincoln and having gone on to score more humanitarian legislation than all of them put together.[81]

Blacks, especially, noted the significance of Johnson's origins. Vernon Jordan, asked in 1972 why, with such a demanding schedule, he found time to attend a conference honoring LBJ, replied that it was "because of what I think to be Lyndon Johnson's commitment to civil rights and really because of the record of achievement that I think unique, that I think was creative and innovative and imaginative." He continued: "And I think that I'm excited about his contributions largely because he, like myself, comes from the South. And I have a feeling that ultimately in the area of race that Southerners will show the way." Charles Evers made that point more vividly. "I admired him because he was a Southerner, and somehow he knew how to handle these Southern rascals," he said. "Those Texas big-hat men that he knew, those Mississippians, Eastland and Stennis; Strom Thurmond, Talmadge, Russell and Long—they had been with him for years. He challenged them. When a man does that, you have to give him credit."[82]

Other commentators, though not discounting the advantage to Johnson of his origins in sensing how to sweet-talk southern legislators, put greater stress on the leverage he got from his fungible sectional identity. Alistair Cooke described him as "a country boy with Southern talk and Western habits," and Tom Wicker wrote that Johnson "was, first, by blood and geography, a Southerner—although by nature, at least as much a Westerner." Even his wife has denied he was a true southerner. "He was a Westerner, a Southwesterner," she once said. "I'm the one who's really from the South." Puzzlement over where to place Johnson left the southern politicians with whom he negotiated addled, as is suggested by a snatch of recollection by Strom Thurmond: "Since he was from the South, although he called Texas from the West—he always spoke of Texas as being a western state; well, it is somewhat both." Terry Sanford's reflections indicate similar disarray. In 1960, he remembered, southerners flocked to LBJ as a son of Dixie. Yet Sanford immediately added, "And of course as soon as Johnson crossed the Mississippi River he was no longer a Southerner and didn't claim to be."[83]

Johnson orchestrated and exploited this confusion about where he came from. As a Texan, he was at liberty to do so. "There are regions of Texas," a historian noted in 1960, "which are Southern or Western apparently at the whim of the local chamber of commerce." Even when he became president, he magnified the befuddlement. "If you said he was from the South," Reston has written, "he would say he was from the West or the other way around." Conflating the sections put Johnson in the catbird seat. "He lived in both worlds," Jim Rowe remarked, "and he could go back and forth." Furthermore, his status as both insider and outsider led at least some southerners to be more accepting of his initiatives on civil rights. "Lyndon's record on the race issue was all right," said Governor Sanford, "partially because he wasn't from the South."[84]

In 1971 the African-American writer Albert Murray developed these insights vividly in setting down a monologue he had heard from an ancient black man in "chinaberry-blue Maytime" of 1969 at "one very special back porch after-supper rocking-chair session in the fig-tree-fresh, damp-clay-scented twilight" of Mobile: "Lyndon Johnson, Lyndon Johnson. Old Lyndon Johnson. They can call him everything but a child of God as long as you please and I still say old

Lyndon Johnson, faults and all. . . . I say old Lyndon Johnson is the one that brought more government benefits to help us out than all the rest of them up there put together all the way back through old Abe Lincoln." He continued: "When they all used to get to making such miration over old Franklin D. I said that's all right about Muscle Shoals and Three Point Two and God bless Miss Eleanor for being as nice as she is and all that, but I said both of them come from up there and I don't care how good they talk you just watch and see if they don't always manage to find some old excuse not to buck the Southern white man. . . . It's going to take one of these old Confederate bushwhackers from somewhere right down through in here to go up against these old Southern white folks."

In his rambling discourse during this first spring of the Nixon presidency, Murray's companion finally came to his point: "So when old Lyndon Johnson come along and got in there on a humble—and, boy that's the onliest way he ever coulda made it into there—I was watching with my fingers crossed because he was the first one from down in here since old Woodrow Wilson and all that old dirt he did us. . . . But now here's what give the whole thing away to me. These white folks down here. Boy don't you never forget they always been the key to everything so far as we concerned. . . . They the very first ones to realize that old Lyndon Johnson meant business when he said the time is here to do something. And didn't nobody have to tell them what that meant because they already knew he was one of them and if they made him mad he subject to do some of that old rowdy cracker cussing right back at them, and some of that old cowboy stuff to boot. When they commence to telling me about how mean he is that's when I tell them . . . that's exactly what we need, some mean old crackers on our side for a change."[85]

EPILOGUE:
THE SOUTH ON THE MOVE

I

Less than three years after Lyndon Johnson died, a little-known ex-governor set his sights on becoming president of the United States. The odds against his succeeding were huge. So obscure that he was called "Jimmy Who?," he held no office. He could claim no experience whatsoever in foreign affairs. Worst of all, he came from Georgia. Save for the controverted example of LBJ, no resident of a Deep South state had been elected president since 1848. To numbers of southerners, his ambition constituted a test of how far the country had come since the age of Roosevelt in accepting the states of the onetime Confederacy as fully accredited members of the United States.

James Earl Carter Jr., "who in the ostentatiously folksy Southern way called himself Jimmy," was a sure enough son of Dixie. Unlike Johnson, this born-again peanut grower from the sleepy village of Plains, Georgia, had no western cast to his background. Though "his New South approach to voters is cooler than the delivery of the hot stump speechifiers of another era," Carter, *Time* noted, "is a Southern farm boy at heart who still knows how to turn sweet potato vines, chop cotton and pull peanuts, and who looks homeward to a hamlet so archetypically Southern that it is almost a parody. Beyond that, he is a bucolic devotee of hunting and bird dogs, stock-car racing and rock music—notably backwoods Georgia's own Allman Brothers."[1]

With good reason, Carter could say on the first page of his autobiography, "I am a Southerner and an American," mentioning "Southerner" first. At Annapolis, he had been hazed mercilessly for defying an order from an upperclassman to sing "Marching Through Georgia." Three of his ancestors had fought with Lee in the Virginia campaigns. The Confederacy's death camp at Andersonville had been located in Carter's county. Northerners may have found that unsettling, but Carter did not dissemble in stating how he felt about Union incursions. At one point, he said, "The last time the Republicans were in Atlanta was 100 years ago. They burned it down."[2]

When during the early winter primary season of 1976 Carter's "Peanut Brigade" braved snowdrifts as far north as the Canadian border, Georgia "snowbunnies," bearing down-home names like Starlet McKendree and Trisha Lee, made a point of thickening their "Southernese, heavily accented with laryngitis," to emphasize how far they had trudged to promote the cause of their former governor. One of the "peachblossoms in the snow," in the phrase of the *Boston Globe*, has set down how canvassers would respond when asked by a Nashua housewife or an Aroostook potato digger what they thought of the New England weather:

> "Oh, we jes' not used to it a-tall," the Georgian could say pitifully, desperately clutching the step railing to stay upright on the ice. "It never even snows in Plains."
>
> "Plains! Are you from Plains?"
>
> "Well, nearly 'bout, jes' over the county line in Smithville. (Oh, catch hold to my hand, I'm 'bout to fall.)"
>
> "Then do you really know Jem-mie Kot-ta?"
>
> "Why, I jes' don't know HOW long my mama and Miss Lillian been frien's."[3]

After Carter beat out a field of northern contenders to win the Democratic presidential nomination in 1976, southerners rejoiced. At a filling station outside Americus, Georgia, an attendant said, "He'll bring the South back into the country, that I can tell you. And . . . we can offer the country something too. Maybe now is our turn, at last." After listening to Carter's acceptance speech, with its maladroit reference to "*Eye*talians," Larry King wrote: "Wellsir, you just can't imagine what that inflection meant to hearts bred and born in Dixie. Ol' Southern boys around the world, recognizing the nuances and shadings of home, lurched to their collective feet, spilling right smart amounts of bourbon and branch water over the rims of their gold goblets or jelly glasses, and with wet eyes huskily proclaimed, 'We ain't *trash* no more.'" In short, wrote Roy Blount, the Democrats, in choosing Carter, had wound up with "a Southern Baptist simple-talking peanut-warehousing grit-eating 'Eyetalian'-saying Cracker."[4]

Carter exploited sectional pride in seeking votes below the Mason-Dixon line. In one radio spot aired on southern stations that a Carter aide acknowledged was "blatant—waving the bloody rebel flag," an announcer declared:

> On November 2, the South is being readmitted to the Union. If that sounds strange, maybe a Southerner can understand. Only a Southerner can understand years of coarse, anti-Southern jokes and unfair comparison. Only a Southerner can understand what it means to be a political whipping-boy. But then only a Southerner can understand what Jimmy Carter as President can mean. It's like this: November 2 is the most important day in our region's history. Are you going to let it pass without having your say? Are you going to let the Washington politicians keep one of our own out of the White House? . . . The South has always been the conscience of America—maybe they'll start listening to us now. Vote for Jimmy Carter on November 2.[5]

One of Carter's chief advisors cautioned him to muffle that message in appealing to a national electorate. In a campaign memo, Hamilton Jordan counseled: "Although the Southern states provide us with a rich base of support, it would be a mistake to appear to be overly dependent on the South for victory in November. . . . To the extent that regional bias exists in this country—and it does—there would be a negative reaction to a candidacy that was perceived as being a captive of the Southern states and/or people. Sad but true. Southern regional pride can be used to great advantage without necessarily alienating potential anti-Southern voters."[6]

Jimmy Carter, however, went out of his way to portray himself as a southerner, and, despite that identification, defeated President Ford in November. An Alabama writer charged that Carter and his crowd, though in more moderate guise than George Wallace, were "only the latest wave of Confederate cadets Dixie has sent out to prolong its battle against the alien, infidel, and conquering North." Carter's victory, said the historian David Lee, was "especially meaningful because he emphasized rather than concealed his Southern heritage." Lee pointed out: "On the night of the Ohio primary he told a cheering Atlanta crowd, 'I'm proud to be a Southerner.' To perplexed reporters who sought a key to his character, Carter suggested, 'those who understand the South would understand a major portion of me.'" Three-fifths of the electoral votes for a man with a Georgia inflection came from the North and West. Yet Carter could not have succeeded if he had not swept all but one of the states of the former Confederacy.[7]

In his first important journey to the South after entering the White House, Carter declared, "I'm proud being an American, but I'm even more proud being a Southerner!" Unlike Lyndon Johnson, who sought protective coloration in the "Harvards" he bragged about recruiting, Carter surrounded himself with a "Georgia Mafia," and of the fourteen officials with cabinet status he appointed, six came from the South and one from a border state. Even when the president's tenure was nearing an end, a southern journalist wrote: "Carter remained irrevocably in psyche, thought, and action a direct product of Southern culture. There remained embedded in his deepest essence that same unapologetic embrace of the Southern attitudes that had always formed his person. . . . Religion and his constant immersion in the verities of homeplace and family and region were mingled into a solution that was as vital as the blood in his veins." On January 14, 1981, during his final week in office, Carter, in a televised address, bade farewell by saying, "I return home to the South where I was born and raised."[8]

Southerners viewed Carter's presence in the White House as sweet redemption. A historian at the University of Georgia speculated that Carter's victory might be "a form of psychological reparation done by other sections of the nation to the South as a kind of late payment for injuries done in the past." The Georgian Griffin Bell, Carter's attorney general, recalled, "There is not anybody my age that wasn't very proud of the fact that we could get somebody from the South elected President and rejoin the union," and a former Atlanta newspaperman wrote that since Carter's election "I have felt more like an American *every* day. . . . Ethnic redneckism was destroyed when he took the oath of office. . . . Damn. Pinch me. This is Jimmy Carter of Plains, Georgia, we're talking about here." Another Atlanta journalist, commenting on the jubilant Carter victory revels in his city, said, "Tell them you were here when the war finally ended." Tom Wicker concluded that "whatever else he may do, Jimmy Carter has removed the last great cause of Southern isolation; and even in the remote little farm towns that dot the Southern countryside, it is already possible to sense that Southerners are coming to believe that they finally belong to something larger than the South."[9]

Political analysts, too, saw Carter's victory as a significant chapter in the relation of the South to the nation. Dewey Grantham of Vanderbilt expressed widespread sentiment in observing that "the very fact that a one-term governor of Georgia could be elected president suggests that sectional acrimony in national politics has lost much of its onetime potency," and the New York City columnist Max Lerner asserted: "The South has been brought back into the presidential history of the United States, from which it was long excluded. . . . Carter's victory will give Southerners a new sense of political confidence, and will soften some of their chip-on-the-shoulder resentments about the national parties."[10]

The South, which since antebellum days had been told to snap to it and fall in line with northern expectations, now found itself a trend-setter. "Big-city reporters and prophets of the electronic media hastened to Confederate south Georgia to soak up the local atmosphere of kudzu, red clay, and fried-everything hospitality," one account noted, and a University of Georgia professor remarked upon a torrent of "articles about Georgia, Georgians, Georgia politics, Georgia social mores, Georgia customs, Georgia speech, Georgia cooking, the Georgia man, the Georgia mind." In the interregnum following the 1976 election, Washington language schools offered crash courses in talking southern. Students "won't have time to master more than a rudimentary vocabulary," one entrepreneur explained. "But I'll guarantee that if a bureaucrat's new boss turns out to be a southerner, he'll be able to carry on a limited conversation." In 1976, or in later years, car radios from Bangor to San Diego played the Nashville sound; Hardee's chain coaxed Yankees to eat barbecue; and, in Seattle, espresso fanciers, fussy about their "coffee and . . . ," queued for Krispy Kreme doughnuts, which could also be found in London's upscale emporium, Harrod's. "My northern-born friends have been celebrating the Democrats' nomination of Jimmy Carter as a signal that the South is ready to return to the Union," wrote the Mississippi-born Harvard historian David Herbert Donald. "It is more accurate to see Carter's nomination as further evidence that, a century after the Civil War and Reconstruction, the United States has finally decided to rejoin the South."[11]

II

A good number of commentators, especially in the South, refused to enter into the euphoria, in part because they read the tea leaves differently. "Much was written in the days following Carter's election about how the nation matured to the point where it was now ready to elect and accept a southerner," said *Newsday*'s Washington bureau chief. "That is true. But a greater truth is that it was the South which matured and accepted the nation." A political scientist approached the question more obliquely. Carter's victory, William Havard said, raised a question: "Did the election actually demonstrate that the South had rejoined the Union? And the ancillary question . . . : if the South has been reunited with the nation, was it readmitted after having been rehabilitated (or 're-constructed') following its long banishment on the grounds of moral and political delinquency, or did it . . . wage a long political war of attrition so successfully that it forced its way in by eventual domination?"[12]

Some observers denied that the election returns demonstrated either that the country had embraced a southerner or that Carter was the choice of the white South. The South and three border states together gave him a plurality of nearly two million, but he ran behind in the popular vote in the rest of the country. The historian Robert Kelley contended that as a "Deep Southerner" Carter was stigmatized as a member of an out group and that, consequently, "his Southern accent, Southern Baptist style, and Southern populist aura almost defeated him, so widely do these diverge from the Northern WASP manner and outlook that seem to have become the basis for a national culture." When Carter told reporters he had "nothing against" communities "trying to maintain the ethnic purity of their neighborhoods," the black mayor of Gary called him a "Frankenstein monster with a Southern drawl." Furthermore, Carter failed to win the ballots of most white voters in the South. "Ethnic southerners were not loyal to their soul brother; what remained of the 'solid South' mystique dissolved in 1976," Jack Temple Kirby has written. "Carter was a scalawag, it would seem, to most of his kind." The erstwhile Georgia governor came close to sweeping the South only because Lyndon Johnson's legislation had greatly expanded the black electorate. "Jimmy Carter," Robert McElvaine pointed out, "would not be President today had the Voting Rights Act not been passed."[13]

Analysts disputed the familiar interpretation of the meaning of the 1976 outcome by advancing yet another contention—that Jimmy Carter's triumph signified little because he was not a representative southerner. One commentator even called Carter a "Yankee from Georgia," a southerner *manqué.* "Brother Billy may have personified the good ole boy," Kirby has remarked, "but Jimmy was anything but: he neither drinks nor smokes; he does not seem gregarious; he is not lazy; he is incisive and tireless." Jody Powell, his press secretary, agreed. "Carter did not fit the southern-pol atmosphere," he has written. "He did not tell racist jokes, even in private, and he did not drink large quantities of bourbon and pat strange women on the fanny. Lastly, he did not particularly enjoy bullshit sessions with the boys." Carter, William Lee Miller insisted, lacked the distinguishing marks of a southerner. Despite his origins, he was a "prosaic Yankee," with the "didactic" intelligence of an engineer; a "Puritan-Yankee deacon" who, bereft of the southern gift of eloquence, carpentered lumpy sentences that appeared to have been "a translation from the German."[14]

The North Carolina–born essayist Edwin M. Yoder Jr. tested Carter against C. Vann Woodward's thesis that the experience of defeat has given southerners a different sensibility from northerners with their optimistic faith in progress and modernity. Meditating on this central theme of Woodward's work, Yoder said of Carter: "We might have expected him to exhibit that sense of historical complexity and tragedy that the historian found to be close to the core of the southern experience. But . . . so far as a sense of history was concerned, Mr. Carter traveled light. It was not so much a sense of tragedy as of rationalism, optimism, excessive deference to popular vanity, the engineer's illusion of a manipulable world, that became the hallmarks of the Carter style. His claim to be a student of Reinhold Niebuhr, hence presumably a sort of historical pessimist, did not sustain exacting scrutiny."[15]

Representative or not, Jimmy Carter absorbed a slew of mean abuse as a southern provincial. He was referred to as "Grits" (the Carter-Mondale ticket was reversed to "Fritz and Grits") and, in an allusion to his occupation, belittled as "peanuts." At the very moment that he was being honored by inauguration as president of the United States of America, a Washington newspaper chose to publish, in Carter's words, "a full-page cartoon depicting an outhouse on the White House lawn, with my mother wearing a sunbonnet and smoking a corncob pipe." One of his advisors complained that Carter was regarded as "an ambassador from Dogpatch," and reporters, said Jody Powell, viewed the president as "a peanut farmer from some piddly-ass little gnat-hole in south Georgia."[16]

Commentators surmise that the ways the president and his southern circle responded, sometimes defensively, sometimes aggressively, account for why Carter ran into so much trouble in trying to govern. The CBS correspondent Lesley Stahl was "dumbfounded" when Jody Powell stared at her, then stuttered, "Look, Lesley, er—uh—we know you're against us. We know what you think about us and that you're, um, on the other side." She has reflected: "As I thought about it that night, I decided that part of my problem was that I wasn't southern. When the president or his Georgia inner circle were criticized as incompetent (Hamilton Jordan was widely known as Hannibal Jerkin), they'd circle the wagons and blame it on 'southern-hating northerners,' which to them included the media. The Georgians succumbed to a tyranny of trivial resentments against the Washington establishment and the press."[17]

Some insiders accepted the indictment of the White House coterie and, indeed, of Carter. His speech writer, Gerald Rafshoon, has said, "When he became President he felt, 'I've got to show Southerners are not dumb. I'm going to defend the South by showing every time how much I know. I'm not going to use metaphors. I'm not going to be folksy.'" Another thoughtful member of the Carter administration commented in a 1981 interview: "I was a Georgian, and it was as if I had ridden up the four-lane highway with cotton along the side. You know, we were going back north to take over. It was the craziest experience. . . . We really had won an incredible victory. We had finally established a level of pride, . . . but also bitterness. Bitterness that existed then and existed throughout the administration and exists today . . . bitterness directed toward those in power who tried to deny it to us." He continued: "I think it undid us. . . . We, as a group, were naïve and not wise to the ways of Washington. It was not Atlanta. It was not Columbus or Macon or Savannah. It took us a heck of a long time to figure it out, which caused great problems for the President. We did not seek out. . . . This hurt us."[18]

By the spring of 1979, after little more than two years as vice president, Walter Mondale, who had initially viewed Carter "as someone who could end the vestiges of the Civil War," had come to a more downbeat judgment. His biographer Steven Gillon writes: "Mondale had hoped that by joining the ticket he could help ease the North-South tensions that had divided the party for over a century. That hope had faded. Now he concluded that the two geographical regions of the party were no longer separated by questions of racial equality but by subtle differences of political style and philosophy. Mondale realized Carter and his Georgia advisors represented a different political tradition from his, and it would take more than friendship and hard work to bridge the gap between them."[19]

III

Many southerners who acknowledged that there had been change thought that the nationalization of the South, if that is what it was, came at a prohibitive cost: the loss of sectional distinctiveness. "The anguish that most of us have observed for some time now," said Flannery O'Connor, "has been caused not by the fact that the South is alienated from the rest of the country, but by the fact that it is not alienated enough, that . . . we are being forced out, not only of our many sins but of our few virtues." In 1979 Mississippi's Willie Morris recalled an occasion in a Manhattan bar when a displaced New Orleans man said: "You fellows are writers, and you have the gall to say you want to change Mississippi? You must be insane. Here you are from a place . . . [with] the most haunting landscape in all the United States . . . and a spoken word that would make a drunk Irishman envious . . . and miscegenation that is the envy of Brazil . . . and a sense of the histrionic that would pale the Old Testament . . . and a past so contorted that it embarrasses the people of Scarsdale . . . and you say you want to *change* Mississippi?" He ended his tirade: "Why if I were you, I'd put up big green signs at every point of entry into Mississippi which said, 'Posted. No Trespassing.'"[20]

Morris himself sounded a protest against the homogenization of his native land that others echoed. "Now Jackson from Highway 55 looms before one like a city devastated by some alien intrusion," he grumbled. "It all seemed to have happened so quickly: the parking lots, motels, franchise stores, pizza parlors, all those accoutrements out at the edge of the great American schizophrenia, a whole beautiful terrain wiped out and vanished. The view could have been of Cleveland, Ohio. . . . My grandparents' house torn down for a parking lot for a shopping center." The novelist Harry Crews joined in this lament: "We were a proud and reticent people, a people who knew that manners were important because manners saved us from ourselves and from each other. Now our manners are gone and our idiom turns up in the *Journal of Popular Culture*. The food we eat comes from McDonald's and our preachers are more interested in sociology than theology. . . . The South . . . has been corrupted all the way to quaint." A biographer of George Wallace concurred. "The South is being etherized," said Marshall Frady, "subtly rendered pastless, memoryless and vague of identity. What we are talking about is the passing of a sensibility—an event perhaps too wispy to define, but no less seismic. . . . The old pipe-organ range of prodigal possibilities for life there—both gentle and barbarous, good and evil—has contracted to the comfortable monotone note of middle C."[21]

Atlanta, which Georgia boosters touted as a showplace, filled other southerners with dismay. "The rebuilding of Atlanta in recent years is an astonishment," wrote Elizabeth Hardwick. "The incredible hotels . . . their fake gold chandeliers, the raw orange of the lobbies, the schlock and kitsch of the architecture, the dead shops, the superfluous fountains dripping over plastic rocks: this creation is close to the vision that made Las Vegas out of a wasteland, and very far from the 'Old South.'" No less dyspeptic, Peirce Lewis fretted that "a new generation of Snopeses bestride the land, alight with the Atlanta Spirit, their carpetbags now made indestructible by Samsonite, their bib overalls discarded in favor of double-knit leisure suits, and the moonshine they once drank disdained for dry Martinis, sipped in air-cooled bars that revolve eternally above the canyons of Peachtree Street."[22]

"Well, the so-called Southern thing is over and done with I think," Walker Percy said. "Nowadays," he observed, a writer was "pretty much looking at the same sort of reality in New Orleans or Birmingham or Atlanta as his counter-part in Cincinnati or Los Angeles." Will Barrett's life style in *The Second Coming* was "socking little balls around the mountains, rattling ice in Tanqueray, riding $35,000 German cars, watching Billy Graham and the Steelers and M*A*S*H on 45-inch Jap TV." In another of his novels, *Lancelot,* a character asks, "Which is worse, to die with T. J. Jackson at Chancellorsville or live with Johnny Carson in Burbank?" In *Signposts in a Strange Land,* Percy declares: "The North did win and did put the South in Arrow collars. The sections are homogenized. Everybody watches the same television programs. In another hundred years, everybody will talk like Art Linkletter." Though there contin-ued to be nods to plantation culture, they were no more genuine than "the Con-federate Chevrolet agency" in *The Last Gentleman* with "salesmen in Reb-colonel hats and red walking canes."[23]

So lugubrious were the grinches that they opened themselves to some gen-tle ribbing. After attending two more of the never-ending symposia on sectional melancholia, one reporter remarked, "This has got to stop—these endless farewells. The South seems to have an incurable impulse for bittersweet good-byes to itself—sad, low murmurings into mauve twilights, adieux to gold dust glories and lost green afternoons." To an inquiry from *Harper's* in 1986, Lee Smith responded:

> You can't tell who's nice anymore, . . . not like you used to could back in the days when you just naturally knew everybody in town and what their daddy did. Now people that you have almost never heard of are running everything. I mean the guy from high school who used to wear the soft brown flattop, you know the one I mean. You just can't remember his name. Or his last name anyway—you *think* his first name was Dave. Dave! What a dumb no-account lackluster name, nothing like Fon-taine B. Barrett IV or Hogface Haines. In high school he wore high-water pants that showed his white socks and short-sleeved plaid shirts or shirts that had a little all-over pattern? and a pen-and-pencil set in a clear plastic case in his breast pocket? Now he's grown up and bought

him some *Miami Vice* clothes and got a portfolio. He's running this town, and nobody even *thinks* to ask who his daddy was.[24]

Most commentators, though, saw little occasion for humor. In 1957 Louis Rubin let out a cry of anguish: "The Southern way of life is now being threatened, as it has not been threatened since the Civil War. . . . I am talking about the quality which makes a region a region, instead of a colorless, standardized set of people and places." The following year, Henry Savage Jr. wrote that it was "irretrievably foreordained that, year by year, the South will be more American and less Southern." The same thoughts were being expressed a generation later. The South, observers groused, was "now just Topeka with more fried food, road kill, heat, and history." The Arkansas editor Harry Ashmore titled his reflections *Epitaph for Dixie,* and an *Esquire* editor summed up the situation by writing, "The South is over. La commedia è finita!"[25]

IV

If Franklin Roosevelt, Harry Truman, and Lyndon Johnson had been permitted to survey the South in the final decades of the twentieth century, they would have found the political landscape disheartening. They had assumed that progressive causes were at a disadvantage below the Mason-Dixon line because voting restrictions and the stifling one-party system prevented or discouraged poor folk, white and black, from going to the polls. If the suffrage were expanded and two-party competition emerged, the Democratic Party and, more particularly, liberal Democratic policies would prevail since elite opponents would be outnumbered. These were the premises behind FDR's condemnation of the poll tax, Truman's 1948 message to Congress, and LBJ's civil rights legislation. The three presidents had succeeded beyond expectations. But the end result was not at all what they had anticipated.

The Voting Rights Act of 1965 promoted by Johnson ushered in an era not of Democratic but of Republican hegemony. When the protagonist of the 1966 novel *The Last Gentleman* returns to his native section, Walker Percy writes, "The South he came home to was different from the South he had left. It was happy, victorious, Christian, rich, patriotic and Republican."[26] In 1968 Hubert Humphrey made the poorest showing in the South of any Democratic presidential nominee since Horatio Seymour in 1868, and in 1972 Richard Nixon swept the section, the first of several occasions that the GOP would do so. The South that Roosevelt had carried each time was "solid" again, but solidly Republican. In 1980 Jimmy Carter lost all of the southern states save his own Georgia, and in 1984, in corralling the whole region, Ronald Reagan took Georgia too. Bill Clinton of Hope, Arkansas, fared better in every part of the country in 1992 than he did in the South, which provided the main electoral base for George Bush who got 108 of his 168 electoral votes there. Eight years later, Bush's son, with the aid of a questionable count in Florida, recorded all of the former Confederacy, plus Kentucky, in his column. Al Gore could not even win his own state of Tennessee.

Since 1964—forty years ago—no Democratic presidential candidate has been able to get a majority of the ballots of white southerners. Though white disaffection in the South had been building since the FDR presidency, and had been exacerbated by Truman's policies, Johnson's civil rights stance was the tipping point. One careful study found that "the principal transformation in the native white electorate occurred between 1964 and 1968." In 1968 the Democrats' share of the southern white vote dipped below 20 percent, and in 1972 Nixon captured so much of what had been the George Wallace following that he wound up with the largest share of southern white ballots any Republican had ever received: an astonishing 79 percent. Carter won only 36 percent of the southern white electorate in 1980, and four years later, with southern whites backing Reagan 71 percent to 29 percent, one analyst reported "a literal white flight from the Democratic Party all across the South." In 1996 Clinton ran twenty points behind on ballots cast by whites in the South at the same time that he was carrying the majority of white voters in the East.[27]

The GOP matched these triumphs in congressional contests, again by luring white voters. When Truman succeeded Roosevelt, the Republicans held no U.S. Senate seats in the South; after the 1994 elections, they had thirteen, outnumbering the Democrats, left with only nine. Their improvement in the House of Representatives was no less spectacular. In 1951 Republicans claimed only 2 percent of southern seats in the House. Of 106 congressional districts in the South, the Republicans as late as 1960 controlled only six. By 1994 they boasted a majority of southern seats in the House. That year the GOP picked up nineteen seats in the South; in 1996, it added six more. "For the rest of the 1990s," wrote an analyst, "the 'party of Lincoln' will increasingly draw its life from the land of Jefferson Davis."[28]

That comment proved to be right on the mark, for the Republicans, once the party of Boston abolitionists, Iowa farmers, and Kansas merchants, finished the twentieth century flying the Confederate battle flag. At a convention of the

Sons of Confederate Veterans in Biloxi, Senator Trent Lott said that "the spirit of Jefferson Davis lives in the 1984 Republican platform." Twelve years later, a Miami columnist wrote: "Might as well designate 'Dixie' as the official party anthem for next month's Republican National Convention. The peckerwoods have taken over the GOP." In 1996 the GOP staged its biggest grassroots social event of the year not in Abe Lincoln country but at Beauvoir, ancestral home of Jefferson Davis in the Mississippi delta.[29]

Washington politics took on an ideological coloration that had not been seen before in the century, not even in the pre-FDR era. Herbert Hoover was a much more progressive figure than any of the modern-day southern Republican true believers, who were well to the right of their party elsewhere. Under Newt Gingrich, they even dared to shut down the national government. Democratic presidents, though not nearly as extreme, pursued policies so far removed from those of recent predecessors that they were likened to Grover Cleveland's. Jimmy Carter initiated deregulation, and his fellow southerner, Bill Clinton, dismantled a vital feature of the Welfare State structure erected by FDR. Michael Lind, who sees "the Southern takeover of American politics" exemplified by "the 'Texanization' of the American right," has written, "From William F. Buckley, Jr., the son of a Texas oil man, to those two other Texas oil men, George H. W. Bush and George W. Bush, conservative thinkers and politicians rooted in the old Texan commodity-exporting oligarchy have redefined what conservatism means in the United States."[30]

Two historians have summed up the outcome of the attempt by Roosevelt, Truman, and Johnson to reconfigure southern politics. "The irony for American liberals is that the political changes they desired actually materialized," Alan Draper has written. "Southern party systems have been realigned and Dixiecrat domination of Congress has been broken. Two-party competition in the South now exists and the Democratic party in Congress is now disciplined and ideologically unified. But the scourge of the South still remains. Southern Democracy has declined only to reappear in a new form as the conservative vanguard of a resurgent Republican party. The old adage, 'Be careful what you wish for. It might come true!' has never been more appropriately or accurately applied than to the case of American liberals and the South." Similarly, Bruce Schulman has concluded that though "Carter's election symbolized the South's reunification with the nation, the entry into the American mainstream that FDR had sought," Roosevelt could not "have imagined the transformation in politics that his program ignited. Ironically, a program designed to nurture intelligent and liberal Democracy in the South would ultimately yield conservative Republicanism."[31]

The three presidents would also have been crestfallen to learn that, in the midst of all the hullabaloo about flush times, large pockets of poverty remained. In San Antonio, where close to one-third of families lived below the poverty line in 1970, Robert Coles found "unpaved, undrained streets; homes without water; homes with outdoor privies," and in Houston in 1978 a *New York Times* correspondent came upon "one-story shacks with rusting tin roofs, peeling paint, and rickety porches on concrete blocks" a few minutes from the imposing high rise "citadels of Exxon and Shell." One of America's most farsighted governors, William Winter of Mississippi, the state with the greatest proportion of its citizens below the poverty line, said, as he was leaving office in 1986, "There remains the other South, largely rural, undereducated, underproductive, and underpaid that threatens to become a permanent shadow of distress and deprivation in a region that less than a decade ago had promised it better days." Of all the measurements of comparative performance, one was especially stark: the South had the country's highest infant mortality rate.[32]

Scholars echoed Governor Winter's bleak appraisal. In 1988, two decades after Lyndon Johnson's tenure ended, Paul Conkin declared: "Despite a closing gap in incomes, despite the Sun Belt phenomena, despite the miracle of air conditioning, the industrial foliage has not changed that much. Wages remain below national averages, fewer workers enjoy the protection of union representation and bargaining, state regulations tend to be more lax than in the North, state-shared welfare transfers are well below national averages, and a whole array of public services remain ill-funded in comparison to those in the North. Thus, not only has industrialism conquered the South but in its worst possible dress." Some years earlier, Charles Roland had remarked: "A statement issued in 1964 by the Federal Department of Health and Welfare is strikingly reminiscent of the report of President Franklin D. Roosevelt's National Emergency Council thirty years ago. The Welfare Department named Tunica County, Mississippi, as the poorest spot in the nation. . . . The South remains the nation's economic problem No. 1."[33]

Racism, too, though much diminished, continued to be endemic. A 1997 study reported "racial prejudice to be . . . markedly higher in the South than the non-South," especially among white males. "Much has been made of the South's transformation," it added. "Whatever shapes it might have taken, a precipitous decline in racial prejudice does not appear to be one of them." In Laurens, a South Carolina mill town with a population 43 percent black, the Redneck Shop sold sweatshirts with the message, "Ain't Racist—Just Never Met a Nigger I Liked." The proprietor was so outrageous that he embarrassed the civic elders; unhappily, though, he was not an aberration but only the end of a spectrum. Jesse Helms, the Republican U.S. senator from North Carolina, was one of several southern politicians who stooped to playing the race card.[34]

A prominent South Carolina Republican, reviewing the book *The Two-Party South*, confessed:

> I look back on the last twenty years of Republicanism in the South and see the progress that the GOP has made. I remember my own bit parts in the drama, and I want to feel pride. Well, I do feel pride, but this other feeling keeps creeping in—shame. And the Lamis book reminds me of it in chapter after chapter—the role of segregationist issues in Claude Kirk's election as governor of Florida, in Bill Brock's Tennessee Senate campaigns, in Albert Watson's ill-fated gubernatorial campaign (I served as campaign manager for that one).
>
> I want to say: But those were insignificant details! Our real pitch was for freedom—free enterprise, freedom from governmental interference in the rights of states, of communities, of businesses. . . .
>
> I can't buy my own line. I was there, and I remember. Denouncing "the bloc vote"; opposing "busing" so long and so loud that rural voters thought we were going to do away with school buses; the lurid leaflets "exposing" the integrationist ties of our Democratic opponents—leaflets we mailed in plain white envelopes to all the white voters in the precincts George Wallace had carried. . . .
>
> Well . . . there's nothing we can do to change history. Racism, often purposely inflamed by many southern Republicans, either because we believed it or because we thought it would win votes, was a major tool in the building of the new Republican party in the South.[35]

Though the region's leaders claimed that the South looked toward the future, the past did not altogether surrender its grip. Helms opposed the nomination of a former U.S. senator as ambassador to New Zealand, in good part because she had led a successful fight against renewing a patent that featured the Confederate flag. Early in 2003 the commander of the Sons of Confederate Veterans called Lincoln "this country's most notorious war criminal . . . this Marxist . . . this monster directly responsible for the killing of 620,000 Americans." When a philanthropist who had raised a million dollars for a Museum of the Confederacy proposed, as a gesture of reconciliation, to erect a statue of Lincoln in Richmond, irate southerners sent viruses to his computers and asked him to contribute to sculpting a statue to the assassin John Wilkes Booth.[36]

More than a century after Fort Sumter, antebellum magic still enchants, and the Lost Cause continues to claim adherents. "When we asked our respondents if there were any Southerners they especially admired," John Shelton Reed reported in an analysis of survey results in 1983, "the most frequent response by far was Robert E. Lee." Bumper stickers on southern cars say DON'T BLAME US. WE VOTED FOR JEFFERSON DAVIS, and cadets at The Citadel go on singing "Dixie." At St. Simons Island in the twenty-first century, each room at an elegant inn is provided with a guidebook to local sites in "the War of Northern Aggression." Though a fabled Mississippi river town was "cluttered . . . with the paraphernalia of contemporaneity," wrote David Cohn, "Natchez will never be part of the world in which it lives. . . . Natchez lives with its dead."[37]

v

Notwithstanding these unexpected disappointments, the three presidents might well have found more to gratify than to displease them. They had wanted the South to become an integral part of the nation, and now, like that Memphis institution, FedEx, the region is linked not only to the rest of America, but also to the world. The South, Peter Applebome wrote in 1996, had "turned out to be not America's insular kingdom of the eccentric, forlorn, or exotic, but a place that had managed to maintain its identity while also putting its fingerprints on almost every aspect of the nation's soul, from race, to politics, to culture, to values." In 2001 another observer concluded that "in many respects, the South that had so long been the backwater of the country today serves as a pacesetter for the nation."[38]

In the decades following the age of Roosevelt, the impoverished South of the Great Depression seemed changed almost beyond recognition. The region came out of World War II, said H. C. Nixon, with "a standard of living for the common man that was undreamt of in its prewar philosophy." After a trip across several states, Walter Prescott Webb reported, "I saw fat cattle on green meadows, better farms and crops, and fresh paint on houses. I saw Southerners wearing good clothes, registering in the best hotels, carrying themselves with confidence into banks and business houses." The novelist Peter La Salle wrote of

Austin: "In the city you sensed that nothing would ever be finished. Forget all that grim news about slowdowns in construction starts in other parts of the country; this was 1980, and this was the Sun Belt. Out here on the south side of town, the low cinnamon dirt hills, peppered with scrub mesquite and prickly pear cactus, were constantly being gouged out for more apartment complexes— more mazes of redwood sides, tinted glass, . . . chlorinated aqua pools, . . . and patio decks cluttered with hibachis." Well before the end of the century, Charlotte had emerged as the country's second leading banking center, more important than Chicago or Boston or San Francisco, and, in contrast to the age of Roosevelt when southerners fled to escape hard times, the section was attracting a million newcomers a year.[39]

Commentators marveled at the transformation. In 1964, the year President Johnson won reelection, a North Carolina State sociologist announced, "The South that you and I knew . . . just three or four decades ago is no more." Eight years later, just before Johnson died, two geographers voiced the same sentiment: "The South is in a state of change. No longer is the stereotype of a languid, agricultural society dominated by a distinct arcadianism accurate." In 1929 Georgia gave twice as many acres to cotton as to pasture; in 1959 pasture outpaced cotton, 4–1. By 1960, David Goldfield has written, "the white fields [had] receded before the green wave of pasture, soybeans, and corn." The census that year ranked both Texas and Florida as more urbanized than Pennsylvania, Ohio, and Michigan. A political scientist itemized the breaks with the past: "Cotton has moved west, cattle have moved east, the farmer has moved to town, the city resident has moved to the suburbs, the Negro has moved north, and the Yankee has moved south." In 1958 Harry Ashmore listed the institutions that for so long had given the South "its unique character": "the agrarian economy, the one-party political system, and legal segregation." Now all three were going or gone.[40]

In an address at Yale University in the 1960s, the Georgia congressman Charles Longstreet Weltner told his northern audience:

When dignitaries visit our region, their speech writers usually have them say, "Thirty years ago, Franklin Delano Roosevelt termed the South . . . the Nation's number one economic problem! Today, thirty years later, I say that the South is the Nation's number one economic opportunity." Then we all applaud. We've heard it before, but we enjoy hearing it again. For, indeed, it is the fact.

Yes, hook-worm and pellagra, the one-crop economy, the one-mule farm, the one-room schoolhouse—all of these are no more. They, along with Scarlett O'Hara, are "Gone With the Wind."[41]

Introducing a new edition of the *Report on Economic Conditions in the South*, which had branded the section with that notorious phrase "number one economic problem," David Carlton and Peter Coclanis wrote: "Whether of southern origin or not, Americans today might well have a difficult time believing that the South was once defined in part as a uniquely poor region in a land of plenty. . . . Younger southerners living in the modern suburbs of Atlanta, or North Carolina's Research Triangle, or Orlando, or the Dallas-Fort Worth 'Metroplex,' can be forgiven for wondering how the South in which they live could ever have been described in such grim terms, or how its problems could have seemed so intractable."[42]

VI

During World War I a venerable Tar Heel statesman, Secretary of Navy Josephus Daniels, had posed for his picture on the portico of the White House with his handsome, lithe, youthful assistant secretary, Franklin Delano Roosevelt, who stood alongside him grinning. Later, in examining the photograph, Daniels said to FDR, who was making his first appearance in Washington, "We are both looking down on the White House, and you are saying to yourself, being a New Yorker, 'Some day I will be living in that house'—while I, being from the South, know I must be satisfied with no such ambition." So altogether different is the situation in America today that southerners of the present generation might well find it hard to believe that those words could ever have been spoken, for in the generation that began with Lyndon Johnson's victory in 1964, the country elected presidents from Texas (thrice), Georgia, and Arkansas.[43]

In 1976, with Jimmy Carter well ahead, C. Vann Woodward, who had dwelled on the burden of southern history, commented in an essay in *Time*, "For nearly a century after the Civil War, the Northeast governed the country, furnished nearly all the Presidents and, for much of the period, presided over a built-in empire, the South and West, its annexed territories. That period may have ended." Over the next two decades, events confirmed Woodward's cautious surmise. Since the Reagan interlude, only southerners have held the highest office. To capture the White House, Democrats required "Bubba-talking" sons of Dixie, said Kevin Phillips. It also helped in bidding for southern votes, he went on, to have a "black-sheep brother": "Good-ole-boy brothers would turn out to be reliable hallmarks of late-twentieth-century Democratic White Houses: Sam Houston Johnson; Billy Carter, who took money from Libya and had a beer—Billy beer—named after him; and finally Roger Clinton, an attention-seeking rock musician who had done time on a drug charge." Many Democrats, who had once taken the Solid South for granted, acknowledged that it could be fatal to have a northerner head the ticket. "The balance of power in America," one analyst concluded, had shifted "away from the Northeast and toward the Southern Rim."[44]

The first George Bush's victory, following those of Lyndon Johnson and Jimmy Carter, signified that three southerners had made it to the White House in a brief period. To be sure, Bush, the preppie son of a quondam U.S. senator from New England, was southern only by migration. When he ran for the U.S. Senate in 1964, the *Washington Star* headlined its account of the Texas race, "Connecticut Yankee Battles Yarborough." After announcing his candidacy, he sought to overcome this liability "of being branded as a carpetbagger, an eastern liberal in oilman's clothing," by distributing flyers saying, "Bush is a Texan by choice, not by chance." As a Texas congressman, furthermore, he had aligned himself with Old South folkways by empathizing with George Wallace supporters. In the White House, his ambiguous sectional identity helped him to reconcile the traditional New England wing of the GOP and Sunbelt Republicans. Bush lasted only one term, but that was because he could not turn aside the challenge of yet another southerner.[45]

In 1992 Democratic convention delegates demonstrated how much the political universe had changed by flouting the rule that tickets must be balanced regionally in choosing a slate of Governor Bill Clinton of Arkansas and Senator Al Gore of Tennessee. "So while the band won't be playing 'Dixie'—no politically incorrect tunes make this show's play list—there is a distinctively Southern air to the outcome," a *Boston Globe* columnist remarked. "There seems to be less trepidation about having two Southerners on the ticket this time than there was about the presence of one in 1976," added another *Globe* correspondent. Furthermore, both of Clinton's rivals—Bush and Ross Perot—made their homes in Texas. Educated outside the South (Georgetown, Yale Law School, Oxford) and married to a Chicago woman who had gone to Wellesley, Clinton did not feel constrained to accept a single sectional identity. During the ensuing campaign, though, he deliberately played up his southern origins. Speaking on a torrid day in Tennessee, he said in the thickest drawl he could muster, "It's hotter than a pickup's windshield."[46]

Clinton won a second term in 1996 by whipping a northerner at the same time that other southerners were fastening their hold on Capitol Hill. "What the South could never do on Civil War battlefields it has managed to do through the ballot box: take control of the country," a writer said. That year the chairmen of both major parties hailed from the deep South: the Republican from Mississippi, the Democrat from South Carolina. Mississippi provided the Senate majority leader, Trent Lott; a Georgian, Newt Gingrich, presided as Speaker of the House. Gingrich's two chief lieutenants came from Texas, as did the chair of the House Ways and Means Committee, while the powerful Senate Armed Services Committee was headed by the erstwhile Dixiecrat Strom Thurmond. "Considering that the nation's four top elected officials . . . were all from the South," commented Alexander Lamis, "northerners might be forgiven for concluding that the South had rejoined the national political mainstream a little too exuberantly!"[47]

The 2000 campaign pitted the southerner Al Gore against the southerner George W. Bush, a contest that would have seemed inconceivable in 1932. At the official opening of Gore's campaign, a Nashville singer warmed up the crowd, and the vice president mounted the stage to the country beat of Shania Twain. "So it was exquisitely appropriate," wrote Diane Roberts, "that in the 2000 presidential election a Tennessean and a Texan strove for the office held for eight years by an Arkansan," with the disputed outcome attracting reporters to Tallahassee, which they saw as a "place . . . as southern as Georgia: tea is sweet unless otherwise specified, everyone says 'y'all,' there are big white houses, Spanish moss, and a Confederate memorial in front of the capitol building." The victory of the Republican, a more authentic Texan than his father, meant that southerners, so long denied any prospect of reaching the White House, had secured a near-monopoly. Noting that since 1964 Texas has produced four presidential candidates (three of them elected), and two vice presidential candidates, one of them Lloyd Bentsen, Michael Lind wrote, "The Lone Star State, having long been known for its exports of cotton, oil, and cattle, was now exporting presidents and would-be presidents."[48]

VII

By far the most significant transformation in southern mores has taken place in race relations. John Shelton Reed underscored the contrast in writing: "Ulrich

Phillips said in the 1920s: The 'cardinal test of a southerner' was the commitment that the South be and remain a white man's country. That was a glaring and obvious distinction. The minute you crossed into the South you were under a different system of laws. Ninety-eight percent of white southerners in 1942 thought black and white children should go to separate schools. But that's not what the South's about any more." David Carlton, too, has stated: "The collapse in the 1960s of Jim Crow and its accompanying siege mentality has made the South a much more open society. . . . The modern South is more hospitable to immigrants, more culturally tolerant, and more accommodating of modernity than ever before. . . . The South has learned that pluralism can be economically energizing." Atlanta, said Jesse Jackson, could thank the civil rights revolution for being able to host CNN, the Braves, and the Olympics.[49]

The region has jettisoned many of the assumptions that had curdled the era in which the three presidents had come of age. The governor of South Carolina called the 1970 election, five years after enactment of LBJ's voting legislation, the first with "racial overtones where the moderates won." He had defeated a vicious demagogue, a Strom Thurmond protégé whose incendiary attack on busing had provoked a white mob to overturn school buses carrying black pupils. Elsewhere in the South, Orval Faubus took a licking, and axe-wielding Lester Maddox gave way to Jimmy Carter. "We have a lot of problems still left concerning race, but we are no longer preoccupied with this problem to the exclusion of others," Carter affirmed. "There is a new dynamic, a new freedom . . . throughout the South." None of the winners campaigned as enthusiasts for racial justice. Instead, they muted the issue, or ignored it, much to the bewilderment of an elderly Georgia farmer who remarked, "Always before, you could tell right easy how somebody stood on the nigras. I don't say it isn't a good thing, but it does make for a mighty peculiar election."[50]

Jimmy Carter's reach for the White House in 1976 proved to be a historic moment. In defeating George Wallace in the North Carolina primary, thereby ending the Alabaman's last hope of becoming the Democratic nominee, Carter emerged as the candidate of a South that had turned its back on racism. In his bid for the presidency, Carter in Mississippi, in the presence of Senators Eastland and Stennis, praised the end of Jim Crow. "I sometimes think that a Southerner of my generation can most fully understand the meaning and the impact of Martin Luther King's life," he said. Carter, commentators remarked, bridged the world of his father, "Mr. Earl," described as "a seigneurial landowner and entrepreneur who did not allow Negroes beyond his back door," and his mother,

"Miz Lillian," who "represented the New South, urging fair . . . treatment for blacks . . . and more attention to the times that are a-changing." Jimmy Carter, in sum, "reflected the mood of much of the contemporary South—a continued reverence for the past with a growing desire to 'get shut' of it."[51]

Roosevelt, Truman, and Johnson understood that the South would continue to be an outcast unless it abandoned folkways that were injurious—to whites as well as blacks—and they employed the powers of the state to coerce recalcitrants into new patterns of behavior. "By accepting the legal direction to obey the Constitution and do what was morally right," wrote Ralph McGill in Johnson's final year in the White House, "the Southern white man was freed to advance his economy, to remove his political system from bondage, and to begin improving the quality of his education so that it would give Southern children equal opportunity . . . with children in the rest of the nation." The civil rights legislation sponsored by Lyndon Johnson, Carter affirmed, was "the greatest thing that ever happened to the South."[52]

"Clearly there is something new in the South," declared Peter Schrag in 1972. He explained: "Jackson, Mississippi, in 1972 is not the same town it was in 1960 or even in 1969. Can one imagine integrated groups of blacks and whites eating in the restaurants of Capitol Street? Can one imagine a black candidate for governor of Mississippi speaking unmolested from the steps of nearly every little county courthouse in the state? Can one imagine the citizens of Sunflower County trying the white killers of a black girl before a jury of nine blacks and three whites? Can one imagine watching the black sheriff of Greene County, Alabama, in a mod Italian suit, inspecting the watermelon crop on a thriving 4,000-acre farm owned by Muslims?"[53]

When a white anti-poverty activist who had worked in Mississippi in the 1960s returned two decades later, the transmutation startled him. "So many of the generation of twenty years ago came to Head Start with swollen bellies, distended navels, and dull eyes," wrote Tony Dunbar. "That first generation is now leaving college or the service and making its way into the mainstream of life." In the midst of the 1962 crisis stirred up by Governor Ross Barnett over the determination of Attorney General Robert Kennedy to enroll the first black student at the University of Mississippi, Ole Miss undergraduates sang:

Never, never, never, never, no-o-o never, never, never,
We will not yield an inch of any field.
Fix us another toddy, ain't yielding to nobody.

Ross's standing like Gibraltar, he shall never falter.

Ask us what we say, it's to hell with Bobby K.

Never shall our emblem go from Colonel Reb to old black Joe.

More recently, though, black and white football players at Ole Miss were exchanging jive handshakes, and a black halfback from Yazoo was elected Colonel Rebel.[54]

Dunbar made a point of looking up a black man in Belzoni whom he had first encountered on his earlier visit. He was told: "You used to call the Ku Klux Klan's name twenty-five years ago and it would make my heart skip a beat. Now it seems like you would say, 'We're gonna chew some bubble gum.' . . . It ain't like it used to be. You say something, the man didn't like it, say if he was white, he'd go get two or three more and they'd come and publicly beat you up or run you away from your family. That didn't exist no more. . . . You don't see any restaurant doors say white only. You don't see no restrooms at service stations now say white only. . . . Things is a hundred percent better than it was."[55]

No one could mistake the change in the political culture in the aftermath of the Franklin Roosevelt–Harry Truman–Lyndon Johnson era. "The baby-kissing backwoodsman who drove his mules up to the courthouse square to quote the Bible, cuss the niggers, and claim the votes is an anachronism," declared the onetime editor of the *Atlanta Constitution,* Reg Murphy, during Carter's campaign. Three years later, Peirce Lewis, who almost certainly had in mind FDR's nemesis, Gene Talmadge, asserted: "Southern politics are better than they used to be. It is hardly possible any longer for some semi-literate mountebank in a rotten borough to get himself elected in perpetuity by chewing the right kind of plug, snapping the right color of galluses, and hollering Nigger at predetermined intervals."[56]

The reverberations in Mississippi registered especially high on the Richter scale. The 1971 gubernatorial contest, Willie Morris declared, was the state's "first in which the old racial phantoms were not raised," and in 1980 Mississippi elected to the governorship William Winter, "an eloquent student of history and literature," who was "not a Snopes, but a Sartoris." The national image of Mississippians in the 1960s, Dunbar noted, "was the balding [white] politicians or sheriff in short sleeves, wearing a skinny black tie and backed up by dogs and joking deputies." No longer. "One is as likely to see blacks as whites behind the office doors in courthouses these days," he said. Coahoma County had an African-American sheriff. When Dunbar was pulled over for speeding, the officers who forced him to the side of the road were "black troopers wearing Mountie hats with gold peanuts on them."[57]

As an unexpected consequence of this transformation, Mississippi and other southern states experienced a surging influx of African Americans. "Before 1970 black migration from the North to the rural South had been a trickle," noted Carol Stack. "After 1970 the northward flow gradually dried up, while the southward migration of black Americans swelled to 50,000 a year." From 1995 to 2000, the South recorded a net gain of 347,000 African Americans with twice as many coming in as leaving. No other section of the country witnessed this pattern. The newcomers found a South strikingly different from the fearsome land of memory. "Mississippi underwent a metamorphosis . . . thanks to the Voting Rights Act," asserted a writer in *The Crisis*. In places such as Holmes County, where there are twice as many blacks as whites, political power had changed hands in a way that once could not have been imagined. "Black southerners who went North to escape the Jim Crow South can now go home again," said Jimmie Lewis Franklin in 1994. "New returnees may encounter difficulty finding Saturday night fish fries, all-week revivals, and church dinner on the grounds. But they still recognize their southern place." Asked why he had no interest in leaving Mississippi, the chief of an all-black police force in the town of Tchula replied, "I'm a Southern boy."[58]

Much of the dramatic change derived from the altered complexion of the electorate. In 1940, only 5 percent of African American adults in the South were registered to vote; by 1971, 59 percent. In the two years after enactment of LBJ's voting rights law, black registration in Mississippi bounded from 7 to 60 percent. With blacks able to go to the polls freely, the number of black officeholders multiplied rapidly. The total of seventy-nine African-American officials elected in the South in 1964 grew to six thousand by 1998. Richmond, the one-time capital of the Confederacy, elected an African-American mayor; so, too, did Scarlett O'Hara's Atlanta. Even George Wallace and Strom Thurmond learned that they needed to cater to black voters.

The expansion of suffrage represented only one phase of the multifold consequences of the dethroning of Jim Crow. Asked in a Southern Focus Poll what was the most important change in their lifetimes, southerners had no doubt of the answer: the new paradigm on race. African Americans understood that the country, north as well as south, had no reason for complacency, but by well over 2–1 most of those responding to the survey thought there had been progress. No one knew better than Andy Young what remained to be done, but, asking,

"What of the dream?" he concluded, "It ain't what we wanted it to be, and it ain't what it ought to be, but, thank God, it ain't what it used to be."[59]

VIII

How did all this come to pass? Some historians have found the answer to that question by concentrating on grassroots activities within the South, especially in the resolve of the civil rights movement. Unquestionably, thousands of civil rights activists, mostly black but sometimes white, behaved with uncommon bravery in sparking insurrections in scores of southern communities. In his memorable voting rights address in 1965, Lyndon Johnson said, "The real hero of this struggle is the American Negro. His actions and protests, his courage to risk safety and even to risk his life, have awakened the conscience of this Nation."[60]

Yet until the federal government stepped in, African Americans had little to show for their efforts. As Sheldon Hackney has observed, "Almost every significant change in the life of the South has been initiated by external powers." In the progressive college community of Chapel Hill, an alliance of intrepid black high school students, University of North Carolina undergraduates, and townspeople labored for months to break the hold of Jim Crow, but failed to persuade the city council to adopt a public accommodations ordinance. Not until the 1964 civil rights act compelled obedience did the segregationists yield. When, immediately after enactment of the 1964 law, the largest cafeteria chain in the South announced that it was desegregating, it explained that it was doing so "rather than buck the federal government." To be sure, federal intervention was sometimes the result of local instigation, notably so in Selma. The lines of influence, though, also ran in the opposite direction. After scrutinizing developments in Georgia, one scholar determined, "In many smaller communities, organized challenges to white supremacy occurred only *after* Lyndon Johnson had signed the Civil Rights Bill."[61]

Both scholars and political activists have recognized how vital the federal government has been as an agent of change. "Left alone," wrote a sociologist in 1966, the South "would have continued into the present" much as it had been for decades past—"an anomaly: a backward area contained within the borders of one of the most developed nations in the world." But thanks in good part to federal intervention, this section of "oppressive rurality," racial castes, and "social isolation" had "lost the option" of resistance to change and "been impelled into a massive social transformation that must bring the region more into line with the rest of the country." More recently, Randy Sanders observed that "significant integration came about primarily through federal coercion," adding: "Many southerners required prodding before stepping outside the circle of racial segregation that had surrounded them all their lives. Jerris Leonard, assistant attorney general for civil rights, found that many school superintendents in the South had desegregation plans in their bottom desk drawers, but were unwilling to use them unless court orders required implementation. 'Often they would tell us, "You must make us do it if you want us to do it."' Pat Watters of the Southern Regional Council made a similar point: 'Many white southerners still need the excuse that they are being forced to do what they know is right about race.'"[62]

No one has summed up these developments better than Dewey Grantham. "The national government has been the principal instrument in the broadening of the southern electorate, in making southerners more politically conscious, and in orienting them toward substantive issues," he has concluded. "It is not too much to say that a political revolution, the end of which is not in sight, has swept the South since the 1930s. The federal government has probably had a greater impact upon the South than upon any other section—whether in the form of TVA, military and space installations, or . . . in the field of civil rights."[63]

Some historians, while agreeing that change in the South came from without, have attributed it to broad socioeconomic trends rather than governmental action, but that explanation leaves a lot unaccounted for. "The transformation of the southern economy did not proceed from unguided market forces alone," Bruce Schulman has written. "Government policy not only regulated private economic decision-making, but also shaped the local political environments in which those decisions were taken." Moreover, modernization of the economy did not automatically result in a more equable social order. The southern political elite found the mechanical cotton picker altogether compatible with racial segregation. It required national political leadership, working in tandem with the civil rights movement, to bring about the demise of the old order. In sum, concluded one study of racial prejudice, "If the issue is outright discrimination, there can be no doubt that the South of today does not resemble the South of yesterday; federal laws guarantee that."[64]

Andrew Young has given vivid testimony with regard to the changes wrought by the most important enactment of the LBJ era, the civil rights law of 1964. When, while the bill was making its way through Congress, he sought to desegregate a motel in St. Augustine, a waitress poured hot coffee over him and his companions at the motel cafe, and the manager poisoned the swimming pool with hydrochloric acid to deter Young from wading in. A week or so later, after the civil rights law had been enacted, Young recalls, "We went back to that same restaurant, and those people were just wonderful. They were apologetic. They said, 'We were just afraid of losing our business. We didn't want to be the only ones to be integrated. But if everybody's got to do it, we've been ready for it a long time. We're so glad the president signed this law.'"[65]

IX

In a special issue, *The Economist* asked, "Is Dixie Dead?" It certainly looked that way. Rednecks had moved to the suburbs and had taken jobs at a new Michelin plant; cotton had been nudged from its throne by soybeans. "If you go to the South expecting on the one hand old classical mansions with Scarlett O'Hara at the bottom of the stairs in a confection of silk and lace and, on the other, the 'nigras' sitting on the porch of their shack in the evening light, savouring the memory of their last dish of possum shanks and chitterlings, you will be disappointed," the British journal said. Still, "live oaks have continued to stand in Savannah; magnolias to blossom in Charleston; cotton to be picked on the black soil of the Mississippi Delta; grits to be served with breakfast in Anniston, Alabama." Above all, southerners remained "markedly different from other Americans" because of "their sense of place." *The Economist* did not think that distinctiveness would last much more than another generation, but at present there was "still that fondness for church-going, neighbor-killing and being back home."[66]

Evidence of the persistence of the past and of southern particularity, John Shelton Reed has observed, "continues to crop up here, there, and everywhere, like grass through concrete." The massive changes "that have swept across the region," he has asserted, "have clearly *not* rendered Southern identity useless and irrelevant, nor have they doomed it to early extinction." Surveys have found sharp differences in values between southerners and the residents of other regions, larger than those between city-dwellers and country folk or between blue-collar and white-collar workers and as great as those between blacks and whites. Strikingly, they were even more marked among the young. "The lists of Southern idiosyncrasies," stated one report, "are endless, the sum of them impossible to describe." Though the population of the South is considerably more diverse today than it was when FDR first took office, there are pockets of northeastern North Carolina where, in the words of one observer, people "look . . . like they did when Sir Walter Raleigh sent his parties ashore."[67]

Numbers of commentators agree that the singularity of the region has not ended. In 1955 V. O. Key Jr., anticipating that "the reality of sectionalism will decline and . . . kindred interests in South and North will become more and more interwoven," still foresaw that when that development took place, "the politics of the South will be Southern—not Midwestern or Northeastern." In a book published in the year following Carter's victory, Carl Degler declared that "neither in the realm of social fact nor in the realm of psychological iden- tity has the South ceased to be distinctive, despite the changes of the twentieth century," and not many years later Carl Abbott noted, "After several decades in which a majority of scholars waited impatiently for the South to converge on national social and economic patterns, specialists in the last fifteen years have re- emphasized the region's unique historical heritage, its continuing cultural differ- ence from other parts of the country, and its irreducible self-consciousness." The South, Diane Roberts remarked more recently, "was supposed to be gone by now, . . . all difference swept away in America's mass-culture tsunami. . . . Psy- chically, the South would be like one of those legendary drowned lands, Ys or Lyonnesse, where at certain times, if you listen carefully, you can hear the church bells, the sounds of the old ways, under the water—but not very distinctly and not very often." Instead, though "many old ways have passed—and thank God for that," the South was still debating familiar questions. "Today," declared the economic historian Gavin Wright in 1999, "the South appears more distinctive than ever." The demise of the South, George Tindall has concluded, is "one of the most prolonged disappearing acts since the decline and fall of Rome."[68]

In truth, observers could as readily find discontinuities as continuities. "Pow- erful forces from outside the Delta are reshaping the life there daily, yet there is a deep cultural bedrock that refuses to give way," wrote Tony Dunbar. "This extraordinary place strikes me as the American face of Zimbabwe, a country sorting out the debris left by the eradication of legal segregation." From the per- spective of a onetime Yankee who had come to regard himself as a native, Peter Applebome remarked: "Looked at one way, it's a place of grace and faith that has purged most of its old sins while maintaining most of its old virtues, a place that for all its bloody past and the ambiguities and unresolved issues of the present offers the nation's best blueprint for racial peace. Looked at another way, it's a Potemkin Village of mirrors and trap doors, where old inequities are cloaked in new forms, a chameleon South changed only on the surface, now pumping old poisons into new veins, a place where even in the most neutered suburbs, what was still lives, beating insistently away like Poe's telltale heart."[69]

Willie Morris, in an essay in *Terrains of the Heart*, summed up the contrasting perceptions sensibly:

> The truth, of course, is that Mississippi has changed phantasmagorically in some ways, and in others it has changed hardly at all. It is a blend of the relentless and the abiding. There are things here now which my grandfather, who was born shortly after the Civil War and who died in 1953, would find unfathomable. All around him he would discover a brisk new world, all growth and deracination and touched with the Yankee dollar.
>
> Yet if my grandfather had been with me on a spring morning of 1980, driving from Jackson northeast to Oxford on the country roads, he would have been witness to the sights of his memory. Off the interstates and removed from the resounding nostrums of the New South, lies our remembered world, the world of my childhood.[70]

FDR, Truman, and Johnson would have welcomed this unresolved outcome, characterized by both change and continuity. Each of the three sought to usher the South into a different future, but none of them wanted to obliterate its past. Neither carpetbaggers nor scalawags, Truman and Johnson took pride in their family heritage of links to the Confederacy and felt deep affection for southern ways. Roosevelt, who held an unreconstructed view of "the tragic era" and who, through his wife, claimed kinship to the Georgia Bullochs, deliberately chose to embed himself in the South, where he built his "Little White House."

The three presidents sought, above all, to end the South's isolation, and since they regarded sectional identity as fungible, they positioned themselves to assume that task. Lyndon Johnson's "great concern," William S. White emphasized, "was truly—it really honestly was— . . . to get rid of what he considered to be sterile and outdated regional abrasions." In his election eve speech at the Houston Astrodome in 1964, Johnson said that after "Franklin Roosevelt, at Warm Springs, saw the effect of Southern poverty, . . . the South found its voice in a new political instrument of union," a "party that united southerners and northerners. . . . That party provided progressive leadership for America in the thirties and forties, and the South began to wake up from its troubled sleep." Johnson, Paul Conkin has concluded, "did more than any other politician to lead the South, not into any promised land, but fully back into a troubled national union."[71]

Johnson's appeal for sectional unity resonated with progressive southerners, and, despite his desolate fear in his final days that, in White's phrase, "the dichotomy . . . of the two nations" would never end, he, along with Roosevelt and Truman, made considerable advances. "What is needed," declared the former Mississippi congressman Frank E. Smith in Johnson's second term, "is not a New South but a South that is inextricably and indefinably a part of the United States." In the generation after Johnson's death, that goal came very close to being reached. "We are beginning to function like a state," said a Georgia legislator, " . . . not like a province."[72]

X

The huge metamorphosis that had come about since young Franklin Roosevelt accompanied his superior on the White House portico had multiple causes, not all of them political, but the contributions of the three presidents merit more attention than they have usually been accorded. "There is loose in the land the notion that political change chiefly results from economic and social factors," Alexander Lamis remarked in exploring "New Directions for Dixie." In fact, he maintained: "After examining carefully the major political changes that have transformed the region, one realizes that they [were] not . . . directly propelled by . . . major socioeconomic changes. . . . Rather, they were tied to actions by politicians on political issues that went to the heart of the political arrangements underpinning the solidly Democratic South. When the national Democratic party moved off of dead center on the question of equal rights for blacks, starting slowly with Harry Truman and ending momentously with Lyndon Johnson, the southern rationale for white unity in the Democratic party collapsed and the region's politics underwent a massive restructuring." Lamis might well have dated this development earlier, for it was in the age of Roosevelt—as a consequence of New Deal programs, abrogation of the two-thirds rule, FDR's cultivation of southern liberals, Eleanor Roosevelt's activities, and the upheaval of World War II—that the first cleavages opened.[73]

Though other people and institutions—Congress, the Supreme Court, the civil servants charged with carrying out programs such as school busing—were important, presidents played indispensable roles. Federal officials could not have administered executive orders if presidents had not issued them—from FDR's FEPC edict to Truman's desegregation of the armed forces ukase to

Johnson's affirmative action directives. It is highly unlikely that Congress would have overcome the hostility of the southern bloc and enacted the landmark civil rights laws of 1964 and 1965 without the leadership of President Johnson. The Supreme Court's first steps toward desegregation owed no little to the initiative of the Justice Department with the approval of President Truman, and the significance of presidential appointees in securing judicial validation of major civil rights laws is suggested by the very name of the seminal Ollie's Barbecue case, *Katzenbach v. McClung*, in which LBJ's attorney general was plaintiff. "By publicly stating that he sought to eliminate racial segregation from the military, Truman broke with prior national policy and altered the course of the debate," a scholarly survey, *Foxholes and Color Lines*, concluded. "His intervention emboldened advocates of racial equality, put supporters of segregation on the defensive, and opened a path leading toward the completion of formal racial integration."[74]

In assessing the impact of the White House, scholars emphasize not only what happens when presidents take charge, but also what the consequences are when, as with Dwight Eisenhower, they do not. "Presidents . . . can profoundly shape and change public attitudes on civil rights," Katherine Tate and Gloria Hampton have written. William O. Douglas, they note, said that if Eisenhower "had gone to the nation and radio telling people to obey the law" after the *Brown* decision, "the cause of desegregation would have been accelerated," for "Ike was a hero and he was worshipped." Instead, he had refused to spend "some of his political capital . . . on the racial cause," Douglas declared, and "Ike's ominous silence on our 1954 decision gave courage to the racists."[75]

Eisenhower failed to act both because he was a closet racist and because he had a Whiggish view of the Oval Office. He found it hard to comprehend what was so wrong about Jim Crow; abhorred "social mingling"; and was shocked by the notion that "a Negro should court my daughter." Eisenhower, who as a general had disapproved of Truman's integration of the armed forces, was, concluded a high-ranking government aide, "neither emotionally nor intellectually in favor of combating segregation." Opposed to a mandatory FEPC and the rest of the Truman program that the white South so fiercely resented, he refused to use the powers of his office to safeguard equal rights save in areas such as military bases that were unquestionably under federal jurisdiction. "I do not believe," he declared, "that prejudice . . . will succumb to compulsion." Attuned to the sensibility of southern whites but not to the aspirations of African Americans, he cautioned his attorney general not to be "another Sumner" and riled black publishers by lecturing them, "You must be patient" without giving them any reason to believe that so long as he was in the White House patience would be rewarded.[76]

Only with the greatest reluctance did Eisenhower permit his attorney general to go through the motions of endorsing the initiative of Truman's officials toward desegregating schools, and when the *Brown* ruling was handed down, he refused to speak out. Shortly before the Supreme Court acted, he said of the foes of integration, "All they are concerned about is to see that their sweet little girls are not required to sit in schools alongside some big overgrown Negroes." When the Court did act, he was appalled. "I am convinced that the Supreme Court decision *set back* progress in the South *at least fifteen years*," he told an advisor. "The fellow who tries to tell me that you can do these things *by force* is just plain *nuts*." With the Court under a barrage of abuse for daring to breach the walls of Jim Crow, Eisenhower would do nothing to ease the transition to a different social order. Asked by a newspaperman two days after the *Brown* ruling whether he had any advice for the South, Eisenhower replied, "Not in the slightest."[77]

Other presidents over the past half century have approached or exceeded Eisenhower's disregard of the interests of African Americans. Though John F. Kennedy said during the 1960 campaign that discrimination in housing could be wiped out with "the stroke of a presidential pen," the White House was flooded with pens before he issued an order so weak that Martin Luther King commented, "If tokenism were our goal, the administration moves us adroitly toward it." Not until his third and final year in office did Kennedy seriously identify himself with the cause of equal rights. Richard Nixon, who forced the resolute chair of the United States Commission on Civil Rights out of office, pursued a "Southern strategy" so tenaciously that John Hope Franklin declared that Nixon would "never be forgiven by blacks" or "by any segment of the population." Gerald Ford mobilized his cabinet to speak out against court-ordered busing. In the 1980 campaign, Reagan callously championed "states' rights" at Philadelphia, Mississippi, where three civil rights workers had been brutally slain, and in office he exhorted Congress not to renew Lyndon Johnson's 1965 Voting Rights Act. Asking a black person to vote for Ronald Reagan, said an NAACP official in 1984, was like urging a chicken to vote for Colonel Sanders. Neither George H. W. Bush, who gained office with the help of racially inflammatory campaign ads, nor his son, who chose Martin Luther King's birthday as the occasion to hobble affirmative action, earned the confidence of

African Americans. George "Dubya" Bush, said the NAACP's Julian Bond, "has selected nominees from the Taliban wing of American politics . . . and chosen Cabinet officials whose devotion to the Confederacy is nearly canine in its uncritical affection." Though Toni Morrison called Bill Clinton the first black president, he gutted federal programs on which impoverished African Americans depended. Surveying his record in 1996, Richard Reeves wrote, "Many members of his own party, the Democrats, sputtering of betrayal, wondered whether they were present at the dismantling of the party's patrimony, the New Deal of Franklin D. Roosevelt."[78]

If this brisk survey indicates that chief executives can affect African Americans, the South, and the nation adversely by their actions and inactions, the performances of FDR, Truman, and Johnson demonstrate that presidents can also have a positive influence. More than one historian has traced the rise of the modern civil rights movement to the yeasty 1930s. Even when Roosevelt acted with no intent of affecting race relations, his large view of government reverberated. Without the Constitutional Revolution of 1937, it would not have been possible for the Supreme Court to validate the Civil Rights Act of 1964 as within the commerce power, even when it was applied to puny neighborhood cafes. Harry Truman went considerably beyond Roosevelt in spotlighting the issue of racial discrimination. "Truman," said Thurgood Marshall, "proved that one man can be bigger than the statutes of his time—more forceful than the lawmakers." Not until Lyndon Johnson took over the Oval Office, though, was the full power of the federal government exerted on behalf of equal rights, notably in the legislation of 1964, 1965, and, unexpectedly, 1968. LBJ's "consistent and courageous support" of open housing legislation, Hugh Graham pointed out, did much to account for "the surprising turnaround" in 1968 when Congress approved a proposal by the president that two years earlier had been seen as "overreaching if not quixotic."[79]

The three presidents may well have had their greatest impact in loosening the terrible grip of the past on the region. "If history has defined the South, writes David Goldfield, "it has also trapped white southerners into sometimes defending the indefensible, holding onto views generally discredited in the rest of the civilized world and holding on the fiercer because of that." No longer— or at least not nearly to the same extent. "For years now," Joseph Persky has observed, "the South has been shedding its history." In the final sentence of his book *Still Fighting the Civil War*, published in 2002, Goldfield said, "History will still matter, because that is the South's immutable distinction, but it will matter differently." The changes the three presidents helped bring about fell well short of solving every problem that had plagued the region in past years, but they did create new opportunities. "For me," writes Hodding Carter III, "what is exciting about the South today is that there is no convincing reason to say that it is fated to go one way or another. Our history is no longer our future, because to a meaningful extent we are free of it for the first time."[80]

To savvy observers at the end of the FDR-Truman-Johnson era, the South appeared a world remade. The Tar Heel Edwin Yoder has written: "I sometimes think with amazement how little my own children, who are of the modern suburban South, know of the region that existed only a few decades ago. If I told them about it—and if they listened, as I once listened to the family storytellers—they would surely think my South as strange and exotic as Xanadu." Even in Xanadu, "ancestral voices" can be heard, but they echo over a transmuted landscape. If the South seceded, *The Economist* in London observed, "it would become the world's fifth biggest economy." In sum, the South in the twenty-first century—indeed the South on Lyndon Johnson's final day in office in 1973—is a very different place from the South Franklin Roosevelt found when he got off the train in a rundown Georgia village in 1923.[81]

NOTES

COHC   Columbia Oral History Collection, Columbia University, New York
FDRL   Franklin D. Roosevelt Library, Hyde Park, N.Y.
HSTL   Harry S. Truman Library, Independence, Mo.
JFKL   John F. Kennedy Library, Boston, Mass.
LBJL   Lyndon B. Johnson Library, Austin, Tex.
LC   Library of Congress, Washington, D.C.
SHC   Southern Historical Collection, University of North Carolina at Chapel Hill, Chapel Hill, N.C.
SOHP   Southern Oral History Project, University of North Carolina at Chapel Hill, Chapel Hill, N.C.

PROLOGUE

1. Thomas J. Knock, *To End All Wars: Woodrow Wilson and the Quest for a New World Order* (New York, 1992), 3; Woodrow Wilson, *Robert E. Lee: An Interpretation* (Chapel Hill, N.C., 1924), 11–12.

2. Leonard Lutwack, *The Role of Place in Literature* (Syracuse, N.Y., 1984), 183; Alvin Toffler, *Future Shock* (New York, 1970), 69, 82; Joseph J. Persky, *The Burden of Dependency: Colonial Themes in Southern Economic Thought* (Baltimore, 1992), 151. See, too, William M. Bevis, "Region, Power, Place," in *Reading the West: New Essays on the Literature of the American West,* ed. Michael Kowalewski (New York, 1996), 21; Joseph A. Amato, *Rethinking Home: A Case for Writing Local History* (Berkeley, Calif., 2002), 2.

3. Jack Temple Kirby, *Media-made Dixie: The South in the American Imagination* (Athens, Ga., 1986), 159–60; Fritz Steele, *The Sense of Place* (Boston, 1981), 8; Walker Percy, *Signposts in a Strange Land* (New York, 1991), 5.

4. Michel Foucault, *Power/Knowledge: Selected Interviews and Other Writings,* ed. Colin Gordon (New York, 1980), 70; John A. Jakle, "Time, Space, and the Geographic Past: A Prospectus for Historical Geography," *American Historical Review* 76 (1971): 1087; Wayne Franklin and Michael

Steiner, "Taking Place: Toward the Regrounding of American Studies," in *Mapping American Culture*, ed. Franklin and Steiner (Iowa City, Iowa, 1992), 8; Allen K. Philbrick, "Perceptions and Technologies as Determinants of Predictions about Earth, 2050," in *Human Geography in a Shrinking World*, ed. Ronald Abler, Donald Janelle, Allen Philbrick, and John Sommer (Belmont, Calif., 1975), 33.

5. Michael Sorkin, "Introduction," in *Variations on a Theme Park*, ed. Sorkin (New York, 1992), xi; Lutwack, *Role of Place*, 183.

6. Franklin and Steiner, "Taking Place," 3–9; Michael A. Godkin, "Identity and Place: Clinical Applications Based on Notions of Rootedness and Uprootedness," 73, and Anne Buttimer, "Home, Reach, and the Sense of Place," 167, in *The Human Experience of Space and Place*, ed. Buttimer and David Seamon (New York, 1980); Carville Earle, *The American Way: A Geographical History of Crisis and Recovery* (Lanham, Md., 2003), 335; Robin W. Winks, "Regionalism in Comparative Perspective," in *Regionalism and the Pacific Northwest*, ed. William G. Robbins, Robert J. Frank, and Richard E. Ross (Corvallis, Ore., 1983), 26; Peter N. Stearns, "Social History Present and Future," *Journal of Social History* 37 (2003): 15. "Knowing who you are," maintained one writer, "is impossible without knowing where you are." Paul Shepard, "Place in American Culture," *North American Review* 262 (fall 1977): 32.

7. Raymond Williams, "Decentralism and the Politics of Place," in *Resources of Hope: Culture, Democracy, Socialism*, ed. Robin Gale (London, 1989), 282.

8. Alexander Pope, "Epistle to Burlington," in *The Poems of Alexander Pope*, ed. John Butt (New Haven, Conn., 1963), 590, quoted in Franklin and Steiner, "Taking Place," 6; D. H. Lawrence, *Studies in Classic American Literature* (New York, 1923), 8–9; Lutwack, *Role of Place*, 141, 2; Steele, *Sense of Place*, 99. One writer, though, alleging that "literary criticism has failed to acknowledge the full physical presence of the American landscape and its local geographies," has called for "a new attention to place in literary studies." Michael Kowalewski, "Writing in Place: The New American Regionalism," *American Literary History* 6 (1994): 180, 182.

9. Annie Dillard, *An American Childhood*, in *Three by Annie Dillard* (New York, 1990), 273; Eudora Welty, *The Eye of the Story: Selected Essays and Reviews* (New York, 1978), 128–29.

10. Frank E. Vandiver, *The Southwest: South or West?* (College Station, Tex., 1975), 13; Scott Romine, "Where Is Southern Literature?: The Practice of Place in a Postsouthern Age," in *South to a New Place: Region, Literature, Culture*, ed. Suzanne W. Jones and Sharon Monteith (Baton Rouge, La., 2002), 23, 39; James C. Cobb, "Community and Identity: Redefining Southern Culture," *Georgia Review* 50 (1996): 11. A 1990 survey found that 68 percent of institutions with Ph.D. programs that responded to a questionnaire reported offering courses in U.S. regional history; in the South, 83 percent did so. Carl Abbott, "Tracing the Trends in U.S. Regional History," *Perspectives* 22 (1990): 4. See, too, Louis D. Rubin Jr., "The American South: The Continuity of Self-Definition," in *The American South: Portrait of a Culture*, ed. Rubin (Baton Rouge, La., 1980), 17.

11. Charlayne Hunter-Gault, *In My Place* (New York, 1992), 232; Jimmie Lewis Franklin, "Black Southerners, Shared Experience, and Place: A Reflection," *Journal of Southern History* 60 (1994): 3. A 1993 study found that black southerners were more disposed than were whites in the region to taking pride in a southern identity. Benjamin Schwarz, "The Idea of the South," *Atlantic Monthly* (December 1997): 122.

12. Michael Clark Steiner, "The Regional Impulse in the United States, 1923–1941" (Ph.D. dis-

sertation, University of Minnesota, 1978), 28, 32; Walter Kollmorgen, "Crucial Deficiencies of Regionalism," *American Economic Review* 35 (1945): 377, 381, 385–86; Jane Jacobs, *The Death and Life of Great American Cities* (New York, 1961), 22; Paul Goodman, *Utopian Essays and Practical Proposals* (New York, 1962), 7; Laurence R. Veysey, "Myth and Reality in Approaching American Regionalism," *American Quarterly* 12 (1960): 31; Richard Maxwell Brown, "The New Regionalism in America, 1970–1981," in *Regionalism and Pacific Northwest,* ed. Robbins, Frank, and Ross, 42, 45, 47; Bruce Clayton, "Southern Intellectuals," in *Debating Southern History: Ideas and Action in the Twentieth Century,* ed. Clayton and John A. Salmond (New York, 1999), 40–41; John Shelton Reed, *One South: An Ethnic Approach to Regional Culture* (Baton Rouge, La., 1982), 33–34, citing Frank Westie.

13. James Gray, quoted in Earl Rovit, "The Region versus the Nation: Critical Battles in the Thirties," *Mississippi Quarterly* 8 (1960): 91; George Core, ed., *Southern Fiction Today: Renascence and Beyond* (Athens, Ga., 1969), 66.

14. Ray Allen Billington, *Frederick Jackson Turner: Historian, Scholar, Teacher* (New York, 1973), 216, 374; Michael C. Steiner, "The Significance of Turner's Sectional Thesis," *Western Historical Quarterly* 10 (1979): 440; Merle E. Curti, "The Section and the Frontier in American History: The Methodological Concepts of Frederick Jackson Turner," in *Methods in Social Science: A Case Book,* ed. Stuart A. Rice (Chicago, 1931), 364; Howard W. Odum, *Southern Regions of the United States* (Chapel Hill, N.C., 1936), 251.

15. Frederick Jackson Turner, "Is Sectionalism in America Dying Away?" in Turner, *The Significance of Sections in American History* (New York, 1932), 313–14; Donald G. Holtgrieve, "Frederick Jackson Turner as a Regionalist," *Professional Geographer* 26 (1974): 159–65; Billington, *Turner,* 381.

16. Richard Hofstadter, *The Progressive Historians: Turner, Beard, Parrington* (New York, 1968), 91; Arthur M. Schlesinger Jr., *A Life in the Twentieth Century: Innocent Beginnings, 1917–1950* (Boston, 2000), 159; Billington, *Turner,* 371, 470–71; William Cronon, "Revisiting the Vanishing Frontier: The Legacy of Frederick Jackson Turner," *Western Historical Quarterly* 28 (1987): 168.

17. Billington, *Turner,* 471; Hofstadter, *Progressive Historians,* 91, 100–101, 153.

18. David Potter, *The South and the Sectional Conflict* (Baton Rouge, La., 1968), 4; David R. Goldfield, "The New Regionalism," *Journal of Urban History* 10 (1984): 176; Raymond D. Gastil, *Cultural Regions of the United States* (Seattle, 1975); Joel Garreau, *The Nine Nations of North America* (Boston, 1981), xiii–xiv; James C. Cobb, "An Epitaph for the North: Reflections on the Politics of Regional and National Identity at the Millennium," *Journal of Southern History* 66 (2000): 16–17. See, too, Dewey W. Grantham Jr., *The Regional Imagination: The South and Recent American History* (Nashville, Tenn., 1979), 229; Allan G. Bogue, *Frederick Jackson Turner: Strange Roads Going Down* (Norman, Okla., 1998), 460.

19. Richard Franklin Bensel, *Sectionalism and American Political Development, 1880–1980* (Madison, Wis., 1984), xix, 17, 411; M. Elizabeth Sanders, *The Regulation of Natural Gas: Policy and Politics, 1938–1978* (Philadelphia, 1981), 14, 196–97; Frederick C. Harris, "Notes on a Native Son: A Foreword," in Hanes Walton Jr., *Reelection: William Jefferson Clinton as a Native-Son Presidential Candidate* (New York, 2000), x; Thomas J. Sugrue, "All Politics Is Local: The Persistence of Localism in Twentieth-Century America," in *The Democratic Experiment: New Directions in American Political History,* ed. Meg Jacobs, William J. Novak, and Julian E. Zelizer (Princeton, N.J., 2003), 302. See, too, Elizabeth Sanders, "Industrial Concentration, Sectional Competition, and Antitrust

Politics in America, 1880–1980," *Studies in American Political Development* 1 (1986): 142–214; Michael S. Lewis-Beck and Tom W. Rice, "Localism in Presidential Elections: The Home State Advantage," *American Journal of Political Science* 27 (1983): 548. In 1970 Ira Sharkansky wrote, "The nationalization of American politics and public policies is more often alleged than demonstrated: it is evident that the nationalizing process has not proceeded so far as to obliterate the regions," for "some of the sharpest differences in public affairs can be found in comparisons of politics from one section of the country to another." Sharkansky found "a development toward both greater regionalism and greater nationalization—complementary movements which may seem odd in juxtaposition." Ira Sharkansky, *Regionalism in American Politics* (Indianapolis, Ind., 1970), 78, 4, 98.

20. David J. Russo, *Families and Communities: A New View of American History* (Nashville, Tenn., 1974), 282; J. Bill Berry, ed., *Located Lives: Place and Idea in Southern Autobiography* (Athens, Ga., 1990), xii; Cleanth Brooks, "Regionalism in American Literature," *Journal of Southern History* 26 (1960): 35, 37.

21. Michael Kammen, "Introduction," in *The Past before Us: Contemporary Historical Writing*, ed. Kammen (Ithaca, N.Y., 1980), 35; Peter H. Smith, "Political History in the 1980s: A View from Latin America," *Journal of Interdisciplinary History* 12 (1981): 3; Sean Wilentz, "On Class and Politics in Jacksonian America," *Reviews in American History* 10 (1982): 51; Paul Goodman, "Putting Some Class Back into Political History: 'The Transformation of Political Culture' and the Crisis in American Political History," *Reviews in American History* 12 (1984): 80. See, too, J. Morgan Kousser, "Restoring Politics to Political History," *Journal of Interdisciplinary History* 12 (1982): 569. "Younger scholars," James T. Patterson has noted, "distance themselves from a once dominant form of political history that had focused on the doings of federal government leaders and institutions. . . . The old adage 'History is past politics, and politics present history' long ago lost its appeal among younger historians interested in America in the twentieth century." James T. Patterson, "Americans and the Writing of Twentieth-Century United States History," in *Imagined Histories: American Historians Interpret the Past*, ed. Anthony Molho and Gordon S. Wood (Princeton, N.J., 1998), 193, 195.

22. Hugh Davis Graham, "The Stunted Career of Public History: A Critique and an Agenda," *Public Historian* 15 (1993): 30. That same year, John Morton Blum found the "guarded hostility" of social historians to political history "in one way curious because the state has continually affected the treatment of questions of race and gender and family." Indeed, he added, "for more than a decade politics has resounded with debate over abortion, affirmative action, family values, and ethnic diversity." John Morton Blum, *Liberty, Justice, Order: Essays on Past Politics* (New York, 1993), 4.

23. Eric Foner, "History in Crisis," *Commonweal*, December 18, 1981, 725; *Raleigh News and Observer*, January 10, 1988; Anthony J. Badger, "Introduction," in *Contesting Democracy: Substance and Structure in American Political History, 1775–2000*, ed. Byron E. Shafer and Badger (Lawrence, Kans., 2001), 1.

24. Joel Silbey, "The State and Practice of American Political History at the Millennium: The Nineteenth Century as a Test Case," *Journal of Policy History* 11 (March 1999): 3; Lewis L. Gould, review of *Contesting Democracy: Substance and Structure in American Political History, 1775–2000*, edited by Byron E. Shafer and Anthony J. Badger, *North Carolina Historical Review* 89 (2002): 491.

25. Steven M. Gillon, "The Future of Political History," *Journal of Policy History* 9 (1997): 241;

Badger, "Introduction," 2. Lawrence Levine has argued that "to accuse contemporary historians of having abandoned politics . . . in favor of parochial, politically correct areas is to have seriously misread the historiography of the last few decades." Instead, he asserts, political history has been reconfigured and enriched. Lawrence W. Levine, "Clio, Canons, and Culture," *Journal of American History* 80 (1993): 864.

26. Gillon, "Future of Political History," 250.

27. *Chronicle of Higher Education,* April 14, 1995, A8; Michael Nelson, "History, Meet Politics," *American Prospect,* June 18, 2001, 36, 37. The OAH panelists were Alan Brinkley, Lizabeth Cohen, Sara Evans, Ronald Formisano, Laura Kalman, and James Patterson. Steven Gillon sparked the planning committee, whose members included, in addition to some of the panelists, William H. Chafe, Hugh Graham, David Kennedy, and Harvard Sitkoff.

28. Wilentz, "Class and Politics," 51; Alice Kessler-Harris, "Social History," in *The New American History,* ed. Eric Foner (Philadelphia, 1990), 178; Peter N. Stearns, "Social and Political History," *Journal of Social History* 16 (1983): 5, 3. For the conviction that "one cannot separate social and political history," see John Garrard, "Social History, Political History and Political Science: The Study of Power," *Journal of Social Science* 16 (spring 1983): 119.

29. Elizabeth Fox-Genovese and Eugene D. Genovese, *Fruits of Merchant Capital: Slavery and Bourgeois Property in the Rise and Expansion of Capitalism* (New York, 1983), 181, 207. There is no reason to suppose, though, that they would approve of what I do in this book, for they deplore the "ossification of the political, best exemplified in its curtailment to a series of electoral figures." Ibid., 208.

30. Tony Judt, "A Clown in Regal Purple: Social History and the Historians," *History Workshop Journal* (spring 1979): 68, 71.

31. David Brian Robertson, "The Return to History and the New Institutionalism in American Political Science," *Social Science History* 17 (1993): 1–2, 20–23; Ira Katznelson and Bruce Pietrykowski, "Rebuilding the American State: Evidence from the 1940s," *Studies in American Political Development* 5 (1991): 304. The Section on Politics and History had been initiated informally two years earlier. Aggregate statistical approaches, asserted a British political scientist, "betrayed the worst excesses of behaviouralism and the dangers of the neglect of history." As a consequence of "the lack of historical perspective," it was "understandable that such a welter of contradictory findings from so many studies invites a reaction close to despair." Dennis Kavanagh, "Why Political Science Needs History," *Political Studies* 39 (1991): 493. See, too, John Dearlove, "Bringing the Constitution Back In: Political Science and the State," *Political Studies* 37 (1989): 527. Even in the heyday of ahistorical behavioralism, not every political scientist accepted its premises. In his Inaugural Lecture at the London School of Economics and Political Science in 1951, Michael Oakeshott declared that "politics are a proper subject for academic study," and, furthermore, that "the study of politics should be an historical study." Michael Oakeshott, *Political Education* (Cambridge, Eng., 1951), 25.

32. Myron Marty, "America Revising," *History Teacher* 15 (1982): 558; Mark Leff, "Revisioning U.S. Political History," *American Historical Review* 100 (1995): 835; Thomas Bender, "Wholes and Parts: The Need for Synthesis in American History," *Journal of American History* 71 (1986): 125; Joanne Meyerowitz, "History and September 11: An Introduction," *Journal of American History* 89 (2002): 415; Meg Jacobs and Julian E. Zelizer, "The Democratic Experiment: New Directions in American Political History," in *Democratic Experiment,* ed. Jacobs, Novak, and Zelizer, 1. I have developed

these arguments at greater length in William E. Leuchtenburg, "The Pertinence of Political History: Reflections on the Significance of the State in America," *Journal of American History* 73 (1986): 585–600. See, too, Sean Wilentz, "Introduction: Teufelsdrockh's Dilemma: On Symbolism, Politics, and History," in *Rites of Power: Symbolism, Ritual, and Politics since the Middle Ages,* ed. Wilentz (Philadelphia, 1985), 8–9. For the importance of political history in German historiography, see George Iggers, *The Social History of Politics: Critical Perspectives in West German Historical Writing since 1945* (New York, 1965), 34.

33. Arthur Schlesinger Jr., "The End of an Era," *Wall Street Journal,* November 20, 1980; *New York Times,* January 21, 1981, January 25, 1995; David Cieply, "Why the State Was Dropped in the First Place: A Prequel to Skocpol's 'Bringing the State Back In,'" *Critical Review: An Interdisciplinary Journal of Politics and Society* 14 (2000): 159; Gordon Craig, "Political History," *Daedalus* 100 (1971): 323; David Thelen, "The Practice of American History," *Journal of American History* 81 (1994): 957.

34. Murray Edelman, *The Symbolic Uses of Politics* (Urbana, Ill., 1964), 1; Lance E. Davis, "It's a Long, Long Road to Tipperary, or Reflections on Organized Violence, Protection Rates, and Related Topics: The New Political History," *Journal of Economic History* 40 (1980): 2; Ellis W. Hawley, "Social Policy and the Liberal State in Twentieth-Century America," in *Federal Social Policy: The Historical Dimension,* ed. Donald T. Critchlow and Ellis W. Hawley (University Park, Pa., 1988), 125; Theda Skocpol, "Bringing the State Back In," *Items* 36 (1982): 1–8. See, too, J. P. Nettl, "The State as a Conceptual Variable," *World Politics* 20 (1968): 559–92; Edward D. Berkowitz, "Social Welfare and the American State," in *Federal Social Policy,* ed. Critchlow and Hawley, 180.

35. Alan Brinkley, "Writing the History of Contemporary America: Dilemmas and Challenges," *Daedalus* 113 (1984): 124–25.

36. Gabriel A. Almond and Sidney Verba, *The Civic Culture: Political Attitudes and Democracy in Five Nations* (Boston, 1965), 46, 64; Fareed Zakaria, "The End of the End of History," *Newsweek,* September 24, 2001, 70.

37. Edward T. Price, "The Central Courthouse Square in the American County Seat," *Geographical Review* 58 (1968): 29, 59; Ross Lockridge, *Raintree County* (Boston, 1948), 380–81.

38. Wayne K. Durrill, "A Tale of Two Courthouses: Civic Space, Political Power and Capitalist Development in a New South Community, 1843–1940," *Journal of Social History* 35 (2002): 661–62; John Brinckerhoff Jackson, *The Southern Landscape Tradition in Texas* (Fort Worth, Tex., 1980), 14. See, too, Robert E. Veselka, *The Courthouse Square in Texas,* ed. Kenneth E. Foote (Austin, Tex., 2000).

39. Conrad M. Arensberg, "American Communities," *American Anthropologist* 57 (1955): 1151; Milton B. Newton Jr., "Settlement Patterns as Artifacts of Social Structure," in *The Human Mirror: Material and Spatial Images of Man,* ed. Miles Richardson (Baton Rouge, La., 1974), 343, 352–53.

40. William Faulkner, *Requiem for a Nun* (New York, 1951), 28, 40. For its place in a South Carolina town in another novel, see Hamilton Basso, *Courthouse Square* (New York, 1936).

41. Peter Gay, *Voltaire's Politics: The Poet as Realist* (Princeton, N.J., 1959), 181; Thomas Carlyle, *On Heroes, Hero-Worship and the Heroic in History* (London, 1841), 1–2; James West Davidson and Mark Hamilton Lytle, *After the Fact: The Art of Historical Detection* (New York, 1982), 300; Sidney Hook, *The Hero in History: A Study in Limitation and Possibility* (New York, 1943), 18–19, 77.

42. Walter Karp, "In Defense of Politics: Against Theorists, Cynics, and the New Historians," *Harper's* 276 (1988): 44; Eric A. Nordlinger, *On the Autonomy of the Democratic State* (Cambridge, Mass., 1981), 2; Don Higginbotham, *George Washington: Uniting a Nation* (Lanham, Md., 2002), 85; Alonzo Hamby, *For the Survival of Democracy: Franklin Roosevelt and the World Crisis of the 1930s* (New York, 2004), xiii.

43. Hook, *Hero in History*, 104, 106, 147, 175.

44. Thomas C. Cochran, "The 'Presidential Synthesis' in American History," *American Historical Review* 53 (1948): 758.

45. Jordan A. Schwarz, *Interregnum of Despair: Hoover, Congress, and the Depression* (Urbana, Ill., 1970), 237. Tony Badger, "The New Deal without FDR: What Biographies of Roosevelt Cannot Tell Us," in *History and Biography: Essays in Honour of Derek Beales*, ed. T. C. W. Blanning and David Cannadine (New York, 1996), 265; *American Heritage* (July/August 1988): 63.

46. Foner, *New American History*, ix.

47. Russell L. Riley, *The Presidency and the Politics of Racial Inequality: Nation-Keeping from 1831 to 1965* (New York, 1999), 3–5.

48. Ibid., 274; William Howard Taft, *Our Chief Magistrate and His Powers* (Durham, N.C., 2002; 1st ed. 1916), 52; William E. Leuchtenburg, "The Twentieth-Century Presidency," in *Perspectives on Modern America: Making Sense of the Twentieth Century*, ed. Harvard Sitkoff (New York, 2001), 29. I was present at the Memphis session at which this statement was made.

49. Badger, "New Deal without FDR," 254.

50. Ibid.; Franklin Forts, "Living with Confederate Symbols," *Southern Cultures* 8 (2002): 67–68.

51. D. W. Meinig, "The Continuous Shaping of America: A Prospectus for Geographers and Historians," *American Historical Review* 83 (1978): 1202; Richard Gray, *Southern Aberrations: Writers of the American South and the Problem of Regionalism* (Baton Rouge, La., 2000), 511; W. Fitzhugh Brundage, "No Deed but Memory," in *Where These Memories Grow: History, Memory, and Southern Identity*, ed. Brundage (Chapel Hill, N.C., 2000), 2–3.

52. Jack Temple Kirby, "The South as Pernicious Abstraction," *Perspectives on the American South: An Annual Review of Society, Politics and Culture*, ed. Merle Black and John Shelton Reed, 2 (1984): 174; Larry J. Griffin, "Southern Distinctiveness, Yet Again, or, Why America Still Needs the South," *Southern Cultures* 6 (2000): 62–63. So far had the South moved from the era of John Randolph of Roanoke and William Yancey that the 2003 gubernatorial election in Louisiana pitted a Cajun woman against the son of immigrants from Punjab.

53. W. J. Cash, *The Mind of the South* (New York, 1960; 1st ed. 1941), vii; David Moltke-Hansen, "Regional Frameworks and Networks: Changing Identities in the Southeastern United States," paper delivered in Germany (1997), 1; Schwarz, "Idea of the South," 120; John B. Boles, ed., *Dixie Dateline: A Journalistic Portrait of the Contemporary South* (Houston, Tex., 1983), 7.

54. John Shelton Reed, "Southerners," in *Harvard Encyclopedia of American Ethnic Groups*, ed. Stephan Thernstrom (Cambridge, Mass., 1980), 944. Reed, *Southerners: The Social Psychology of Sectionalism* (Chapel Hill, N.C., 1983), 27; Elizabeth Fox-Genovese and Eugene D. Genovese, "Surveying the South: A Conversation with John Shelton Reed," *Southern Cultures* 7 (2001): 92.

55. Gastil, *Cultural Regions*, 175; David Goldfield, *Still Fighting the Civil War: The American South and Southern History* (Baton Rouge, La., 2002), 307. See, too, Karsten Hülsemann, "Greenfields in

the Heart of Dixie: How the American Auto Industry Discovered the South," in *The Second Wave: Southern Industrialization from the 1940s to the 1970s*, ed. Philip Scranton (Athens, Ga., 2001), 220.

56. *Guinn v. United States*, 238 U.S. 347 (1915); *McLaurin v. Oklahoma State Regents for Higher Education*, 339 U.S. 637 (1950).

57. Core, *Southern Fiction Today*, 64–65; David L. Carlton, "The American South and the American Manufacturing Belt," in *The South, the Nation, and the World: Perspectives on Southern Economic Development*, ed. Carlton and Peter A. Coclanis (Charlottesville, Va., 2003), 177; H. Brandt Ayers, "You Can't Eat Magnolias," in *You Can't Eat Magnolias*, ed. Ayers and Thomas H. Naylor (New York, 1972), 5–6.

58. William Faulkner, *Absalom, Absalom!* (New York, 1936), 361; William Howarth, "Writing Upside Down: Voice and Place in Southern Autobiography," in *Located Lives*, ed. Berry, 3; Carl N. Degler, "Thesis, Antithesis, Synthesis: The South, the North, and the Nation," *Journal of Southern History* 53 (1987): 3.

59. Mary Hood et al., "A Stubborn Sense of Place: Writers and Writings on the South," *Harper's* 273 (1986): 36.

60. Joe P. Dunn and Howard L. Preston, eds., *The Future South: A Historical Perspective for the Twenty-first Century* (Urbana, Ill., 1991), 170.

61. The Virginian was George Poland, quoted in *Raleigh News and Observer*, December 30, 1992.

62. John Shelton Reed, "For Dixieland: The Sectionalism of *I'll Take My Stand*," in *A Band of Prophets: The Vanderbilt Agrarians after Fifty Years*, ed. William C. Havard and Walter Sullivan (Baton Rouge, La., 1982), 59; Pat Conroy, *The Prince of Tides* (New York, 1986), 1; Alan Sillitoe, "A Sense of Place," *Geographical Magazine* 47 (1975): 689; Elizabeth Hardwick, "Southern Literature: The Cultural Assumptions of Regionalism," in *Southern Literature: Heritage and Promise*, ed. Philip Castille and William Osborne (Memphis, Tenn., 1983), 17–18.

63. Core, *Southern Fiction Today*, 68.

64. Peirce Lewis, "Defining a Sense of Place," *Southern Quarterly* 17 (1979): 24; Peter Applebome, *Dixie Rising: How the South Is Shaping American Values, Politics and Culture* (New York, 1996), 18–19; Degler, "Thesis," 3.

1. FDR: GEORGIA SQUIRE

1. Frank Freidel, *Franklin D. Roosevelt: The Apprenticeship* (Boston, 1952), 28–29.

2. *Atlanta Constitution*, April 12, 1985.

3. Samuel I. Rosenman, ed., *The Public Papers and Addresses of Franklin D. Roosevelt*, 13 vols. (New York, 1938–50), 2: 490; Richard Thayer Goldberg, *The Making of Franklin D. Roosevelt: Triumph over Disability* (Cambridge, Mass., 1981), 91. Virginia Foster Durr recalled: "Mrs. Roosevelt . . . would often . . . tell the same little tale over with the same little laugh. She told all the Southerners repeatedly that her grandmother came from Georgia and was a Bullock. Well, that's the family that Bullock County is named for. . . . I bet she told that tale fifty times. She was trying to identify with the Southerners." Hollinger F. Barnard, ed., *Outside the Magic Circle: The Autobiography of Virginia Foster Durr* (University, Ala., 1985), 183. The name is actually spelled "Bulloch."

4. *Public Papers*, 7: 611–12; Hugh Gregory Gallagher, *FDR's Splendid Deception* (New York, 1985),

14; William Warren Rogers Jr., "The Death of a President, April 12, 1945: An Account from Warm Springs," *Georgia Historical Quarterly* 75 (1991): 107; Ruth Stevens, *"Hi-Ya Neighbor"* (New York, 1947), 30.

5. Lee Rowe OH, "Warm Springs Interviews," Rexford G. Tugwell MSS, Box 75; F. P. Henderson, "FDR at Warm Springs," *Marine Corps Gazette* 66 (1982): 57; Frank Freidel, *Franklin D. Roosevelt: The Ordeal* (Boston, 1954), 198; Kenneth S. Davis, *FDR: The Beckoning of Destiny* (New York, 1972), 810; Theo Lippman Jr., *The Squire of Warm Springs: FDR in Georgia, 1924–1945* (Chicago, 1977), 232–35; Daisy Bonner OH, Martin Gibson OH, "Warm Springs Interviews," Tugwell MSS, Box 75; "Franklin D. Roosevelt at Warm Springs, Georgia," Tugwell MSS, Box 75. Roosevelt wrote his distant cousin Daisy Suckley in 1934 of Warm Springs: "Some day you must see that spot—you would like the great pines & the red earth." Geoffrey C. Ward, ed., *Closest Companion: The Unknown Story of the Intimate Friendship between Franklin Roosevelt and Margaret Suckley* (Boston, 1995), 16. Roosevelt found possum hard to take. He remembered with distaste an occasion in 1913 in Brunswick, Georgia: "There we had lukewarm possum soup and it wouldn't have been good even if it were hot, followed by some fried possum and then some baked possum." Charles F. Palmer, "Confidential Memorandum Regarding Dinner at White House Monday Evening, May 17, 1937," Palmer MSS, 5, Box 129. For the Warm Springs story, Lippman's account is indispensable, and I am happy to acknowledge my large debt to it.

6. Bill Ellison in *Columbus (Ga.) Enquirer,* April 13, 1945, clipping, Scrapbook, Franklin D. Roosevelt Museum Archives.

7. "Franklin D. Roosevelt at Warm Springs, Georgia," Rexford G. Tugwell MSS, Box 75; K. S. Davis, *FDR: Beckoning of Destiny,* 811; Ward quoted in WGBH, "Draft of FDR, Program One," proposal for television series on Franklin D. Roosevelt. Warm Springs, writers later noted, was the one place in the country where he "could drop the exhausting pretense of having two good legs." *Washington Post,* May 2, 1997.

8. Paul K. Conkin, "It All Happened in Pine Mountain Valley," *Georgia Historical Quarterly* 47 (1963): 1; K. S. Davis, *FDR: Beckoning of Destiny,* 808–9; Henry A. Wallace COHC, 407 (courtesy of Jordan Schwarz); Rexford G. Tugwell, *The Brains Trust* (New York, 1968), 89.

9. Turnley Walker, *Roosevelt and the Warm Springs Story* (New York, 1953), 208.

10. Donald Scott Carmichael, ed., *F.D.R. Columnist: The Uncollected Columns of Franklin D. Roosevelt* (Chicago, 1947), 11–12.

11. Rogers, "Death of a President," 107; Frank Freidel, *F.D.R. and the South* (Baton Rouge, La., 1965), 2.

12. Blanche Wiesen Cook, "Eleanor Roosevelt and the South: 1994 Elson Lecture," *Atlanta History* 38 (1995): 34; David McCullough, *Mornings on Horseback* (New York, 1981), 46–55; Blanche Wiesen Cook, *Eleanor Roosevelt: Volume 1, 1884–1933* (New York, 1992), 28–29; Lilian Rixey, *Bamie: Theodore Roosevelt's Remarkable Sister* (New York, 1963), 12–13; Joseph P. Lash, *Eleanor and Franklin: The Story of Their Relationship, Based upon Eleanor Roosevelt's Private Papers* (New York, 1971), 3, 5. Jonathan Daniels later reflected, "Mrs. Roosevelt disliked the South; she said that the Spanish moss was a ghostly thing and sent chills up and down her spine." Jonathan Daniels ER OH, 28.

13. Evelyn Winchell in *Columbus (Ga.) Enquirer,* April 14, 1945, clipping, Scrapbook, Franklin D. Roosevelt Museum Archives; Stevens, *"Hi-Ya Neighbor,"* 37; *Gainesville (Ga.) Eagle,* August 21, 1930,

clipping, Democratic National Committee Papers, Box 888; *Atlanta Constitution*, June 18, 1933, photocopy, FDRL PPF 604.

14. "Franklin D. Roosevelt at Warm Springs, Georgia," Rexford G. Tugwell MSS, Box 75; *Public Papers*, 2: 491, 502, 8: 180; Lippman, *Squire of Warm Springs*, 149, 153; Robert A. Caro, *The Years of Lyndon Johnson: The Path to Power* (New York, 1982), 526; Wilma Dykeman and James Stokely, *Seeds of Southern Change: The Life of Will Alexander* (Chicago, 1962), 307. Italics have been added. In 1937 Roosevelt characterized himself as "a Dutchess County, New York and Meriwether County, Georgia, farmer." FDR to Hendrik Willem van Loon, February 2, 1937, in *Franklin D. Roosevelt and Conservation, 1911–1945*, ed. Edgar B. Nixon (Hyde Park, N.Y., 1957), 10.

15. *Public Papers*, 1: 886–89; Virginia Van der Veer Hamilton, *Lister Hill: Statesman from the South* (Chapel Hill, N.C., 1987), 70. Italics added on "neighbors." When in 1937 Roosevelt was inducted into the University of Georgia chapter of Phi Beta Kappa, he exhorted student delegates, one of them Morris Abram, to preserve the homes of people who had been important in the nation's past, in particular the ancestral home of Alexander Stephens, the vice president of the Confederacy. *New York Times*, March 23, 1937; William B. Rhoads, "Franklin D. Roosevelt and the Architecture of Warm Springs," *Georgia Historical Quarterly* 67 (1983): 70–71.

16. Claude Bowers, *The Tragic Era: The Revolution after Lincoln* (Cambridge, Mass., 1929), v–vi; Bowers, *My Life: The Memoirs of Claude Bowers* (New York, 1962), 249–50, 210; *New York Times*, September 18, 1937.

17. Lippman, *Squire of Warm Springs*, 85–86.

18. Ibid., 88–89. White sharecroppers Roosevelt interrogated gave the same answers.

19. "Extemporaneous Remarks by the President on the Occasion of the Dedication of the Eleanor Roosevelt Schoolhouse," Warm Springs, Georgia, March 18, 1937, FDRL PPF 4474. See, too, S. L. Smith MS. Diary, Fisk University Archives, Julius Rosenwald Fund Collection, Box 129; S. L. Smith, "FDR and the Last Rosenwald School," S. L. Smith MSS, Nashville, Tennessee, privately held. I am indebted to Thomas W. Hanchett for copies of these documents.

20. JoAnn Deakin Carpenter, "Olin D. Johnston, the New Deal and the Politics of Class in South Carolina, 1934–1938" (Ph.D. dissertation, Emory University, 1987), 73–74; George Lee Simpson Jr., *The Cokers of Carolina: A Social Biography of a Family* (Chapel Hill, N.C., 1956), 210; J. B. Shannon, "Presidential Politics in the South," in *The Southern Political Scene, 1938–1948*, ed. Taylor Cole and John H. Hallowell (Gainesville, Fla., 1948), 466.

21. Frank Freidel, "The South and the New Deal," in *The New Deal and the South*, ed. James C. Cobb and Michael Namorato (Jackson, Miss., 1984), 23; Jordan A. Schwarz, *The New Dealers: Power Politics in the Age of Roosevelt* (New York, 1993), 90.

22. Kaye Lanning Minchew, "Shaping a Presidential Image: FDR in Georgia," *Georgia Historical Quarterly* 83 (1999): 747, 750; Clark Howell Jr. to C. H. Scott, n.d. [November 1932], FDRL PPF 604; Frank Freidel, *Franklin D. Roosevelt: The Triumph* (Boston, 1956), 174; Gilbert C. Fite, *Richard B. Russell, Jr.: Senator from Georgia* (Chapel Hill, N.C., 1991), 99–100, 111–12; *Boston Globe*, September 27, 1931, excerpt, Gilbert Fite Files. See, too, Isaac K. Hay OH, 30; Chappelle Matthews OH, 11–12; John Carlton OH, 40, Richard B. Russell MSS. The president of Oglethorpe University invited Roosevelt to give what proved to be a major address at a commencement held at Atlanta's Fox Theatre because his residence in Warm Springs had led the state to adopt him as a "sec-

ond native son." Paul Stephen Hudson, "A Call for 'Bold Persistent Experimentation': FDR's Oglethorpe University Commencement Address, 1932," *Georgia Historical Quarterly* 77 (1994): 364.

23. Douglas L. Smith, *The New Deal in the Urban South* (Baton Rouge, La., 1988), 43; Harllee Branch to FDR, March 12, 1931, FDRL PPF 2653; Fay Webb Gardner MS. Diary, October 15, 1931, January 15, 1932; Tracy E. Danese, *Claude Pepper and Ed Ball: Politics, Purpose, and Power* (Gainesville, Fla., 2000), 111; Winfred Bobo Moore Jr., "New South Statesman: The Political Career of James Francis Byrnes, 1911–1941" (Ph.D. dissertation, Duke University, 1975), 105; John Dean Minton, *The New Deal in Tennessee, 1932–1938* (New York, 1979), 6. See, too, Carroll Kilpatrick, ed., *Roosevelt and Daniels: A Friendship in Politics* (Chapel Hill, N.C., 1952), 105–6; Kenneth McKellar to FDR, April 7, 1932, McKellar MSS; William D. Miller, *Mr. Crump of Memphis* (Baton Rouge, La., 1964), 173. "You will get the entire delegation from North Carolina," a prominent attorney told him. Aubrey Lee Brooks, *A Southern Lawyer: Fifty Years at the Bar* (Chapel Hill, N.C., 1950), 138. Cordell Hull of Tennessee, who organized southern backing for Roosevelt in 1932, stressed among FDR's advantages his part-time residence in Georgia. David Leon Chandler, *The Natural Superiority of Southern Politicians: A Revisionist History* (Garden City, N.Y., 1977), 199. See, too, Frank W. Buxton to E. M. House, October 15, 1931, House MSS, Series 1, Box 23. In December 1931 Grover Hall's *Montgomery Advertiser* became the first Alabama paper to come out for Roosevelt. When FDR was driven up Dexter Avenue in 1933, he tipped his hat as he passed the *Advertiser* building. Daniel Webster Hollis III, *An Alabama Newspaper Tradition: Grover C. Hall and the Hall Family* (University, Ala., 1983), 61–62.

24. Stephan Lesher, *George Wallace: American Populist* (Reading, Mass., 1994), 28; Jack Bass and Marilyn W. Thompson, *Ol' Strom: An Unauthorized Biography of Strom Thurmond* (Atlanta, 1998), 44; Harmon Dean Shaw Jr., "Mississippi and the Election of 1932" (M.A. essay, Mississippi State University, 1965), 32; Herman Talmadge SOHP, A–347. "The Sidewalks of New York" was actually Al Smith's theme song, not FDR's, but Wallace makes his point. In these years, it should be noted, the Wallaces were regarded as relatively liberal.

25. James Farley OH, Graff MSS, Box 3; Norman D. Brown, "Garnering Votes for 'Cactus Jack': John Nance Garner, Franklin D. Roosevelt, and the 1932 Democratic Nomination for President," *Southwestern Historical Quarterly* 104 (2000): 183; Christopher M. Finan, *Alfred E. Smith: The Happy Warrior* (New York, 2002), 286; Schwarz, *Interregnum of Despair,* 190; George Wolfskill and John A. Hudson, *All But the People: Franklin D. Roosevelt and His Critics, 1933–39* (New York, 1969), 257. In 1932, one historian later noted, "Southern leaders and the Southern masses were strong for Roosevelt's nomination, and without that support his nomination would have been impossible." William G. Carleton, "The Conservative South—A Political Myth," *Virginia Quarterly Review* 22 (1946): 185. See, too, Cordell Hull, *The Memoirs of Cordell Hull* (New York, 1948), 153.

26. Douglas L. Fleming, "The New Deal in Atlanta: A Review of the Major Programs," *Atlanta Historical Journal* 30 (1986): 23; Jennifer Fox, "Hail to the Chief: Presidential Visits to Atlanta," *Atlanta History* 36 (1992): 42; Fred Powledge in *Atlanta Journal,* October 10, 1960, drawing on 1932 account, clipping, Scrapbook, Franklin D. Roosevelt Museum Archives. A San Antonio church began Sunday School with a rendition of "Onward Christian Soldiers" in FDR's honor. Donald W. Whisenhunt, *The Depression in Texas: The Hoover Years* (New York, 1983), 67. For Texas, see, too, William Robert "Bob" Poage OH, 275.

27. *Atlanta Constitution,* November 9, 1932; Charles Wallace Collins, *Whither Solid South? A Study in Politics and Race Relations* (New Orleans, 1947), 249. A former governor of Arkansas made fifty-six speeches for FDR in 1932. Charles Brough to FDR, November 9, 1932, Brough MSS, Box 11. See, too, Joseph T. Robinson to James A. Farley, August 26, 1932, Robinson MSS, Box 40.

28. Thomas H. Coode, "Walter Chandler as Congressman," *West Tennessee Historical Society Papers* 29 (1975): 25; David D. Lee, *Tennessee in Turmoil: Politics in the Volunteer State, 1920–1932* (Memphis, Tenn., 1979), 147. Davidson County (Nashville), which had been won by Hoover in 1928, voted 3–1 for FDR. Don H. Doyle, *Nashville since the 1920s* (Knoxville, Tenn., 1985), 87. From Texas as early as September, Wilson's former attorney general had assured him, "There is no ground for apprehension as to any southern or border state." Thomas W. Gregory to FDR, September 2, 1932, Gregory MSS, Box 8. In Kentucky, Fayette County (Lexington), which Hoover had carried by an emphatic 2–1 in 1928, gave FDR a comfortable margin. James Duane Bolin, "The Human Side: Politics, the Great Depression, and the New Deal in Lexington, Kentucky, 1929–35," *Register of the Kentucky Historical Society* 90 (1992): 266.

29. Jack Irby Hayes Jr., "South Carolina and the New Deal, 1932–1938" (Ph.D. dissertation, University of South Carolina, 1972), 44.

30. Michael S. Holmes, "From Euphoria to Cataclysm: Georgia Confronts the Great Depression," *Georgia Historical Quarterly* 58 (1974): 328; Barbara Barksdale Clowse, *Ralph McGill: A Biography* (Macon, Ga., 1998), 75; Lippman, *Squire of Warm Springs,* 157; Charles F. Palmer, "Confidential Memorandum." See, too, Clark Howell Jr. to FDR, November 8, 1932, FDRL PPF 604. Roosevelt did not acknowledge that Georgia Democrats, too, were voting ancestral loyalties deriving from the era of slavery and secession. In 1932 Fulton County (Atlanta) gave FDR 19,044, Hoover a miserable 1940.

31. Douglas Lee Fleming, "Atlanta, the Depression, and the New Deal" (Ph.D. dissertation, Emory University, 1984), 131; Holmes, "From Euphoria to Cataclysm," 328; *Atlanta Constitution,* March 5, 1933, clipping, Scrapbook, Franklin D. Roosevelt Museum Archives; Stevens, *"Hi-Ya Neighbor,"* 50: Lawrence Camp, speech made at Sylvester, Georgia, December 5, 1935, FDRL PPF 5781. Italics added. See, too, *Columbus (Ga.) Ledger Enquirer,* March 31, 1938, clipping, FDRL PPF 200B (43). In his inaugural address in January 1937, Governor E. D. Rivers of Georgia declared: "I tender from the Democrats of Georgia to President Franklin D. Roosevelt . . . our supreme love and loyalty. He, a part-time Georgian amongst us, went forth to render for our party . . . very wonderful service. . . . Happy indeed are we because of his overwhelming victory last November." *Atlanta Constitution,* January 13, 1937, photocopy, Ruby Webb Collection of E. D. Rivers material.

32. Albert Gore, *Let the Glory Out: My South and Its Politics* (New York, 1972), 41; Richard Norton Smith, *An Uncommon Man: The Triumph of Herbert Hoover* (New York, 1984), 191. In South Carolina in 1935, fifty thousand Charlestonians turned out to hail FDR. Marvin Leigh, "Burnett Rhett Maybank and the New Deal in South Carolina, 1931–1941" (Ph.D. dissertation, University of North Carolina at Chapel Hill, 1967), 86.

33. *Atlanta Constitution,* October 9, 1935; Louis Turner Griffith and John Erwin Talmadge, *Georgia Journalism, 1763–1950* (Athens, Ga., 1951), 326–37; Sam Nunn, "Foreword," in *My Fellow Americans: Presidential Addresses That Shaped History,* by James C. Humes (New York, 1992), ix; Bessie

Fowler, interviewed by Christy Gresham, Bindas Oral History Project, West Georgia College, Carrollton, Ga. (courtesy of Kenneth J. Bindas).

34. Ferrol Sams Jr., "God as Elector: Religion and the Vote," in *The Prevailing South: Life and Politics in a Changing Culture,* ed. Dudley Clendinen (Atlanta, 1988), 50, 52. See, too, Howard N. Mead, "Russell vs. Talmadge: Southern Politics and the New Deal," *Georgia Historical Quarterly* 65 (1981): 31, 43. Among the alphabet agencies were the WPA (Works Progress Administration), the NRA (National Recovery Administration), the CCC (Civilian Conservation Corps), and the AAA (Agricultural Adjustment Administration).

35. Martha H. Swain, *Pat Harrison: The New Deal Years* (Jackson, Miss., 1978), 36, 57, 79; Swain, "A New Deal for Mississippi Women, 1933–1943," *Journal of Mississippi History* 46 (1984): 191; Roger D. Tate Jr., "Easing the Burden: The Era of Depression and New Deal in Mississippi" (Ph.D. dissertation, University of Tennessee, Knoxville, 1978), 163. "Relief from summer dust came for the first time in the hundred years of the town's existence when the WPA blacktopped the two main streets," recalled a Mississippian who was later elected to Congress. Indeed, "the days of WPA, NYA, and the distribution of surplus food commodities were the first that Sidon ever knew without sharp pockets of poverty and even just plain hunger in some corners of the community." Frank E. Smith, *Congressman from Mississippi* (New York, 1964), 21–22. See, too, James W. Loewen and Charles Sallis, eds., *Mississippi: Conflict and Change* (New York, 1974), 240.

36. Federal Writers' Project, *These Are Our Lives: As Told by the People and Written by Members of the Federal Writers' Project of the Works Progress Administration in North Carolina, Tennessee, and Georgia* (Chapel Hill, N.C., 1939); Dorothy De Moss, "Resourcefulness in the Financial Capital: Dallas, 1929–1933," in *Texas Cities in the Great Depression,* by Robert C. Cotner et al. (Austin, Tex., 1973), 133; Patrick J. Maney, *The Roosevelt Presence: A Biography of Franklin Delano Roosevelt* (New York, 1992), 71. "A worker in Texas with a poor opinion on the New Deal was a rarity," a historian has noted. Lionel Patenaude, "The New Deal: Its Effect on the Social Fabric of Texas Society, 1933–1938," *Social Science Journal* 14 (1977): 51. See, too, Monroe Billington and Cal Clark, "Texas Clergymen, Franklin D. Roosevelt, and the New Deal," *Locus* 4 (1991): 30; Orval Faubus SOHP, 4; Billy Hall Wyche, "Southern Industrialists View Organized Labor in the New Deal Years, 1933–1941," *Southern Studies* 19 (1980): 159; Cliff Kuhn, "Reminiscences: Interviews with Atlanta New Deal Social Workers," *Atlanta Historical Journal* 30 (1986): 115; Linda Reed, *Simple Decency and Common Sense: The Southern Conference Movement, 1938–1963* (Bloomington, Ind., 1991), 69–70; Merlin G. Cox, "David Sholtz: New Deal Governor of Florida," *Florida Historical Quarterly* 43 (1964): 148–49; address of A. Frank Lever to Roosevelt for Re-Election Club of Darlington, South Carolina, September 14, 1935, Asbury Francis Lever MSS, Speech Series, Folder 80; Monroe Billington, "The Alabama Clergy and the New Deal," *Alabama Review* 32 (1979): 215. "If Roosevelt had announced himself the spiritual godchild of Lenin, the southern editor would have swallowed his embarrassment and let out an earnest whoop," one commentator said. John D. Allen, "Journalism in the South," in *Culture in the South,* ed. W. T. Couch (Chapel Hill, N.C., 1934), 146.

37. Federal Writers' Project, *These Are Our Lives,* 210; Eric F. Goldman, *Rendezvous with Destiny* (New York, 1952), 345.

38. John Temple Graves, *The Fighting South* (New York, 1943), 114; Dykeman and Stokely, *Seeds*

of Southern Change, 191–92; *Louisville Herald-Post,* March 13, 1935, clipping FDRL OF 175 Coal, Box 2. See, too, Thomas D. Clark and Albert D. Kirwan, *The South since Appomattox: A Century of Regional Change* (New York, 1967), 235; Olin D. Johnston to FDR, March 19, 1935, FDRL PPF 2361.

39. James Seay Brown Jr., ed., *Up before Daylight: Life Histories from the Alabama Writers' Project, 1938–1939* (Tuscaloosa, Ala., 1997), 42; Julia Kirk Blackwelder, *Women of the Depression: Caste and Culture in San Antonio, 1929–1939* (College Station, Tex., 1984), 13; Jack Temple Kirby, *Rural Worlds Lost: The American South, 1920–1960* (Baton Rouge, La., 1987), 56–57; D. L. Fleming, "Atlanta, the Depression and the New Deal," 131; Larry F. Whatley, "The Works Progress Administration in Mississippi," *Journal of Mississippi History* 30 (1968): 40; Pete Daniel, *Standing at the Crossroads: Southern Life since 1900* (New York, 1986), 222–23.

40. Wayne Greenhaw, *Elephants in the Cottonfields: Ronald Reagan and the New Republican South* (New York, 1982), 1–5.

41. Bruce Bliven, "In the Land of Cotton," *New Republic,* March 21, 1934, 155.

42. Cash, *Mind of the South,* 364–65.

43. Helen Fuller, "The Ring Around the President," *New Republic,* October 25, 1943, 564; Marian D. Irish, "The Southern One-Party System and National Politics," *Journal of Politics* 4 (1942): 86.

44. John Morton Blum, *From the Morgenthau Diaries: Years of Crisis, 1928–1938* (Boston, 1959), 292.

45. George E. Mowry, *Another Look at the Twentieth-Century South* (Baton Rouge, La., 1973), 46; John Sparkman LBJL OH, 1: 33; John Sparkman OH, Richard B. Russell MSS, 4; Freidel, *F.D.R. and the South,* 51.

46. Ben Robertson, *Red Hills and Cotton: An Upcountry Memory* (New York, 1942), 286–87. The Supreme Court justice was James F. Byrnes.

47. Dewey W. Grantham Jr., *The Life and Death of the Solid South: A Political History* (Lexington, Ky., 1988), 104; Robert A. Lively, "The South and Freight Rates: Political Settlement of an Economic Argument," *Journal of Southern History* 14 (1948): 357–84; Lively, *The South in Action: A Sectional Crusade against Freight Rate Discrimination* (Chapel Hill, N.C., 1949), 24–25; H. Clarence Nixon, "The New Deal and the South," *Virginia Quarterly Review* 19 (1943): 331; John Sparkman SOHP, 4–6. Scholars later concluded that the freight rate differentiation was not nearly as significant as was believed at the time.

48. Mrs. Lewis Stuyvesant Chanler to FDR, n.d. [June 1936]; FDR to Mrs. Chanler, July 1, 1936, FDRL PPF 3669; Arthur M. Schlesinger Jr., *The Coming of the New Deal* (Boston, 1959), 378.

49. *Public Papers,* 8: 182–84. See, too, Clarence Poe, *My First 80 Years* (Chapel Hill, N.C., 1963), 244. In setting TVA policy, David Lilienthal began with the premise that the rundown farm lands could not be expected to compete with the rich soil of northern and western states, but that power from the Tennessee river could make the region competitive. Willson Whitman, *David Lilienthal* (New York, 1948), 28–29.

50. Thomas H. Greer, *What Roosevelt Thought: The Social and Political Ideas of Franklin D. Roosevelt* (East Lansing, Mich., 1958), 36, 143; Lippman, *Squire of Warm Springs,* 146–49.

51. Dykeman and Stokely, *Seeds of Southern Change,* 215. Alexander wrote the book in collaboration with Edwin R. Embree.

52. *Memphis Commercial Appeal,* October 13, 1940, clipping, Theodore G. Bilbo MSS, Box 1012; Caro, *Path to Power,* 471–72. A black man from Johnson City, Tennessee, wrote, "May it be said to your credit Mr. President that you have been more generous toward the South with funds from the public treasury . . . than any President of the past." William H. Carriger to FDR, March 29, 1938, FDRL PPF 200B (43). "Federal money," noted one account, was "a regional free lunch. It cost the South little because most southerners did not earn enough money to pay federal income taxes. A study of the first Congressional District of Texas during the 1930s, for example, estimated that less than two-thirds of one percent of its citizens paid federal income taxes." Earl Black and Merle Black, *The Rise of Southern Republicans* (Cambridge, Mass., 2002), 56. See, too, Ernest McPherson Lander Jr., *A History of South Carolina, 1865–1960* (Chapel Hill, N.C., 1960), 75.

53. Harold M. Goldstein, "Regional Barriers in the Utilization of Federal Aid: The Southeast in the 1930's," *Quarterly Review of Economics and Business* 7 (1967): 65; Leonard J. Arrington, "Western Agriculture and the New Deal," *Agricultural History* 44 (1970): 344; Fred Bateman and Jason E. Taylor, "Franklin Roosevelt, Federal Spending, and the Postwar Southern Economic Rebound," *Essays in Economic and Business History* 20 (2002): 81–82.

54. Anthony J. Badger, *Prosperity Road: The New Deal, Tobacco, and North Carolina* (Chapel Hill, N.C., 1980), 64–65.

55. George McJimsey, *The Presidency of Franklin Delano Roosevelt* (Lawrence, Kans., 2000), 41; "Reactions of the Country to the Passage of the Muscle Shoals Bill," *Public Utility Fortnightly* 11 (1933): 724–29; Minton, *New Deal in Tennessee,* 100–101; *Knoxville Journal,* February 28, 1936, reported in *Index of TVA News,* February 29, 1936, Arthur E. Morgan MSS. With Knoxville, headquarters of the TVA, "thriving on the payrolls of thousands of government employees," noted a writer for the *New York Times Magazine,* "little of the depression psychology so prevalent in New York is felt here." Russell B. Porter, "TVA's Empire Grows Amid Controversy," *New York Times Magazine,* April 17, 1938, 2. See, too, "Knoxvillians to Send Big Telegram of Thanks to F.D.R.," Norris Today," clipping, n.d. [1934], Scrapbook, TVA Technical Library. Founded in 1934, the American Liberty League was an archconservative organization financed and led by the du Pont interests. Recent scholarship has questioned whether the long-term benefits of the TVA are so demonstrable. Michael J. McDonald and John Muldowny, *TVA and the Dispossessed: The Resettlement of Population in the Norris Dam Area* (Knoxville, Tenn., 1982), 266–69.

56. J. I. Hayes, "South Carolina and the New Deal," 467, 432; Bryant Simon, "A Fabric of Defeat: The Politics of South Carolina Textile Workers in State and Nation, 1920–1938" (Ph.D. dissertation, University of North Carolina at Chapel Hill, 1992), 162; Frederick Sullens, "Mississippi," *Review of Reviews* (January 1936): 39.

57. Robert R. Reynolds to Haywood Robbins Jr., March 2, 1936; Robbins to Wallace Winbourne, March 17, 1936; Robbins to Marvin H. McIntyre, September 17, 1936, all in Robbins MSS, Box 1; *Public Papers,* 5: 343; *Charlotte News,* September 10, 1936, clipping, Robbins Scrapbook, Box 2.

58. Josiah W. Bailey to Marvin McIntyre, September 14, 1936, FDRL OF 300, Box 27.

59. Speech of Senator William L. Hill before the Florida Democratic Club of Washington, D.C., October 21, 1936, R. Walton Moore MSS, Box 17.

60. Lionel V. Patenaude, *Texans, Politics and the New Deal* (New York, 1983), 110; Kenneth B. Ragsdale, *The Year America Discovered Texas: Centennial '36* (College Station, Tex., 1987), 246;

Maury Maverick, "The South Is Rising," *Nation,* June 17, 1936, 772. In Houston in June 1936 the president drew the largest crowd in the city's history. E. Thomas Lovell, "Houston's Reaction to the New Deal, 1932–1936" (M.A. essay, University of Houston, 1964), 194.

61. A. Cash Koeniger, "The New Deal and the States: Roosevelt Versus the Byrd Organization in Virginia," *Journal of American History* 68 (1982): 879; Carter Glass to J. A. Zeigler, August 3, 1936, Glass MSS, Box 347–48; William Anderson, *The Wild Man from Sugar Creek: The Political Career of Eugene Talmadge* (Baton Rouge, La., 1975), 149; Francis Shackelford to Edward S. Corwin, July 8, 1936, Corwin MSS, Box 2; Herman E. Talmadge with Mark Royden Winchell, *Talmadge: A Political Legacy, A Politician's Life: A Memoir* (Atlanta, 1987), 36. In heavily rural Seminole County, which Talmadge had swept 4–1 in 1934, Roosevelt outpolled the Georgia governor in every precinct.

62. Virginia Van der Veer Hamilton, *Hugo Black: The Alabama Years* (Baton Rouge, La., 1972), 272; John Temple Graves, "The South Still Loves Roosevelt," *Nation,* July 1, 1939, 11, 13; Lyle W. Dorsett, *Franklin D. Roosevelt and the City Bosses* (Port Washington, N.Y., 1977), 39; Kevin P. Phillips, *The Emerging Republican Majority* (New Rochelle, N.Y., 1969), 261, 217; Swain, *Pat Harrison,* 146; Grantham, *Life and Death of Solid South,* 103, 117; *Jackson Daily News,* October 29, 1940, *Jackson Clarion Ledger,* October 30, 1940, *Memphis Commercial Appeal,* November 16, 1944, clippings, Theodore G. Bilbo MSS, Box 1012; Miller, *Mr. Crump,* 282; Alvin LeRoy Hall, "James H. Price and Virginia Politics, 1878 to 1943" (Ph.D. dissertation, University of Virginia, 1970), 329. When a British traveler, Sir Arthur Willert, reached Athens, Georgia, in March 1936, he set down his thoughts on his journey through the Southeast: "The South apt to be more for F.D.R. than the North. In spite of State Rights. Reason for this it is more Liberal. . . . Most of the intellectuals in the South are for F.D.R. Another reason for this is that they are poorer. Also his farm policy is popular in what is essentially an agricultural area." Sir Arthur Willert MS. Notebook, March 2, 1936, Willert MSS, Box 24. In the four elections in which FDR ran for the presidency, votes for him in only two Louisiana parishes fell under 60 percent. Perry H. Howard, "Louisiana: Resistance and Change," in *The Changing Politics of the South,* ed. William C. Havard (Baton Rouge, La., 1972), 544. See, too, John H. Bankhead MSS, Box 4.

2. THE FDR COALITION

1. Charles H. Martin, "Negro Leaders, the Republican Party and the Election of 1932," *Phylon* 32 (1971): 88; Harvard Sitkoff, *A New Deal for Blacks: The Emergence of Civil Rights as a National Issue: The Depression Decade* (New York, 1978), 40–41; Jervis Anderson, *A. Philip Randolph: A Biographical Portrait* (New York, 1973), 260; Raymond Wolters, *Negroes and the Great Depression: The Problem of Economic Recovery* (Westport, Conn., 1970); Paula F. Pfeffer, *A. Philip Randolph: Pioneer of the Civil Rights Movement* (Baton Rouge, La., 1990), 33–34; Nancy J. Weiss, *Farewell to the Party of Lincoln* (Princeton, N.J., 1983). On a Caribbean cruise in 1912, when he was a member of the New York legislature, he wrote home, in a letter intended for Eleanor, about "a naked nigger boy." Geoffrey C. Ward, *A First-Class Temperament: The Emergence of Franklin Roosevelt* (New York, 1989), 173. "With race as with so many things, Franklin's real private views proved maddeningly elusive," Ward has written. He combined unfailing courtesy and compassion toward blacks with occasional lapses into residual racism. Ibid., 766–67n. Roosevelt, another historian has observed,

"hardly seemed to care at all about race relations." Roger Biles, *The South and the New Deal* (Lexington, Ky., 1994), 118. So incensed was a young black woman by FDR's failure to acknowledge in an address in Chapel Hill that the University of North Carolina admitted only white students that for the first time in her life she wrote a letter to a president. "We are as much political refugees from the South as any of the Jews in Germany," Pauli Murray told him. "Have you raised your voice loud enough against the burning of our people?" Pauli Murray, *Song in a Weary Throat: An American Pilgrimage* (New York, 1987), 111. For a charge by the leading GOP black politician that the little patronage African Americans had received from FDR had gone mostly to "Psalm-singing Rosenwald workers," see Perry W. Howard to chairman and members of the Republican National Committee, July 22, 1935, William Lemke MSS, Box 12.

2. David E. Lilienthal LBJL OH, 22; Swain, *Pat Harrison*, 253; Geoffrey C. Ward, *Before the Trumpet: Young Franklin Roosevelt, 1882–1905* (New York, 1985), 215–16; Roy Wilkins, with Tom Mathews, *Standing Fast: The Autobiography of Roy Wilkins* (New York, 1984), 127; Joseph P. Lash, *Dealers and Dreamers: A New Look at the New Deal* (New York, 1988), 415.

3. Jonathan Daniels, Eleanor Roosevelt Oral History Project, 19; John Frederick Martin, *Civil Rights and the Crisis of Liberalism: The Democratic Party, 1945–1976* (Boulder, Colo., 1979), 61. Before releasing a pro forma message to the annual convention of the NAACP in 1935, Steve Early turned it over to the Democratic National Committee to be "checked carefully, considering the possible political reaction from the standpoint of the South." Nancy J. Weiss, *The National Urban League, 1910–1940* (New York, 1974), 266.

4. Sitkoff, *New Deal for Blacks*, 50–55; John P. Davis, "The Negro and TVA," National Association for the Advancement of Colored People, August, 1935, Robert Wagner MSS; Davis, "A Black Inventory of the New Deal," *Crisis* 42 (1935): 141–42; Arthur F. Raper, "The Southern Negro and the NRA," *Georgia Historical Quarterly* 64 (1980): 128; Charles H. Houston and John P. Davis, "TVA: Lily-White Reconstruction," *Crisis* 41 (1934): 290–91; Biles, *South and the New Deal*, 111; Genna Rae McNeil, *Groundwork: Charles Hamilton Houston and the Struggle for Civil Rights* (Philadelphia, 1983), 96; Guy B. Johnson, "Does the South Owe the Negro a New Deal?" *Social Forces* 13 (1934): 101; Henry Lee Moon, *Balance of Power: The Negro Vote* (Garden City, N.Y., 1949), 37. See, too, Nancy L. Grant, *TVA and Black Americans: Planning for the Status Quo* (Philadelphia, 1990); Melissa Walker, "African Americans and TVA Reservoir Property Removal: Race in a New Deal Program," *Agricultural History* 72 (1998): 417–28; Douglas C. Abrams, "Irony of Reform: North Carolina Blacks and the New Deal," *North Carolina Historical Review* 66 (1989): 150; Randy J. Sparks, "'Heavenly Houston' or 'Hellish Houston'?" *Southern Studies* 25 (1986): 363. For evidence that opposition to the presence of blacks in CCC camps was not limited to the South, see Ellicottville Home Bureau to Daniel Reed, October 11, 1937, Reed MSS, Box 14. The upstate New York congressman replied: "I believe you will find that these colored camps are deliberately put in Republican counties as a form of punishment to those who support the opposing party. . . . These arbitrary and tyrannical acts are typical of the philosophy of the New Deal." Reed to Mrs. Frank Russon, October 20, 1937, Reed MSS, Box 14. For a rebuttal of the NAACP charges, see Donald Richberg to Eleanor Roosevelt, October 23, 1934, Richberg MSS, Box 2.

5. James F. Byrnes to W. W. Alexander, October 9, 1937, Byrnes MSS; Memo, Lindsay Warren MSS, Box 10.

6. Dennis S. Nordin, *The New Deal's Black Congressman: A Life of Arthur Wergs Mitchell* (Columbia, Mo., 1997), 139–40; Eleanor Roosevelt to Walter White, May 2, 1934, Robert Wagner MSS.

7. Sitkoff, *New Deal for Blacks*, 283–88; Walter White to Edward P. Costigan, June 8, 1934; White to FDR, May 6, 1935, Costigan MSS, Vertical File 3; Fred Greenbaum, "The Anti-Lynching Bill of 1935: The Irony of Equal Justice—Under Law," *Journal of Human Relations* 15 (1967): 76. One of the cosponsors of antilynching legislation in Congress recalled, "I got very little support from the White House . . . either in the first or the second term." Joseph Gavagan COHC, 46. Roosevelt blamed both the southern filibusterers and the northern liberals for creating a stalemate that was delaying enactment of his program. George C. Rable, "The South and the Politics of Antilynching Legislation, 1920–1940," *Journal of Southern History* 51 (1985): 211. There had long been an active campaign by certain white southerners against lynching. See Jacquelyn Dowd Hall, *Revolt against Chivalry: Jessie Daniel Ames and the Women's Campaign against Lynching* (New York, 1979); Will W. Alexander COHC, 1: 241; Mrs. W. B. Newell to Carter Glass, April 23, 1935, Glass MSS, Box 321. The papers of Senator Tom Connally of Texas contain numerous justifications of lynching. A Houston attorney protested that proponents of antilynching legislation "pawn the safety of the American school girl and house-wife for the hope of securing political consideration from the negro." Thomas B. Lewis to Tom Connally, January 24, 1939, Connally MSS, Box 126. Connally himself circularized his southern colleagues to find out if there were instances where the Tuskegee Institute had reported lynchings when they had not occurred. See especially Connally to Charles Andrews, February 9, 1939; Andrews to Connally, March 13, 15, 1939, Connally MSS, Box 126.

8. Walter White, *A Man Called White: The Autobiography of Walter White* (New York, 1948), 169–70.

9. Dykeman and Stokely, *Seeds of Southern Change,* 254.

10. Mary McLeod Bethune, "My Secret Talks with FDR," *Ebony* (April 1949): 44.

11. Barry Bingham to Francis P. Miller, November 28, 1938, Brooks Hays MSS, University of Arkansas, Box 42; *Congressional Record,* 75th Cong., 1st sess., August 12, 1937, copy in Claude Pepper MSS, Series 203A, Box 1; Richard Polenberg, *War and Society: The United States, 1941–1945* (Philadelphia, 1972), 192; Louis Coleridge Kesselman, *The Social Politics of FEPC: A Study in Reform Pressure Movements* (Chapel Hill, N.C., 1948), 169; Patricia Sullivan, *Days of Hope: Race and Democracy in the New Deal Era* (Chapel Hill, N.C., 1996), 164; Sitkoff, *New Deal for Blacks,* 45. On Pepper, see, too, *Miami Herald,* n.d., clipping, Thomas G. Corcoran MSS, Box 208. For the limits to William T. Couch's racial liberalism, see Kenneth R. Janken, "African-American Intellectuals Confront the 'Silent South': The *What the Negro Wants* Controversy," *North Carolina Historical Review* 70 (1993): 153–79. Maury Maverick traced his "conversion" on the rights of blacks to something he recalled FDR's saying to him in the 1940s: "Maury, I would like to interest you in the Black Man's burden. Don't worry too much about the White Man's burden—just look out for the human race." Richard B. Henderson, *Maury Maverick: A Political Biography* (Austin, Tex., 1970), 295. Maybe that conversation took place, but the tale sounds improbable.

12. Freidel, *F.D.R. and the South,* 35–36; Rembert W. Patrick, "The Deep South, Past and Present," in *The Deep South in Transformation: A Symposium,* ed. Robert B. Highsaw (University, Ala., 1964), 143.

13. Kenneth Robert Janken, *White: The Biography of Walter White, Mr. NAACP* (New York, 2003),

227; "The Roosevelt Record," *Crisis* (November 1940): 343; Richard Robbins, *Sidelines Activist: Charles S. Johnson and the Struggle for Civil Rights* (Jackson, Miss., 1996), 69–70.

14. Ronald E. Marcello, "Senator Josiah Bailey, Harry Hopkins, and the WPA: A Prelude to the Conservative Coalition," *Southern Studies* 22 (1983): 324; Edwin Hoffman, "The Genesis of the Modern Movement for Equal Rights in South Carolina, 1930–1939," *Journal of Negro History* 44 (1959): 361; Abrams, "Irony of Reform," 164; Pat Watters and Reese Cleghorn, *Climbing Jacob's Ladder: The Arrival of Negroes in Southern Politics* (New York, 1967), 12; Arthur F. Raper, *Preface to Peasantry: A Tale of Two Black Belt Counties* (Chapel Hill, N.C., 1936), 243; J. Anderson, *A. Philip Randolph*, 242–43. See, too, Ann Wells Ellis, "Uncle Sam Is My Shepherd: The Commission on Interracial Cooperation and the New Deal in Georgia," *Atlanta Historical Journal* 30 (1986): 58–60; Michael S. Holmes, "The Blue Eagle as 'Jim Crow Bird': The NRA and Georgia's Black Workers," *Journal of Negro History* 57 (1972): 281; David Levering Lewis, "The Origins and Causes of the Civil Rights Movement," in *The Civil Rights Movement in America*, ed. Charles W. Eagles (Jackson, Miss., 1986), 5; Marc W. Kruman, "Quotas for Blacks: The Public Works Administration and the Black Construction Worker," *Labor History* 16 (1975): 48; Karen L. Kalmar, "Southern Black Elites and the New Deal: A Case Study of Savannah, Georgia," *Georgia Historical Quarterly* 65 (1981): 341, 353.

15. Anthony J. Badger, *The New Deal: The Depression Years, 1933–40* (New York, 1989), 253; William J. Brophy, "Black Texans and the New Deal," in *The Depression in the Southwest*, ed. Donald W. Whisenhunt (Port Washington, N.Y., 1980), 118; John A. Salmond, *The Civilian Conservation Corps, 1933–1942: A New Deal Case Study* (Durham, N.C., 1967), 91–101. Some of these operations, besides sustaining black families in the Great Depression, enlarged the civic authority of blacks in the South. One survey of southern history has concluded, "By educating southern people through agencies like the Farm Security Administration and the insuring of Negro voting in the AAA crop-control elections, the New Deal brought tenants and sharecroppers, both white and black, into participation in decisions affecting their community." Clark and Kirwan, *South since Appomattox*, 240–41.

16. Minutes of the fourth meeting of the interdepartmental group concerned with the special problem of Negroes, June 1, 1934, Leon Henderson MSS, Box 7; Sitkoff, *New Deal for Blacks*, 69; Donald S. Howard, *The WPA and Federal Relief Policy* (New York, 1943), 285–96; Wolters, *Negroes and the Great Depression*, 70–71; Hugh Davis Graham, *The Civil Rights Era: Origins and Development of National Policy, 1960–1972* (New York, 1990), 10. For Roosevelt's efforts to persuade Governor Bibb Graves of Alabama to commute the sentences of the "Scottsboro Boys," see James Goodman, *Stories of Scottsboro* (New York, 1994), 317.

17. Kruman, "Quotas for Blacks," 37–49; Michael S. Holmes, "The New Deal and Georgia's Black Youth," *Journal of Southern History* 38 (1972): 452, 444–50; Arthur Raper and Ira DeA. Reid, "Old Conflicts in the New South," *Virginia Quarterly Review* 16 (1940): 227; Karen Ferguson, *Black Politics in New Deal Atlanta* (Chapel Hill, N.C., 2002), 91. See, too, Irving Bernstein, *A Caring Society: The New Deal, the Worker, and the Great Depression* (Boston, 1985), 287.

18. Garth Pauley, *The Modern Presidency and Civil Rights: Rhetoric on Race from Roosevelt to Nixon* (College Station, Tex., 2001), 18; Sitkoff, *New Deal for Blacks*, 77, 66; Matthew Holden Jr., "Race and Constitutional Change in the Twentieth Century: The Role of the Executive," in *African Amer-*

icans and the Living Constitution, ed. John Hope Franklin and Genna Rae McNeil (Washington, D.C., 1995), 128. See, too, Walter White to FDR, November 17, 1939, FDRL OF 41, Box 114.

19. Morton Sosna, *In Search of the Silent South: Southern Liberals and the Race Issue* (New York, 1977), 66–67, 74.

20. John B. Kirby, *Black Americans in the Roosevelt Era: Liberalism and Race* (Knoxville, Tenn., 1980), 84; Allida M. Black, "Championing a Champion: Eleanor Roosevelt and the Marian Anderson 'Freedom Concert,'" *Presidential Studies Quarterly* 20 (1990): 719–36; Black, "A Reluctant but Persistent Warrior: Eleanor Roosevelt and the Early Civil Rights Movement," in *Women in the Civil Rights Movement: Trailblazers and Torchbearers, 1941–1965,* ed. Vicki L. Crawford, Jacqueline Anne Rouse, and Barbara Woods (Bloomington, Ind., 1990), 233–49.

21. *Crisis* 41 (January 1934): 20; Walter White to Charles West, January 10, 1934, Edward P. Costigan MSS, Vertical File 3; Frank Freidel, *Franklin D. Roosevelt: A Rendezvous with Destiny* (Boston, 1990), 247; Robert L. Zangrando, *The NAACP Crusade against Lynching, 1909–1950* (Philadelphia, 1980), 118–27. It should be noted that when Roosevelt spoke out against lynching in 1933, he was moved to do so not by yet another outrage against blacks but because the governor of California had defended the lynching of two whites. Donald L. Grant, *The Way It Was in the South: The Black Experience in Georgia* (New York, 1993), 331.

22. Sitkoff, *New Deal for Blacks,* 134; Stetson Kennedy, *Southern Exposure* (Garden City, N.Y., 1946), 359; Brooks Hays, *A Southern Moderate Speaks* (Chapel Hill, N.C., 1959), 21–22; Frederic D. Ogden, *The Poll Tax in the South* (University, Ala., 1958), 225, 245. "I think the South agrees with you and me," he wrote Aubrey Williams in late March 1938. "One difficulty is that three-quarters of the whites in the South cannot vote—poll tax etc." Steven F. Lawson, *Black Ballots: Voting Rights in the South, 1944–1969* (New York, 1976), 57.

23. Monroe Billington, "Freedom to Serve: The President's Committee on Equality of Treatment and Opportunity in the Armed Forces, 1949–1950," *Journal of Negro History* 51 (1966): 268; Pauley, *Modern Presidency,* 28; Carl T. Rowan, *Dream Makers, Dream Breakers: The World of Justice Thurgood Marshall* (Boston, 1993), 99. Marshall, Rowan found in interviewing him at length, "badmouthed" FDR "wherever he got the chance." Among his statements was the allegation that on the antilynching bill, "Roosevelt never said one word in favor of it." Not so. Ibid., 130–31.

24. Mary Martha Thomas, "The Mobile Homefront during the Second World War," *Gulf Coast Historical Quarterly* 1 (1986): 70–71; David Robertson, *Sly and Able: A Political Biography of James F. Byrnes* (New York, 1994), 334; Clete Daniel, *Chicano Workers and the Politics of Fairness: The FEPC in the Southwest, 1941–1945* (Austin, Tex., 1991), 187; Adolph J. Sabath MS. Autobiography, Sabath MSS. In permanent form, the "C" in FEPC was to stand not for *Committee* but for *Commission.* A leading student of the subject has concluded, "Although FEPC's progress with the federal agencies and private contractors was modest at best, it is perhaps remarkable under the circumstances that as much was accomplished by so few." Merl E. Reed, "FEPC and the Federal Agencies in the South," *Journal of Negro History* 65 (1980): 54. See, too, M. Reed, "The FEPC, the Black Worker, and the Southern Shipyards," *South Atlantic Quarterly* 74 (1975): 446–67.

25. Hortense Powdermaker, *After Freedom: A Cultural Study in the Deep South* (New York, 1939), 139.

26. Walter Lord, *The Past That Would Not Die* (New York, 1965), 44–45.

27. Guido van Rijn, *Roosevelt's Blues: African-American Blues and Gospel Songs on FDR* (Jackson, Miss., 1997), 96–101.

28. David R. Goldfield, *Black, White, and Southern: Race Relations and Southern Culture, 1940 to the Present* (Baton Rouge, La., 1990), 30–31; Doug McAdam, *Political Process and the Development of Black Insurgency, 1930–1970* (Chicago, 1982), 108–9.

29. J. Saunders Redding, *No Day of Triumph* (New York, 1942), 260.

30. Gunnar Myrdal, *An American Dilemma: The Negro Problem and Modern Democracy* (New York, 1944), 74; Moon, *Balance of Power,* 21; Alex Haley, "Preface," in *Prevailing South,* ed. Clendinen.

31. Will Danis to FDR, 11, 1932, in "Letters to Their President: Mississippians to Franklin D. Roosevelt, 1932–1933," ed. William T. Schmidt, *Journal of Mississippi History* 40 (1978): 252; Weiss, *National Urban League,* 265.

32. John L. Robinson, *Living Hard: Southern Americans in the Great Depression* (Washington, D.C., 1981), 103; Donald R. Matthews and James W. Prothro, *Negroes and the New Southern Politics* (New York, 1966), 377–78.

33. Grantham, *Regional Imagination,* 147; Chalmers Archer Jr., *Growing Up Black in Rural Mississippi: Memories of a Family, Heritage of a Place* (New York, 1992), 105; Theodore Rosengarten, *All God's Dangers: The Life of Nate Shaw* (New York, 1974), 373; J. S. Brown, *Up before Daylight,* 173–78.

34. Anthony Barry Miller, "Palmetto Politician: The Early Political Career of Olin D. Johnston, 1896–1945" (Ph.D. dissertation, University of North Carolina at Chapel Hill, 1976), 273; Sitkoff, *New Deal for Blacks,* 94; *United States News,* June 9, 1944, 22. At the Democratic national convention in Chicago in 1944, South Carolina blacks, while pressing their claims for recognition, refused to do anything that might impair FDR's prospects. They angrily rejected an offer to have all their expenses paid by the rabidly anti-Roosevelt newspaper publisher, Colonel Robert McCormick, and they refrained from carrying their demand for acceptance to the floor, lest it provoke a walkout of southern whites that would damage the president. Miles S. Richards, "The Progressive Democrats in Chicago, July 1944," *South Carolina Historical Magazine* 102 (2001): 219–37. A former Hoover official noted: "A banker from Richmond came out of his bank with a friend the day after the election. A couple of niggers were leaning against the wall of the bank sunning themselves. The banker overheard one of them say, 'Who did you vote for?' The other one answered, 'I voted for Roosevelt. Who did you?' The first one said, 'Oh, I voted for Roosevelt too. I guess he was the only candidate.'" But the second one denied this. He said, 'No, you're wrong. I heard the white folks had a candidate too.'" William R. Castle Jr. MS. Diary, January 7, 1941. See, too, Larry W. Dunn, "Knoxville Negro Voting and the Roosevelt Revolution, 1928–1936," *East Tennessee Historical Society's Publications* 43 (1971): 92; Blair T. Hunt, "Cold Facts and Figures on Why Negroes Should Vote for President Roosevelt," 1944, Walter Chandler MSS.

There remained, though, an undercurrent of discontent. In a novel published later by the black writer Chester Himes, one character says of FDR, "You know he's our friend. You know yourself if it hadn't been for Roosevelt—" but another character breaks in to rebut: "Roosevelt! Roosevelt! All he ever done for the nigger was to put him on relief. . . . You is Roosevelt-happy like the other niggers. Roosevelt! How he done it I do not know—starve you niggers and made you love 'im." Chester Himes, *Lonely Crusade* (New York, 1947), 55. More idiosyncratic was the attitude of Zora Neale

Hurston, who had been entitled by the Federal Writers' Project in Florida. Six months after Roosevelt's death, she wrote a friend, "That dear, departed, crippled-up so-and-so was the Anti-Christ long spoken of. I never dreamed that so much hate and negative forces could be un-leashed on the world until I wintered and summered under his dictatorship." Zora Neale Hurston to Tracy L'Engle Angas, October 24, 1945, L'Engle Angas MSS, Box 2: Correspondence.

35. Don C. Reading, "New Deal Activity and the States, 1933–1939," *Journal of Economic History* 33 (1973): 793; Pete Daniel, "The Transformation of the Rural South, 1930 to the Present," *Agricultural History* 55 (1981): 246–47; Gilbert C. Fite, *Cotton Fields No More: Southern Agriculture, 1865–1980* (Lexington, Ky., 1984), 134–36; J. T. Kirby, *Rural Worlds Lost,* 58. See, too, Numan V. Bartley, "The New Deal as a Turning Point in Southern History," in *New Deal and the South,* ed. Cobb and Namorato, 138; Edward C. Banfield, "Ten Years of the Farm Tenant Purchase Program," *Journal of Farm Economics* 31 (1949): 469–86.

36. James A. Hodges, *New Deal Labor Policy and the Southern Cotton Textile Industry, 1933–1941* (Knoxville, Tenn., 1986), 198; J. L. Robinson, *Living Hard,* 10.

37. Raper, *Preface to Peasantry,* 272; Rexford G. Tugwell, *FDR: Architect of an Era* (New York, 1967), 148; Lee J. Alston and Joseph P. Ferrie, *Southern Paternalism and the American Welfare State: Economics, Politics, and Institutions in the South, 1865–1965* (Cambridge, Eng., 1999), 55; Wayne Flynt, *Poor but Proud: Alabama's Poor Whites* (Tuscaloosa, Ala., 1989), 294, 319; J. William Harris, *Deep Souths: Delta, Piedmont, and Sea Island Society in the Age of Segregation* (Baltimore, 2001), 300; Anthony J. Badger, "The New Deal and the Localities," in *The Growth of Federal Power in American History,* ed. R. Jeffreys-Jones and Bruce Collins (Edinburgh, 1983), 11.

38. Roy V. Scott and J. G. Shoalmire, *The Public Career of Cully A. Cobb: A Study in Agricultural Leadership* (Jackson, Miss., 1973), 234; Flynt, *Poor But Proud,* 319–20; David E. Conrad, *The Forgotten Farmers: The Story of Sharecroppers in the New Deal* (Westport, Conn., 1982), 176; Lawrence J. Nelson, "Welfare Capitalism on a Mississippi Plantation in the Great Depression," *Journal of Southern History* 50 (1984): 229; Monroe Lee Billington, *The Political South in the Twentieth Century* (New York, 1975), 67. See, too, Phillip J. Wood, *Southern Capitalism: The Political Economy of North Carolina, 1880–1980* (Durham, N.C., 1986), 136; Anthony P. Dunbar, *Against the Grain: Southern Radicals and Prophets, 1929–1959* (Charlottesville, Va., 1981), 130; E. F. (Ed) Chesnutt, "Rural Electrification in Arkansas, 1935–1940: The Formative Years," *Arkansas Historical Quarterly* 46 (1987): 215–60; David Goldfield, *Cotton Fields and Skyscrapers: Southern City and Region, 1607–1980* (Baton Rouge, La., 1982), 140.

39. FDR to Edward M. House, November 21, 1933, in *F.D.R.: His Personal Letters, 1928–1945,* ed. Elliott Roosevelt, 2 vols. (New York, 1950), 1: 372; Katharine DuPre Lumpkin, *The South in Progress* (New York, 1940), 166; *Public Papers,* 4: 473.

40. Paul E. Mertz, *New Deal Policy and Southern Rural Poverty* (Baton Rouge, La., 1978), 106–64; Gardner Jackson to H. L. Mitchell, January 15, 1936, Southern Tenant Farmers Union MSS, Box 1; Donald H. Grubbs, *Cry from the Cotton: The Southern Tenant Farmers' Union and the New Deal* (Chapel Hill, N.C., 1971), 140–57; Sidney Baldwin, *Poverty and Politics: The Rise and Decline of the Farm Security Administration* (Chapel Hill, N.C., 1968), 162–67. See, too, H. Clarence Nixon, "Farm Tenancy to the Forefront," *Southwest Review* 22 (1936): 14; Donald Holley, *Uncle Sam's Farmers: The New Deal Communities in the Lower Mississippi Valley* (Urbana, Ill., 1975), 98–102. When

members of the Southern Tenant Farmers' Union (STFU) were assaulted in Arkansas, Roosevelt, while avoiding a direct confrontation with the powerful Arkansas senator Joseph T. Robinson, urged the governor to end this "cruel and inhuman treatment." His advisor Rex Tugwell, generally regarded as much more radical than FDR, drafted a letter to send to Norman Thomas that included the observation that the tribulations of the STFU were "beyond the scope of Federal interference"; the president struck it out. Grubbs, *Cry from the Cotton*, 99–116. One writer has concluded that "the New Deal raised more than 20,000,000 white and Negro tenant farmers of the South from the legal and economic prostration they had suffered over years past." Henry Allen Bullock, "Urbanism and Race Relations," in *The Urban South*, ed. Rupert B. Vance and Nicholas J. Demerath (Chapel Hill, N.C., 1954), 228.

41. "The Journey to Arkansas on the President's Special," Brooks Hays MSS, University of Arkansas, Box 39; H. C. Nixon, "New Deal and South," 324; Thomas D. Clark, *The Emerging South* (New York, 1961), 52.

42. Marian D. Irish, "The Proletarian South," *Journal of Politics* 2 (1940): 245; John A. Salmond, *The General Textile Strike of 1934: From Maine to Alabama* (Columbia, Mo., 2002), 180; J. I. Hayes, "South Carolina and New Deal," 404; Bruce J. Schulman, *From Cotton Belt to Sunbelt: Federal Policy, Economic Development, and the Transformation of the South, 1938–1980* (New York, 1991), 26–31.

43. John W. Hevener, *Which Side Are You On? The Harlan County Coal Miners, 1931–39* (Urbana, Ill., 1978), 153–66.

44. Charles H. Martin, "Southern Labor Relations in Transition: Gadsden, Alabama, 1930–1943," *Journal of Southern History* 47 (1981): 567–68; Douglas Flamming, *Creating the Modern South: Millhands and Managers in Dalton, Georgia, 1884–1984* (Chapel Hill, N.C., 1992), 195–96, 229. Section 7(a) of the National Industrial Recovery Act recognized the right to collective bargaining. In 1935 the U.S. Supreme Court invalidated that law, but that same year the right was incorporated in the National Labor Relations Act (the Wagner Act). See, too, H. C. Nixon, "New Deal and South," 327; Calvin B. Hoover and B. U. Ratchford, *Economic Resources and Policies of the South* (New York, 1951), 412. In Chattanooga, the election of FDR and the emergence of the New Deal revitalized the labor movement, which had been devastated by the Great Depression. Charles L. Fontenay, *Estes Kefauver: A Biography* (Knoxville, Tenn., 1980), 72. A study of another Tennessee city found: "The New Deal changed relations between Nashville's employers and labor as much as it changed the city's streets, buildings, parks, airfields, and housing. Before the New Deal, labor in Tennessee had suffered a long history of losing battles against employers, who were often aided by the state." Doyle, *Nashville since the 1920s*, 99.

45. Alexander Heard, *A Two-Party South?* (Chapel Hill, N.C., 1952), 17; Grantham, *Life and Death of Solid South*, 102. One man wrote Joseph T. Robinson of Arkansas, "My dear Senator, as a Southerner I must admit that I am becoming rather weary of the South being the tail to the dog of the Northern Democratic machine." I. H. Wise to Robinson, February 8, 1937, Robinson MSS, Box 225.

46. Proceedings of the Democratic National Committee, October 29, 1947, J. Howard McGrath MSS, Box 71; W. D. Miller, *Mr. Crump*, 173; James A. Farley, *Behind the Ballots: The Personal History of a Politician* (New York, 1938), 116–19; Homer Cummings to E. M. House, July 14, 1932, House MSS, Series 1, Box 34; Harold F. Bass Jr., "Presidential Party Leadership and Party Reform: Franklin

D. Roosevelt and the Abrogation of the Two-Thirds Rule," *Presidential Studies Quarterly* 18 (1988): 308. Though the South had less than one-third of the delegates at Democratic national conventions, a united South anticipated that it could pick up the few remaining votes it needed to block an objectionable candidate. Edward McChesney Sait, *American Parties and Elections*, rev. ed. (New York, 1939), 585.

47. Arthur M. Schlesinger Jr., *The Politics of Upheaval* (Boston, 1960), 581; James A. Farley OH, University of Kentucky; *New York Times*, June 27, 1936.

48. *New York Times*, June 25, 1936; *Washington Post*, June 26, 1936; James A. Farley LBJL OH, 24; Blair Moody in the *Detroit News*, June 26, 1936, clipping, Blair Moody Scrapbooks.

49. *New York Times*, June 25, 1936; typescript of address by Joseph E. Ransdell, n.d. [July 1937], Ransdell MSS, Folder 21, Box 3; George Fort Milton to William G. McAdoo, July 8, 1936, McAdoo MSS, Box 20; Bass, "Presidential Party Leadership," 310–11. See, too, Burnet R. Maybank to T. R. Waring, May 25, 1944, Maybank MSS.

50. Robert F. Hunter, "Carter Glass, Harry Byrd, and the New Deal, 1932–1936," *Virginia Social Science Journal* 4 (1969): 99; Kilpatrick, ed., *Roosevelt and Daniels*, 162–63. See, too, Thomas T. Spencer, "Bennett Champ Clark and the 1936 Presidential Campaign," *Missouri Historical Review* 75 (1981): 203. As a sop to the South, the resolution repealing the two-thirds rule also instructed the Democratic National Committee to devise a new plan of representation at future conventions that would take into consideration the ballots cast in elections, a feature intended to benefit a section known for its high Democratic percentages.

51. *Baltimore News-Post*, April 29, 1936, clipping, Henry Breckinridge MSS, Box 22; J. B. Hodges to E. Noble Calhoun, January 1, 1938, Hodges MSS; Josiah Bailey to R. R. King, August 10, 1936, Bailey MSS, Senatorial Series, Political National Papers, Box 475; Josiah Bailey to J. O. Carr, May 9, 1938, Bailey MSS, Box 476. "The Democratic Party in the South," wrote the former head of the NRA in a syndicated column in 1938, had been "kicked all over the lot by this Administration." Hugh S. Johnson in *Fort Worth Press*, March 31, 1938, in Albert B. Chandler MSS.

52. Alfred Steinberg, *Sam Johnson's Boy: A Close-Up of the President from Texas* (New York, 1968), 426; Collins, *Whither Solid South?* 251. For the subsequent effort to get the Democrats to reward the Solid South for its fidelity, see John Temple Graves II, Memorandum on the Need of a Reapportionments of Delegates to Democratic National Conventions, Gordon Gray MSS, Folder 41.

53. John Temple Graves, "The Solid South Is Cracking," *American Mercury* 56 (1943): 401; "The WHY of States Rights," *Southern Fireside* (October 1949): 39.

54. James F. Byrnes, *All in One Lifetime* (New York, 1958), 50; Robert A. Garson, *The Democratic Party and the Politics of Sectionalism, 1941–1948* (Baton Rouge, La., 1974), 8.

3. LIBERALIZING DIXIE

1. David E. Lilienthal, *The Journals of David E. Lilienthal*, 7 vols. (New York, 1964–83), 1: 64. Bruce Schulman has written: "Zeal to reform the South, rather than dissipating, emerged in earnest during Roosevelt's second term. It was not so much that the New Deal withered . . . as that it headed south. Decrying the South's economic backwardness and political conservatism, the Roosevelt administration launched a series of aggressive programs to reorder the southern economy. A

generation of young liberal southerners entered the national government to preside over these policies during the Roosevelt and Truman administrations." Schulman, *From Cotton Belt*, viii. Schulman dates this development "after 1938," but it actually began in 1937, as he makes clear elsewhere in his important book.

2. Allan A. Michie and Frank Ryhlick, *Dixie Demagogues* (New York, 1939), 75; Tate, "Easing the Burden," 168. One of the most important advocates of the Social Security bill credited Harrison with saving the legislation from death in committee. Martha Swain, "Pat Harrison and the Social Security Act of 1935," *Southern Quarterly* 15 (1976): 6–7.

3. Martha Swain oral history interview of Turner Catledge, Catledge MSS; Joseph Alsop and Stewart Alsop, *The Reporter's Trade* (New York, 1958), 20. When in 1957 five senators were chosen for the Hall of Fame, a Republican senator from South Dakota said he thought Pat Harrison should have been one of the five. "Senator Francis Case Reports," May 13, 1957, Case MSS.

4. J. G. Shoalmire oral history interview of Turner Catledge, Catledge MSS; Martha Swain, "The Lion and the Fox: The Relationship of President Franklin D. Roosevelt and Senator Pat Harrison," *Journal of Mississippi History* 38 (1976): 343; Polly Davis, "Court Reform and Alben W. Barkley's Election as Majority Leader," *Southern Quarterly* 15 (1976): 26; Harold L. Ickes, *The Secret Diary of Harold L. Ickes*, 3 vols. (New York, 1953–54), 2: 164.

5. Alben Barkley, *That Reminds Me—* (Garden City, N.Y., 1954), 16, 64, 77–78; *New York Herald Tribune*, July 22, 1937; Cal Tinney, "Man of the Week—Senator Barkley," *Boston Herald*, July 17, 1937, clipping, Joseph T. Robinson Scrapbooks; J. G. Shoalmire interview of Turner Catledge, Catledge MSS; *United States News*, July 5, 1937, 11, clipping, Alben Barkley Scrapbooks; "Border-State Balance," *Richmond News-Leader*, July 22, 1937. An Alabama writer later contended that a vote was switched by pressure from "a federal official in Washington" who made "use of the Negro vote" as a threat, since Barkley favored antilynching legislation and Harrison was opposed. Russell Kent in *Birmingham News*, July 22, 1937.

6. George Morris in *Memphis Commercial Appeal*, July 18, 1937, clipping Alben Barkley Scrapbooks, Barkley MSS; O. R. Altman, "First Session of the Seventy-fifth Congress, Jan. 5, 1937, to Aug. 21, 1937," *American Political Science Review* 31 (1937): 1075; *Orlando Morning Sentinel*, July 16, 1937. See, too, Felix Frankfurter to C. C. Burlingham, August 16, 1937, Frankfurter MSS, Box 34. The ideological division did not constitute an absolutely perfect fit. The liberal Claude Pepper backed Harrison. *Miami Herald*, n.d., clipping, Thomas G. Corcoran MSS, Box 208; Pepper to J. B. Hodges, July 27, 1937, Hodges MSS, Box 128.

7. Ulric Bell in *Louisville Courier-Journal*, July 15, 1937, clipping, Alben Barkley Scrapbooks, Barkley MSS; Swain, *Pat Harrison*, 157; Edward Keating MS. Diary, July 17–18, 1937; *Philadelphia Record*, July 22, 1937, Alben Barkley Scrapbooks, Barkley MSS; Joseph Tumulty to Pat Harrison, July 16, 1937, Tumulty MSS, Box 63; John Bankhead to James F. Byrnes, July 24, 1937, Byrnes MSS (courtesy of Martha Swain). Harrison even drew support from the very far right. The Vigilantes and Affiliated Organizations U.S.A. to "Dear Congressman," July 20, 1937, Sam Hobbs MSS.

8. *New York Times*, July 16, 1937; Swain, *Pat Harrison*, 156.

9. Byrnes, *All in One Lifetime*, 99; James F. Byrnes to John H. Bankhead, July 22, 1937, Byrnes MSS; Ickes, *Secret Diary*, 2: 170, 174; Grace Tully, *F.D.R. My Boss* (New York, 1949), 225; James A. Farley COHC, 22; James A. Farley, *Jim Farley's Story: The Roosevelt Years* (New York, 1948), 92; James

A. Farley OH, University of Kentucky; interview by the author with James A. Farley, New York, April 24, 1974.

10. *Time,* August 2, 1937, 10; *New York Herald Tribune,* July 22, 1937; *Washington Post,* July 22, 1937; Barkley, *That Reminds Me—,* 156.

11. Unidentified clipping; *Washington Daily News,* August 8, 1938, clippings, Alben Barkley Scrapbooks.

12. Thomas G. Corcoran, "Rendezvous with Democracy: The Memoirs of 'Tommy the Cork,'" Corcoran MSS, Box 586A; Turner Catledge to Joseph W. Alsop, November 9, 1937, Alsop MSS, LC, Box 2. See, too, Howard Ball, "Justice Hugo L. Black: A Magnificent Product of the South," *Alabama Law Review* 36 (1985): 791–834; E. C. Boswell to Chauncey Sparks, August 7, 1937, Sparks MSS, Box 2; Charles F. Roos to John J. Sparkman, July 29, 1937, Sparkman MSS.

13. *Detroit News,* May 16, 1937; W. W. Ball MS. Diary, April 13, 1937.

14. Ickes, *Secret Diary,* 2: 196; H. M. Weldon to Richard B. Russell Jr., August 14, 1937, Russell MSS, 4 B 37; Edward Keating MS. Diary, August 12, 1937; E. David Cronon, "A Southern Progressive Looks at the New Deal," *Journal of Southern History* 24 (1958): 171–72; Josiah W. Bailey to James F. Byrnes, December 21, 1938, Byrnes MSS, Folder 30. A former Republican congressman from Virginia wrote Roosevelt that he discerned no real opposition in the South to the president's objectives but did find that there was a fuss about "the ku-klux matter pertaining to Senator Black, which is being made a lot of down South at the present time." C. Bascom Slemp to FDR, September 15, 1937, Slemp MSS, Box 32. On the other hand, one of the original Brain Trusters, Adolf Berle, observed: "Since the nomination, and although a good many Southern newspapers disapproved of it, their own people have brought pressure on them to get behind and support a Southern Supreme Court justice." A. A. Berle Jr. MS. Diary, September 14, 1937.

15. Hamilton, *Lister Hill,* 76–84; Joseph Keenan to James Roosevelt, December 11, 1937, James Roosevelt MSS, Box 12; Bibb Graves to FDR, January 4, 1938, FDRL OF 300, Box 10; John Edward Hopper, "The Purge: Franklin D. Roosevelt and the 1938 Democratic Nominations" (Ph.D. dissertation, University of Chicago, 1966), 47–48. Hopper's quotation on Heflin's backers came from an article by Paul Y. Anderson. Hopper concluded that "Roosevelt's share" of Hill's victory "was considerable, perhaps crucial." Hopper, "Purge," 114.

16. L. Patrick Hughes, "West Texas Swing: Roosevelt Purge in the Land of the Lone Star?" *West Texas Historical Association Year Book 1999,* 48; Maury Maverick to Thomas G. Corcoran, June 25, 1938, Corcoran MSS, Box 205; Hopper, "Purge," 129–30; Henderson, *Maury Maverick,* 179. Both Maverick and Johnson, though, went down to defeat. See Maury Maverick to Oswald Garrison Villard, August 8, 1938, Villard MSS.; William E. Leuchtenburg, *In the Shadow of FDR: From Harry Truman to George W. Bush* (Ithaca, N.Y., 2001), 128–30. For the contention that FDR did not do enough for Texas liberals, see Hughes, "West Texas Swing," 50, and Vernon Allen Fagin, "Franklin D. Roosevelt, Liberalism in the Democratic Party, and the 1938 Congressional Elections: The Urge to Purge" (Ph.D. dissertation, University of California, Los Angeles, 1979), 192–93.

17. M. Philips Price, *America after Sixty Years: The Travel Diaries of Two Generations of Englishmen* (London, 1936), 207–8.

18. *Public Papers,* 7: 164–68.

19. Ross T. McIntire, *White House Physician* (New York, 1946), 107; *Time,* April 4, 1938, 10; *Greens-*

boro (N.C.) Daily News, March 25, 1938, clipping; *Chattanooga Free Press,* n.d., clipping; T. H. McKeown to FDR, March 29, 1938; Guy G. Moore to FDR, March 28, 1938; Gladys S. Martin to FDR, March 26, 1938, FDRL PPF 200B (43).

20. *Atlanta Constitution,* August 12, 1938; Farley, *Jim Farley's Story,* 127–28.

21. *Charlotte Observer,* March 26, 1938, clipping; *Chattanooga Free Press,* n.d. [c. March 25, 1938], clipping, FDRL PPF 200B (43).

22. Edgar B. Dunlap to Marguerite LeHand, March 26, 1938, enclosing George Barrett to Dunlap, March 24, 1938, FDRL PPF 5274; Chester M. Morgan, *Redneck Liberal: Theodore G. Bilbo and the New Deal* (Baton Rouge, La., 1985), 73. See, too, G. R. Brigham to Editor, *Time,* April 2, 1938, FDRL PPF 200B (43).

23. "When Roosevelt Decides to Speak His Mind," *Augusta (Ga.) Herald,* March 25, 1938, clipping, FDRL PPF 200B (43).

24. N. M. Leonard to FDR, March 27, 1938; Walter Richard Irving to FDR, March 24, 1938; G. H. Pennington to FDR, n.d. [March 1938], FDRL PPF 200B (43). See, too, Aubrey Williams to FDR, March 24, 1938; Claude Pepper to FDR, March 25, 1938, FDRL PPF 200B (43); John A. Salmond, *Miss Lucy of the CIO: The Life and Times of Lucy Randolph Mason, 1882–1959* (Athens, Ga., 1988), 153.

25. Arnold A. McKay to Marvin H. McIntyre, March 24, 1938; T. H. McKeown to FDR, March 29, 1938, FDRL PPF 200B (43). Some of FDR's correspondents who got his talk not from the newspapers but by hearing it over the airwaves regarded it not as an assault on the South but as a most welcome sermon. The sister of a southern legislator told Roosevelt how glad she was that lightning and thunder had relented so that she could hear him clearly on the radio. "That was a most encouraging message you sent out to the people of Georgia," she said. And a Concord, North Carolina man wrote: "As a native of that section my heart was thrilled indeed at what I picked up on the radio. Mr. President. I am a young textile worker but I have the same desires as my more fortunate brothers on higher planes of living." Mrs. E. S. Sherrill to FDR, March 23, 1938; Thomas R. Loggans to FDR, March 21, 1938, FDRL PPF 200B (43).

26. Joseph L. Morrison, *Governor O. Max Gardner: A Power in North Carolina and New Deal Washington* (Chapel Hill, N.C., 1971), 184.

27. John Egerton, *Shades of Gray: Dispatches from the Modern South* (Baton Rouge, La., 1991), 154; Ickes, *Secret Diary,* 2: 342. Hopper, "Purge," 55. Pepper backed the wages and hours bill only after seeing to it that Florida businessmen were exempted from having to meet basic standards.

28. Hopper, "Purge," 59; Ric A. Kabat, "From New Deal to Red Scare: The Political Odyssey of Senator Claude D. Pepper" (Ph.D. dissertation, Florida State University, 1995), 71–75; Claude Pepper MS. Diary, December 20, 1937. Three weeks earlier, following dinner with Roosevelt at the White House, Pepper had noted in his diary, "He spoke very seriously about the possibility of his going out to defeat the reactionary Senators next year, naming George, Smith." Ibid., November 28, 1937.

29. J. B. Shannon, "Presidential Politics in the South: 1938, I," *Journal of Politics* 1 (1939): 150; *New York Times,* February 7, 1938; *Washington Post,* February 7, 1938; *Miami Herald,* n.d., clipping; Claude Pepper to FDR, September 10, 1937, Thomas G. Corcoran MSS, Box 208; Claude Pepper to FDR, May 4, 1938, FDRL PPF 4773; Claude Pepper MS. Diary, May 18, 1938. For a complaint by Pep-

per's chief rival against Jimmy Roosevelt's meddling in the Florida race, see J. Mark Wilcox to FDR, February 7, 1938, FDRL OF 300 (Florida).

30. Thomas G. Corcoran, memo, n.d., Joseph Lash MSS, Box 68; James C. Cobb, "The Big Boy Has Scared the Lard Out of Them," *Research Studies* 43 (1975): 124; Dowell E. Patterson, "Notes on Senatorial Campaign in Georgia," FDRL PSF 151; Glen Moore, "An Analysis of Georgia's 1938 Senate Race," *Proceedings and Papers of the Georgia Association of Historians* 6 (1985): 87; Roy Edward Fossett, "The Impact of the New Deal on Georgia Politics, 1933–1941" (Ph.D. dissertation, University of Florida, 1960), 278. Apparently, George had second thoughts about his "traitor" comment because, though this epithet appeared in his press release of a radio address, he did not use the word on the air.

31. Walter George to FDR, June 27, 1938, FDRL PSF 151.

32. FDR to Walter George, June 29, 1938, FDRL PSF 151.

33. Farley, *Jim Farley's Story,* 133–34; Isaac K. Hay OH, 45, Richard B. Russell MSS; Moore, "Analysis," 89; Fagin, "Franklin D. Roosevelt," 225; *Atlanta Constitution,* August 11, 1938. Toward the end of July, a New Deal official reported that if the president said emphatically "that he wants Camp elected there is a fine chance that he will be." Clark Foreman, memorandum for Mr. Corcoran, July 27, 1937, Thomas G. Corcoran MSS, Box 247. George had a very good idea of what FDR's intervention portended. "Unquestionably, one of my opponents was put in the race by the President," he wrote Senator Bailey. "The President will probably take pleasure in giving me a kick down stairs on his visit to the State. What the reaction will be I am not able to foresee." Walter F. George to Josiah Bailey, July 21, 1938, Bailey MSS, Box 476.

34. *Public Papers,* 7: 471–75.

35. Ibid., 260–95.

36. James P. Fleissner, "August 11, 1938: A Day in the Life of Senator Walter F. George," *Journal of Southern Legal History* 9 (2001): 63–70; Thomas L. Stokes, *Chip off My Shoulder* (Princeton, N.J., 1940), 496; *Atlanta Constitution,* August 12, 1938.

37. Fleissner, "August 11, 1938," 71–87; *Public Papers,* 7: 467–70. Roosevelt may well have been aware that Barnesville was notoriously anti-union, and that may have affected his remarks. Shortly before he spoke, a southern woman, who said that she had been raised to rely upon the southern tradition of chivalry toward ladies, wrote him that a year earlier a mob of vigilantes led by prominent businessmen had kidnapped her and dumped her 60 miles out of town with a warning not to return to attempt to organize a union local. The whole episode, she said, was observed by the mayor of Barnesville and the chief of police. Billye Bailey to FDR, July 9, 1938, Lucy Randolph Mason MSS, Box 1.

38. *Time,* August 22, 1938, 19–20; McIntire, *White House Physician,* 107; Cobb, "Big Boy," 125; Fossett, "Impact of New Deal on Georgia," 291. The governor of North Carolina, O. Max Gardner, who guided George on strategy in the campaign, had counseled him to shake Roosevelt's hand after the president denounced him and then utter a statesmanlike sentence, for FDR was too powerful to be attacked directly. Morrison, *Governor O. Max Gardner,* 184–85.

39. James C. Cobb, "Not Gone, But Forgotten: Eugene Talmadge and the 1938 Purge Campaign," *Georgia Historical Quarterly* 59 (1975): 204; Fagin, "Franklin D. Roosevelt," 261; Talmadge with Winchell, *Talmadge,* 39; Fleissner, "August 11, 1938," 55–57.

40. *Atlanta Constitution,* August 16, 1938; Moore, "Analysis," 87; Richard Polenberg, "The Decline of the New Deal, 1937–1940," in *The New Deal: The National Level,* ed. John Braeman, Robert H. Bremner, and David Brody (Columbus, Ohio, 1975), 258; Lippman, *Squire of Warm Springs,* 170; Luther Harmon Zeigler Jr., "Senator Walter George's 1938 Campaign," *Georgia Historical Quarterly* 43 (1959): 333; Raymond Clapper, "Roosevelt Tries the Primaries," *Current History* 49 (October 1938): 16; Margaret Mitchell to Norma and Herschel Brickell, September 4, 1938, in *Margaret Mitchell's Gone with the Wind Letters,* ed. Richard Harwell (New York, 1976), 224; Cobb, "Not Gone," 204–5. Mitchell added: "Roosevelt lost an awful lot of personal popularity by that Barnesville speech endorsing Camp. And more popularity by forgetting to throw the switch that was to turn on the electricity into that section of rural Georgia. He'd been invited for the purpose of throwing the switch and after he got through lambasting George it slipped his mind." Her comments, though, have to be put in the context of her remarking that Camp's supporters included "everybody who was sucking a Government tit or hoping to suck one if they could bump another sucker out of the way," and her saying of Talmadge's entrance into the race, "We are afraid he may split the conservative vote." Ibid., 224–25. One friend later recalled "Margaret's vituperative denunciations of FDR and all his works." Clifford Dowdey, quoted in Darden Asbury Pyron, *Southern Daughter: The Life of Margaret Mitchell* (New York, 1991), 438. For Georgia's opposition to the purge, see, too, Spence M. Grayson OH, 27, Richard B. Russell MSS; James C. Cobb, "Eugene Talmadge and the Purge: The Georgia Senatorial Campaign of 1938" (M.A. essay, University of Georgia, 1972), 72. Polls revealed that the president's attack had bolstered George's position, yet had done nothing to lessen FDR's popularity in Georgia. Cobb, "Big Boy," 126.

41. Daniel W. Hollis, "'Cotton Ed Smith'—Showman or Statesman?" *South Carolina Historical Magazine* 71 (1970): 236, 256, 251–52; Mary Louise Gehring, "'Cotton Ed' Smith: The South Carolina Farmer in the United States Senate," in *The Oratory of Southern Demagogues,* ed. Cal M. Logue and Howard Dorgan (Baton Rouge, La., 1981), 144–45; Simon, "Fabric of Defeat," 429; Miller, "Palmetto Politician," 308; interview with Farley Smith, Tanglewood Plantation, December 9, 1962, William D. Workman Jr. MSS, Box 22. See, too, *Columbia (S.C.) Record,* March 26, 1937, clipping, Scrapbook 1937, Olin D. Johnston MSS.

42. Simon, "Fabric of Defeat," 434–35; unidentified clipping, n.d. [August 1938], Scrapbook 1938, Olin D. Johnston MSS; James F. Byrnes to Bernard M. Baruch, August 16, 1938, Byrnes MSS. As Simon demonstrates, there is more than one version of Roosevelt's remarks as the train whistle sounded, but there is no dispute about the essence of them. Smith had said, "If, by way of illustration, a man could live on fifty cents a day in South Carolina and a dollar and a half in New England," that differential should not be changed by statute. He did not actually say that a man could live on fifty cents a day. James F. Byrnes to Bernard M. Baruch, August 16, 1938, Byrnes MSS.

43. Interview with Farley Smith; *The State* (Columbia, S.C.), May 17, 1938, clipping, Scrapbook 1938, Olin D. Johnston MSS; *Berkeley (S.C.) Democrat,* June 15, 1938, *Union (S.C.) Daily Times,* June 30, 1938, clippings, Edgar A. Brown MSS, Scrapbook 4; Nadine Cohodas, *Strom Thurmond and the Politics of Southern Change* (New York, 1993), 66; "This Man Brown," pamphlet, Edgar A. Brown MS, Folder L836; *Greenville (S.C.) News,* August 3, 1938, clipping, Scrapbook 1938, Olin D. Johnston MSS.

44. Olin D. Johnston, radio address, August 22, 1938, Johnston MSS, Speeches, Box 1.

45. *Columbia (S.C.) Record,* August 29, 1936, clipping, Edgar A. Brown MSS, Scrapbook 4; Travis Dayhuff, "The 1938 'Purge' Campaign in South Carolina and Southern Political Culture in the New Deal Era" (M.A. thesis, University of Tennessee, Knoxville, 1994), 47–48. Before Brown withdrew, pollsters assessed his strength at 13 percent, compared to Johnston's 36 percent and Smith's 51 percent. *New York Times,* August 30, 1938, clipping, Edgar A. Brown MSS, Scrapbook 4.

46. Dowell E. Patterson, "Notes on Senatorial Campaign in South Carolina," FDRL PSF 151; V. O. Key, with Alexander Heard, *Southern Politics in State and Nation* (New York, 1949), 139; *Public Papers,* 7: 477; John D. Stark, *Damned Upcountryman: William Watts Ball* (Durham, N.C., 1968), 181–83; Harry S. Ashmore, *Hearts and Minds: The Anatomy of Racism from Roosevelt to Reagan* (New York, 1982), 20–22.

47. Hollis, "'Cotton Ed Smith,'" 254; *Beaufort Gazette,* September 1, 1938, clipping, Scrapbook 1938, Olin D. Johnston MSS; L. A. Crowell Jr. to FDR, August 31, 1938, FDRL OF 300 South Carolina (courtesy of Travis Dayhuff); *Lexington (S.C.) Dispatch News,* September 1, 1938, clipping, Edgar A. Brown MSS, Scrapbook 4; William J. Cooper Jr. and Thomas E. Terrill, *The American South: A History* (New York, 1990), 684.

48. Harry S. Ashmore, *Civil Rights and Wrongs: A Memoir of Race and Politics, 1944–1994* (New York, 1994), 9; James F. Byrnes to Bernard M. Baruch, August 16, 1938, Byrnes MSS, Folder 20.

49. Cobb, "Not Gone," 197; Farley, *Jim Farley's Story,* 144. For Barkley's victory over Happy Chandler, see Hopper, "Purge," 101–3; Charlton Ogburn to FDR, October 20, 1938, Frances Perkins MSS; Brady M. Stewart to FDR, May 23, 1938, copy in Robert F. Wagner MSS, Personal File, Box 689, Folder 156; *Louisville Courier-Journal,* August 7–9, 1938; John Ed Pearce, *Divide and Dissent: Kentucky Politics, 1930–1963* (Lexington, Ky., 1987), 45. See, too, Edgar A. Brown to R. G. Thach, September 8, 1938, Brown MSS, Folder L837. After the ballots were counted, commentators minimized the significance of FDR's intervention, for, they said, Barkley's victory had never been in doubt. During the campaign, however, conservatives had anticipated a Chandler win. American Liberty League Memorandum No. 215, July 8, 1938, Pierre S. du Pont MSS, Box 3. A prominent Chandler supporter, the acting governor, wrote in his newspaper diary: "He gave Kentuckians some advice about senatorial campaigns that I do not believe they are going to take." *Richmond (Ky.) Daily Register,* August 8, 1938, clipping, Keen Johnson MSS, Box 31. One writer has concluded: "In the final analysis, Barkley's victory resulted from the enduring popularity of the New Deal. Kentucky voters expressed their approval of the Roosevelt program by overwhelmingly supporting Barkley in 1938 as they had supported the president two years earlier. . . . Roosevelt's Kentucky visit, although not decisive in the election, generated state pride in Barkley's position of national leadership and his friendship with the popular president." Walter L. Hixson, "The 1938 Kentucky Senate Election: Alben W. Barkley, 'Happy' Chandler, and the New Deal," *Register of the Kentucky Historical Society* 80 (1982): 327–28. For a protest by Chandler's campaign chairman against the use of federal machinery on behalf of Barkley, see Brady M. Stewart to FDR, May 23, 1938, in Robert F. Wagner MSS, Personal Files, Box 689, Folder 156. The victory in Kentucky, though, was offset by the results in Maryland where Roosevelt failed to unseat Senator Millard Tydings. Roosevelt and his circle made a fainthearted and poorly executed effort to oust Howard W. Smith in Virginia, but Smith trounced the weak New Deal candidate. For the impact of FDR on Elmer Thomas's victory in Oklahoma, which some writers view as a southern state, see T. P. Gore to Elmer Thomas,

July 21, 1938, Thomas MSS, Political Campaigns—Correspondence and Papers, 1938. Ball rejoiced in the South Carolina results: "As for old Smith, monstrous wind-bag, he has been invaluable—we have used him for the undoing of Blease and now of Roosevelt who is an edition de luxe of Blease." W. W. Ball to "Sara," September 2, 1938, Ball MSS.

50. L. Reed, *Simple Decency*, 10; Randall Lee Patton, "Southern Liberals and the Emergence of a 'New South,' 1938–1950" (Ph.D. dissertation, University of Georgia, 1990), 28; Clark Foreman, "The Decade of Hope," *Phylon* 12 (1951): 139; Laurence Hewes, *Boxcar in the Sand* (New York, 1957), 64; *South Today* (1942): 51.

51. Thomas A. Krueger, *And Promises to Keep: The Southern Conference for Human Welfare, 1938–1948* (Nashville, Tenn., 1967), 13; Steve Davis, "The South as 'The Nation's No. 1 Economic Problem': The NEC Report of 1938," *Georgia Historical Quarterly* 62 (1978): 120–21; memorandum of conversation between Lowell Mellett and Sidney Hyman, August 8, 1949, Papers of the Franklin D. Roosevelt Memorial Foundation, Box 23.

52. Clifford and Virginia Durr LBJL OH, 14–16; *Kiplinger Washington Letter*, August 13, 1938; Capus M. Waynick in the *High Point Enterprise*, July 19, 1938, clipping, Frank P. Graham MSS, Series 1.1, Box 10.

53. Message, FDRL OF 788, Box 3. Italics added.

54. F. Garvin Davenport Jr., *The Myth of Southern History: Historical Consciousness in Twentieth-Century Southern Literature* (Nashville, Tenn., 1970), 91–92; Williams Haynes, *Southern Horizons* (New York, 1946), 1; *New York Times*, July 7, 1938; David L. Carlton and Peter A. Coclanis, *Confronting Southern Poverty in the Great Depression: The Report on Economic Conditions of the South with Related Documents* (Boston, 1996), 19–20.

55. *Textile Bulletin*, July 7, 1938, 14–15; Kennedy, *Southern Exposure*, 2. (I have rearranged the order of the sentence in the *Textile Bulletin* quotation.) This sentiment was not universal, however. The governor of Arkansas called FDR's request for a study "the first positive step taken to readmit the South to the union," and Lister Hill declared: "The President has again and again . . . demonstrated his friendship for the south. His ordering of the economic survey and his remarks with reference to it shows just how splendid and sincere that friendship is." Somewhat surprisingly, even Senator McKellar said that he was "glad the President is having a study made." *Greenville (S.C.) News*, July 10, 1938, clipping, Scrapbook 1938, Olin D. Johnston MSS. Noting that the South had been called "Economic Problem No. 1," a southern editor commented, "I am afraid it is more than that. I fear—I hope foolishly—that not merely in its executive offices, but out on the gullied hills, something strange, too native to be fascism, is breeding in the sun." Jonathan Daniels, "Democracy Is Bread," *Virginia Quarterly Review* 14 (1938): 482. The issue of the *Textile Bulletin* was sent to Graham by an admirer who scrawled a penciled note signed simply "a Cotton Mill Worker." Frank Porter Graham MSS, Series 1.1, Box 10.

56. National Emergency Council, *Report to the President on the Economic Conditions of the South* (Washington, D.C., 1938); "Southern Waste Land," *Nation*, August 20, 1938, 169.

57. National Emergency Council, *Report*.

58. Numan V. Bartley, "Writing About the Post–World War II South," *Georgia Historical Quarterly* 68 (1984): 2–3; Walter Prescott Webb, *Divided We Stand* (New York, 1937); Edward Shapiro, "The Southern Agrarians and the Tennessee Valley Authority," *American Quarterly* 29 (winter 1970):

795; Maury Maverick, "Let's Join the United States," *Virginia Quarterly Review* 15 (1939): 64–65; George B. Tindall, "The 'Colonial Economy' and the Growth Psychology: The South in the 1930's," *South Atlantic Quarterly* 64 (1965): 473. Shapiro's quotations came from Donald Davidson and other agrarians. The report was drafted in Cliff Durr's living room. John A. Salmond, *The Conscience of a Lawyer: Clifford J. Durr and American Civil Liberties, 1899–1975* (Tuscaloosa, Ala., 1990), 55. In submitting the report, Mellett warned the president, "Do not read it for literature, for it is not that." Still, an effort had been made "to have it unimpeachable as to facts," and though he did not think that the goal of rendering it comprehensible to any reader had been completely achieved, "there is very little hard reading in the report." Lowell Mellett to FDR, August 6, 1938, FDRL OF 788, Box 3.

59. Richard H. King, *A Southern Renaissance: The Cultural Awakening of the American South, 1930–1955* (New York, 1980), 50; Persky, *Burden of Dependency*, 128, 130; Arthur F. Raper and Ira De A. Reid, *Sharecroppers All* (Chapel Hill, N.C., 1941), 265; Clarence H. Danhof, "Four Decades of Thought on the South's Economic Problems," in *Essays in Southern Economic Development*, ed. Melvin L. Greenhut and W. Tate Whitman (Chapel Hill, N.C., 1964), 7–68, especially 50. See, too, Persky, "Regional Colonialism and the Southern Economy," *Review of Radical Political Economics* 4 (1972): 70–79.

60. Clayton, "Southern Intellectuals," in *Debating Southern History*, ed. Clayton and Salmond, 40; Carlton and Coclanis, *Confronting Southern Poverty*, 6; George B. Tindall, "The Significance of Howard W. Odum to Southern History: A Preliminary Estimate," *Journal of Southern History* 24 (1958): 285, 306; R. Alan Lawson, *The Failure of Independent Liberalism, 1930–1941* (New York, 1971), 142. Tindall has written, "Possibly the Odumesque regionalism of the thirties, which attracted so much attention at the time, was really, as one sociologist has described it, a means of exorcising the evil spirits of sectionalism, and may now be seen as a sort of way station on the twentieth-century Road to Reunion." George B. Tindall, "The Status and Future of Regionalism—A Symposium," *Journal of Southern History* 26 (1960): 23–24.

61. George L. Simpson, "Howard W. Odum and American Regionalism," *Social Forces* 34 (1955): 101. Odum, *Southern Regions*, 253, 255, 259, 353; R. M. Brown, "New Regionalism," in *Regionalism and Pacific Northwest*, ed. Robbins, Frank, and Ross, 40.

62. David L. Carlton and Peter A. Coclanis, "Another 'Great Migration' from Region to Race in Southern Liberalism, 1938–1945," *Southern Cultures* 3 (1997): 37–38, 45.

63. "Southern Waste Land," *Nation,* August 20, 1938, 169.

64. Lippman, *Squire of Warm Springs,* 147–48; Shannon, "Presidential Politics in the South," 469; Charles P. Roland, "The South, America's Will-o-the-Wisp Eden," *Louisiana History* 11 (1970): 114; Paul M. Gaston, *The New South Creed: A Study in Southern Mythmaking* (New York, 1970), 222–23. See, too, C. Vann Woodward, "Hillbilly Realism," *Southern Review* 4 (1939): 677; Fitzgerald Hall, Comments on the Report on Economic Conditions of the South, September 7, 1938, Frank Porter Graham MSS, Series 1.1, Box 10.

65. Garet Garrett, "The Problem South," *Saturday Evening Post,* October 8, 1938, 86; S. Davis, "The South," 127–28; Marian E. Strobel, "FDR and the Nation's 'No. 1 Economic Problem': 1938" (M.A. essay, Duke University, 1971), 21; L. Reed, *Simple Decency,* 6.

66. *Greenville (S.C.) News,* July 10, 1938, clipping, Scrapbook 1938, Olin D. Johnston MSS; Lind-

ley S. Butler and Alan D. Watson, eds., *The North Carolina Experience: An Interpretive and Documentary History* (Chapel Hill, N.C., 1984), 403; *Charleston News and Courier*, August 12, 1938; Irish, "Proletarian South," 252. See, too, "Giving the South a Bad Name," *Charleston News and Courier*, August 14, 1938.

67. Federal Writers' Project, *These Are Our Lives*, 11, 15.

68. C. K. De Busk to Sam H. Jones, December 5, 1942, Jones MSS; William T. Polk, *Southern Accent: From Uncle Remus to Oak Ridge* (New York, 1953), 219–22; John Temple Graves, "Revolution in the South," *Virginia Quarterly Review* 26 (1950): 193; W. R. Poage LBJL OH, 2: 6. In the late 1930s, a textbook on southern history later noted crossly, "the South was being used as 'the issue' in national politics. To dramatize it, photographers came with cameras to peer into the lined faces of the lowly. Mrs. Eleanor Roosevelt visited and inspected the croppers' shacks; Secretary of Labor Frances Perkins made an unfortunate remark about Southerners being without shoes." William B. Hesseltine and David L. Smiley, *The South in American History* (Englewood Cliffs, N.J., 1960), 535, quoted in Strobel, "FDR." Odum himself later wrote, "The realistic researches into the resources, deficiencies, and needs of the South, and then the action of the New Deal administration, caused the nation to rediscover the South as a peculiar example of backwardness and later of badness, and to undertake to remake it overnight." Howard W. Odum, "Social Change in the South," *Journal of Politics* 10 (1948): 252.

69. Schulman, *From Cotton Belt*, 50–52; *Congressional Record*, 76th Cong., 1st sess., A3903; Carlton and Coclanis, *Confronting Southern Poverty*, 8–9.

70. James A. Hodges, "George Fort Milton and the New Deal," *Tennessee Historical Quarterly* 36 (1977): 401; Gerald Johnson column reprinted as advertisement in *Charlotte Observer*, October 9, 1938, in Lowell Mellett MSS, Box 11. A group of twelve southern editors embraced the report as the "key to the doorway of opportunity" for their region. "What about the South?" *Washington Daily News*, August 23, 1938.

71. Charles W. Eagles, *Jonathan Daniels and Race Relations: The Evolution of a Southern Liberal* (Knoxville, Tenn., 1982), 66; Jonathan Daniels, *A Southerner Discovers the South* (New York, 1938), 345; Patricia Sullivan, "Gideon's Southern Soldiers: New Deal Politics and Civil Rights Reform, 1933–1948" (Ph.D. dissertation, Emory University, 1983), 32. Thomas Corcoran, memorandum for the president, August 1, 1938; S. E. Early for Mellett, n.d., FDRL PSF 151; FDR to Mr. Forster for Lowell Mellett, August 9, 1938, via naval communications, FDRL OF 788, Box 3; *Public Papers*, 7: 471–75.

72. Sosna, *In Search of Silent South*, 89–90; Robin D. G. Kelley, *Hammer and Hoe: Alabama Communists during the Great Depression* (Chapel Hill, N.C., 1990), 128; Clifford and Virginia Durr LBJL OH, 20; Barnard, *Outside the Magic Circle*, 119–21; Sullivan, "Gideon's Southern Soldiers," 52–53. See, too, Virginia Durr SOHP, 1–5; Clark Foreman to Tom Krueger, June 17, 1963, Southern Conference for Human Welfare Papers, Atlanta University, 19–A–B–1 (3).

73. W. T. Couch to Isaac Copeland, June 21, 1971, Kenneth Douty MSS; Sarah Newman Shouse, *Hillbilly Realist: Herman Clarence Nixon of Possum Trot* (University, Ala., 1986), 1–3, 74, 120; H. Clarence Nixon, *Forty Acres and Steel Mules* (Chapel Hill, N.C., 1938), 96; L. Reed, *Simple Decency*, 8. The SCHW, one scholar has noted, "was not . . . merely the southern analogue to national liberal groups." It "existed precisely because southerners and many national liberals thought that the

South had . . . unique problems that required unique solutions. Many southerners perceived their region as a 'poor relation' in an affluent nation, a 'nation within a nation' in many respects, with a different culture and a dependent economy." Randall L. Patton, "The Popular Front Alternative: Clark H. Foreman and the Southern Conference for Human Welfare, 1938–1948," in *Georgia in Black and White: Explorations in the Race Relations of a Southern State, 1865–1950,* ed. John C. Inscoe (Athens, Ga., 1994), 228. See, too, H. C. Nixon to Brooks Hays, July 27, 1938, National Policy Committee MSS, Box 3; Raper and Reid, "Old Conflicts in New South," 225.

74. W. T. Couch, "Southerners Inspect the South," *New Republic,* December 14, 1938, 168; Nell Irvin Painter, *The Narrative of Hosea Hudson: His Life as a Negro Communist in the South* (Cambridge, Mass., 1979), 288. In late July, Nixon reported, "Clark Foreman has been interviewed in Atlanta with a view to hooking up the conference with the recent work of the President's Committee on Southern economic problems." H. C. Nixon to Brooks Hays, July 27, 1938, Hays MSS, University of Arkansas, Box 42. Charles S. Johnson said the meeting had been "inspired . . . by the devastating government report on the region's . . . plight," and the presiding officer, Judge Louise O. Charlton, called it "the answer" to the *Report.* Charles S. Johnson, "More Southerners Discover the South," *Crisis* 46 (1939): 14; Kenneth Douty, "The Southern Conference for Human Welfare: A Report," 9, Douty MSS.

75. H. C. Nixon to Brooks Hays, July 27, 1938, Hays MSS, University of Arkansas, Box 42; Daniel Joseph Singal, *The War Within: From Victorian to Modernist Thought in the South, 1919–1945* (Chapel Hill, N.C., 1982), 292; Myrdal, *An American Dilemma,* 469; "Southern Conference for Human Welfare: Plans and Purposes," in Louise O. Charlton and Luther Patrick to Myles Horton, August 13, 1938, Highlander Research and Education Center MSS, Box 70. The secretary of the Communist Party in Alabama claimed that the Southern Conference had been "anticipated" by the head of the Party, Earl Browder, who had urged "all progressives" to "rally around" the *Report* and, indeed, "that the Southern Conference was a brilliant confirmation of the line of the democratic front advanced by Comrade Browder at the Tenth Convention." Rob F. Hall, "The Southern Conference for Human Welfare," *Communist* 18 (1939): 57, 60. In 1939 Browder himself testified that the SCHW was a Party "transmission belt." Shouse, *Hillbilly Realist,* 189.

76. Virginia Durr SOHP, 83; Diane McWhorter, *Carry Me Home: Birmingham, Alabama, the Climactic Battle of the Civil Rights Revolution* (New York, 2001), 50; William A. Nunnelley, *Bull Connor* (Tuscaloosa, Ala., 1991), 30; Shouse, *Hillbilly Realist,* 179.

77. Pauli Murray, Eleanor Roosevelt Oral History Project, 18; Virginia Durr SOHP, 24; Tarleton Collier in *Atlanta Georgian,* November 25, 1938, clipping, Arthur Raper MSS, 2: 37 (4), Folder 946. For skepticism about the legend, see John Egerton, *Speak Now against the Day: The Generation before the Civil Rights Movement in the South* (New York, 1994), 193–94; George Stoney SOHP (interviewed by John Egerton), 25–26. For yet another version of where Mrs. Roosevelt placed her chair, see Tamara K. Hareven, *Eleanor Roosevelt: An American Conscience* (New York, 1975), 118.

78. Barnard, *Outside the Magic Circle,* 121, 127.

79. The group became preoccupied with internal quarrels. Even Frank Porter Graham, who was far more willing than other southern liberals to tolerate Communists, was denounced by them as a "tool of Wall Street" and a "lackey of the mill barons." In later years, many southern liberals sundered their ties with the organization. The founding convention chair, Louise Charlton, upon re-

signing in 1941, wrote, "I am afraid . . . we are being used as pawns in a much deeper game." Shouse, *Hillbilly Realist*, 193. At its Nashville convention in 1942, the SCHW drove away still more advocates of civil rights in the South when Paul Robeson demanded the freeing from federal prison of "a great prophet, Earl Browder." Merl E. Reed, "The Nashville Convention of the Southern Conference for Human Welfare, 1942," *Alabama Review* 37 (1984): 58–59. Ralph McGill asserted: "The Southern Conference for Human Welfare did degenerate into a Communist front outfit. . . . [Jim Dombrowski] and Clark Foreman . . . betrayed Mark Ethridge and Barry Bingham by an ardent bit of fellow traveling with the Communists who were in it." McGill to Aubrey Williams, December 10, 1953, McGill MSS, Series 2, Box 5. See, too, Frank McCallister to Clark Foreman, May 4, 1942; James A. Dombrowski to Roger Baldwin, May 27, 1942, Dombrowski MSS, Box 17; "Memorandum on the Southern Conference for Human Welfare," in Joseph L. Rauh Jr. to Mrs. Gifford Pinchot, July 15, 1947, Rauh MSS, Box 41; H. L. Mitchell COHC, 119–22; Alexander Heard SOHP, 16; Jonathan Daniels COHC, 106. Williams himself called Foreman "a pompous stupid mess." Williams to McGill, December 16, 1953, idem. Even his staunch advocate Virginia Durr felt called upon to say of Foreman: "I am sorry Clark made a poor impression and I do think he gives impressions that he does not mean to. I do not think he is the strong arrogant type at all." Virginia Durr to Jessica Mitford, n.d. [1957], Mitford MSS, Box 22. Foreman himself concluded that "the Southern Conference went down in '48 on the shoals of Wallace. It went all out in the Wallace campaign and when that was such a fiasco there was nothing for us to do but to fold up." Clark Foreman SOHP, 66.

80. FDR to Judge Louise O. Charlton, FDRL PPF 5664.

81. FDR to Frank P. Graham, April 12, 1940, FDRL PPF 5664. See, too, FDR to Frank P. Graham, March 28, 1942, Carl and Anne Braden MSS, Box 18.

82. John A. Salmond, "Aubrey Williams: Atypical New Dealer?" in *New Deal*, ed. Braeman, Bremner, and Brody, 236; Salmond, "Postscript to the New Deal: The Defeat of the Nomination of Aubrey W. Williams as Rural Electrification Administrator in 1945," *Journal of American History* 61 (1974): 420; Leonard Dinnerstein, "The Senate's Rejection of Aubrey Williams as Rural Electrification Administrator," *Alabama Review* 21 (1968): 141–43; Dan T. Carter, *The Politics of Rage: George Wallace, the Origins of the New Conservatism, and the Transformation of American Politics* (New York, 1995), 274; Hamilton, *Lister Hill*, 132. See, too, Carl Elliott Sr. and Michael D'Orso, *The Cost of Courage: The Journey of an American Congressman* (New York, 1992), 66–67; Salmond, *Miss Lucy*, 177–78. The biographer of the most prominent liberal in Arkansas has written: "Not only did F.D.R. become the president Brooks wanted, bringing the New Deal to America, but he would be a real friend to Brooks Hays. He would keep Brooks in federal jobs throughout the Depression, he would protect Brooks from the eastern Arkansas 'Bourbons' who would have destroyed him, and he would have made him a federal judge in 1936 had Arkansas Senator Hattie Caraway not blocked Brooks's nomination." James T. Baker, *Brooks Hays* (Macon, Ga., 1989), 48.

83. John M. Matthews, "Dissenters and Reformers: Some Southern Liberals between the World Wars," in *Developing Dixie: Modernization in a Traditional Society*, ed. Winfred B. Moore Jr., Joseph F. Tripp, and Lyon G. Tyler Jr. (New York, 1988), 172; Claude Pepper SOHP, 8. John Sparkman characterized himself as a "TVA liberal," which implied, Anthony Badger has pointed out, he had learned "that the federal government . . . could regenerate an entire region," and hence that "fed-

eral government assistance was to be the answer to the region's problems." Anthony J. Badger, "Whatever Happened to Roosevelt's New Generation of Southerners?" in *The Roosevelt Years: New Perspectives on American History, 1933–1945,* ed. Robert A. Garson and Stuart S. Kidd (Edinburgh, 1999), 128. "By the late 1930s," Fred Hobson has noted, Gerald Johnson "viewed the South from afar, with great interest, even fascination, but not as the preoccupation it had been before. It had ceased being that when Franklin D. Roosevelt entered the White House and Johnson turned his energies to a defense of the New Deal. The last forty years of his life would be given to reflections on American politics and culture in a larger sense." Hobson, "Introduction," in *South-Watching: Selected Essays by Gerald W. Johnson,* ed. Hobson (Chapel Hill, N.C., 1983), xxiv.

84. Sosna, *In Search of Silent South,* 66, 71, 204.

4. INTIMATIONS OF A COMING STORM

1. R. A. Garson, *Democratic Party,* 2; Cash, *Mind of the South,* 364.

2. Gore, *Let the Glory Out,* 53, 45–46; Whitman, *Lilienthal,* 28; Donald Davidson, "Where Regionalism and Sectionalism Meet," *Social Forces* 13 (1934): 26–27; Paul Conkin, *The Southern Agrarians* (Knoxville, Tenn., 1988), 151–52; Swain, *Pat Harrison,* 253; H. Clarence Nixon, *Lower Piedmont Country* (New York, 1946), 122.

3. James P. Johnson, *The Politics of Soft Coal: The Bituminous Industry from World War I through the New Deal* (Urbana, Ill., 1979), 187; Daniels, *Southerner Discovers South,* 282. See, too, James E. Fickle, "The S.P.A. and the N.R.A.: A Case Study of the Blue Eagle in the South," *Southwestern Historical Quarterly* 79 (1956): 275; Robert J. Norrell, "Labor at the Ballot Box: Alabama Politics from the New Deal to the Dixiecrat Movement," *Journal of Southern History* 57 (1991): 214–19; S. G. Harwood to Carter Glass, February 26, 1934, Glass MSS, Box 328.

4. George Brown Tindall, *The Disruption of the Solid South* (New York, 1972), 30–31.

5. Dewey W. Grantham Jr., *The Democratic South* (Athens, Ga., 1963), 74. See, too, Grantham, *Life and Death of the Solid South,* 114. Similarly, George Tindall has written: "Roosevelt increasingly acquired enemies. Nearly every program to which the New Deal addressed itself seemed inadvertently designed to raise sectional opposition. New Deal crop limitations antagonized the cotton trade, NRA codes and labor standards annoyed industrialists, relief policies raised the question of regional wage differentials. Sectional feeling, which had strengthened the coalitions of Bryan and Wilson, plagued Roosevelt as it had plagued his party in the 1920s. Unlike Wilson's New Freedom, Roosevelt's New Deal challenged the social and economic power structures of the South, and thereby provoked an opposition such as Wilson never had—and created a loyalty among the rank and file such as Wilson never had." Tindall, *Disruption of Solid South,* 30.

6. Graves, *Fighting South,* 114.

7. Richard Lowitt and Maurine Beasley, eds., *One Third of a Nation: Lorena Hickok Reports on the Great Depression* (Urbana, Ill., 1981), 215; Richard N. Current, *Northernizing the South* (Athens, Ga., 1983), 106; Raper, *Preface to Peasantry,* 237; Raper, "Southern Negro," 133; Cooper and Terrill, *American South,* 675; Holmes, "Blue Eagle as 'Jim Crow Bird,'" 279. See, too, Billington and Clark, "Texas Clergymen," 31; John Faulkner, *My Brother Bill: An Affectionate Reminiscence* (New York, 1963), 206.

8. Sullivan, *Days of Hope,* 159; Winfred B. Moore Jr., "The Unrewarding Stone: James F. Byrnes

and the Burden of Race, 1908–1944," in *The South Is Another Land: Essays on the Twentieth-Century South*, ed. Bruce Clayton and John A. Salmond (Westport, Conn., 1987), 16; *Greenville (S.C.) Observer*, n.d., reprint in James F. Byrnes MSS, Folder 17. See, too, Robert W. Dubay, "Mississippi and the Proposed Federal Anti-Lynching Bills of 1937–38," *Southern Quarterly* 7 (1968): 73–89; Nicholas Lemann, *The Promised Land: The Great Migration and How It Changed America* (New York, 1991), 48; Franck Roberts Havenner OH, 94.

9. W. B. Moore, "New South Statesman," 208; Sitkoff, *New Deal for Blacks*, 296, 98.

10. *New York Times*, June 26, 1936.

11. Virginius Dabney, *Below the Potomac: A Book about the New South* (New York, 1942), 33; Alexander P. Lamis, *The Two-Party South*, expanded ed. (New York, 1988), 7–8.

12. A. Cash Koeniger, "The Politics of Independence: Carter Glass and the Elections of 1936," *South Atlantic Quarterly* 80 (1981): 102, 104; Richard Polenberg, "Roosevelt, Carter, and Executive Reorganization: Lessons of the 1930s," *Presidential Studies Quarterly* 9 (1979): 43; Francis Pickens Miller, *Man from the Valley: Memoirs of a 20th-Century Virginian* (Chapel Hill, N.C. 1971), 154. See, too, R. Walton Moore to C. O'Conor Goolrick, October 2, 1936, Moore MSS, Box 17. Even the most prominent Roosevelt man in Virginia made a point of saying, "I am not the great New Dealer that some of these correspondents indicate." James H. Price to Fontaine Johnson, August 24, 1937, Price MSS, Box 1.

13. W. Anderson, *Wild Man*, 118, 117, 134.

14. Elliott and D'Orso, *Cost of Courage*, 118; D. L. Grant, *Way It Was*, 351; John Gunther, *Inside U.S.A.* (New York, 1947), 777; Sarah McCulloh Lemmon, "Governor Eugene Talmadge and the New Deal," in *Studies in Southern History*, ed. J. Carlyle Sitterson (Chapel Hill, N.C., 1957), 158–63; *New York Times*, September 29, 1935. Talmadge's attitude reflected a strong antimetropolis sentiment. He would tell rural voters, "Come see me at the mansion after I'm elected, and we'll set on the front porch and piss over the rail at them city bastards." *Time*, September 27, 1976, 46.

15. Lemmon, "Governor Eugene Talmadge," 154; W. Anderson, *Wild Man*, 103; Jane Walker Herndon, "Ed Rivers and Georgia's 'Little New Deal,'" *Atlanta Historical Journal* 30 (1986): 98. See, too, Allen Lumpkin Henson, *Red Galluses: A Story of Georgia Politics* (Boston, 1945), 266. Henson offers an altogether unpersuasive defense of Talmadge. In 1936, Talmadge called the Warm Springs Foundation "a racket, being disguised under the name of charity, by the President of the United States." Wolfskill and Hudson, *All But the People*, 14.

16. Michael S. Holmes, *The New Deal in Georgia: An Administrative History* (Westport, Conn., 1975), 85, 235; Richard Hyatt, *Zell: The Governor Who Gave Georgia HOPE* (Macon, Ga., 1997), 253.

17. Rufus Jarman, "Wool-Hat Dictator," *Saturday Evening Post*, June 27, 1942, 112; *Congressional Intelligence*, February 4, 1936, Louis Brandeis MSS, Reel 51; Anderson, *Wild Man*, 138; Schlesinger, *Politics of Upheaval*, 522; George Norris Green, *The Establishment in Texas Politics: The Primitive Years, 1938–1957* (Westport, Conn., 1979), 59. The meeting had been touted as, in the words of *News-Week*, "the hottest battle for Democratic principles since shells plopped on Fort Sumter!" But, in fact, Macon's Municipal Auditorium was only half-filled, and the turnout of delegates fell far short of what had been promised. Furthermore, straw vote surveys showed that the citizens of Macon approved of FDR by a whopping 5–2. *News-Week*, February 8, 1936, 11–13.

18. Gore, *Let the Glory Out*, 62; Clayton Rand, *Ink on My Hands* (New York, 1940), 345; Wolfskill

and Hudson, *All But the People,* 257; L. Reed, *Simple Decency,* 53; Morrison, *Governor O. Max Gardner,* 176. One historian has seen 1937 as the year that South Carolina turned against the New Deal. J. I. Hayes, "South Carolina and New Deal," 139. For further evidence of rising hostility, see Lawrence J. Nelson, "New Deal and Free Market: The Memphis Meeting of the Southern Commissioners of Agriculture, 1937," *Journal of Southern History* 40 (1981): 225–38; Lee J. Alston and Joseph P. Ferrie, "Resisting the Welfare State: Southern Opposition to the Farm Security Administration," *Research in Economic History 1985* (Supplement 4): 83–120; "The Truth about the Coalition Manifesto," Arthur Vandenberg MSS, Vol. 10; Frank Gannett to Louis J. Taber, October 20, 1937, Gannett MSS, Box 16. When Coke Stevenson, who would later be governor of Texas, received a copy of *Roosevelt's Red Record,* he responded that it was "an excellent publication." Patenaude, *Texans, Politics and New Deal,* 113.

19. *Fayette-Chronicle,* September 28, 1937, in *The Attitude of the Southern White Press Toward Negro Suffrage, 1932–1940,* ed. Rayford W. Logan (Washington, D.C., 1940), 37; James T. Patterson, *Congressional Conservatism and the New Deal: The Growth of the Conservative Coalition in Congress, 1933–1939* (Lexington, Ky., 1967), 257; Miller, "Palmetto Politician," 292. In November 1937 the former Republican senator from New Hampshire, George Moses, wrote Glass: "You and I have often discussed realignment but you have always raised the color question. This condition no longer exists. Jim Farley and the Roosevelt largess have made the colored vote in the North impregnably Democratic. Therefore, with the color line obliterated, why cannot those of us who are free, white and twenty-one get together and do a job as effective as Mussolini did when he made his march upon Rome?" James T. Patterson, "The Failure of Party Realignment in the South, 1937–1939," *Journal of Politics* 27 (1965): 605.

20. Josiah W. Bailey to R. G. Cherry, March 1, 1938, Cherry MSS, Personal Papers, Box 104; Strobel, "FDR," 32; J. B. Cranfill to Bailey, March 17, 1938, Bailey MSS, Box 476.

21. Josiah W. Bailey to H. G. Gulley, May 25, 1938; Bailey to Harry Byrd, June 27, 1938, Bailey MSS, Box 476. In his letter to Gulley, Bailey not only badly misspelled the name of Tommy Corcoran, but could not even get straight the name of the NAACP, which Walter White headed. Robert Vann was a prominent black editor and politician in Pennsylvania.

22. Schulman, *From Cotton Belt,* 57–58. Gore, *Let the Glory Out,* 57; John Ray Skates, "From Enchantment to Disillusionment: A Southern Editor Views the New Deal," *Southern Quarterly* 5 (1967): 377; Leon C. Phillips, "A Southern Democrat Renounces the New Deal Party," *Manufacturers' Record* 112 (August 1943): 32–33, 60; Polenberg, "Decline of New Deal," 253; James A. Farley to Claude Bowers, July 30, 1937, Bowers MSS 2; Swain, *Pat Harrison,* 164; Schulman, *From Cotton Belt,* 55. See, too, Charles A. Fell to Dear Sir, n.d. [September 1937], Chauncey Sparks MSS, Box 2; J. L. Camp Jr. to Allard H. Gasque, June 25, 1937, Gasque MSS, Box 5.

23. James F. Byrnes OH, Robert D. Graff MSS, Box 3; Byrnes, *All in One Lifetime,* 103; Chandler, *Natural Superiority,* 326; Vance Johnson, "The Old Deal Democrats," *American Mercury* 59 (1944): 51, 57. See, too, Marvin Jones OH, 11, Richard B. Russell MSS. Relations between the president and Senator George never warmed beyond a chilly formality. When Roosevelt needed George's support for the lend-lease bill in 1941, the question arose of whether George would go to the White House if FDR bade him to come. George remarked, "When Franklin Roosevelt sends for Walter George, I shall not go; when the President of the United States sends for the Chairman

of the Senate Committee on Foreign Relations, I shall go." Selma Borchardt to Ralph McGill, March 12, 1948; Walter George to McGill, April 3, 1948, McGill MSS, Series 2, Box 3. Early in 1939, the U.S. Senate spiked Roosevelt's efforts to undercut the Byrd machine in Virginia by rejecting one of his nominees for the very first time and by the largest margin for turning down a presidential nomination in the history of the republic. Koeniger, "New Deal and the States," 890; Alvin L. Hall "Politics and Patronage: Virginia's Senators and the Roosevelt Purges of 1938," *Virginia Magazine of History and Biography* 82 (1974): 345. Chastened by his experience in the purge campaigns, Roosevelt pulled back. When Pat Harrison scolded him for supporting the suffrage reformers in Arkansas, the president replied, "At no time and in no manner did I even suggest federal legislation of any kind to deprive states of their rights directly or indirectly to impose the poll tax," and the following year he rejected a plea to assist a repeal movement in Tennessee because, he claimed, he made it a practice of not intervening "in campaigns on state issues." S. F. Lawson, *Black Ballots,* 57. Yet in a radio message from the White House in the fall of 1944 Roosevelt was still urging abolition of all restrictions on the right to vote. Neil A. Wynn, *The Afro-American and the Second World War* (New York, 1976), 113.

24. James R. Sweeney, "'Sheep without a Shepherd': The New Deal Faction in the Virginia Democratic Party," *Presidential Studies Quarterly* 29 (1999): 451; John Connally, with Mickey Herskowitz, *In History's Shadow: An American Odyssey* (New York, 1993), 76–77. See, too, Jonathan James Wolfe, "Virginia in World War II" (Ph.D. dissertation, University of Virginia, 1971), 24; Francis Earle Lutz, *Richmond in World War II* (Richmond, Va., 1951), 342. James A. Farley drew some southern backing in seeking to take the nomination away from his former chief. An Illinois congressman told the president "that Jim is being misled by some of the Southern gentlemen." Adolph J. Sabath MS. Autobiography, Sabath MSS.

25. G. N. Green, *Establishment in Texas Politics,* 29–30; Bernard F. Donahoe, *Private Plans and Public Dangers* (Notre Dame, Ind., 1965), 183; Hollis, "'Cotton Ed Smith,'" 255; J. B. Shannon, "Presidential Politics in the South," *Journal of Politics* 10 (1948): 473. Of the eight leading newspapers in Tennessee, only one backed Roosevelt in 1940. Thomas E. Coode, "The Presidential Election of 1940 as Reflected in the Tennessee Metropolitan Press," *East Tennessee Historical Society's Publications* 40 (1968): 83.

26. Sam H. Jones, "Will Dixie Bolt the New Deal?" *Saturday Evening Post,* March 6, 1943, 20–21, 42, 45; V. Johnson, "Old Deal Democrats," 50. The head of the Washington bureau of the *Nashville Tennessean* responded to Jones's article by pointing out that it was not the governor's business allies but New Dealers who had led the fight to end freight rate discrimination. He noted that a TVA study published in 1937 had first focused attention on the problem; that "a Roosevelt-appointed Interstate Commerce Commission" had begun to redress grievances in 1939; and "a New Deal congress" had enacted the 1940 law barring discrimination in rate-setting. *Nashville Tennessean,* March 13, 1943, clipping, Sam H. Jones MSS. See, too, Paul C. Light, *The President's Agenda: Domestic Policy Choice from Kennedy to Reagan,* rev. ed. (Baltimore, 1991), 119.

27. Tindall, *Emergence,* 707; A. B. Moore, "One Hundred Years of Reconstruction in the South," *Journal of Southern History* 9 (1943): 161; Carroll Kilpatrick, "Will the South Secede?" *Harper's* 186 (1943): 419; Arthur J. Kaul, "Hazel Brannon Smith and the *Lexington Advertiser,*" in *The Press and Race: Mississippi Journalists Confront the Movement,* ed. David R. Davies (Jackson, Miss., 2001), 237.

See, too, C. Calvin Smith, *War and Wartime Changes: The Transformation of Arkansas, 1940–1945* (Fayetteville, Ark., 1986), 79; *Union Republican*, June 10, 1943, cited in Jonathan Houghton (draft, Ph.D. dissertation on Republican Party in North Carolina, University of North Carolina at Chapel Hill). For resentment at the hiring of blacks in formerly whites-only jobs in cotton mills, see "Pittsylvania County Virginia Racial Tensions," Jonathan W. Daniels MSS, Folder 426a.

28. *Smith v. Allwright*, 321 U.S. 649 (1944); Peter Molyneaux, *The South's Political Plight* (Dallas, Tex., 1948), 8–9; C. Calvin Smith, "The Politics of Evasion: Arkansas' Reaction to *Smith v. Allwright*, 1944," *Journal of Negro History* 67 (1982): 45, 47–48. See, too, John L. McClellan to Mr. and Mrs. John A. Lipton, April 4, 1944, McClellan MSS, File 175, Drawer A. The Molyneaux book was published by the Calhoun Clubs of the South. After the 1942 midterm elections, which dealt a severe blow to the administration, Ed Pauley, secretary of the Democratic National Committee, reported to the White House: "The Southern Democrats generally are extremely bitter concerning the fact that the so-called poll tax legislation was brought to the floor. The situation is most explosive in Mississippi and Louisiana, but it is deep . . . everywhere in the South." Edwin W. Pauley to Grace Tully, December 14, 1942, FDRL OF 300. See, too, Gould Lincoln, "The Political Mill," *Ohio State Journal*, April 14, 1944, John Daniel Zook MSS, Box 2.

29. James A. Nuechterlein, "The Politics of Civil Rights: The FEPC, 1941–46," *Prologue* 10 (1978): 183–84.

30. E. H. Crump to Kenneth McKellar, March 2, 1942, McKellar MSS; Ellett Lawrence in *Pages* (June–July 1943): 1, published in Greenwood, Mississippi; James C. Cobb, *The Most Southern Place on Earth: The Mississippi Delta and the Roots of Regional Identity* (New York, 1992), 202; E. J. Thornhill to Burnet R. Maybank, August 14, 1942, Maybank MSS; Kennedy, *Southern Exposure*, 86. When Jonathan Daniels went to work at the White House, his brother instructed him to "tell Papa to keep Mama at home" and silent on racial questions. Eagles, *Jonathan Daniels and Race Relations*, 95. Jonathan Daniels himself later recalled: "Right in the middle of the war . . . she wanted me to go down to Atlanta and take the 'white' and 'colored' signs off the restrooms." He ignored her because if her instruction had been carried out "I would've raised such a stink as never was." Daniels ER OH, 48. In the spring of 1944, Byrnes relayed to a confidant that he had said to FDR: "Some time ago I told you, Mr. President, it would be a good thing if you could keep your wife from talking on the negro question until the convention. Her speech in Baltimore is hurting some of your friends who are trying to help." According to Byrnes, the president responded: "You know, Mrs. Roosevelt just does not understand the South. I have spent a lot of time there in my life, and I appreciate the problems of the people there, but life is too short to try to get Mrs. Roosevelt to see them." Walter J. Brown, *James F. Byrnes of South Carolina: A Remembrance* (Macon, Ga., 1992), 183.

31. *Richmond Times-Dispatch*, August 12, 1942, clipping, Thomas R. Waring Jr., MSS; Howard W. Odum, *Race and Rumors of Race: Challenge to American Crisis* (Chapel Hill, N.C., 1943), 73–81, 87; R. Phillip Stone II, "A Battle for Their Rights: Race and Reaction in South Carolina, 1940–1945," *Proceedings of the South Carolina Historical Association 1999*, 37; Junius L. Allison to Howard W. Odum, December 4, 1942, Odum MSS, Box 58; Timothy B. Tyson, *Radio Free Dixie: Robert F. Williams and the Roots of Black Power* (Chapel Hill, N.C., 1999), 31–32. For a report of Eleanor Clubs in Pensacola, see Harley Cobb to University of Florida, February 2, 1943, Odum MSS, Box 58. See,

too, Sandra K. Behel, "The Mississippi Home Front during World War II: Tradition and Change" (Ph.D. dissertation, Mississippi State University, 1989), 107–8.

32. Robert A. Hill, ed., *The FBI's RACON: Racial Conditions in the United States during World War II* (Boston, 1995), 289, 56; Odum, *Race,* 87. Ralph McGill reported on a woman "outraged because her cook, who had worked for twenty years at wages from three to five dollars a week, quit and 'just sat on her porch and rocked' when her two sons went into the army and began sending home allotment checks." Ralph McGill, *The South and the Southerner* (Boston, 1963), 170.

33. Virginius Dabney to John Temple Graves, June 13, 1942, Dabney MSS 7690a, Box 7; Emile B. Ader, *The Dixiecrat Movement: Its Role in Third Party Politics* (Washington, D.C., 1955), 9.

34. L. L. Martin to Frank C. Walker, December 11, 1943; Jesse Taylor to Frank C. Walker, November 23, 1943, Democratic National Committee Papers, Box 1157; G. N. Green, *Establishment in Texas Politics,* 50–51.

35. Selden Menefee, *Assignment: U.S.A.* (New York, 1943), 44–45; Gunther, *Inside U.S.A.,* 845; David L. Cohn, "How the South Feels," *Atlantic Monthly* 173 (1944): 49.

36. Roger Biles, *Memphis in the Great Depression* (Knoxville, Tenn., 1986), 82; R. A. Garson, *Democratic Party,* 92, 104–5. In 1944 the Ku Klux Klan distributed a cartoon in which the president was depicted saying to his wife: "You kiss the niggers, and I'll kiss the Jews, / And we'll stay in the White House as long as we choose." FDR had the last word, though. Pressed by the Bureau of Internal Revenue's agent in Atlanta in 1944 to pay back taxes, the KKK disbanded. The Imperial Wizard, asked to account for the downfall of the Order, said, "It was that nigger-lover Roosevelt and that Jew Morgenthau who was his Secretary of the Treasury who did it!" Wyn Craig Wade, *The Fiery Cross: The Ku Klux Klan in America* (New York, 1986), 275.

37. *Washington Times-Herald,* June 10, 1944, clipping, Theodore G. Bilbo MSS, Box 1012; Paul G. Borron to Governor Sam Jones, July 20, 1944, Sam H. Jones MSS. The restlessness of southern Democrats in 1944 caused party leaders considerable concern. For the attitude of the North Dakota Democratic national committeeman, see D. G. Kelly to J. F. T. O'Connor, February 1, 1944, O'Connor MSS, Vol. 20. In June 1944, the Alabama party chairman circularized the members of the State Democratic Executive Committee with a memo saying that, given the strain under which Roosevelt was laboring, it was imperative for the Democratic national convention to nominate "some strong, outstanding Southern man" for vice president. In addition, "our Delegates should fight hard for the restoration of the Two-Thirds Rule." Gessner T. McCorvey to The Members of the State Democratic Executive Committee of Alabama, June 24, 1944, in Sam H. Jones MSS.

38. Forrest Davis, "The Fourth Term's Hair Shirt," *Saturday Evening Post,* April 8, 1944, 9; Carter Glass to Harry F. Byrd, August 30, 1935, Glass MSS, Box 341; Frank R. Kent, "Roosevelt's Bid for Dictatorship," *American Mercury* 43 (1938): 405; Harry Flood Byrd Jr. to Virginius Dabney, November 21, 1944, Dabney MSS, Box 5; J. J. Kramer to Sam Houston Jones, May 13, 1944, Jones MSS. FDR's press secretary was so excited by a report toward the end of the 1944 campaign that Glass favored the president's reelection that he phoned the Virginia senator to find out if it was true. When in a voice that was barely audible Glass confirmed the statement, his wife broke in to say "he is voting for the President," then instructed the senator, "Tell him loud." "Yes," Glass said more forcefully. Memorandum from Walter Brown to Steve Early, October 31, 1944; telephone conver-

sation between Senator Carter Glass and Mr. Stephen T. Early, November 3, 1944, Early MSS, Box 6. Byrd declined to speak for Roosevelt in 1944 because, he said, he was too busy harvesting apples.

39. Independent party materials in Sam H. Jones MSS; Sam M. Johnston to Gessner T. McCorvey, August 30, 1944, in Sam H. Jones MSS. In the spring of 1943, Alabama Governor Frank M. Dixon had reported that "the governors who attended were, to a man, opposed to a fourth term." Frank M. Dixon to Lloyd C. Griscom, March 29, 1943, Dixon MSS, Box 1. In 1942 Governor Dixon had refused to sign a contract to furnish war materiel to the federal government because the agreement contained a nondiscrimination clause. Clark Foreman, "Race Tension in the South," *New Republic,* September 21, 1942, 340.

40. W. I. Brown, *Byrnes,* 191, 197; Lander, *History of South Carolina,* 175; *Charleston News and Courier,* July 10, 1944.

41. "Cosmopolitan Provincial: The Delta and the World According to David L. Cohn," manuscript of an autobiography edited by James C. Cobb; Weaver E. Gore OH; Roy H. Ruby, "The Presidential Election of 1944 in Mississippi: The Bolting Electors" (M.A. essay, Mississippi State University, 1966); Thomas Sancton, "White Supremacy—Crisis or Plot?" *Nation,* July 31, 1948, 126; "Memorandum of Telephone Conversation with F.D.R. on Tuesday, July 18, 1944," James F. Byrnes MSS, Folder 7; F. E. Smith, *Congressman from Mississippi,* 75; Sarah F. Ratliff, "The Career of Thomas Lowry Bailey" (M.S. essay, Mississippi State College, 1952), 56–62. See, too, Frank E. Smith OH, 33. I am indebted to Professor Cobb for sending pertinent excerpts of the Cohn memoir to me.

42. Frank Goodwyn, *Lone-Star Land: Twentieth-Century Texas in Perspective* (New York, 1955), 252; Gunther, *Inside U.S.A.,* 844.

43. G. N. Green, *Establishment in Texas Politics,* 45–52; Alvin J. Wirtz to Harold L. Ickes, May 25, 1944, copy in Eleanor Bontecou MSS, Box 3; George A. Butler, "To Southern Democrats," February 14, 1944, in Sam H. Jones MSS; *Time,* June 5, 1944, 21–22; Charles W. Stephenson, "The Democrats of Texas and Texas Liberalism, 1944–1960: A Study in Political Frustration" (M.A. essay, Southwest Texas State College, 1967), 2–3; D. B. Hardeman and Donald C. Bacon, *Rayburn: A Biography* (Austin, Tex., 1987), 296; George N. Green, "The Far Right Wing in Texas Politics, 1930s–1960s" (Ph.D. dissertation, Florida State University, 1966), 50; Connally, *In History's Shadow,* 112. In commenting on these developments in Texas, one scholar has asserted that "the southern states' rights movement, heavily financed by oil and electric power, from its inception has been a creature of the northern financial groups whose colonial empire the South has been." Robert Engler, *The Politics of Oil* (New York, 1961), 354.

44. Seth Shepard McKay, *Texas Politics, 1906–1944: With Special Reference to the German Counties* (Lubbock, Tex., 1952), 434–35, 438, 457; William Jean Tolleson, "The Rift in the Texas Democratic Party, 1944" (M.A. essay, University of Texas, 1953), 35–42, 118–19; Goodwyn, *Lone-Star Land,* 281; Jonathan Daniels MS. Diary, June 13, 1944. New Dealers did not trust the imperious banker, who was called "Jesus Jones." See, too, Coke R. Stevenson OH, 117. The struggle on behalf of FDR had an enduring effect. "It was the first time that we even got to know who the other liberals were," one of the leaders later said. "That was the beginning of the modern Texas liberal movement." Chandler Davidson, *Race and Class in Texas Politics* (Princeton, N.J., 1990), 159. On the other hand, nearly a quarter of a century later a onetime Texas governor said, "The Democratic Party of Texas

has never *fully* recovered from that split that began in 1944." Price Daniel OH, University of North Texas. The interview took place in 1967.

45. Walter Chandler to Lem Tate Sr., October 30, 1944, Chandler MSS; Robert Edward Ficken, "The Democratic Party and Domestic Politics during World War II" (Ph.D. dissertation, University of Washington, 1973), 130; W. D. Miller, *Mr. Crump,* 305; Allen Drury, *A Senate Journal, 1943–1945* (New York, 1963), 281; W. D. Workman Jr., *The Bishop from Barnwell: The Political Life and Times of Senator Edgar A. Brown* (Columbia, S.C., 1963), 134, 313. See, too, Burnet R. Maybank to W. J. Cormack, April 21, 1944, Maybank MSS. Subduing bifactionalism in Louisiana in quadrennial elections, "the force of Franklin Roosevelt's personality overrode all other concerns in presidential politics," one scholar has written. "No matter how far apart reformers and Longites stood on various other issues, they found common ground in their general support of Roosevelt's presidential campaigns." Jerry Purvis Sanson, *Louisiana during World War II* (Baton Rouge, La., 1999), 34. See, too, Martin A. Hutchinson to L. M. Robinette, May 26, 1944, Hutchinson MSS, Box 6; Josephus Daniels, *Shirt-Sleeve Diplomat* (Chapel Hill, N.C., 1947), 465.

46. John Temple Graves, "This Morning," November 11, 1944, clipping, Chauncey Sparks MSS, Scrapbook 8; R. A. Garson, *Democratic Party,* 113. The Democratic candidate for governor of North Carolina responded to a heckler who criticized him for backing FDR: "I would rather support a first-rate man for the fourth term than a fourth-rate man for a first term." Quoted in Frank Porter Graham to FDR, November 3, 1944, FDRL PPF 530.

47. J. Oliver Emmerich, *Two Faces of Janus: The Saga of Deep South Change* (Jackson, Miss., 1973), 77; Theodore G. Bilbo to Edward A. Keeler, June 11, 1944; Bilbo to Walter Lowenthal, June 7, 1944, Bilbo MSS, Box 1114. John Bricker of Ohio was the Republican vice presidential candidate in 1944. In the 1946 filibuster against an FEPC bill, Bilbo denied that FDR favored such a measure and criticized those who sought to link the late president to it. Robert J. Bailey, "Theodore G. Bilbo and the Fair Employment Practices Controversy: A Southern Senator's Reaction to a Changing World," *Journal of Mississippi History* 42 (1980): 39. Bilbo's detestation of Eleanor Roosevelt never abated. "No man in American history deserved more honor than Franklin D. Roosevelt," he later told his colleagues, but he had hoped that when FDR died, his wife, after more than twelve years of trying to run the government, would finally be content to "keep her proboscis out of controversial questions." He added, "If this good woman had given one-half of the attention to the rearing and directing of the lives and affairs of her brood that she has given trying to force recognition and social equality for the Negro in America, she would not today be embarrassed with headline stories about some of her off-spring." Statement, n.d., Theodore G. Bilbo MSS, Box 1095.

48. George Rothwell Brown, "The Political Parade," *New York Journal-American,* November 14, 1944, clipping, Sam H. Jones MSS; John U. Barr to L. D. Nuchols, November 20, 1944, in Sam H. Jones MSS; H. G. Nicholas, ed., *Washington Despatches, 1941–1945: Weekly Political Reports from the British Embassy* (Chicago, 1981), 456. The account was quite likely written by Isaiah Berlin. A short while later, the young historian Richard Hofstadter went so far as to say of the situation in 1944: "The state of ideological tension in the party was even stronger than in 1860." Hofstadter, "From Calhoun to the Dixiecrats," *Social Research* 16 (1949): 143.

49. McIntire, *White House Physician,* 240; Michael F. Reilly as told to William J. Slocum, *Reilly of the White House* (New York, 1947), 225–28; James MacGregor Burns, *Roosevelt: The Soldier of Free-*

dom, 1940–1945 (New York, 1970), 599; Margaret Suckley MS. Diary, March 31—April 12, 1945; Robert H. Ferrell, *The Dying President: Franklin D. Roosevelt, 1944–1945* (Columbia, Mo., 1998), 117; Elizabeth Shoumatoff, "FDR: The Last Photo," *American Heritage* 38 (1987): 103; William D. Hassett, *Off the Record with F.D.R., 1942–1945* (New Brunswick, N.J., 1958), 333.

50. Bernard Asbell, *When F.D.R. Died* (London, 1962), 179; Kathryn W. Kemp, "Warm Springs Recollections from the Graham Jackson Papers," *Atlanta Historical Journal* 29 (1985): 68–69.

51. George W. Andrews OH, 20; A. Merriman Smith, *Thank You, Mr. President: A White House Notebook* (New York, 1946), 194–95.

52. *Buffalo News,* April 14, 1935.

53. Drury, *Senate Journal,* 141.

54. Gore, *Let the Glory Out,* 65; Robert S. McElvaine, *The Great Depression: America, 1929–1941* (New York, 1984), 116.

55. F. E. Smith, *Congressman from Mississippi,* 39; Ben Beagle and Ozzie Osborne, *J. Lindsay Almond: Virginia's Reluctant Rebel* (Roanoke, Va., 1984), 127; Sherrill, *Gothic Politics,* 18; Hardeman and Bacon, *Rayburn,* 309.

56. Samuel Lubell, *White and Black: Test of a Nation* (New York , 1964), 67–68.

5. BORDER-STATE DEMOCRAT

1. HST to Margaret Truman, November 10, 1941, in *Letters from Father,* ed. Margaret Truman (South Yarmouth, Mass., 1981), 49–50.

2. Merle Miller, *Plain Speaking: An Oral History of Harry S. Truman* (New York, 1974), 59; "My Most Interesting Ancestor" and "The Truman Family," Mary Ethel Noland MSS, Box 5; Bennett Roach, "President Truman's Whistle Stop Here 40 Years Ago," *Shelbyville Sentinel-News,* September 28, 1988, clipping, Truman Family Genealogy HSTL; Bailey Fulton Davis Sr., "President Truman's Ancestors in Kentucky," Truman Family Genealogy, HSTL; Franklin D. Mitchell, "The Southern Confederate Heritage of Harry S. Truman"; Jonathan Daniels, *The Man of Independence* (Philadelphia, 1950), 34.

3. Research notes used in connection with writing *The Man of Independence,* Jonathan Daniels MSS, HSTL, 4: 197; James I. Loeb HSTL OH, 73; F. D. Mitchell, "Southern Confederate Heritage"; David McCullough, *Truman* (New York, 1992), 53. M. Miller, *Plain Speaking,* 75–76.

4. Albert Castel, "The Bloodiest Man in American History," *American Heritage* 11 (1960): 22–24, 97–99. "To most slaveholders Quantrill was a hero and in memory, in after years in Jackson County, he would acquire a romantic glow, an aura like that of no other figure of the war, as if he had been the very soul of Old South gallantry in service of the Cause," David McCullough has written. "In reality, he came from Ohio. Nor had he ever shown any southern sympathies or convictions, until the killing began." McCullough, *Truman,* 23. The border war, he adds, "was like some horrible chapter out of the Middle Ages, with gangs of brigand horsemen roaming the land." Ibid., 27.

5. Bert Cochran, *Harry Truman and the Crisis Presidency* (New York, 1973), 24; M. Miller, *Plain Speaking,* 62; Robert Underhill, *The Truman Persuasions* (Ames, Iowa, 1948), 17; Margaret Truman, *Harry S Truman* (London, 1973), 49–50. McCullough raises some doubts about Grandmother Truman's account of Lane's raid. McCullough, *Truman,* 30–31.

6. F. D. Mitchell, "Southern Confederate Heritage"; M. Miller, *Plain Speaking,* 78; B. Cochran, *Harry Truman,* 24. After the war, George Caleb Bingham, though a steadfast Unionist, painted *Order No. 11* in protest.

7. M. Miller, *Plain Speaking,* 74–75; F. D. Mitchell, "Southern Confederate Heritage."

8. M. Truman, *Harry S Truman,* 45; Tom C. Clark HSTL OH (Jerry N. Hess interview), 12–13; Alonzo L. Hamby, "The Mind and Character of Harry S. Truman," in *The Truman Presidency,* ed. Michael J. Lacey (Cambridge, 1984), 22; "President Truman calling from Key West, Florida," March 10, 1951, notes and transcripts of Johnson conversations, LBJ MSS, LBJL.

9. Hamby, "Mind and Character," in *Truman Presidency,* ed. Lacey, 23; M. Truman, *Harry S Truman,* 49; Mary Martha Truman to Nancy Bentley, May 10, 1883, Bentley MSS, Box 1; Robert H. Ferrell, ed., *The Autobiography of Harry S. Truman* (Boulder, Colo., 1980), 28; M. Miller, *Plain Speaking,* 46.

10. Clark Clifford, with Richard Holbrooke, *Counsel to the President: A Memoir* (New York, 1991), 73; B. Cochran, *Harry Truman,* 24–25; Alonzo Fields, *My 21 Years in the White House* (New York, 1961), 127; Capus Miller Waynick MS. Diary, June 1949. There is more than one version of the Lincoln bed story. A Texas congressman once remarked that Truman's mother "was one of these old-time Southern-supremacy individuals and was inclined to speak out quite freely. And she was very much against much of the reform that Mr. Truman later supported." W. R. Poage OH, 814–15.

11. F. D. Mitchell, "Southern Confederate Heritage"; Edward T. Folliard HSTL OH, 16; M. Miller, *Plain Speaking,* 408.

12. *Memoirs by Harry S. Truman,* 2 vols. (Garden City, N.Y., 1955–56), 2: 184; Jonathan Daniels COHC, 133; J. F. Martin, *Civil Rights and the Crisis of Liberalism,* 91; McCullough, *Truman,* 29, 33–34; research notes used in connection with writing *The Man of Independence,* part 1, Jonathan Daniels MSS, HSTL. Jim Crow Chiles apparently got his name not from his racist behavior but from a country dance that he carried off with abandon. In later years, Truman had an idealized view of race relations in his childhood. He wrote, "No color line was drawn. Nearly every family had a negro cook and a yard man, who was a negro. . . . Their children played with the white children and there was no color line." "Early 1900's and Late 1890's," handwritten memo, n.d., HSTL Harry S. Truman's Personal Notes Desk File.

13. Richard Kirkendall, "Truman and the South"; F. D. Mitchell, "Southern Confederate Heritage"; William E. Pemberton, *Harry S. Truman: Fair Dealer and Cold Warrior* (Boston, 1989), 113; Monte M. Poen, ed., *Letters Home by Harry Truman* (New York, 1984), 106; *Kansas City Star,* April 10, 1983; Richard Lawrence Miller, *Truman: The Rise to Power* (New York, 1985), 325; Alonzo L. Hamby, "'The Modest and Capable Western Statesman': Harry S. Truman in the United States Senate, 1935–1940," *Congress and the Presidency* 17 (1990): 115.

14. F. D. Mitchell, "Southern Confederate Heritage"; Kari Frederickson, "'The Slowest State' and 'Most Backward Community': Racial Violence in South Carolina and Federal Civil-Rights Legislation, 1946–1948," *South Carolina Historical Magazine* 98 (1997): 178; James Giglio, "Harry S. Truman and the Multifarious Ex-Presidency," *Presidential Studies Quarterly* 12 (1982): 251. The identification of Truman with the South was widespread. In a secret message to Molotov in 1944, Andrei Gromyko characterized him as a "Southern Democrat." Gromyko to V. M. Molotov, July 24, 1944, Molotov MSS, Archives of Russian Foreign Policy (courtesy of Vladimir Pechatnov).

15. Robert J. Donovan, *Conflict and Crisis: The Presidency of Harry S. Truman, 1945–1948* (New York, 1977), 31; Robert H. Ferrell, ed., *Truman in the White House: The Diary of Eben A. Ayers* (Columbia, Mo., 1991), 88–89, 145; Curtis D. MacDougall, *Gideon's Army* (New York, 1965), 388; McCullough, *Truman,* 110. He was even capable of referring to his haberdashery partner, Eddie Jacobson, as a "Jew clerk" and apparently never invited him to his home. *Kansas City Star,* April 10, 1983. In the 1944 campaign, at a restaurant in San Francisco's Chinatown, Truman allegedly said, "Those Chinese are wonderful, they are the only colored people I trust." Robert W. Kenny, "My First Forty Years in California Politics, 1922–1962," Kenny MSS (courtesy of John D. Weaver). According to another account, Truman, when asked to pose for pictures with black politicians in Minneapolis in 1944, said, "Well now, I have no objection to having my picture taken with a nigger, but you know, I was put on this ticket to sort of offset Roosevelt in some ways." This episode may have happened, but the story is suspect for it comes from a leftwing politician hostile to Truman and was reported in a book by a supporter of Truman's opponent in the 1948 campaign, Henry Wallace. MacDougall, *Gideon's Army,* 387–88.

16. John Thomas Truman to Anderson Shipp Truman, February 1, 1860, October 8, 1861, Truman Family Letters, Box 1.

17. John T. Truman to Anderson Shipp Truman, September 19, 1864; Edmund Armstead Truman to Anderson Shipp Truman, November 4, 1860, Truman Family Letters, Box 1.

18. M. Truman, *Harry S Truman,* 392.

19. Josiah Gregg, *Commerce of the Prairies,* ed. Max L. Moorhead (Norman, Okla., 1954), 23; Paul C. Nagel, *Missouri: A Bicentennial History* (New York, 1977), 6, 10; Alonzo Hamby, "The Temperament of Harry S. Truman: An Interview with Alonzo Hamby," *The Woodrow Wilson Center Report* 4 (1992): 12.

20. Robert H. Ferrell, ed., *Dear Bess: The Letters from Harry to Bess Truman, 1910–1959* (New York, 1983), 324–25; Richard Kirkendall, "Truman and Missouri," *Missouri Historical Review* 81 (1987): 140; Robert H. Ferrell, *Truman and Pendergast* (Columbia, Mo., 1999), 33.

21. Paul Nafe and Grace Clayton Banta, "Truman's Kentucky Background," *Louisville Courier-Journal,* June 3, 1945, Truman Family Genealogy, HSTL; Harold Gosnell MS., Chapter 1, 23, Gosnell MSS, Box 1. Truman's cousin said that "the scalping story was a myth." "My Most Interesting Ancestor," Mary Ethel Noland MSS, Box 5.

22. Bernard De Voto, *Year of Decision, 1846* (Boston, 1943); research notes used in connection with writing *The Man of Independence,* part 1, Jonathan Daniels MSS, HSTL; Daniels, *Man of Independence,* 40.

23. Richard L. Strout HSTL OH, 21–23; M. Miller, *Plain Speaking,* 65.

24. M. Truman, *Harry S Truman,* 22; Jonathan Daniels HSTL OH, 77; Lilienthal, *Journals,* 2: 433–34; A. G. Mezerik, *The Revolt of the South and the West* (New York, 1946), 198; Underhill, *Truman Persuasions,* 14; George E. Allen, *Presidents Who Have Known Me* (New York, 1950), 126, 136, 167. Truman himself once wrote of his childhood "in the country districts of the middle west." "Early 1900's and late 1890's," handwritten memo, n.d., HSTL Harry S. Truman's Personal Notes Desk File. As a vice presidential nominee in 1944, Truman, a historian has noted, was "perceived as a midwestern New Dealer." After his nomination, though, Truman described himself as a "pro-

gressive Southerner," one who was "not interested one whit in questions of 'white supremacy.'" Gary A. Donaldson, *Truman Defeats Dewey* (Lexington, Ky., 1998), 236.

25. John Morton Blum, *V Was for Victory: Politics and American Culture during World War II* (New York, 1976), 290; Alonzo L. Hamby, "Harry S. Truman," in *The American Presidents*, ed. Melvin I. Urofsky (New York, 2000), 359; Kirkendall, "Truman and Missouri," 128; Kirkendall, "Truman's Path to Power," *Social Science* 43 (1968): 69; Albert Edmund Trombly, "Little Dixie," quoted in Lawrence O. Christensen, "Missouri: The Heart of the Nation," in *Heartland: Comparative Histories of the Midwestern States*, ed. James H. Madison (Bloomington, Ind., 1988), 90; Robert M. Crisler, "The Regional Status of Little Dixie in Missouri and Little Egypt in Illinois," *Journal of Geography* 49 (1950): 337–43; Christensen, "Missouri," 89; James Q. Wilson, quoted in J. Christopher Schnell, Richard J. Collings, and David W. Dillard, "The Political Impact of the Depression on Missouri, 1929–1940," *Missouri Historical Review* 85 (1991): 131.

26. Larry Grothaus, "Kansas City Blacks, Harry Truman and the Pendergast Machine," *Missouri Historical Review* 69 (1974): 72, 82; Thomas D. Wilson, "Chester A. Franklin and Harry S. Truman: An African-American Conservative and the 'Conversion' of the Future President," *Missouri Historical Review* 88 (1993): 58; Larry Henry Grothaus, "The Negro in Missouri Politics, 1890–1941" (Ph.D. dissertation, University of Missouri-Columbia, 1970), 145.

27. Wilson, "Chester A. Franklin," 60–61; Wilkins with Mathews, *Standing Fast,* 193; Harold F. Gosnell, *Truman's Crises: A Political Biography of Harry S. Truman* (Westport, Conn., 1980), 108. See, too, Hamby, "Mind and Character," in *Truman Presidency,* ed. Lacey, 30–31. Hamby has said: "As a local politician, as soon as he had to run for countywide office, he learned to work with black political leaders in Kansas City. Later, as a candidate for the U.S. Senate from Missouri, he worked with black political leaders in both Kansas City and St. Louis. Certainly from early on Truman accepted blacks as one of the legitimate interest groups of the Democratic party." "Temperament of Harry S. Truman," 14.

28. Samuel Lubell, *The Future of American Politics,* 3rd ed. (New York, 1965), 26; Zangrando, *NAACP Crusade,* 152; Gladys King Burns, "The Alabama Dixiecrat Revolt of 1948" (M.A. essay, Auburn University, 1965), 12; Walter White, "The President Means It," David K. Niles MSS, Box 27. In 1935, though, Truman was one of four senators who switched his vote to end an antilynching effort. Greenbaum, "Anti-Lynching Bill," 83.

29. M. Miller, *Plain Speaking,* 155; R. L. Miller, *Truman: Rise to Power,* 328–29.

30. Carleton Kent HSTL OH, 118; J. F. Martin, *Civil Rights and the Crisis of Liberalism,* 66; Kirkendall, "Truman and the South," 2; Donovan, *Conflict and Crisis,* 30. One of the most conspicuous foes of the legislation was William Borah, the Republican senator from Idaho. "Borah just made a wonderful speech on the anti-lynching bill," Truman wrote in January 1938. "I'll tell my mother to read the *Record* today. She'll agree entirely with him on it. So do I, but I may have to vote for the bill." R. L. Miller, *Truman: Rise to Power,* 326. "As senator in 1935–1944," his generally admiring biographer Robert Ferrell has written, "Truman showed no major signs of racial consciousness." Robert H. Ferrell, *Harry S. Truman: A Life* (Columbia, Mo., 1994), 292.

31. Kirkendall, "Truman and the South," 4; Mary G. Ramsey to HST, April 1, 1943, HSTL Senatorial File, Box 89; Robert S. Page to Harry F. Byrd, May 17, 1944, HSTL Senatorial File, Box 105;

C. W. Latimer to HST, March 8, 1944; HST to Latimer, March 13, 1944, HSTL Senatorial File, Box 102.

32. W. White, *A Man Called White*, 266; Sean J. Savage, *Truman and the Democratic Party* (Lexington, Ky., 1997), 19; Kirkendall, "Truman and the South," 4; Jasper Berry Shannon, *Toward a New Politics in the South* (Knoxville, Tenn., 1949), 52; William P. Helm, *Harry Truman: A Political Biography* (New York, 1947), 226; Frank McNaughton and Walter Hehmeyer, *This Man Truman* (New York, 1945), 151–52. To northern Democrats, Byrnes had three shortcomings: he was a conservative, a racist, and a lapsed Catholic. Two writers who interviewed Bob Hannegan, the Democratic Party chairman, have offered his account of the critical meeting of Democratic politicians with FDR: "Hannegan pointed to the geographic advantage Truman could bring to the ticket. Hailing from a border state, Truman could not be considered a southerner and therefore posed little threat to alienate black and civil rights constituencies. At the same time, though, Missouri was considered close enough to the South to attract some southern votes." Thomas F. Eagleton and Diane L. Duffin, "Bob Hannegan and Harry Truman's Vice Presidential Nomination," *Missouri Historical Review* 90 (1996): 272. The Mississippi delegation had recorded itself as "opposed to any candidate not in sympathy with the customs of the Old South" and insistent upon a "conservative Southern Democrat for vice-presidential nominee." Ratliff, "Career of Thomas Lowry Bailey," 56.

33. "Support from South Gives Impetus to Truman Drive," *New Orleans Times-Picayune*, July 21, 1944; Frank W. Boykin to J. Vivian Truman, June 25, 1945, C. Jasper Bell MSS, Folder 678; Sam H. Jones to Harry S. Truman, July 29, 1944, Sam H. Jones MSS.

34. Boss Crump refused to bring Tennessee in line for Truman in 1944, in part because he thought the Missouri senator was too liberal on race. Dorsett, *Franklin D. Roosevelt and the City Bosses*, 42.

35. Joseph L. Morrison, *Josephus Daniels: The Small-d Democrat* (Chapel Hill, N.C., 1966), 241; John T. Barker to William Logan Martin, August 14, 1944, in Barker to HST, August 18, 1944, HSTL Senatorial File, Box 92. In an even greater exaggeration of Truman's military lineage, a *Washington Post* reporter recalled, "The South . . . knew that his grandparents had fought in the Confederacy." Edward T. Folliard HSTL OH, 11. For the identification, "Harry Truman, son of a Confederate father," see *Time*, October 11, 1948, 25. As recently as 1992, a historian called Truman "the son of a Confederate soldier." Frank B. Atkinson, *The Dynamic Dominion: Realignment and the Rise of Virginia's Republican Party since 1945* (Fairfax, Va., 1992), 22. Truman's father was only nine at the time of the firing on Fort Sumter.

36. Clyde Hoey to R. A. Doughton, August 12, 1944, Hoey MSS, Box 2; Kirkendall, "Truman and the South," 5; William C. Berman, *The Politics of Civil Rights in the Truman Administration* (Columbus, Ohio, 1970), 21; A. G. Grayson, "North Carolina and Harry Truman, 1944–1948," *Journal of American Studies* 9 (1975): 286n.

37. R. A. Garson, *Democratic Party*, 124; W. C. Berman, *Politics of Civil Rights*, 19, quoting the *Pittsburgh Courier*.

38. Kirkendall, "Truman and the South," 5; *Chicago Herald American*, October 26, 1944, clipping, Victor Messall MSS, Box 7; Matthew J. Connelly HSTL OH, 107. When FDR's running mate endorsed a Democratic candidate for Congress in California despite the fact that he had once been a kleagle of the KKK, the chairman of the Republican National Committee, Herbert Brownell Jr.,

declared, "The New Deal's dependence on the support of . . . even elements as un-American as the Ku Klux Klan has finally been emphasized in all its ugliness by Senator Harry S. Truman." Press release, October 24, 1944, John Daniel Zook MSS, Box 21. According to an account attributed to the *Kansas City Star*'s editor Roy Roberts, Truman, informed that he needed to join the KKK if he hoped to get anywhere in politics, forked over the initiation fee. The recruiter then told him, "When you get in the Klan, Harry, you can't do any favors for any Catholics or Jews." The story concludes: "Harry is supposed to have said . . . you know Battery D was mostly Catholic boys and his partner was a Jew, and he was going to do whatever he could for them. And the fellow said, 'Well, here's your money back.'" Frank Holeman HSTL OH, 32–33. See, too, Gosnell, *Truman's Crises,* 74. In reprisal, the KKK passed out sample ballots noting next to Truman's name, when he was a candidate for a county office, that he had been endorsed by "two Roman Catholic Political Bosses." Alonzo Hamby, *Man of the People: The Life of Harry S. Truman* (New York, 1995), 114. There is no evidence that the Klan's notorious hostility to blacks played any part in his renunciation.

39. Michael Carter, *Baltimore Afro-American,* transcript of interview, August 9, 1944, HSTL Senatorial Papers, Box 94.

40. James H. Rowe Jr. HSTL OH, 18–20; Gosnell, *Truman's Crises,* 208; Brenda L. Heaster, "Who's on Second?" *Missouri Historical Review* 80 (1986): 165; Asbell, *When F.D.R. Died,* 61.

41. Walter Sillers Jr. to James O. Eastland, April 15, 1945, Sillers MSS, 33:16; Donovan, *Conflict and Crisis,* 33. See, too, McNaughton and Hehmeyer, *This Man Truman,* 162.

42. Richard S. Kirkendall, *A History of Missouri, 1919 to 1953* (Columbia, Mo., 1986), 377; *Richmond Times-Dispatch,* April 17, 1945.

43. Richard M. Dalfiume, *Desegregation of the U.S. Armed Forces: Fighting on Two Fronts, 1939–1953* (Columbia, Mo., 1969), 142; Pauley, *Modern Presidency,* 31. See, too, Donald R. McCoy and Richard T. Ruetten, *Quest and Response: Minority Rights and the Truman Administration* (Lawrence, Kans., 1973), 13.

44. McCoy and Ruetten, *Quest and Response,* 24. Truman named another southerner, Fred Vinson, secretary of the treasury (and later chief justice of the United States). For belief in the white South that Truman had gotten off to a good start, see Virginius Dabney to John Temple Graves, April 20, 1945, Dabney MSS 7690a, Box 7.

45. HST to Adolph J. Sabath, June 5, 1945, HSTL OF 40 Miscellaneous, June 1945, Folder 1; Merl E. Reed, *Seedtime for the Modern Civil Rights Movement: The President's Committee on Fair Employment Practice, 1941–1946* (Baton Rouge, La., 1991), 167–68; Dudley G. Roe to HST, June 6, 1945; HST to Roe, June 8, 1945, HSTL OF 40 Miscellaneous, June 1945, Folder 1; R. A. Garson, *Democratic Party,* 137–38. Truman acted at the request of Walter White. Donovan, *Conflict and Crisis,* 32. For commendation by a southerner of Truman's letter, see Aubrey Williams to HST, June 26, 1945, HSTL PPF 1726.

46. Frank McNaughton to Don Bermingham, June 8, 1945, memo on FEPC, photocopy, Harold F. Gosnell MSS, Box 13; Frank W. Boykin to HST, June 29, 1945, HSTL OF 40 Miscellaneous, June 1945, Folder 1.

47. Kesselman, *Social Politics of FEPC,* 213–14; Grayson, "North Carolina and Harry Truman," 289; Donovan, *Conflict and Crisis,* 123. See, too, Robert A. Garson, "The Alienation of the South:

A Crisis for Harry S. Truman and the Democratic Party, 1945–1948," *Missouri Historical Review* 64 (1970): 454. In December 1945, Truman sent a directive requiring examination of government personnel policies, for it had come to his attention "that a considerable number of loyal and qualified employees have been refused transfer and reemployment . . . solely because of race and creed. This condition is a violation of civil service rules which have been issued by the President." Those in charge of personnel, he said, had to "assure" him that their procedures were nondiscriminatory. Desmond King, "'The Longest Road to Equality': The Politics of Institutional Desegregation under Truman," *Journal of Historical Sociology* 6 (1993): 126.

48. McCoy and Ruetten, *Quest and Response*, 31; Gunther, *Inside U.S.A.*, 851; Robert Louis Pritchard, "Southern Politics and the Truman Administration: Georgia as a Test Case" (Ph.D. dissertation, University of California, Los Angeles, 1970), 90. "Industrial crisis" is an allusion to the record number of workers who went out on strike in 1946, with headline-grabbing stoppages at General Motors and in the steel industry. Southerners were also unhappy with the ceiling on cotton prices proposed by the Office of Price Administration. "Rift with Southern Democrats," *United States News and World Report,* January 25, 1946, 32. In the spring of 1946, a candidate for the gubernatorial nomination in South Carolina referred to Truman as "that stupid accident in the White House." James G. Banks, "Strom Thurmond and the Revolt against Modernity" (Ph.D. dissertation, Kent State University, 1970), 62.

49. Walter White to HST, December 19, 1945, HSTL OF 40 (1945), Box 196; Paul Seabury, *The Waning of Southern Internationalism* (Princeton, N.J., 1957), 2; R. A. Garson, *Democratic Party,* 169–70. Truman did, however, write a public letter in August 1946 stating that "discrimination, like a disease, must be attacked wherever it appears." McCoy and Ruetten, *Quest and Response,* 43.

50. Draft of statement by the president to the President's Committee on Civil Rights, David K. Niles MSS, Box 26; David R. Goldfield, *Promised Land: The South since 1945* (Arlington Heights, Ill., 1987), 43. The two southern members were Frank Porter Graham and Dorothy Tilly.

51. W. White, *A Man Called White,* 330–31; Walter White, "The President Means It," David K. Niles MSS, Box 27; John H. McCray, "The Isaac Woodward Story," McCray MSS, Box 7; Wallace H. Warren, "'The Best People in Town Won't Talk': The Moore's Ford Lynching of 1946 and Its Cover-Up," in *Georgia in Black and White,* ed. Inscoe, 266–88; *Atlanta Journal,* May 31, 1992; W. White, "The President Means It"; Gunther, *Inside U.S.A.,* 777–78; Hamby, *Man of the People,* 365–66. For a cautionary note on the Isaac Woodward episode, see Robert K. Carr, *Federal Protection of Civil Rights: Quest for a Sword* (Ithaca, N.Y., 1947), 161. More than one writer has suggested that Truman already knew of the terrible events, and, before this meeting, had made up his mind to act. The evidence is inconclusive.

52. Michael R. Gardner, *Harry Truman and Civil Rights: Moral Courage and Political Risks* (Carbondale, Ill., 2002), 17–18.

53. Donovan, *Conflict and Crisis,* 244–45; W. White, *A Man Called White,* 331–32; Zangrando, *NAACP Crusade,* 178. "The absence of a mass public outcry for racial reform meant that the Truman administration felt little pressure to enact measures that would move the nation away from its culture of racial division," two scholars have pointed out. W. H. Knight and Adrien Wing, "Weep Not, Little Ones: An Essay to Our Children," in *African Americans,* ed. Franklin and McNeil, 213.

54. Informal remarks of the president to the Members of the President's Committee on Civil Rights, David K. Niles MSS, Box 26; McCoy and Ruetten, *Quest and Response*, 80.

55. William E. Juhnke, "President Truman's Committee on Civil Rights: The Interaction of Politics, Protest, and Presidential Advisory Commission," *Presidential Studies Quarterly* 19 (1989): 593–610. The scholar was Robert Cushman, who gave me my first serious introduction to American government when I was a freshman at Cornell.

56. Jack M. Bloom, *Class, Race, and the Civil Rights Movement* (Bloomington, Ind., 1987), 78.

57. W. White, "President Means It"; Leslie W. Dunbar, *A Republic of Equals* (Ann Arbor, Mich., 1966), 13–14.

58. Jonathan Daniels COHC, 153–54. As Desmond King has written, "Debates about whether Truman 'really cared' about civil rights or was narrowly 'political' in motivation are both arid and unilluminating. What matters is that he applied a mechanism sufficiently powerful to investigate and expose the institutions and values sustaining institutional segregation, which oppressed the largest minority in the U.S. Exposure was necessarily the catalyst to termination." D. King, "'Longest Road to Equality,'" 128.

59. Paul Gordon Lauren, *Power and Prejudice: The Politics and Diplomacy of Racial Discrimination* (Boulder, Colo., 1988), 188; Mary L. Dudziak, "Desegregation as a Cold War Imperative," *Stanford Law Review* 41 (1988): 88, 81, 94–95; Bloom, *Class, Race, and Civil Rights Movement*, 78; Moon, *Balance of Power*, 9.

60. Dennis K. Merrill, *Documentary History of the Truman Presidency* (Bethesda, Md., 1995), 11: 757; Daniels, *Man of Independence*, 336; George M. Elsey HSTL OH, 449–50; W. C. Berman, *Politics of Civil Rights*, 58–59; Dalfiume, *Desegregation of U.S. Armed Forces*, 137–38; R. A. Garson, *Democratic Party*, 186–201. Asked to explain Truman's commitment to civil rights as president, Alonzo Hamby replied: "The key, aside from party politics, to Truman's decision was a belief that came naturally from his democratic background, which was that everyone deserved an equal chance in life. And he became president when black veterans . . . were returning more assertive than they might have been if they never had left the rural South." Hamby, "Temperament of Harry S. Truman," 14.

61. Daniel P. Parker, "The Political and Social Views of Harry S. Truman" (Ph.D. dissertation, University of Pennsylvania, 1951), 12; Ferrell, *Dear Bess*, 286; Frederickson, "'Slowest State,'" 184; Zangrando, *NAACP Crusade*, 178; H. C. Brearley, "The Negro's New Belligerency," *Phylon* 5 (1944): 339–45; Merrill, *Documentary History*, 11: 124. In setting up the civil rights committee, Truman, one scholar has noted, was "acting perhaps as much as a veteran as a humanitarian." Stuart J. Little, "More Than Race: Strom Thurmond, the States' Rights Democrats, and Postwar Political Ideology," *Southern Studies* 4 (1993): 116.

62. Richard Kluger, *Simple Justice: The History of Brown v. Board of Education and Black America's Struggle for Equality* (New York, 1977), 250.

63. Garson, "Alienation of the South," 464; Donovan, *Conflict and Crisis,* 333; *New York Times,* June 30, 1947; Gardner, *Harry Truman,* 30.

64. W. White, *A Man Called White,* 348–49; W. C. Berman, *Politics of Civil Rights,* 61–63; Pauley, *Modern Presidency,* 33, 44–45.

65. Clement E. Vose, *Caucasians Only: The Supreme Court, the NAACP, and the Restrictive*

Covenant Cases (Berkeley, Calif., 1947), 171; R. A. Garson, *Democratic Party*, 221; Barbara Dianne Savage, *Broadcasting Freedom: Radio, War, and the Politics of Race, 1938–1948* (Chapel Hill, N.C., 1999), 226.

66. Juhnke, "President Truman's Committee," 602. Juhnke sheds new light on this much-discussed topic. Truman's address came at a significant time. In the nation's capital, Constance McLaughlin Green has written, "the segregationist triumph looked assured in mid-1947. The *Star* remarked that 'the Confederacy, which was never able to capture Washington during the course of that war, now holds it as a helpless pawn.'" Constance McLaughlin Green, *The Secret City: A History of Race Relations in the Nation's Capital* (Princeton, N.J., 1967), 278–79.

67. The President's Committee on Civil Rights, *To Secure These Rights: The Report of the President's Committee on Civil Rights* (Washington, D.C., 1947); Arnold Shankman, "Dorothy Tilly and the Fellowship of the Concerned," in *From the Old South to the New: Essays on the Transitional South*, ed. Walter J. Fraser Jr. and Winfred B. Moore Jr. (Westport, Conn., 1981), 243. Frank Porter Graham thought the committee went too far in calling for federal intervention to end segregated facilities. The states, he maintained, should be left to work out the problem, even though it would be a "slow process." Jake Wade, typescript of article, Frank Porter Graham MSS, Box 35.

68. McCoy and Ruetten, *Quest and Response*, 86; Merrill, *Documentary History*, 11: 753; HST to John S. Dickey, November 3, 1947, Dickey MSS. As note 2 indicates, the sobriquet, "The Man of Independence," derives from Jonathan Daniels. Shortly after the report was issued, the President's Commission on Higher Education recommended ending racial segregation in America's colleges and universities.

6. SCOURGING THE SCALAWAG

1. Daniel M. Zimmerman to Burnet R. Maybank, July 16, 1947, Maybank MSS.

2. Thomas R. Waring Jr. to William A. Brower, October 8, 1947, Waring MSS.

3. Mark Ethridge to Jonathan Daniels, March 11, 1946, Daniels MSS, Series 1.4, Folder 526; Jonathan Daniels, "Southern Rebels 1947 Version," Daniels MSS, 2.2.2 Folder 2443. After the defeat of Arnall, who had spearheaded a movement to eliminate the poll tax, the father of a moderate southern publisher wrote him, "The clouds are hovering low all over Georgia today, for on yesterday the voters of this state nominated Eugene Talmadge for governor over one of the best men in the state. I can't understand why so many people, many of them men of intelligence and good citizens, could support a man with the record Talmadge has." The victories of Talmadge in Georgia and of Bilbo in Mississippi, he said, showed "that our people are possessed with racial hatred." Kevin Stoker, "Liberal Journalism in the Deep South: Harry M. Ayers and the 'Bothersome' Race Question," *Journalism History* 27 (2001): 29.

4. Gail Williams O'Brien, *The Color of the Law: Race, Violence and Justice in the Post–World War II South* (Chapel Hill, N.C., 1999); Dorothy Beeler, "Race Riot in Columbia, Tennessee, February 25–27, 1946," *Tennessee Historical Quarterly* 39 (1980): 49–61; James Albert Burran III, "Racial Violence in the South during World War II" (Ph.D. dissertation, University of Tennessee, 1977), 229–54; Paul F. Bumpas, closing argument, October 4, 1946, Bumpas Family MSS, Series 2, Folder 12. Civil rights advocates drew some sustenance from the verdict of a jury in another county acquit-

ting all but two of twenty-five blacks prosecuted by the Columbia authorities. Charges against these two were subsequently dismissed. In a separate action, a black man was convicted of attempted murder in the shooting of a highway patrolman. For the Truman administration's response to developments in Columbia, see Tom C. Clark to Horace Frierson, March 21, 1946, Hollywood Democratic Committee MSS, Box 6. One southerner said, "My belief is that people in other sections are beginning to regard the South with a cold distaste that is worse than hatred." A. G. Mezerik, "Dixie Inventory," *Nation*, January 10, 1948, 42.

5. *Time*, October 11, 1948, 25; Kevin M. Kruse, "North Carolinians' Reaction to Truman's Civil Rights Program (1947–1948)" (Senior honors thesis, University of North Carolina at Chapel Hill, 1994); William D. Barnard, *Dixiecrats and Democrats: Alabama Politics, 1942–1950* (University, Ala., 1974), 104; Monroe Billington, "Civil Rights, President Truman and the South," *Journal of Negro History* 58 (1973): 131–32.

6. John B. McDaniel to HST, October 31, 1947; Rev. A. C. Shuler to HST, October 30, 1947, all in HSTL OF 596–A; Gardner, *Harry Truman*, 62. For a complaint that not enough action was being taken in Georgia against the report, see James C. Davis to Herman Talmadge, December 9, 1947, Davis MSS, PC 11–A, Box 1.

7. James H. Rowe Jr. HSTL OH, 27–29; Ken Hechler, *Working with Truman: A Personal Memoir of the White House Years* (New York, 1982), 62; confidential memorandum for the president, November 19, 1947, Clark Clifford MSS, Political File, Box 23.

8. J. Barton Starr, "Birmingham and the 'Dixiecrat' Convention of 1948," *Alabama Historical Quarterly* 32 (1970): 24–25; W. C. Berman, *Politics of Civil Rights*, 83; R. A. Garson, *Democratic Party*, 228; Stark, *Damned Upcountryman*, 214.

9. Eben A. Ayers MS. Diary, January 23, 1948; Clifford with Holbrooke, *Counsel to the President*, 205; Irwin Ross, *The Loneliest Campaign* (New York, 1968), 64. See, too, Robert K. Carr to Charles E. Wilson, January 26, 1948, Carr MSS, Box 11.

10. Matthew J. Connelly HSTL OH, 269; Frank McNaughton to Don Bermingham, February 6, 1948, McNaughton MSS, Box 13; Donaldson, *Truman Defeats Dewey*, 116; Pritchard, "Southern Politics," 111; Goldfield, *Promised Land*, 55; Robert Sherrill, *Gothic Politics in the Deep South: Stars of the New Confederacy* (New York, 1968), 145; Kari Frederickson, *The Dixiecrat Revolt and the End of the Solid South, 1932–1968* (Chapel Hill, N.C., 2001), 77.

11. Frederickson, *Dixiecrat Revolt*, 77; Merrill, *Documentary History*, 11: 14; R. H. Cochran to Charles G. Hamilton, February 11, 1948. See, too, Thurman Sensing, "Down South," Southern States Industrial Council No. 186, February 15, 1948, R. Gregg Cherry MSS, Governor's Papers, Box 52.

12. W. S. Pritchard to John H. Kerr, February 20, 1948; Kerr to Pritchard, February 25, 1943, Kerr MSS, Box 27; Kruse, "North Carolinians' Reaction."

13. To The Two Southern Residents of The Civil Rights (?) Committee, February 8, 1948, Dorothy Rogers Tilly MSS; Helena Huntington Smith, "Mrs. Tilly's Crusade," *Collier's*, December 30, 1950, 65, 67.

14. Leonard Ray Teel, *Ralph Emerson McGill: Voice of the Southern Conscience* (Knoxville, Tenn., 2001); Ralph McGill, "Will the South Ditch Truman?" *Saturday Evening Post*, May 22, 1948, 17; Anthony Lake Newberry, "Without Urgency or Ardor: The South's Middle-of-the-Road Liberals and

Civil Rights, 1945–1960" (Ph.D. dissertation, Ohio University, 1982), 134–35. Truman, a Georgia congressman charged, proposed to "set up an Ogpu or Gestapo in the South." Henderson Lanham, "Your Congressman Reports," 1948, Lanham MSS, Box 50.

15. Banks, "Strom Thurmond," III; Frederickson, *Dixiecrat Revolt*, 77; *Newsweek*, February 16, 1948, 26. See, too, *Augusta Courier*, February 9, 1948, R. Gregg Cherry MSS, Governor's Papers, Box 52.

16. *Time*, March 15, 1948, 29; Carl T. Rowan, *South of Freedom* (Baton Rouge, La., 1997), 147.

17. *Jackson Daily News*, February 5, 1948; *Jackson Clarion Ledger*, October 20, 1958, Walter Sillers Jr. MSS, 86: 5.

18. William M. Colmer, "The South, the Democratic Party, the So-Called Civil Rights Program," typescript, Colmer MSS, Box 425; Philip A. Grant Jr., "The Mississippi Congressional Delegation and the Formation of the Conservative Coalition, 1937–1940," *Journal of Mississippi History* 50 (1988): 24; Billington, "Civil Rights," 133; Kenneth H. Williams, "Mississippi and Civil Rights, 1945–1954" (Ph.D. dissertation, Mississippi State University, 1985), 140; *Providence Journal*, February 23, 1948, clipping, J. Howard McGrath MSS, Box 59; William M. Colmer OH, University of Southern Mississippi, 53–64. The "tragic part" of Truman's message, said another Mississippi congressman, was that it assumed that Negroes were mistreated in the South when, in fact, southerners had been "extra lenient" with them. *The State* (Columbia, S.C.), February 4, 1948.

19. John Bell Williams, "The President's Infamous Civil Rights Program," Williams MSS, R033–B019–S2–10383; Richard D. Chesteen, "'Mississippi Is Gone Home!': A Study of the 1948 Mississippi States' Rights Bolt," *Journal of Mississippi History* 32 (1970): 48; *Congressional Record*, 80th Cong., 2nd sess., 976. A Natchez attorney wrote his friend, the Speaker of the Mississippi House of Representatives, "If Mr. Truman's Civil Rights Committee can make a deal with the Almighty to remove from the Negro that ineradicable odor that the Almighty endowed him with for all time then I might feel more favorable to the removal of the so-called Jim Crow restrictions." C. F. Engle to Walter Sillers Jr., February 10, 1948, Sillers MSS, 106: 25.

20. Key with Heard, *Southern Politics*, 330; unidentified clipping in Mamie Serio to J. Howard McGrath, February 11, 1948, McGrath MSS, Box 22; L. Howard Vaughan and David R. Deener, *Presidential Politics in Louisiana, 1952* (New Orleans, 1954), 56; *New York Times*, February 13, 1948; Resolution Adopted by Mississippi Conference of Democrats, Mississippi State Democratic Executive Committee MSS. In a front-page editorial a week before the Jackson meeting, Hodding Carter denounced Truman's program as "symptomatic of a widespread and unfortunate reliance upon Federal authority as a cureall." *New York Times*, February 13, 1948. Carter was regarded as one of the most liberal editors in the South, but he insisted: "Few people, White or Black, who live in the South want to see segregation abolished. As we have said repeatedly, such an idea is both unrealistic and dangerous to inter-racial progress." Dorothy C. Kinsella, O.S.F., "Southern Apologists: A Liberal Image" (Ph.D. dissertation, St. Louis University, 1971), 355.

21. John U. Barr, "For White Men and Women Everywhere," R. Gregg Cherry MSS, Governor's Papers, Box 52; *Gastonia Gazette*, February 7, 1948, clipping, Scrapbook 34, R. Gregg Cherry MSS, Personal Papers.

22. *Time*, October 11, 1948, 25; Grayson, "North Carolina and Harry Truman," 294; Donovan, *Conflict and Crisis*, 354; Seth Shepard McKay, *Texas and the Fair Deal, 1945–1952* (San Antonio, Tex., 1954), 247; Vaughan and Deener, *Presidential Politics in Louisiana*, 55–56; *Raleigh News and Observer*,

February 9, 1948, Scrapbook 34, R. Gregg Cherry MSS, Personal Papers; Jack Redding, *Inside the Democratic Party* (Indianapolis, Ind., 1958), 134; "Motion of J. Strom Thurmond, Wakulla Springs Lodge, February 7, 1948," William D. Workman Jr., MSS, Box 22; Thomas Koehler-Shepley, "Robert Mc C Figg Jr.: South Carolina's Lawyers' Lawyer" (M.A. essay, University of South Carolina, 1994), 30.

23. Donovan, *Conflict and Crisis,* 353–54; Goldfield, *Promised Land,* 54; Robert C. Ruark, quoted in Clarence Ervin Landrum, "The States' Rights Democratic Movement of 1948" (M.A. essay, Wofford College, 1950), 45–46; Milton D. Stewart to Robert K. Carr, February 10, 1948, Carr MSS, Box 4. See, too, Jules Abels, *Out of the Jaws of Victory* (New York, 1959), 10; George W. Andrews to G. M. Edwards, February 19, 1948, Andrews MSS, Box 5.

24. *Charleston News and Courier,* February 20, 1948, clipping, Burnet R. Maybank Scrapbook; Zachary Karabell, *The Last Campaign: How Harry Truman Won the 1948 Election* (New York, 2000), 45.

25. Hugh M. Gloster, "The Southern Revolt," *Crisis* 55 (1948): 137; Ward M. Morton, "Report on Arkansas Politics in 1948," *Southwestern Social Science Quarterly* 30 (June 1949): 36; John E. Borsos, "Support for the National Democratic Party in South Carolina during the Dixiecrat Revolt of 1948" (M.A. essay, University of South Carolina, 1987), 11–12; *Time,* March 1, 1948, 12; *Washington Post,* February 20, 1948, Clark Clifford MSS, Political File, Box 21; Bass and Thompson, *Ol' Strom,* 102–3; Jim Lester, *A Man for Arkansas: Sid McMath and the Southern Reform Tradition* (Little Rock, Ark., 1976), 96; Ross, *Loneliest Campaign,* 65; Ronald F. Stinnett, *Democrats, Dinners, and Dollars: A History of the Democratic Party, Its Dinners, Its Ritual* (Ames, Iowa, 1967), 178; Garson, "Alienation of the South," 469; Tom C. Clark HSTL OH (Jerry N. Hess interview), 160–62; speech by Harry F. Byrd, February 19, 1948, Jefferson Day Dinner, Richmond, Va., Byrd MSS, Box 368; Donovan, *Conflict and Crisis,* 353–54.

26. "Transcript of Conference of Southern Governors with Senator J. Howard McGrath, Chairman of the Democratic National Committee, Monday, February 23, 1948," J. Howard McGrath MSS, Box 59; *Newsweek,* March 4, 1948, 18; J. Redding, *Inside the Democratic Party,* 136; Samuel C. Brightman HSTL OH, 30; Abels, *Out of the Jaws of Victory,* 13; Key with Heard, *Southern Politics,* 331; *Providence Journal,* February 24, 1948, clipping, J. Howard McGrath MSS, Box 59. "The race issue is by no means the sole cause of the great division in Democratic ranks," noted a Little Rock newspaper. "It is no accident that those who are loudest now in denouncing Mr. Truman are the same Southern Democrats who have also taken issue with him and with his predecessor on many other matters—labor legislation, price controls, public power, federal spending, etc." Key with Heard, *Southern Politics,* 339n. See, too, Edward T. Folliard HSTL OH, 60; A. Willis Robertson to Virginius Dabney, April 5, 1952, Dabney MSS 7690e, Box 1. When Truman vetoed an antilabor bill, nine of Georgia's ten members in the House voted to override. Yet there was no serious breach with Truman until his civil rights message. On issues such as farm legislation and federal aid to education, Truman had the backing of Richard Russell.

27. *Newsweek,* March 4, 1948, 18; Frederickson, *Dixiecrat Revolt,* 80–81; Frank McNaughton to Don Bermingham and Girvin, February 20, 1948, McNaughton MSS; John A. Kirk, *Redefining the Color Line: Black Activism in Little Rock, Arkansas, 1940–1970* (Gainesville, Fla., 2002), 57. See, too, *Laurel (Miss.) Leader-Call,* March 8, 1948, photocopy in William M. Colmer MSS, Box 318; W. J. Bryan Dorn to S. K. Grayson, February 25, 1948, Dorn MSS.

28. J. Harvie Wilkinson III, *Harry Byrd and the Changing Face of Virginia Politics, 1945–1966* (Charlottesville, Va., 1968), 79–80; James R. Sweeney, "The Golden Silence: The Virginia Democratic Party and the Presidential Election of 1948," *Virginia Magazine of History and Biography* 82 (1974): 351–58; Frank McNaughton to David Hulburd, February 27, 1948, McNaughton MSS, Box 13; James Randolph Roebuck Jr., "Virginia in the Election of 1948" (M.A. essay, University of Virginia, 1969), 30. Though Byrd had called Truman's message a "devastating broadside at the dignity of Southern traditions and institutions," he wrote the chief Washington correspondent of the *New York Times:* "The officials at Richmond became so enthusiastic that they actually introduced a bill to prohibit electors in Virginia for both Truman and Wallace, but I was successful today in having the bill amended, as, of course, their electors should have a right to get on the ballot." Harry F. Byrd to Arthur Krock, February 27, 1948, Krock MSS, Box 19. A former Republican official, however, noted, "Even as sane a man as Harry Byrd says that if Congress enacts the laws Truman wants it will lead to bloodshed." William R. Castle Jr. MS. Diary, March 9, 1948. One scholar has written: "Clearly, Senator Byrd was intimately involved in attempting to blackmail the national party into rejecting President Truman's renomination or at least watering down the civil rights platform by threatening to withhold Virginia's support from the party. It constituted nothing less than a brazen attempt to deny Virginians an opportunity to cast their ballots for whomever they pleased." Ronald L. Heinemann, *Harry Byrd of Virginia* (Charlottesville, Va., 1996), 256.

29. Burns, "Alabama Dixiecrat Revolt," 29–34, 64, 76; Frank McNaughton to Don Bermingham, February 6, 1948; McNaughton to David Hulburd, February 27, 1948, McNaughton MSS, Box 13; J. W. Fulbright to A. B. Priddy, February 28, 1948, Fulbright MSS, BCN 48, F1; *Montgomery Advertiser,* March 26, 1948, typescript, Aubrey Williams MSS, Box 58; *Newsweek,* March 5, 1946, 15. See, too, Edmund Blair to Marion Rushton, February 22, 1948, Rushton MSS, Box 211; "Talmadgeites Reject Truman," *Atlanta Constitution,* February 25, 1948, clipping, M. E. Thompson Scrapbooks. Crump said of Truman: "In his scheming, cold-blooded effort to outdo Henry Wallace and Governor Dewey of New York for the Negro vote, he has endeavored to reduce the South to a country of crawling cowards." Gloster, "Southern Revolt," 137.

30. Ben Green, *Before His Time: The Untold Story of Harry Moore, America's First Civil Rights Martyr* (New York, 1999), 75; Tom P. Brady, "The South at Bay," Brookhaven, Miss., March 6, 1948, Palmer Bradley MSS, Box 2; Garson, "Alienation of the South," 470n. See, too, Kent Barnett Germany, "Rise of the Dixiecrats: Louisiana's Conservative Defection from the National Democratic Party, 1944–1948" (M.A. essay, Louisiana Technical University, 1994), 47–48.

31. Bass and Thompson, *Ol' Strom,* 87; *New York Times,* March 14, 1948. See, too, Minutes of a Meeting of the Mississippi State Democratic Executive Committee Held on March 1, 1948, Mississippi State Democratic Executive Committee MSS; Horace C. Wilkinson to Kenneth McKellar, March 18, 1948, McKellar MSS; Fielding Wright to Strom Thurmond, March 19, 1948, Wright-Thurmond MSS; *Montgomery Advertiser,* March 19, 1948, clipping, Chauncey Sparks MSS, Box 10; address, March 17, 1948, J. Strom Thurmond MSS, Speeches, Box 2; Senator Harlan J. Bushfield, "Farm Views from the Capitol," March 15, 1948, Bushfield MSS. "Truman's Committee . . . the infamous 'Civil Rights Thing,'" a San Antonio man wrote Dwight Eisenhower, "was composed mainly if not entirely of Jewish Rabbis, Jew lawyers, Left Wingers, New Dealers and Communist-minded." Austin F. Hancock to Dwight D. Eisenhower, March 8, 1948, copy in William Langer

MSS, Box 211. In the last week of March, a national magazine reported: "From Vicksburg, Miss., to Columbia, S.C., a member of the Board of Editors of *U.S. News and World Report* found the South ablaze with talk about Mr. Truman's civil-rights program." "Gauging the South's Revolt," *U.S. News and World Report*, March 26, 1948, 22.

32. Glenn Feldman, *From Demagogue to Dixiecrat: Horace Wilkinson and the Politics of Race* (Lanham, Md., 1995), 131–34. Samuel M. Dowling to George Andrews, March 1, 1948, Andrews MSS, Box 5; Burns, "Alabama Dixiecrat Revolt," 105; Gloster, "Southern Revolt," 137; Pritchard, "Southern Politics," 139; "The South and the Democratic Convention," *University of Chicago Round Table* (June 13, 1948): 4.

33. Hamilton, *Lister Hill*, 154–55; *St. Louis Post-Dispatch*, March 28, 1948, photocopy, Clark Clifford MSS, Political File, Box 21; Wat Arnold, "Weekly News Letter No. 46," March 26, 1948, Arnold MSS, Folder 4; address by Lister Hill, March 11, 1948; *Montgomery Advertiser*, March 24, 1948, Chauncey Sparks MSS, Box 10. In running for the position of alternate delegate to the 1948 Democratic national convention, young George Wallace passed around campaign cards reading: "Unalterably opposed to the nomination of Harry S. Truman and so-called Civil Rights Program." Marshall Frady, *Wallace*, enlarged and updated edition (New York, 1976), 141.

34. *New York Times*, May 9, 1948; Harry F. Byrd Sr. to William M. Tuck, March 22, 1948, Byrd MSS, Box 191; Harry F. Byrd Sr. to E. R. Combs, March 31, 1948, Byrd MSS, Box 185.

35. *Mobile Register*, c. April 1, 1948, clipping, Marion Rushton MSS, Box 214.

36. Mary Heaton Vorse, "The South Has Changed," *Harper's* 199 (1949): 31; *The States' Righter*, April 1948; Bass and Thompson, *Ol' Strom*, 104; *The State* (Columbia, S.C.), May 20, 1948, Strom Thurmond Scrapbooks, Winthrop University; statement by Senator Maybank, n.d., Maybank MSS; Eugene Connor to Marion Rushton, April 26, 1948, Rushton MSS, Box 211. See, too, *Anderson (S.C.) Independent*, May 14, 1948, clipping, Burnet R. Maybank MSS; Douglas Southall Freeman to Harry F. Byrd, May 21, 1948, Freeman MSS, Box 85. "This Civil Rights measure of his certainly stirred up a hornet's nest all over the States and in Texas as well," Sam Rayburn acknowledged. He thought, though, that Americans should not be "pounding each other," but should be concentrating their attention on international affairs where "President Truman has been a good leader." Rayburn to Grover Sellers, March 26, 1948, Rayburn MSS.

37. John Anthony Tuggle, "The Dixiecrats as a 'Stepping-Stone' to Two-Party Politics for Mississippi" (M.A. essay, University of Southern Mississippi, 1994), 48–49.

38. Address by J. Strom Thurmond, Jackson, Mississippi, May 10, 1948, Progressive Party MSS, Box 38; *Newsweek*, May 24, 1948, 23; *New York Times*, May 11, 1948. Roosevelt had, in fact, endorsed the FEPC and antilynching legislation, and had sought to remove the poll tax. He had not, however, been nearly as outspoken on civil rights as Truman.

39. E. H. Crump to Kenneth McKellar, May 10, 1948, McKellar MSS; T. H. McRorie to HST, May 19, 1948, Clyde Hoey MSS, Box 39; Anonymous to R. Gregg Cherry, n.d. [1948], Cherry MSS, Governor's Papers, Box 52.

40. Clifford, *Counsel to the President*, 207. W. C. Berman, *Politics of Civil Rights*, 94–96; R. A. Garson, *Democratic Party*, 265; Barton J. Bernstein, "The Ambiguous Legacy: The Truman Administration and Civil Rights," in *Politics and Policies of the Truman Administration*, ed. Bernstein (Chicago, 1970), 286. The aide was Philleo Nash. Another of Truman's assistants has contended,

"The strategy was to dampen the controversy, keep the South in line until after the election, and then proceed to enact the much stronger program the President had enunciated in his February message to Congress." Hechler, *Working with Truman*, 80.

41. Eben A. Ayers MS. Diary, February 23, 1948; Ferrell, ed., *Truman in the White House*, 244–45; Burns, "Alabama Dixiecrat Revolt," 90–91; Rayford Logan MS. Diary, February 17, 1948; *Washington Post*, March 9, 1948.

42. *Washington Post*, March 5, 1948, March 10, 1948, clippings, Stephen J. Spingarn MSS, Box 40; Starr, "Birmingham and the 'Dixiecrat' Convention," 23, 26; Sherie Mershon and Steven Schlossman, *Foxholes and Color Lines: Desegregating the U.S. Armed Forces* (Baltimore, 1998), 177; B. Cochran, *Harry Truman*, 230; Frank McNaughton to Don Bermingham, March 5, 26, 1948, McNaughton MSS, Box 13. See, too, Edward T. Folliard HSTL OH, 11.

43. *Washington Post*, October 10, 1948, clipping, Stephen J. Spingarn MSS, Box 40. See, too, *Jackson Clarion-Ledger*, June 8, 1944, Theodore G. Bilbo MSS, Box 1012; Paul T. David, ed., *Presidential Nominating Politics in 1952: The South* (Baltimore, 1954), 225.

44. Thomas Sancton, "White Supremacy—Crisis or Plot?" *Nation*, July 31, 1948, 127; *Cong. Rec.*, 80th Cong., 2nd sess., 976, 1193–99. Truman had "turned his back on the loyal South," charged Burnet Maybank. "The South WAS his friend. The Southern states voted for him for vice-president. . . . I cannot see what we in the South have done to deserve such treatment." *Columbia (S.C.) Record*, February 24, 1948, clipping, Burnet R. Maybank Scrapbook.

45. Lesher, *George Wallace*, 77; W. J. Brown, *James F. Byrnes*, 355–56. See, too, Shannon, *Toward a New Politics*, 52.

46. Address by Governor Beauford H. Jester, Texas Democratic Barbecue, April 20, 1948, LBJ MSS, LBJA Famous Names, Box 5; McKay, *Texas and Fair Deal*, 249–50.

47. J. F. Martin, *Civil Rights and the Crisis of Liberalism*, 82.

48. Joseph C. Goulden, ed., *Mencken's Last Campaign: H. L. Mencken on the 1948 Election* (Washington, D.C., 1976), 41, 44, 48.

49. Abels, *Out of the Jaws of Victory*, 89; Lesher, *George Wallace*, 81; Germany, "Rise of the Dixiecrats," 69. Truman got thirteen of North Carolina's thirty-two votes, which turned out to be the ones that pushed him beyond the number he needed to be nominated on the first ballot. Jonathan Daniels later said, "I was one of a very small group of North Carolinians who voted for the nomination of Truman in '48, and when we came back, we were all bunched together as nigger lovers." Jonathan Daniels COHC, 132. The rebels drew small comfort from the choice of a southerner—(again from a border state) Alben Barkley of Kentucky, as the president's running mate.

50. McCoy and Ruetten, *Quest and Response*, 125; Charles J. Greene HSTL OH, 20.

51. Frederickson, *Dixiecrat Revolt*, 118–19; Clifford, *Counsel to the President*, 218–19; Robert H. Ferrell, ed., *Off the Record: The Private Papers of Harry S. Truman* (New York, 1980), 143.

52. *Montgomery Advertiser*, July 15, 1948, clipping, William J. Primm MSS, Box 2; Joseph L. Rauh Jr., Eleanor Roosevelt Oral History Project, 25–26; James I. Loeb HSTL OH, 38–39. The threat that Henry Wallace's Progressives might lure black voters from the Democrats probably played some part in the eagerness for a strong civil rights plank, but there is no evidence that it had any considerable effect on Truman. Dewey was also a source of some concern on this issue, for, as governor of New York, he had put through an FEPC.

53. *Time,* July 26, 1948, 13; *Newsweek,* July 26, 1948, 21; "A Gettysburg for Dixie," *Richmond Times-Dispatch,* July 15, 1948; Frederickson, *Dixiecrat Revolt,* 118; Landrum, "States' Rights Democratic Movement of 1948," 78; William Manchester, *The Glory and the Dream: A Narrative History of America, 1932–1972* (Boston, 1974), 456; Goulden, ed., *Mencken's Last Campaign,* 60. At the 1948 convention, a political scientist later observed, "the Democratic party violated an implicit compact with its southern wing to ignore the racial issue and could not be counted on any longer as the unequivocal defender of white supremacy in the South." Paul Allen Beck, "Partisan Dealignment of the Postwar South," *American Political Science Review* 71 (1977): 486.

54. *Montgomery Advertiser,* July 15, 1948, clipping, William J. Primm MSS, Box 2.

55. Abels, *Out of the Jaws of Victory,* 91–92; Donovan, *Conflict and Crisis,* 406; Ralph McGill to Hardy Lott, August 26, 1948, McGill MSS, Series 2, Box 3; Burns, "Alabama Dixiecrat Revolt," 162; Julian M. Pleasants, "Claude Pepper, Strom Thurmond, and the 1948 Presidential Election in Florida," *Florida Historical Quarterly* 76 (1998): 453. One of the Alabamians who remained behind was George Wallace. Nunnelley, *Bull Connor,* 34. A Mississippi liberal who would serve several terms in Congress stated subsequently, "The people who were planning to walk out in Mississippi were scared to death that there was going to be a compromise on the civil rights plank, and they wouldn't have an excuse to walk out. . . . They already had the plans to go to Birmingham." Frank E. Smith OH. A Democratic Party official later said of the strong civil rights plank: "We knew that it was going to be adopted, we knew that some of the southern people would walk out, so we put a copy of the Bill of Rights over the door where they would walk out, so they would be walking out under that." Samuel C. Brightman HSTL OH, 61.

56. Susan Weill, *In a Madhouse's Din: Civil Rights Coverage by Mississippi's Daily Press, 1948–1968* (Westport, Conn., 2002), 30, 28, 32.

57. Gore, *Let the Glory Out,* 66–67; Gessner T. McCorvey to Herman Talmadge, September 21, 1948, in Marion Rushton MSS, Box 21. "The Dixiecrat revolt," observed a political scientist, "may be considered . . . as pursuing a politics of revenge, but one aimed not at the alienation of region from party but rather the opposite: the purification of party so as to promote the reuniting of region and party on terms laid down mostly by the region." Allan P. Sindler, "The South in Political Transition," in *The South in Continuity and Change,* ed. John C. McKinney and Edgar T. Thompson (Durham, N.C., 1965), 303. In an address in Baltimore, Thurmond said that the Dixiecrats would see to it that the "tides" of the Democratic Party "will flow like muddy water over the sands and rocks and be purified. The impurities of that party—Harry Truman and all his followers—will be deposited like sediment on the banks." Greenhaw, *Elephants in the Cottonfields,* 221. A contemporary account pointed out: "There is no fear of losing patronage, since no one believes Truman will be elected anyway." Helen Fuller, "The New Confederacy," *New Republic,* November 1, 1948, 10, 12.

58. Ann Mathison McLaurin, "The Role of the Dixiecrats in the 1948 Election" (Ph.D. dissertation, University of Oklahoma, 1972), 172; James M. Stayer, "A History of the Presidential Campaign of 1948" (M.A. essay, University of Virginia, 1958), 179; Feldman, *From Demagogue to Dixiecrat,* 144; Frederickson, *Dixiecrat Revolt,* 142.

59. *Birmingham News-Age-Herald,* July 18, 1948; John M. Coski, "The Confederate Battle Flag in Historical Perspective," in *Confederate Symbols in the Contemporary South,* ed. J. Michael Martinez, William D. Richardson, and Ron McNinch-Su (Gainesville, Fla., 2000), 109.

60. "Frank M. Dixon Keynote Speech," Birmingham, Ala., July 17, 1948, William M. Colmer MSS, Box 318; Declaration of Principles, Birmingham, Alabama Convention of States Rights Democrats, July 17, 1948, J. Strom Thurmond MSS, Speeches, Box 2.

61. Alberta Lachicotte, *Rebel Senator: Strom Thurmond of South Carolina* (New York, 1967), 43; *New York Times,* July 18, 1948; Abels, *Out of the Jaws of Victory,* 98; *Birmingham News-Age-Herald,* July 18, 1948; *Jackson (Miss.) Clarion-Ledger,* July 18, 1948; *Birmingham News,* July 17, 1948. See, too, Fielding L. Wright, as told to Howard Suttle, "Give the Government Back to the People," *American Magazine* 146 (July 1948): 36; *Birmingham News-Age-Herald,* July 18, 1948.

62. Starr, "Birmingham and 'Dixiecrat' Convention," 34; *New York Times,* July 18, 1948; W. D. Barnard, *Dixiecrats and Democrats,* 116; *Birmingham News,* July 18, 1948; Stayer, "History," 181.

63. W. D. Barnard, *Dixiecrats and Democrats,* 101; Ader, *Dixiecrat Movement,* 14; Sancton, "White Supremacy" *Nation,* July 31, 1948, 97; Lowell Mellett story, unidentified source, n.d. [summer 1948], Clark Clifford MSS, Political File, Box 21; Perry H. Howard, "Louisiana: Resistance and Change," in *Changing Politics,* ed. Havard, 547–48; Numan V. Bartley, *The Rise of Massive Resistance: Race and Politics in the South during the 1950's* (Baton Rouge, La., 1969), 34; Frederickson, *Dixiecrat Revolt,* 1. The ideology of the Dixiecrats, one scholar concluded, "was promulgated by a distinct social class, the middle class and/or upper middle class which derives its income from new industries and branches of established northern industries which have arisen in the South. . . . The ideology was rooted . . . in a desire to defend the economic system as it now exists against changes which the progressive utopia might achieve." Sarah McCulloh Lemmon, "The Ideology of the 'Dixiecrat' Movement," *Social Forces* 30 (1951): 171.

64. O. Douglas Weeks, "Texas: Land of Conservative Expansiveness," in *Changing Politics,* ed. Havard, 212; Gessner T. McCorvey to Homer D. Cobb, October 22, 1948, in Marion Rushton MSS, Box 212; Jonathan Daniels SOHP, 217.

65. "Morning Spot," Terry Sanford MSS, Series 1.2, Folder 21.

66. Key with Heard, *Southern Politics,* 10; Frederickson, *Dixiecrat Revolt,* 143.

67. Germany, "Rise of the Dixiecrats," 123; *Anderson (S.C.) Daily Mail,* October 21, 1948, clipping; Associated Press bulletin, October 26, 1948, Thomas R. Waring Jr., MSS.

68. Karabell, *Last Campaign,* 59.

69. Overton Brooks to Sam Rayburn, November 9, 1948, Rayburn MSS; *Alabama Journal,* September 8, 1948, clipping, William J. Primm MSS, Box 2.

70. David M. Tucker, *Memphis since Crump: Bossism, Blacks, and Civic Reformers, 1948–1968* (Knoxville, Tenn., 1980), 57; Bruce J. Dierenfield, *Keeper of the Rules: Congressman Howard W. Smith of Virginia* (Charlottesville, Va., 1987), 123; Charles R. Hill to M. J. Menefee, July 14, 1948, Menefee MSS, Box 6; Howard E. Covington Jr. and Marion A. Ellis, *Terry Sanford: Politics, Progress, and Outrageous Ambitions* (Durham, N.C., 1999), 96; Doughton himself wrote, "Mr. Truman is unpopular and a part of the platform despised by Southern Democrats and confidentially I shall not be surprised if he loses North Carolina." R. L. Doughton to Thad F. Wasielewski, July 26, 1948, Doughton MSS, Box 44.

71. Billie Mayfield to Palmer Bradley, July 28, 1948, Bradley MSS, Box 1; *Houston Press,* August 11, 1948, clipping, Strom Thurmond Scrapbooks, Winthrop University. The attorney general of Virginia in 1948 later remembered that after he made a firm commitment to Truman, Senator Byrd

"called me on the mat and gave me the devil about it." J. Lindsay Almond JFKL OH, 17–18. The governor of Alabama, Jim Folsom, endorsed Truman and backed litigation to give the people of his state the opportunity to vote for the choice of the Democratic national convention, but nothing came of that effort. George E. Sims, *The Little Man's Big Friend: James E. Folsom in Alabama Politics, 1946–1958* (University, Ala., 1985), 102–3. "The Democrats made a mistake when they named Truman for vice-president," one observer remarked. "The South demanded that Truman be nominated. The South had their way—they got Truman. Now they don't want him." William G. Owens, Statement on 1948 Election, n.d. [Fall 1948], Usher L. Burdick MSS, Box 17.

72. Tuggle, "Dixiecrats," 70; Marion Rushton to Grover C. Hall, July 23, 1948, Rushton MSS, Box 211; W. D. Barnard, *Dixiecrats and Democrats,* 120; Donald S. Strong, "Alabama: Transition and Alienation," in *Changing Politics,* ed. Havard, 459–60; Perry H. Howard, *Political Tendencies in Louisiana,* rev. and expanded ed. (Baton Rouge, La., 1971), 306; R. A. Garson, *Democratic Party,* 274; Abels, *Out of the Jaws of Victory,* 96. For hostility to Truman in Texas, see "Purge of Dixiecrats," *Newsweek,* September 27, 1948, 19; J. W. Jackson, "Texas Politics in 1948," *Southwest Social Science Quarterly* 30 (1949): 48. In Texas, even the Democratic National Committeeman bolted to the Dixiecrats.

7. THE LIBERAL NATIONALIST

1. W. McNeil Lowry HSTL OH, 56–57; Weill, *Madhouse's Din,* 22, 31; R. A. Garson, *Democratic Party,* 290. See, too, "States Rights vs. Totalitarianism," August 4, 1948, John Bell Williams MSS, R033–B019–S2–10383. "If damn fool Democrats in other sections want to eat, drink and sleep with negroes that is their business," wrote the influential editor of a Jackson paper. "We can only deplore their degeneracy and declare we will have none of it." Weill, *Madhouse's Din,* 34.

2. Renwick C. Kennedy, "The Cracker Boy's Vote," *Christian Century,* October 27, 1948, 1143.

3. Edyth Gilbert Barton to HST, July 27, 1948; Mrs. Alex J. McAllister to HST, September 12, 1948, HSTL OF 596—A. When in Arkansas Brooks Hays backed the Truman ticket, he got so much criticism, his biographer writes, that "his Sunday school class even threatened to change its name from the Brooks Hays class to something more in keeping with its segregationist philosophy." J. T. Baker, *Brooks Hays,* 148.

4. Gardner, *Harry Truman,* 119.

5. Walter Millis, ed., *The Forrestal Diaries* (New York, 1951), 458; Susan M. Hartmann, *Truman and the 80th Congress* (Columbia, Mo., 1971), 207; Jonathan Daniels to "Charlie," November 23, 1948, HSTL OF 93—B, Box 442; Robert H. Ferrell, *Harry S. Truman and the Modern American Presidency* (Boston, 1983), 102–3.

6. Ernest W. Roberts to HST, n.d., HSTL PSF Personal "C" (Civil Rights), Box 306; Ferrell, ed., *Off the Record,* 146–47. I have corrected errors in the Roberts letter that are distracting.

7. Ferrell, ed., *Off the Record,* 146–47. Though Truman says "one of his eyes," the sergeant, in fact, lost both eyes. "As the Democratic convention neared," noted one report, "Mr. Truman appeared to be wooing rebellious Democrats with shameless ardor. . . . Soon afterward, Mr. Truman resumed a fighting posture." James A. and Nancy F. Wechsler, "The Road Ahead for Civil Rights: The President's Report One Year Later," *Commentary* 6 (1948): 299.

8. *Public Papers of the Presidents of the United States: Harry S. Truman, 1945* (Washington, D.C., 1961), 409; Kenneth M. Birkhead HSTL OH, 59; Phillip McGuire, *Taps for a Jim Crow Army: Letters from Black Soldiers in World War II* (Santa Barbara, Calif., 1983), 250; Thomas R. Brooks, *Walls Come Tumbling Down: A History of the Civil Rights Movement, 1940–1970* (Englewood Cliffs, N.J., 1974), 73; Weill, *Madhouse's Din*, 24; Tuggle, "Dixiecrats," 73–74; E. W. Kenworthy HSTL OH, 14–15; *Baltimore Sun,* January 16, 1950, Gordon Gray MSS, Scrapbook 6; Morris J. MacGregor Jr., *Integration of the Armed Forces, 1940–1965* (Washington, D.C., 1981), 313. In neither his executive order on discrimination in the armed forces nor his edict on discrimination in federal employment did he allude to segregation. National Association for the Advancement of Colored People, American Jewish Congress, "Civil Rights in the United States in 1948: A Balance Sheet of Group Relations," copy in Wat Abbitt MSS. For flaws in the president's edict on desegregating the armed forces, see Ruth P. Morgan, *The President and Civil Rights: Policy-Making by Executive Order* (New York, 1970), 21.

9. John Franklin Carter [Jay Franklin], "What Truman Really Thinks of Negroes," *Negro Digest* 7 (1949): 11; Roebuck, "Virginia," 60; Herbert Shapiro, *White Violence and Black Response: From Reconstruction to Montgomery* (Amherst, Mass., 1988), 389.

10. Harry Ashmore OH, Patricia Sullivan Interviews, 9; "President Truman's Orders," *The Crisis* 55 (1948): 264; John H. McCray to Dear Co-Worker, August 16, 1948, McCray MSS, Box 7. A prominent black activist has recalled: "As I grew up in Grand Rapids, there were really only two figures, in the larger world, that I cared about and only one issue. The people were Harry Truman and Jackie Robinson, and the issue was race." R. Wilkins, *A Man's Life,* 47. In Florida, the black activist Harry Moore, who has been called "America's first civil rights martyr," enthusiastically backed Truman, who had "stuck his neck out farther for the Negro race than any president." B. Green, *Before His Time,* 75. See, too, H. D. Price, *The Negro and Southern Politics: A Chapter of Florida History* (New York, 1957).

11. "Should the President Call Congress back?" Johannes Hoeber HSTL OH, 89; Samuel I. Rosenman HSTL OH, 88; James I. Loeb HSTL OH, 41–42; McCoy and Ruetten, *Quest and Response,* 134–35. See, too, Philip H. Vaughan, "President Truman's Committee on Civil Rights: The Urban Implications," *Missouri Historical Review* 66 (1972): 427–28; John Franklin Carter HSTL OH, 40.

12. McCullough, *Truman,* 677; *Public Papers, 1948,* 818–27; Jonathan Daniels HSTL OH, 142–44. "I got Gerald Johnson, as one of my favorite historians, to write the address in which he compared Truman to Johnson, Jackson and Polk, without ever saying that he compared him," Jonathan Daniels later said. "He made them an old ripsnorting speech, and the visit to the South was . . . a tremendous success and broke a lot of ice in the South. We carried the state for Truman that fall." Jonathan Daniels COHC, 152. I have rearranged the order of sentences. See, too, Jonathan Daniels SOHP, 218.

13. *Raleigh News and Observer,* October 31, 1948.

14. *Time,* October 11, 1948, 25; press release, October 29, 1948, Charter Heslep MSS, Box 2; *New York Times,* October 30, 1948.

15. Steven M. Gillon, *Politics and Vision: The ADA and American Liberalism, 1947–1985* (New York, 1987), 47; Allen Morris, "Cracker Politics," September 18, 1948, clipping, Scrapbook, Morris MSS,

Box 245; Claude Pepper MS. Diary, August 11, 19, 1948; David, *Presidential Nominating Politics*, 18; Heinemann, *Harry Byrd*, 262–63; *Newsweek*, October 25, 1948, 32. See, too, James B. Gardner, "Political Leadership in a Period of Transition: Frank G. Clement, Albert Gore, Estes Kefauver, and Tennessee Politics, 1948–1956" (Ph.D. dissertation, Vanderbilt University, 1978), 136. The White House correspondent for the *New York Daily News* later recalled that he "thought that probably Truman would lose the southern states because I knew, coming out of the South, . . . something about the intense dislike of Truman down there." Charles J. Greene HSTL OH, 28.

16. Julius E. Thompson, *Percy Greene and the Jackson Advocate: The Life and Times of a Radical Conservative Black Newspaperman, 1897–1977* (Jefferson, N.C., 1994), 41. When Jim Folsom filed suit to compel Alabama's electors to cast their ballots for Truman, the *Montgomery Advertiser* called him "this berserk peckerwood, otherwise the 48th Governor of Alabama" and railed against "the blind staggers and lunges of this lost and bewildered man" (an allusion to Folsom's alcoholism). *Montgomery Advertiser*, November 6, 1948, clipping, William J. Primm MSS, Box 2.

17. Heinemann, *Harry Byrd*, 263; Stayer, "History," 188.

18. Earl Black and Merle Black, *The Vital South: How Presidents Are Elected* (Cambridge, Mass., 1992), 145; Morton, "Report on Arkansas," 37; James Roebuck, "Virginia and the Election of 1948: Prelude to Massive Resistance," *Valley Forge Journal* 6 (1992): 101; Emile B. Ader, "Why the Dixiecrats Failed," *Journal of Politics* 15 (1953): 360. In addition to winning the four states, Thurmond received the vote of one defiant elector from Tennessee.

19. Clark and Kirwan, *South since Appomattox*, 294; "Southwide Workshops Draft Civil Rights Program," *New South* 3 (1948): 1–2, 7; Anthony Champagne, *Congressman Sam Rayburn* (New Brunswick, N.J., 1984), 19; Covington and Ellis, *Terry Sanford*, 98; Joseph L. Bernd, "Georgia: Static and Dynamic," in *Changing Politics*, ed. Havard, 316–17. From Key West, a supporter wired the president: "Happy to inform you that Monroe County where you have your Little White House gave you 3742 votes against 740 votes for your opponents." Earl Adams to HST, November 2, 1948, HSTL OF 300–Florida, Box 977.

20. William M. Ramsey to J. Howard McGrath, February 22, 1948, McGrath MSS, Box 22; Tuggle, "Dixiecrats," 75; Alexander S. Leidholdt, *Editor for Justice: The Life of Louis I. Jaffé* (Baton Rouge, La., 2002), 443; Vincent Fitzpatrick, *Gerald Johnson: From Southern Liberal to National Conscience* (Baton Rouge, La., 2002), 197; Marie Morris Nitschke, "Virginius Dabney of Virginia: Portrait of a Southern Journalist in the Twentieth Century" (Ph.D. dissertation, Emory University, 1987), 189; *Raleigh News and Observer*, May 11, 1948, quoted in Kruse, "North Carolinians' Reaction." One white southerner who rejoiced in Truman's victory was Eudora Welty. Suzanne Marrs, "'The Huge Fateful Stage of the Outside World': Eudora Welty's Life in Politics," in *Eudora Welty and Politics: Did the Writer Crusade?* ed. Harriet Pollack and Suzanne Marrs (Baton Rouge, La., 2001), 70. Despite his distaste for the Dixiecrats, Dabney did not endorse Truman.

21. Cabell Phillips, *The Truman Presidency: The History of a Triumphant Succession* (New York, 1966), 223; Germany, "Rise of the Dixiecrats," 82; G. E. Allen, *Presidents Who Have Known Me*, 175. A prominent Virginia Democrat thought Truman had done "a splendid job." Martin A. Hutchinson to William M. Kemper, August 5, 1948, Hutchinson MSS, Box 11. For expressions of pleasure by Burnet Maybank and Olin Johnston in Truman's victory, see unidentified clipping, n.d. [November 1948], Burnet R. Maybank Scrapbook. See, too, Aubrey Williams to Fielding Wright, Feb-

ruary 25, 1948, Williams MSS, Box 35; Roger L. Simmons to HST, August 1, 1948, HSTL PSF 56; Wallace C. Porter to Oscar L. Chapman, November 8, 1948, Chapman MSS, Box 84; Harry S. Ashmore, "The South's Year of Decision," *Southern Packet* 4 (1948): 3; Brian Lewis Crispell, *Testing the Limits: George Armistead Smathers and Cold War America* (Athens, Ga., 1999), 36; Harry F. Byrd Sr. to William M. Tuck, July 21, 1948, Byrd MSS, Box 191. In Louisiana, a hotbed of rebellion, Governor-elect Earl Long announced that he was backing Truman, and in late September, Alabama's Jim Folsom endorsed the president. He was the only governor of a former Confederate state to do so publicly. Raymond B. Wells, "The States' Rights Movement of 1948: A Case Study" (M.A. essay, Mississippi State University, 1965), 48; Jim Folsom SOHP, 16. For the view that the southern attacks actually helped Truman, see Milton D. Stewart to George M. Elsey, February 11, 1948, Elsey MSS, Box 104.

22. McCoy and Ruetten, *Quest and Response,* 149; Alonzo L. Hamby, *Beyond the New Deal: Harry S. Truman and American Liberalism* (New York, 1973), 314; *Public Papers, 1949,* 439.

23. Ralph McGill to Walter Winchell et al., November 4, 1948, McGill MSS, Series 2, Box 3.

24. Robert J. Donovan, *Tumultuous Years: The Presidency of Harry S. Truman, 1949–1953* (New York, 1982), 21; Manchester, *Glory and Dream,* 482; Westbrook Pegler, "The State of the Nation," clipping, n.d. [1950?], Strom Thurmond Scrapbooks, Winthrop University; Lachicotte, *Rebel Senator,* 61; Tyler Abell, ed., *Drew Pearson Diaries, 1949–1959* (New York, 1974), 14; Eric F. Goldman, *The Crucial Decade—And After: America, 1945–1960* (New York, 1960), 91–92; Eben A. Ayers MS. Diary, November 5, 1948. Truman, did, though, name Thurmond to be a brigadier general in the Army Reserve. Francis H. Heller, *The Truman White House: The Administration of the Presidency, 1949–1953* (Lawrence, Kans., 1980), 82.

25. F. P. Miller, *Man from the Valley,* 197; Glen Jeansonne, *Leander Perez: Boss of the Delta* (Baton Rouge, La., 1977), 184–85; Philip H. Vaughan, "The Truman Administration's Fair Deal for Black America," *Missouri Historical Review* 70 (1976): 293; *Public Papers, 1949,* 169–70; Monte M. Poen, ed., *Strictly Personal and Confidential: The Letters Harry Truman Never Mailed* (Boston, 1982), 103. Truman directed an aide to send a less "abrupt" response than the one the president had drafted. In 1950, Thurmond and Wright were left off a list of governors invited to lunch with President Truman. *Washington Post,* June 17, 1950, clipping, L. Mendel Rivers MSS, LC, Box 52. For Truman's continued willingness to appoint southerners to high posts, see Martin L. Friedman HSTL OH, 39–40; McLaurin, "Role of Dixiecrats," 272.

26. "Meeting with President Truman," National Citizens' Council on Civil Rights, Report, January 1949, W. W. Waymack MSS, Box 85; MacDougall, *Gideon's Army,* 386; *Washington Post,* January 6, 1949, clipping, Stephen J. Spingarn MSS, Box 40; Gardner, *Harry Truman,* 148; Zangrando, *NAACP Crusade,* 201.

27. Hays, *Southern Moderate Speaks,* 33–34; Moon, *Balance of Power,* 201, 205; Frederickson, *Dixiecrat Revolt,* 192; Wade, *Fiery Cross,* 297. For Hays's ideas for compromises on civil rights, see Hays to Ralph McGill, November 10, 1948, McGill MSS, Series 2, Box 3; Helen Gahagan Douglas, transcription for KFMV Los Angeles, February 4, 1949, Charles B. Deane MSS, Box 25. At a White House staff meeting in the spring of 1949, though, the president said that civil rights bills should not be permitted to jeopardize foreign policy legislation. Ferrell, ed., *Truman in the White House,* 301–2.

28. Billington, "Civil Rights, President Truman and the South," 137; L. Reed, *Simple Decency*, 155; D. M. Giangreco and Kathryn Moore, *Dear Harry . . . Truman's Mailroom, 1945–1953: The Truman Administration through Correspondence with "Everyday Americans"* (Mechanicsburg, Pa., 1999), 216.

29. Glenn Feldman, *Politics, Society, and the Klan in Alabama, 1915–1949* (Tuscaloosa, Ala., 1999), 312; R. B. Chandler to Tom Connally, June 12, 1950, Connally MSS, Box 278; Albert Gore, "Harry Truman: The Man and the President," Huntington, W.Va., May 6, 1949, Gore MSS, House Speeches, Box 10; Walter Sillers to Palmer Bradley, December 6, 1949, Bradley MSS, Box 1; Billington, "Civil Rights," 138.

30. Jere L. Crook to HST, July 4, 1949, HSTL OF 596–A.

31. "Line-Up Against the President: Congress Set to Block Most of 'Fair Deal,'" *U.S. News and World Report*, March 25, 1949, 20–21; Wilkins with Mathews, *Standing Fast*, 203; Gardner, *Harry Truman*, 151; "Should President Truman's Civil Rights Program Be Adopted?" *University of Chicago Round Table* (February 6, 1949): 6–7, 11.

32. Scott Fowler, "Congress Blocks the Civil Rights Program," *Commentary* 9 (1950): 398–99; Zangrando, *NAACP Crusade*, 204; MDH to *Jacksonville Journal*, January 11, 1949, clipping, Fuller Warren MSS, Box 425; Steinberg, *Sam Rayburn*, 252. In 1949, too, the Alabama editor John Temple Graves denounced Truman's "civil force measures." John Temple Graves, "This Afternoon," *Birmingham Post*, August 16, 1949, clipping, Virginius Dabney MSS 7690–M, Box 8.

33. W. D. Barnard, *Dixiecrats and Democrats*, 140–41; "Views of the Southern Press," *Southern Weekly* 50 (June 28, 1950): 7; Jeansonne, *Leander Perez*, 174.

34. *New York Times*, June 1, 1950; Roger P. Leemhuis, "Olin Johnston Runs for the Senate, 1938 to 1962," *South Carolina Historical Association Proceedings* 56 (1986): 64; Luther Brady Faggart, "Defending the Faith: The 1950 U.S. Senate Race in South Carolina" (M.A. essay, University of South Carolina, 1992), 46–47, 62–63; Bryant Simon, "Race Reactions: African American Organizing, Liberalism, and White Working-Class Politics in Postwar South Carolina," in *Jumpin' Jim Crow: Southern Politics from Civil War to Civil Rights*, ed. Jane Dailey, Glenda Elizabeth Gilmore, and Bryant Simon (Princeton, N.J., 2000), 251; Frederickson, *Dixiecrat Revolt*, 202; poster, n.d. [1950], Strom Thurmond Scrapbooks, Winthrop University; *Southern Weekly* 50 (June 28, 1950): 1; Samuel Lubell, "Has Truman Lost the South?" *Look*, October 24, 1950, 129. In the 1950 senatorial contest in North Carolina, Frank Porter Graham's forces praised "the progressive leadership which President Truman is giving to the nation" whereas Willis Smith condemned "Truman socialism." Cary Committee for Graham, clipping, FDRL OF 300—North Carolina, Box 981. In November 1950, in an address in Memphis, John Temple Graves reported more antagonism toward Truman in the South, the heartland of the Democratic Party, than in any other section. *The States' Righter*, December 15, 1950.

35. Price Daniel OH, North Texas University, 85–87, 107–8; "Statement of Attorney General Price Daniel Re President Truman's Tidelands Speech," Daniel MSS, Box 59.

36. G. N. Green, *Establishment in Texas Politics*, 108, 142–43; Lindsy Escoe Pack, "The Political Aspects of the Texas Tidelands Controversy" (Ph.D. dissertation, Texas A & M University, 1979), 114–15. See, too, "President's Outburst on the Tidelands," *Fort Worth Star-Telegram*, May 20, 1952, Thomas A. Pickett MSS, Box 2; Price Daniel Sr. LBJL OH, 12; Maury Maverick Jr. SOHP, 32; Ernest R. Bartley, *The Tidelands Oil Controversy: A Legal and Historical Analysis* (Austin, Tex., 1953),

229; Jerry Flemmons, *Amon: The Life of Amon Carter, Sr. of Texas* (Austin, Tex., 1978), 475. Not all southerners opposed Truman on the tidelands. Alabama Senators Lister Hill and John Sparkman and Governor Sidney McMath of Arkansas were among those who agreed with his stand. Engler, *Politics of Oil,* 355; *Louisville Courier-Journal,* n.d. [1948], clipping, McMath MSS, Box 13.

37. Hamilton, *Lister Hill,* 183; William M. Boyd, "Southern Politics, 1948–1952," *Phylon* 13 (1952): 232; James R. Sweeney, "Revolt in Virginia: Harry Byrd and the 1952 Presidential Election," *Virginia Magazine of History and Biography* 86 (1978): 182. See, too, "The South's Plan to Beat Truman," *U.S. News and World Report,* November 30, 1951, 29, 31; Harry F. Byrd, address, Selma, Alabama, November 1, 1951, copy in Herman E. Talmadge MSS, Senatorial Early Office Series, Box 39; George Rothwell Brown, "The Political Parade," clipping, n.d. [1951], Spessard Holland MSS, Florida State University. In order to build support for his controversial policy in Korea, however, Truman wooed southern Democrats. He even covertly invited Richard Russell to take over the majority leadership. Hamby, *Beyond the New Deal,* 442.

38. Catherine A. Barnes, *Journey from Jim Crow: The Desegregation of Southern Transit* (New York, 1983), 72–74; Kluger, *Simple Justice,* 558–59. For an illuminating discussion of the role of the Truman administration in filing the *amicus* briefs, see Dudziak, "Desegregation," 103–4n. In Truman's first term, the administration had involved itself in *Shelley v. Kraemer* to outlaw restrictive covenants. Never before had the government stepped into a civil rights case in which it had no direct interest. Mary L. Dudziak, *Cold War Civil Rights: Race and the Image of American Democracy* (Princeton, N.J., 2000), 90–91.

39. John Robert Greene, *The Crusade: The Presidential Election of 1952* (Lanham, Md., 1985), 12; Peter R. Henriques, "John S. Battle and Virginia Politics, 1948–1953" (Ph.D. dissertation, University of Virginia, 1971), 263, 266; Wilkinson, *Harry Byrd,* 88, 84. See, too, Anna Holden, "Race and Politics: Congressional Elections in the Fifth District of Georgia, 1946 to 1952" (M.A. essay, University of North Carolina at Chapel Hill, 1955), 150–51.

40. Feldman, *From Demagogue to Dixiecrat,* 164; Frederickson, *Dixiecrat Revolt,* 225; O. Douglas Weeks, *Texas Presidential Politics in 1952* (Austin, Tex., 1953), 16–17; Sam Kinch and Stuart Long, *Allan Shivers: The Pied Piper of Texas Politics* (Austin, Tex., 1973), 77; Pritchard, "Southern Politics," 314. See, too, Orval Eugene Faubus, *Down from the Hills* (Little Rock, Ark., 1980), 6.

41. Philip A. Grant Jr., "Editorial Reaction to the 1952 Presidential Candidacy of Richard B. Russell," *Georgia History Quarterly* 57 (1973): 167–77; Hamby, *Man of the People,* 602.

42. John Bartlow Martin, *Adlai Stevenson of Illinois: The Life of Adlai E. Stevenson* (Garden City, N.Y., 1976), 652. At their national convention in 1952, the Democrats approved a civil rights plank that was somewhat stronger than the one that had led to the walkout in 1948, yet there was no Dixiecrat defection. It appears that the 1952 platform was acceptable only because Harry Truman was not directly associated with it. He was not a candidate, and there was no clause praising this "traitor" to Dixie for his courage on civil rights. (Truman himself had no thought of compromise. When he heard there was a plan afoot to weaken the party's civil rights plank, he told Senator Humphrey, "If that convention tries to disavow all I have worked for in the last seven years, I'll come out there and announce that I'll run for another term.") McCoy and Ruetten, *Quest and Response,* 323–25; McKay, *Texas and Fair Deal,* 392.

43. Egerton, *Speak Now against the Day,* 577; James F. Byrnes, address, October 21, 1952,

Charleston, S.C., William D. Workman Jr., MSS, Box 21; statement by Governor James F. Byrnes at press-radio conference on September 18, 1952, Herman E. Talmadge MSS, Senatorial Early Office Series, Box 39; Philip A. Grant Jr., "Eisenhower and the 1952 Republican Invasion of the South: The Case of Virginia," *Presidential Studies Quarterly* 20 (1990): 288; Allan P. Sindler, "The Unsolid South: A Challenge to the Democratic Party," in *The Uses of Power: 7 Cases in American Politics,* ed. Alan F. Westin (New York, 1962), 268; Peter R. Henriques, "The Byrd Organization Crushes a Liberal Challenge, 1950–1953," *Virginia Magazine of History and Biography* 87 (1979): 26; Gardner, *Harry Truman,* 210–14.

44. Heard, *Two-Party South?* 21; Lubell, "Has Truman Lost the South?" 129; James F. Byrnes, introduction of General Eisenhower, Columbia, S.C., September 30, 1952, William D. Workman Jr. MSS, Box 21; Grayson, "North Carolina and Harry Truman," 300; Arjen Westerhoff, "Politics of Protest: Strom Thurmond and the Development of the Republican Southern Strategy, 1948–1972" (M.A. essay, Smith College, 1997), 22.

45. Nunnelley, *Bull Connor,* 54; Giglio, "Harry S. Truman," 245, 250; Andrew J. Dunar, "Truman on Civil Rights: A Post-Presidential Perspective," paper delivered at Southern Historical Association meeting (November 1995), 2; Hamby, *Man of the People,* 631. "I read with disgust Truman's speech," one woman wrote Senator Gore in 1958. "Of all people HE should be the last to make that speech." Kate Steele to Albert Gore, February 28, 1958, Gore MSS, "Civil Rights." Less than half a year after Truman took office, Jonathan Daniels recorded an episode at a gathering on Jefferson Island: "President told a story that when he was sixteen years old somebody told him and he believed it that [the] way to solve race problem was to let women become mulattos and octoroons and then they wouldn't breed. 'Like mules,' a Senator said. 'Yes,' said HST. 'That's the point.'" Jonathan Daniels MS. Diary, September 23, 1945.

46. Brian Urquhart, *Ralph Bunche: An American Life* (New York, 1993), 438.

47. Dean Acheson to HST, April 14, 1960; HST to Acheson, April 20, 1960; Acheson to HST, June 28, 1960, Acheson MSS, Yale University, Box 31; Harris Wofford to Harry Truman, April 20, 1960, Dean Acheson MSS, Box 92; Dunar, "Truman on Civil Rights," 2, 5–6, 8. Acheson told Wofford that he had "scolded" Truman for his comments on the sit-ins, adding, "I hope and believe that H.S.T. will make amends but they won't mend the harm he has done." Acheson to Wofford, April 28, 1960, Acheson MSS, Box 92.

48. *Des Moines Register,* September 12, 1963.

49. *New York Herald Tribune,* September 10, 1963; *New Orleans Times-Picayune,* September 15, 1963; unidentified clipping in T. C. Almon to HST, September 23, 1963, HSTL PPGF, Box 194; Stephen M. Young, *Tales Out of Congress* (Philadelphia, 1964), 22–23. Accounts of his talk differ in minor detail.

50. *New York Post,* April 12, 1965, clipping, HSTL Post Presidential Files, Box 300; *New York Times,* April 15, 1965.

51. Ted McCurdy to HST, April 15, 1965; George Hall to HST, September 13, 1961, HSTL Post-Presidential Files, Box 300; *Daytona Beach Morning Journal,* April 13, 1965, clipping, HSTL PPGF, Box 161.

52. Clipping, n.d. [1955 or 1956], SCHW MSS, Box 83. In the 1950s, he backed the *Brown* decision and the effort of liberal congressmen to deny funds to states that sanctioned segregation. In

the fall of 1953, after receiving overwhelmingly enthusiastic receptions in two places, Truman had written Acheson, "I don't know what the world is coming to when people in Arkansas and southeast Missouri, which is about the same as the deep South, turn out like that for an Ex-President, who has told them where to get off on Civil Rights." Ferrell, ed., *Off the Record,* 297. Truman, like FDR, had a "little White House" in the South, but Key West was so atypical that it did not begin to have the effect on him that the Warm Springs domicile exerted on Roosevelt.

53. Carl T. Rowan to Augusta Shannon, April 19, 1960, Rowan MSS, Subgroup 6, Series 4, Subseries 1, Box 2; Watson, "Papers," 638.

8. THE LONE COWPOKE FROM DIXIE

1. Caro, *Path to Power,* 449; Michael Davie, *LBJ: A Foreign Observer's Viewpoint* (New York, 1966), 5. See, too, Ronnie Dugger, *The Politician* (New York, 1982), 140. Roosevelt must have meant the first southern president of the modern era, since there had been a number of southern presidents, particularly in the early years of the republic. "Lyndon Johnson will always be memorable because he was our last frontiersman-President," wrote Joseph Alsop. *Washington Post,* January 26, 1973.

2. Tom Wicker, *JFK and LBJ: The Influence of Personality upon Politics* (New York, 1968), 152; Jonathan Daniels, *Frontier on the Potomac* (New York, 1946), 73. An INS correspondent also alluded to Johnson's "frontier heritage and background." John William Theis LBJL OH, 7. As late as 1970, a newspaper referred to his "Texas accent, . . . his frontier aura, his Southern origin." "A Complex Man," *Christian Science Monitor,* January 3, 1970, clipping, Museum of Television and Radio Archives.

3. Lyndon Baines Johnson, *The Vantage Point: Perspectives of the Presidency, 1963–1969* (New York, 1971), 155.

4. Dugger, *Politician,* 407; Andrew Sparks, "President Johnson's Georgia Ancestors," *Atlanta Journal and Constitution Magazine,* clipping, LBJL, 6; Wright Patman LBJL OH, 2: 7 (italics added).

5. *Public Papers, 1963–64,* 1: 650; Dugger, *Politician,* 407. See, too, Rebekah Baines Johnson, "The Johnsons: Descendants of John Johnson, A Revolutionary Soldier of Georgia: A Genealogical History," LBJA Subject File, LBJL, Box 72.

6. Robert Dallek, *Lone Star Rising: Lyndon B. Johnson and His Times, 1908–1960* (New York, 1991), 17.

7. Dugger, *Politician,* 407, 27; Rebekah Baines Johnson, *A Family Album* (New York, 1965), 30; Caro, *Path to Power,* 153. In 1956 he had boasted, "Both of my grandparents fought on the Confederate side in the War Between the States." Mark Stern, "Lyndon Johnson and Richard Russell: Institutions, Ambitions and Civil Rights," *Presidential Studies Quarterly* 21 (1991): 692. See, too, *Binghamton (N.Y.) Sunday Press,* June 5, 1960, clipping, LBJL Senate Political Files, Box 253.

8. Merle Miller, *Lyndon: An Oral Biography* (New York, 1980), 50–51; Ruth Montgomery, *Mrs. LBJ* (New York, 1964), 3; Jan Jarboe Russell, *Lady Bird: A Biography of Mrs. Johnson* (New York, 1999), 26–32; *Washington Star,* September 17, 1967, clipping, Katie Louchheim MSS, Box 20; Lady Bird Johnson to Virginia Durr, May 1, 1961, Durr MSS, LBJL. Lister Hill pointed out that "some of her family came from right across the Alabama River in Autauga County. We're on one side of

the river and Autauga County is on the other side." Lister Hill LBJL OH, 16. See, too, Wright Patman LBJL OH, 2: 9; *Birmingham Post-Herald,* March 25, 1964, clipping, Southern Collection, Birmingham Public Library.

9. Caro, *Path to Power,* 153; LBJ to Mrs. S. E. Johnson, August 20, 1937, LBJ MSS, Family Correspondence, Box 1. Dugger, *Politician,* 465, 220–21; Bill Davidson, "Lyndon Johnson: Can a Southerner be Elected President?" *Look,* August 18, 1959, 66; Eric F. Goldman, *The Tragedy of Lyndon Johnson* (New York, 1969), 289; James H. Rowe Jr., LBJL OH, 18.

10. Allen Ellender LBJL OH, 18; James Reston, *Deadline: A Memoir* (New York, 1991), 308; Timothy G. Smith, ed., *Merriman Smith's Book of Presidents: A White House Memoir* (New York, 1972), 35–36; James H. Rowe Jr. LBJL OH, 4: 5. The congressman was Warren Magnuson. Lady Bird Johnson said of her husband's relationship to Abe Fortas, "I think it mattered to Lyndon that he came from the South." Laura Kalman, *Abe Fortas: A Biography* (New Haven, Conn., 1990), 204.

11. *Washington Post,* April 1, 1965, clipping, Family Correspondence, LBJL, Box 2; Christie L. Bourgeois, "Stepping over Lines: Lyndon Johnson, Black Texans, and the National Youth Administration, 1935–1937," *Southwestern Historical Quarterly* 91 (1987): 151.

12. Neil R. McMillen, commentary on "The Death of a Friendship: Richard Russell and Lyndon Johnson," Southern Historical Association meeting (November 1989); Emmette S. Redford LBJL OH, 2: 14; Monroe Billington, "Lyndon B. Johnson and Blacks: The Early Years," *Journal of Negro History* 62 (1977): 27; Stanford Dyer, "Lyndon B. Johnson and the Politics of Civil Rights, 1935–1960: The Art of 'Moderate' Leadership" (Ph.D. dissertation, Texas A & M, 1978), 43–50; Carol A. Weisenberger, *Dollars and Dreams: The National Youth Administration in Texas* (New York, 1994), 134; Dugger, *Politician,* 216; George Reedy, *Lyndon B. Johnson: A Memoir* (New York, 1982), 39. Robert Caro has challenged the prevailing contention that Johnson was free of bigotry. He also has concluded that the NYA in Texas had the poorest record in the country with regard to granting blacks a fair share of aid in schooling. Caro, *The Years of Lyndon Johnson: Master of the Senate* (New York, 2002), 712–14, 731. It is difficult to know how to square Caro's evidence with the enthusiasm of blacks for Johnson's performance. One writer has said that, contrary to the notion that Johnson "always moved with the political winds" and advocated civil rights only when it was expedient, he had "a hidden agenda to address the problem of minorities. . . . Johnson's record demonstrates an active and genuine commitment to extend to blacks their share of the National Youth Administration. He did it in a covert and paternalistic way, but he made a consistent and relatively successful effort." Bourgeois, "Stepping Over Lines," 169. In Johnson's very first year in Congress, he secured approval for a nearly half-million-dollar housing project for black and Mexican-American families in Austin. Dyer, "Lyndon B. Johnson," 59–60. Long's record on race, it should be noted, was not nearly so exemplary as it has often been said to have been. See Glen Jeansonne, "Huey Long and Racism," *Louisiana History* 33 (1992): 265–82.

13. Frank Cormier, *LBJ: The Way He Was* (Garden City, N.Y., 1977), 145; Hubert Humphrey, *The Education of a Public Man* (New York, 1976), 163; William S. White, "Who *Is* Lyndon Johnson?" *Harper's* 216 (1958): 56; Robert L. Riggs, "The South *Could* Rise Again: Lyndon Johnson and Others," in *Candidates 1960: Behind the Headlines in the Presidential Race,* ed. Eric Sevareid (New York, 1959), 316. In introducing Johnson on the Mercer University campus in the fall of 1964, Herman Talmadge said that save for the eighteen "Southern Senators," LBJ had been the best senator for

the South. Excerpts of Remarks of Senator Herman E. Talmadge, October 14, 1960, Howard W. Smith MSS, Box 204.

14. George Reedy LBJL OH, Tape 2: 18; Maury Maverick Jr., "The Hill Country of Lyndon Johnson," *New Republic*, March 14, 1964, 12; Emmette S. Redford LBJL OH, 2: 9; Kittie Clyde Leonard LBJL OH, 14; McMillen, Commentary on "Death of a Friendship." Johnson, Paul Conkin has written, "was in many respects identifiably southern, but it may be equally important that he was never part of the inner South. . . . Lyndon Johnson was a clear representative of the outer South. He came from the hill country of Texas, an area with few blacks and where sturdy Germans made up the only important minority. He had almost no hangups about race, even as he echoed conventional racial stereotypes." Conkin, "Lyndon Johnson and the Outer South," in *Is There a Southern Political Tradition?* ed. Charles W. Eagles (Jackson, Miss., 1996), 151–52, 156. "Architecture in the city of Fredericksburg," one guidebook has noted, "has little relation to the way of life on the Southern plantation." Drury B. Alexander, "Homes in the Hills," in *A President's Country: A Guide to the Hill Country of Texas*, ed. Jack Maguire (Austin, Tex., 1964), 58. For data showing that modern-day Texas is questionably southern, see John Shelton Reed, *The Enduring South: Subcultural Persistence in Mass Society* (Chapel Hill, N.C., 1986), 14–17.

15. Stanley Walker, "Is Texas 'South,' 'West,' Both or More?" *New York Times Magazine*, April 12, 1959, 35; William C. Pool, Emmie Craddock, and David E. Conrad, *Lyndon Baines Johnson: The Formative Years* (San Marcos, Tex., 1965), 5, quoting Walter Prescott Webb, *The Great Plains* (New York, 1935), 8; Vandiver, *Southwest*, 21.

16. Maverick, "Hill Country," 12; W. W. Newcomb and Gerald Raun, "Where the Deer and the Paisano Play," in *A President's Country*, ed. Maguire, 45–49; Hugh Sidey, *A Very Personal Presidency: Lyndon Johnson in the White House* (New York, 1968), 22; Bill Porterfield, *LBJ Country* (Garden City, N.Y., 1965), 46.

17. Hubert Humphrey LBJL OH, Interview 2: 9; Carl Solberg, *Hubert Humphrey—A Biography* (New York, 1984), 163; interview, Nicholas deB. Katzenbach, April 13, 1989; Liz Carpenter, *Ruffles and Flourishes* (Garden City, N.Y., 1970), 14; Caro, *Master of the Senate*, xviii; Michael Davie, "A Briton Scans Our Obsession," *Washington Post*, June 18, 1963, clipping, Bess Furman MSS, Box 44. See, too, Tom C. Clark HSTL OH (Jerry N. Hess interview), 202. As vice president, Johnson appointed Webb, the premier historian of the land beyond the 98th meridian, to his staff. Melody Webb, "Lyndon Johnson: The Last Frontier President," *Journal of the West* 34 (1995): 74.

18. Tom Wicker, "With Johnson on the Ranch: The President, Observed at Home, Reveals Image of a Westerner," *New York Times*, January 5, 1964; Thomas G. Wicker LBJL OH, 59; Paul H. Douglas LBJL OH, 1; James H. Rowe Jr., LBJL OH, 18. Paul B. Johnson Jr. LBJL OH, 3; Riggs, "South *Could* Rise Again," in *Candidates 1960*, ed. Sevareid, 319. "The Great Southwest," wrote the San Antonio congressman Maury Maverick in 1937, "is the land of my fathers. The old South, on the other hand, seems to me to be the land of my forefathers, a strange and distant illusion." Maury Maverick, *A Maverick American* (New York, 1937), 224. James H. Rowe Jr., LBJL OH, 18.

19. Reedy, *Lyndon B. Johnson*, 75; Dugger, *Politician*, 41, 141–44; Caro, *Master of the Senate*, 647; Cormier, *LBJ*, 110; D. B. Hardeman OH. As late as 1964, his capsule campaign biography, which made no mention of the South, stated, "He was born in a small, weather-beaten clapboard house

in Stonewall, Texas, in 1908, when Texas—and indeed the whole West, was frontier country." "New Johnson Biography," Wayne L. Hays MSS, Box 20.

20. Hal K. Rothman, *LBJ's Texas White House: "Our Heart's Home"* (College Station, Tex., 2001), 58, 77–78.

21. M. Miller, *Lyndon,* 59; Cormier, *LBJ,* 19; Evelyn Lincoln, *Kennedy and Johnson* (New York, 1968), 14.

22. Stewart Alsop, "Lyndon Johnson: How Does He Do It?" *Saturday Evening Post,* January 24, 1959, 38.

23. M. Miller, *Lyndon,* 403–4; Richard S. "Cactus" Pryor LBJL OH, 9. Johnson did not abandon his western identification even after he became vice president. Asked why Jacqueline Kennedy was on the fateful trip to Dallas in 1963 when she did not usually accompany the president on political expeditions, Johnson replied, "I think she had a curiosity about the Western background here. . . . We had planned to have a little Western show for her, horses and things that we thought she would like." Walter Cronkite interview of LBJ, 1969, Burton Benjamin MSS, Box 20.

24. Reedy, *Lyndon B. Johnson,* 154; Joseph Kraft, *Profiles in Power* (New York, 1966), 11; Doris Kearns, *Lyndon Johnson and the American Dream* (New York, 1991), 127. Johnson's notion of the call of the wild was also suspect. A Georgia governor regarded forays at the LBJ Ranch as "about the plushest hunting he had ever done." Harold Paulk Henderson, *Ernest Vandiver: Governor of Georgia* (Athens, Ga., 2000), 201.

25. Jim Bishop, *A Day in the Life of President Johnson* (New York, 1967), 184; Steinberg, *Sam Johnson's Boy,* 535.

26. LBJ Library Audio Visual Collections, "LBJ Humor"; James E. McMillan, ed., *The Ernest W. McFarland Papers: The United States Senate Years, 1940–1952* (Prescott, Ariz., 1995), 397; Robert Spivack, "The New President," *New York Herald Tribune,* December 1, 1963, clipping, James H. Rowe Jr., MSS, Box 100; Paul K. Conkin, *Big Daddy from the Pedernales: Lyndon Baines Johnson* (Boston, 1986), 7.

27. William S. White, "Johnson, the Ablest Leader," *Washington Evening Star,* June 13, 1958, clipping, A. Willis Robertson MSS, Box 212, Folder 12.

28. Paul Christensen, *West of the American Dream: An Encounter with Texas* (College Station, Tex., 2001), 26; Theodore White, "Texas: Land of Wealth and Fear," *Reporter,* June 8, 1954, 35; Odum, *Southern Regions,* 5; Howard W. Odum, "Regionalism vs. Sectionalism in the South's Place in the National Economy," *Social Forces* 12 (1934): 345; *Dallas Morning News,* May 23, 1999; Eugene Genovese, *The Political Economy of Slavery: Studies in the Economy and Society of the Slave South* (Middletown, Conn., 1989), 30; Walter L. Buenger, "Texas and the South," *Southwestern Historical Quarterly* 103 (2000): 314–18. "Significantly, Texas seceded before Arkansas, North Carolina, Tennessee, and Virginia," Buenger has pointed out. "By the early 1890s Confederate mythology, a cotton-based economy, a common culture based on evangelical Protestantism, racial violence, and ties of friendship and kinship linked Texans more firmly than ever to the South." Walter L. Buenger, *The Path to a Modern South: Northeast Texas between Reconstruction and the Great Depression* (Austin, Tex., 2001), xvi. A geographer has written that "the South finally fades away as one approaches the famous 100th Meridian," and Texas, in particular, "presents some vexing taxonomic and cartographic

questions." Wilbur Zelinsky, *The Cultural Geography of the United States* (Englewood Cliffs, N.J., 1992), 124.

29. Mary McGrory, "Lyndon Johnson—Tall Texas Marshal," *America* 100 (January 10, 1959): 418; *Time*, July 18, 1960, 10; G. William Whitehurst MS. Diary, January 7, 1969; Conkin, *Big Daddy*, 1, 7. Johnson, said a White House correspondent, "was . . . self-conscious about his Texas origins—more so than any other Texan I've ever known." Helen Thomas, *Dateline: White House* (New York, 1975), 40.

30. Transcript of BBC World Service, April 11, 1965, Richard Rovere MSS, Box 5; Emma Jean Walker, "The Contemporary Texan: An Examination of Major Additions to the Mythical Texan in the Twentieth Century" (Ph.D. dissertation, University of Texas, 1966), 166–68.

31. Gertrude Harris Cook, "The Heritage of Lyndon B. Johnson," LBJL; Steinberg, *Sam Johnson's Boy*, 19.

32. William Humphrey, *No Resting Place* (New York, 1989), 9.

33. Dugger, *Politician*, 74; *Austin American-Statesman Sunday Magazine*, December 2, 1928, clipping, LBJ MSS, Family Correspondence, Box 2; Caro, *Path to Power*, 44; Hugh Sidey, "The Presidency," *Life*, May 31, 1968, 32B; Sidey, *Very Personal Presidency*, 23; Peter B. Benchley LBJL OH, 23–24. A Texas newspaperman recalled: "Some people said he had an ancestor at the Alamo, and of course they made a lot of that. . . . Then he made a joke out of it. He said he was talking about the Alamo, a saloon at Laredo, Texas. Something like that." Bascom Timmons LBJL OH, 20.

34. Kearns, *Lyndon Johnson*, xv.

35. M. Miller, *Lyndon*, 89; Dugger, *Politician*, 251. In the late 1950s Johnson compared the *Sputnik* challenge to the Alamo. Just as the Mexicans had been defeated, so, too, would the Russians be overcome. Caro, *Master of the Senate*, 24.

36. Caro, *Path to Power*, 4, 21; Theodore H. White, *The Making of the President, 1964* (New York, 1965), 36; Conkin, *Big Daddy*, 3; Sidey, *Very Personal Presidency*, 21; Steinberg, *Sam Johnson's Boy*, 16–17; Cormier, *LBJ*, 19. The many versions of Johnson's grandmother's heroics vary in detail.

37. Caro, *Path to Power*, 665; *Time*, June 22, 1953, 21; Larry L. King, "My Hero LBJ," *Harper's* 233 (1966): 54; Cormier, *LBJ*, 16–17; Caro, *Master of the Senate*, 118, 426; *Public Papers, 1968*, 1109. See, too, Lincoln, *Kennedy and Johnson*, 16, 75. When an interviewer began a question to a Texas congressman by stating that it "was often said of Lyndon Johnson that he was more a citizen of Washington, D.C. than of Texas," the congressman broke in to respond, "I never thought that was true of Lyndon. Lyndon made a tremendous effort to hold his ties at home." W. R. Poage OH, 59.

38. Harry Middleton, "The Lion in Winter: LBJ in Retirement," in *Lyndon Johnson Remembered: An Intimate Portrait of the Presidency*, ed. Thomas W. Cowger and Sherwin J. Markham (Lanham, Md., 2003), 151–52.

39. Key with Heard, *Southern Politics*, 254; Thurgood Marshall LBJL OH, 6. Marshall added, "And that his record wasn't that bad. But I do remember that other people in NAACP hit the ceiling." See, too, Nicholas deB. Katzenbach LBJL OH, 1: 5–6; Lady Bird Johnson OH, 5, Richard B. Russell MSS; Bascom Timmons LBJL OH, 16. "Although only one Texan in eight is black," one study has noted, "racial attitudes were shaped by the experience shared with other southern states in the Civil War and Reconstruction. In east Texas from 1882 to 1943, there were 551 lynchings of African Americans." Jack Bass and Walter DeVries, *The Transformation of Southern Politics: Social*

Change and Political Consequence since 1945 (New York, 1976), 306. "The Southwest," wrote the well-known geographer, D. W. Meinig, "is a distinctive place to the American mind but a somewhat blurred place on American maps, which is to say that everyone knows that there is a Southwest but that there is little agreement as to just where it is." Michael J. Riley, "Constituting the Southwest, Contesting the Southwest, Reinventing the Southwest," *Journal of the Southwest* 36 (1994): 221.

40. Reedy, *Lyndon B. Johnson*, 154.

41. Jeff Shesol, *Mutual Contempt: Lyndon Johnson, Robert Kennedy, and the Feud that Defined a Decade* (New York, 1997), 29; Dyer, "Lyndon B. Johnson," 46; Conkin, *Big Daddy*, 62–63; Richard Wilson, quoted in Dugger, *Politician*, 358–59.

42. Reedy, *Lyndon B. Johnson*, 154; Harry McPherson, *A Political Education* (Boston, 1972), 177; Henry Brandon, *Special Relationships: A Foreign Correspondent's Memoirs from Roosevelt to Reagan* (New York, 1988), 243. Lady Bird Johnson, though, once said: "Lyndon didn't even want the sun to set before he got out of Washington when sessions of Congress ended. He'd rush right back to our ranch here in Texas." Charles L. Sanders, "LBJ and Civil Rights: An Interview with Lady Bird Johnson," *Ebony* (March 1974): 161.

43. M. Miller, *Lyndon*, 68; A. Willis Robertson, LBJL OH, 9; Richard Bolling LBJL OH, 6. Miller quotes Russell Morton Brown's recollection of Connally's words. Brown says that the remarks were occasioned by Johnson's voting against a southern filibuster, but since Johnson was at this time in the House, whose rules did not permit a filibuster, that feature of Brown's story at least is inaccurate.

44. Michael C. Janeway, "Lyndon Johnson and the Rise of Conservatism in Texas" (Senior thesis, Harvard University, 1952), 62; T. H. White, *Making of the President, 1964*, 252–53; Schwarz, *New Dealers*, 250.

45. Statement, August 19, 1948, quoted in *Houston Post*, research memo, John Tower MSS NA 51; Booth Mooney, *The Politicians, 1945–1960* (Philadelphia, 1970), 266; T. H. White, *Making of the President, 1964*, 253n. In 1948, Johnson, despite his avowed hostility to civil rights legislation, carried African-American precincts, in part because of memory of his past behavior, in part because of his association with FDR, in part because he quietly promoted projects such as a new black hospital, and in part because his opponent offered even less. The editor of the black newspaper in Houston said of Johnson: "Though he is no angel, he is about as good as we have seen in the race." Subsequently, the editor added: "Coke has been as cold to Negroes as a snake all of his life. Lyndon has been supported by Negroes throughout his political career and has shown himself to be as nearly a statesman as the South has produced." Patrick Cox, "'Nearly a Statesman': LBJ and Texas Blacks in the 1948 Election," *Social Science Quarterly* 74 (1993): 241–63.

46. *Congressional Record*, 81st Cong., 1st Sess., 2042–49; Robert A. Caro, *The Years of Lyndon Johnson: Means of Ascent* (New York, 1990), xvii; Rowland Evans and Robert D. Novak, *Lyndon B. Johnson: The Exercise of Power* (New York, 1966), 43.

47. Jeter D. Steger II to LBJ, May 19, 1949; Lulu B. White to LBJ, March 9, 1949; LBJ to Bob Lowdon Jr., March 19, 1949; LBJ to Paul T. Spellman, March 19, 1949, LBJ MSS, Senate files, Box 214.

48. Hal E. Tindall to LBJ, April 1, 1949, quoted in Billington, "Lyndon B. Johnson and Blacks," 38; Dyer, "Lyndon B. Johnson," 80–81.

49. LBJ to James H. Rowe Jr., March 15, 1949, Senate files, LBJL, Box 214.

50. Bobby Baker, with Larry L. King, *Wheeling and Dealing: Confessions of a Capitol Hill Operator* (New York, 1978), 40–41.

51. Walter White to Adlai Stevenson, February 19, 1953, copy in Richard B. Russell MSS, Political Series; Steinberg, *Sam Johnson's Boy*, 436; Roy Wilkins LBJL OH, 1.

52. Baker with King, *Wheeling and Dealing*, 70–71; Arthur M. Schlesinger Jr., *A Thousand Days: John F. Kennedy in the White House* (Boston, 1965), 10–11. In April 1949, one black editor wrote Johnson, "I believe you are a captive of the political mold and traditions of Texas and the South, and that you don't dare even think courageously on this question . . . but you are still about as good a man as we've got up there from Texas." Carolyn M. Johnson, "A Southern Response to Civil Rights: Lyndon Baines Johnson and Civil Rights Legislation 1956–1960" (M.A. essay, University of Houston, 1975), 26.

53. Fite, *Russell*, 268; Thomas M. Gaskin, "Lyndon B. Johnson and Senator Richard B. Russell: Death of a Friendship," paper delivered at Southern Historical Association meeting (November 1989); Lady Bird Johnson OH, 4, Richard B. Russell MSS; Chappelle Matthews OH, 54–55, Russell MSS; Steinberg, *Sam Johnson's Boy*, 289; William H. Darden LBJL OH, 6. "Johnson was our enemy all of the years that he was Senate Majority Leader," recalled the secretary of the Leadership Conference on Civil Rights. "We never regarded him as an ally at all." Charles and Barbara Whalen, *The Longest Debate: A Legislative History of the 1964 Civil Rights Act* (Cabin John, Md., 1985), 75.

54. Robert Parker, with Richard Rashke, *Capitol Hill in Black and White* (New York, 1986), 16.

55. McPherson, *Political Education*, 138.

56. Fite, *Russell*, 268–69, 302, 309–10; Gilbert C. Fite, "Richard B. Russell and Lyndon B. Johnson: The Story of a Strange Friendship," *Missouri Historical Review* 83 (1989): 130.

57. David C. Williams, "The Legend of Lyndon Johnson," *Progressive* 21 (1957): 22; Clinton P. Anderson, with Milton Viorst, *Outsider in the Senate: Senator Clinton Anderson's Memoirs* (New York, 1970), 128–29. Yet in another place in the same book Anderson wrote, "Lyndon and I were both Southwesterners." Ibid., 299. Richard Nixon later said, "I don't think Johnson made a move on any very major issue without talking to Dick Russell." Richard Milhous Nixon OH, 16, Russell MSS. One of the foremost political scientists of his generation remarked on Johnson's situation as majority leader: "Even had he not had political and personal ties to the Southern wing of the party, he could hardly have avoided being drawn toward the Southerners in any effort to develop the semblance of a program likely to be acceptable to most Senate Democrats." David B. Truman, *The Congressional Party: A Case Study* (New York, 1959), 315.

58. *New York Times*, March 12, 1956; T. Harry Williams, "Huey, Lyndon, and Southern Radicalism," *Journal of American History* 60 (1973): 283; Caro, *Master of the Senate*, 786; John Egerton, *The Americanization of Dixie: The Southernization of America* (New York, 1974), 134; copy of address by Clarence Mitchell in Earle C. Clements to Lyndon B. Johnson, January 27, 1958, Clements MSS, Box 192. The first draft of the manifesto had been even stronger. Brent J. Aucoin, "The Southern Manifesto and Southern Opposition to Desegregation," *Arkansas Historical Quarterly* 55 (1996): 180–81.

59. G. N. Green, *Establishment in Texas Politics*, 190; Robert J. Robertson, "Congressman Jack Brooks, the Civil Rights Act of 1964, and the Desegregation of Public Accommodations and Facilities in Southeast Texas: A Preliminary Inquiry," *Texas Gulf Historical and Biographical Record* 35

(1999): 21–22; Albert Gore Sr. SOHP, 2: 48–49; Doris Fleeson, "Lyndon Johnson and the Mani-festo," *Chattanooga Times,* March 16, 1956, Estes Kefauver MSS, Series 5g, Box 5; John C. Stennis LBJL OH, 9; Fite, *Russell,* 336; M. Miller, *Lyndon,* 187; Baker with King, *Wheeling and Dealing,* 71. When the Arkansas editor Harry Ashmore asked the South Carolina senator Olin Johnston to try to dissuade Strom Thurmond from drafting the manifesto because it would embarrass moderates such as John Sparkman, Johnston replied, "Oh hell, it ain't any use for anybody to talk to Strom. The trouble with Strom is he believes that shit!" Harry Ashmore LBJL OH, 6–7. Thurmond him-self later recalled that when the southern senators approached Johnson about signing the manifesto, he explained that as majority leader he could not do so. Strom Thurmond LBJL OH, 11. For the drafting of the manifesto, see Price Daniel OH, 185–87. For why Gore refused to sign, see Gore to Russell M. D. Bruce and Leroy Ward, March 29, 1956, Gore MSS, "Segregation" folder. "What Lyndon Johnson, Estes Kefauver, Albert Gore, Jim Wright and Charles Deane objected to in the Manifesto," Tony Badger has observed, "was the fact that it stirred up . . . white sentiment and cre-ated the false hope that the court could be defied. What they wanted instead was token compli-ance, to leave the matter to local men and women of good will of both races." Significantly, Gore, Wright, and Dante Fascell refused to lend their names to the manifesto; voted for the mild 1957 civil rights bill; but voted against the far-reaching 1964 measure. Tony Badger, "Southerners Who Re-fused to Sign the Southern Manifesto," paper delivered at Organization of American Historians meeting (April 1997), 18–19. In a speech on the Senate floor in 1954, Johnson declared: "The deci-sion is an accomplished fact. . . . It cannot be overruled now, and it is possible that it can never be overruled. Second, the Supreme Court in its ruling has recognized the complexity of the problem. It has delayed the actual decree that will turn a general ruling into a specific order." Stern, "Lyndon Johnson and Richard Russell," 691–92. Characteristically, Johnson later remembered, "I was the one southern Senator that didn't sign the Manifesto." Walter Cronkite, Last Interview of LBJ, c. 1972, Burton Benjamin MSS, Box 21.

60. Steinberg, *Sam Johnson's Boy,* 434; Carl Sanders LBJL OH, 2; J. F. Martin, *Civil Rights and the Crisis of Liberalism,* 137; LBJ to Palmer Bradley, May 15, 1956, Bradley MSS, Box 2.

61. *New York Times,* March 12, May 13, 1956; *Baltimore Sun,* April 11, 1956; *Lubbock (Tex.) Morn-ing Advocate,* May 2, 1956; *Washington Star,* May 26, 1956, clippings, Estes Kefauver MSS; Booth Mooney LBJL OH, 2: 22. See, too, dispatch to Editors of *Time,* April 6, 1956, John L. Steele MSS. Johnson, a liberal observer reported, "held a press conference indicating that his candidacy was a serious one. . . . Lyndon probably wanted to name or at least veto the Vice Presidential candidate, to exercise strong influence in the platform against a vigorous civil rights plank and also to name the new Chairman of the Democratic National Committee." Robert R. Nathan, "Some Observa-tions and Highlights on the Democratic National Convention in Chicago," August 16, 1956, Joseph L. Rauh Jr. MSS, Box 29. Embattled Texas liberals, though they recognized that Johnson was an improvement on rightwingers, could not summon up much enthusiasm for him. One of them ex-plained that they "favored a weekend romance with Lyndon, but didn't want to marry him." Ann Fears Crawford, *Frankie: Mrs. R. D. Randolph and Texas Liberal Politics* (Austin, Tex., 2000), 46.

62. Louis Heren, *No Hail, No Farewell* (New York, 1970), 19; Caro, *Path to Power,* 535; Joe B. Frantz, "Opening a Curtain: The Metamorphosis of Lyndon B. Johnson," *Journal of Southern His-tory* 45 (1979): 5–6; Helen Gahagan Douglas LBJL OH, 43; Gerald S. and Deborah H. Strober,

"Let Us Begin Anew": An Oral History of the Kennedy Presidency (New York, 1993), 5. An Associated Press White House correspondent later said, "Lyndon once told me he didn't think he'd ever live long enough for a Texan to be President of the United States." Jack Bell JFKL OH, 35. See, too, Wicker, *JFK and LBJ,* 152; Robert E. Baskin LBJL OH, 14.

63. James H. Rowe Jr. LBJL OH, 2: 7; Baker with King, *Wheeling and Dealing,* 44.

64. James H. Rowe Jr., to LBJ, June 28, 1955, Rowe MSS, Box 99. Curiously, Rowe later claimed that he had cautioned Johnson against seeking the vice presidential nomination. James H. Rowe Jr. LBJL OH, 1: 35.

65. Caro, *Master of the Senate,* 788, 829; John L. Steele, "A Kingmaker or a Dark Horse?" *Life,* June 25, 1956, 124; Conkin, *Big Daddy,* 149; Stewart Alsop, "Matter of Fact," *Washington Post,* May 9, 1956, clipping, Estes Kefauver MSS; Theodore H. White, *The Making of the President, 1960* (New York, 1961), 43.

66. Baker with King, *Wheeling and Dealing,* 42; Gaskin, "Lyndon B. Johnson and Senator Richard B. Russell"; Karen Kalmar Johnson, "Lyndon Johnson and Richard Russell: Southerners at War over the Great Society," paper delivered at Southern Historical Association meeting (November 1989); Walter C. Hornaday LBJL OH, 23–24; Joseph L. Rauh Jr. LBJL OH, 1: 10. Robert Caro maintains that Johnson did attend some of the caucuses. *Master of the Senate,* 219–20. His evidence, though, is not conclusive.

67. William H. Darden LBJL OH, 14; Hubert H. Humphrey LBJL OH, Tape One, 2, 6.

68. W. S. White, "Who *Is* Lyndon Johnson?" 55; William S. White, *The Responsibles* (New York, 1972), 257. In the fall of 1955 Johnson wrote the editor-in-chief of the Scripps-Howard Newspapers to take exception to a story about a "Southern coalition scheme of Senator Lyndon Johnson." There was "no such scheme," he insisted. "I am not in the business of forming any coalition whatsoever." LBJ to Walker Stone, October 28, 1955, Stone MSS, Box 6.

69. Douglass Cater LBJL OH, 1: 3, 5; Lemann, *Promised Land,* 137.

70. Robert Dallek, *Flawed Giant: Lyndon Johnson and His Times, 1961–1973* (New York, 1998), 24; McPherson LBJL OH, 6: 1–2; McPherson, *Political Education,* 138.

71. Lemann, *Promised Land,* 137; *Washington Post,* November 13, 1988; Richard Bolling, *House Out of Order* (New York, 1965), 183. "We are going to have the civil rights controversy with us for many years," he wrote early in 1957. "However it may have started, it has now gone beyond the point where it can be called off." Stern, "Lyndon Johnson and Richard Russell," 693.

72. Caro, *Master of the Senate,* 842; J. W. Anderson, *Eisenhower, Brownell, and the Congress: The Tangled Origins of the Civil Rights Bill of 1956–1957* (University, Ala., 1964), 139; Robert Branyon and R. Alton Lee, "Lyndon Johnson and the Art of the Possible," *Southwestern Social Science Quarterly* 45 (1964): 218–19. Less than a year after the election, Johnson wrote that "there must be action" on civil rights if the Democratic Party hoped to get ahead. Lyndon B. Johnson to Arthur Schlesinger Jr., June 21, 1957, Schlesinger MSS, Box P–17.

73. *Washington Post and Times Herald,* May 7, 1956, clipping, Estes Kefauver MSS; G. N. Green, *Establishment in Texas Politics,* 173; George Fuermann, *Reluctant Empire* (Garden City, N.Y., 1957), 68. In 1956, Johnson was, in fact, pushing for elimination of the poll tax. LBJ to James O. Eastland, March 15, 1956, copy in Everett Dirksen MSS, Alpha File.

74. Parker with Rashke, *Capitol Hill,* 81; M. Miller, *Lyndon,* 207. See, too, Timothy Thurber, "'The

Politics of Consensus': Hubert Humphrey and Civil Rights, 1952–1957" (M.A. essay, University of North Carolina at Chapel Hill, 1991); Lloyd Bentsen OH, Sam Rayburn Library, 3.

75. *Augusta Courier,* February 4, 1957, clipping, Earle C. Clements MSS, Box 192. At a time when almost no progress was being made on racial integration and blacks could not vote in the Deep South, a congressman from the "progressive" state of North Carolina wrote, "It looks as if the country has gone crazy about the subject of civil rights. I don't know of any people who are being mistreated in this country at the present time." Carl T. Durham to W. N. Jefferies, February 25, 1957, Durham MSS, Folder 451. See, too, "A Guide for Action in 1957," *American Nationalist,* Erwin A. Holt MSS, Folder 2.

76. Philip Graham to LBJ, December 20, 1956, copy, James H. Rowe Jr., MSS, Box 99; Ashmore, *Hearts and Minds,* 308.

77. Caro, *Master of the Senate,* 656; James Rowe Jr., "Lyndon Johnson, Civil Rights and 1960," July 3, 1957, Rowe MSS, Box 99. For misperceptions about the Stars and Bars, see Coski, "Confederate Battle Flag," in *Confederate Symbols,* ed. Martinez, Richardson and McNinch-Su.

78. Mark Stern, *Calculating Visions: Kennedy, Johnson, and Civil Rights* (New Brunswick, N.J., 1992), 133; David Halberstam, *The Powers That Be* (New York, 1979), 307–8; Thomas G. Wicker LBJL OH, 6; Wilkins with Mathews, *Standing Fast,* 243. See, too, Katharine Graham, *Personal History* (New York, 1997), 238.

79. Conkin, "Lyndon Johnson," 159; Tris Coffin, "How Lyndon Johnson Engineered Compromise on Civil Rights Bill," *New Leader,* August 5, 1957, 3.

80. Caro, *Master of the Senate,* 916, 934; Carolyn M. Johnson, "Southern Response to Civil Rights, 97, 98, 115; LBJ to Mrs. Sam E. Johnson, July 24, 1957, LBJ MSS, Family Correspondence, Box 1.

81. Irving Bernstein, *Guns or Butter: The Presidency of Lyndon Johnson* (New York, 1996), 46. George Reedy to Michael L. Gillette, June 2, 1982, Reedy LBJL OH, Interview 10.

82. Howard Shuman, "Senate Rules and the Civil Rights Bill: A Case Study," *American Political Science Review* 51 (1957): 974; Frank Ikard LBJL OH, 23–24; Sherrill, *Gothic Politics,* 251n.; Crispell, *Testing the Limits,* 117; Kearns, *Lyndon Johnson,* 150; Caro, *Master of the Senate,* 954.

83. "Statement Made by Senate Democratic Leader Lyndon B. Johnson," August 7, 1957, Senate files, LBJL Box 290.

84. LBJ to E. W. Austin, July 6, 1957, LBJ MSS, Senate Files, Box 290; Kearns, *Lyndon Johnson,* 151; Carl Brauer, *John F. Kennedy and the Second Reconstruction* (New York, 1977), 10; Fite, *Russell,* 44; M. Miller, *Lyndon,* 208–9. See, too, Roger Biles, *Crusading Liberal: Paul H. Douglas of Illinois* (DeKalb, Ill., 2002), 120.

85. Shuman, "Senate Rules," 975; *Exclusive,* July 24, 1957, 1; Allida Black, *Casting Her Own Shadow: Eleanor Roosevelt and the Shaping of Postwar Liberalism* (New York, 1996), 117; Fite, *Russell,* 341; Eleanor Roosevelt to LBJ, August 17, 1957, in *It Seems to Me: Selected Letters of Eleanor Roosevelt,* ed. Leonard C. Schlup and Donald W. Whisenhunt (Lexington, Ky., 2001), 227; Parker with Rashke, *Capitol Hill,* 83. "In its final form," one historian has noted, "the act disappointed liberals more than it upset the southerners." Gary W. Reichard, "Democrats, Civil Rights, and Electoral Strategies in the 1950's," *Congress and the Presidency* 13 (1986): 67. A North Carolina congressman commented, "As bad as this bill was as originally proposed, we can all be thankful that it did not go as far as Mr. Truman when he urged the adoption of an FEPC law." Johnson, said the *Chattanooga News-Free*

Press, had been "adept" at saving the South from the worst features of the original bill. *Chattanooga News-Free Press*, August 2, 1957, clipping, Stanley F. Reed MSS, Box 330; Charles Raper Jonas to T. C. Heyward, July 26, 1957, Jonas MSS, Folder 50. For opposition to the jury trial amendment to the bill, see William P. Rogers to Joseph C. O'Mahoney, August 6, 1957, Sherman Adams MSS, Series 8, Box 8. For the majority leader's defense of the amendment, see LBJ to Aubrey Williams, August 5, 1957, James Dombrowski MSS, Box 1. A national columnist attributed the weakness of the law to the fact that the man in charge of the legislation had been the "errand boy for Senator Richard B. Russell, who put Lyndon Johnson in the post of leadership." Thomas Stokes quoted in Fite, "Richard B. Russell and Lyndon B. Johnson," 132.

86. Communications to Dwight D. Eisenhower, press release, August 19, 1957, Bernard Shanley MSS.

87. Caro, *Master of the Senate*, 893; Conkin, *Big Daddy*, 140–42; Kearns, *Lyndon Johnson*, 151; James C. Davis, statement on television, August 28, 1957; Weekly Television Program, August 25, 1957, Graham Barden MSS, Box 195; George Reedy, Interview 11, LBJL OH, 26.

88. Marvin Caplan, *Farther Along: A Civil Rights Memoir* (Baton Rouge, La., 1999), 189; T. R. Brooks, *Walls Come Tumbling Down*, 137–38; Eugene McCarthy, *Up 'Til Now: A Memoir* (New York, 1987), 58. A labor union bulletin concluded, "While the bill is tragically weak, it does represent the possibility of some good." *IUE-AFL CIO Civil Rights Bulletin* 6 (July—August 1957): 2, copy in Brent Spence MSS, 1957.

89. Kearns, *Lyndon Johnson*, 150; Kathleen Louchheim LBJL OH, 10–11; Timothy Thurber (draft, Ph.D. dissertation on Hubert Humphrey and civil rights, University of North Carolina at Chapel Hill).

90. William S. White, *The Professional: Lyndon B. Johnson* (Boston, 1964), 128; John Stennis LBJL OH, 9–10.

91. William Colmer OH, 69–70; Allen Ellender LBJL OH, 7, 12. See, too, L. H. Fountain LBJL OH, 3; Frank R. Kent, "The Game of Politics," clipping, *Washington News*, September, 22, 1957, Earle Clements MSS, Box 192; Lester Maddox, *Speaking Out: The Autobiography of Lester Garfield Maddox* (Garden City, N.Y., 1975), 56; J. Evetts Haley, *A Texan Looks at Lyndon: A Study in Illegitimate Power* (Canyon, Tex., 1964), 178.

92. John A. Goldsmith, *Colleagues: Richard B. Russell and His Apprentice, Lyndon B. Johnson* (Washington, D.C., 1993), 65; Mr. and Mrs. Gene B. Fleming to LBJ, July 20, 1957; Katherine Thompson to editor, *Fort Worth Star Telegram*, n.d., clipping in LBJ to Katherine Thompson, September 17, 1957; Webb B. Joiner to LBJ, July 3, 1957; LBJL Senate Legislative Files, Box 290; Joe Caldwell to LBJ, August 16, 1957, Martin Dies MSS, Box 102. See, too, Jeff Roche, "The Emergence of a Conservative Ideology: Texas Panhandle Politics in the Sixties," *Mid-America* 81 (1999): 233.

9. SOUTHERNER WITH A NATIONAL FACE

1. T. H. White, *Making of the President 1964*, 253.

2. S. F. Lawson, *Black Ballots*, 183; Caro, *Master of the Senate*, 1008–9; *New York Times*, September 2, 1957; David L. Chappell, *Inside Agitators: White Southerners in the Civil Rights Movement* (Baltimore, 1994), 153.

3. A. Willis Robertson to Virginius Dabney, January 5, 1958, Dabney MSS 7690e, Box 1; Sarah Hart Brown, *Standing against Dragons: Three Southern Lawyers in an Era of Fear* (Baton Rouge, La., 1998), 160–61; *Washington Star,* August 26, 1958; unidentified clipping, n.d. [1959], Scrapbook, Roy V. Harris MSS; Riggs, "South *Could* Rise Again," in *Candidates 1960,* ed. Sevareid, 314. See, too, *Columbia (S.C.) Record,* August 23, 1958, reprint, Edgar A. Brown MSS, Folder L925. For Johnson's resentment of the Lawrence column, see LBJ to David Lawrence, September 6, 1958, Lawrence MSS, Box 62.

4. Virginia Durr to Jessica Mitford, October 27, 1959, Mitford MSS, Box 22; Floyd B. McKissick in *Lyndon Baines Johnson and the Uses of Power,* ed. Bernard J. Firestone and Robert C. Vogt (New York, 1988), 181–82. For southern resentment at Johnson's actions in 1959, see Mrs. Sam H. Davis to John Dowdy, July 10, 1959, Dowdy MSS, Box 180; Jodie Aldridge to Albert Gore, March 25, 1959, "Civil Rights" folder, Gore MSS.

5. Stern, "Lyndon Johnson and Richard Russell," 697; Dyer, "Lyndon B. Johnson," 185; Dallek, *Lone Star Rising,* 563; *Newsweek,* March 14, 1960, 30; "South Grows a Crop of Machiavellis," *Florida Times Union,* February 17, 1960, clipping, Richard B. Russell MSS, Series 6, Political Subseries E: Lyndon Johnson. See, too, Edwin E. Willis, "The Rigged Civil Rights Bill," March 7, 1960, Graham Barden MSS, Box 202. A powerful southern congressman who opposed the legislation said with a straight face, "Frankly I have never known of any violation of voting rights in my home state of Arkansas." Extension of Remarks of Honorable Wilbur D. Mills, April 4, 1960, Mills MSS, Box 784.

6. Herman L. Driskell to LBJ, February 19, 1960, Richard B. Russell MSS; Lester Maddox LBJL OH, 6, 10.

7. C. W. Blalock to Richard B. Russell, February 20, 1960; W. R. Simpson to Russell, n.d. [February 1960], Russell MSS, Series 6, Political Subseries E: Lyndon Johnson. Senator Spessard L. Holland of Florida charged that Johnson's tactic of round-the-clock sessions was an effort to "wear out Southern Senators" by "cruel and inhuman treatment." *Atlanta Constitution,* March 8, 1960, clipping, Spessard L. Holland MSS, Emory University. In attacking civil rights legislation, South Carolina Congressman L. Mendel Rivers warned of "bloodshed." "Civil Wrongs Proposals," *Rivers Reports from Washington,* March 26, 1960, Rivers MSS, LC, Box 10.

8. *Beaumont Enterprise,* February 26, 1960, clipping, LBJL Senate Political Files, Box 254; transcript of interview of Lyndon B. Johnson by Walter Cronkite, December 1, 1971, Burton Benjamin MSS, Box 21. In this conversation, Johnson conflated the 1957 and 1960 struggles.

9. Memorandum to Senator John L. McClellan from Pat Baker, "How the Senate Toned Down the Civil Rights Bill," McClellan MSS; Fite, *Russell,* 347; J. F. Martin, *Civil Rights and the Crisis of Liberalism,* 166; S. F. Lawson, *Black Ballots,* 246; Robert Edward Hayes, "Senatorial Voting Behavior with Regard to the 'Southern Interest'" (Ph.D. dissertation, University of Colorado, 1964), 1; F. Edward Hebert LBJL OH, 18; *Newsweek,* March 14, 1960, 29; Daniel Berman, *A Bill Becomes a Law: The Civil Rights Act of 1960* (New York, 1962), 55. See, too, Harry Byrd Jr. SOHP, 15–16. Noting that Congress had enacted "what can only by courtesy be called a civil rights bill," Paul Douglas pointed out that "Senator Ellender of Louisiana has hailed the bill as 'a Southern victory.'" Paul H. Douglas, "The 1960 Voting Rights Bill: The Struggle, the Final Results, and the Reasons," *Journal of Intergroup Relations* 1 (1960): 82. For the problem created for Johnson by Midwestern senators

who voted with the South, see Francis Case to Helen Rex Shroyer, March 17, 1960, Case MSS, File No. 11, Drawer 41.

10. *Wall Street Journal,* July 10, 1959. Roy Wilkins later said of Johnson: "I suppose he began to run for President when he was three, and he knew he had to make a break with his Southern roots at some point." Wilkins with Mathews, *Standing Fast,* 297. "What could stop him?" asked a *Newsweek* correspondent in 1959. "For one thing, Johnson comes from the wrong part of the country. Not since the Civil War has either party nominated a Southerner for President." So Johnson was trying "to take this geographical curse from his ambitions." Samuel Shaffer, "Can a Southerner Win?" *Newsweek,* March 30, 1959, 29. In the late summer of 1959, Claude Pepper wrote Johnson, his favorite for the Democratic nomination, "Whether your association with the South, although Texas is really in the Southwest, in spite of your magnificent and liberal record, would prevent your nomination, I don't know." Pepper to LBJ, September 14, 1959, Pepper MSS, Series 401B, Box 76.

11. Virginius Dabney, *Across the Years: Memories of a Virginian* (Garden City, N.Y., 1978), 257; Selig S. Harrison, "Lyndon Johnson's World," *New Republic,* June 13, 1960, 15; L. B. Johnson, *Vantage Point,* 90; Baker with King, *Wheeling and Dealing,* 45. "I am in no sense a candidate for the presidency," Johnson wrote a columnist early in 1959." LBJ to Marquis Childs, January 29, 1959, Childs MSS, Box 4.

12. Robert Sherrill, *The Accidental President* (New York, 1967), 4; Richard B. Russell to Price Daniel, November 18, 1959, Russell MSS.

13. Memo, Pre-Presidential Memos, LBJL, Box 6. See, too, Gerald W. Siegel LBJL OH, 2: 6.

14. *Congressional Quarterly,* August 17, 1959, copy in Arthur Krock MSS, Box 30; *The New Mexican,* December 30, 1959, copy in Claude Pepper MSS, Series 401B, Box 76. New Mexico Senator Clinton Anderson later said: "We had known Lyndon pretty well up here because we had some western saddles and six or seven horses, and he'd go out there and ride. So I was friendly to him." Clinton P. Anderson JFKL OH, 23.

15. George Reedy LBJL OH, Tape 2: 18–19; T. H. White, *Making of the President, 1960,* 43.

16. *Newsweek,* February 15, 1960, 26; unidentified, undated clipping, probably 1958, in LBJ MSS, LBJA Famous Names, Box 3; Mooney, *Politicians,* 323. "Geographically and in other ways, Johnson is indeed a Southern politician," declared a leading weekly. *Saturday Evening Post,* January 24, 1959. See, too, Republican National Committee, *Battle Line,* February 19, 1959, Joseph L. Rauh Jr. MSS, Box 36. A former member of Johnson's Senate staff recalled that "along the way somebody . . . recognized that it was possible for the Senator properly to claim himself as a Southwesterner, and then, therefore, as a Westerner, and to try to shed himself of the burden . . . of a Southerner." Gerald W. Siegel LBJL OH, 2: 6.

17. George Reedy LBJL OH, Interview 9: 29.

18. Robert E. Baskin LBJL OH, 9; Thomas G. Abernethy OH, 111; William H. Jordan Jr. LBJL OH, 1: 12; Herman Talmadge SOHP, 2: 29. When an interviewer in 1974 called Lyndon Johnson "the last Southerner to be elected president," George Wallace replied, "Of course, Lyndon, you know, called himself a Westerner." George Wallace SOHP, 45.

19. James Jackson Kilpatrick, "Lyndon Johnson: Counterfeit Confederate," *Human Events,* August 25, 1960, 374.

20. *Shreveport Journal,* n.d. [February 1960], clipping, John G. Tower MSS, Box NA 51. Sectional

identity was a touchy matter. A decade earlier, a prominent editor had written indignantly, "Arkansas is a Southern state, not a western state . . . even though it is west of the Mississippi river." J. N. Heiskell to Ward Greene, August 7, 1948, Heiskell MSS, Series 2, Box 2, File 9.

21. James F. Byrnes to John D. Long, September 16, 1960, Byrnes MSS.

22. *Memphis Commercial Appeal,* February 14, 1960, clipping, Estes Kefauver MSS, Series 5H, Box 12.

23. D. Robertson, *Sly and Able,* 535; *New York Times,* February 14, 1960; Harry McPherson LBJL OH, Interview 1, Tapes 1–6. *Staunton (Va.) News Leader,* October 12, 1959, A. Willis Robertson MSS.

24. Price Daniel to Harry Flood Byrd, October 26, 1959, Byrd MSS, Box 243; A. Willis Robertson to J. Lindsay Almond Jr., October 21, 1959, Robertson MSS, Box 123, Folder 87; James W. Ely, *The Crisis of Conservative Virginia: The Byrd Organization and the Politics of Massive Resistance* (Knoxville, Tenn., 1976), 148–49; James R. Sweeney, "Whispers in the Golden Silence: Harry F. Byrd, Sr., John F. Kennedy, and Virginia Democrats in the 1960 Election," *Virginia Magazine of History and Biography* 99 (1991): 12.

25. Louis Harris and Associates, Inc., "A Study of Voter Preferences in North Carolina"; "A Study of the Presidential Election of 1960 in South Carolina," June 1960, JFKL Pre-Presidential, Box 818. A Democratic county chairman said that of those mentioned for the presidential nomination Johnson was "the best of the lot, but leaves a lot to be desired, especially if you are a Southerner." Nicholas Evan Sarantakes, "Lyndon Johnson, Foreign Policy, and the Election of 1960," *Southwestern Historical Quarterly* 103 (1999): 151. For additional evidence that Johnson was the South's candidate in 1960, see Albert Gore Sr. JFKL OH, 7; Le Roy Collins JFKL OH, 24. Ross Barnett, though, told Mississippi's senators when they wanted him to go to Johnson's hotel room at the 1960 convention, "That is one man I cannot support." Ross Barnett JFKL OH, 8–9.

26. Terry Sanford LBJL OH, 1: 4, 21. Sanford remarked, "Of course as soon as Johnson crossed the Mississippi River he was no longer a Southerner and didn't claim to be." Ibid., 4.

27. Riggs, "South *Could* Rise Again," in *Candidates 1960,* ed. Sevareid, 280–81. Theodore White has said that, like Al Smith who in 1928 was the first credible Catholic aspirant for the presidency, Johnson in 1960 "also represented a minority, perhaps the most embittered in the nation—the Southern whites; and he was the first representative of them to be considered seriously for the Presidency in over a century." T. H. White, *Making of the President, 1960,* 131.

28. Bill Davidson, "Lyndon Johnson," 64, 66; Frantz, "Opening a Curtain," 6–7. See, too, O. Douglas Weeks, *Texas in the 1960 Presidential Election* (Austin, Tex., 1961).

29. Booth Mooney, *The Lyndon Johnson Story* (New York, 1964), 97; Riggs, "South *Could* Rise Again," in *Candidates 1960,* ed. Sevareid, 294; Haley, *A Texan Looks at Lyndon,* 195.

30. Willard Edwards, "Lyndon the Great: Johnson of Texas Runs for President," *Human Events* 17 (May 19, 1960): 1; Reedy, *Lyndon B. Johnson,* 116–17; Bill Davidson, "Texas Political Powerhouse: Lyndon Johnson," *Look,* August 4, 1959, 40; Herbert Parmet, *JFK: The Presidency of John F. Kennedy* (New York, 1983), 13. In 1959 an Indiana man wrote the chairman of the Democratic Advisory Council, "If you let Sam Rayburn and Lyndon Johnson run everything, us Liberals are going to be in trouble in 1960." J. A. Beery to Paul M. Butler, September 14, 1959, Butler MSS, Box 2.

31. Helen Fuller, *Year of Trial: Kennedy's Crucial Decisions* (New York, 1962), 4; M. Miller, *Lyndon,*

197; Theodore Sorensen, *Kennedy* (New York, 1965), 128. The Pennsylvania boss David Lawrence later said of Johnson: "You see, the problem at that time, the thought of nominating a southerner in '60 was just out of the question. He couldn't win, or at least we felt that way. Maybe we were wrong. But he was getting very few votes in the North, very few delegates." David L. Lawrence JFKL OH, 27. See, too, Richard Bolling LBJL OH, 15; "A Cowboy Hat in the Presidential Ring?" *Milwaukee Journal*, February 2, 1959, clipping, Joseph L. Rauh Jr. MSS, Box 36. An editorial in one black publication in 1960, though, stated: "Please don't think we are crazy, but this newspaper would like to see Lyndon B. Johnson nominated for President DESPITE the fact that he is from the South (Texas)." *Philadelphia Tribune*, March 22, 1960, clipping, Senate Political Files, LBJL, Box 254. "I have read in the papers that Senator Johnson is considered too southern; that he will not carry the northern states," a New Yorker wrote. "That is pure fabrication. Senator Johnson is an American— and a great one, at that." Dorothy L. Airheart to Sam Rayburn, June 28, 1960, Rayburn MSS. See, too, *Washington Star*, November 1, 1959, clipping, Theodore Sorensen MSS, Box 24.

32. Americans for Democratic Action MSS, Microfilm Reel III (Series 6, No. 96), a pamphlet drawing upon a memorandum from Vi Gunther to Bill Taylor, March 1, 1960; Samuel H. Beer to "Dear Delegate," June 30, 1960, Joseph L. Rauh Jr. MSS, Box 29. Texas liberals also regarded LBJ as suspect. "There was no way I could have made peace with Lyndon," one of them explained. "This went back a long ways, back to the 1940s. I thought Lyndon was a scoundrel." A. F. Crawford, *Frankie*, 77.

33. "Texas 'Country Boy' Johnson Leaves Many at U.N. Bewildered," *St. Louis Post-Dispatch*, November 19, 1958, copy in Americans for Democratic Action MSS, Microfilm Reel III (Series 6, No. 96).

34. Ashmore, *Hearts and Minds*, 307, quoting Liebling, *The Earl of Louisiana;* T. H. White, *Making of the President 1960*, 132. When the co-chair of the Citizens for Johnson Committee sought to rally Democratic delegates in northern states, she was met with gales of derisive laughter. India Edwards, *Pulling No Punches: Memoirs of a Woman in Politics* (New York, 1977), 227.

35. Fulbright to R. B. McCallum, January 14, 1960, Fulbright MSS, BCN 105, F54; Herbert S. Parmet, *Jack: The Struggles of John F. Kennedy* (New York, 1980), 500; M. Miller, *Lyndon*, 239; Lincoln, *Kennedy and Johnson*, 28; Tom Wagy, *Governor LeRoy Collins of Florida: Spokesman of the New South* (University, Ala., 1985), 146, 235. See, too, Carroll Kilpatrick LBJL OH, 5.

36. Dyer, "Lyndon B. Johnson," 199; *New York Times*, January 22, 1960; T. H. White, *Making of the President 1960*, 135; Jonathan Daniels LBJL OH, 18; Davie, *LBJ*, 62–63. In 1960 Terry Sanford reasoned that he should back Kennedy rather than Johnson because "I don't want to throw my vote away on a person that's not going to win anyhow just for the sake of keeping faith with the Old South." Terry Sanford LBJL OH, 1: 15.

37. Beagle and Osborne, *J. Lindsay Almond*, 144; Lamis, *Two-Party South*, 318; Steinberg, *Sam Johnson's Boy*, 531. See, too, David L. Lawrence JFKL OH, 7; Arthur Krock JFKL OH, 24; J. Lindsay Almond LBJ OH, 17; Oren Harris JFKL OH, 19; Hale Boggs JFKL OH, 22–24; Ed Gossett LBJL OH, 16–17. Kennedy, according to Tip O'Neill, said, "I want him badly. With him we can carry Texas. We may be able to break the South." John Aloysius Farrell, *Tip O'Neill and the Democratic Century* (Boston, 2001), 182. Quite apart from the need to forge a sectional alliance, Kennedy, as William S. White pointed out, "realized that the tableau presented to the country of so much raw urban Catholic power" by the big city bosses such as Chicago's Richard Daley who had secured

his nomination made it advisable to call upon Johnson, "a member of the fundamentalist Protestant Church of Christ and a man of rural roots, to help redress the balance." White, *The Making of a Journalist* (Lexington, Ky., 1986), 177. Four years later, Johnson told Jim Rowe of his encounter with the Democratic presidential nominee: "Kennedy sat down and had a cold one with me. He said, 'Now I want you to understand. I know you don't believe in a lot of this integration in this platform. But you've got to go with it the whole hog or I don't want you to go.'" Michael Beschloss, ed., *Taking Charge: The Johnson White House Tapes, 1963–1964* (New York, 1997), 485.

38. Eugene "Gene" Worley LBJL OH, 26; Steinberg, *Sam Johnson's Boy*, 530; Fuller, *Year of Trial*, 9; David Lawrence, "Garner on Kennedy-Johnson Ticket," *Washington Evening Star,* August 4, 1970, clipping Lawrence MSS, Box 64; M. Miller, *Lyndon*, 248. Rayburn yielded after Hale Boggs told him that Johnson could carry Louisiana for the ticket, and Governor Almond of Virginia said it was the only way the Democrats could hope to win his state. Arthur Krock, Private Memorandum, September 22, 1960, Krock MSS, Box 22.

39. Evans and Novak, *Lyndon B. Johnson*, 287. See, too, Jack Valenti, *A Very Human President* (New York, 1975), 16; T. H. Williams, "Huey, Lyndon, and Southern Radicalism," 284. One prominent Kentucky politician later said: "To the surprise of I would guess 90 percent or 95 percent of the people of this country, he accepted the vice-presidency." George W. Robinson, ed., *Bert Combs the Politician: An Oral History* (Lexington, Ky., 1991), 125. According to Carl Albert, Kerr told Johnson, "If you take that, I will take my rifle and I will shoot you right between the eyes." But after Sam Rayburn pointed out to Kerr that in running for reelection in Bible Belt Oklahoma on a ticket headed by a Massachusetts Catholic he would find it much easier with a Texas Campbellite on the ticket, Kerr phoned Johnson and said, "If you don't take this thing, I am going to shoot you between the eyes." Carl Albert OH, 3, Sam Rayburn MSS. A Virginia state senator was relieved that Johnson accepted because, if he had not, the vice presidential nomination would have gone to a northern liberal such as Hubert Humphrey. *Danville Commercial Appeal,* July 18, 1960, clipping, W. C. (Dan) Daniel MSS. Richard Russell, though, was acutely unhappy. Robert Battey Troutman Jr. OH, 20.

40. Lawrence Wright, *In the New World: Growing Up with America, 1960–1984* (New York, 1988), 24; Mark Stern, "Lyndon Johnson and the Democrats' Civil Rights Strategy," *Humboldt Journal of Social Relations* 16 (1990): 10; James W. Hilty, *Robert Kennedy: Brother Protector* (Philadelphia, 1997), 159; Roy Wilkins LBJL OH, 4; James Farmer LBJL OH, 1: 2; Bayard Rustin LBJL OH, 1: 2; Anne C. Loveland, *Lillian Smith: A Southerner Confronting the South* (Baton Rouge, La., 1986), 219. Joe Rauh strongly opposed the choice of Johnson for the vice presidential nomination on the grounds "that the Democratic party shouldn't have for Vice President a gas and oil, anti–civil rights senator" who, additionally, "was not qualified for the presidency" because "he had no capacity on the world front." Joseph L. Rauh Jr. LBJL OH, 2: 23–24. Rauh to Abram J. Chayes, July 25, 1960, Rauh MSS, Box 29. See, too, A. Philip Randolph LBJL OH, 10; M. Miller, *Lyndon*, 264; Stewart E. McClure to Kenneth Birkhead, August 26, 1960, David D. Lloyd MSS, Box 42; Fuller, *Year of Trial*, 12. Blacks strung together a picket line to oppose Johnson's nomination as vice president, but called it off after Congressman Dawson reminded them of the majority leader's role in enacting the 1957 and 1960 laws.

41. Elizabeth Rowe LBJL OH, Tape 1: 15–16.

42. James Rowe Jr., Memorandum for Senator Lyndon Johnson: "The Dilemma of Lyndon Johnson," August 24, 1960, Rowe MSS, Box 100.

43. Lee Edwards, *Goldwater: The Man Who Made a Revolution* (Washington, D.C., 1995), 135; T. White, *Making of the President, 1960*, 268; Grantham, *Life and Death of Solid South*, 150; William H. Jordan Jr. LBJL OH, 2: 5–6.

44. Lincoln, *Kennedy and Johnson*, 124; James Reston Jr., *The Lone Star: The Life of John Connally* (New York, 1989), 196–97.

45. Robert Battey Troutman Jr. OH, 22–23.

46. *Greensboro Record*, October 11, 1960; *Winston-Salem Journal*, October 11, 1960, clippings, Terry Sanford MSS; Lincoln, *Kennedy and Johnson*, 126; Leonard Baker, *The Johnson Eclipse: A President's Vice Presidency* (New York, 1966), 80; David Burner, *John F. Kennedy and a New Generation* (Glenview, Ill., 1988), 51; Fuller, *Year of Trial*, 13.

47. Steinberg, *Sam Johnson's Boy*, 540; *Charlotte Observer*, October 11, 1960; *Shelby (N.C.) Daily Star*, October 11, 1960, clipping, Terry Sanford MSS; unidentified clipping, October 1, 1960, Scrapbook, John W. Davis MSS; Montgomery, *Mrs. LBJ*, 96. Sam Houston, the first president of the Texas republic, had earlier been governor of Tennessee.

48. Eugene W. Jones, ed., *The Texas Country Editor: H. M. Baggarly Takes a Grass-Roots Look at National Politics* (Cleveland, Ohio, 1966), 198; *Raleigh News and Observer*, October 11, 1960; Walt Dantoff in *Charlotte Observer*, October 9, 1960, clippings, Terry Sanford MSS.

49. *Raleigh Times*, October 11, 1960, clipping, Terry Sanford MSS; Dallek, *Lone Star Rising*, 583; Black and Black, *Vital South*, 80; *Charlotte Observer*, August 15, 1960, clipping, Luther H. Hodges MSS, Box 24.

50. Fuller, *Year of Trial*, 13; *Winston-Salem Journal*, October 11, 1960, clipping, Terry Sanford MSS; Lincoln, *Kennedy and Johnson*, 125.

51. Mooney, *Politicians*, 350; Lincoln, *Kennedy and Johnson*, 128; Steinberg, *Sam Johnson's Boy*, 535.

52. Mooney, *Politicians*, 350; James A. Michener, *Report of the County Chairman* (New York, 1961), 186.

53. Brauer, *John F. Kennedy*, 54, 56; *Dixie News*, Columbia (S.C.), 1960, Olin D. Johnston MSS, Campaign files; excerpts from speech of Governor Ernest F. Hollings, Democratic Party Reconvention, August 15, 1960, Olin D. Johnston MSS, Campaign files.

54. Kilpatrick, "Lyndon Johnson," 373, 376; Lincoln, *Kennedy and Johnson*, 125; Dallek, *Lone Star Rising*, 586.

55. Mooney, *Politicians*, 349; Andrew McDowd Secrest, "In Black and White: Press Opinion and Race Relations in South Carolina, 1954–1964" (Ph.D. dissertation, Duke University, 1971), 275; Lang W. Anderson to Olin D. Johnston, August 26, 1960, Johnston MSS, Campaign files; Willie Morris, *North Toward Home* (Boston, 1967), 237n. In 1960, Barry Goldwater told a responsive Hattiesburg audience that Lyndon Johnson was a "counterfeit Confederate." Guy Paul Lord, "Mississippi Republicanism and the 1960 Presidential Election," *Journal of Mississippi History* 40 (1978): 41. See, too, L. J. Worrell to J. Strom Thurmond, September 1, 1960; J. R. Hanahan to Thurmond, August 22, 1960, Thurmond MSS, Subject Correspondence, Box 26; Roy V. Harris, "Strictly Personal," *Augusta (Ga.) Courier*, August 8, 1960, copy in Harris to Richard B. Russell, August 24, 1960, Russell

MSS, Political Series; Howard P. Baucum to George A. Smathers, August 23, 1960, Smathers MSS, Box 27.

56. Mr. and Mrs. W. C. Hardy to Price Daniel, July 30, 1960, Daniel MSS, Box 533; Mary Kimbrough to Price Daniel, July 31, 1960, Daniel MSS, Box 532; J. J. Kilpatrick, "Lyndon Johnson," 376. Stanley Marcus, *Minding the Store: A Memoir* (Denton, Tex., 1974), 252; Committee for the South, Houston, Texas, Edgar A. Brown MSS, Folder L925; *The Texas Councilor,* June 5, 1960, 1. One Texas delegate, irate at his senator for accepting second spot on the ticket, said, "They crammed a civil rights plank down our throats, nominated a liberal for president and then asked us to help sell the deal to the South with Johnson's aid." Ann Fears Crawford and Jack Keever, *John B. Connally: Portrait in Power* (Austin, Tex., 1973), 73–74n.

57. Warren Leslie, *Dallas Public and Private* (New York, 1964), 133–38; Badger, "Southerners Who Refused," 6–7; Montgomery, *Mrs. LBJ,* 98–99; Reston Jr., *Lone Star,* 198–99; Steinberg, *Sam Johnson's Boy,* 543; Charles McDowell Jr., *Campaign Fever* (New York, 1965), 220, 222–23; *Dallas Times-Herald,* November 4, 1960; *Dallas Morning News,* November 5, 7, 1960; Jim Wright to Edith Green, December 17, 1963, Bruce Alger MSS, Box 29; Robert K. Walsh HSTL OH, 177; Jim Schutze, *The Accommodation: The Politics of Race in an American City* (Secaucus, N.J., 1986), 142; Marie Smith, *The President's Lady: An Intimate Biography of Mrs. Lyndon B. Johnson* (New York, 1964), 126. For the background in the 1950s, see William G. Carleton, "How Fascist-Minded Is the Southwest?" typescript, n.d., Carleton MSS.

58. Wright, *New World,* 24–28; Lawrence Wright, "Was Dallas a City of Hate?" *Dallas* (November 1988): 62–67, 93–103; Evans and Novak, *Lyndon B. Johnson,* 320; Luther Hodges JFKL OH, 9; Clinton P. Anderson JFKL OH, 32. One prominent Democrat recalled: "Johnson was very popular that night in New York because of the Dallas incident. I think it made more votes there than it did in Texas." Jim Grant Bolling JFKL OH, 17. Since the sources are so partisan, it is very difficult to reconstruct the episode with confidence. Alger claimed that Johnson "trumped it up." Bruce Alger OH, 39. He further maintained, "I did not even see Mrs. Johnson." Alger to Edith Green, December 12, 1963, Bruce Alger MSS, Box 29. His protestations are implausible, but the version of Johnson and his friends invites scrutiny too. Many Dallasites, it should be noted, were justifiably incensed by a newspaper ad that listed them as supporters of Johnson when they had never consented to have their names used and, in fact, opposed the Democratic ticket.

59. George Reedy LBJL OH, 16: 73–74.

60. Fuller, *Year of Trial,* 15–16; James O. Eastland LBJL OH, 8; Allan Shivers LBJL OH, 25. "He made the difference in the 1960 campaign," Senator Stennis later asserted. "He carried enough of the South anyway to make the difference." John C. Stennis LBJL OH, 23. Rowe wrote him, "You should be gratified by the comments, . . . particularly the Eastern press. They have all said that without the South Kennedy clearly would have been beaten and without Lyndon Johnson Kennedy would not have got the South." James Rowe Jr. to LBJ, November 14, 1960, Rowe MSS, Box 100. See, too, Brauer, *John F. Kennedy,* 58; Terry Sanford LBJL OH, 1: 27. During the campaign, Governor Buford Ellington told a Nashville rally: "When those famous initials of LBJ were put on the Democratic ballot, it was the same thing as taking out a fidelity bond that Tennessee will be back in the Democratic column next November, and the South will be there too!" *Gilmer (Tex.) Mirror,*

August 4, 1960, clipping, JFKL Pre-Presidential Papers, Box 987. But as it turned out, the Kennedy-Johnson ticket lost Tennessee. Some southern voters, Louisiana's Senator Ellender later explained, stayed with the Democrats in 1960 because they thought that Johnson, though they were "very much disappointed" in him, would not pursue civil rights so tenaciously once he was in national office. Allen Ellender JFKL OH, 12.

61. William F. Nichols OH, 142; Grantham, *Life and Death of Solid South,* 152.

62. Morris, *North Toward Home,* 234; Smith, *President's Lady,* 126; Jack Brooks LBJL OH, 1: 21. See, too, A. Willis Robertson LBJL OH, 8; Robert E. Baskin LBJL OH, 22; Wilbur J. Mills LBJL OH, 6; Thomas G. Wicker LBJL OH, 14; O. C. Fisher LBJL OH, 20; Kinch and Long, *Allan Shivers,* 214. The ticket lost Dallas, Houston, Amarillo, and other cities and a good deal of East Texas, but Johnson's traditional strength in areas such as southwestern Texas and the mobilization of labor in cities such as Fort Worth and Galveston pulled the Democrats through. Roger M. Olien, *From Token to Triumph: The Texas Republicans since 1920* (Dallas, Tex., 1982), 73. "I *know* they would not have carried Texas if Johnson had not been on the ticket," Allan Shivers maintained. "They didn't carry it by many votes as it was." Allan Shivers OH, Sam Rayburn Library, 39. Johnson also drew votes as a southwesterner, notably in New Mexico, which Kennedy carried by only 2300 votes. "If Lyndon Johnson hadn't been on the ticket with him," Clinton Anderson has written, "I'm sure he'd have lost New Mexico." Anderson with Viorst, *Outsider in the Senate,* 305–6. If Johnson had not been on the slate, Herman Talmadge said, Kennedy would have lost Georgia. Herman Talmadge LBJL OH, 11. Arthur Schlesinger Jr., though, has reflected: "I think it was felt that Johnson did very well in the campaign, and was enormously helpful. However, I've never believed the theory that had Johnson not been on the ticket, Kennedy would not have won. I think that he would not have carried Texas without Johnson, but he could have lost Texas and still won comfortably. But Johnson certainly helped." Arthur M. Schlesinger Jr. LBJL OH, 6–7. For the idiosyncratic view that Johnson was "not being very, very helpful" to the Kennedy ticket in Texas, see Joseph Kraft JFKL OH, 7.

63. Morris, *North Toward Home,* 237; *Greensboro (N.C.) Daily News,* February 15, 1963, clipping in Luther H. Hodges to LBJ, February 20, 1963, LBJ MSS, LBJA Famous Names, Box 5; T. H. Williams, "Huey, Lyndon, and Southern Radicalism," 284; William S. White LBJL OH, Tape 1: 25; Fuller, *Year of Trial,* 21; Fite, *Russell,* 33; Conkin, *Big Daddy,* 162.

64. Baker with King, *Wheeling and Dealing,* 138–39.

65. Taylor Branch, *Parting the Waters: America in the King Years, 1954–63* (New York, 1988), 863–64; Frady, *Wallace,* 129.

66. Harold C. Fleming, with Virginia Fleming, *The Potomac Chronicle: Public Policy and Civil Rights from Kennedy to Reagan* (Athens, Ga., 1996), 13; Conkin, "Lyndon Johnson," 161; Hodding Carter LBJL OH, 2; Nancy J. Weiss, *Whitney M. Young, Jr., and the Struggle for Civil Rights* (Princeton, N.J., 1989), 146–47. Russell later said that it was during the vice presidency that Johnson parted ways with him. Goldsmith, *Colleagues,* 91.

67. Lyndon Baines Johnson, *A Time for Action: A Selection from the Speeches and Writings of Lyndon B. Johnson, 1953–64* (New York, 1964), 84; Dallek, *Flawed Giant,* 36.

68. L. B. Johnson, *Time for Action,* 124–27.

69. Transcript of Edison Dictaphone Recording of Conversation between Lyndon Johnson and

Ted Sorensen, June 3, 1963, Office Files of George Reedy, LBJL, Box 1; Michael P. Riccards, "Rare Counsel: Kennedy, Johnson and the Civil Rights Bill of 1963," *Presidential Studies Quarterly* 11 (1981): 395–98; Rowland Evans and Robert Novak, "Inside Report: Lyndon Leaves the South," *Washington Post,* August 27, 1963.

70. Dallek, *Flawed Giant,* 13, 25, 42; Sorensen, *Kennedy,* 266; Benjamin C. Bradlee, *Conversations with Kennedy* (New York, 1975), 217–18.

71. Unidentified clipping, October 25, 1963, Jake More MSS, Box 3; A. C. Greene, *Dallas U.S.A.* (Austin, Tex., 1984), 106–7; G. N. Green, "Far Right Wing," 269; David Richards, *Once upon a Time in Texas: A Liberal in the Lone Star State* (Austin, Tex., 2002), 30, 32; Pierre Salinger, *With Kennedy* (Garden City, N.Y., 1966), 1; Kenneth P. O'Donnell and David F. Powers, with Joe McCarthy, *"Johnny, We Hardly Knew Ye": Memories of John Fitzgerald Kennedy* (Boston, 1972), 25. The wife of a Texas congressman later recalled that she had told a dinner companion just prior to Kennedy's assassination, "If you can, persuade the President not to go to Dallas. I don't think it's going to be so terrible, but you know they spit on Bird Johnson and they do so many insulting things in Dallas. I just don't want our President insulted." Libbie Moody Thompson OH, 21.

72. William Manchester, *The Death of a President, November 20–November 25, 1963* (New York, 1967), 3; O'Donnell and Powers, with McCarthy, *"Johnny, We Hardly Knew Ye,"* 3–5; Patrick Cox, *Ralph W. Yarborough: The People's Senator* (Austin, Tex., 2001), 189; Chris Cravens, "Edwin A. Walker and the Right Wing in Dallas, 1960–1966" (M.A. essay, Southwest Texas State University, 1991), 155. See, too, Carolyn Ann Carney, "The 'City of Hate': Anti-Communist and Conservative Attitudes in Dallas, Texas, 1950–1964" (M.A. essay, University of Texas at Arlington, 1994), 17; Steven Dwight Holley, "The Dallas *Morning News* and the *Times-Herald* and the Image of Dallas in the Decade after the Kennedy Assassination" (M.A. essay, University of Texas, 1974), 25. In October, the chairman of the National Draft Goldwater Committee had claimed that rising Goldwater strength was "forcing Kennedy to make political trips throughout the United States." Peter O'Donnell Jr. to Goldwater State Chairmen, Key Goldwater People, Progress Report No. 3, October 10, 1963, John Tower MSS. For resentment of Vice President Johnson in Texas, see Gore Vidal, "A Liberal Meets Mr. Conservative," *Life,* June 9, 1961, 106–18, typescript and interview notes, Vidal MSS, Boxes 10, 34. After the assassination, Texans joined in the denunciation of Dallas. One Texas congressman recalled that "people from all over the state" who were gathered in Austin "didn't talk so much about Oswald as they talked about the city of Dallas . . . and that Dallas was a place where nobody's life was safe." They "seemed to be more interested in condemning Dallas than they did in any other feature of the murder." W. R. Poage OH, 1136–37. Toward the end of his life, Johnson reflected: "Dallas has always been a nightmare for me. I've never discussed it. Kennedy thought our election was in danger. His purpose was to raise $1 million and get identification with Texas to carry the state." "LBJ Reminisces: The Fatal Trip to Dallas," *Among Friends of LBJ* 27 (1983): 4.

10. NIGRA, NIGRA, NIGRA

1. Lubell, *White and Black,* 154; E. F. Goldman, *Tragedy of Lyndon Johnson,* 181. See, too, Charles Longstreet Weltner, *Southerner* (Philadelphia, 1966), 67.

2. Lubell, *White and Black,* 153–55. Albert Gore later wrote: "Twentieth century South finally had

a President—a Southerner, born and bred—I liked that." Gore, *Let the Glory Out,* 166. See, too, "Johnson for Softer Bill on Rights, Says Georgian," unidentified clipping, n.d. [1963], Scrapbook, John W. Davis MSS. Not all white southerners were pleased by Johnson's ascendancy, however. "As far as the South is concerned," commented the *Charlotte Observer,* "Lyndon Johnson's accession to the presidency was a hard blow to those who hoped to see a genuine two-party system emerge in Dixie in a few years." *Charlotte Observer,* January 4, 1964, clipping, John Grenier MSS, Box 3. South Carolina congressmen deplored Johnson's endorsement of civil rights in his address to Congress in November 1963. *Greenville (S.C.) News,* November 28, 1963, Scrapbook, Robert T. Ashmore MSS.

3. Simeon Booker, "Blacks Remember Civil Rights Role of Lyndon B. Johnson," *Jet,* February 8, 1973, 15–16; John Dittmer, *Local People: The Struggle for Civil Rights in Mississippi* (Urbana, Ill., 1994), 211; Mary King, *Freedom Song: A Personal Story of the 1960s Civil Rights Movement* (New York, 1987), 242; *New York Herald Tribune,* February 29, 1964, clipping, Fred Schwengel MSS, Box 252; Roger Wilkins, *A Man's Life: An Autobiography* (New York, 1982), 132; L. B. Johnson, *Vantage Point,* 18; Kearns, *Lyndon Johnson,* 170. Lawrence F. O'Brien, who had been trying to put Kennedy's civil rights bill through Congress, was one of many who were apprehensive. "Early in Johnson's presidency," he remembered, "I wondered if he had a real deep, gut commitment to civil rights being a Southerner with strong Southern ties." Lawrence F. O'Brien, *No Final Victories: A Life in Politics—From John F. Kennedy to Watergate* (Garden City, N.Y., 1974), 173–74; *USA Today,* November 21, 2003; *Wisconsin State Journal,* November 22, 2003.

4. Kirkpatrick Sale, *Power Shift: The Rise of the Southern Rim and Its Challenge to the Eastern Establishment* (New York, 1975), 134; Richard Byrne, "Lyndon Agonistes," *American Prospect* 15 (August 2004): 47–48. For further evidence of anxiety that Johnson, as a southerner, would scuttle Kennedy's civil rights bill, see Robert D. Loevy, *To End All Segregation: The Politics of the Passage of the Civil Rights Act of 1964* (Lanham, Md., 1990), 83–84.

5. Taylor Branch, *Pillar of Fire: America in the King Years, 1963–65* (New York, 1998), 178; Louis E. Lomax, "A Negro View: Johnson Can Free the South," *Look,* March 10, 1964, 34.

6. Lerone Bennett Jr., "What Negroes Can Expect from President Lyndon Johnson," *Ebony,* January 19, 1964, 82–84.

7. Kluger, *Simple Justice,* 759; *New York Herald Tribune,* February 29, 1964, typescript, William Miller MSS; Joel Rosenstein, "Lyndon B. Johnson and the 1964 Civil Rights Act" (Senior honors thesis, University of North Carolina at Chapel Hill, 1993), 72.

8. Bill D. Moyers, "Epilogue: Second Thoughts," in *Lyndon Baines Johnson,* ed. Firestone and Vogt, 352–53. See, too, Buford Ellington LBJL OH, 1: 11–12.

9. Jon Margolis, *The Last Innocent Year: America in 1964: The Beginning of the "Sixties"* (New York, 1999), 187; Richard N. Goodwin, *Remembering America: A Voice from the Sixties* (Boston, 1988), 257–58; Dyer, "Lyndon B. Johnson," 197; *Public Papers of the Presidents: Lyndon B. Johnson, 1963–64* (Washington, D.C., 1965), 9 (emphasis added). One of LBJ's aides recalls that when the final draft of the president's speech was completed, Johnson gave it to his daughter Lynda to read and she found a word that was used only in Texas and the South. "Father," she said, "tomorrow you're going to be speaking to the world. I think we should change this word." He did. M. Miller, *Lyndon,* 338.

10. *Public Papers, 1968–69,* 1: 482; Lemann, *Promised Land,* 326; Lesher, *George Wallace,* 328.

11. Nicolaus Mills, *Like a Holy Crusade: Mississippi 1964—The Turning of the Civil Rights Movement in America* (Chicago, 1992), 100–110; T. R. Brooks, *Walls Come Tumbling Down*, 245n.; Benjamin Muse, *The American Negro Revolution: From Nonviolence to Black Power, 1963–1967* (Bloomington, Ind., 1968), 144–45; Burke Marshall LBJL OH, 39. Though many had feared that Johnson's coming to power would mean a diminished will, Marshall eventually concluded, surprisingly and unpersuasively, that LBJ's "greatest weakness" was that "he turned to force."

12. Caplan, *Farther Along*, 213; James C. Harvey, *Black Civil Rights during the Johnson Administration* (Jackson, Miss., 1973), 9; Weiss, *Whitney M. Young, Jr.*, 148; James Farmer LBJL OH, 2: 25; Ramsey Clark LBJL OH, 3: 19; Arnold Aronson to Cooperating Organizations, Memo No. 16, December 2, 1963, Leadership Conference on Civil Rights MSS, Box 1. Two days after Johnson succeeded Kennedy, Bayard Rustin wrote an article in which, he later recalled, he said "that I didn't think people ought to be fearful; . . . that perhaps a Southerner would be able to do more than a Yankee, particularly with a Boston accent, to get some things done in Congress." Bayard Rustin LBJL OH, 1: 8. "For the moment," King's biographer, David Levering Lewis, has said, "Martin believed that cruel chance had devised the ultimate civil rights weapon, a presidential voice that spoke in a drawl." David L. Lewis, *King: A Critical Biography* (New York, 1970), 237.

13. Evans and Novak, *Lyndon B. Johnson*, 379; Kearns, *Lyndon Johnson*, 191; *Newsweek*, March 2, 1964, 20; Dittmer, *Local People*, 211.

14. Jack Bass, *Unlikely Heroes* (New York, 1981), 146; *Atlanta Constitution*, January 8, 1964; Dallek, *Flawed Giant*, 114; David William Brooks OH, 50; Rowland Evans and Robert Novak, "Inside Report," *Washington Post*, December 19, 1963.

15. Religious Action Center, Union of American Hebrew Congregations, Report to Social Action Leaders in New York: Status of Civil Rights Legislation, January 21, 1964, Leadership Conference on Civil Rights MSS, Box A–2; Lomax, "Negro View," 34.

16. Jack Valenti, "Lyndon Johnson: An Awesome Engine of a Man," in *Lyndon Johnson Remembered*, ed. Cowger and Markham, 39–40; "Notes on Meeting: President Johnson, Clarence Mitchell, and Joe Rauh, January 21, 1964," Joseph L. Rauh Jr. MSS, Box 26; Conkin, *Big Daddy*, 215; *New York Times*, July 2, 1989; Dallek, *Flawed Giant*, 113, 118. William Scranton, the governor of Pennsylvania, was being considered for the Republican presidential nomination in 1964. I have merged two separate Valenti accounts, which differ only slightly in phrasing. What was "very painful" for her husband, Lady Bird Johnson later said, was that he had to join "with a bunch of strangers" to defeat "the friends of our lifetime and of our heritage—people for whom Lyndon had just towering respect" such as Dick Russell. C. L. Sanders, "LBJ and Civil Rights," 160.

17. *Public Papers, 1963–64*, 1: 112, 116; Branch, *Pillar of Fire*, 210; Jonathan Rosenberg and Zachary Karabell, *Kennedy, Johnson, and the Quest for Justice: The Civil Rights Tapes* (New York, 2003), 256–80; Beschloss, *Taking Charge*, 123; James Farmer LBJL OH, 2: 1, 25; Milton Viorst, *Fire in the Streets: America in the 1960s* (New York, 1979), 432; Carl T. Rowan, *Breaking Barriers: A Memoir* (Boston, 1991), 245–47.

18. *Dallas Morning News*, April 6, 1964, copy, Don Short MSS; A. Willis Robertson to Virginius Dabney, May 8, 1964, Dabney MSS 7690e, Box 2; A. Willis Robertson LBJL OH, 31.

19. Wright Patman LBJL OH, Side One, 1: 1.

20. C. L. Sanders, "LBJ and Civil Rights," 158.

21. Reston, *Lone Star*, 294; Goodwin, *Remembering America*, 316; Kearns, *Lyndon Johnson*, 232.

22. Johnson, "Lyndon Johnson and Richard Russell." Russell may have realized that he was only one in a line of men Johnson claimed as his daddy. See Leuchtenburg, *In the Shadow of FDR*, 121–22.

23. John Carlton OH, 35; John Stennis OH, 13, both in Richard B. Russell MSS.

24. T. H. White, *Making of the President, 1964*, 177; M. Miller, *Lyndon*, 369; Peter Evans Kane, "The Senate Debate on the 1964 Civil Rights Act" (Ph.D. dissertation, Purdue University, 1967), 229.

25. "Washington Report," December 18, 1963, John Stennis MSS; L. H. Hollingsworth to Alton Lennon, March 18, 1964, Lennon MSS; Raymond Meredith to Edmund S. Muskie, January 15, 1964, Edmund S. Muskie Archives, Box 66; Hodding Carter LBJL OH, 17; Harry S. Dent, *The Prodigal South Returns to Power* (New York, 1978), 7. The phrase "turncoat son-of-a-bitch" is Hodding Carter's paraphrase of the sentiment he encountered. When interviewed later for an oral history program, a Mississippi congressman said: "I hate to put on here about Lyndon. . . . Johnson just was not himself when he was president. . . . He was a phony if one ever lived." Thomas G. Abernethy OH, 109.

26. James F. Owens to O. C. Fisher, December 2, 1963, Fisher MSS, Box 387; Mrs. Charles F. Farmer to O. C. Fisher, March 17, 1964; Mrs. Eva Belling to O. C. Fisher, July 21, 1964, Fisher MSS, Box 387. Johnson's sponsorship of the civil rights bill, a Texas congressman who viewed the legislation as "vicious" recalled, "made it rather embarrassing for us, and it made it hard for us to try to give the cooperation we wanted to to the president and, at the same time, to keep in line with the feeling of our constituents at home." W. R. Poage to Mrs. Walker Jones, June 29, 1964, Poage MSS, Box 362; W. R. Poage OH, 1171. Other Texas congressmen, though, had a different attitude.

27. Erle Johnston, *Mississippi's Defiant Years, 1953–1973: An Interpretive Documentary with Personal Experiences* (Forest, Miss., 1990), 243; Joseph L. Rauh Jr., "The Role of the Leadership Conference on Civil Rights in the Civil Rights Struggle of 1963–1964," in *The Civil Rights Act of 1964: The Passage of the Law that Ended Racial Segregation*, ed. Robert D. Loevy (Albany, N.Y., 1997), 61; Rosenstein, "Lyndon B. Johnson," 68; O. C. Fisher to Ed C. Burris, February 7, 1964, Fisher MSS, Box 387; Robert Mann, *The Walls of Jericho: Lyndon Johnson, Hubert Humphrey, Richard Russell and the Struggle for Civil Rights* (New York, 1996), 473; John L. McClellan to Homer Nunnally, June 11, 1964, McClellan MSS, File 177, Drawer C.

28. Stern, "Lyndon Johnson," 17; Andrew Young, *An Easy Burden: The Civil Rights Movement and the Transformation of America* (New York, 1996), 298.

29. Virginia Durr to "Maggie," n.d., Durr MSS, LBJL.

30. John R. Knaggs, *Two-Party Texas: The John Tower Era, 1961–1984* (Austin, Tex., 1986), 49; L. B. Johnson, *Vantage Point*, 38. See, too, Ralph McGill to Jack Valenti, March 31, 1966, McGill MSS. Seven Democrats from former Confederate states—four from Texas, two from Tennessee, plus Claude Pepper of Florida—voted for the 1964 civil rights bill. *Washington Post*, n.d. [1964], clipping, Clarence J. Brown MSS, Box 65. Johnson exploited his southern antecedents to win support for the legislation. A president from Texas, he told the chairman of the House Rules Committee, Howard W. Smith, needed the backing of the South. Roy Earl Young, "Presidential Leadership and Civil Rights Legislation, 1963–64" (Ph.D. dissertation, University of Texas, 1969), 306.

31. Jody Carlson, *George C. Wallace and the Politics of Powerlessness: The Wallace Campaigns for the Presidency, 1964–1976* (New Brunswick, N.J., 1981), 34; Barry Goldwater, *The Conscience of a Conservative* (Shepherdsville, Ky., 1960), 31–37; Democratic National Committee, "What Goldwater Said, 1953–1964," 226; Goldwater, with Jack Casserly, *Goldwater* (New York, 1988), 173; Stewart Alsop, "Can Goldwater Win in '64?" *Saturday Evening Post,* August 24, 1963, 24; *New York Times,* April 2, 1964, clipping, Hubert Humphrey MSS, Senatorial, Civil Rights, 1964; Everett M. Dirksen, "Goldwater Nomination," July 15, 1964, Dirksen MSS, Alpha File; Richard Rovere, draft of article "American Letter," *Encounter* 23 (1964): 51, Rovere MSS, Box 11; Bob Short, *Everything Is Pickrick: The Life of Lester Maddox* (Macon, Ga., 1999), 168–69. An Arizona senator noted that Goldwater had "bragged . . . about having voted for desegregation at the Sky Chief Restaurant at the Phoenix Municipal Airport . . . while he was on the Phoenix City Council." Ernest McFarland to Wilton E. Hall, October 27, 1940, McFarland MSS, Box 142. The head of the Phoenix branch of the NAACP stated that, though blacks had supported Goldwater in 1952 in order to oust a Democratic senator with a poor civil rights record, Goldwater "then 'went to Mississippi' and became the reactionary that he is." Release, September 18, 1964, Carl and Anne Braden MSS, Box 50. The Republican candidate's views on civil rights were all too liberal for the head of the American Nazi Party. "Goldwater, the Jew," he said, was "the darling of . . . the Kosher Conservatives" and an advocate of race mixing. Lincoln Rockwell, "The Barry Goldwater Record," Wesley George Fritz MSS, Folder 84.

32. "Glossary of Goldwater Opinionata," January 1964, Edmund Muskie Archives, Box 64; Betty E. Chmaj, "Paranoid Patriotism: The Radical Right and the South," *Atlantic Monthly* (November 1962): 94; Alsop, "Can Goldwater Win?" 24; Robert MacNeil MSS, Box 11.

33. Rosenberg and Karabell, *Kennedy, Johnson, and the Quest for Justice,* 318; Rick Perlstein, *Before the Storm: Barry Goldwater and the Unmaking of the American Consensus* (New York, 2001), 363–64; G. D. Shorey Jr. to F. Clifton White, May 20, 1965, White MSS, Ashland, Box 25; Black and Black, *Vital South,* 129.

34. Democratic National Committee, "What Goldwater Said, 1953–1964," 515; Lamis, *Two-Party South,* 18; The San Francisco Ministers Union, "The Civil Rights Records of Lyndon Johnson and Barry Goldwater," F. Clifton White MSS, Ashland; *Washington Post,* August 12, 1964, clipping, Hale Boggs MSS. One longtime Johnson friend reversed the Maryland Republican's charge. At a forum in Montgomery, Alabama, Clifford Durr called Goldwater "an Arizona Carpetbagger dressed in gray." S. H. Brown, *Standing against Dragons,* 209. Though the Goldwater movement is often portrayed as a rebellion of the West against the eastern seaboard, only 18.1 percent of the Arizona senator's early support came from the West, in contrast to 43.8 percent from southern and border states. His backers were more racist than Johnson's supporters, but what especially defined them was less advocacy of segregation than hostility to federal intervention to end segregation. James McEvoy III, "The American Right in the National Election of 1964" (Ph.D. dissertation, University of Michigan, 1968), 84–96. See, too, *Florence (S.C.) Morning News,* October 20, 1964, clipping, John McMillan MSS, Box 8; William E. Miller, "Memorandum," n.d., Miller MSS, Box 68; Robert P. Kingsbury to John Rhodes, June 12, 1964, Rhodes MSS, 88th Congress, Box 15; Scrapbook, Carl T. Hayden MSS, Box 779; Stephen Shadegg, *What Happened to Goldwater? The Inside Story of the 1964 Republican Campaign* (New York, 1965), 213–15; Neil R. McMillen, *The Citizens' Council: Organized Resistance to the Second Reconstruction, 1954–64* (Urbana, Ill., 1971), 351; *Des Moines Register,*

June 13, 1964, clipping, Bourke Hickenlooper MSS, Box 9A; Beschloss, *Taking Charge,* 457n. In 1963 Goldwater had told a Republican gathering: "I believe the most stupid, irresponsible suggestion I have ever heard put forward is the argument that the Republican party should soft-pedal its efforts in the South because a determined effort in that area might give the party a racist tinge." Barry Goldwater, address, Republican Men's Club, Bartlesville, Oklahoma, September 13, 1963, Robert MacNeil MSS, Box 11. He insisted: "Republican influence in the South is growing in direct proportion to the South's moderation on the race issue." For Goldwater's views on civil rights, see "Q & A: Barry Goldwater Speaks Out on the Issues," Michael V. Di Salle MSS, Box 344. A North Carolina Goldwater enthusiast, irate at Senator Dirksen for lining up Republican support to the civil rights bill, asked him scornfully, "How many Negro votes do you think the Republican Party is going to get no matter what you do?" John A. Wilkinson to Everett M. Dirksen, June 3, 1964, copy in John G. Tower MSS, Box 442.

35. T. H. White, *Making of the President, 1964,* 235–36, 332–33n; Robert D. Novak, *The Agony of the G.O.P., 1964* (New York, 1965), 201; Bill Hunter, "To Delegates and Alternates of the South Carolina Delegation," n.d. [1964], Charles Boineau MSS, Box 1; *The State* (Columbia, S.C.), July 11, 1964, clipping, Gregory D. Shorey MSS, Box 1; Facts on File, *1964 News Dictionary* (New York, 1965), 73–74; typescript of article for the *New Yorker,* October 3, 1964, Richard Rovere MSS, Box 9.

36. John C. Topping Jr., John R. Lazarek, and William H. Linder, *Southern Republicanism and the New South* (Cambridge, Mass., 1966), 15; Wilkins with Mathews, *Standing Fast,* 303. Early in 1964, Goldwater declared: "I am completely opposed to segregation. It is not only a Southern problem. It is the world's one big major problem. This is God's master plan—when we can live together all over this world in brotherhood, we'll have peace." Notes, Robert MacNeil MSS, Box 11. He said this, though, not in the South but in Nashua, New Hampshire, where he was trying to win a critical primary in a contest with liberal challengers.

37. James Charles Cobb, "Politics in a New South City: Augusta, Georgia, 1946–1971" (Ph.D. dissertation, University of Georgia, 1975), 150; George F. Gilder and Bruce K. Chapman, *The Party That Lost Its Head* (New York, 1966), 62; George C. Roberts, "The 1964 Presidential Election in Arkansas," in *The 1964 Presidential Election in the Southwest,* ed. John M. Claunch (Dallas, Tex., 1966), 85; Roy Harris SOHP, 5–6. See, too, Reg Murphy SOHP, 19; Jimmy Carter SOHP, 2. Goldwater's "appeal," commented the southern editor Mark Ethridge, was "to the ardent segregationist." Ethridge to W. E. Chilton III, July 20, 1964, Ethridge MSS, Folder 74.

38. Richard H. Rovere, *The Goldwater Caper* (New York, 1965), 140–41; typescript of article for the *New Yorker,* October 3, 1964, Rovere MSS, Box 9; Strout, *TRB,* 271. "Nowhere is Barry Goldwater supported with more fervor than in this colorful old port city where the Civil War began," reported Haynes Johnson from Charleston. "At the center of their emotional feeling stands the only issue of consequence here—the issue of race. . . . The support for Goldwater means avid backing of rabid segregationists. As a result a climate of hatred and extremism does exist in South Carolina. Without the race issue, Johnson would carry South Carolina easily. Some astute Carolinians even think he would win by as much as 3 to 1." *Washington Star,* October 22, 1964, excerpted in F. Clifton White MSS, Ashland. A white woman who served on the Atlanta school board wrote in her diary: "Philosophy and religion as well as politics are implicated in the upcoming election between Lyndon Johnson and Barry Goldwater. . . . Republicans in the South think Goldwater will

restore states' rights, which they understand to mean every black back in his or her place—preferably back in the cotton fields or in the kitchens of the 'white folks.'" Sara Mitchell Parsons, *From Southern Wrongs to Civil Rights: The Memoir of a White Civil Rights Activist* (Tuscaloosa, Ala., 2000), 110.

39. Margolis, *Last Innocent Year,* 334; Lesher, *George Wallace,* 307; *Orlando Sentinel,* January 5, 1964, clipping, John Grenier MSS, Box 1; Houghton, draft, Ph.D. dissertation on the Republican Party in North Carolina. See, too, *Columbus (Ga.) Enquirer,* January 10, 1964, clipping, Scrapbook, Roy V. Harris MSS; Bob Currie to John L. McClellan, May 18, 1964, McClellan MSS, File 45, Drawer E. For Barnett's defection, see clipping, UPI dispatch, September 13, 1964, Barry Goldwater Scrapbooks. Conservatives frequently invoked memories of Reconstruction against reformers, but Senator Olin Johnston of South Carolina charged that Goldwater, "a self-styled saviour of the South," was, in fact, an "infamous interloper" who had contributed to the NAACP to desegregate Arizona schools. Though "he speaks with honey in his mouth," the South Carolina senator said, Goldwater "aims a shotgun at our hearts." Olin Johnston, press release, October 1960, Ernest McFarland MSS, Box 142. See, too, James Conaway, *Judge: The Life and Times of Leander Perez* (New York, 1973), 141.

40. Hale Boggs LBJL OH, 2: 13; transcript of BBC Home Service, June 16, 1964, Richard Rovere MSS, Box 5; typescript of article for the *New Yorker,* October 3, 1964, Richard Rovere MSS, Box 9; Hale Boggs LBJL OH, 2: 13; Pat Watters, *The South and the Nation* (New York, 1969), 242–43; Virginia Durr to Hugo and Elizabeth Black, October 12, 1964, Virginia Durr MSS, Box 1. In Southside Virginia, where there was a powerful white backlash, supporters of the Johnson ticket, one observer reported, "were ridiculed, maligned and otherwise intimidated." Robert D. Partridge to Luther Hodges, November 24, 1964, Hodges MSS, Folder 791. A Houston man wrote Harry Truman, "President Johnson has run out on the South 100%." Anon. to Harry S. Truman, July 2, 1964, HSTL PPGF, Box 194.

41. Jimmy Carter, *An Hour before Daylight: Memories of a Rural Boyhood* (New York, 2001), 267; William F. Nichols OH, 143; Roman Heleniak, "Lyndon Johnson in New Orleans," *Louisiana History* 21 (1980): 274; Jeansonne, *Leander Perez,* 50; Sherrill, *Gothic Politics,* 35. See, too, Oren Harris LBJL OH, 44; "Johnson Quotes," n.d., Lester Maddox MSS, Box 8.

42. Memorandum, F. Clifton White MSS, Ashland, October 1964; Grantham, *Life and Death of Solid South,* 160; Shirley Tucker, ed., *Mississippi from Within* (New York, 1965), 45. See, too, address by Governor Paul B. Johnson to state Democratic convention, July 28, 1964; Address to the Reconvened State Democratic Convention, Paul B. Johnson MSS. John Brademas, the Indiana congressman who made an outstanding record as a liberal Democrat, has recalled an occasion in 1964 at the height of the Goldwater campaign when he introduced himself to a man identified as a fellow Democrat. "Good evening, sir," Brademas said. "I understand that you and I are the only two people in the state of Mississippi tonight who are going to vote for Lyndon Johnson for president." The man smiled, then replied, "You don't think I'm gonna vote for no Jew, do you?" John Brademas, Address at a Ceremony Marking the Centennial of the Birth of William Faulkner, Oxford, Miss., September 25, 1997 (courtesy of John Brademas). See, too, Alan Draper, *Conflict of Interests: Organized Labor and the Civil Rights Movement in the South, 1954–1968* (Ithaca, N.Y., 1994), 142–43.

43. Margolis, *Last Innocent Year,* 295; Beschloss, *Taking Charge,* 515–16, 523, 470; interview, Joseph

Rauh, Anne Romaine MSS, 34; Richard Rovere, Memo of a Conversation with the President at the White House, October 1, 1964, Rovere MSS, Box 17; Arthur I. Waskow, Notes on the Democratic National Convention, Atlantic City, August 1964, Confidential, Howard Zinn MSS, Box 1. A business newsletter reported, "The big news in a convention that provided little in the way of surprises was LBJ's *divorce* from the Old South." *Babson's Washington Forecast* 51 (August 31, 1964): 1, Walter Sillers Jr. MSS, 104: 2.

44. Perlstein, *Before the Storm*, 429; Black and Black, *Vital South*, 203.

45. Branch, *Pillar of Fire*, 473, 468; Beschloss, *Taking Charge*, 531. Noting that in his memoirs Johnson offered a picture of himself as "Hamlet, a man tortured by the call of public duty on one hand and a rending aversion on the other to anything smacking of ambition or interfering with family, grandchildren, fireside or ranch," J. Kenneth Galbraith commented, "It is hard to believe how badly LBJ always wanted to escape from the distractions of politics and public office. In point of fact, no one will." Especially startling, Galbraith observed, was the notion that at the Atlantic City convention in 1964 Johnson contemplated not running, "a state of the presidential mind that, in our innocence, none of us along the boardwalk ever suspected." John Kenneth Galbraith, *A View from the Stands: Of People, Politics, Military Power and the Arts* (Boston, 1986), 335. Galbraith wrote this before transcripts of LBJ's phone conversations became available. Skepticism about Johnson's intentions, however, is always in order.

46. Wicker, *JFK and LBJ*, 176; John H. Kessel, *The Goldwater Coalition: Republican Strategies in 1964* (Indianapolis, Ind., 1968), 229; T. H. White, *Making of the President, 1964*, 353.

47. Carpenter, *Ruffles and Flourishes*, 149–50.

48. Carl Sanders LBJL OH, 9; Nancy Kegan Smith, "Private Reflections on a Public Life: The Papers on Lady Bird Johnson at the LBJ Library," *Presidential Studies Quarterly* 20 (1990): 742; Liz Carpenter Files (Whistle Stop), LBJL, Box 12.

49. Memo, "The Lady Bird Special," LBJ MSS, President, EX TR July 1, 1968, Box 2; Carpenter, *Ruffles and Flourishes*, 143–44; Marjorie Hunter, "Public Servant Without Pay: The First Lady," *New York Times Magazine*, clipping, Katie Louchheim MSS, Box 20.

50. Carpenter, *Ruffles and Flourishes*, 156–57. The president employed that same quotation from Lee a few days later. Helen Fuller, "The Powerful Persuaders: Lady Bird's Trip Through the South," *New Republic*, October 24, 1964, 11.

51. Russell, *Lady Bird*, 255; Barbara Howar, *Laughing All the Way* (New York, 1973), 111; *Washington Star*, January 12, 1969, clipping, Katie Louchheim MSS, Box 20; Herman Talmadge LBJL OH, 21.

52. Russell, *Lady Bird*, 258; M. Miller, *Lyndon*, 397. For the heckling of Lady Bird Johnson in South Carolina, see *Daily Telegraph and Morning Post* (London), October 9, 1964, clipping, Liz Carpenter files, LBJL, Box 12.

53. M. Miller, *Lyndon*, 397; Howar, *Laughing All the Way*, 111. Justice Black wrote his sister-in-law, "Lady Bird . . . is such a genuinely fine person. . . . It takes pretty callous and prejudiced people to treat her as she was treated by a small minority in South Carolina." Hugo Black to Virginia Durr, October 19, 1964, Virginia Durr MSS, Box 1. A number of South Carolinians were embarrassed. One woman, displaying a Johnson banner, said, "We could weep." *Newsweek*, October 19, 1964, 31.

54. "Mrs. Johnson's Charleston Speech," Liz Carpenter Files (Whistle Stop) LBJL, Box 12.

55. Steinberg, *Sam Johnson's Boy*, 712; Carpenter, *Ruffles and Flourishes*, 168; M. Miller, *Lyndon*, 397;

Washington Star, March 25, 1964, clipping, Katie Louchheim MSS, Box 20; Virginia Durr to Hugo and Elizabeth Black, October 12, 1964, Virginia Durr MSS, Box 1; Paul B. Johnson Jr. LBJL OH, 47–48; Lady Bird Johnson to Paul B. Johnson, October 27, 1964, Paul B. Johnson MSS. See, too, Lindy Boggs with Katherine Hatch, *Washington through a Purple Veil: Memoirs of a Southern Woman* (New York, 1994), 192.

56. H. Thomas, *Dateline,* 54; Carpenter, *Ruffles and Flourishes,* 144, 165–66; Howar, *Laughing All the Way,* 110. In calling Johnson the first southern-born president in a century, Boggs forgot about Woodrow Wilson. He would have been accurate if he had said the first in that period who was also a resident of a southern state, for Wilson had gone to the White House from the governorship of New Jersey. Boggs had voted against the 1964 Civil Rights Act, but in New Orleans in November he was to gain 93 percent of the ballots of African Americans, who recognized that he was willing to go as far as he dared to on civil rights. In 1965 he was one of only six southern congressmen recorded for the voting rights bill. Chandler Davidson, *Biracial Politics: Conflict and Coalition in the Metropolitan South* (Baton Rouge, La., 1972), 214; Allen Rosenzweig, "The Influence of Class and Race on Political Behavior in New Orleans, 1960–1967" (M.A. essay, University of Oklahoma, 1967), 230. "It was a great adventure for me," she said afterward. "I shall never forget those thousands of friendly faces, the banners, the bands, and the youngsters up on the box cars." Lady Bird Johnson to Le Roy Collins, October 23, 1964, Collins MSS, Florida State University, Tallahassee.

57. *Public Papers, 1963–1964,* 1278, 1282; M. Miller, *Lyndon,* 397.

58. Curtis Wilkie, *Dixie: A Personal Odyssey Through Events That Shaped the Modern South* (New York, 2001), 151; Henry H. (Joe) Fowler, Memorandum for the President, September 29, 1964, James H. Rowe Jr., MSS, Box 146; *Newsweek,* October 19, 1964, 29; Heleniak, "Lyndon Johnson in New Orleans," 272; L. B. Johnson, *Vantage Point,* 109. In the spring of 1964, the wife of a White House staff member, the historian Eric Goldman, recorded in her diary: "E reports Pres expects the election to be hard fight. Very much worried about White backlash." Joanna Goldman MS. Diary, May 12, 1964, Eric Goldman MSS, Series 1, Box 6. Less than two months before the election, the Alabamian Hugo Black wrote a former U.S. Senate and Supreme Court colleague, "It does look to me as if the South is likely to go Republican." Hugo Black to Sherman Minton, September 17, 1964, Black MSS, Box 61.

59. Branch, *Pillar of Fire,* 514; *Public Papers, 1963–64,* 1282–83. For Congressman Boggs's syrupy introduction promising "that the South is not thinking about turning its back on our President, our neighbor from Texas," see typescript, Hale Boggs MSS.

60. Cormier, *LBJ,* 125; Valenti, *Very Human President,* 206; *Public Papers, 1963–64,* 1285–86; L. B. Johnson, *Vantage Point,* 109.

61. *Public Papers, 1963–64,* 1286; T. H. White, *Making of the President, 1964,* 363–64; Carpenter, *Ruffles and Flourishes,* 170; Vaughn Davis Bornet, *The Presidency of Lyndon B. Johnson* (Lawrence, Kans., 1983), 114. The unnamed senator was Joseph Weldon Bailey. Though Bailey was U.S. senator from Texas, Johnson was referring not to that state, but to Mississippi where Bailey was born and grew up. The Sam Rayburn anecdote was not on the Teleprompter; the passionate tale came not from his speech writers but from the president. David Zarefsky, "Subordinating the Civil Rights Issue: Lyndon Johnson in 1964," *Southern Speech Communication Journal* 48 (1983): 109. One writer has maintained, after listening to an audio tape, that Johnson used the pronunciation *Negro.* Hele-

niak, "Lyndon Johnson in New Orleans," 274. Others assert that the word was *Nigger,* but that the press was wary of printing that pejorative term. It has, in any event, become commonplace to refer to the address as the "Nigra, Nigra, Nigra speech."

62. Valenti, *Very Human President,* 207; Manchester, *Glory and the Dream,* 1030; Carpenter, *Ruffles and Flourishes,* 170; M. Miller, *Lyndon,* 398; Cormier, *LBJ,* 125.

63. T. H. White, *Making of the President, 1964,* 363; Reedy, *Lyndon B. Johnson,* xiv; M. Miller, *Lyndon,* 397. A confidential Goldwater campaign memo reported: "President Johnson's visit to New Orleans on October 9 and his speeches here did him a lot of good." "Louisiana Report," October 16, 1964, F. Clifton White MSS, Ashland, Box 28.

64. Roy Peter Clark and Raymond Arsenault, eds., *The Changing South of Gene Patterson: Journalism and Civil Rights, 1960–1968* (Gainesville, Fla., 2002), 165–66; Hale Boggs LBJL OH, 2: 10; Herman Talmadge LBJL OH, 19; George Goodwin, "The Morning After," in Joseph M. Bowman to Perry Barber, November 9, 1964, LBJ MSS GEN PL/ST 9, 4/6/68, Box 42; Charles Longstreet Weltner, address, n.d., Yale University, Weltner MSS, Box 4; Fite, *Russell,* 419–20; Ralph McGill to LBJ, November 6, 1964, McGill MSS, 5, Box 59; Bruce E. Altschuler, *LBJ and the Polls* (Gainesville, Fla., 1990), 23; Sarah Van V. Woolfolk, "Alabama Attitudes Toward the Republican Party in 1868 and 1964," *Alabama Review* 20 (1967): 31–32. Goldwater ran strongly in the same parts of Georgia that had been attracted to Thurmond in 1948. Numan V. Bartley, *From Thurmond to Wallace: Political Tendencies in Georgia, 1948–1968* (Baltimore, 1970), 61. An Alabama congressman and his wife wrote after the election: "There was no way to vote for Lyndon Johnson in Alabama, because he was not on the ticket. I know that is hard for anybody to believe; it certainly was for me." Ocllo and Frank W. Boykin to John McCormack, Carl Albert, and Hale Boggs, December 19, 1964, Boggs MSS. A local Republican official reported on Monroe County, Alabama: "We picked up quite a few votes from people who considered Johnson a turncoat." John S. Moore to John Grenier, November 18, 1964, Grenier MSS, Box 5. See, too, Powell Moore LBJL OH, 4; *Atlanta Constitution,* November 6, 1964; Bernard Cosman, *Five States for Goldwater: Continuity and Change in Southern Presidential Voting Patterns* (University, Ala., 1966); Donald Thomas Wolfe, "Southern Strategy: Race, Region, and Republican Presidential Politics, 1964 and 1968" (Ph.D. dissertation, The Johns Hopkins University, 1974). For the strength of George Wallace in the rural South, see Stephen S. Birdsall, "Preliminary Analysis of the 1968 Wallace Vote in the Southeast," *Southeastern Geographer* 9 (1969): 58.

65. Matthews and Prothro, *Negroes and the New Southern Politics,* 369; Walker Percy, "Mississippi: The Fallen Paradise," *Harper's* 230 (1965): 169–70, 172. One analyst has written of the Goldwater showing in Mississippi, "To say that it was 95 percent of the white vote would not be far wrong." Harry Holloway, *The Politics of the Southern Negro: From Exclusion to Big City Organization* (New York, 1969), 53. One survey found that 96 percent of Mississippi disapproved of civil rights legislation, compared to 54 percent of all southerners. Samuel G. Patterson, "The Political Cultures of the American States," *Journal of Politics* 30 (1968): 197–98.

66. "The South and Senator Goldwater's Siren Song," Editorial, WDSU-TV and WDSU-Radio, Hale Boggs MSS; Bernard Cosman and Robert J. Huckshorn, eds., *Republican Politics: The 1964 Campaign and Its Aftermath for the Party* (New York, 1968), 62–63; Paul Casdorph, *A History*

of the Republican Party in Texas, 1865–1965 (Austin, Tex., 1965), 245; John C. McGlennon, "Virginia's Changing Party Politics, 1976–1986," in *The South's New Politics: Realignment and Dealignment,* ed. Robert H. Swansbrough and David M. Brodsky (Columbia, S.C., 1988), 57. "Given the fact that Goldwater wooed the South so straightforwardly, and injected the new and potent ingredient of clear party differentiation on civil rights into the 1964 picture," the "retrogression" from the Eisenhower-Nixon era was "astonishing," a team of political scientists concluded. Philip E. Converse, P. R. Clauson, and Warren E. Miller, "Electoral Myth and Reality: The 1964 Election," *American Political Science Review* 59 (1965): 328–29.

67. *Waycross Journal-Herald,* n.d. [October 1964], clipping, LBJ MSS GEN PL/ST 9, 4/6/68, Box 42; Black and Black, *Vital South,* 202; Numan V. Bartley, "Comments," in Ernest McPherson Lander Jr. and Richard J. Calhoun, *Two Decades of Change: The South since the Supreme Court Desegregation Decision* (Columbia, S.C., 1975), 23; Hale Boggs to Randolph Feltus, July 31, 1964, Boggs MSS; Wilkinson, *Harry Byrd,* 252–54. One North Carolina congressman, after strongly opposing Johnson's 1964 civil rights legislation, nonetheless wrote a constituent that fall, "I feel that President Johnson has many high qualifications for continuing his leadership of our country." Alton Lennon to Mrs. I. M. Scott, October 6, 1964, Lennon MSS. Save for Strom Thurmond, no southern senator endorsed Goldwater, and even Orval Faubus wound up backing Johnson. Stanley Kelley Jr., "The Presidential Campaign," in *The National Election of 1964,* ed. Milton C. Cummings Jr. (Washington, D.C., 1966), 68. See, too, Edgar A. Brown to LBJ, November 9, 1964, Brown MSS, Folder L928; Ely, *Crisis of Conservative Virginia,* 177; Ralph Eisenberg, "Virginia: The Emergence of Two-Party Politics," in *Changing Politics,* ed. Havard, 63; John Shaw Billings MS. Diary, November 3, 1964.

68. William E. Pemberton, *Exit with Honor: The Life and Presidency of Ronald Reagan* (Armonk, N.Y., 1998), 52; Bruce A. Campbell, "Change in the Southern Electorate," *American Journal of Political Science* 21 (1977): 38.

69. Aaron Henry LBJL OH, Tape 2: 10; Everett Carll Ladd Jr., "Negro Politics in the South: An Overview," in *Negro Politics in America,* ed. Harry A. Bailey Jr. (Columbus, Ohio, 1967), 244; Houghton, draft, Ph.D. dissertation on the Republican Party in North Carolina, University of North Carolina at Chapel Hill; Wilkinson, *Harry Byrd,* 181, 186; Thomas R. Morris and Neil Bradley, "Virginia," in *Quiet Revolution in the South: The Impact of the Voting Rights Act, 1965–1990,* ed. Chandler Davidson and Bernard Grofman (Princeton, N.J., 1994), 275. In a black precinct in Raleigh, Johnson got 1045, Goldwater 4. Capus Waynick, "The Race Issue in the 1964 State Campaign," Luther Hodges MSS, Folder 789. In Virginia, Johnson recorded 99 percent of the African-American vote, carrying Richmond's precinct 16 by 2138 to 14. In the Jefferson Park precinct of Newport News, he rang up 1325 votes; Goldwater got none. Bass and DeVries, *Transformation of Southern Politics,* 350. See, too, D. M. Tucker, *Memphis since Crump,* 149; Alwyn Barr, *Black Texans: A History of Negroes in Texas, 1528–1971* (Austin, Tex., 1973), 178–79; Clark and Kirwan, *South since Appomattox,* 302–3; Watters and Cleghorn, *Climbing Jacob's Ladder,* 37. For the importance of black ballots in Arkansas in 1964, see Irving J. Spitzberg Jr., *Racial Politics in Little Rock, 1954–1964* (New York, 1987), 162–63.

70. David S. Castle, "Goldwater's Presidential Candidacy and Political Realignment," *Presiden-*

tial Studies Quarterly 20 (1990): 103–10; Jimmy Carter SOHP, 22; Black and Black, *Vital South,* 156; Holloway, *Politics of the Southern Negro,* 53; Strout, *TRB,* 273. Carter used the word *bridesmaid,* but he clearly meant to say *bride.* He also stated that Johnson gave up on the South in 1964, which was not so.

71. *Washington Post,* July 13, 1988.

II. THE AGONY OF VICTORY

1. F. Edward Hebert LBJL OH, 48; Kay Mills, *This Little Light of Mine: The Life of Fannie Lou Hamer* (New York, 1993), 143; Goodwin, *Remembering America,* 344–45; Chandler, *National Superiority,* 354.

2. Rowan, *Breaking Barriers,* 249; *Public Papers of the Presidents: Lyndon Johnson, 1965* (Washington, D.C., 1966), 281–87; John Lewis, with Michael D'Orso, *Walking with the Wind: A Memoir of the Movement* (New York, 1998), 339–40; Dean Rusk, as told to Richard Rusk, *As I Saw It,* ed. Daniel Papp (New York, 1990), 588.

3. David J. Garrow, *Protest at Selma: Martin Luther King, Jr., and the Voting Rights Act of 1965* (New Haven, Conn., 1978), 133; Harris Wofford, *Of Kennedys and Kings: Making Sense of the Sixties* (New York, 1980), 186; Bayard Rustin and Tom Kahn, "Johnson So Far: Civil Rights," *Commentary* 39 (1965): 44; Richard Lentz, *Symbols, the News Magazines, and Martin Luther King* (Baton Rouge, La., 1990), 161; Joseph A. Califano Jr., *The Triumph and Tragedy of Lyndon Johnson: The White House Years* (New York, 1991), 58.

4. Goodwin, *Remembering America,* 310; C. T. Vivian in *Voices of Freedom: An Oral History of the Civil Rights Movement from the 1950s through the 1980s,* ed. Henry Hampton and Steve Fayer, with Sarah Flynn (New York, 1990), 236.

5. Parker with Rashke, *Capitol Hill in Black and White,* 185–86; Herman Talmadge LBJL OH, 34; Caro, *Master of the Senate,* 868. After the 1964 election, Senator Russell wrote: "President Johnson and I have been intimates for a number of years and I hope that, now that he has received an overwhelming mandate from the people, he will shake off the termite left-wingers, the ADAers and the Reuthers and go back to the Jeffersonian principles that have made our country great." Richard B. Russell to R. F. Morris, November 23, 1964, Russell MSS, Political Series.

6. Sherrill, *Gothic Politics,* 237–38; John A. Andrew III, *Lyndon Johnson and the Great Society* (Chicago, 1998), 38; Bass and Thompson, *Ol' Strom,* 220; Virginius Dabney to Harry F. Byrd, April 2, 1965, Dabney MSS 7690–M, Box 3. In his campaign for governor of Georgia in 1966, Lester Maddox denounced Johnson's "racist, 'We Shall Overcome' attitude." Earl Black, *Southern Governors and Civil Rights: Racial Segregation as a Campaign Issue in the Second Reconstruction* (Cambridge, Mass., 1976), 69. Incensed by Johnson's advocacy of voting rights legislation, a Norfolk woman who had always voted Democrat wrote her congressman, "We are sick and tired of him trying to pass laws cramming ideas originated with King, Powell, Wilkins and the rest of the troublemakers . . . putting our feet on the road to a Mongrel Nation." Elizabeth Downing to Porter Hardy Jr., March 16, 1965, Hardy MSS. When in 1967 Johnson opposed a maneuver by Senator Sam Ervin against a new civil rights measure, Ervin complained, "A bill sponsored in good faith by a Southerner ap-

parently cannot see the light of day." Steven F. Lawson, *In Pursuit of Power: Southern Blacks and Electoral Politics, 1965–1982* (New York, 1985), 81. Barbara Howar, a North Carolinian who was an intimate of the Johnson family, recalls her North Carolina mother saying to her: "I've had about enough of those tacky Johnsons. . . . They aren't even *real* southerners." Howar, *Laughing All the Way*, 23. For southern resentment of Johnson's civil rights legislation in 1968, see correspondence in William Cato Cramer MSS.

7. Lesher, *George Wallace*, 332; Anna Permaloff and Carl Grafton, *Political Power in Alabama: The More Things Change . . .* (Athens, Ga., 1995), 214–15. Of the seventeen Democratic votes cast against the Voting Rights Act, all came from the South. *Washington Star*, August 5, 1965, clipping, O. C. Fisher MSS, Box 387.

8. Wilkins with Mathews, *Standing Fast*, 156; Valenti, *Very Human President*, 395; Louis Martin LBJL OH, 22. A prominent black lawyer in Selma later said, "When you have a white Southerner who is *for* you he understands the landscape—like Lyndon Johnson did." Haynes Johnson, *Divided We Fall: Gambling with History in the Nineties* (New York, 1994), 378. "You spoke words that will go down in history of the great Presidents of our nation," Wilkins wrote him. Roy Wilkins to LBJ, n.d., Wilkins MSS, Box 7. "We were as well protected as a shipment of gold from Ft. Knox—thanks to President Johnson," one of the leaders of the Selma-Montgomery march, Ralph Abernathy, recalled. Ralph David Abernathy, *And the Walls Came Tumbling Down: An Autobiography* (New York, 1989), 348.

9. Willie Morris, *New York Days* (Boston, 1993), 163; Herbert Block, *The Herblock Gallery* (New York, 1968), 12; L. B. Johnson, *Vantage Point*, 162; *New York Times*, June 25, 1964, clipping, Hubert Humphrey MSS, Senatorial, Civil Rights, 1964; Dallek, *Flawed Giant*, 215; clipping, July 12, 1965, Ellis Berry MSS, Box 505; Peter Goldman, *Report from Black America* (New York, 1970), 22–23; Dallek, *Flawed Giant*, 515–16; *1968 News Dictionary*, 62; Ashmore, *Civil Rights and Wrongs*, 198. In the spring of 1964, Joanna Goldman noted in her diary, "Every day produces some further incident of LBJ totally wrapping himself up in Texans, things southern, etc." Joanna Goldman MS. Diary, May 12, 1964, Eric Goldman MSS, Series 1, Box 6.

10. Clayborne Carson, *In Struggle: SNCC and the Black Awakening of the 1960s* (Cambridge, Mass., 1981), 256; Merriman Smith, "Backstairs at the White House," *Philadelphia Bulletin*, September 27, 1967, clipping, Office Files of Fred Panzer: LBJ Criticism, Box 402, LBJL; James Farmer LBJL OH, 2: 27; Lewis with D'Orso, *Walking with the Wind*, 340; Rowan, *Breaking Barriers*, 276. One account notes the "profound skepticism of President Johnson" felt by civil rights workers in the Deep South. Mary Aickin Rothschild, *A Case of Black and White: Northern Volunteers and the Southern Freedom Summers, 1964–1965* (Westport, Conn., 1982), 179. An angry black in the child development program in Mississippi called the president "Lynchum B. Johnson." Quoted in Polly Greenberg, *The Devil Has Slippery Shoes: A Biased Biography of the Child Development Group of Mississippi* (New York, 1969), 513. In 1967 black protesters from Harlem, blaming Johnson for the delay in enacting a rat eradication bill, handed Capitol police in Washington a brown rat, explaining before television cameras, "His name is Lyndon." Thomas Byrne Edsall with Mary D. Edsall, *Chain Reaction: The Impact of Race, Rights, and Taxes on American Politics* (New York, 1992), 65. An observer of a Freedom Summer event in Mississippi recorded that Stokely Carmichael told a class, "Trouble w

LBJ is he thinks he's to lead and we're to follow." Notes by Jane Stembridge about a class held by Stokely Carmichael, Allard Lowenstein MSS, Box 32. For Johnson's difficulties with another minority group, see Julie Leininger Pycior, "From Hope to Frustration: Mexican Americans and Lyndon Johnson in 1967," *Western Historical Quarterly* 24 (1993): 468–94.

11. Dallek, *Flawed Giant,* 111; Beschloss, *Taking Charge,* 185–86; Robert Kastenmeier interview, August 23, 1967, Anne Romaine MSS; Roger Wilkins in *Voices of Freedom,* ed. Hampton and Fayer, 384; Kearns, *Lyndon Johnson,* 305.

12. Robert Kastenmeier interview, August 23, 1967, Anne Romaine MSS; Aaron Henry with Constance Curry, *The Fire Ever Burning* (Jackson, Miss., 2000), 186–87; Lewis with D'Orso, *Walking with the Wind,* 280–82; Jack Irby Hayes Jr., *Dan Daniel and the Persistence of Conservatism in Virginia* (Macon, Ga., 1997), 105; "Recommendations of the Special Equal Rights Committee to the Democratic National Convention," February 1, 1967, Aaron Henry MSS, Series 2, Box 5; Michael Paul Sistrom, "Authors of the Liberation: The Mississippi Freedom Democrats and the Redefinition of Politics" (Ph.D. dissertation, University of North Carolina at Chapel Hill, 2002). One of the leaders of the MFDP later said, "We always had to underplay our potential strength so that Lyndon Johnson didn't smash us." Ed King OH, Anne Romaine MSS, SHC, 262.

13. Jonathan Rosenberg and Zachary Karabell, eds., *Kennedy, Johnson, and the Quest for Justice: The Civil Rights Tapes* (New York, 2003), 250; Beschloss, *Taking Charge,* 433; Branch, *Pillar of Fire,* 471.

14. Howell Raines, *My Soul Is Rested: Movement Days in the Deep South Remembered* (New York, 1977), 337; Goodwin, *Remembering America,* 342–43.

15. *Public Papers, 1965,* 635–40; Lee Rainwater and William L. Yancey, *The Moynihan Report and the Politics of Controversy* (Cambridge, Mass., 1967), 1–15; Stephen C. Keadey, draft of Ph.D. dissertation on Lyndon B. Johnson and civil rights, 1965–68, University of North Carolina at Chapel Hill.

16. Califano, *Triumph and Tragedy,* 62–70; James W. Button, *Black Violence: Political Impact of the 1960s Riots* (Princeton, N.J., 1978), 30–32. In 1964 the Justice Department intervened in only one school desegregation case; in 1967, in 109. In 1966 the black journalist Carl Rowan wrote, "The history books may say that Lyndon Baines Johnson's real contribution . . . was the way he browbeat the executive branch to make equality of opportunity a fact." From June 1964 to June 1965, Rowan noted, more than half of new federal employees were black, a good number of them in high-paid jobs. Carl T. Rowan to Bob Blakely, February 13, 1966, Rowan MSS, Subgroup 4, Series 5, Box 7.

17. Califano, *Triumph and Tragedy,* 58–59.

18. Lewis L. Gould, *1968: The Election that Changed America* (Chicago, 1993), 13–14; Califano, *Triumph and Tragedy,* 276; *New York Times,* May 11, 1967, clipping, Dan Carter MSS, Box 5; Steven F. Lawson, *Civil Rights Crossroads: Nation, Community, and the Black Freedom Struggle* (Lexington, Ky., 2003), 43; Stephen Keadey, draft of Ph.D. dissertation on Lyndon B. Johnson and civil rights, 1965–68, University of North Carolina at Chapel Hill. In promoting the 1964 civil rights bill, the ranking Republican on the House Judiciary Committee had sought to win over undecided members by pointing out that the legislation did not cover housing. "Analysis of Civil Rights Bill H.R. 7152," April 20, 1964, William McCulloch MSS, Box 43. For disapproval of the housing bill from the president of Rich's in Atlanta, see Harold Brockey to Evelyn Lincoln, March 18, 1968, Lincoln MSS, Box 40. Lawson, an acute critic of the shortcomings of liberal attitudes toward race, has written,

"As the civil rights coalition diminished in size and white reactionary forces grew, Johnson refused to order a major retreat on the legislative front." Steven F. Lawson, "Civil Rights," in *Exploring the Johnson Years,* ed. Robert A. Divine (Austin, Tex., 1981), 106.

19. Emily Stoper, *The Student Nonviolent Coordinating Committee: The Growth of Radicalism in a Civil Rights Organization* (Brooklyn, N.Y., 1989), 45; A. Young, *Easy Burden,* 369–70; James R. Ralph Jr., *Northern Protest: Martin Luther King, Jr., Chicago, and the Civil Rights Movement* (Cambridge, Mass., 1993), 173–75, 193; Resolution of the Board of Directors, Southern Christian Leadership Conference, Jackson, Miss., August 11, 1968, Chicago Urban League MSS, Box 169; Mills, *This Little Light of Mine,* 217; James Forman, *The Making of Black Revolutionaries* (New York, 1972), 547; Cleveland Sellers with Robert Terrell, *The River of No Return: The Autobiography of a Black Militant and the Life and Death of SNCC* (New York, 1973), 199; Julius Lester, *Look Out, Whitey! Black Power's Gon' Get Your Mama!* (New York, 1968), 16, 23, 133. At a retrospective on Freedom Summer in 1979, "many conference speakers," noted Anthony Lewis, "sounded a theme of betrayal and the main targets of their denunciations were not the old segregationists of Mississippi but the Northern liberals and especially the Kennedy and Johnson administrations." Anthony Lewis, "Winds of Change," *New York Times,* November 5, 1979; John R. Salter Jr. to Lewis, November 10, 1979, Mississippi "Freedom Summer" Reviewed Conference MSS. See, too, "Both Sides Critical of 'Rights' Bill," *Jackson Clarion Ledger,* June 7, 1966, clipping, Ed King MSS, Box 4. As late as 1966, only 35 percent of African Americans disapproved of the Vietnam War, but opposition rose in 1967 when the government altered its standards to induct disproportionate numbers of racial minorities. Brenda Gayle Plummer, *Rising Wind: Black Americans and U.S. Foreign Affairs, 1935–1960* (Chapel Hill, N.C., 1996), 318.

20. Arthur M. Schlesinger Jr., *Robert Kennedy and His Times* (Boston, 1978), 623.

21. Ira Mothner, "The Texanization of Washington," *Look,* April 6, 1965, 30–34; Daniel P. Moynihan, "The President and the Negro: The Moment Lost," *Commentary* 43 (1967): 35.

22. Beschloss, *Taking Charge,* 105; *New York Herald Tribune,* March 20, 1964, clipping, Hubert Humphrey MSS, Senatorial, Civil Rights, 1964; Davie, *LBJ,* 27; Randy Roberts and James S. Olson, *A Line in the Sand: The Alamo in Blood and Memory* (New York, 2001), 284. In the midst of a highly favorable appraisal of LBJ's presidency published in 1967, one of the original members of FDR's brain trust observed that "Mr. Johnson's limitations are obvious." They were those of "a dogged, roughhewn Texas politician." Adolf Berle, "LBJ's Record Will Show He Did His Damnedest," *Washington Post,* November 26, 1967, clipping, Le Roy Collins MSS, Box 389. See, too, Edward W. Chester, "Lyndon Baines Johnson, An American 'King Lear': A Critical Evaluation of His Newspaper Obituaries," *Presidential Studies Quarterly* 21 (1991): 320.

23. Richard Harwood and Haynes Johnson, *Lyndon* (New York, 1973), 52; Beschloss, *Taking Charge,* 310–11; Bradlee, *Conversations with Kennedy,* 273; Richard H. Rovere, *Arrivals and Departures: A Journalist's Memoirs* (New York, 1976), 138–39; Califano, *Triumph and Tragedy,* 279.

24. Patricia Sullivan, ed., *Freedom Writer: Virginia Foster Durr, Letters from the Civil Rights Years* (New York, 2003), 304; Larry Berman, "Lyndon Johnson's Presidential Leadership: Paths Chosen and Opportunities Lost," paper delivered at conference on leadership in the modern presidency, Princeton University (April 1987), 12; Reedy, *Lyndon B. Johnson,* 55. See, too, transcript of interview of Lyndon B. Johnson by Walter Cronkite, 1969, Burton Benjamin MSS, Box 21.

25. L. B. Johnson, *Time for Action*, 85.

26. Dallek, *Flawed Giant*, 98; Kevin Phillips, *American Dynasty: Aristocracy, Fortune, and the Politics of Deceit in the House of Bush* (New York, 2004), 297. Philip Geyelin, *Lyndon B. Johnson and the World* (New York, 1966), 7; Dugger, *Politician*, 41.

27. Wicker, *JFK and LBJ*, 196; Dallek, *Flawed Giant*, 90–91; John Herbers, *The Lost Priority: What Happened to the Civil Rights Movement in America?* (New York, 1970), 191; Alistair Cooke, *Talk about America* (New York, 1969), 95.

28. Dugger, *Politician*, 35; Neal R. Peirce and Jerry Hagstrom, *The Book of America: Inside 50 States Today* (New York, 1983), 623. See, too, Susan Prendergast Schoelwer with Tom W. Glaser, *Alamo Images: Changing Perceptions of a Texas Experience* (Dallas, Tex., 1985), 166, 168; William Physick Zuber, *My Eighty Years in Texas*, ed. Janis Boyle Mayfield (Austin, Tex., 1971), 251. There is no hard evidence that Travis ever did draw a line, but some authorities have said that the facts do not matter. No amount of scholarship can ever erode the "Grand Canyon cut into the bedrock of human emotions and heroical impulses" by that tale, J. Frank Dobie contended. Edward Tabor Linenthal, "'A Reservoir of Spiritual Power': Patriotic Faith at the Alamo in the Twentieth Century," *Southwestern Historical Quarterly* 91 (1988): 516. See, too, Walter Lord, *A Time to Stand* (New York, 1961), 204. The man who skulked away, Moses Rose, was a war-weary veteran of the Napoleonic wars. "Rose is the old order, being both Jewish and European," a scholar has noted. "In the mythology, he is similar to Judas in the Gospels who, though initially part of Christ's inner circle, abandons Christ and his disciples in their darkest hour." Holly Beachley Brear, *Inherit the Alamo: Myth and Ritual at an American Shrine* (Austin, Tex., 1995), 27, 40. In recent years, the pilgrimage to the Alamo, which began in 1926, has had a new feature. The marchers begin their trek at the San Antonio Vietnam Memorial.

29. David Halberstam, *The Best and the Brightest* (New York, 2001), 604; Hugh Sidey, "The Presidency," *Life*, May 31, 1968, 32B; October 10, 1969, 4.

30. Roberts and Olson, *Line in the Sand*, 281. In Vietnam, Sheldon Hackney has noted, "the United States was led by a southern president, a southern secretary of state, and a southern commanding general." Sheldon Hackney, "The Contradictory South," *Southern Cultures* 7 (2001): 67.

31. Roberts and Olson, *Line in the Sand*, 281; Evan Anders, "Light at the End of the Tunnel: Evaluating the Major Biographies of Lyndon Johnson," *Southwestern Historical Quarterly* 98 (1994): 307–8. Kevin Phillips has maintained, "He did not just escalate the war, he Texified it." Phillips, *American Dynasty*, 298.

32. Steinberg, *Sam Johnson's Boy*, 20; Sidey, *Very Personal Presidency*, 240. It is curious that Johnson would associate the Texas hero Travis with the enemy in Hanoi.

33. Gould, *1968*, 12; Bill Moyers, "Flashbacks," *Newsweek*, February 10, 1975, 76; Halberstam, *The Best and the Brightest* (New York, 1972), 435 (2001 ed., 603); Jack W. Germond, *Fat Man in a Middle Seat: Forty Years of Covering Politics* (New York, 1999), 74. Tom Wicker thought that LBJ's western heritage was "a very important part" of his attitude toward Vietnam. "Kind of a tall-in-the-saddle sort of attitude. 'They're not going to push us around.'" Thomas G. Wicker LBJL OH, 59. See, too, Rowan, *Breaking Barriers*, 271. "It was very much in character for Lyndon Johnson to identify the peasantry of Southeast Asia with the rural laborers of the South," Randall Woods has written. Furthermore, Johnson's aides charged that Senator Fulbright opposed the war because he

analogized U.S. troops to carpetbaggers, regarded Vietnam as "his ancestral plantation," and did not believe that white boys should die to help a dark-skinned race. Randall Bennett Woods, "Dixie's Dove: J. William Fulbright, the Vietnam War, and the American South," *Journal of Southern History* 60 (1994): 536–37. Lillian Smith broke with her liberal friends over the Vietnam War because, unlike them, she did not question his good intentions in Southeast Asia. The reason liberals detested him, she concluded, was that he was southern. Loveland, *Lillian Smith,* 246. When the press carried a story that Bayard Rustin had endorsed Johnson in 1968, pacifists denounced him and he issued a formal disavowal. Rustin MSS, Box 25.

34. John Bell Williams to Benjamin K. Pullen, September 3, 1965, Williams MSS, R033–B017–S3–10382; Dallek, *Flawed Giant,* 442; Short, *Everything Is Pickrick,* 169; Bass and Thompson, *Ol' Strom,* 221. At the same time that Johnson was being upbraided by black militants, the columnist James J. Kilpatrick was denouncing the 1968 fair housing law as a reward for looting and burning. "Congress," he wrote, "invited the black militants to return, torch in hand, to see what else can be got while the going is good." James J. Kilpatrick in *Washington Evening Star,* April 16, 1968, clipping, Ellis Berry MSS, Box 505. For disapproval by South Carolina congressmen of Johnson's State of the Union address in 1968, see *Greenville (S.C.) News,* January 18, 1968, clipping, Scrapbook, Robert T. Ashmore MSS.

35. John L. Garner to Ray Roberts, June 11, 1966; Mrs. H. A. White to Roberts, n.d. [1966], Ray Roberts MSS, Box 19. A Texas congressman phrased his objection quaintly: "I thought he was much too premature in civil rights." Eugene "Gene" Worley LBJL OH, 35.

36. A. F. S. to James T. Broyhill, June 23, 1966; D. L. to Broyhill, August 31, 1966, Broyhill MSS, Congressional Series, Subseries 1, Box 35.

37. Egerton, *Americanization of Dixie,* 133. From 1964 to 1968, party preferences in the North remained constant, but in that brief period the proportion of whites in the South who called themselves Independents doubled—from 18 to 36 percent. E. M. Schreiber, "Where the Ducks Are: Southern Strategy versus Fourth Party," *Public Opinion Quarterly* 35 (1971): 160. See, too, John Grenier SOHP, 34–35; John R. Petrocik, "Realignment: New Party Coalitions and the Nationalization of the South," *Journal of Politics* 49 (1987): 357. By tarring Le Roy Collins as a Lyndon Johnson man, Edward Burney became the first Republican U.S. senator from Florida since Reconstruction. Peter D. Klingman, *Neither Dies nor Surrenders: A History of the Republican Party in Florida, 1867–1970* (Gainesville, Fla., 1984), 182.

38. Steven F. Lawson, "Mixing Moderation with Militancy: Lyndon Johnson and African-American Leadership," in *The Johnson Years, Volume 3: LBJ at Home and Abroad,* ed. Robert A. Divine (Lawrence, Kans., 1994), 82, 105; S. F. Lawson, *Civil Rights Crossroads,* 52, 56; S. F. Lawson, *Black Ballots,* 328; Degler, "Thesis, Antithesis, Synthesis, 11.

39. Moyers, "Epilogue: Second Thoughts," in *Lyndon Baines Johnson,* ed. Firestone and Vogt, 353.

40. Harry Middleton, "Lion in Winter," in *Lyndon Johnson Remembered,* ed. Cowger and Markman, 156; Dallek, *Flawed Giant,* 621–22.

41. Ted Poston, *Draft of History,* ed. Kathleen A. Hauke (Athens, Ga.), 182–85.

42. Lewis Bowman and Guy Peters, "Alabama," in *Explaining the Vote: Presidential Choices in the Nation and States, 1968,* by David M. Kovenock et al. (Chapel Hill, N.C., 1973), 492. The Urban League's Whitney Young scoffed at liberals who forgot about Johnson's "impressive record of ac-

complishing what they have been fighting for for years" and were working "themselves into a lather over Vietnam." S. F. Lawson, *Civil Rights Crossroads*, 46.

43. Juan Williams, *Thurgood Marshall: American Revolutionary* (New York, 1998), 343; Marvin Caplan, "Civil Rights: Reunion at LBJ's," *Congress Bi-Weekly* 40 (January 26, 1973): 5; Robert C. Rooney, ed., *Equal Opportunity in the United States: A Symposium on Civil Rights* (Austin, Tex., 1973), 128. See, too, Carl T. Rowan, "Was LBJ the Greatest Civil Rights President Ever?" *Ebony* (December 1990): 76. Asked whether he regarded Lyndon Johnson as "the greatest civil rights president we ever had," Thurgood Marshall replied, "In my book he was." Rowan, *Dream Makers, Dream Breakers*, 415.

CONCLUSION

1. John Smith, *The Generall Historie of Virginia, New England, and the Summer Isles* (London, 1624), Fifth Booke; draft of address by Franklin D. Roosevelt, not delivered, November 1934, FDRL PPF 1820 (courtesy of Bruce Dennett); Max Lerner, *America as a Civilization: Life and Thought in the United States Today* (New York, 1957), 103; Edward L. Ayers, "Why Place Still Matters," conference paper, University of Virginia, Charlottesville, Va. (June 1999), 20–21; John Lewis Gaddis, *The Landscape of History: How Historians Map the Past* (New York, 2002), 33.

2. James G. Gimpel and Jason E. Schuknecht, "Reconsidering Political Regionalism in the American States," *State Politics and Policy Quarterly* 2 (2002): 326; Ayers, "Why Place Still Matters," 20; John Quinterno, "Going Beyond the Economy . . . ," Raleigh *News and Observer*, October 24, 2003. Robert M. Pierce has pointed out: "Systematic voting research dates back to the 1920's and perceptual studies from the 1940's. However, little of this work, conducted primarily by political scientists, has dealt with how the candidate's regional origins contribute to the mental image a voter has of him." Robert M. Pierce, "Jimmy Carter and the New South: The View from New York," *Perspectives on the American South 2*, 182.

3. Norval D. Glenn and J. L. Simmons, "Are Regional Cultural Differences Diminishing?" *Public Opinion Quarterly* 31 (1967): 180; Pierce, "Jimmy Carter," 187–88; *Raleigh News and Observer*, October 18, 2000. "American social science has paid scant attention to the possibility of regional diversity in the country's population," noted Andrew Greeley in 1974. Yet "no one can travel across America and fail to note the substantial differences in different regions of the country. That sociologists ignored these differences suggests how powerful the homogenization ideology is." Andrew M. Greeley, *Ethnicity in the United States: A Preliminary Reconnaissance* (New York, 1974), 253.

4. FDR to Rev. John Jeter Hurt, March 5, 1929, Hurt MSS (privately held, courtesy of Christie Hurt); Henry A. Wallace COHC, 407 (courtesy of Jordan Schwarz); Conkin, *Big Daddy*, 7; Kent Germany, "'I'm Not Lying about That One': Manhood, LBJ, and the Politics of Speaking Southern," *Miller Center Report* 58 (2002): 32. The TVA was "important," George McJimsey has written, "because it represented more clearly than any other New Deal measure Franklin Roosevelt's vision of American society. Roosevelt pictured Americans identified by some specific and distinct characteristic—in this instance, place." George McJimsey, *The Presidency of Franklin Delano Roosevelt* (Lawrence, Kans., 2000), 41.

5. Ayers, "You Can't Eat Magnolias," in *You Can't Eat Magnolias*, ed. Ayers and Naylor, 10–11;

"Roosevelt's Visit to Alabama," *Lafayette (Ala.) Sun,* January 25, 1933, clipping, Southern Collection, Birmingham Public Library; C. M. Morgan, *Redneck Liberal,* 190.

6. Samuel I. Rosenman to Frank C. Walker, March 8, 1950, Walker MSS, Box 123; Wilkins, *Standing Fast,* 192.

7. North Carolinian quoted in Houghton, draft, Ph.D. dissertation on Republican Party in North Carolina; Lee White, in *"Let Us Begin Anew,"* ed. Strober and Strober, 293; Eric F. Goldman to Mrs. Jessie Hunter, July 15, 1965, Goldman MSS, Series 1, Box 59; Fred Powledge, *Journeys through the South: A Rediscovery* (New York, 1979), 7; Dallek, *Lone Star Rising,* 583.

8. Lippman, *Squire of Warm Springs,* 240.

9. *Public Papers,* 3: 273; Lippman, *Squire of Warm Springs,* 149; *Public Papers,* 10: 423–24.

10. Gallagher, *FDR's Splendid Deception,* 214.

11. "Franklin D. Roosevelt at Warm Springs, Georgia," Rexford G. Tugwell MSS, Box 75; remarks of R. G. Tugwell at Warm Springs, January 30, 1957; Henry H. Revill, remarks, Warm Springs, April 12, 1955, Franklin D. Roosevelt Museum Archives. His physician at the White House, Vice Admiral Ross T. McIntire, claimed that "the story of a farmer who had been ruined by bank failure, told to him at Warm Springs, had much to do with the law insuring bank deposits." McIntire, *White House Physician,* 89. In fact, though, Roosevelt resisted that proposition almost to the very end.

12. Rexford G. Tugwell, *In Search of Roosevelt* (Cambridge, Mass., 1972), 18; Tugwell, *Brains Trust,* 92.

13. Alfred Steinberg, *Sam Rayburn: A Biography* (New York, 1975), 130; Workman, *Bishop from Barnwell,* 78; *Public Papers,* 7: 463. Rayburn insisted that Roosevelt was mistaken, that he had first given FDR the idea.

14. Neal R. Peirce, *The Deep South States of America: People, Politics, and Power in the Seven Deep South States* (New York, 1974), 39; H. C. Nixon, *Lower Piedmont Country,* 212; Lorena Hickok to Harry Hopkins, February 10, 1934, in *One Third of a Nation,* ed. Lowitt and Beasley, 185.

15. Dabney, *Below the Potomac,* 58.

16. George Brown Tindall, *The Emergence of the New South, 1913–1945* (Baton Rouge, La., 1967), 695; "The Deep South Looks Up," *Fortune* 28 (1943): 95; Morton Sosna, "More Important than the Civil War?: The Impact of World War II on the South," in *Perspectives on the American South* 4 (1987): 145–61; Numan V. Bartley, "The Southern Conference and the Shaping of Post–World War II Southern Politics," in *Developing Dixie,* ed. Moore, Tripp, and Tyler, 182. "No event in Mobile's history would bring more dramatic change to the city than World War II," said a history of the Alabama port. Melton McLaurin and Michael Thomason, *Mobile: The Life and Times of a Great Southern City* (Woodland Hills, Calif., 1981), n.p. See, too, William T. Schmidt, "The Impact of Camp Shelby in World War II on Hattiesburg, Mississippi," *Journal of Mississippi History* 39 (1977): 42; Lewis M. Killian, *White Southerners,* rev. ed. (Amherst, Mass., 1985), 50–51. For a challenge to the prevailing view that the war transformed the South, see Roger W. Lotchin and David R. Long, "World War II and the Transformation of Southern Urban Society: A Reconsideration," *Georgia Historical Quarterly* 83 (1999): 29–57.

17. William R. Majors, *The End of Arcadia: Gordon Browning and Tennessee Politics* (Memphis, Tenn., 1982), 84; Lionel V. Patenaude, "Texas and the New Deal," in *Depression in Southwest,* ed. Whisenhunt, 101; James M. Smallwood, *The Great Recovery: The New Deal in Texas* (Boston, 1983),

40. In Kentucky, George T. Blakey has noted, coal miners unionized bloody Harlan County, to-bacco farmers benefited from the AAA, the REA lit up remote mountain homes, CCC camps dot-ted the state, the TVA built its biggest dam near Paducah, and "bourbon distilleries resumed oper-ation with the ending of prohibition." Blakey, "Kentucky Youth and the New Deal," *Filson Club History Quarterly* 60 (1986): 37.

18. Hamilton, *Lister Hill*, 81.

19. Tate, "Easing the Burden," 197; Badger, *New Deal*, 281.

20. Fossett, "Impact of New Deal on Georgia Politics," 337; Edward Chan Sieg, *Eden on the Marsh: An Illustrated History of Savannah* (Savannah, Ga., 1985), 107.

21. Eliot Wigginton, "The Mountains: A Different Mix of Politics," in *Prevailing South*, ed. Clendinen, 157.

22. Anthony J. (Tony) Badger, "How Did the New Deal Change the South?" in *Looking Inward, Looking Outward: From the 1930s through the 1940s*, ed. Steve Ickringill (Amsterdam, 1990), 166; Roger Biles, "The New Deal in Dallas," *Southwestern Historical Quarterly* 95 (1991): 3; Biles, *Memphis in Great Depression*, 121–24; Gaston, *New South Creed*, 231; Fite, *Cotton Fields No More*, 173. See, too, Howard N. Rabinowitz, "The Weight of the Past versus the Promise of the Future: Southern Race Relations in Historical Perspective," in *Future South*, ed. Dunn and Preston, 109.

23. Gaston, *New South Creed*, 231; Arthur Raper, "Is There 'A New South'?" *New Republic*, August 18, 1952, 9; Arthur Raper, talk to History Honor Society, University of North Carolina at Chapel Hill (January 29, 1974); M. L. Billington, *Political South in the Twentieth Century*, 68.

24. Dewey W. Grantham Jr., "An American Politics for the South," in *The Southerner as American*, ed. Charles Grier Sellers Jr. (New York, 1966), 162. See, too, Grantham, *Life and Death of Solid South*, 112–13; and, for a judicious summing-up, Grantham, *The South in Modern America: A Region at Odds* (New York, 1994), 137–38.

25. Douglas F. Dowd, "A Comparative Analysis of Economic Development in the American West and South," *Journal of Economic History* 16 (1956): 563; Frank E. Smith, *Look Away from Dixie* (Baton Rouge, La., 1965), 87–88; Ralph McGill, *The South and the Southerner* (Boston, 1963), 15; Lyndon B. Johnson, address, May 30, 1959, Hyde Park, N.Y., FDRL, Addresses Relating to Franklin D. Roosevelt. See, too, Harold H. Martin, *Ralph McGill, Reporter* (Boston, 1973), 40.

26. Schwarz, *New Dealers*, 322; Robert S. McElvaine, "New Deal Cultural Programs," in *Encyclopedia of Southern Culture*, ed. Charles R. Wilson and William Ferris (Chapel Hill, N.C., 1989), 649; Bartley, "Writing About the Post–World War II South," 3.

27. Roland, "The South, America's Will-o-the-Wisp Eden," 114.

28. William E. Leuchtenburg, "The Presidents Come to Chapel Hill," *Carolina Comments* 42 (1994): 59–60; *Daily Tar Heel*, December 6, 1938.

29. Key with Heard, *Southern Politics*, 645; Joseph M. Ray, "The Influence of the Tennessee Valley Authority on Government in the South," *American Political Science Review* 43 (1949): 932; Virginia Van der Veer Hamilton, "Lister Hill, Hugo Black, and the Albatross of Race," *Alabama Law Review* 36 (1985): 849; James R. Soukup, Clifton McCleskey, and Harry Holloway, *Party and Factional Division in Texas* (Austin, Tex., 1964), 91, 168. "The New Deal," one scholar has said, "was indeed a watershed period in Texas politics." Kenneth E. Hendrickson Jr., "Texas Politics since the New Deal," in *Texas through Time: Evolving Interpretations*, ed. Walter L. Buenger and Robert A.

Calvert (College Station, Tex., 1991), 251. "The Rooseveltian New Deal introduced many important changes into the Border State political arena" also, one analyst has noted. No longer could the Bourbons count on mining towns and cities to supply the votes to subdue liberal candidates. John H. Fenton, *Politics in the Border States: A Study of the Patterns of Political Organization, and Political Change, Common to the Border States: Maryland, West Virginia, Kentucky and Missouri* (New Orleans, La., 1957), 209. "Senator Claghorn," an imaginary figure on a popular radio comedy hour, drew laughs each week because of his absurdly antiquated commitment to the Old South.

30. Frederickson, *Dixiecrat Revolt*, 8.

31. Moon, *Balance of Power*, 181–82; J. B. Kirby, *Black Americans in the Roosevelt Era*, 221; Pauley, *Modern Presidency*, 18; Walter Bridgforth Floter OH.

32. Harris, *Deep Souths*, 293; Denton L. Watson, "The Papers of the '101st Senator': Clarence Mitchell Jr. and Civil Rights," *Historian* 64 (2002): 631; Patricia Sullivan, "Southern Reformers, the New Deal and the Movement's Foundation," in *New Directions in Civil Rights Studies*, ed. Armstead L. Robinson and Patricia Sullivan (Charlottesville, Va., 1991), 82–83.

33. Le Roy Collins LBJL OH, 6; Robert J. Norrell, "One Thing We Did Right: Reflections on the Movement," in *New Directions*, ed. Robinson and Sullivan, 67.

34. Brinkley, "New Deal and Southern Politics," in *New Deal and the South*, ed. Cobb and Namorato, 112–14.

35. Ibid. Chester Morgan, too, has asserted that the most important influence of the New Deal came "outside the South, as Roosevelt transformed the Democratic party into a powerful and effective liberal coalition that . . . made possible the civil rights movement and the consequent revolution in southern politics." Morgan, *Redneck Liberal*, 252.

36. Schwarz, *New Dealers*, 214, 322; FDR to Hattie Caraway, December 20, 1937, Caraway MSS.

37. *Public Papers*, 3: 272, 274; *New York Times*, September 18, 1937.

38. Mezerik, *Revolt of South and West*, 96. See, too, McElvaine, "New Deal Cultural Programs," 650. The objection to freight rate discrimination raised by a TVA report was that it erected "barriers against the free flow of commerce which are hampering . . . the normal development of the Nation as a whole." *House Document 264,* 75th Cong., 1st Sess. (1937), iv, cited in Lively, *South in Action,* 24–25.

39. Hoover and Ratchford, *Economic Resources and Policies*, 51, 60; Schulman, *From Cotton Belt*, 15; Biles, *South and New Deal*, 157. For the impact of the war, see John R. Skates Jr., "World War II as a Watershed in Mississippi History," *Journal of Mississippi History* 37 (1975): 131–42; Charles W. Johnson and Charles O. Jackson, *City Behind a Fence: Oak Ridge, Tennessee, 1942–1946* (Knoxville, Tenn., 1981); John T. Westbrook, "Twilight of Southern Regionalism," *Southwest Review* 42 (1957): 231–34; Elise Hopkins Stephens, *Historic Huntsville: A City of New Beginnings* (Woodland Hills, Calif., 1984), 118.

40. Salmond, "Postscript to New Deal," 420; C. Bascom Slemp to FDR, September 15, 1937, copy in Thomas G. Corcoran MSS, Box 203; H. Clarence Nixon, "New Deal and the South," 321. See, too, Daniel Roper, *Fifty Years of Public Life* (Durham, N.C., 1941), 270; B. Robertson, *Red Hills and Cotton,* 272–73; Lippman, *Squire of Warm Springs,* 3–4.

41. Roy Parker Jr., "Roosevelt's Enduring Legacy in the South," *Fayetteville (N.C.) Times*, January 30, 1982. See, too, Hale Boggs address, October 1964, Boggs MSS.

42. McCullough, *Truman,* 53; Nagel, *Missouri,* 93. Alonzo Hamby has noted: "He grew up in a

town in which blacks just did not vote, even though blacks voted in Kansas City." Hamby, "Temperament of Harry S. Truman," 14.

43. *The Political Bandwagon* 8 (1991): 8; unidentified clipping, October 1, 1948, Mrs. J. Richard Allison Scrapbook.

44. Kirkendall, *History of Missouri*, 383, 402; Ferrell, ed., *Off the Record*, 146–47.

45. Pauley, *Modern Presidency*, 36; Kluger, *Simple Justice*, 249–50.

46. McCoy and Ruetten, *Quest and Response*, 321–22; Lee Nichols, *Breakthrough on the Color Front* (Colorado Springs, Colo., 1993), 130, 187.

47. J. F. Martin, *Civil Rights*, 78; Ferrell, *Harry S. Truman and Modern American Presidency*, 97–98.

48. W. C. Berman, *Politics of Civil Rights*, 197; Giangreco and Moore, *Dear Harry*, 76–78; C. Vann Woodward, *The Strange Career of Jim Crow*, 3rd rev. ed. (New York, 1974), 135; James Farmer, *Lay Bare the Heart: An Autobiography of the Civil Rights Movement* (New York, 1985), 159.

49. Branch, *Parting the Waters*, 66; Francis M. Wilhoit, *The Politics of Massive Resistance* (New York, 1973), 21; Leslie Dunbar, "The Changing Mind of the South: The Exposed Nerve," *Journal of Politics* 17 (1964): 14; S. F. Lawson, *Black Ballots*, 137.

50. W. C. Berman, *Politics of Civil Rights*, 60–61; Bernstein, "Ambiguous Legacy," 302.

51. Thomas Borstelmann, *The Cold War and the Color Line: American Race Relations in the Global Arena* (Cambridge, Mass., 2001), 48–49, 60. For a much more negative assessment of Truman's record, see Carol Anderson, *Eyes off the Prize: The United Nations and the African American Struggle for Human Rights, 1944–1955* (New York, 2003).

52. Strom Thurmond SOHP, 6; Gerald R. Webster, "Demise of the Solid South," *Geographical Review* 82 (1992): 48. See, too, Grantham, *Regional Imagination*, 212; Albert Gore SOHP, 2: 1–3; Claude Pepper, "The Influence of the Deep South upon the Presidential Election of 1952," *Georgia Review* 6 (1952): 127–28; Grayson, "North Carolina and Harry Truman," 298; Stanley D. Brunn, *Geography and Politics in America* (New York, 1974), 72.

53. William M. Colmer, "Congressional Sidelights," April 15, 1959, Colmer MSS, Box 381; Jeansonne, *Leander Perez*, 174. The moderate congressman Brooks Hays went down to defeat in 1958 after his opponent told Arkansas voters, "Mr. Hays is a Harry Truman Democrat and I am an Orval Faubus Democrat." Brooks Hays LBJL OH, 1: 2. See, too, Donald S. Strong, "Durable Republicanism in the South," in *Change in the Contemporary South*, ed. Allan P. Sindler (Durham, N.C., 1963), 176.

54. M. Miller, *Plain Speaking*, 155–56.

55. *Public Papers, 1948*, 818–27.

56. *New York Times*, June 30, 1947; W. C. Berman, *Politics of Civil Rights*, 64.

57. Mitchell, "Southern Confederate Heritage"; Richard Bolling HSTL OH, 149. Truman's cousin has written of her ancestors: "These good people did not regret that their darkies had gained their freedom. They knew that that was as it should be." "My Most Interesting Ancestor," Mary Ethel Noland MSS, Box 5.

58. HST to William M. Greene, June 13, 1950, HSTL OF 896, Box 1557; Margaret Truman, ed., *Where the Buck Stops: The Personal and Private Writings of Harry S. Truman* (New York, 1989), 322, 340.

59. Tom C. Clark HSTL OH (Jerry N. Hess interview), 141.

60. L. B. Johnson, *Vantage Point*, 568; *Public Papers, 1963–64*, 1513.

61. *Public Papers, 1963–64,* 1513; L. B. Johnson, *Vantage Point,* 95; transcript of interview of Lyndon B. Johnson by Walter Cronkite, 1969, Burton Benjamin MSS, Box 21. Jim Rowe later reflected, "I think he always had this complex that the South was discriminated against, the southerners and the Texans, whether it was by the intellectuals or by the rest of the country." James H. Rowe Jr. LBJL OH, 1: 18.

62. *New York Times,* May 11, 1967, clipping, Dan Carter MSS, Box 5; Michael Beschloss, ed., *Reaching for Glory: Lyndon Johnson's Secret White House Tapes, 1964–1965* (New York, 2001), 387; Barbara Garson, *MacBird!* (New York, 1967), 60; Frady, *Wallace,* 143; Connally, with Herskowitz, *In History's Shadow,* 203; P. Sullivan, ed., *Freedom Writer,* 368, 391; Watters, *South and Nation,* 240. Years later, Senator Sam Ervin of North Carolina continued to express displeasure with Johnson's role in pressing for "civil rights bills, they were really civil-wrong bills, mostly." Samuel J. Ervin Jr. OH, Richard B. Russell MSS. When Martin Luther King was assassinated, one publication wrote, "President Johnson went all the way and degraded the Flag by ordering that it be flown at half-mast for this agitator," a man who had been "a staunch and faithful worker for the communist cause." *Liberty Letter,* May 1968, Ellis Berry MSS, Box 505.

63. Clark and Arsenault, eds., *Changing South,* 236–37, 263.

64. Larry L. King, "An Epitaph for LBJ," *Harper's* 236 (1968): 14, 16; Lewis Chester, Godfrey Hodgson, and Bruce Page, *An American Melodrama: The Presidential Campaign of 1968* (New York, 1969), 776; Leo Janos, "The Last Days of the President: LBJ in Retirement," *Atlantic* (July 1973): 41; T. H. Williams, "Huey, Lyndon, and Southern Radicalism," 293.

65. William S. White LBJL OH, 1: 10–11. See, too, W. S. White, *Responsibles,* 218.

66. *Public Papers, 1963–64,* 9; Fuller, "Powerful Persuaders," 11; Kessel, *Goldwater Coalition,* 224; *Public Papers, 1963–64,* 647–48. I have altered capitalization for greater clarity.

67. Cormier, *LBJ,* 78; Allan Wolk, *The Presidency and Black Civil Rights: Eisenhower to Nixon* (Rutherford, N.J., 1971), 232–33n. See, too, Paul Southwick, memorandum for Henry Wilson, July 18, 1963, Office Files of Fred Panzer: Southern States (General), Box 492, LBJL.

68. *Public Papers, 1968–69,* 1107–9.

69. Lemann, *Promised Land,* 182; Herbers, *Lost Priority,* 191. "President Johnson," Le Roy Collins later reflected, "saw, really, that his opportunity to establish a position in history and be a great man" lay in taking strong leadership in race relations. Le Roy Collins SOHP, 36.

70. Wicker, *JFK and LBJ,* 176; E. F. Goldman, *Tragedy,* 289; James H. Rowe Jr., LBJL OH, 18.

71. *Public Papers, 1963–64,* 1450. Johnson was convinced that he was the first southerner in the twentieth century to reach the White House. So persuaded was he that he had blazed a new path that he asked Bill Moyers to have the Library of Congress undertake an investigation to demonstrate that Woodrow Wilson was not truly a southerner. Lemann, *Promised Land,* 137.

72. Wicker, *JFK and LBJ,* 176; *Time,* July 29, 1991, 6; T. H. White, *Making of the President 1964,* 376. See, too, A. Leon Higginbotham Jr., LBJL OH, 22; Cecil L. Eubanks, "Contemporary Southern Politics: Present State and Future Possibilities," in *Contemporary Southern Politics,* ed. James F. Lea (Baton Rouge, La., 1988), 290.

73. Confidential Memo on Turner Catledge's Conversation with President Johnson, Arthur Krock MSS, Box 30; Wicker, *JFK and LBJ,* 170–71.

74. Wicker, *JFK and LBJ,* 175; S. F. Lawson, *Black Ballots,* 328.

75. W. S. White, *Responsibles,* 258. For Byrd's insistence that Virginia's delegation be instructed for Johnson, see J. Lindsay Almond JFKL OH, 11.

76. Fite, *Russell,* 375; Russell to Charles Sussman, January 5, 1960, Russell MSS, Series 6, Political Subseries E: Lyndon Johnson; UPI dispatch, June 17, 1960, Senate Political Files, LBJL, Box 254; Dent, *Prodigal South,* 61; *Orangeburg (S.C.) Times and Democrat,* April 9, 1960, clipping, LBJL Senate Political Files, Box 254; *Time,* April 25, 1960, 23; Luther H. Hodges LBJL OH, 2–3. See, too, Hodges JFKL OH, 3; W. R. Poage to Charles Sussman, January 13, 1960, Poage MSS, Box 1394; Alton Lennon to Martha J. Swain, February 6, 1964, Lennon MSS; *Savannah Morning News,* May 14, 1960, clipping, Russell MSS, Political Series. For Senator McClellan of Arkansas, the question of whom to endorse in 1960 required no thought. "I supported Johnson of course," he later said. "He was a southerner." John McClellan OH, Earle C. Clements Oral History Project, University of Kentucky, 7.

77. Wolk, *Presidency and Black Civil Rights,* 233n; Tom C. Clark HSTL OH (Jerry N. Hess interview), 141; Strober and Strober, *"Let Us Begin Anew,"* 482, 285.

78. Germany, "'I'm Not Lying,'" 32; E. W. Kenworthy, quoted in *The Road to the White House: The Story of the 1964 Election by the Staff of the New York Times,* ed. Harold Faber (New York, 1965), 244; John F. Stacks, *Scotty: James B. Reston and the Rise and Fall of American Journalism* (Boston, 2003), 235.

79. Lillian Smith to Alice Shoemaker, October 30, 1965, in *How Am I to Be Heard? Letters of Lillian Smith,* ed. Margaret Rose Gladney (Chapel Hill, N.C., 1993), 330.

80. Gaskin, "Lyndon B. Johnson and Senator Richard B. Russell"; Frantz, "Opening a Curtain," 25; Clifford and Virginia Durr LBJL OH, 52; Salmond, *Conscience of a Lawyer,* 208; William M. Lunch, *The Nationalization of American Politics* (Berkeley, Calif., 1987), 25. Frank Smith has written, "The Civil Rights Act of 1964 has been more than a Magna Carta for Negro citizens; it has freed the Southern white moderate from the oppressive restrictions which have so effectively silenced him heretofore." F. E. Smith, *Look Away,* 12.

81. C. Vann Woodward, "Look Away, Look Away," *Journal of Southern History* 59 (1993): 489.

82. Interview of Vernon Jordan Jr., 1972, Burton Benjamin MSS, Box 20; Charles Evers, *Evers* (New York, 1971), 127–28.

83. Cooke, *Talk about America,* 94; Dugger, *Politician,* 21; C. L. Sanders, "LBJ and Civil Rights," 161; Strom Thurmond LBJL OH, 6–7; Terry Sanford LBJL OH, 1: 4–5.

84. William B. Hesseltine, "Sectionalism and Regionalism in American History," *Journal of Southern History* 26 (1960): 33; Reston, *Deadline,* 302; James H. Rowe Jr., LBJL OH, 2: 9; Terry Sanford LBJL OH, 1: 21.

85. Albert Murray, *South to a Very Old Place* (New York, 1971), 175–78. "Muscle Shoals" refers to the site, long a source of controversy, which evolved into the TVA. "3.2" was the proportion of alcohol in beer that was legalized in 1933. "Woodrow Wilson and all that old dirt he did us" alludes to Wilson's imposition of Jim Crow on the national government in Washington.

EPILOGUE

1. Jules Witcover, *Marathon* (New York, 1977), 113; *Time,* September 27, 1976, 46.

2. Jimmy Carter, *Why Not the Best?* (Nashville, Tenn., 1975), 9; Numan V. Bartley, "Jimmy Carter and the Politics of the New South," *The Forum Series* (St. Louis, 1979), 3; Reg Murphy and Hall

Gulliver, *The Southern Strategy* (New York, 1971), 173. Explaining why he backed Carter, an Alabama congressman said, "There was a feeling of kinship by virtue that we were Southern born and bred." William Nichols OH.

3. Genelle Jennings, *Into the Jaws of Politics: The Charge of the Peanut Brigade* (Huntsville, Ala., 1979), 23.

4. Robert Coles, "Jimmy Carter: Agrarian Rebel?" *New Republic,* June 26, 1976, 19; Larry King, "We Ain't Trash No More!" *Esquire* (November 1976): 88; Roy Blount Jr., *Crackers: This Whole Many-Angled Thing of Jimmy, More Carters, Ominous Little Animals, Sad-Singing Women, My Daddy and Me* (New York, 1980), 4.

5. Martin Schram, *Running for President, 1976: The Carter Campaign* (New York, 1977), 332.

6. Witcover, *Marathon,* 520.

7. Johnny Greene, "The Dixie Smile," *Harper's* (September 1976): 14; David D. Lee, "The South and the American Mainstream: The Election of Jimmy Carter," *Georgia Historical Quarterly* 61 (1977): 7–8.

8. Clayton Fritchey, "Carter: Misreading the Grass Roots," *Washington Post,* August 13, 1979; William Lee Miller, *Yankee from Georgia: The Emergence of Jimmy Carter* (New York, 1978), 26; Phil Garner, "Once There Was a President," *Atlanta Weekly,* January 18, 1981, 23.

9. Phinizy Spalding, "Georgia and the Election of Jimmy Carter," *Georgia Historical Quarterly* 61 (1977): 13–14; Griffin Bell, Miller Center Interview, Jimmy Carter Library, 6; Garner, "Once There Was a President," 12, quoting Theo Lippman; Robert Akerman, "Those Who Really Won," November 8, 1976, quoting David Norden, clipping, Le Roy Collins MSS; Russell Carter, "A Native Son Led the Way: Jimmy Carter and the Modern South," in *The Southern State of Mind,* ed. Jan Norby Gretlund (Columbia, S.C., 1999), 154. See, too, W. L. Miller, *Yankee from Georgia,* 35; John Shelton Reed, James Kohls, and Carol Hanchette, "The Dissolution of Dixie and the Changing Shape of the South," *Social Forces* 69 (1990): 222.

10. Grantham, *Regional Imagination,* 228; Henry Paolucci, *"The South and the Presidency": From Reconstruction to Carter, A Long Day's Task* (Whitestone, N.Y., 1978), 9.

11. Thomas L. Connelly and Barbara L. Bellows, *God and General Longstreet: The Lost Cause and the Southern Mind* (Baton Rouge, La., 1982), 139; Spalding, "Georgia," 13; Michael Montgomery, "The Southern Accent—Alive and Well," *Southern Cultures* (Inaugural Issue, 1993): 62; Killian, *White Southerners,* 155. Integration of the South into the nation made it harder for southern politicians to argue persuasively that they were victims of regional prejudice, as the experience of Bill Clinton revealed. "Despite the First Lady's suggestion of an anti-Arkansas conspiracy," James C. Cobb of the University of Georgia observed slyly, "little seemed to be made of the southern origins of the peerless presidential practitioner of white-trash culture." Cobb, "Epitaph for the North," 17.

12. Schram, *Running for President,* 362; William C. Havard Jr., "Southern Politics: Old and New Style," in *American South,* ed. Rubin, 44.

13. Robert Kelley, "Ideology and Political Culture from Jefferson to Nixon," *American Historical Review* 82 (1977): 560; Burton I. Kaufman, *The Presidency of James Earl Carter, Jr.* (Lawrence, Kans., 1993), 13–14; Kirby, *Media-made Dixie,* 172; Robert S. McElvaine, "Old Times There Are Not Forgotten: A Personal View of the 'New South,'" *Midwest Quarterly* 19 (1978): 249.

14. W. L. Miller, *Yankee from Georgia,* 30–38; Kirby, *Media-made Dixie,* 172; Jody Powell, *The Other Side of the Story* (New York, 1984), 207.

15. Edwin M. Yoder Jr., "Thoughts on the Dixiefication of Dixie," in *Dixie Dateline: A Journalistic Portrait of the Contemporary South,* ed. John B. Boles (Houston, Tex., 1983), 162–63.

16. Jimmy Carter, *Keeping Faith: Memoirs of a President* (New York, 1982), 23; Loyis Martin, Exit Interview, Jimmy Carter Library, 4–5; Powell, *Other Side of the Story,* 207.

17. Lesley Stahl, *Reporting Live* (New York, 1999), 86.

18. Gerald Rafshoon, Miller Center Interview, 23; James McIntyre, Miller Center Interview, Jimmy Carter Library, 25.

19. Steven M. Gillon, *The Democrats' Dilemma: Walter F. Mondale and the Liberal Legacy* (New York, 1992), 165, 171, 257.

20. Charles P. Roland, "The Ever-Vanishing South," *Journal of Southern History* 48 (1982): 19; Willie Morris, "A Sense of Place and the Americanization of Mississippi," *Southern Quarterly* 17 (1979): 3.

21. Morris, "Sense of Place," 10–11; Mary Hood et al., "Stubborn Sense of Place," 39–40; Applebome, *Dixie Rising,* 14. See, too, Marshall Frady, *Southerners: A Journalist's Odyssey* (New York, 1980), 284. As far back as 1935, a southern writer had stated, "If any of the traditions of the old South are still usable, by all means we should keep them. Is not one Middle West enough?" Jay B. Hubbell, "Southern Magazines," in *Culture in the South,* ed. Couch, 181.

22. Hardwick, "Southern Literature," in *Southern Literature,* ed. Castille and Osborne, 22; Lewis, "Defining Sense of Place," 26.

23. Richard Gray, *Writing the South: Ideas of an American Region* (Cambridge, 1986), 236–55; Walker Percy, *The Second Coming* (New York, 1980), 19; Percy, *Lancelot* (New York, 1977), 158; Percy, *Signposts,* 81; Percy, *The Last Gentleman* (New York, 1966), 261.

24. Joseph Cumming Jr., "A Final Farewell," *Georgia* 15 (1972): 35; Mary Hood et al., "Stubborn Sense of Place," 38.

25. Louis D. Rubin Jr., "An Image of the South," in *The Lasting South: Fourteen Southerners Look at Their Home,* ed. Rubin and James Jackson Kilpatrick (Chicago, 1957), 2, 13–14; Henry Savage Jr., *Seeds of Time: The Background of Southern Thinking* (New York, 1959), 274; Applebome, *Dixie Rising,* 13; Joseph B. Cumming Jr., "Been Down Home So Long It Looks Like Up to Me," *Esquire* (August 1971): 84. See, too, John Shelton Reed, "The Same Old Stand?" in *Why the South Will Survive,* by Fifteen Southerners (Athens, Ga., 1981), 20; John C. McKinney and Linda Brookover Bourque, "The Changing South: National Incorporation of a Region," *American Sociological Review* 36 (1971): 409.

26. Percy, *Last Gentleman,* 185.

27. Beck, "Partisan Dealignment," 484; Gray, *Writing the South,* 223. For skepticism about the impact of civil rights on party identification, see Bruce A. Campbell, "Patterns of Change in the Partisan Loyalties of Native Southerners: 1952–1972," *Journal of Politics* 39 (1977): 730–63. GOP gains were also the result of developments largely unrelated to racial cleavages, such as the migration to the South of northern Republicans. Even when race was pertinent, desertion of the Democrats did not always reflect racism, though it frequently did. Rather, once the Democrats ceased to be the guardians of white supremacy, southerners were liberated to vote as they did elsewhere in the coun-

try, and urban businessmen, suburban housewives, and others gravitated to the Republicans in country club Richmond as they did in Grosse Pointe.

28. David W. Rohde, "The Inevitability and Solidity of the 'Republican Solid South,'" *American Review of Politics* 17 (1996): 28; Gray, *Southern Aberrations*, 352.

29. Applebome, *Dixie Rising*, 121; Ron Nixon, "The Dixiefication of America," *Southern Exposure* 24 (1996): 19–20.

30. Michael Lind, *Made in Texas: George W. Bush and the Southern Takeover of American Politics* (New York, 2003), x. Kevin Phillips characterized what he regarded as the infamous behavior of the two Bushes as "Mayberry Machiavellianism." Phillips, *American Dynasty*, 145.

31. Alan Draper, "Be Careful What You Wish For . . . : American Liberals and the South," *Southern Studies* 4 (1993): 319; Schulman, *From Cotton Belt*, 205.

32. Goldfield, *Cotton Fields and Skyscrapers*, 130–51; Schulman, *From Cotton Belt*, 204.

33. Paul K. Conkin, "The South in Southern Agrarianism," in *The Evolution of Southern Culture*, ed. Numan V. Bartley (Athens, Ga., 1988), 143; Roland, "Will-o-the-Wisp Eden," 117.

34. James H. Kuklinski, Michael D. Cobb, and Martin Gilens, "Racial Attitudes and the 'New South,'" *Journal of Politics* 59 (1997): 323, 330; Martin Fletcher, *Almost Heaven: Travels through the Backwoods of America* (London, 1998), 71–72.

35. Hastings Wyman Jr., in *Southern Politics in the 1990s*, ed. Alexander P. Lamis (Baton Rouge, La., 1999), 6.

36. *Charlotte Observer*, February 12, 2003; *Richmond Times-Dispatch*, December 26, 2002.

37. J. S. Reed, *Southerners*, 85; Applebome, *Dixie Rising*, 317, 308.

38. Applebome, *Dixie Rising*, 22; Augustus B. Cochran III, *Democracy Heading South: National Politics in the Shadow of Dixie* (Lawrence, Kans., 2001), 225.

39. Randy Sanders, *Mighty Peculiar Elections: The New South Gubernatorial Campaigns of 1970 and the Changing Politics of Race* (Gainesville, Fla., 2002), 12; Walter Prescott Webb, "The South's Future Prospect," in *The Idea of the South: Pursuit of a Central Theme*, ed. Frank E. Vandiver (Chicago, 1964), 69; Peter La Salle, *Strange Sunlight* (Austin, Tex., 1984), 49.

40. Selz C. Mayo, "Social Change, Social Movements and the Disappearing Sectional South," *Social Forces* 43 (1964): 1–2; Goldfield, *Cotton Fields and Skyscrapers*, 142; Stanley D. Brunn and Gerald L. Ingalls, "The Emergence of Republicanism in the Urban South," *Southeastern Geographer* 12 (1972): 133; William C. Havard, "The South: A Shifting Perspective," in *Changing Politics*, ed. Havard, 17; Harry S. Ashmore, *An Epitaph for Dixie* (New York, 1958), 15.

41. Charles Longstreet Weltner, address, New Haven, Conn., n.d., Weltner MSS, Box 4.

42. Carlton and Coclanis, *Confronting Southern Poverty*, 1.

43. Josephus Daniels, *The Wilson Era: Years of Peace, 1910–1917* (Chapel Hill, N.C., 1944), 129.

44. C. Vann Woodward, "The South Tomorrow," *Time*, September 27, 1976, 99; Phillips, *American Dynasty*, 82; Sale, *Power Shift*, 6. See, too, Robert Estall, "The Changing Balance of the Northern and Southern Regions of the United States," *Journal of American Studies* 14 (1980): 365–86.

45. *Washington Star*, October 29, 1964, in F. Clifton White MSS, Ashland, Box 28; John Robert Greene, *The Presidency of George Bush* (Lawrence, Kans., 2000), 16; Herbert S. Parmet, *George Bush: The Life of a Lone Star Yankee* (New York, 1997), 102.

46. David Nyhan, "In a New York State of Mind," *Boston Globe*, July 16, 1992; *Boston Globe*, July

13, 12, 1992. "I have to admit that one of the reasons I voted for Clinton is that he is from the South," a South Carolinian confided as Inauguration Day approached. "And the reason I am convinced he will screw up is that he is from the South." *Washington Post,* January 10, 1993.

47. R. Nixon, "Dixiefication of America," 19; Michael Lind, "The Southern Coup," *New Republic,* June 19, 1995, 20; Lamis, *Southern Politics in the 1990s,* 404.

48. Diane Roberts, "The South of the Mind," in *South to a New Place,* ed. Jones and Monteith, 372; Lind, *Made in Texas,* ix.

49. Fox-Genovese and Genovese, "Surveying the South," 77–78; Carlton, "American South," in *South, Nation, World,* ed. Carlton and Coclanis, 177; Gavin Wright, "The Civil Rights Revolution as Economic History," *Journal of Economic History* 59 (1999): 283.

50. R. Sanders, *Mighty Peculiar Elections,* 5, 173, 12, 175.

51. Black and Black, *Vital South,* 333; Patrick Anderson, *Electing Jimmy Carter: The Campaign of 1976* (Baton Rouge, La., 1994), 173; *Time,* September 27, 1976, 46.

52. R. Sanders, *Mighty Peculiar Elections,* 13; Black and Black, *Vital South,* 333.

53. Peter Schrag, "A Hesitant New South: Fragile Promise on the Last Frontier," *Saturday Review,* February 12, 1972, 52.

54. Tony Dunbar, *Delta Time: A Journey through Mississippi* (New York, 1990), xvi, 48, 184; Morris, "Sense of Place," 7–8.

55. Dunbar, *Delta Time,* 46.

56. Lewis, "Defining a Sense of Place," 25; Reg Murphy, "Not since Jefferson and Madison . . . ," *Saturday Review,* n.s. 3 (September 4, 1976), 8.

57. Willie Morris, *Terrains of the Heart and Other Essays on Home* (Oxford, Miss., 1981), 13–14; Dunbar, *Delta Time,* xvi, 69–70.

58. Carol Stack, *Call to Home: African Americans Reclaim the Rural South* (New York, 1996), xiii; *Raleigh News and Observer,* October 31, 2003; J. L. Franklin, "Black Southerners," 17–18; David L. Langford, "Going Back Home to the South," *Crisis* 101 (April 1994): 35, 40.

59. *Social Science Newsletter* (September 1992): 1; Garner, "Once There Was," 25.

60. *Public Papers, 1965,* 1: 287–91.

61. Sheldon Hackney, "Southern Violence," *American Historical Review* 74 (1969): 924–25; John Ehle, *The Free Men* (New York, 1965), 327; Facts on File, *1964 News Dictionary,* 72; Stephen G. N. Tuck, *Beyond Atlanta: The Struggle for Racial Equality in Georgia, 1940–1980* (Athens, Ga., 2001), 2. Emphasis added.

62. Leonard Reissman, "Social Development and the American South," *Journal of Social Issues* 22 (1966): 101–2; R. Sanders, *Mighty Peculiar Elections,* 13.

63. Dewey W. Grantham Jr., "The South and the Reconstruction of American Politics," *Journal of American History* 53 (1966): 244.

64. Schulman, *From Cotton Belt,* vii; Kuklinski, Cobb, and Gilens, "Racial Attitudes," 328.

65. Goldfield, *Still Fighting,* 254.

66. "Is Dixie Dead? A Survey of the American South," *The Economist,* March 17, 1979, 5–6, 27.

67. J. S. Reed, "Same Old Stand?" 20; J. S. Reed, *Southerners,* 108; Current, *Northernizing the South,* 117; J. S. Reed, "Southerners," in *Harvard Encyclopedia,* ed. Thernstrom, 947; *Raleigh News and Observer,* December 28, 1998.

68. V. O. Key Jr., "The Erosion of Sectionalism," *Virginia Quarterly Review* 31 (1955): 162–63; Carl Degler, *Place over Time: The Continuity of Southern Distinctiveness* (Baton Rouge, 1977), 126; Carl Abbott, "The End of the Southern City," in *Perspectives on the American South* 4 (1987): 187; Roberts, "South of the Mind," in *South to a New Place,* ed. Jones and Monteith, 363, 373; G. Wright, "Civil Rights Revolution," 285; George B. Tindall, *The Ethnic Southerners* (Baton Rouge, 1976), ix. In Arthurian legend, and in several versions of Tristan and Iseult, Lyonnesee is a land, reaching from Cornwall to the Scilly Isles, that sank into the sea.

69. Dunbar, *Delta Time,* xx; Applebome, *Dixie Rising,* 20.

70. Morris, *Terrains of the Heart,* 12–13.

71. William S. White LBJL OH, 1: 10–11; *Public Papers, 1968–69,* 1108; Conkin, "Lyndon Johnson," 166.

72. William S. White LBJL OH, 1: 10–11; F. E. Smith, *Look Away from Dixie,* 9; Clark and Arsenault, eds., *Changing South,* 165.

73. Alexander P. Lamis, "The Future of Southern Politics: New Directions for Dixie," in *Future South,* ed. Dunn and Preston, 51, 53.

74. *Katzenbach v. McClung,* 379 U.S. 294 (1964); Mershon and Schlossman, *Foxholes and Color Lines,* 158.

75. Katherine Tate and Gloria J. Hampton, "Changing Hearts and Minds: Racial Attitudes and Civil Rights," in *Legacies of the 1964 Civil Rights Act,* ed. Bernard Grofman (Charlottesville, Va., 2000), 186.

76. Robert Fredrick Burk, *The Eisenhower Administration and Black Civil Rights* (Knoxville, Tenn., 1985), 16, 262, 135, 214, 238; Arthur Larson, *Eisenhower: The President Nobody Knew* (New York, 1968), 128.

77. *New York Times,* March 15, 1977 (as reported by Earl Warren); Emmet Hughes, *The Ordeal of Power* (New York, 1963), 201; Sherman Adams, *Firsthand Report* (New York, 1961), 331; Burk, *Eisenhower Administration,* 201.

78. R. P. Morgan, *The President and Civil Rights,* 69–75; *Maine Sunday Telegram,* July 11, 2004; Richard Reeves, *Running in Place: How Bill Clinton Disappointed America* (Kansas City, Mo., 1996), xiv.

79. Rowan, *Dream Makers, Dream Breakers,* 348; H. Graham, *Civil Rights Era,* 272.

80. Goldfield, *Still Fighting the Civil War,* 318–19; Persky, *Burden of Dependency,* 148; Hodding Carter, "The South and the World: A Dissenting Postscript," in *Dixie Dateline,* ed. Boles, 170.

81. Edwin M. Yoder Jr., "Thoughts on the Dixiefication of Dixie," in *Dixie Dateline,* ed. Boles, 159; John Peet, "A Survey of the American South," *The Economist* 10 (December 1994), Supplement: 4.

BIBLIOGRAPHY

MANUSCRIPTS

Aandahl, Fred. State Historical Society of North Dakota, Bismarck, N.D.

Abbitt, Wat. University of Richmond, Richmond, Va.

Acheson, Dean. HSTL.

————. Yale University, New Haven, Conn.

Adams, Sherman. Dartmouth College, Hanover, N.H.

Alger, Bruce. Dallas Public Library, Texas/Dallas History and Archives Division, Dallas, Tex.

Allen-Angier Family. Duke University, Durham, N.C.

Allison, Mrs. J. Richard. South Caroliniana Library, University of South Carolina, Columbia, S.C.

Allred, Jimmie. University of Houston, Houston, Tex.

Americans for Democratic Action. State Historical Society of Wisconsin, Madison, Wis.

Amlie, Thomas. State Historical Society of Wisconsin, Madison, Wis.

Andrews, Charles O. P. K. Yonge Library of Florida History, University of Florida, Gainesville, Fla.

Andrews, George W. Auburn University, Auburn, Ala.

Angas, Tracy L'Engle. P. K. Yonge Library of Florida History, University of Florida, Gainesville, Fla.

Arnold, Wat. Western Historical Manuscripts Collection, University of Missouri, Columbia, Mo.

Ashburn, Karl Everett. Duke University, Durham, N.C.

Ashmore, Harry. University of Arkansas at Little Rock, Little Rock, Ark.

Ashmore, Robert T. South Caroliniana Library, University of South Carolina, Columbia, S.C.

Ashwander Case Files. Tennessee Valley Authority, Technical Library, Knoxville, Tenn.

Ayers, Eben A. HSTL.

Ayers, Harry. University of Alabama, University, Ala.

Bailey, Josiah W. Duke University, Durham, N.C.

Ball, William Watts. Duke University, Durham, N.C.

Bankhead, John H. State of Alabama Department of Archives and History, Montgomery, Ala.

Bankhead, Tallulah. State of Alabama Department of Archives and History, Montgomery, Ala.

Bankhead, William. State of Alabama Department of Archives and History, Montgomery, Ala.

Barden, Graham A. Duke University, Durham, N.C.

Barkley, Alben W. University of Kentucky, Lexington, Ky.

Barnett, Ross. Mississippi Department of Archives and History, Jackson, Miss.

Bell, C. Jasper. Western Historical Manuscripts Collection, University of Missouri, Columbia, Mo.

Benjamin, Burton. State Historical Society of Wisconsin, Madison, Wis.

Bennett, Charles E. P. K. Yonge Library of Florida History, University of Florida, Gainesville, Fla.

Benson, Elmer. Minnesota Historical Society, St. Paul, Minn.

Bentley, Nancy. HSTL.

Bentsen, Lloyd. Sam Rayburn Library, Bonham, Tex.

Berry, Ellis. Black Hills State University, Spearfish, S.D.

Bilbo, Theodore G. Mississippi Department of Archives and History, Jackson, Miss.

————. University of Southern Mississippi, Hattiesburg, Miss.

Billings, John Shaw. South Caroliniana Library, University of South Carolina, Columbia, S.C.

Black, Hugo. LC.

Bland, Schuyler Otis. Earl Gregg Swem Library, The College of William and Mary, Williamsburg, Va.

Boggs, Hale. Tulane University, New Orleans, La.

Boineau, Charles. South Caroliniana Library, University of South Carolina, Columbia, S.C.

Bolling, Richard. Western Historical Manuscripts Collection, University of Missouri, Columbia, Mo.

Bontecou, Eleanor. HSTL.

Bowers, Claude. Indiana University, Bloomington, Ind.

Braden, Carl and Anne. State Historical Society of Wisconsin, Madison, Wis.

Bradley, Palmer. Houston Metropolitan Research Center, Houston Public Library, Houston, Tex.

Brandeis, Louis. University of Louisville Law School, Louisville, Ky.

Breckinridge, Henry. LC.

Brooks, Overton. Louisiana State University, Baton Rouge, La.

Brough, Charles. University of Arkansas, Fayetteville, Ark.

Brown, Clarence J. Ohio Historical Society, Columbus, Ohio.

Brown, Edgar A. Clemson University, Clemson, S.C.

Broyhill, James T. Appalachian Collection, Appalachian State University, Boone, N.C.

Bryant, Henry Edward Cowan. SHC.

Bumpas Family MSS. SHC.

Bunche, Ralph J. Vanderbilt University, Nashville, Tenn.

Burch, Dean. Arizona Historical Society, Tucson, Ariz.

Burdick, Usher. University of North Dakota, Grand Forks, N.D.

Burleson, Albert. LC.

Burns, Gladys King. State of Alabama Department of Archives and History, Montgomery, Ala.

Bushfield, Harlan J. South Dakota State Historical Society, Pierre, S.D.

Butler, Paul M. University of Notre Dame, South Bend, Ind.

Byrd, Harry F., Jr. University of Virginia, Charlottesville, Va.

Byrd, Harry Flood, Sr. University of Virginia, Charlottesville, Va.

Byrnes, James F. Clemson University, Clemson, S.C.

Caraway, Hattie. University of Arkansas, Fayetteville, Ark.

Carleton, William. P. K. Yonge Library of Florida History, University of Florida, Gainesville, Fla.

Carpenter, Liz. LBJL.

Carr, James Ozborn. SHC.

Carr, Robert K. Oberlin College Archives, Oberlin, Ohio.

Carter, Dan. Emory University, Atlanta, Ga.

Carter, Jimmy. Jimmy Carter Library, Atlanta, Ga.

Case, Francis. Dakota Wesleyan University, Mitchell, S.D.

———. South Dakota State Historical Society, Pierre, S.D.

Castle, William R., Jr. Houghton Library, Harvard University, Cambridge, Mass.

Catledge, Turner. Mississippi State University, Mississippi State, Miss.

Chadwick, Stephen. University of Washington, Seattle, Wash.

Chambers, Lenoir. SHC.

Chandler, Albert B. University of Kentucky, Lexington, Ky.

Chandler, Walter. Memphis/Shelby County Archives, Memphis, Tenn.

Chapman, Oscar L. HSTL.

Cherry, R. Gregg. North Carolina State Archives, Raleigh, N.C.

Chicago Urban League. University of Illinois at Chicago, Chicago, Ill.

Childs, Marquis. State Historical Society of Wisconsin, Madison, Wis.

Clark, Grenville. Dartmouth College, Hanover, N.H.

Clayton, William Lockhart. Rice University, Houston, Tex.

Clements, Earle C. University of Kentucky, Lexington, Ky.

Clifford, Clark. HSTL.

Clipping Files, Southern Collection. Birmingham Public Library, Birmingham, Ala.

Cocke, Philip Charles. SHC.

Cole, William P. Maryland Historical Society, Baltimore, Md.

Collins, Le Roy. Florida State University, Tallahassee, Fla.

———. University of South Florida, Tampa, Fla.

Collins, Ross. LC.

Colmer, William M. University of Southern Mississippi, Hattiesburg, Miss.

Connally, Tom. LC.

Cooley, Harold D. SHC.

Cooper, John Sherman. University of Kentucky, Lexington, Ky.

Corcoran, Thomas G. LC.

Corwin, Edward S. Princeton University, Princeton, N.J.

Couch, William T. SHC.

Cox, Allen Eugene. Mississippi State University, Mississippi State, Miss.

Cramer, William Cato. University of Tampa, Tampa, Fla.

Cummings, Homer S. University of Virginia, Charlottesville, Va.

Dabney, Virginius. University of Virginia, Charlottesville, Va.

Daniel, Price. Sam Houston Regional Library and Research Center, Liberty, Tex.

Daniel, W. C. (Dan). Averett College, Danville, Va.

Daniels, Jonathan. HSTL.

——. SHC.

Daniels, Josephus. LC.

Davidson, Donald. Vanderbilt University, Nashville, Tenn.

Davis, Charles Hall. University of Virginia, Charlottesville, Va.

Davis, John W. Richard B. Russell Memorial Library, Athens, Ga.

Davis, Westmoreland. University of Virginia, Charlottesville, Va.

Deane, Charles B. Southern Baptist Historical Collection, Wake Forest University, Winston-Salem, N.C.

Democratic National Committee. FDRL.

Dickey, John. Dartmouth College, Hanover, N.H.

Dies, Martin. Sam Houston Regional Library and Research Center, Liberty, Tex.

Dirksen, Everett M. Dirksen Congressional Center, Pekin, Ill.

Di Salle, Michael V. Ohio Historical Society, Columbus, Ohio.

Dixon, Frank M. Alabama Department of Archives and History, Montgomery, Ala.

Dodd, William E. LC.

Dombrowski, James. State Historical Society of Wisconsin, Madison, Wis.

Dorn, W. J. Bryan. South Caroliniana Library, University of South Carolina, Columbia, S.C.

Doughton, Robert L. SHC.

Douty, Kenneth. SHC.

Dowdy, John. Baylor University Collection of Political Materials, Waco, Tex.

Drewry, Patrick Henry. University of Virginia, Charlottesville, Va.

Du Pont, Pierre S. Eleutherian Mills Historical Library, Hagley Museum and Library, Wilmington, Del.

Durham, Carl T. SHC.

Durr, Clifford. Alabama Department of Archives and History, Montgomery, Ala.

Durr, Clifford and Virginia. LBJL.

Durr, Virginia. Alabama Department of Archives and History, Montgomery, Ala.

Early, Stephen T. FDRL.

Ellender, Allen J. Nicholls State University, Thibodaux, La.

Elsey, George M. HSTL.

Ethridge, Mark. SHC.

Farley, James A. LC.

Fisher, O. C. Baylor University Collection of Political Materials, Waco, Tex.

Fite, Gilbert. Richard B. Russell Memorial Library, University of Georgia, Athens, Ga.

Fleming, Harold. LC.

Frank, Jerome N. Yale University, New Haven, Conn.

Franklin D. Roosevelt Memorial Foundation. FDRL.

Franklin D. Roosevelt Museum Archives. Warm Springs, Ga.

Freeman, Douglas Southall. LC.

Freidel, Frank. FDRL.

Fulbright, J. W. University of Arkansas, Fayetteville, Ark.

Furman, Bess. LC.

Gannett, Frank E. Cornell University Collection of Regional History, Ithaca, N.Y.

Gardner, Fay Webb. Gardner-Webb College, Boiling Springs, N.C.

Gardner, O. Max. SHC.

Garner, John Nance. Archives, University of Texas Library, Austin, Tex.

Gasque, Allard H. South Caroliniana Library, University of South Carolina, Columbia, S.C.

George, Wesley Critz. SHC.

Glass, Carter. University of Virginia, Charlottesville, Va.

Goldwater, Barry. Arizona Historical Foundation, Tempe, Ariz.

Gosnell, Harold F. HSTL.

Gossett, Ed Lee. Baylor University Collection of Political Materials, Waco, Tex.

Graff, Robert D. FDRL.

Graham, Frank Porter. SHC.

Gray, Gordon. SHC.

Green, Robert A. "Lex." P. K. Yonge Library of Florida History, University of Florida, Gainesville, Fla.

Gregory, Thomas W. LC.

Grenier, John. Auburn University, Auburn, Ala.

Gruening, Ernest H. Alaska and Polar Regions Department, University of Alaska, Fairbanks, Alaska.

Gudger, Lamar. Western Carolina University, Cullowhee, N.C.

Hall, Grover C. Alabama Department of Archives and History, Montgomery, Ala.

Hancock, Frank. East Carolina University, Greenville, N.C.

Harden, John William. SHC.

Hardy, Porter, Jr. Randolph Macon College, Ashland, Va.

Harris, Roy V. Richard B. Russell Memorial Library, University of Georgia, Athens, Ga.

Harrison, Pat. Mississippi State University, Mississippi State, Miss.

———. University of Mississippi, Oxford, Miss.

Hart, James. University of Virginia, Charlottesville, Va.

Hayden, Carl T. Arizona State University, Tempe, Ariz.

Hays, Brooks. JFKL.

———. Southern Baptist Historical Collection, Wake Forest University, Winston-Salem, N.C.

———. University of Arkansas, Fayetteville, Ark.

Hays, Wayne L. Ohio University, Athens, Ohio.

Hebert, F. Edward. Tulane University, New Orleans, La.

Heiskell, J. N. University of Arkansas at Little Rock, Little Rock, Ark.

Hemphill, Robert V. South Caroliniana Library, University of South Carolina, Columbia, S.C.

Henderson, Leon. FDRL.

Hendricks, Joseph E. P. K. Yonge Library of Florida History, University of Florida, Gainesville, Fla.

Henry, Aaron. Wayne State University, Detroit, Mich.

Herlong, A. Sydney, Jr. P. K. Yonge Library of Florida History, University of Florida, Gainesville, Fla.

Heslep, Charter. HSTL.

Hickenlooper, Bourke B. Herbert Hoover Presidential Library, West Branch, Iowa.

Highlander Research and Education Center. State Historical Society of Wisconsin, Madison, Wis.

Hill, Lister. Alabama Department of Archives and History, Montgomery, Ala.

Hilles, Charles D. Yale University, New Haven, Conn.

Hobbs, Sam. University of Alabama, University, Ala.

Hodges, James B. P. K. Yonge Library of Florida History, University of Florida, Gainesville, Fla.

Hodges, Luther. SHC.

Hoey, Clyde. Duke University, Durham, N.C.

Holland, Spessard. Emory University, Atlanta, Ga.

———. Florida State University, Tallahassee, Fla.

———. P. K. Yonge Library of Florida History, University of Florida, Gainesville, Fla.

Holt, Erwin A. SHC.

Hoover, Herbert. Herbert Hoover Presidential Library, West Branch, Iowa.

Hopkins, Harry. FDRL.

House, E. M. Yale University, New Haven, Conn.

Hoyt, James A. South Caroliniana Library, University of South Carolina, Columbia, S.C.

Humphrey, Hubert. Minnesota Historical Society, St. Paul, Minn.

Hunter, Thomas Lomax. University of Virginia, Charlottesville, Va.

Hutchinson, Martin A. University of Virginia, Charlottesville, Va.

Hyde, Henry Morrow. University of Virginia, Charlottesville, Va.

Ickes, Harold L. LC.

Jaffé, Louis I. University of Virginia, Charlottesville, Va.

Jeter, Edwin R. South Caroliniana Library, University of South Carolina, Columbia, S.C.

Johnson, Guy Benton. SHC.

Johnson, Keen. Eastern Kentucky University, Richmond, Ky.

Johnson, Lyndon B. LBJL.

Johnson, Paul B. University of Southern Mississippi, Hattiesburg, Miss.

Johnston, Olin D. South Caroliniana Library, University of South Carolina, Columbia, S.C.

———. State of South Carolina Archives, Columbia, S.C.

Jonas, Charles Raper. SHC.

Jones, Jesse H. LC.

Jones, Sam H. Tulane University, New Orleans, La.

Keating, Edward. University of Colorado, Boulder, Colo.

Kefauver, Estes. University of Tennessee, Knoxville, Tenn.

Kennedy, John F. JFKL.

Kenny, Robert W. University of California, Los Angeles, Calif.

Kent, Frank R. Maryland Historical Society, Baltimore, Md.

Kerr, John Hosea. SHC.

Krock, Arthur. Princeton University, Princeton, N.J.

Lanham, Henderson. Richard B. Russell Memorial Library, University of Georgia, Athens, Ga.

Lawrence, David. Princeton University, Princeton, N.J.

Leadership Conference on Civil Rights. State Historical Society of Wisconsin, Madison, Wis.

Lennon, Alton. University of North Carolina at Wilmington, Wilmington, N.C.

Lerner, Max. Yale University, New Haven, Conn.

Lever, Asbury Francis. Clemson University, Clemson, S.C.

Lewis, David J. Duke University, Durham, N.C.

Lilienthal, David E. Princeton University, Princeton, N.J.

Lincoln, Evelyn. JFKL.

Lloyd, David D. HSTL.

Loftin, Scott M. P. K. Yonge Library of Florida History, University of Florida, Gainesville, Fla.

Logan, Marvel Mills. University of Kentucky, Lexington, Ky.

Logan, Rayford. LC.

Long, Breckinridge. LC.

Louchheim, Katie. LC.

Love, Thomas B. Dallas Historical Society, Dallas, Tex.

Lowenstein, Allard. SHC.

Mackoy Family. University of Kentucky, Lexington, Ky.

MacNeil, Robert. State Historical Society of Wisconsin, Madison, Wis.

McAdoo, William G. LC.

McCord, Jim. Tennessee State Library and Archives, Nashville, Tenn.

McCray, John H. South Caroliniana Library, University of South Carolina, Columbia, S.C.

McCulloch, William. Ohio Northern University Law School, Ada, Ohio.

McFarland, Ernest. McFarland State Historic Park, Florence, Ariz.

McGill, Ralph. Emory University, Atlanta, Ga.

McGrath, J. Howard. HSTL.

McKellar, Kenneth D. Memphis/Shelby County Archives, Memphis, Tenn.

McMath, Sidney. University of Arkansas, Fayetteville, Ark.

McMillan, John. South Caroliniana Library, University of South Carolina, Columbia, S.C.

McNaughton, Frank. HSTL.

McSwain, John J. Duke University, Durham, N.C.

Maddox, Lester. Richard B. Russell Memorial Library, Athens, Ga.

Martin, John Sanford. Duke University, Durham, N.C.

Mason, Lucy Randolph. Duke University, Durham, N.C.

Matthews, D. R. (Billy). P. K. Yonge Library of Florida History, University of Florida, Gainesville, Fla.

Maverick, Maury. Archives, University of Texas Library, Austin, Tex.

Maybank, Burnet R. College of Charleston, Charleston, S.C.

———. South Caroliniana Library, University of South Carolina, Columbia, S.C.

———. State of South Carolina Archives, Columbia, S.C.

Mellett, Lowell. FDRL.

Menefee, Marvin J. University of Virginia, Charlottesville, Va.

Messall, Victor. HSTL.

Miller, Francis Pickens. University of Virginia, Charlottesville, Va.

Miller, William E. Cornell University Collection of Regional History, Ithaca, N.Y.

Mills, Wilbur D. Hendrix College, Conway, Ark.

Milton, George Fort. LC.

Mississippi Freedom Summer Collection. Tougaloo College, Tougaloo, Miss.

Mississippi State Democratic Executive Committee. Mississippi Department of Archives and History, Jackson, Miss.

Mitchell, Samuel Chiles. SHC.

Mitford, Jessica. Ohio State University, Columbus, Ohio.

Moody, Blair. Michigan Historical Collections, University of Michigan, Ann Arbor, Mich.

Moore, R. Walton. FDRL.

More, Jake. University of Iowa, Iowa City, Iowa.

Morgan, Arthur E. Antioch College, Yellow Springs, Ohio.

Morris, Allen. Florida State University, Tallahassee, Fla.

Morton, Thruston B. University of Kentucky, Lexington, Ky.

Museum of Television and Radio Archives. New York.

Muskie, Edmund S. Bates College, Lewiston, Maine.

Nash, Philleo. HSTL.

National Association for the Advancement of Colored People. LC.

National Policy Committee. LC.

Niles, David K. HSTL.

Noland, Mary Ethel. HSTL.

O'Connor, J. F. T. Bancroft Library, University of California, Berkeley, Calif.

Odum, Howard. SHC.

O'Mahoney, Joseph C. University of Wyoming, Laramie, Wyo.

O'Neal, Edward A. State of Alabama Department of Archives and History, Montgomery, Ala.

Overton, John H. Louisiana State University, Baton Rouge, La.

Owsley, Frank. Vanderbilt University, Nashville, Tenn.

Palmer, Charles F. Emory University, Atlanta, Ga.

Panzer, Fred A. LBJL.

Parker, John J. SHC.

Peabody, George Foster. LC.

Pegler, Westbrook. Herbert Hoover Presidential Library, West Branch, Iowa.

Pepper, Claude. The Archives Branch, Washington National Records Center, Suitland, Md.

————. Florida State University Claude Pepper Library, Tallahassee, Fla.

————. P. K. Yonge Library of Florida History, University of Florida, Gainesville, Fla.

————. Privately held.

Perkins, Frances. Columbia University, New York.

Peterson, James Hardin. P. K. Yonge Library of Florida History, University of Florida, Gainesville, Fla.

Pickett, Thomas A. Baylor University Collection of Political Materials, Waco, Tex.

Pilcher, J. L. Richard B. Russell Memorial Library, University of Georgia, Athens, Ga.

Pittman, Key. LC.

Poage, W. R. Baylor University Collection of Political Materials, Waco, Tex.

Price, James H. Washington and Lee University, Lexington, Va.

Primm, William J. Duke University, Durham, N.C.

Progressive Party. University of Iowa, Iowa City, Iowa.

Ramsey, D. Hiden. SHC.

Ransdell, Joseph E. Louisiana State University, Baton Rouge, La.

Raper, Arthur. SHC.

Rauh, Joseph L., Jr. LC.

Rayburn, Sam. Sam Rayburn Library, Bonham, Tex.

Reed, Stanley. University of Kentucky, Lexington, Ky.

Rhodes, John. Arizona State University, Tempe, Ariz.

Rivers, E. D. Ruby Webb Collection, Richard B. Russell Memorial Library, Athens, Ga.

Rivers, L. Mendel. The Citadel, Charleston, S.C.

Robbins, Haywood. University of North Carolina at Charlotte, Charlotte, N.C.

Roberts, Ray. Texas A & M University at Commerce, Commerce, Tex.

Robertson, A. Willis. College of William and Mary, Williamsburg, Va.

Robinson, Joseph T. University of Arkansas, Fayetteville, Ark.

Romaine, Anne. SHC.

————. State Historical Society of Wisconsin, Madison, Wis.

Roosevelt, Franklin D. FDRL.

Roosevelt, James. FDRL.

Roper, Daniel C. Duke University, Durham, N.C.

Rovere, Richard. State Historical Society of Wisconsin, Madison, Wis.

Rowan, Carl T. Oberlin College, Oberlin, Ohio.

Rowe, James H., Jr. FDRL.

Rushton, Marion. Alabama Department of Archives and History, Montgomery, Ala.

Russell, Richard B., Jr. Richard B. Russell Memorial Library, University of
Georgia, Athens, Ga.

Sabath, Adolph J. Tulane University, New Orleans, La.

Samford, T. D. SHC.

Sanford, Terry. SHC.

Schlesinger, Arthur, Jr. JFKL.

Schwellenbach, Lewis B. LC.

Schwengel, Frederick. University of Iowa, Iowa City, Iowa.

Shanley, Bernard. Seton Hall University, South Orange, N.J.

Sheppard, Morris. Archives, University of Texas Library, Austin, Tex.

Shorey, Gregory D. South Caroliniana Library, University of South Carolina,
Columbia, S.C.

Short, Don. Dickinson State College, Dickinson, N.D.

Sillers, Walter, Jr. Delta State University, Cleveland, Miss.

Slemp, C. Bascom. University of Virginia, Charlottesville, Va.

Smathers, George. P. K. Yonge Library of Florida History, University of Florida, Gainesville, Fla.

Smith, Howard W. University of Virginia, Charlottesville, Va.

Sorensen, Theodore. JFKL.

Southern Conference for Human Welfare. Atlanta University, Atlanta, Ga.

————. Tuskegee University, Tuskegee, Ala.

Southern Politics Collection. Vanderbilt University, Nashville, Tenn.

Southern Regional Council. Atlanta University, Atlanta, Ga.

Southern Tenant Farmers Union. SHC.

Sparkman, John. University of Alabama, University, Ala.

Sparks, Chauncey. Alabama Department of Archives and History, Montgomery, Ala.

Spence, Brent. University of Kentucky, Lexington, Ky.

Spingarn, Stephen J. HSTL.

Stanley, A. O. University of Kentucky, Lexington, Ky.

States Rights Scrapbook. Mississippi Department of Archives and History, Jackson, Miss.

Steele, John L. LBJL.

Stennis, John. Mississippi State University, State University, Miss.

Stone, Walker. State Historical Society of Wisconsin, Madison, Wis.

Suckley, Margaret. FDRL.

Swearingen, Mack. Cornell University Collection of Regional History, Ithaca, N.Y.

Talmadge, Herman E. Richard B. Russell Memorial Library, Athens, Ga.

Taylor, George C. Regional Archives Branch, Federal Records Center, East Point, Ga.

Tennessee Valley Authority Ashwander Case Scrapbooks. TVA Technical Library, Knoxville, Tenn.

Thomas, Elmer. University of Oklahoma, Norman, Okla.

Thompson, M. E. Emory University, Atlanta, Ga.

Thurmond, J. Strom. Clemson University, Clemson, S.C.

————. South Caroliniana Library, University of South Carolina, Columbia, S.C.

————. Winthrop University, Rock Hill, S.C.

Tilly, Dorothy Rogers. Emory University, Atlanta, Ga.

Tower, John G. Southwestern University, Georgetown, Tex.

Trammell, Park. Park Trammell Public Library, Lakeland, Fla.

Truman, Harry S. HSTL.

Truman Family Genealogy. HSTL.

Truman Family Letters. HSTL.

Tucker, Cornelia Dabney. South Caroliniana Library, University of South Carolina, Columbia, S.C.

Tugwell, Rexford G. FDRL.

Tumulty, Joseph. LC.

Turner, Thomas O. University of Kentucky, Lexington, Ky.

Underwood, Thomas R. University of Kentucky, Lexington, Ky.

Vandenberg, Arthur H. Clements Library, University of Michigan, Ann Arbor, Mich.

Vidal, Gore. State Historical Society of Wisconsin, Madison, Wis.

Vinson, Fred M. University of Kentucky, Lexington, Ky.

Wadsworth, James W. LC.

Wagner, Robert. Georgetown University, Washington, D.C.

Walker, Frank. University of Notre Dame, South Bend, Ind.

Walsh, David I. College of the Holy Cross, Worcester, Mass.

Waring, Thomas R., Jr. South Carolina Historical Society, Charleston, S.C.

Warren, Fuller. Florida State University, Tallahassee, Fla.

———. P. K. Yonge Library of Florida History, University of Florida, Gainesville, Fla.

Warren, Lindsay. SHC.

Watts, John C. University of Kentucky, Lexington, Ky.

Waymack, W. W. State Historical Society of Iowa, Iowa City, Iowa.

Waynick, Capus Miller. East Carolina University, Greenville, N.C.

Weaver, Zebulon. Western Carolina University, Cullowhee, N.C.

Webb, Edwin Yates. SHC.

Weltner, Charles Longstreet. Atlanta Historical Society, Atlanta, Ga.

White, F. Clifton. Cornell University Collection of Regional History, Ithaca, N.Y.

———. John M. Ashbrook Center for Public Affairs, Ashland University, Ashland, Ohio.

White, Theodore H. Harvard University Archives, Cambridge, Mass.

Whitehurst, G. William. Washington and Lee University, Lexington, Va.

Whitener, Basil Lee. Duke University, Durham, N.C.

Wilkins, Roy. LC.

Willert, Sir Arthur. Yale University, New Haven, Conn.

Williams, Aubrey. FDRL.

———. HSTL.

Williams, John J. University of Delaware, Newark, Del.

Willis, Edwin E. Southwestern Archives and Manuscripts Collection, Lafayette, La.

Wilson, Samuel M. University of Kentucky, Lexington, Ky.

Winston, Robert W. SHC.

Woodrum, Clifton. Roanoke City Library, Roanoke, Va.

Woodson, Urey. University of Kentucky, Lexington, Ky.

Workman, William D., Jr. South Caroliniana Library, University of South Carolina, Columbia, S.C.

Wright-Thurmond Correspondence. Mississippi Department of Archives and History, Jackson, Miss.

Zook, John Daniel. Ohio Historical Society, Columbus, Ohio.

ORAL HISTORIES

Abernethy, Thomas G. University of Southern Mississippi, Hattiesburg, Miss.

Alexander, Will. COHC.

Alger, Bruce. Dallas Public Library, Dallas, Tex.

Almond, J. Lindsay. JFKL.

———. LBJL.

Anderson, Clinton P. JFKL.

Andrews, George W. Auburn University, Auburn, Ala.

Ashmore, Harry. LBJL.

———. Patricia Sullivan Interviews, Emory University, Atlanta, Ga.

———. SOHP.

Barkley, Alben W. (Sidney Shalett interview). HSTL.

Barnett, Ross. JFKL.

Baskin, Robert E. LBJL.

Bell, Griffin. Miller Center Interview, Jimmy Carter Library, Atlanta, Ga.

Bell, Jack. JFKL.

Benchley, Peter B. LBJL.

Bentley, Nancy. HSTL.

Biemiller, Andrew J. HSTL.

Birkhead, Kenneth M. HSTL.

Boggs, Hale. JFKL.

Bolling, Jim Grant. JFKL.

Bolling, Richard. HSTL.

———. LBJL.

Bolton, Paul. LBJL.

Bonner, Daisy. FDRL.

Brightman, Samuel C. HSTL.

Brooks, David William. Richard B. Russell Memorial Library, University of Georgia, Athens, Ga.

Busby, Horace. JFKL.

Byrd, Harry A., Jr. SOHP.

Byrnes, James F. Robert D. Graff MSS, FDRL.

Carlton, John. Richard B. Russell Memorial Library, University of Georgia, Athens, Ga.

Carter, Hodding. LBJL.

Carter, Jimmy. SOHP.

Carter, John Franklin. HSTL.

Cater, Douglass. LBJL.

Catledge, Turner (recorded at the University of Southern Mississippi). Mississippi State University, State University, Miss.

Clark, Ramsey. LBJL.

Clark, Tom (Jerry N. Hess interview). HSTL.

———. LBJL.

Clayton, William Lockhart. COHC.

Clements, Earle C. LBJL.

Collins, Le Roy. JFKL.

———. LBJL.

———. SOHP.

Collins, Linton M. Richard B. Russell Memorial Library, University of Georgia, Athens, Ga.

Colmer, William. University of Southern Mississippi, Hattiesburg, Miss.

Connelly, Matthew J. HSTL.

Dabney, Virginius. SOHP.

Daniel, Price. LBJL.

———. University of North Texas, Denton, Tex.

Daniels, Jonathan. COHC.

———. Eleanor Roosevelt Oral History Project, FDRL.

———. HSTL.

———. LBJL.

———. SOHP.

Darden, William H. LBJL.

Deason, Willard. LBJL.

Douglas, Helen Gahagan. LBJL.

Douglas, Paul H. LBJL.

Dugger, Ronnie. SOHP.

Durr, Clifford and Virginia. LBJL.

Durr, Virginia. COHC.

———. SOHP.

Dutton, Frederick. JFKL.

Eastland, James O. LBJL.

Ellender, Allen. JFKL.

———. LBJL.

Ellington, Buford. LBJL.

Elsey, George M. HSTL.

Ervin, Samuel J., Jr. Richard B. Russell Memorial Library, University of Georgia, Athens, Ga.

Ewing, Oscar R. HSTL.

Farley, James A. COHC.

———. University of Kentucky, Lexington, Ky.

———. LBJL.

Farmer, James. JFKL.

———. LBJL.

Faubus, Orval. SOHP.

Fisher, O. C. LBJL.

Floter, Walter Bridgforth. Southern Politics Collection, Vanderbilt University, Nashville, Tenn.

Folliard, Edward T. HSTL.

Folsom, Jim. SOHP.

Foreman, Clark. SOHP.

Fountain, L. H. LBJL.

Franklin, John Hope. COHC.

Friedman, Martin L. HSTL.

Gibson, Martin. FDRL.

Gideon, Sim. LBJL.

Gore, Albert, Sr. JFKL.

———. SOHP.

Gore, Weaver E. Southern Politics Collection, Vanderbilt University, Nashville, Tenn.

Grayson, Spence M. Richard B. Russell Memorial Library, University of Georgia, Athens, Ga.

Greene, Charles J. HSTL.

Grenier, John. SOHP.

Hardeman, D. B. Southern Politics Collection, Vanderbilt University, Nashville, Tenn.

Harris, Oren. JFKL.

———. LBJL.

Harris, Roy. SOHP.

Havenner, Franck Roberts. Bancroft Library, University of California, Berkeley, Calif.

Hay, Isaac K. Richard B. Russell Memorial Library, University of Georgia, Athens, Ga.

Hays, Brooks. LBJL.

Heard, Alexander. SOHP.

Hebert, F. Edward. LBJL.

Henry, Aaron. LBJL.

———. SOHP.

Higginbotham, A. Leon, Jr. LBJL.

Hill, Lister. LBJL.

Hirshberg, Harry. LBJL.

Hodges, Luther H. JFKL.

———. LBJL.

Hoeber, Johannes. HSTL.

Holeman, Frank. HSTL.

Holt, Thad. FDRL.

Hornaday, Walter C. LBJL.

Howerton, H. V. Southern Politics Collection, Vanderbilt University, Nashville, Tenn.

Humphrey, Hubert H. LBJL.

Ikard, Frank. LBJL.

———. University of North Texas, Denton, Tex.

Johnson, Guy. SOHC.

Johnson, Lady Bird. LBJL.

———. Richard B. Russell Memorial Library, University of Georgia, Athens, Ga.

Johnson, Paul B., Jr. LBJL.

Jones, Marvin. LBJL.

———. Richard B. Russell Memorial Library, University of Georgia, Athens, Ga.

Jordan, Barbara. LBJL.

Jordan, William H., Jr. LBJL.

Junkin, John R. Mississippi Department of Archives and History, Jackson, Miss.

Katzenbach, Nicholas deB. LBJL.

Kent, Carleton. HSTL.

Kenworthy, E. W. HSTL.

Kilpatrick, Carroll. LBJL.

King, Ed. Anne Romaine MSS, SHC.

Kraft, Joseph. JFKL.

Krock, Arthur. JFKL.

Kytle, Calvin. SOHP.

Latimer, Gene. LBJL.

Lawrence, David L. JFKL.

Leonard, Kittie Clyde. LBJL.

Loeb, James I. HSTL.

Louchheim, Kathleen. LBJL.

Lowry, W. McNeil. HSTL.

Maddox, Lester. LBJL.

Manatos, Mike. LBJL.

Marshall, Burke. LBJL.

Marshall, Thurgood. LBJL.

Martin, Louis. LBJL.

Martin, Loyis. Exit Interview, Jimmy Carter Library, Atlanta, Ga.

Matthews, Chappelle. Richard B. Russell Memorial Library, University of Georgia, Athens, Ga.

Maverick, Maury, Jr. SOHP.

McIntyre, James. Miller Center Interview, Jimmy Carter Library, Atlanta, Ga.

Mills, Wilbur J. Former Members of Congress, LC.

———. LBJL.

Mitchell, H. L. COHC.

Mooney, Booth. LBJL.

Moore, Powell. LBJL.

Murphy, Reg. SOHP.

Murray, Pauli. Eleanor Roosevelt Oral History Project, FDRL.

Nichols, William F. Auburn University, Auburn, Ala.

Niles, David K. HSTL.

Nixon, H. C. Southern Politics Collection, Vanderbilt University, Nashville, Tenn.

Nixon, Richard. Richard B. Russell Memorial Library, University of Georgia, Athens, Ga.

Nixon, Robert G. HSTL.

Noland, Mary Ethel. HSTL.

Pearson, Drew. LBJL.

Pepper, Claude. SOHP.

Poage, William Robert "Bob." Baylor University Collection of Political Materials, Waco, Tex.

Powell, Jody. Miller Center Interview, Charlottesville, Va.

Pryor, Richard S. "Cactus." LBJL.

Quill, Daniel J. LBJL.

Rafshoon, Gerald. Miller Center Interview, Jimmy Carter Library, Atlanta, Ga.

Randolph, A. Philip. LBJL.

Rather, Mary. LBJL.

Rauh, Joseph L., Jr. Anne Romaine MSS, SHC.

———. Eleanor Roosevelt Oral History Project, FDRL.

———. JFKL.

Redford, Emmette S. LBJL.

Reedy, George. LBJL.

Robertson, Willis. LBJL.

Rosenman, Samuel I. HSTL.

Rovere, Richard H. LBJL.

Rowe, Elizabeth. LBJL.

Rowe, James H., Jr. HSTL.

———. LBJL.

Rowe, Lee. FDRL.

Rustin, Bayard. LBJL.

Sanders, Carl. LBJL.

Sanford, Terry. LBJL.

Schlesinger, Arthur M., Jr. LBJL.

Shelton, Polk and Nell. LBJL.

Shivers, Allan. LBJL.

———. University of North Texas, Denton, Tex.

———. Sam Rayburn Library, Bonham, Tex.

Sidey, Hugh. LBJL.

Siegel, Gerald W. LBJL.

Smith, Frank E. University of Southern Mississippi, Hattiesburg, Miss.

Sparkman, John. LBJL.

———. Richard B. Russell Memorial Library, University of Georgia, Athens, Ga.

———. SOHP.

Spingarn, Stephen J. HSTL.

Stennis, John. LBJL.

———. Richard B. Russell Memorial Library, University of Georgia, Athens, Ga.

Stevenson, Coke R. University of North Texas, Denton, Tex.

Stone, Sam V. LBJL.

Stoney, George. SOHP.

Strout, Richard L. HSTL.

Sweeney, Robert L. HSTL.

Talmadge, Herman. LBJL.

———. SOHP

Taylor, Hobart, Jr. LBJL.

Taylor, Hobart, Sr. LBJL.

Thomason, R. E. LBJL.

Thompson, Libbie Moody. Rosenberg Library, Galveston, Tex.

Thurmond, Strom. LBJL.

———. SOHP.

Timmons, Bascom. LBJL.

Troutman, Robert Battey, Jr. Richard B. Russell Memorial Library, University of Georgia, Athens, Ga.

Tully, Grace. LBJL.

Vandiver, Samuel Ernest, Jr. Richard B. Russell Memorial Library, University of Georgia, Athens, Ga.

Wallace, George C. LBJL.

———. SOHP.

Wallace, Henry A. COHC.

Walsh, Robert K. HSTL.

Weaver, George L. P. LBJL

Weaver, Robert C. LBJL.

White, William S. LBJL.

Wicker, Thomas G. LBJL.

Wild, Claude. LBJL.

Wilkins, Josephine. Southern Politics Collection, Vanderbilt University, Nashville, Tenn.

Wilkins, Roy. LBJL.

Williams, John Bell. University of Southern Mississippi, Hattiesburg, Miss.

Worley, Eugene. LBJL.

Wright, James C., Jr. LBJL.

Young, Whitney, Jr. LBJL.

BOOKS

Abell, Tyler, ed. *Drew Pearson Diaries, 1949–1959.* New York, 1974.

Abels, Jules. *Out of the Jaws of Victory.* New York, 1959.

Abernathy, Ralph David. *And the Walls Came Tumbling Down: An Autobiography.* New York, 1989.

Abler, Ronald, Donald Janelle, Allen Philbrick, and John Sommer, eds. *Human Geography in a Shrinking World.* Belmont, Calif., 1975.

Adams, Sherman. *Firsthand Report.* New York, 1961.

Ader, Emile B. *The Dixiecrat Movement: Its Role in Third Party Politics.* Washington, D.C., 1955.

Allen, George E. *Presidents Who Have Known Me.* New York, 1950.

Almond, Gabriel A., and Sidney Verba. *The Civic Culture: Political Attitudes and Democracy in Five Nations.* Boston, 1965.

Alsop, Joseph, and Stewart Alsop. *The Reporter's Trade.* New York, 1958.

Alston, Lee J., and Joseph P. Ferrie. *Southern Paternalism and the American Welfare State: Economics, Politics, and Institutions in the South, 1865–1965.* Cambridge,1999.

Altschuler, Bruce E. *LBJ and the Polls.* Gainesville, Fla., 1990.

Amato, Joseph A. *Rethinking Home: A Case for Writing Local History.* Berkeley, Calif., 2002.

Anderson, Carol. *Eyes off the Prize: The United Nations and the African American Struggle for Human Rights, 1944–1955.* New York, 2003.

Anderson, Clinton P., with Milton Viorst. *Outsider in the Senate: Senator Clinton Anderson's Memoirs.* New York, 1970.

Anderson, J. W. *Eisenhower, Brownell, and the Congress: The Tangled Origins of the Civil Rights Bill of 1956–1957.* University, Ala., 1964.

Anderson, Jervis. *A. Philip Randolph: A Biographical Portrait.* New York, 1973.

Anderson, Patrick. *Electing Jimmy Carter: The Campaign of 1976.* Baton Rouge, La., 1994.

Anderson, William. *The Wild Man from Sugar Creek: The Political Career of Eugene Talmadge.* Baton Rouge, La., 1975.

Andrew, John A., III. *Lyndon Johnson and the Great Society.* Chicago, 1998.

————. *The Other Side of the Sixties: Young Americans for Freedom and the Rise of Conservative Politics.* New Brunswick, N.J., 1997.

Applebome, Peter. *Dixie Rising: How the South Is Shaping American Values, Politics and Culture.* New York, 1996.

Archer, Chalmers, Jr. *Growing Up Black in Mississippi: Memories of a Family, Heritage of a Place.* New York, 1992.

Asbell, Bernard. *When F.D.R. Died.* London, 1962.

Ashmore, Harry S. *Civil Rights and Wrongs: A Memoir of Race and Politics, 1944–1994.* New York, 1994.

————. *An Epitaph for Dixie.* New York, 1958.

————. *Hearts and Minds: The Anatomy of Racism from Roosevelt to Reagan.* New York, 1982.

Atkinson, Frank B. *The Dynamic Dominion: Realignment and the Rise of Virginia's Republican Party since 1945.* Fairfax, Va., 1992.

Ayers, Edward L., ed. *All Over the Map: Rethinking American Regions.* Baltimore, 1996.

Ayers, H. Brandt, and Thomas H. Naylor, eds. *You Can't Eat Magnolias.* New York, 1972.

Badger, Anthony J. *The New Deal: The Depression Years, 1933–1940.* New York, 1989.

————. *North Carolina and the New Deal.* Raleigh, N.C., 1981.

————. *Prosperity Road: The New Deal, Tobacco, and North Carolina.* Chapel Hill, N.C., 1980.

Bailey, Harry A., Jr., ed. *Negro Politics in America.* Columbus, Ohio, 1967.

Baker, Bobby, with Larry L. King. *Wheeling and Dealing: Confessions of a Capitol Hill Operator.* New York, 1978.

Baker, James T. *Brooks Hays.* Macon, Ga., 1989.

Baker, Leonard. *The Johnson Eclipse: A President's Vice Presidency.* New York, 1966.

Baldwin, Sidney. *Poverty and Politics: The Rise and Decline of the Farm Security Administration.* Chapel Hill, N.C., 1968.

Barkley, Alben. *That Reminds Me—.* Garden City, N.Y., 1954.

Barnard, Hollinger F., ed. *Outside the Magic Circle: The Autobiography of Virginia Foster Durr.* University, Ala., 1985.

Barnard, William D. *Dixiecrats and Democrats: Alabama Politics, 1942–1950.* University, Ala., 1974.

Barnes, Catherine A. *Journey from Jim Crow: The Desegregation of Southern Transit.* New York, 1983.

Barr, Alwyn. *Black Texans: A History of Negroes in Texas, 1528–1971.* Austin, Tex., 1973.

Bartley, Ernest R. *The Tidelands Oil Controversy: A Legal and Historical Analysis.* Austin, Tex., 1953.

Bartley, Numan V. *From Thurmond to Wallace: Political Tendencies in Georgia, 1948–1968.* Baltimore, 1970.

————. *The New South, 1945–1980.* Baton Rouge, La., 1995.

————. *The Rise of Massive Resistance: Race and Politics in the South during the 1950's.* Baton Rouge, La., 1969.

————, ed. *The Evolution of Southern Culture.* Athens, Ga., 1988.

Bass, Jack. *Unlikely Heroes.* New York, 1981.

Bass, Jack, and Marilyn W. Thompson. *Ol' Strom: An Unauthorized Biography of Strom Thurmond.* Atlanta, 1998.

Bass, Jack, and Walter DeVries. *The Transformation of Southern Politics: Social Change and Political Consequence since 1945.* New York, 1976.

Beagle, Ben, and Ozzie Osborne. *J. Lindsay Almond: Virginia's Reluctant Rebel.* Roanoke, Va., 1984.

Belknap, Michal R., ed. *Civil Rights, the White House and the Justice Department, 1945–1968, Vol. 2: Presidential Committees and White House Conferences.* New York, 1991.

Bensel, Richard Franklin. *Sectionalism and American Political Development, 1880–1980.* Madison, Wis., 1984.

Berman, Daniel. *A Bill Becomes a Law: The Civil Rights Act of 1960.* New York, 1962.

Berman, William C. *The Politics of Civil Rights in the Truman Administration.* Columbus, Ohio, 1970.

Bernstein, Irving. *A Caring Society: The New Deal, the Worker, and the Great Depression.* Boston, 1985.

————. *Guns or Butter: The Presidency of Lyndon Johnson.* New York, 1996.

Berry, Jason. *Amazing Grace: With Charles Evers in Mississippi.* New York, 1973.

Berry, J. Bill, ed. *Located Lives: Place and Idea in Southern Autobiography*, Athens, Ga., 1990.

Beschloss, Michael, ed. *Reaching for Glory: Lyndon Johnson's Secret White House Tapes, 1964–1965.* New York, 2001.

———. *Taking Charge: The Johnson White House Tapes, 1963–1964.* New York, 1997.

Beyle, Thad B., and Merle Black. *Politics and Policy in North Carolina.* New York, 1975.

Biles, Roger. *Crusading Liberal: Paul H. Douglas of Illinois.* DeKalb, Ill., 2002.

———. *Memphis in the Great Depression.* Knoxville, Tenn., 1986.

———. *A New Deal for the American People.* DeKalb, Ill., 1991.

———. *The South and the New Deal.* Lexington, Ky., 1994.

Billington, Monroe Lee. *The Political South in the Twentieth Century.* New York, 1975.

Billington, Ray Allen. *Frederick Jackson Turner: Historian, Scholar, Teacher.* New York, 1973.

Bishop, Jim. *A Day in the Life of President Johnson.* New York, 1967.

Black, Allida. *Casting Her Own Shadow: Eleanor Roosevelt and the Shaping of Postwar Liberalism.* New York, 1996.

Black, Earl. *Southern Governors and Civil Rights: Racial Segregation as a Campaign Issue in the Second Reconstruction.* Cambridge, Mass., 1976.

Black, Earl, and Merle Black. *The Rise of Southern Republicans.* Cambridge, Mass., 2002.

———. *The Vital South: How Presidents Are Elected.* Cambridge, Mass., 1992.

Blackwelder, Julia Kirk. *Women of the Depression: Caste and Culture in San Antonio, 1929–1939.* College Station, Tex., 1984.

Bloom, Jack M. *Class, Race, and the Civil Rights Movement.* Bloomington, Ind., 1987.

Blount, Roy, Jr. *Crackers: This Whole Many-Angled Thing of Jimmy, More Carters, Ominous Little Animals, Sad-Singing Women, My Daddy and Me.* New York, 1980.

Blum, John Morton. *From the Morgenthau Diaries: Years of Crisis, 1928–1938.* Boston, 1959.

———. *Liberty, Justice, Order: Essays on Past Politics.* New York, 1993.

———. *V Was for Victory: Politics and American Culture during World War II.* New York, 1976.

Boggs, Lindy, with Katherine Hatch. *Washington through a Purple Veil: Memoirs of a Southern Woman*. New York, 1994.

Bogue, Allan G. *Frederick Jackson Turner: Strange Roads Going Down*. Norman, Okla., 1998.

Boles John B., ed. *Dixie Dateline: A Journalistic Portrait of the Contemporary South*. Houston, Tex., 1983.

Boles, John B., and Evelyn Thomas Nolen, eds. *Interpreting Southern History: Historiographical Essays in Honor of Sanford W. Higginbotham*. Baton Rouge, La., 1987.

Bolling, Richard. *House Out of Order*. New York, 1965.

Bornet, Vaughn Davis. *The Presidency of Lyndon B. Johnson*. Lawrence, Kans., 1983.

Borstelmann, Thomas. *Apartheid's Reluctant Uncle: The United States and Southern Africa in the Early Cold War*. New York, 1993.

———. *The Cold War and the Color Line: American Race Relations in the Global Arena*. Cambridge, Mass., 2001.

Bowers, Claude. *My Life: The Memoirs of Claude Bowers*. New York, 1962.

———. *The Tragic Era: The Revolution after Lincoln*. Cambridge, Mass., 1929.

Bradlee, Benjamin C. *Conversations with Kennedy*. New York, 1975.

Braeman, John, Robert H. Bremner, and David Brody, eds. *The New Deal: The National Level*. Columbus, Ohio, 1975.

———. *The New Deal: The State and Local Levels*. Columbus, Ohio, 1975.

Branch, Taylor. *Parting the Waters: America in the King Years, 1954–63*. New York, 1988.

———. *Pillar of Fire: America in the King Years, 1963–65*. New York, 1998.

Brandon, Henry. *Special Relationships: A Foreign Correspondent's Memoirs from Roosevelt to Reagan*. New York, 1988.

Brauer, Carl. *John F. Kennedy and the Second Reconstruction*. New York, 1977.

Brear, Holly Beachley. *Inherit the Alamo: Myth and Ritual at an American Shrine*. Austin, Tex., 1995.

Brooks, Aubrey Lee. *A Southern Lawyer: Fifty Years at the Bar*. Chapel Hill, N.C., 1950.

Brooks, Thomas R. *Walls Come Tumbling Down: A History of the Civil Rights Movement, 1940–1970*. Englewood Cliffs, N.J., 1974.

Brown, James Seay, Jr., ed. *Up before Daylight: Life Histories from the Alabama Writers' Project, 1938–1939*. Tuscaloosa, Ala., 1997.

Brown, Sarah Hart. *Standing against Dragons: Three Southern Lawyers in an Era of Fear.* Baton Rouge, La., 1998.

Brown, Walter J. *James F. Byrnes of South Carolina: A Remembrance.* Macon, Ga., 1992.

Brunn, Stanley D. *Geography and Politics in America.* New York, 1974.

Buenger, Walter L. *The Path to a Modern South: Northeast Texas between Reconstruction and the Great Depression.* Austin, Tex., 2001.

Buenger, Walter L., and Robert A. Calvert. *Texas through Time: Evolving Interpretations.* College Station, Tex., 1991.

Burk, Robert Fredrick. *The Eisenhower Administration and Black Civil Rights.* Knoxville, Tenn., 1985.

Burner, David. *John F. Kennedy and a New Generation.* Glenview, Ill., 1988.

Burns, James MacGregor. *Roosevelt: The Soldier of Freedom, 1940–1945.* New York, 1970.

Butler, Lindley S., and Alan D. Watson, eds. *The North Carolina Experience: An Interpretive and Documentary History.* Chapel Hill, N.C., 1984.

Buttimer, Anne, and David Seamon, eds. *The Human Experience of Space and Place.* New York, 1980.

Button, James W. *Black Violence: Political Impact of the 1960s Riots.* Princeton, N.J., 1978.

Byrnes, James F. *All in One Lifetime.* New York, 1958.

Califano, Joseph A., Jr. *The Triumph and Tragedy of Lyndon Johnson: The White House Years.* New York, 1991.

Caplan, Marvin. *Farther Along: A Civil Rights Memoir.* Baton Rouge, La., 1999.

Carlson, Jody. *George C. Wallace and the Politics of Powerlessness: The Wallace Campaigns for the Presidency, 1964–1976.* New Brunswick, N.J., 1981.

Carlton, David L., and Peter A. Coclanis. *Confronting Southern Poverty in the Great Depression: The Report on Economic Conditions of the South with Related Documents.* Boston, 1996.

———, eds. *The South, the Nation, and the World: Perspectives on Southern Economic Development.* Charlottesville, Va., 2003.

Carlyle, Thomas. *On Heroes, Hero-Worship and the Heroic in History.* London, 1841.

Carmichael, Donald Scott, ed. *F.D.R. Columnist: The Uncollected Columns of Franklin D. Roosevelt.* Chicago, 1947.

Caro, Robert A. *The Years of Lyndon Johnson: Master of the Senate.* New York, 2002.

———. *The Years of Lyndon Johnson: Means of Ascent.* New York, 1990.

————. *The Years of Lyndon Johnson: The Path to Power.* New York, 1982.

Carpenter, Liz. *Ruffles and Flourishes.* Garden City, N.Y., 1970.

Carr, Robert K. *Federal Protection of Civil Rights: Quest for a Sword.* Ithaca, N.Y., 1947.

Carson, Clayborne. *In Struggle: SNCC and the Black Awakening of the 1960s.* Cambridge, Mass., 1981.

Carter, Dan. *From George Wallace to Newt Gingrich: Race in the Conservative Counterrevolution, 1963–1994.* Baton Rouge, La., 1996.

————. *The Politics of Rage: George Wallace, the Origins of the New Conservatism, and the Transformation of American Politics.* New York, 1995.

Carter, Hodding. *The South Strikes Back.* Garden City. N.Y., 1959.

Carter, Jimmy. *An Hour before Daylight: Memories of a Rural Boyhood.* New York, 2001.

————. *Keeping Faith: Memoirs of a President.* New York, 1982.

————. *Southern Legacy.* Baton Rouge, La., 1950.

————. *Why Not the Best?* Nashville, Tenn., 1975.

Casdorph, Paul. *A History of the Republican Party in Texas, 1865–1965.* Austin, Tex., 1965.

Cash, W. J. *The Mind of the South.* New York, 1960; 1st ed., 1941.

Champagne, Anthony. *Congressman Sam Rayburn,* New Brunswick, N.J., 1984.

Chandler, David Leon. *The Natural Superiority of Southern Politicians: A Revisionist History.* Garden City, N.Y., 1977.

Chappell, David L. *Inside Agitators: White Southerners in the Civil Rights Movement.* Baltimore, 1994.

Chester, Lewis, Godfrey Hodgson, and Bruce Page. *An American Melodrama: The Presidential Campaign of 1968.* New York, 1969.

Christensen, Paul. *West of the American Dream: An Encounter with Texas.* College Station, Tex., 2001.

Clark, Roy Peter, and Raymond Arsenault, eds. *The Changing South of Gene Patterson: Journalism and Civil Rights, 1960–1968.* Gainesville, Fla., 2002.

Clark, Thomas D. *The Emerging South.* New York, 1961.

Clark, Thomas D., and Albert D. Kirwan. *The South since Appomattox: A Century of Regional Change.* New York, 1967.

Claunch, John M., ed. *The 1964 Presidential Election in the Southwest.* Dallas, Tex., 1966.

Clayton, Bruce, and John A. Salmond, eds. *Debating Southern History: Ideas and Action in the Twentieth Century.* New York, 1999.

————, eds. *The South Is Another Land: Essays on the Twentieth-Century South.* Westport, Conn., 1987.

Clendinen, Dudley, ed. *The Prevailing South: Life and Politics in a Changing Culture.* Atlanta, 1988.

Clifford, Clark, with Richard Holbrooke. *Counsel to the President: A Memoir.* New York, 1991.

Clowse, Barbara Barksdale. *Ralph McGill: A Biography.* Macon, Ga., 1998.

Cobb, James C. *Industrialization and Southern Society, 1877–1984.* Lexington, Ky., 1984.

————. *The Most Southern Place on Earth: The Mississippi Delta and the Roots of Regional Identity.* New York, 1992.

————. *Redefining Southern Culture: Mind and Identity in the Modern South.* Athens, Ga., 1999.

————. *The Selling of the South: The Southern Crusade for Industrial Development, 1936–1980.* Baton Rouge, La., 1982.

Cobb, James C., and Michael Namorato, eds. *The New Deal and the South.* Jackson, Miss., 1984.

Cobb, James C., and Charles R. Wilson, eds. *Perspectives on the American South: An Annual Review of Society, Politics, and Culture.* Vol. 4. New York, 1987.

Cochran, Augustus B., III. *Democracy Heading South: National Politics in the Shadow of Dixie.* Lawrence, Kans., 2001.

Cochran, Bert. *Harry Truman and the Crisis Presidency.* New York, 1973.

Cohodas, Nadine. *Strom Thurmond and the Politics of Southern Change.* New York, 1993.

Cole, Taylor, and John H. Hallowell, eds. *The Southern Political Scene, 1938–1948.* Gainesville, Fla., 1948.

Collins, Charles Wallace. *Whither Solid South? A Study in Politics and Race Relations.* New Orleans, 1947.

Conaway, James. *Judge: The Life and Times of Leander Perez.* New York, 1973.

————. *The Texans.* New York, 1976.

Conkin, Paul K. *Big Daddy from the Pedernales: Lyndon Baines Johnson.* Boston, 1986.

————. *The Southern Agrarians.* Knoxville, Tenn., 1988.

Connally, John, with Mickey Herskowitz. *In History's Shadow: An American Odyssey.* New York, 1993.

Connelly, Thomas L., and Barbara L. Bellows. *God and General Longstreet: The Lost Cause and the Southern Mind.* Baton Rouge, La., 1982.

Conrad, David E. *The Forgotten Farmers: The Story of Sharecroppers in the New Deal.* Westport, Conn., 1982.

Conroy, Pat. *The Prince of Tides.* New York, 1986.

Cook, Blanche Wiesen. *Eleanor Roosevelt, Volume 1, 1884–1933.* New York, 1992.

Cooke, Alistair. *Talk about America.* New York, 1968.

Cooper, William J., Jr., and Thomas E. Terrill. *The American South: A History.* New York, 1990.

Core, George, ed. *Southern Fiction Today: Renascence and Beyond.* Athens, Ga., 1969.

Cormier, Frank. *LBJ: The Way He Was.* Garden City, N.Y., 1977.

Cosman, Bernard. *Five States for Goldwater: Continuity and Change in Southern Presidential Voting Patterns.* University, Ala., 1966.

Cosman, Bernard, and Robert J. Huckshorn, eds. *Republican Politics: The 1964 Campaign and Its Aftermath for the Party.* New York, 1968.

Cotner, Robert C., et al. *Texas Cities and the Great Depression.* Austin, Tex., 1973.

Couch, W. T., ed. *Culture in the South.* Chapel Hill, N.C., 1934.

Covington, Howard E., Jr., and Marion A. Ellis. *Terry Sanford: Politics, Progress, and Outrageous Ambitions.* Durham, N.C., 1999.

Cowger, Thomas W., and Sherwin J. Markham, eds. *Lyndon Johnson Remembered: An Intimate Portrait of the Presidency.* Lanham, Md., 2003.

Cox, Patrick. *Ralph W. Yarborough: The People's Senator.* Austin, Tex., 2001.

Crawford, Ann Fears. *Frankie: Mrs. R. D. Randolph and Texas Liberal Politics.* Austin, Tex., 2000.

Crawford, Ann Fears, and Jack Keever. *John B. Connally: Portrait in Power.* Austin, Tex., 1973.

Crawford, Vicki L., Jacqueline Anne Rouse, and Barbara Woods, eds. *Women in the Civil Rights Movement: Trailblazers and Torchbearers, 1941–1965.* Bloomington, Ind., 1990.

Crispell, Brian Lewis. *Testing the Limits: George Armistead Smathers and Cold War America.* Athens, Ga., 1999.

Critchlow, Donald T., and Ellis W. Hawley, eds. *Federal Social Policy: The Historical Dimension.* University Park, Pa., 1988.

Cummings, Milton C., Jr., ed. *The National Election of 1964.* Washington, D.C., 1966.

Current, Richard N. *Northernizing the South.* Athens, Ga., 1983.

Dabbs, James McBride. *Who Speaks for the South?* New York, 1964.

Dabney, Virginius. *Across the Years: Memories of a Virginian.* Garden City, N.Y., 1978.

———. *Below the Potomac: A Book about the New South.* New York, 1942.

Dailey, Jane, Glenda Elizabeth Gilmore, and Bryant Simon, eds. *Jumpin' Jim Crow: Southern Politics from Civil War to Civil Rights.* Princeton, N.J., 2000.

Dalfiume, Richard M. *Desegregation of the U.S. Armed Forces: Fighting on Two Fronts, 1939–1953.* Columbia, Mo., 1969.

Dallek, Robert. *Flawed Giant: Lyndon Johnson and His Times, 1961–1973.* New York, 1998.

———. *Lone Star Rising: Lyndon Johnson and His Times, 1908–1960.* New York, 1991.

Danese, Tracy E. *Claude Pepper and Ed Ball: Politics, Purpose, and Power.* Gainesville, Fla., 2000.

Daniel, Clete. *Chicano Workers and the Politics of Fairness: The FEPC in the Southwest, 1941–1945.* Austin, Tex., 1991.

Daniel, Pete. *Breaking the Land: The Transformation of Cotton, Tobacco, and Rice Cultures since 1880.* Urbana, Ill., 1985.

———. *Standing at the Crossroads: Southern Life since 1900.* New York, 1986.

Daniels, Jonathan. *Frontier on the Potomac.* New York, 1946.

———. *The Man of Independence.* Philadelphia, 1950.

———. *A Southerner Discovers the South.* New York, 1938.

Daniels, Josephus. *Shirt-Sleeve Diplomat.* Chapel Hill, N.C., 1947.

———. *The Wilson Era: Years of Peace, 1910–1917.* Chapel Hill, N.C. 1944.

Davenport, F. Garwin, Jr. *The Myth of Southern History: Historical Consciousness in Twentieth-Century Southern Literature.* Nashville, Tenn., 1970.

David, Paul T., ed. *Presidential Nominating Politics in 1952: The South.* Baltimore, 1954.

Davidson, Chandler. *Biracial Politics: Conflict and Coalition in the Metropolitan South.* Baton Rouge, La., 1972.

———. *Race and Class in Texas Politics.* Princeton, N.J. 1990.

Davidson, Chandler, and Bernard Grofman, eds. *Quiet Revolution in the South: The Impact of the Voting Rights Act, 1965–1990.* Princeton, N.J., 1994.

Davidson, James West, and Mark Hamilton Lytle. *After the Fact: The Art of Historical Detection.* New York, 1982.

Davie, Michael. *LBJ: A Foreign Observer's Viewpoint.* New York, 1966.

Davis, Kenneth S. *FDR: The Beckoning of Destiny.* New York, 1972.

Degler, Carl. *Place over Time: The Continuity of Southern Distinctiveness.* Baton Rouge, 1977.

Dent, Harry S. *The Prodigal South Returns to Power.* New York, 1978.

De Voto, Bernard. *Year of Decision, 1846.* Boston, 1943.

Dierenfield, Bruce J. *Keeper of the Rules: Congressman Howard W. Smith of Virginia.* Charlottesville, Va., 1987.

Dillard, Annie. *An American Childhood.* In *Three by Annie Dillard.* New York, 1990.

Dittmer, John. *Local People: The Struggle for Civil Rights in Mississippi.* Urbana, Ill., 1994.

Donahoe, Bernard F. *Private Plans and Public Dangers.* Notre Dame, Ind., 1965.

Donaldson, Gary A. *Truman Defeats Dewey.* Lexington, Ky., 1998.

Donovan, Robert J. *Conflict and Crisis: The Presidency of Harry S. Truman, 1945–1948.* New York, 1977.

———. *Tumultuous Years: The Presidency of Harry S. Truman, 1949–1953.* New York, 1982.

Dorsett, Lyle W. *Franklin D. Roosevelt and the City Bosses.* Port Washington, N.Y., 1977.

Doyle, Don H. *Nashville since the 1920s.* Knoxville, Tenn., 1985.

Draper, Alan. *Conflict of Interests: Organized Labor and the Civil Rights Movement in the South, 1954–1968.* Ithaca, N.Y., 1994.

Drury, Allen. *A Senate Journal, 1943–1945.* New York, 1963.

Dudziak, Mary L. *Cold War Civil Rights: Race and the Image of American Democracy.* Princeton, N.J., 2000.

Dugger, Ronnie. *The Politician.* New York, 1982.

Dulaney, W. Marvin, and Kathleen Underwood, eds. *Essays on the American Civil Rights Movement by John Dittmer, George C. Wright, and W. Marvin Dulaney.* College Station, Tex., 1993.

Dunbar, Anthony P. (Tony). *Against the Grain: Southern Radicals and Prophets, 1929–1959.* Charlottesville, Va., 1981.

———. *Delta Time: A Journey through Mississippi.* New York, 1990.

Dunbar, Leslie W. *A Republic of Equals.* Ann Arbor, Mich., 1966.

Dunn, Joe P., and Howard L. Preston, eds. *The Future South: A Historical Perspective for the Twenty-first Century.* Urbana, Ill., 1991.

Dykeman, Wilma, and James Stokely. *Seeds of Southern Change: The Life of Will Alexander.* Chicago, 1962.

Eagles, Charles W. *Jonathan Daniels and Race Relations: The Evolution of a Southern Liberal.* Knoxville, Tenn., 1982.

———, ed. *The Civil Rights Movement in America.* Jackson, Miss., 1986.

Earle, Carville. *The American Way: A Geographical History of Crisis and Recovery.* Lanham, Md., 2003.

———. *Geographical Inquiry and American Historical Problems.* Stanford, Calif., 1992.

Edelman, Murray. *The Symbolic Uses of Politics.* Urbana, Ill., 1964.

Edsall, Thomas Byrne, with Mary D. Edsall. *Chain Reaction: The Impact of Race, Rights, and Taxes on American Politics.* New York, 1992.

Edwards, India. *Pulling No Punches: Memoirs of a Woman in Politics.* New York, 1977.

Edwards, Lee. *Goldwater: The Man Who Made a Revolution.* Washington, D.C., 1995.

Egerton, John. *The Americanization of Dixie: The Southernization of America.* New York, 1974.

———. *A Mind to Stay Here: Profiles from the South.* New York, 1970.

———. *Shades of Gray: Dispatches from the Modern South.* Baton Rouge, La., 1991.

———. *Speak Now against the Day: The Generation before the Civil Rights Movement in the South.* New York, 1994.

Ehle, John. *The Free Men.* New York, 1965.

Elliff, John Thomas. *The United States Department of Justice and Individual Rights, 1937–1962.* New York, 1987.

Elliott, Carl, Sr., and Michael D'Orso. *The Cost of Courage: The Journey of an American Congressman.* New York, 1992.

Ely, James W. *The Crisis of Conservative Virginia: The Byrd Organization and the Politics of Massive Resistance.* Knoxville, Tenn., 1976.

Emmerich, J. Oliver. *Two Faces of Janus: The Saga of Deep South Change.* Jackson, Miss., 1973.

Engler, Robert. *The Politics of Oil.* New York, 1961.

Evans, Rowland, and Robert D. Novak. *Lyndon B. Johnson: The Exercise of Power.* New York, 1966.

Evers, Charles. *Evers.* New York, 1971.

Faber, Harold, ed. *The Road to the White House: The Story of the 1964 Election by the Staff of the New York Times.* New York, 1965.

Facts on File. *1964 News Dictionary.* New York, 1965.

Fairclough, Adam. *To Redeem the Soul of America: The Southern Christian Leadership Conference and Martin Luther King, Jr.* Athens, Ga., 1987.

Farley, James A. *Behind the Ballots: The Personal History of a Politician.* New York, 1938.

————. *Jim Farley's Story: The Roosevelt Years.* New York, 1948.

Farmer, James. *Lay Bare the Heart: An Autobiography of the Civil Rights Movement.* New York, 1985.

Farrell, John Aloysius. *Tip O'Neill and the Democratic Century.* Boston, 2001.

Faubus, Orval Eugene. *Down from the Hills.* Little Rock, Ark., 1980.

Faulkner, John. *My Brother Bill: An Affectionate Reminiscence.* New York, 1963.

Federal Writers' Project. *These Are Our Lives: As Told by the People and Written by Members of the Federal Writers' Project of the Works Progress Administration in North Carolina, Tennessee, and Georgia.* Chapel Hill, N.C., 1939.

Feldman, Glenn. *From Demagogue to Dixiecrat: Horace Wilkinson and the Politics of Race.* Lanham, Md., 1995.

————. *Politics, Society, and the Klan in Alabama, 1915–1949.* Tuscaloosa, Ala., 1999.

Fenton, John H. *Politics in the Border States: A Study of the Patterns of Political Organization, and Political Change, Common to the Border States: Maryland, West Virginia, Kentucky and Missouri.* New Orleans, 1957.

Ferguson, Karen. *Black Politics in New Deal Atlanta.* Chapel Hill, N.C., 2002.

Ferrell, Robert H. *Choosing Truman: The Democratic Convention of 1944.* Columbia, Mo., 1994.

————. *The Dying President: Franklin D. Roosevelt, 1944–1945.* Columbia, Mo., 1998.

————. *Harry S. Truman: A Life.* Columbia, Mo., 1994.

————. *Harry S. Truman and the Modern American Presidency.* Boston, 1983.

————. *Truman and Pendergast.* Columbia, Mo., 1999.

————, ed. *The Autobiography of Harry S. Truman.* Boulder, Colo., 1980.

————, ed. *Dear Bess: The Letters from Harry to Bess Truman, 1910–1959.* New York, 1983.

————, ed. *Off the Record: The Private Papers of Harry S. Truman.* New York, 1980.

————, ed. *Truman in the White House: The Diary of Eben A. Ayers.* Columbia, Mo., 1991.

Fifteen Southerners. *Why the South Will Survive.* Athens, Ga., 1981.

Finan, Christopher M. *Alfred E. Smith: The Happy Warrior.* New York, 2002.

Firestone, Bernard J., and Robert C. Vogt, eds. *Lyndon Baines Johnson and the Uses of Power.* New York, 1988.

Fite, Gilbert C. *Cotton Fields No More: Southern Agriculture, 1865–1980.* Lexington, Ky., 1984.

————. *Richard B. Russell, Jr.: Senator from Georgia.* Chapel Hill, N.C., 1991.

Fitzpatrick, Vincent. *Gerald Johnson: From Southern Liberal to National Conscience.* Baton Rouge, La., 2002.

Flamming, Douglas. *Creating the Modern South: Millhands and Managers in Dalton, Georgia, 1884–1984.* Chapel Hill, N.C., 1992.

Fleming, Harold C., with Virginia Fleming. *The Potomac Chronicle: Public Policy and Civil Rights from Kennedy to Reagan.* Athens, Ga., 1996.

Flemmons, Jerry. *Amon: The Life of Amon Carter, Sr. of Texas.* Austin, Tex., 1978.

Fletcher, Martin. *Almost Heaven: Travels through the Backwoods of America.* London, 1998.

Flynt, Wayne. *Poor but Proud: Alabama's Poor Whites.* Tuscaloosa, Ala., 1989.

Foner, Eric, ed. *The New American History.* Philadelphia, 1990.

Fontenay, Charles L. *Estes Kefauver: A Biography.* Knoxville, Tenn., 1980.

Forman, James. *The Making of Black Revolutionaries.* New York, 1972.

Foucault, Michel. *Power/Knowledge: Selected Interviews and Other Writings.* Edited by Colin Gordon. New York, 1980.

Fox-Genovese, Elizabeth, and Eugene D. Genovese. *Fruits of Merchant Capital: Slavery and Bourgeois Property in the Rise and Expansion of Capitalism.* New York, 1983.

Frady, Marshall. *Southerners: A Journalist's Odyssey.* New York, 1980.

————. *Wallace.* Enlarged and updated edition. New York, 1976.

Franklin, Jimmie Lewis. *Back to Birmingham: Richard Arrington, Jr. and His Times.* Tuscaloosa, Ala., 1989.

Franklin, John Hope, and Genna Rae McNeil, eds. *African Americans and the Living Constitution.* Washington, D.C., 1995.

Franklin, Wayne, and Michael Steiner, eds. *Mapping American Culture.* Iowa City, Iowa, 1992.

Fraser, Walter J., Jr., and Winfred B. Moore, Jr., eds. *From the Old South to the New: Essays on the Transitional South.* Westport, Conn., 1981.

Frederickson, Kari. *The Dixiecrat Revolt and the End of the Solid South, 1932–1968.* Chapel Hill, N.C., 2001.

Freidel, Frank. *F.D.R. and the South.* Baton Rouge, La., 1965.

———. *Franklin D. Roosevelt: The Apprenticeship.* Boston, 1952.

———. *Franklin D. Roosevelt: The Ordeal.* Boston, 1954.

———. *Franklin D. Roosevelt: A Rendezvous with Destiny.* Boston, 1990.

———. *Franklin D. Roosevelt: The Triumph.* Boston, 1956.

Fuermann, George. *Reluctant Empire.* Garden City, N.Y., 1957.

Fuller, Helen. *Year of Trial: Kennedy's Crucial Decisions.* New York, 1962.

Gaddis, John Lewis. *The Landscape of History: How Historians Map the Past.* New York, 2002.

Galbraith, John Kenneth. *A View from the Stands: Of People, Politics, Military Power and the Arts.* Boston, 1986.

Gallagher, Hugh Gregory. *FDR's Splendid Deception.* New York, 1985.

Gardner, Michael R. *Harry Truman and Civil Rights: Moral Courage and Political Risks.* Carbondale, Ill., 2002.

Garreau, Joel. *The Nine Nations of North America.* Boston, 1981.

Garrow, David J. *Protest at Selma: Martin Luther King, Jr., and the Voting Rights Act of 1965.* New Haven, Conn., 1978.

Garson, Barbara. *MacBird!* New York, 1967.

Garson, Robert A. *The Democratic Party and the Politics of Sectionalism, 1941–1948.* Baton Rouge, La., 1974.

Gastil, Raymond D. *Cultural Regions of the United States.* Seattle, 1975.

Gaston, Paul M. *The New South Creed: A Study in Southern Mythmaking.* New York, 1970.

Gay, Peter. *Voltaire's Politics: The Poet as Realist.* Princeton, N.J., 1959.

Genovese, Eugene. *The Political Economy of Slavery: Studies in the Economy and Society of the Slave South.* Middletown, Conn., 1989.

Germond, Jack W. *Fat Man in a Middle Seat: Forty Years of Covering Politics.* New York, 1999.

Geyelin, Philip. *Lyndon B. Johnson and the World.* New York, 1966.

Giangreco, D. M., and Kathryn Moore. *Dear Harry . . . Truman's Mailroom, 1945–1953: The Truman Administration through Correspondence with "Everyday Americans."* Mechanicsburg, Pa., 1999.

Gilder, George F., and Bruce K. Chapman. *The Party That Lost Its Head.* New York, 1966.

Gillon, Steven M. *The Democrats' Dilemma: Walter F. Mondale and the Liberal Legacy.* New York, 1992.

———. *Politics and Vision: The ADA and American Liberalism, 1947–1985.* New York, 1987.

Gladney, Margaret Rose, ed. *How Am I to Be Heard?: Letters of Lillian Smith.* Chapel Hill, N.C., 1993.

Goldberg, Richard Thayer. *The Making of Franklin D. Roosevelt: Triumph over Disability.* Cambridge, Mass., 1981.

Goldberg, Robert Alan. *Barry Goldwater.* New Haven, Conn., 1995.

Goldfield, David R. *Black, White, and Southern: Race Relations and Southern Culture, 1940 to the Present.* Baton Rouge, La., 1990.

———. *Cotton Fields and Skyscrapers: Southern City and Region, 1607–1980.* Baton Rouge, La., 1982.

———. *Promised Land: The South since 1945.* Arlington Heights, Ill., 1987.

———. *Still Fighting the Civil War: The American South and Southern History.* Baton Rouge, La., 2002.

Goldman, Eric F. *The Crucial Decade—And After: America 1945–1960.* New York, 1960.

———. *Rendezvous with Destiny.* New York, 1952.

———. *The Tragedy of Lyndon Johnson.* New York, 1969.

Goldman, Peter. *Report from Black America.* New York, 1970.

Goldsmith, John A. *Colleagues: Richard B. Russell and His Apprentice, Lyndon B. Johnson.* Washington, D.C., 1993.

Goldwater, Barry M. *The Conscience of a Conservative.* Shepherdsville, Ky., 1960.

———. *With No Apologies: The Personal and Political Memoirs of United States Senator Barry M. Goldwater.* New York, 1979.

Goldwater, Barry M., with Jack Casserly. *Goldwater.* New York, 1988.

Goodman, James. *Stories of Scottsboro.* New York, 1994.

Goodman, Paul. *Utopian Essays and Practical Proposals.* New York, 1962.

Goodwin, Richard N. *Remembering America: A Voice from the Sixties.* Boston, 1988.

Goodwyn, Frank. *Lone-Star Land: Twentieth-Century Texas in Perspective.* New York, 1955.

Gore, Albert. *Let the Glory Out: My South and Its Politics.* New York, 1972.

Gosnell, Harold F. *Truman's Crises: A Political Biography of Harry S. Truman.* Westport, Conn., 1980.

Gould, Lewis W. *1968: The Election that Changed America.* Chicago, 1993.

Goulden, Joseph C., ed. *Mencken's Last Campaign: H. L. Mencken on the 1948 Election.* Washington, D.C., 1976.

Graham, Hugh Davis. *The Civil Rights Era: Origins and Development of National Policy, 1960–1972.* New York, 1990.

———. *Crisis in Print: Desegregation and the Press in Tennessee.* Nashville, Tenn., 1967.

Graham, Katharine. *Personal History.* New York, 1997.

Grant, Donald L. *The Way It Was in the South: The Black Experience in Georgia.* Edited by Jonathan Grant. New York, 1993.

Grant, Nancy L. *TVA and Black Americans: Planning for the Status Quo.* Philadelphia, 1990.

Grantham, Dewey W., Jr. *The Democratic South.* Athens, Ga., 1963.

———. *The Life and Death of the Solid South: A Political History.* Lexington, Ky., 1988.

———. *The Regional Imagination: The South and Recent American History.* Nashville, Tenn., 1979.

———. *The South in Modern America: A Region at Odds.* New York, 1994.

Graves, John Temple. *The Fighting South.* New York, 1943.

Gray, Richard. *Southern Aberrations: Writers of the American South and the Problem of Regionalism.* Baton Rouge, La., 2000.

———. *Writing the South: Ideas of an American Region.* Cambridge, 1986.

Greeley, Andrew M. *Ethnicity in the United States: A Preliminary Reconnaissance.* New York, 1974.

Green, Ben. *Before His Time: The Untold Story of Harry Moore, America's First Civil Rights Martyr.* New York, 1999.

Green, Constance McLaughlin. *The Secret City: A History of Race Relations in the Nation's Capital.* Princeton, N.J., 1967.

Green, George Norris. *The Establishment in Texas Politics: The Primitive Years, 1938–1957.* Westport, Conn., 1979.

Greenberg, Cheryl Lynn, ed. *A Circle of Trust: Remembering SNCC.* New Brunswick, N.J., 1998.

Greenberg, Polly. *The Devil Has Slippery Shoes: A Biased Biography of the Child Development Group of Mississippi.* New York, 1969.

Greene, A. C. *Dallas U.S.A.* Austin, Tex., 1984.

Greene, John Robert. *The Crusade: The Presidential Election of 1952.* Lanham, Md., 1985.

———. *The Presidency of George Bush.* Lawrence, Kans., 2000.

Greenhaw, Wayne. *Elephants in the Cottonfields: Ronald Reagan and the New Republican South.* New York, 1982.

Greer, Thomas H. *What Roosevelt Thought: The Social and Political Ideas of Franklin D. Roosevelt.* East Lansing, Mich., 1958.

Gregg, Josiah. *Commerce of the Prairies.* Edited by Max L. Moorhead. Norman, Okla., 1954.

Gretlund, Jan Nordby, ed. *The Southern State of Mind.* Columbia, S.C., 1999.

Griffith, Louis Turner, and John Erwin Talmadge. *Georgia Journalism, 1763–1950.* Athens, Ga., 1951.

Grofman, Bernard. *Legacies of the 1964 Civil Rights Act.* Charlottesville, Va., 2000.

Grubbs, Donald H. *Cry from the Cotton: The Southern Tenant Farmers' Union and the New Deal.* Chapel Hill, N.C., 1971.

Gunther, John. *Inside U.S.A.* New York, 1947.

Halberstam, David. *The Best and the Brightest.* New York, 1972; rev. ed., 2001.

———. *The Powers That Be.* New York, 1979.

Haley, J. Evetts. *A Texan Looks at Lyndon: A Study in Illegitimate Power.* Canyon, Tex., 1964.

Hall, Jacquelyn Dowd. *Revolt against Chivalry: Jessie Daniel Ames and the Women's Campaign against Lynching.* New York, 1979.

Hamby, Alonzo L. *Beyond the New Deal: Harry S. Truman and American Liberalism.* New York, 1973.

———. *For the Survival of Democracy: Franklin Roosevelt and the World Crisis of the 1930s.* New York, 2004.

———. *Man of the People: The Life of Harry S. Truman.* New York, 1995.

Hamilton, Virginia Van Der Veer. *Hugo Black: The Alabama Years.* Baton Rouge, La., 1972.

———. *Lister Hill: Statesman from the South.* Chapel Hill, N.C., 1987.

Hampton, Henry, and Steve Fayer, eds., with Sarah Flynn. *Voices of Freedom: An Oral History of the Civil Rights Movement from the 1950s through the 1980s.* New York, 1990.

Hardeman, D. B., and Donald C. Bacon. *Rayburn: A Biography.* Austin, Tex., 1987.

Hareven, Tamara K. *Eleanor Roosevelt: An American Conscience.* New York, 1975.

Harris, J. William. *Deep Souths: Delta, Piedmont, and Sea Island Society in the Age of Segregation.* Baltimore, 2001.

Harris, Seale. *Death of National Democratic Party: The Truth About Truman Big-City-Machine-Labor-Socialist Party.* Birmingham, Ala., 1952.

Hartmann, Susan M. *Truman and the 80th Congress.* Columbia, Mo., 1971.

Harvey, James C. *Black Civil Rights during the Johnson Administration.* Jackson, Miss., 1973.

Harwell, Richard, ed. *Margaret Mitchell's Gone With the Wind Letters*. New York, 1976.

Harwood, Richard, and Haynes Johnson. *Lyndon*. New York, 1973.

Hassett, William D. *Off the Record with F.D.R., 1942–1945*. New Brunswick, N.J., 1958.

Havard, William C., ed. *The Changing Politics of the South*. Baton Rouge, La., 1972.

Hayes, Jack Irby, Jr. *Dan Daniel and the Persistence of Conservatism in Virginia*. Macon, Ga., 1997.

Haynes, Williams. *Southern Horizons*. New York, 1946.

Hays, Brooks. *Politics Is My Parish*. Baton Rouge, La., 1981.

———. *A Southern Moderate Speaks*. Chapel Hill, N.C., 1959.

Heard, Alexander. *A Two-Party South?* Chapel Hill, N.C., 1952.

Hechler, Ken. *Working with Truman: A Personal Memoir of the White House Years*. New York, 1982.

Heinemann, Ronald L. *Harry Byrd of Virginia*. Charlottesville, Va., 1996.

Heller, Francis H. *The Truman White House: The Administration of the Presidency, 1949–1953*. Lawrence, Kans., 1980.

Helm, William P. *Harry Truman: A Political Biography*. New York, 1947.

Hemphill, Paul. *Leaving Birmingham: Notes of a Native Son*. New York, 1993.

Henderson, Harold Paulk. *Ernest Vandiver: Governor of Georgia*. Athens, Ga., 2000.

———. *The Politics of Change in Georgia: A Political Biography of Ellis Arnall*. Athens, Ga., 1991.

Henderson, Richard B. *Maury Maverick: A Political Biography*. Austin, Tex., 1970.

Henry, Aaron, with Constance Curry. *The Fire Ever Burning*. Jackson, Miss., 2000.

Henson, Allen Lumpkin. *Red Galluses: A Story of Georgia Politics*. Boston, 1945.

Herbers, John. *The Lost Priority: What Happened to the Civil Rights Movement in America?* New York, 1970.

Heren, Louis. *No Hail, No Farewell*. New York, 1970.

Hesseltine, William B., and David L. Smiley. *The South in American History*. Englewood Cliffs, N.J., 1960.

Hevener, John W. *Which Side Are You On? The Harlan County Coal Miners, 1931–39*. Urbana, Ill., 1978.

Hewes, Laurence. *Boxcar in the Sand.* New York, 1957.

Higginbotham, Don. *George Washington: Uniting a Nation.* Lanham, Md., 2002.

Highsaw, Robert B., ed. *The Deep South in Transformation: A Symposium.* University, Ala., 1964.

Hill, Robert A., ed. *The FBI's RACON: Racial Conditions in the United States during World War II.* Boston, 1995.

Hilty, James W. *Robert Kennedy: Brother Protector.* Philadelphia, 1997.

Himes, Chester. *Lonely Crusade.* New York, 1947.

Hobson, Fred. *Tell About the South: The Southern Rage to Explain.* Baton Rouge, La., 1983.

——, ed. *South-Watching: Selected Essays by Gerald W. Johnson.* Chapel Hill, N.C., 1983.

Hodges, James A. *New Deal Labor Policy and the Southern Cotton Textile Industry, 1933–1941.* Knoxville, Tenn., 1986.

Hofstadter, Richard. *The Progressive Historians: Turner, Beard, Parrington.* New York, 1968.

Holley, Donald. *Uncle Sam's Farmers: The New Deal Communities in the Lower Mississippi Valley.* Urbana, Ill., 1975.

Hollis, Daniel Webster, III. *An Alabama Newspaper Tradition: Grover C. Hall and the Hall Family.* University, Ala., 1983.

Holloway, Harry. *The Politics of the Southern Negro: From Exclusion to Big City Organization.* New York, 1969.

Holmes, Michael S. *The New Deal in Georgia: An Administrative History.* Westport, Conn., 1975.

Hook, Sidney. *The Hero in History: A Study in Limitation and Possibility.* New York, 1943.

Hoover, Calvin B., and B. U. Ratchford. *Economic Resources and Policies of the South.* New York, 1951.

Howar, Barbara. *Laughing All the Way.* New York, 1973.

Howard, Donald S. *The WPA and Federal Relief Policy.* New York, 1943.

Howard, Perry H. *Political Tendencies in Louisiana.* Rev. and expanded ed. Baton Rouge, La., 1971.

Hughes, Emmet. *The Ordeal of Power.* New York, 1963.

Hull, Cordell. *The Memoirs of Cordell Hull.* New York, 1948.

Humes, James C. *My Fellow Americans: Presidential Addresses That Shaped History.* New York, 1992.

Humphrey, Hubert. *The Education of a Public Man.* New York, 1976.

Humphrey, William. *No Resting Place.* New York, 1989.

Hunter-Gault, Charlayne. *In My Place.* New York, 1992.

Hyatt, Richard. *Zell: The Governor Who Gave Georgia HOPE.* Macon, Ga., 1997.

Ickes, Harold L. *The Secret Diary of Harold L. Ickes.* 3 vols. New York, 1953–54.

Iggers, George. *The Social History of Politics: Critical Perspectives in West German Historical Writing since 1945.* New York, 1985.

Inscoe, John C., ed. *Georgia in Black and White: Explorations in the Race Relations of a Southern State, 1865–1950.* Athens, Ga., 1994.

Jackson, John Brinckerhoff. *The Southern Landscape Tradition in Texas.* Fort Worth, 1980.

Jacobs, Jane. *The Death and Life of Great American Cities.* New York, 1961.

Jacobs, Meg, William J. Novak, and Julian E. Zelizer, eds. *The Democratic Experiment: New Directions in American Political History.* Princeton, N.J., 2003.

Jacoway, Elizabeth, Dan T. Carter, Lester C. Lamon, and Robert C. McMath, Jr. *The Adaptable South: Essays in Honor of George Brown Tindall.* Baton Rouge, La., 1991.

Janken, Kenneth Robert. *White: The Biography of Walter White, Mr. NAACP.* New York, 2003.

Jeansonne, Glen. *Gerald L. K. Smith: Minister of Hate.* Baton Rouge, La., 1997.

———. *Leander Perez: Boss of the Delta.* Baton Rouge, La., 1977.

Jennings, Genelle. *Into the Jaws of Politics: The Charge of the Peanut Brigade.* Huntsville, Ala., 1979.

Johnson, Charles W., and Charles O. Jackson. *City Behind a Fence: Oak Ridge, Tennessee, 1942–1946.* Knoxville, Tenn., 1981.

Johnson, Haynes. *Divided We Fall: Gambling with History in the Nineties.* New York, 1994.

Johnson, James P. *The Politics of Soft Coal: The Bituminous Industry from World War I through the New Deal.* Urbana, Ill., 1979.

Johnson, Lyndon Baines. *A Time for Action: A Selection from the Speeches and Writings of Lyndon B. Johnson, 1953–64.* New York, 1964.

———. *The Vantage Point: Perspectives of the Presidency, 1963–1969.* New York, 1971.

Johnson, Rebekah Baines. *A Family Album.* New York, 1965.

Johnston, Erle. *Mississippi's Defiant Years, 1953–1973: An Interpretive Documentary with Personal Experiences.* Forest, Miss., 1990.

Jones, Eugene W., ed. *The Texas Country Editor: H. M. Baggarly Takes a Grass-Roots Look at National Politics.* Cleveland, Ohio, 1966.

Jones, Suzanne W., and Sharon Monteith, eds. *South to a New Place: Region, Literature, Culture.* Baton Rouge, La., 2002.

Kalman, Laura. *Abe Fortas: A Biography.* New Haven, Conn., 1990.

Kammen, Michael, ed. *The Past before Us: Contemporary Historical Writing.* Ithaca, N.Y., 1980.

Karabell, Zachary. *The Last Campaign: How Harry Truman Won the 1948 Election.* New York, 2000.

Kaufman, Burton I. *The Presidency of James Earl Carter, Jr.* Lawrence, Kans., 1993.

Kearns, Doris. *Lyndon Johnson and the American Dream.* New York, 1991.

Keever, Crawford. *John B. Connally: Portrait in Power.* Austin, Tex., 1973.

Kelley, Robin D. G. *Hammer and Hoe: Alabama Communists during the Great Depression.* Chapel Hill, N.C., 1990.

Kennedy, Stetson. *Southern Exposure.* Garden City, N.Y., 1946.

Kessel, John H. *The Goldwater Coalition: Republican Strategies in 1964.* Indianapolis, Ind., 1968.

Kesselman, Louis Coleridge. *The Social Politics of FEPC: A Study in Reform Pressure Movements.* Chapel Hill, N.C., 1948.

Key, V. O., Jr., with Alexander Heard. *Southern Politics in State and Nation.* New York, 1949.

Killian, Lewis M. *White Southerners.* Rev. ed. Amherst, Mass., 1985.

Kilpatrick, Carroll, ed. *Roosevelt and Daniels: A Friendship in Politics.* Chapel Hill, N.C., 1952.

Kinch, Sam, and Stuart Long. *Allan Shivers: The Pied Piper of Texas Politics.* Austin, Tex., 1973.

King, Mary. *Freedom Song: A Personal Story of the 1960s Civil Rights Movement.* New York, 1987.

King, Richard H. *A Southern Renaissance: The Cultural Awakening of the American South, 1930–1955.* New York, 1980.

Kirby, Jack Temple. *Media-made Dixie: The South in the American Imagination.* Athens, Ga., 1986.

———. *Rural Worlds Lost: The American South, 1920–1960.* Baton Rouge, La., 1987.

———. *Westmoreland Davis: Virginia Planter-Politician, 1859–1942.* Charlottesville, Va., 1968.

Kirby, John B. *Black Americans in the Roosevelt Era: Liberalism and Race.* Knoxville, Tenn., 1980.

Kirk, John A. *Redefining the Color Line: Black Activism in Little Rock, Arkansas, 1940–1970.* Gainesville, Fla., 2002.

Kirkendall, Richard S. *A History of Missouri, 1919 to 1953.* Columbia, Mo., 1986.

Klingman, Peter D. *Neither Dies nor Surrenders: A History of the Republican Party in Florida, 1867–1970.* Gainesville, Fla., 1984.

Klinkner, Philip A., with Rogers M. Smith. *The Unsteady March: The Rise and Decline of Racial Equality in America.* Chicago, 1999.

Kluger, Richard. *Simple Justice: The History of Brown v. Board of Education and Black America's Struggle for Equality.* New York, 1977.

Knaggs, John R. *Two-Party Texas: The John Tower Era, 1961–1984.* Austin, Tex., 1986.

Kneebone, John T. *Southern Liberal Journalists and the Issue of Race, 1920–1944.* Chapel Hill, N.C., 1986.

Knock, Thomas J. *To End All Wars: Woodrow Wilson and the Quest for a New World Order.* New York, 1992.

Kovenock, David M., et al. *Explaining the Vote: Presidential Choices in the Nation and States, 1968.* Chapel Hill, N.C., 1973.

Kraft, Joseph. *Profiles in Power.* New York, 1966.

Krueger, Thomas A. *And Promises to Keep: The Southern Conference for Human Welfare, 1938–1948.* Nashville, Tenn., 1967.

Lacey, Michael J., ed. *The Truman Presidency.* Cambridge, 1984.

Lachicotte, Alberta. *Rebel Senator: Strom Thurmond of South Carolina.* New York, 1967.

Lamis, Alexander P., ed. *Southern Politics in the 1990s.* Baton Rouge, La., 1999.

———. *The Two-Party South.* Expanded ed. New York, 1988.

Lander, Ernest, Jr. *A History of South Carolina, 1865–1960.* Chapel Hill, N.C., 1960.

Lander, Ernest McPherson, Jr., and Richard J. Calhoun, eds. *Two Decades of Change: The South since the Supreme Court Desegregation Decision.* Columbia, S.C., 1975.

Larson, Arthur. *Eisenhower: The President Nobody Knew.* New York, 1968.

Lash, Joseph P. *Dealers and Dreamers: A New Look at the New Deal.* New York, 1988.

———. *Eleanor and Franklin: The Story of Their Relationship, Based upon Eleanor Roosevelt's Private Papers.* New York, 1971.

Lauren, Paul Gordon. *Power and Prejudice: The Politics and Diplomacy of Racial Discrimination.* Boulder, Colo., 1988.

Lawrence, D. H. *Studies in Classic American Literature.* New York, 1923.

Lawson, R. Alan. *The Failure of Independent Liberalism, 1930–1941.* New York, 1971.

Lawson, Steven F. *Black Ballots: Voting Rights in the South, 1944–1969.* New York, 1976.

———. *Civil Rights Crossroads: Nation, Community, and the Black Freedom Struggle.* Lexington, Ky., 2003.

———. *In Pursuit of Power: Southern Blacks and Electoral Politics, 1965–1982.* New York, 1985.

Lea, James F., ed. *Contemporary Southern Politics.* Baton Rouge, La., 1988.

Lee, David D. *Tennessee in Turmoil: Politics in the Volunteer State, 1920–1932.* Memphis, Tenn., 1979.

Leidholdt, Alexander S. *Editor for Justice: The Life of Louis I. Jaffé.* Baton Rouge, La., 2002.

Lemann, Nicholas. *The Promised Land: The Great Migration and How It Changed America.* New York, 1991.

Lentz, Richard. *Symbols, the News Magazines, and Martin Luther King.* Baton Rouge, La., 1990.

Lerner, Max. *America as a Civilization: Life and Thought in the United States Today.* New York, 1957.

Lesher, Stephan. *George Wallace: American Populist.* Reading, Mass., 1994.

Leslie, Warren. *Dallas Public and Private.* New York, 1964.

Lester, Jim. *A Man for Arkansas: Sid McMath and the Southern Reform Tradition.* Little Rock, Ark., 1976.

Lester, Julius. *Look Out, Whitey! Black Power's Gon' Get Your Mama!* New York, 1968.

Leuchtenburg, William E. *In the Shadow of FDR: From Harry Truman to George W. Bush.* Ithaca, N.Y., 2001.

Lewis, David L. *King: A Critical Biography.* New York, 1970.

Lewis, John, with Michael D'Orso. *Walking with the Wind: A Memoir of the Movement.* New York, 1998.

Light, Paul C. *The President's Agenda: Domestic Policy Choice from Kennedy to Reagan.* Rev. ed. Baltimore, 1991.

Lilienthal, David E. *The Journals of David E. Lilienthal.* 7 vols. New York, 1964–83.

Lincoln, Evelyn. *Kennedy and Johnson.* New York, 1968.

Lind, Michael. *Made in Texas: George W. Bush and the Southern Takeover of American Politics.* New York, 2003.

Lippman, Theo, Jr. *The Squire of Warm Springs: FDR in Georgia, 1924–1945.* Chicago, 1977.

Lively, Robert A. *The South in Action: A Sectional Crusade against Freight Rate Discrimination.* Chapel Hill, N.C., 1949.

Lockridge, Ross. *Raintree County.* Boston, 1948.

Loevy, Robert D. *To End All Segregation: The Politics of the Passage of the Civil Rights Act of 1964.* Lanham, Md., 1990.

Loewen, James W., and Charles Sallis, eds. *Mississippi: Conflict and Change.* New York, 1974.

Logan, Rayford W., ed. *The Attitude of the Southern White Press toward Negro Suffrage, 1932–1940.* Washington, D.C., 1940.

Logue, Calvin M., and Howard Dorgan, eds. *The Oratory of Southern Demagogues.* Baton Rouge, La., 1981.

Lord, Walter. *The Past That Would Not Die.* New York, 1965.

———. *A Time to Stand.* New York, 1961.

Loveland, Anne C. *Lillian Smith: A Southerner Confronting the South.* Baton Rouge, La., 1986.

Lowitt, Richard, and Maurine Beasley, eds. *One Third of a Nation: Lorena Hickok Reports on the Great Depression.* Urbana, Ill., 1981.

Lubell, Samuel. *The Future of American Politics.* 3rd ed. New York, 1965.

———. *Revolt of the Moderates.* New York, 1956.

———. *White and Black: Test of a Nation.* New York, 1964.

Lumpkin, Katharine DuPre. *The South in Progress.* New York, 1940.

Lunch, William M. *The Nationalization of American Politics.* Berkeley, Calif., 1987.

Lutwack, Leonard. *The Role of Place in Literature.* Syracuse, N.Y., 1984.

Lutz, Francis Earle. *Richmond in World War II.* Richmond, Va., 1951.

MacDougall, Curtis D. *Gideon's Army.* New York, 1965.

MacGregor, Morris J., Jr. *Integration of the Armed Forces, 1940–1965.* Washington, D.C., 1981.

Maddox, Lester. *Speaking Out: The Autobiography of Lester Garfield Maddox.* Garden City, N.Y., 1975.

Maguire, Jack, ed. *A President's Country: A Guide to the Hill Country of Texas.* Austin, Tex., 1964.

Majors, William R. *The End of Arcadia: Gordon Browning and Tennessee Politics.* Memphis, Tenn., 1982.

Manchester, William. *The Death of a President, November 20–November 25, 1963.* New York, 1967.

———. *The Glory and the Dream: A Narrative History of America, 1932–1972.* Boston, 1974.

Maney, Patrick J. *The Roosevelt Presence: A Biography of Franklin Delano Roosevelt.* New York, 1992.

Mann, Robert. *The Walls of Jericho: Lyndon Johnson, Hubert Humphrey, Richard Russell and the Struggle for Civil Rights.* New York, 1996.

Marcus, Stanley. *Minding the Store: A Memoir.* Denton, Tex., 1974.

Margolis, Jon. *The Last Innocent Year: America in 1964: The Beginning of the "Sixties."* New York, 1999.

Martin, Harold H. *Ralph McGill, Reporter.* Boston, 1973.

Martin, John Bartlow. *Adlai Stevenson of Illinois: The Life of Adlai E. Stevenson.* Garden City, N.Y., 1976.

Martin, John Frederick. *Civil Rights and the Crisis of Liberalism: The Democratic Party, 1945–1976.* Boulder, Colo., 1979.

Matthews, Donald R., and James W. Prothro. *Negroes and the New Southern Politics.* New York, 1966.

Maverick, Maury. *A Maverick American.* New York, 1937.

McAdam, Doug. *Political Process and the Development of Black Insurgency, 1930–1970.* Chicago, 1982.

McCarthy, Eugene. *Up 'Til Now: A Memoir.* New York, 1987.

McCoy, Donald R., and Richard T. Ruetten. *Quest and Response: Minority Rights and the Truman Administration.* Lawrence, Kans., 1973.

McCullough, David. *Mornings on Horseback.* New York, 1981.

———. *Truman.* New York, 1992.

McDonald, Michael J., and John Muldowny. *TVA and the Dispossessed: The Resettlement of Population in the Norris Dam Area.* Knoxville, Tenn., 1982.

McDowell, Charles, Jr. *Campaign Fever.* New York, 1965.

McElvaine, Robert S. *The Great Depression: America, 1929–1941.* New York, 1984.

McGill, Ralph. *The South and the Southerner.* Boston, 1963.

McGuire, Phillip. *Taps for a Jim Crow Army: Letters from Black Soldiers in World War II.* Santa Barbara, Calif., 1983.

McIntire, Ross T. *White House Physician.* New York, 1946.

McJimsey, George. *The Presidency of Franklin Delano Roosevelt*. Lawrence, Kans., 2000.

McKay, Seth Shepard. *Texas and the Fair Deal, 1945–1952*. San Antonio, Tex., 1954.

———. *Texas Politics, 1906–1944: With Special Reference to the German Counties*. Lubbock, Tex., 1952.

———. *W. Lee O'Daniel and Texas Politics, 1938–1942*. Lubbock, Tex., 1944.

McKinney, John C., and Edgar T. Thompson, eds. *The South in Continuity and Change*. Durham, N.C., 1965.

McLaurin, Melton, and Michael Thomason. *Mobile: The Life and Times of a Great Southern City*. Woodland Hills, Calif., 1981.

McMahon, Kevin J. *Reconsidering Roosevelt on Race: How the Presidency Paved the Way for Brown*. Chicago, 2004.

McMillan, James E., ed. *The Ernest W. McFarland Papers: The United States Senate Years, 1940–1952*. Prescott, Ariz., 1995.

McMillen, Neil R. *The Citizens' Council: Organized Resistance to the Second Reconstruction, 1954–64*. Urbana, Ill., 1971.

———. *Dark Journey: Black Mississippians in the Age of Jim Crow*. Urbana, Ill., 1989.

———, ed. *Remaking Dixie: The Impact of World War II on the American South*. Jackson, Miss., 1997.

McNaughton, Frank, and Walter Hehmeyer. *This Man Truman*. New York, 1945.

McNeil, Genna Rae. *Groundwork: Charles Hamilton Houston and the Struggle for Civil Rights*. Philadelphia, 1983.

McPherson, Harry. *A Political Education*. Boston, 1972.

McWhorter, Diane. *Carry Me Home: Birmingham, Alabama, the Climactic Battle of the Civil Rights Revolution*. New York, 2001.

Merrill, Dennis K., ed. *Documentary History of the Truman Presidency*. Bethesda, Md., 1995.

Mershon, Sherie, and Steven Schlossman. *Foxholes and Color Lines: Desegregating the U.S. Armed Forces*. Baltimore, 1998.

Mertz, Paul E. *New Deal Policy and Southern Rural Poverty*. Baton Rouge, La., 1978.

Mezerik, A. G. *The Revolt of the South and the West*. New York, 1946.

Michener, James A. *Report of the County Chairman*. New York, 1961.

Michie, Allan A., and Frank Ryhlick. *Dixie Demagogues*. New York, 1939.

Miller, Francis Pickens. *Man from the Valley: Memoirs of a 20th-Century Virginian.* Chapel Hill, N.C., 1971.

Miller, Merle. *Lyndon: An Oral Biography.* New York, 1980.

———. *Plain Speaking: An Oral Biography of Harry S. Truman.* New York, 1974.

Miller, Richard Lawrence. *Truman: The Rise to Power.* New York, 1985.

Miller, William D. *Mr. Crump of Memphis.* Baton Rouge, La., 1964.

Miller, William "Fishbait," as told to Frances Spatz Leighton. *Fishbait: The Memoirs of the Congressional Doorkeeper.* Englewood Cliffs, N.J., 1977.

Miller, William Lee. *Yankee from Georgia: The Emergence of Jimmy Carter.* New York, 1978.

Millis, Walter, ed. *The Forrestal Diaries.* New York, 1951.

Mills, Kay. *This Little Light of Mine: The Life of Fannie Lou Hamer.* New York, 1993.

Mills, Nicolaus. *Like a Holy Crusade: Mississippi 1964—The Turning of the Civil Rights Movement in America.* Chicago, 1992.

Minton, John Dean. *The New Deal in Tennessee, 1932–1938.* New York, 1979.

Mitchell, Franklin D. *Harry S. Truman and the News Media: Contentious Relations, Belated Respect.* Columbia, Mo., 1998.

Molyneaux, Peter. *The South's Political Plight.* Dallas, Tex., 1948.

Montgomery, Ruth. *Mrs. LBJ.* New York, 1964.

Moon, Henry Lee. *Balance of Power: The Negro Vote.* Garden City, N.Y., 1949.

Mooney, Booth. *The Lyndon Johnson Story.* New York, 1964.

———. *The Politicians, 1945–1960.* Philadelphia, 1970.

———. *Roosevelt and Rayburn: A Political Partnership.* Philadelphia, 1971.

Moore, Winfred B., Jr., Joseph F. Tripp, and Lyon G. Tyler, Jr., eds. *Developing Dixie: Modernization in a Traditional Society.* New York, 1988.

Morgan, Chester M. *Redneck Liberal: Theodore G. Bilbo and the New Deal.* Baton Rouge, La., 1985.

Morgan, Ruth P. *The President and Civil Rights: Policy-Making by Executive Order.* New York, 1970.

Morris, Willie. *New York Days.* Boston, 1993.

———. *North Toward Home.* Boston, 1967.

———. *Terrains of the Heart and Other Essays on Home.* Oxford, Miss., 1981.

———, ed. *The South Today: 100 Years after Appomattox.* New York, 1965.

Morrison, Joseph L. *Governor O. Max Gardner: A Power in North Carolina and New Deal Washington.* Chapel Hill, N.C., 1971.

———. *Josephus Daniels: The Small-d Democrat.* Chapel Hill, N.C., 1966.

Mowry, George. *Another Look at the Twentieth-Century South*. Baton Rouge, La., 1973.

Murphy, Reg, and Hal Gulliver. *The Southern Strategy*. New York, 1971.

Murray, Albert. *South to a Very Old Place*. New York, 1971.

Murray, Pauli. *Song in a Weary Throat: An American Pilgrimage*. New York, 1987.

Muse, Benjamin. *The American Negro Revolution: From Nonviolence to Black Power, 1963–1967*. Bloomington, Ind., 1968.

Myrdal, Gunnar. *An American Dilemma: The Negro Problem and Modern Democracy*. New York, 1944.

Nagel, Paul C. *Missouri: A Bicentennial History*. New York, 1977.

National Emergency Council. *Report to the President on the Economic Conditions of the South*. Washington, D.C., 1938.

Nicholas, H. G., ed. *Washington Despatches, 1941–1945: Weekly Political Reports from the British Embassy*. Chicago, 1981.

Nichols, Lee. *Breakthrough on the Color Front*. Colorado Springs, Colo., 1993.

Nixon, Edgar B., ed. *Franklin D. Roosevelt and Conservation, 1911–1945*. Hyde Park, N.Y., 1957.

Nixon, H. Clarence. *Forty Acres and Steel Mules*. Chapel Hill, N.C., 1938.

———. *Lower Piedmont Country*. New York, 1946.

Nordin, Dennis S. *The New Deal's Black Congressman: A Life of Arthur Wergs Mitchell*. Columbia, Mo., 1997.

Nordlinger, Eric A. *On the Autonomy of the Democratic State*. Cambridge, Mass., 1981.

Novak, Robert D. *The Agony of the G.O.P., 1964*. New York, 1965.

Nunnelley, William A. *Bull Connor*. Tuscaloosa, Ala., 1991.

O'Brien, Gail Williams. *The Color of the Law: Race, Violence, and Justice in the Post–World War II South*. Chapel Hill, N.C., 1999.

O'Brien, Lawrence F. *No Final Victories: A Life in Politics—From John F. Kennedy to Watergate*. Garden City, N.Y., 1974.

O'Brien, Michael. *The Idea of the American South, 1920–1941*. Baltimore, 1979.

———. *Rethinking the South: Essays in Intellectual History*. Baltimore, 1987.

O'Donnell, Kenneth P., and David F. Powers, with Joe McCarthy. *"Johnny, We Hardly Knew Ye": Memories of John Fitzgerald Kennedy*. Boston, 1972.

Odum, Howard W. *Race and Rumors of Race: Challenge to American Crisis*. Chapel Hill, N.C., 1943.

———. *Southern Regions of the United States*. Chapel Hill, N.C., 1936.

Ogden, Frederic D. *The Poll Tax in the South*. University, Ala., 1958.

Olien, Roger M. *From Token to Triumph: The Texas Republicans since 1920*. Dallas, Tex., 1982.

O'Reilly, Kenneth. *Nixon's Piano: Presidents and Racial Politics from Washington to Clinton*. New York, 1995.

Painter, Nell Irvin. *The Narrative of Hosea Hudson: His Life as a Negro Communist in the South*. Cambridge, Mass., 1979.

Paolucci, Henry. *"The South and the Presidency": From Reconstruction to Carter, A Long Day's Task*. Whitestone, N.Y., 1978.

Parker, Robert T., with Robert Rashke. *Capitol Hill in Black and White*. New York, 1986.

Parmet, Herbert S. *George Bush: The Life of a Lone Star Yankee*. New York, 1997.

———. *Jack: The Struggles of John F. Kennedy*. New York, 1980.

———. *JFK: The Presidency of John F. Kennedy*. New York, 1983.

Parris, Guichard, and Lester Brooks. *Blacks in the City: A History of the National Urban League*. Boston, 1971.

Parsons, Sara Mitchell. *From Southern Wrongs to Civil Rights: The Memoir of a White Civil Rights Activist*. Tuscaloosa, Ala., 2000.

Patenaude, Lionel V. *Texans, Politics and the New Deal*. New York, 1983.

Patterson, James T. *Congressional Conservatism and the New Deal: The Growth of the Conservative Coalition in Congress, 1933–1939*. Lexington, Ky., 1967.

———. *The New Deal and the States: Federalism in Transition*. Princeton, N.J., 1969.

Pauley, Garth E. *The Modern Presidency and Civil Rights: Rhetoric on Race from Roosevelt to Nixon*. College Station, Tex., 2001.

Pearce, John Ed. *Divide and Dissent: Kentucky Politics, 1930–1963*. Lexington, Ky., 1987.

Peirce, Neal R. *The Deep South States of America: People, Politics, and Power in the Seven Deep South States*. New York, 1974.

Peirce, Neal R., and Jerry Hagstrom. *The Book of America: Inside 50 States Today*. New York, 1983.

Pemberton, William E. *Exit with Honor: The Life and Presidency of Ronald Reagan*. Armonk, N.Y., 1998.

———. *Harry S. Truman: Fair Dealer and Cold Warrior*. Boston, 1989.

Pepper, Claude Denson, with Hays Gorey. *Pepper: Eyewitness to a Century*. New York, 1987.

Percy, Walker. *Lancelot*. New York, 1977.

———. *The Last Gentleman*. New York, 1966.

———. *The Second Coming.* New York, 1980.

———. *Signposts in a Strange Land.* New York, 1991.

Perlstein, Rick. *Before the Storm: Barry Goldwater and the Unmaking of the American Consensus.* New York, 2001.

Permaloff, Anne, and Carl Grafton. *Political Power in Alabama: The More Things Change . . .* Athens, Ga., 1995.

Persky, Joseph J. *The Burden of Dependency: Colonial Themes in Southern Economic Thought.* Baltimore, 1992.

Pfeffer, Paula F. *A. Philip Randolph: Pioneer of the Civil Rights Movement.* Baton Rouge, La., 1990.

Phillips, Cabell. *The Truman Presidency: The History of a Triumphant Succession.* New York, 1966.

Phillips, Kevin P. *American Dynasty: Aristocracy, Fortune, and the Politics of Deceit in the House of Bush.* New York, 2004.

———. *The Emerging Republican Majority.* New Rochelle, N.Y., 1969.

Pitre, Merline. *In Struggle against Jim Crow: Lulu B. White and the NAACP, 1900–1957.* College Station, Tex., 1999.

Plummer, Brenda Gayle. *Rising Wind: Black Americans and U.S. Foreign Affairs, 1935–1960.* Chapel Hill, N.C., 1996.

Poe, Clarence. *My First 80 Years.* Chapel Hill, N.C., 1963.

Poen, Monte M., ed. *Letters Home by Harry Truman.* New York, 1984.

———. *Strictly Personal and Confidential: The Letters Harry Truman Never Mailed.* Boston, 1982.

Polenberg, Richard. *War and Society: The United States, 1941–1945.* Philadelphia, 1972.

Polk, William T. *Southern Accent: From Uncle Remus to Oak Ridge.* New York, 1953.

Pool, William C., Emmie Craddock, and David E. Conrad. *Lyndon Baines Johnson: The Formative Years.* San Marcos, Tex., 1965.

Porterfield, Bill. *LBJ Country.* Garden City, N.Y., 1965.

Poston, Ted. *Draft of History.* Edited by Kathleen A. Hauke. Athens, Ga., 2000.

Potter, David. *The South and the Sectional Conflict.* Baton Rouge, La., 1968.

Powdermaker, Hortense. *After Freedom: A Cultural Study in the Deep South.* New York, 1939.

Powell, Jody. *The Other Side of the Story.* New York, 1984.

The President's Committee on Civil Rights. *To Secure These Rights: The Report of the President's Committee on Civil Rights.* Washington, D.C., 1947.

Price, H. D. *The Negro and Southern Politics: A Chapter of Florida History.* New York, 1957.

Price, M. Philips. *America after Sixty Years: The Travel Diaries of Two Generations of Englishmen.* London, 1936.

Pyron, Darden Asbury. *Southern Daughter: The Life of Margaret Mitchell.* New York, 1991.

Rae, Nicol C. *The Decline and Fall of the Liberal Republicans from 1952 to the Present.* New York, 1989.

————. *Southern Democrats.* New York, 1994.

Ragsdale, Kenneth B. *The Year America Discovered Texas: Centennial '36.* College Station, Tex., 1987.

Raines, Howell. *My Soul Is Rested: Movement Days in the Deep South Remembered.* New York, 1977.

Rainwater, Lee, and William L. Yancey. *The Moynihan Report and the Politics of Controversy.* Cambridge, Mass., 1967.

Ralph, James R., Jr. *Northern Protest: Martin Luther King, Jr., Chicago, and the Civil Rights Movement.* Cambridge, Mass., 1993.

Rand, Clayton. *Ink on My Hands.* New York, 1940.

Raper, Arthur F. *Preface to Peasantry: A Tale of Two Black Belt Counties.* Chapel Hill, N.C., 1936.

Raper, Arthur F., and Ira De A. Reid. *Sharecroppers All.* Chapel Hill, N.C. 1941.

Redding, J. Saunders. *No Day of Triumph.* New York, 1942.

Redding, Jack. *Inside the Democratic Party.* Indianapolis, Ind., 1958.

Reed, John Shelton. *The Enduring South: Subcultural Persistence in Mass Society.* Chapel Hill, N.C., 1986.

————. *One South: An Ethnic Approach to Regional Culture.* Baton Rouge, La., 1982.

————. *Southerners: The Social Psychology of Sectionalism.* Chapel Hill, N.C., 1983.

Reed, Linda. *Simple Decency and Common Sense: The Southern Conference Movement, 1938–1963.* Bloomington, Ind., 1991.

Reed, Merl E. *Seedtime for the Modern Civil Rights Movement: The President's Committee on Fair Employment Practice, 1941–1946.* Baton Rouge, La., 1991.

Reedy, George. *Lyndon B. Johnson: A Memoir.* New York, 1982.

Rees, Matthew. *From the Deck to the Sea: Blacks and the Republican Party.* Wakefield, N.H., 1991.

Reeves, Richard. *Running in Place: How Bill Clinton Disappointed America.* Kansas City, Mo., 1996.

Reilly, Michael F., as told to William J. Slocum. *Reilly of the White House.* New York, 1947.

Reston, James. *Deadline: A Memoir.* New York, 1991.

Reston, James, Jr. *The Lone Star: The Life of John Connally.* New York, 1989.

Richards, David. *Once upon a Time in Texas: A Liberal in the Lone Star State.* Austin, Tex., 2002.

Riley, Russell L. *The Presidency and the Politics of Racial Inequality: Nation-Keeping from 1831 to 1965.* New York, 1999.

Rixey, Lilian. *Bamie: Theodore Roosevelt's Remarkable Sister.* New York, 1963.

Robbins, Richard. *Sidelines Activist: Charles S. Johnson and the Struggle for Civil Rights.* Jackson, Miss., 1996.

Roberts, Randy, and James S. Olson. *A Line in the Sand: The Alamo in Blood and Memory.* New York, 2001.

Robertson, Ben. *Red Hills and Cotton: An Upcountry Memory.* New York, 1942.

Robertson, David. *Sly and Able: A Political Biography of James F. Byrnes.* New York, 1994.

Robinson, Armstead L., and Patricia Sullivan, eds. *New Directions in Civil Rights Studies.* Charlottesville, Va., 1991.

Robinson, George W., ed. *Bert Combs the Politician: An Oral History.* Lexington, Ky., 1991.

Robinson, John L. *Living Hard: Southern Americans in the Great Depression.* Washington, D.C., 1981.

Rooney, Robert C., ed. *Equal Opportunity in the United States: A Symposium on Civil Rights.* Austin, Tex., 1973.

Roosevelt, Elliott, ed. *F.D.R.: His Personal Letters, 1928–1945.* 2 vols. New York, 1950.

Roper, Daniel. *Fifty Years of Public Life.* Durham, N.C., 1941.

Rosenberg, Jonathan, and Zachary Karabell. *Kennedy, Johnson, and the Quest for Justice: The Civil Rights Tapes.* New York, 2003.

Rosengarten, Theodore. *All God's Dangers: The Life of Nate Shaw.* New York, 1974.

Rosenman, Samuel I., ed. *The Public Papers and Addresses of Franklin D. Roosevelt.* 13 vols. New York, 1938–50.

Ross, Irwin. *The Loneliest Campaign.* New York, 1968.

Rothman, Hal K. *LBJ's Texas White House: "Our Heart's Home."* College Station, Tex., 2001.

Rothschild, Mary Aickin. *A Case of Black and White: Northern Volunteers and the Southern Freedom Summers, 1964–1965.* Westport, Conn., 1982.

Rovere, Richard H. *Arrivals and Departures: A Journalist's Memoirs.* New York, 1976.

———. *The Goldwater Caper.* New York, 1965.

Rowan, Carl T. *Breaking Barriers: A Memoir.* Boston, 1991.

———. *Dream Makers, Dream Breakers: The World of Justice Thurgood Marshall.* Boston, 1993.

———. *South of Freedom.* Baton Rouge, La., 1997.

Rubin, Louis D., Jr., ed. *The American South: Portrait of a Culture.* Baton Rouge, La., 1980.

Rusk, Dean, as told to Richard Rusk. *As I Saw It.* Edited by Daniel S. Papp. New York, 1990.

Russell, Jan Jarboe. *Lady Bird: A Biography of Mrs. Johnson.* New York, 1999.

Russo, David J. *Families and Communities: A New View of American History.* Nashville, Tenn., 1974.

Sait, Edward McChesney. *American Parties and Elections.* Rev. ed. New York, 1939.

Sale, Kirkpatrick. *Power Shift: The Rise of the Southern Rim and Its Challenge to the Eastern Establishment.* New York, 1975.

Salinger, Pierre. *With Kennedy.* Garden City, N.Y., 1966.

Salmond, John A. *The Civilian Conservation Corps, 1933–1942: A New Deal Case Study.* Durham, N.C., 1967.

———. *The Conscience of a Lawyer: Clifford J. Durr and American Civil Liberties, 1899–1975.* Tuscaloosa, Ala., 1990.

———. *The General Textile Strike of 1934: From Maine to Alabama.* Columbia, Mo., 2002.

———. *Miss Lucy of the CIO: The Life and Times of Lucy Randolph Mason, 1882–1959.* Athens, Ga., 1988.

Sanders, M. Elizabeth. *The Regulation of Natural Gas: Policy and Politics, 1938–1978.* Philadelphia, 1981.

Sanders, Randy. *Mighty Peculiar Elections: The New South Gubernatorial Campaigns of 1970 and the Changing Politics of Race.* Gainesville, Fla., 2002.

Sanson, Jerry Purvis. *Louisiana during World War II.* Baton Rouge, La., 1999.

Savage, Barbara Dianne. *Broadcasting Freedom: Radio, War, and the Politics of Race, 1938–1948.* Chapel Hill, N.C., 1999.

Savage, Henry, Jr. *Seeds of Time: The Background of Southern Thinking.* New York, 1959.

Savage, Sean J. *Truman and the Democratic Party.* Lexington, Ky., 1997.

Scher, Richard K. *Politics in the New South: Republicanism, Race, and Leadership in the Twentieth Century.* New York, 1992.

Schlesinger, Arthur M., Jr. *The Coming of the New Deal.* Boston, 1959.

——. *A Life in the Twentieth Century: Innocent Beginnings, 1917–1950.* Boston, 2000.

——. *The Politics of Upheaval.* Boston, 1960.

——. *Robert Kennedy and His Times.* Boston, 1978.

——. *A Thousand Days: John F. Kennedy in the White House.* Boston, 1965.

Schlup, Leonard C., and Donald W. Whisenhunt, eds. *It Seems to Me: Selected Letters of Eleanor Roosevelt.* Lexington, Ky., 2001.

Schoelwer, Susan Prendergast, with Tom W. Glaser. *Alamo Images: Changing Perceptions of a Texas Experience.* Dallas, Tex., 1985.

Schram, Martin. *Running for President, 1976: The Carter Campaign.* New York, 1977.

Schulman, Bruce J. *From Cotton Belt to Sunbelt: Federal Policy, Economic Development, and the Transformation of the South, 1938–1980.* New York, 1991.

Schutze, Jim. *The Accommodation: The Politics of Race in an American City.* Secaucus, N.J., 1986.

Schwarz, Jordan A. *The Interregnum of Despair: Hoover, Congress, and the Depression.* Urbana, Ill., 1970.

——. *The New Dealers: Power Politics in the Age of Roosevelt.* New York, 1993.

Scott, Roy V., and J. G. Shoalmire. *The Public Career of Cully A. Cobb: A Study in Agricultural Leadership.* Jackson, Miss., 1973.

Seabury, Paul. *The Waning of Southern Internationalism.* Princeton, N.J., 1957.

Sellers, Charles Grier, Jr., ed. *The Southerner as American.* New York, 1966.

Sellers, Cleveland, with Robert Terrell. *The River of No Return: The Autobiography of a Black Militant and the Life and Death of SNCC.* New York, 1973.

Sevareid, Eric, ed. *Candidates 1960: Behind the Headlines in the Presidential Race.* New York, 1959.

Shadegg, Stephen. *What Happened to Goldwater? The Inside Story of the 1964 Republican Campaign.* New York, 1965.

Shafer, Byron E., and Anthony J. Badger, eds. *Contesting Democracy: Substance and Structure in American Political History, 1775–2000.* Lawrence, Kans., 2001.

Shannon, Jasper Berry. *Toward a New Politics in the South*. Knoxville, Tenn., 1949.

Shapiro, Herbert. *White Violence and Black Response: From Reconstruction to Montgomery*. Amherst, Mass., 1988.

Sharkansky, Ira. *Regionalism in American Politics*. Indianapolis, Ind., 1970.

Sherrill, Robert. *The Accidental President*. New York, 1967.

———. *Gothic Politics in the Deep South: Stars of the New Confederacy*. New York, 1968.

Shesol, Jeff. *Mutual Contempt: Lyndon Johnson, Robert Kennedy, and the Feud that Defined a Decade*. New York, 1997.

Short, Bob. *Everything Is Pickrick: The Life of Lester Maddox*. Macon, Ga., 1999.

Shouse, Sarah Newman. *Hillbilly Realist: Herman Clarence Nixon of Possum Trot*. University, Ala., 1986.

Sidey, Hugh. *A Very Personal Presidency: Lyndon Johnson in the White House*. New York, 1968.

Sieg, Edward Chan. *Eden on the Marsh: An Illustrated History of Savannah*. Savannah, Ga., 1985.

Simpson, George Lee, Jr. *The Cokers of Carolina: A Social Biography of a Family*. Chapel Hill, N.C., 1956.

Sims, George E. *The Little Man's Big Friend: James E. Folsom in Alabama Politics, 1946–1958*. University, Ala., 1985.

Sindler, Allan P., ed. *Change in the Contemporary South*. Durham, N.C., 1963.

Singal, Daniel Joseph. *The War Within: From Victorian to Modernist Thought in the South, 1919–1945*. Chapel Hill, N.C., 1982.

Sitkoff, Harvard. *A New Deal for Blacks: The Emergence of Civil Rights as a National Issue: The Depression Decade*. New York, 1978.

Smallwood, James M. *The Great Recovery: The New Deal in Texas*. Boston, 1983.

Smith, A. Merriman. *Thank You, Mr. President: A White House Notebook*. New York, 1946.

Smith, C. Calvin. *War and Wartime Changes: The Transformation of Arkansas, 1940–1945*. Fayetteville, Ark., 1986.

Smith, Douglas L. *The New Deal in the Urban South*. Baton Rouge, La., 1988.

Smith, Frank E. *Congressman from Mississippi*. New York, 1964.

———. *Look Away from Dixie*. Baton Rouge, La., 1965.

Smith, Marie. *The President's Lady: An Intimate Biography of Mrs. Lyndon B. Johnson*. New York, 1964.

Smith, Richard Norton. *An Uncommon Man: The Triumph of Herbert Hoover*. New York, 1984.

Smith, Timothy G., ed. *Merriman Smith's Book of Presidents: A White House Memoir.* New York, 1972.

Solberg, Carl. *Hubert Humphrey—A Biography.* New York, 1984.

Sorensen, Theodore C. *Kennedy.* New York, 1965.

Sorkin, Michael, ed. *Variations on a Theme Park.* New York, 1992.

Sosna, Morton. *In Search of the Silent South: Southern Liberals and the Race Issue.* New York, 1977.

Soukup, James R., Clifton McCleskey, and Harry Holloway. *Party and Factional Division in Texas.* Austin, Tex., 1964.

Southern, David W. *Gunnar Myrdal and Black-White Relations: The Use and Abuse of An American Dilemma, 1944–1969.* Baton Rouge, La., 1987.

Spitzberg, Irving J., Jr. *Racial Politics in Little Rock, 1954–1964.* New York, 1987.

Stack, Carol. *Call to Home: African Americans Reclaim the Rural South.* New York, 1996.

Stacks, John F. *Scotty: James B. Reston and the Rise and Fall of American Journalism.* Boston, 2003.

Stahl, Lesley. *Reporting Live.* New York, 1999.

Stark, John D. *Damned Upcountryman: William Watts Ball.* Durham, N.C., 1968.

Steed, Robert P., Laurence W. Moreland, and Tod A. Baker, eds. *The Disappearing South? Studies in Regional Change and Continuity.* Tuscaloosa, Ala., 1990.

Steele, Fritz. *The Sense of Place.* Boston, 1981.

Steinberg, Alfred. *Sam Johnson's Boy: A Close-Up of the President from Texas.* New York, 1968.

———. *Sam Rayburn: A Biography.* New York, 1975.

Stephens, Elise Hopkins. *Historic Huntsville: A City of New Beginnings.* Woodland Hills, Calif., 1984.

Stern, Mark. *Calculating Visions: Kennedy, Johnson, and Civil Rights.* New Brunswick, N.J., 1992.

Stevens, Ruth. *"Hi-Ya Neighbor."* New York, 1947.

Stinnett, Ronald F. *Democrats, Dinners, and Dollars: A History of the Democratic Party, Its Dinners, Its Ritual.* Ames, Iowa, 1967.

Stokes, Thomas L. *Chip off My Shoulder.* Princeton, N.J., 1940.

Stoper, Emily. *The Student Nonviolent Coordinating Committee: The Growth of Radicalism in a Civil Rights Organization.* Brooklyn, N.Y., 1989.

Strober, Gerald S. and Deborah H. *"Let Us Begin Anew": An Oral History of the Kennedy Presidency.* New York, 1993.

Suggs, Henry Lewis. *P. B. Young, Newspaperman: Race, Politics, and Journalism, 1910–1962.* Charlottesville, Va., 1988.

Sullivan, Patricia. *Days of Hope: Race and Democracy in the New Deal Era.* Chapel Hill, N.C., 1996.

———, ed. *Freedom Writer: Virginia Foster Durr, Letters from the Civil Rights Years.* New York, 2003.

Swain, Martha H. *Pat Harrison: The New Deal Years.* Jackson, Miss., 1978.

Swansbrough, Robert H., and David M. Brodsky, eds. *The South's New Politics: Realignment and Dealignment.* Columbia, S.C., 1988.

Taft, William Howard. *Our Chief Magistrate and His Powers.* Durham, N.C., 2001 (1st ed., 1916).

Talmadge, Herman E., with Mark Royden Winchell. *Talmadge: A Political Legacy, A Politician's Life: A Memoir.* Atlanta, 1987.

Teel, Leonard Ray. *Ralph Emerson McGill: Voice of the Southern Conscience.* Knoxville, Tenn., 2001.

Thomas, Helen. *Dateline: White House.* New York, 1975.

Thomas, Samuel W., ed. *Barry Bingham: A Man of His Word.* Lexington, Ky., 1993.

Thompson, Edgar T., ed. *Perspectives on the South: Agenda for Research.* Durham, N.C., 1967.

Thompson, Julius E. *Percy Greene and the Jackson Advocate: The Life and Times of a Radical Conservative Black Newspaperman, 1897–1977.* Jefferson, N.C., 1994.

Tillett, Paul, ed. *Inside Politics: The National Conventions, 1960.* Dobbs Ferry, N.Y., 1962.

Tindall, George Brown. *The Disruption of the Solid South.* New York, 1972.

———. *The Emergence of the New South, 1913–1945.* Baton Rouge, La., 1967.

———. *The Ethnic Southerners.* Baton Rouge, La., 1976.

Toffler, Alvin. *Future Shock.* New York, 1970.

Topping, John C., Jr., John R. Lazarek, and William H. Linder. *Southern Republicanism and the New South.* Cambridge, Mass., 1966.

Truman, David B. *The Congressional Party: A Case Study.* New York, 1959.

Truman, Harry S. *Memoirs by Harry S. Truman.* 2 vols. Garden City, N.Y., 1955–56.

Truman, Margaret. *Harry S Truman*. London, 1973.

———, ed. *Letters from Father*. South Yarmouth, Mass., 1981.

———, ed. *Where the Buck Stops: The Personal and Private Writings of Harry S. Truman*. New York, 1989.

Tuck, Stephen G. N. *Beyond Atlanta: The Struggle for Racial Equality in Georgia, 1940–1980*. Athens, Ga., 2001.

Tucker, David M. *Memphis since Crump: Bossism, Blacks, and Civic Reformers, 1948–1968*. Knoxville, Tenn., 1980.

Tucker, Shirley, ed. *Mississippi from Within*. New York, 1965.

Tugwell, Rexford, G. *The Brains Trust*. New York, 1968.

———. *FDR: Architect of an Era*. New York, 1967.

———. *In Search of Roosevelt*. Cambridge, Mass., 1972.

Tully, Grace. *F.D.R. My Boss*. New York, 1949.

Turner, Frederick Jackson. *The Significance of Sections in American History*. New York, 1932.

Tyson, Timothy B. *Radio Free Dixie: Robert F. Williams and the Roots of Black Power*. Chapel Hill, N.C., 1999.

Underhill, Robert. *The Truman Persuasions*. Ames, Iowa, 1948.

Urquhart, Brian. *Ralph Bunche: An American Life*. New York, 1993.

Valenti, Jack. *A Very Human President*. New York, 1975.

Vance, Rupert B., and Nicholas J. Demerath, eds. *The Urban South*. Chapel Hill, N.C., 1954.

Vandiver, Frank E., ed. *The Idea of the South: Pursuit of a Central Theme*. Chicago, 1964.

———. *The Southwest: South or West?* College Station, Tex., 1975.

Van Rijn, Guido. *Roosevelt's Blues: African-American Blues and Gospel Songs on FDR*. Jackson, Miss., 1997.

Vaughan, L. Howard, and David R. Deener. *Presidential Politics in Louisiana, 1952*. New Orleans, 1954.

Veselka, Robert E. *The Courthouse Square in Texas*. Edited by Kenneth E. Foote. Austin, Tex., 2000.

Viorst, Milton. *Fire in the Streets: America in the 1960s*. New York, 1979.

Vose, Clement E. *Caucasians Only: The Supreme Court, the NAACP, and the Restrictive Covenant Cases*. Berkeley, Calif., 1947.

Wade, Wyn Craig. *The Fiery Cross: The Ku Klux Klan in America*. New York, 1986.

Wagy, Tom. *Governor LeRoy Collins of Florida: Spokesman of the New South.* University, Ala., 1985.

Walker, Turnley. *Roosevelt and the Warm Springs Story.* New York, 1953.

Ward, Brian, and Tony Badger, eds. *The Making of Martin Luther King and the Civil Rights Movement.* New York, 1996.

Ward, Geoffrey C. *Before the Trumpet: Young Franklin Roosevelt, 1882–1905.* New York, 1985.

———. *A First-Class Temperament: The Emergence of Franklin Roosevelt.* New York, 1989.

———, ed. *Closest Companion: The Unknown Story of the Intimate Friendship between Franklin Roosevelt and Margaret Suckley.* Boston, 1995.

Watters, Pat. *The South and the Nation.* New York, 1969.

Watters, Pat, and Reese Cleghorn. *Climbing Jacob's Ladder: The Arrival of Negroes in Southern Politics.* New York, 1967.

Webb, Walter Prescott. *Divided We Stand.* New York, 1937.

Weeks, O. Douglas. *Texas in the 1960 Presidential Election.* Austin, Tex., 1961.

———. *Texas Presidential Politics in 1952.* Austin, Tex., 1953.

Weill, Susan. *In a Madhouse's Din: Civil Rights Coverage by Mississippi's Daily Press, 1948–1968.* Westport, Conn., 2002.

Weisenberger, Carol A. *Dollars and Dreams: The National Youth Administration in Texas.* New York, 1994.

Weiss, Nancy J. *Farewell to the Party of Lincoln.* Princeton, N.J., 1983.

———. *The National Urban League, 1910–1940.* New York, 1974.

———. *Whitney M. Young, Jr., and the Struggle for Civil Rights.* Princeton, 1989.

Weltner, Charles Longstreet. *Southerner.* Philadelphia, 1966.

Welty, Eudora. *The Eye of the Story: Selected Essays and Reviews.* New York, 1978.

Whalen, Charles and Barbara. *The Longest Debate: A Legislative History of the 1964 Civil Rights Act.* Cabin John, Md., 1985.

Whisenhunt, Donald W. *The Depression in Texas: The Hoover Years.* New York, 1983.

———, ed. *The Depression in the Southwest.* Port Washington, N.Y., 1980.

White, Owen P. *Texas: An Informal Biography.* New York, 1945.

White, Theodore H. *The Making of the President, 1960.* New York, 1961.

———. *The Making of the President, 1964.* New York, 1965.

White, Walter. *A Man Called White: The Autobiography of Walter White.* New York, 1948.

White, William S. *The Making of a Journalist.* Lexington, Ky., 1986.

———. *The Professional: Lyndon B. Johnson.* Boston, 1964.

———. *The Responsibles.* New York, 1972.

Whitman, Willson. *David Lilienthal.* New York, 1948.

Wicker, Tom. *JFK and LBJ: The Influence of Personality upon Politics.* New York, 1968.

Wilentz, Sean, ed. *Rites of Power: Symbolism, Ritual, and Politics since the Middle Ages.* Philadelphia, 1985.

Wilhoit, Francis M. *The Politics of Massive Resistance.* New York, 1973.

Wilkie, Curtis. *Dixie: A Personal Odyssey through Events That Shaped the Modern South.* New York, 2001.

Wilkins, Roger. *A Man's Life: An Autobiography.* New York, 1982.

Wilkins, Roy, with Tom Mathews. *Standing Fast: The Autobiography of Roy Wilkins.* New York, 1984.

Wilkinson, J. Harvie, III. *Harry Byrd and the Changing Face of Virginia Politics, 1945–1966.* Charlottesville, Va., 1968.

Williams, Juan. *Thurgood Marshall: American Revolutionary.* New York, 1998.

Wilson, Woodrow. *Robert E. Lee: An Interpretation.* Chapel Hill, N.C., 1924.

Witcover, Jules. *Marathon.* New York, 1977.

Wofford, Harris. *Of Kennedys and Kings: Making Sense of the Sixties.* New York, 1980.

Wolfskill, George, and John A. Hudson. *All But the People: Franklin D. Roosevelt and His Critics, 1933–39.* New York, 1969.

Wolk, Allan. *The Presidency and Black Civil Rights: Eisenhower to Nixon.* Rutherford, N.J., 1971.

Wolters, Raymond. *Negroes and the Great Depression: The Problem of Economic Recovery.* Westport, Conn., 1970.

Wood, Phillip J. *Southern Capitalism: The Political Economy of North Carolina, 1880–1980.* Durham, N.C., 1986.

Woodruff, Nan Elizabeth. *America Congo: The African American Freedom Struggle in the Delta.* Cambridge, Mass., 2003.

Woodward, C. Vann. *The Future of the Past.* New York, 1989.

———. *The Strange Career of Jim Crow.* 3rd rev. ed. New York, 1974.

Workman, W. D., Jr. *The Bishop from Barnwell: The Political Life and Times of Senator Edgar A. Brown.* Columbia, S.C., 1963.

Wright, Lawrence. *In the New World: Growing Up with America, 1960–1984.* New York, 1988.

Wynn, Neil A. *The Afro-American and the Second World War.* New York, 1976.

Young, Andrew. *An Easy Burden: The Civil Rights Movement and the Transformation of America.* New York, 1996.

Young, Stephen M. *Tales Out of Congress.* Philadelphia, 1964.

Zangrando, Robert L. *The NAACP Crusade against Lynching, 1909–1950.* Philadelphia, 1980.

Zelinsky, Wilbur. *The Cultural Geography of the United States.* Englewood Cliffs, N.J., 1992.

Zuber, William Physick. *My Eighty Years in Texas.* Edited by Janis Boyle Mayfield. Austin, Tex., 1971.

PUBLISHED ESSAYS AND ARTICLES

Abbott, Carl. "The End of the Southern City." In *Perspectives on the American South: An Annual Review of Society, Politics, and Culture.* Vol. 4, edited by James C. Cobb and Charles R. Wilson. New York, 1987.

Abrams, Douglas C. "Irony of Reform: North Carolina Blacks and the New Deal." *North Carolina Historical Review* 66 (1989): 149–78.

Ader, Emile B. "Why the Dixiecrats Failed." *Journal of Politics* 15 (1953): 356–69.

Alsop, Stewart. "Can Goldwater Win in '64?" *Saturday Evening Post,* August 24, 1963, 19–24.

———. "Lyndon Johnson: How Does He Do It?" *Saturday Evening Post,* January 24, 1959, 13–14, 38, 43.

Alston, Lee J., and Joseph P. Ferrie. "Resisting the Welfare State: Southern Opposition to the Farm Security Administration." *Research in Economic History 1985* (Supplement 4): 83–120.

Anders, Evan. "Light at the End of the Tunnel: Evaluating the Major Biographies of Lyndon Johnson." *Southwestern Historical Quarterly* 98 (1994): 297–320.

Arensberg, Conrad M. "American Communities." *American Anthropologist* 57 (1955): 1143–62.

Arrington, Leonard J. "Western Agriculture and the New Deal." *Agricultural History* 44 (1970): 338–47.

Ashmore, Harry S. "The South's Year of Decision." *Southern Packet* 4 (1948): 1–3.

Aucoin, Brent J. "The Southern Manifesto and Southern Opposition to Desegregation." *Arkansas Historical Quarterly* 55 (1996): 173–93.

Badger, Anthony J. (Tony). "Fatalism, Not Gradualism: Race and the Crisis of Southern Liberalism, 1945–1965." In *The Making of Martin Luther King and the Civil Rights Movement,* edited by Brian Ward and Tony Badger. New York, 1996.

———. "How Did the New Deal Change the South?" In *Looking Inward, Looking Outward: From the 1930s through the 1940s,* edited by Steve Ickringill. Amsterdam, 1990.

———. "The New Deal and the Localities." In *The Growth of Federal Power in American History,* edited by R. Jeffreys-Jones and Bruce Collins. Edinburgh, 1983.

———. "The New Deal without FDR: What Biographies of Roosevelt Cannot Tell Us." In *History and Biography: Essays in Honour of Derek Beales,* edited by T. C. W. Blanning and David Cannadine. New York, 1996.

———. "Whatever Happened to Roosevelt's New Generation of Southerners?" In *The Roosevelt Years: New Perspectives on American History, 1933–1945,* edited by Robert A. Garson and Stuart S. Kidd. Edinburgh, 1999.

Bailey, Robert J. "Theodore G. Bilbo and the Fair Employment Practices Controversy: A Southerner's Reaction to a Changing World." *Journal of Mississippi History* 42 (1980): 27–42.

Ball, Howard. "Justice Hugo L. Black: A Magnificent Product of the South." *Alabama Law Review* 36 (1985): 791–834.

Banfield, Edward C. "Ten Years of the Farm Tenant Purchase Program." *Journal of Farm Economics* 31 (1949): 469–86.

Bartley, Numan V. "Another New South?" *Georgia Historical Quarterly* 55 (1981): 119–37.

———. "Jimmy Carter and the Politics of the New South." *The Forum Series* (St. Louis, 1979).

———. "The South and Sectionalism in American Politics." *Journal of Politics* 38 (1976): 239–57.

———. "Writing about the Post–World War II South." *Georgia Historical Quarterly* 68 (1984): 1–18.

Bass, Harold F., Jr. "Presidential Party Leadership and Party Reform: Franklin D. Roosevelt and the Abrogation of the Two-Thirds Rule." *Presidential Studies Quarterly* 18 (1988): 303–17.

Bateman, Fred, and Jason E. Taylor. "Franklin Roosevelt, Federal Spending, and the Postwar Southern Economic Rebound." *Essays in Economic and Business History* 20 (2002): 71–83.

Beck, Paul Allen. "Partisan Dealignment of the Postwar South." *American Political Science Review* 71 (1977): 477–96.

Beeler, Dorothy. "Race Riot in Columbia, Tennessee, February 25–27, 1946." *Tennessee Historical Quarterly* 39 (1980): 49–61.

Bender, Thomas. "Wholes and Parts: The Need for Synthesis in American History." *Journal of American History* 71 (1986): 120–36.

Bennett, Lerone, Jr. "What Negroes Can Expect from President Lyndon Johnson." *Ebony*, January 19, 1964, 81–84.

Bernstein, Barton J. "The Ambiguous Legacy: The Truman Administration and Civil Rights." In *Politics and Policies of the Truman Administration*, edited by Bernstein. Chicago, 1970.

Bevis, William M. "Region, Power, Place." In *Reading the West: New Essays on the Literature of the American West*, edited by Michael Kowalewski. New York, 1996.

Biles, Roger. "The New Deal in Dallas." *Southwestern Historical Quarterly* 95 (1991): 1–19.

———. "The Persistence of the Past: Memphis in the Great Depression." *Journal of Southern History* 52 (1986): 183–212.

———. "The Urban South in the Great Depression." *Journal of Southern History* 56 (1990): 71–100.

Billington, Monroe. "The Alabama Clergy and the New Deal." *Alabama Review* 32 (1979): 214–25.

———. "Civil Rights, President Truman and the South." *Journal of Negro History* 58 (1973): 127–39.

———. "Freedom to Serve: The President's Committee on Equality of Treatment and Opportunity in the Armed Services, 1949–1950." *Journal of Negro History* 51 (1966): 262–74.

———. "Lyndon B. Johnson and Blacks: The Early Years." *Journal of Negro History* 62 (1977): 26–42.

Billington, Monroe, and Cal Clark. "Texas Clergymen, Franklin D. Roosevelt, and the New Deal." *Locus* 4 (1991): 23–39.

Birdsall, Stephen S. "Preliminary Analysis of the 1968 Wallace Vote in the Southeast." *Southeastern Geographer* 9 (1969): 55–66.

Black, Allida M. "Championing a Champion: Eleanor Roosevelt and the Marian Anderson 'Freedom Concert.'" *Presidential Studies Quarterly* 20 (1990): 719–36.

———. "Eleanor Roosevelt and the Wartime Campaign against Jim Crow." *Social Education* 60 (1996): 284–86.

Blackwelder, Julia Kirk. "Letters from the Great Depression: A Tour through a Collection of Letters to an Atlanta Newspaperwoman." *Southern Exposure* 6 (1978): 73–77.

Blakey, George T. "Kentucky Youth and the New Deal." *Filson Club History Quarterly* 60 (1986): 37–68.

Bliven, Bruce. "In the Land of Cotton." *New Republic*, March 21, 1934, 152–55.

Bolin, James Duane. "The Human Side: Politics, the Great Depression, and the New Deal in Lexington, Kentucky, 1929–35." *Register of the Kentucky Historical Society* 90 (1992): 256–83.

Booker, Simeon. "Blacks Remember Civil Rights Role of Lyndon B. Johnson." *Jet*, February 8, 1973, 15–16.

Bourgeois, Christie L. "Stepping over Lines: Lyndon Johnson, Black Texans, and the National Youth Administration, 1935–1937." *Southwestern Historical Quarterly* 91 (1987): 149–72.

Boyd, William M. "Southern Politics, 1948–1952." *Phylon* 13 (1952): 226–35.

Branyon, Robert, and R. Alton Lee. "Lyndon Johnson and the Art of the Possible." *Southwestern Social Science Quarterly* 45 (1964): 213–25.

Brearley, H. C. "The Negro's New Belligerency." *Phylon* 5 (1944): 339–45.

Brent, Joseph E. "The Civil Works Administration in Western Kentucky: Work Relief's Dress Rehearsal under Fire." *Filson Club History Quarterly* 63 (1993): 259–76.

Brinkley, Alan. "Writing the History of Contemporary America: Dilemmas and Challenges." *Daedalus* 113 (1984): 121–41.

Brooks, Cleanth. "Regionalism in American Literature." *Journal of Southern History* 26 (1960): 35–43.

Brown, Norman D. "Garnering Votes for 'Cactus Jack': John Nance Garner, Franklin D. Roosevelt, and the 1932 Democratic Nomination for President." *Southwestern Historical Quarterly* 104 (2000): 149–88.

Brown, Richard Maxwell. "The New Regionalism in America, 1970–1981." In *Regionalism and the Pacific Northwest*, edited by William G. Robbins, Robert J. Frank, and Richard E. Ross. Corvallis, Ore., 1983.

Brundage, W. Fitzhugh. "No Deed but Memory." In *Where These Memories Grow: History, Memory, and Southern Identity*, edited by Brundage. Chapel Hill, N.C., 2000.

Brunn, Stanley D., and Gerald L. Ingalls. "The Emergence of Republicanism in the Urban South." *Southeastern Geographer* 12 (1972): 133–56.

Buenger, Walter L. "Texas and the South." *Southwestern Historical Quarterly* 103 (2000): 308–24.

Byrne, Richard. "Lyndon Agonistes." *American Prospect* 15 (August 2004): 46–49.

Campbell, Bruce A. "Change in the Southern Electorate." *American Journal of Political Science* 21 (1977): 37–64.

———. "Patterns of Change in the Partisan Loyalties of Native Southerners: 1952–1972." *Journal of Politics* 39 (1977): 730–63.

Carleton, William G. "The Conservative South—A Political Myth." *Virginia Quarterly Review* 22 (1946): 179–92.

Carlton, David L., and Peter A. Coclanis. "Another 'Great Migration': From Region to Race in Southern Liberalism, 1938–1945." *Southern Cultures* 3 (1997): 37–62.

Carter, Hodding. "The South and the World: A Dissenting Postscript." In *Dixie Dateline: A Journalistic Portrait of the Contemporary South,* edited by John B. Boles. Houston, Tex., 1983.

Carter, John Franklin [Jay Franklin]. "What Truman Really Thinks of Negroes." *Negro Digest* 7 (1949): 10–14.

Castel, Albert. "The Bloodiest Man in American History." *American Heritage* 11 (1960): 22–24, 97–99.

Castle, David S. "Goldwater's Presidential Candidacy and Political Realignment." *Presidential Studies Quarterly* 20 (1990): 103–10.

Chesnutt, E. F. (Ed). "Rural Electrification in Arkansas, 1935–1940: The Formative Years." *Arkansas Historical Quarterly* 46 (1987): 215–60.

Chesteen, Richard D. "'Mississippi Is Gone Home!': A Study of the 1948 Mississippi States'Rights Bolt." *Journal of Mississippi History* 32 (1970): 43–59.

Chester, Edward W. "Lyndon Baines Johnson, An American 'King Lear': A Critical Evaluation of His Newspaper Obituaries." *Presidential Studies Quarterly* 21 (1991): 319–31.

Chmaj, Betty E. "Paranoid Patriotism: The Radical Right and the South." *Atlantic Monthly* 210 (1962): 91–97.

Christensen, Lawrence M. "Missouri: The Heart of the Nation." In *Heartland: Comparative Histories of the Midwestern States,* edited by James H. Madison. Bloomington, Ind., 1988.

Cieply, David. "Why the State Was Dropped in the First Place: A Prequel to Skocpol's 'Bringing the State Back In.'" *Critical Review: An Interdisciplinary Journal of Politics and Society* 14 (2000): 157–213.

Clapper, Raymond. "Roosevelt Tries the Primaries." *Current History* 49 (October 1938): 16–19.

Cobb, James C. "The Big Boy Has Scared the Lard Out of Them." *Research Studies* 43 (1975): 123–26.

———. "Community and Identity: Redefining Southern Culture." *Georgia Review* 50 (1966): 9–24.

———. "An Epitaph for the North: Reflections on the Politics of Regional and National Identity at the Millennium." *Journal of Southern History* 66 (2000): 3–24.

———. "Not Gone, But Forgotten: Eugene Talmadge and the 1938 Purge Campaign." *Georgia Historical Quarterly* 59 (1975): 197–209.

———. "'Somebody Done Nailed Us on the Cross': Federal Farm and Welfare Policy and the Civil Rights Movement in the Mississippi Delta." *Journal of American History* 77 (1990): 912–36.

Cochran, Thomas C. "The 'Presidential Synthesis' in American History." *American Historical Review* 53 (1948): 748–59.

Cohn, David L. "How the South Feels." *Atlantic Monthly* 173 (1944): 47–51.

Coles, Robert. "Jimmy Carter: Agrarian Rebel?" *New Republic,* June 26, 1976, 14–19.

Conkin, Paul K. "It All Happened in Pine Mountain Valley." *Georgia Historical Quarterly* 47 (1963): 1–42.

———. "Lyndon Johnson and the Outer South." In *Is There a Southern Political Tradition?* edited by Charles W. Eagles. Jackson, Miss., 1996.

Converse, Philip E., P. R. Clauson, and Warren E. Miller. "Electoral Myth and Reality: The 1964 Election." *American Political Science Review* 59 (1965): 321–36.

Coode, Thomas H. "The Presidential Election of 1940 as Reflected in the Tennessee Metropolitan Press." *East Tennessee Historical Society's Publications* 40 (1968): 83–100.

———. "Walter Chandler as Congressman." *West Tennessee Historical Society Papers* 29 (1975): 25–37.

Cook, Blanche Wiesen. "Eleanor Roosevelt and the South: 1994 Elson Lecture." *Atlanta History* 38 (1995): 34–40.

Coski, John M. "The Confederate Battle Flag in Historical Perspective." In *Confederate Symbols in the Contemporary South,* edited by J. Michael Martinez, William D. Richardson, and Ron McNinch-Su. Gainesville, Fla., 2000.

Couch, W. T. "Southerners Inspect the South." *New Republic,* December 14, 1938, 168–69.

Cox, Merlin G. "David Sholtz: New Deal Governor of Florida." *Florida Historical Quarterly* 43 (1964): 142–52.

Cox, Patrick. "'Nearly a Statesman': LBJ and Texas Blacks in the 1948 Election." *Social Science Quarterly* 74 (1993): 241–63.

Craig, Gordon. "Political History." *Daedalus* 100 (1971): 323–38.

Crisler, Robert M. "The Regional Status of Little Dixie in Missouri and Little Egypt in Illinois." *Journal of Geography* 49 (1950): 337–43.

Cronon, E. David. "A Southern Progressive Looks at the New Deal." *Journal of Southern History* 24 (1958): 151–76.

Cronon, William. "Revisiting the Vanishing Frontier: The Legacy of Frederick Jackson Turner." *Western Historical Quarterly* 28 (1987): 157–76.

Cumming, Joseph. "A Final Farewell." *Georgia* 15 (1972): 35–36, 48, 52.

———. "Been Down So Long It Looks Like Up to Me." *Esquire* (August 1971): 84–85, 90, 110, 114.

Curti, Merle E. "The Section and Frontier in American History: The Methodological Concepts of Frederick Jackson Turner." In *Methods in Social Science: A Case Book,* edited by Stuart E. Rice. Chicago, 1931.

Danhof, Clarence H. "Four Decades of Thought on the South's Economic Problems." In *Essays in Southern Economic Development,* edited by Melvin L. Greenhut and W. Tate Whitman. Chapel Hill, N.C., 1964.

Daniel, Pete. "Going among Strangers: Southern Reactions to World War II." *Journal of American History* 77 (1990): 886–911.

———. "The Transformation of the Rural South, 1930 to the Present." *Agricultural History* 55 (1981): 231–47.

Daniels, Jonathan. "Democracy Is Bread." *Virginia Quarterly Review* 14 (1938): 481–90.

Davidson, Bill. "Lyndon Johnson: Can a Southerner Be Elected President?" *Look,* August 18, 1959, 63–71.

———. "Texas Political Powerhouse: Lyndon Johnson." *Look,* August 4, 1959, 38–46.

Davidson, Donald. "Where Regionalism and Sectionalism Meet." *Social Forces* 13 (1934): 23–31.

Davis, Forrest. "The Fourth Term's Hair Shirt." *Saturday Evening Post,* April 8, 1944, 9–11.

Davis, John P. "A Black Inventory of the New Deal." *Crisis* 42 (1935): 141–42.

Davis, Lance E. "It's a Long, Long Road to Tipperary, or Reflections on Organized Violence, Protection Rates, and Related Topics: The New Political History." *Journal of Economic History* 40 (1980): 1–16.

Davis, Polly. "Court Reform and Alben W. Barkley's Election as Majority Leader." *Southern Quarterly* 15 (1976): 15–31.

Davis, Steve. "The South as 'The Nation's No. 1 Economic Problem': The NEC Report of 1938." *Georgia Historical Quarterly* 62 (1978): 119–32.

Dearlove, John. "Bringing the Constitution Back In: Political Science and the State." *Political Studies* 37 (1989): 521–39.

Degler, Carl N. "Thesis, Antithesis, Synthesis: The South, the North, the Nation." *Journal of Southern History* 53 (1987): 3–18.

Dinnerstein, Leonard. "The Senate's Rejection of Aubrey Williams as Rural Electrification Administrator." *Alabama Review* 21 (1968): 133–43.

Donaldson, Gary A. "The Wardman Park Group and Campaign Strategy in the Truman Administration, 1946–1948." *Missouri Historical Review* 86 (1992): 282–94.

———. "Who Wrote the Clifford Memo? The Origins of Campaign Strategy in the Truman Administration." *Presidential Studies Quarterly* 23 (1993): 747–54.

Douglas, Paul H. "The 1960 Voting Rights Bill: The Struggle, the Final Results, and the Reasons." *Journal of Intergroup Relations* 1 (1960): 82–86.

Dowd, Douglas F. "A Comparative Analysis of Economic Development in the American West and South." *Journal of Economic History* 16 (1956): 558–74.

Draper, Alan. "Be Careful What You Wish For . . . : American Liberals and the South." *Southern Studies* 4 (1993): 309–23.

Dubay, Robert W. "Mississippi and the Proposed Federal Anti-Lynching Bills of 1937–38." *Southern Quarterly* 7 (1968): 73–89.

Dudziak, Mary L. "Desegregation as a Cold War Imperative." *Stanford Law Review* 41 (1988): 61–120.

Dunbar, Leslie. "The Changing Mind of the South: The Exposed Nerve." *Journal of Politics* 17 (1964): 3–21.

Dunn, Larry W. "Knoxville Negro Voting and the Roosevelt Revolution, 1928–1936." *East Tennessee Historical Society's Publications* 43 (1971): 71–93.

Durrill, Wayne K. "A Tale of Two Courthouses: Civil Space, Political Power, and Capitalist Development in a New South Community, 1843–1940." *Journal of Social History* 35 (2002): 659–81.

Eagleton, Thomas F., and Diane L. Duffin. "Bob Hannegan and Harry Truman's Vice Presidential Nomination." *Missouri Historical Review* 90 (1996): 265–83.

Edwards, Willard. "Lyndon the Great: Johnson of Texas Runs for President." *Human Events* 17 (May 19, 1960): 1–3.

Ellis, Ann Wells. "Uncle Sam Is My Shepherd: The Commission on Interracial Cooperation and the New Deal in Georgia." *Atlanta Historical Journal* 30 (1986): 47–63.

Estall, Robert. "The Changing Balance of the Northern and Southern Regions of the United States." *Journal of American Studies* 14 (1980): 365–86.

Fickle, James E. "The S.P.A. and the N.R.A.: A Case Study of the Blue Eagle in the South." *Southwestern Historical Quarterly* 79 (1956): 253–78.

Fishel, Leslie H., Jr. "The Negro in the New Deal Era." *Wisconsin Magazine of History* 48 (1964): 111–26.

Fite, Gilbert C. "Richard B. Russell and Lyndon B. Johnson: The Story of a Strange Friendship." *Missouri Historical Review* 83 (1989): 125–38.

Fleissner, James P. "August 11, 1938: A Day in the Life of Senator Walter F. George." *Journal of Southern Legal History* 9 (2001): 55–101.

Fleming, Douglas L. "The New Deal in Atlanta: A Review of the Major Programs." *Atlanta Historical Journal* 30 (1986): 23–45.

Foner, Eric. "History in Crisis." *Commonweal,* December 18, 1981, 723–26.

Foreman, Clark. "The Decade of Hope." *Phylon* 12 (1951): 137–50.

———. "Race Tension in the South." *New Republic,* September 21, 1942, 340–42.

Formisano, Ronald P. "The Concept of Political Culture." *Journal of Interdisciplinary History* 31 (2001): 393–426.

———. "The New Political History." *International Journal of Social Education* 1 (1986): 5–21.

Forts, Franklin. "Living with Confederate Symbols." *Southern Cultures* 8 (2002): 60–75.

Fowler, Scott. "Congress Blocks the Civil Rights Program." *Commentary* 9 (1950): 397–406.

Fox, Jennifer. "Hail to the Chief: Presidential Visits to Atlanta." *Atlanta History* 36 (1992): 36–48.

Fox-Genovese, Elizabeth, and Eugene D. Genovese. "Surveying the South: A Conversation with John Shelton Reed." *Southern Cultures* 7 (2001): 76–93.

Frady, Marshall. "Cooling Off with LBJ." *Harper's* 238 (1969): 65–72.

Franklin, Jimmie Lewis. "Black Southerners, Shared Experience, and Place: A Reflection." *Journal of Southern History* 60 (1994): 3–18.

Frantz, Joe B. "Opening a Curtain: The Metamorphosis of Lyndon B. Johnson." *Journal of Southern History* 45 (1979): 3–26.

Fredrickson, Kari. "'The Slowest State' and 'Most Backward Community': Racial Violence in South Carolina and Federal Civil-Rights Legislation, 1946–1948." *South Carolina Historical Magazine* 98 (1997): 177–202.

Fuller, Helen. "The New Confederacy." *New Republic,* November 1, 1948, 10–14.

———. "The Powerful Persuaders: Lady Bird's Trip through the South." *New Republic,* October 24, 1964, 11–12.

———. "The Ring around the President." *New Republic,* October 25, 1943, 563–65.

Garrard, John. "Social History, Political History and Political Science: The Study of Power." *Journal of Social History* 16 (spring 1983): 105–21.

Garrett, Garet. "The Problem South." *Saturday Evening Post,* October 8, 1938, 23, 85–91.

Garson, Robert A. "The Alienation of the South: A Crisis for Harry S. Truman and the Democratic Party, 1945–1948." *Missouri Historical Review* 64 (1970): 448–71.

Germany, Kent. "'I'm Not Lying about that One': Manhood, LBJ, and the Politics of Speaking Southern." *Miller Center Report* 58 (2002): 32–39.

Giglio, James. "Harry S. Truman and the Multifarious Ex-Presidency." *Presidential Studies Quarterly* 12 (1982): 239–55.

Gillon, Steven M. "The Future of Political History." *Journal of Policy History* 9 (1997): 240–55.

Gimpel, James G., and Jason E. Schuknecht, "Reconsidering Political Regionalism in the American States." *State Politics and Policy Quarterly* 2 (2002): 325–52.

Glenn, Norval D., and J. L. Simmons. "Are Regional Cultural Differences Diminishing?" *Public Opinion Quarterly* 31 (1967): 176–93.

Gloster, Hugh. "The Southern Revolt." *Crisis* 55 (1948): 137–39, 155–56.

Goldstein, Harold M. "Regional Barriers in the Utilization of Federal Aid: The Southeast in the 1930's." *Quarterly Review of Economics and Business* 7 (1967): 65–70.

Goldfield, David. "The New Regionalism." *Journal of Urban History* 10 (1984): 163–76.

Goodman, Paul. "Putting Some Class Back into Political History: 'The Transformation of Political Culture' and the Crisis in American Political History." *Reviews in American History* 12 (1984): 80–88.

Gould, Lewis L. Review of *Contesting Democracy: Substance and Structure in American Political History, 1775–2000,* edited by Byron E. Shafer and Anthony J. Badger. *North Carolina Historical Review* 89 (2002): 491.

Graham, Hugh Davis. "The Stunted Career of Public History: A Critique and an Agenda." *Public Historian* 15 (1993): 15–37.

Grant, Philip A., Jr. "Editorial Reaction to the 1952 Presidential Candidacy of Richard B. Russell." *Georgia Historical Quarterly* 57 (1973): 167–78.

————. "Eisenhower and the 1952 Republican Invasion of the South: The Case of Virginia." *Presidential Studies Quarterly* 20 (1990): 285–93.

————. "The Mississippi Congressional Delegation and the Formation of the Conservative Coalition, 1937–1940." *Journal of Mississippi History* 50 (1988): 21–28.

————. "The 1948 Presidential Election in Virginia: Augury of the Trend Towards Republicanism." *Presidential Studies Quarterly* 8 (1978): 319–28.

Grantham, Dewey W., Jr. "Interpreters of the Modern South." *South Atlantic Quarterly* 63 (1964): 521–29.

————. "Regional Claims and National Purposes: The South and the New Deal." *Atlanta History* 38 (1994): 5–17.

————. "The Regional Imagination: Social Scientists and the American South. "*Journal of Southern History* 34 (1968): 3–32.

————. "The South and the Reconstruction of American Politics." *Journal of American History* 53 (1966): 227–46.

Graves, John Temple. "Revolution in the South." *Virginia Quarterly Review* 26 (1950): 190–203.

————. "The Solid South Is Cracking." *American Mercury* 56 (1943): 401–6.

————. "The South Still Loves Roosevelt." *Nation,* July 1, 1939, 11–13.

Grayson, A. G. "North Carolina and Harry Truman, 1944–1948." *Journal of American Studies* 9 (1975): 283–300.

Greenbaum, Fred. "The Anti-Lynching Bill of 1935: The Irony of Equal Justice—Under Law."*Journal of Human Relations* 15 (1967): 72–85.

Greene, Johnny. "The Dixie Smile." *Harper's* (September 1976): 14–19.

Griffin, Larry J. "Southern Distinctiveness, Yet Again, or, Why America Still Needs the South." *Southern Cultures* 6 (2000): 47–72.

Grothaus, Larry. "Kansas City Blacks, Harry Truman and the Pendergast Machine." *Missouri Historical Review* 69 (1974): 65–82.

Hackney, Sheldon. "The Contradictory South." *Southern Cultures* 7 (2001): 65–80.

———. "The South as a Counterculture." *American Scholar* 42 (1973): 283–93.

———. "Southern Violence." *American Historical Review* 74 (1969): 906–25.

Hall, Alvin L. "Politics and Patronage: Virginia's Senators and the Roosevelt Purges of 1938." *Virginia Magazine of History and Biography* 82 (1974): 331–50.

Hall, Tomiko Brown. "The Gentleman's White Supremacist: J. Strom Thurmond, the Dixiecrat Campaign, and the Evolution of Southern Politics." *Southern Historian* 16 (1995): 61–86.

Hamby, Alonzo L. "Harry S. Truman." In *The American Presidents*, edited by Melvin I. Urofsky. New York, 2000.

———. "'The Modest and Capable Western Statesman': Harry S. Truman in the United States Senate, 1935–1940." *Congress and the Presidency* 17 (1990): 109–29.

———. "The Temperament of Harry S. Truman: An Interview with Alonzo Hamby." *The Woodrow Wilson Center Report* 4 (1992).

———. "Truman vs. Dewey: The 1948 Election." *Wilson Quarterly* 12 (1988): 48–65.

Hamilton, Virginia Van der Veer. "Lister Hill, Hugo Black, and the Albatross of Race." *Alabama Law Review* 36 (1985): 845–60.

Hardwick, Elizabeth. "Southern Literature: The Cultural Assumptions of Regionalism." In *Southern Literature: Heritage and Promise*, edited by Philip Castille and William Osborne. Memphis, Tenn., 1983.

Harris, Frederick C. "Notes on a Native Son: A Foreword." In *Reelection: William Jefferson Clinton as a Native-Son Presidential Candidate*, edited by Hanes Walton Jr. New York, 2000.

Harrison, Selig S. "Lyndon Johnson's World." *New Republic*, June 13, 1960, 15–23.

Heaster, Brenda L. "Who's on Second?" *Missouri Historical Review* 80 (1986): 156–75.

Heleniak, Roman. "Local Reaction to the Great Depression in New Orleans, 1929–1933." *Louisiana History* 10 (1969): 289–306.

————. "Lyndon Johnson in New Orleans." *Louisiana History* 21 (1980): 263–75.

Henderson, F. P. "FDR at Warm Springs." *Marine Corps Gazette* 66 (1982): 54–58.

Henriques, Peter R. "The Byrd Organization Crushes a Liberal Challenge, 1950–1953." *Virginia Magazine of History and Biography* 87 (1979): 3–29.

Herndon, Jane Walker. "Ed Rivers and Georgia's 'Little New Deal.'" *Atlanta Historical Journal* 30 (1986): 97–105.

Hesseltine, William B. "Sectionalism and Regionalism in American History." *Journal of Southern History* 26 (1960): 25–34.

Hixson, Walter L. "The 1938 Kentucky Senate Election: Alben W. Barkley, 'Happy' Chandler, and the New Deal." *Register of the Kentucky Historical Society* 80 (1982): 309–29.

Hodges, James A. "George Fort Milton and the New Deal." *Tennessee Historical Quarterly* 36 (1977): 383–409.

Hoffman, Edwin. "The Genesis of the Modern Movement for Equal Rights in South Carolina, 1930–1939." *Journal of Negro History* 44 (1959): 346–69.

Hofstadter, Richard. "From Calhoun to the Dixiecrats." *Social Research* 16 (1949): 135–50.

Hollis, Daniel W. "'Cotton Ed Smith'—Showman or Statesman?" *South Carolina Historical Magazine* 71 (1970): 235–56.

Holmes, Michael S. "The Blue Eagle as 'Jim Crow Bird': The NRA and Georgia's Black Workers." *Journal of Negro History* 57 (1972): 276–83.

————. "From Euphoria to Cataclysm: Georgia Confronts the Great Depression." *Georgia Historical Quarterly* 58 (1974): 313–30.

————. "The New Deal and Georgia's Black Youth." *Journal of Southern History* 38 (1972): 443–60.

Holtgrieve, Donald G. "Frederick Jackson Turner as a Regionalist." *Professional Geographer* 26 (1974): 159–65.

Hood, Mary, et al. "A Stubborn Sense of Place: Writers and Writings on the South." *Harper's* 273 (1986): 35–45.

Houston, Charles H., and John P. Davis. "TVA: Lily-White Reconstruction." *Crisis* 41 (1934): 290–91.

Hudson, Paul Stephen. "A Call for 'Bold Persistent Experimentation': FDR's Oglethorpe University Commencement Address, 1932." *Georgia Historical Quarterly* 78 (1994): 361–75.

Hughes, L. Patrick. "West Texas Swing: Roosevelt Purge in the Land of the Lone Star?" *West Texas Historical Association Year Book, 1999:* 41–53.

Hülsemann, Karsten. "Greenfields in the Heart of Dixie: How the American Auto Industry Discovered the South." In *The Second Wave: Southern Industrialization from the 1940s to the 1970s,* edited by Philip Scranton. Athens, Ga., 2001.

Hunter, Robert F. "Carter Glass, Harry Byrd, and the New Deal, 1932–1936." *Virginia Social Science Journal* 4 (1969): 91–103.

Irish, Marian D. "The Proletarian South." *Journal of Politics* 2 (1940): 231–58.

———. "The Southern One-Party System and National Politics." *Journal of Politics* 4 (1942): 80–94.

Jackson, J. W. "Texas Politics in 1948." *Southwest Social Science Quarterly* 30 (1949): 45–48.

Jakle, John A. "Time, Space, and the Geographic Past: A Prospectus for Historical Geography." *American Historical Review* 76 (1971): 1084–1103.

Janken, Kenneth R. "African-American Intellectuals Confront the 'Silent South': The *What the Negro Wants* Controversy." *North Carolina Historical Review* 70 (1993): 153–79.

Janos, Leo. "The Last Days of the President: LBJ in Retirement." *Atlantic* (July 1973): 35–41.

Jarman, Rufus. "Wool-Hat Dictator." *Saturday Evening Post,* June 27, 1942, 20–21, 109, 111–12.

Jeansonne, Glen. "Huey Long and Racism." *Louisiana History* 33 (1992): 265–82.

Johnson, Guy B. "Does the South Owe the Negro a New Deal?" *Social Forces* 13 (1934): 100–103.

Johnson, Vance. "The Old Deal Democrats." *American Mercury* 59 (1944): 50–57.

Jones, Sam H. "Will Dixie Bolt the New Deal?" *Saturday Evening Post,* March 6, 1943, 20–21, 42, 45.

Judt, Tony. "A Clown in Regal Purple: Social History and the Historians." *History Workshop Journal* (spring 1979): 66–94.

Juhnke, William E. "President Truman's Committee on Civil Rights: The Interaction of Politics, Protest, and Presidential Advisory Commission." *Presidential Studies Quarterly* 19 (1989): 593–610.

Kalmar, Karen L. "Southern Black Elites and the New Deal: A Case Study of Savannah, Georgia." *Georgia Historical Quarterly* 65 (1981): 341–55.

Karp, Walter. "In Defense of Politics: Against Theorists, Cynics, and the New Historians." *Harper's* 276 (1988): 41–49.

Katznelson, Ira, Kim Geiger, and Daniel Kryder. "Limiting Liberalism: The Southern Veto in Congress, 1933–1950." *Political Science Quarterly* 108 (1993): 283–306.

Katznelson, Ira, and Bruce Pietrykowski. "Rebuilding the American State: Evidence from the 1940s." *Studies in American Political Development* 5 (1991): 301–39.

Kaul, Arthur J. "Hazel Brannon Smith and the *Lexington Advertiser.*" In *The Press and Race: Mississippi Journalists Confront the Movement,* edited by David R. Davies. Jackson, Miss., 2001.

Kavanagh, Dennis. "Why Political Science Needs History." *Political Studies* 39 (1991): 479–95.

Kelley, Robert. "Ideology and Political Culture from Jefferson to Nixon." *American Historical Review* 82 (1977): 531–62.

Kemp, Kathryn W. "Warm Springs Recollections from the Graham Jackson Papers." *Atlanta Historical Journal* 29 (1985): 63–71.

Kent, Frank R. "Roosevelt's Bid for Dictatorship." *American Mercury* 43 (1938): 404–11.

Key, V. O., Jr. "The Erosion of Sectionalism." *Virginia Quarterly Review* 31 (1955): 161–79.

Kilpatrick, Carroll. "Will the South Secede?" *Harper's* 186 (1943): 415–21.

Kilpatrick, James Jackson. "Lyndon Johnson: Counterfeit Confederate." *Human Events,* August 25, 1960, 373–76.

King, Desmond. "'The Longest Road to Equality': The Politics of Institutional Desegregation under Truman." *Journal of Historical Sociology* 6 (1993): 119–63.

King, Larry L. "An Epitaph for LBJ." *Harper's* 236 (1968): 14–22.

———. "My Hero LBJ." *Harper's* 233 (1966): 51–66.

———. "We Ain't Trash No More!" *Esquire,* November 1976, 88–90, 152–56.

Kirby, Jack Temple. "The South as Pernicious Abstraction." *Perspectives on the American South: An Annual Review of Society, Politics and Culture,* edited by Merle Black and John Shelton Reed, 2 (1984): 167–79.

Kirkendall, Richard. "Truman and Missouri." *Missouri Historical Review* 81 (1987): 127–40.

———. "Truman's Path to Power." *Social Science* 43 (1968): 67–73.

Koeniger, A. Cash. "The New Deal and the States: Roosevelt Versus the Byrd Organization in Virginia." *Journal of American History* 68 (1982): 876–96.

———. "The Politics of Independence: Carter Glass and the Elections of 1936." *South Atlantic Quarterly* 80 (1981): 95–106.

Kollmorgen, Walter. "Crucial Deficiencies of Regionalism." *American Economic Review* 35 (1945): 377–89.

Kousser, J. Morgan. "Restoring Politics to Political History." *Journal of Interdisciplinary History* 12 (1982): 569–95.

Kowalewski, Michael. "Writing in Place: The New American Regionalism." *American Literary History* 6 (1994): 171–83.

Kruman, Marc W. "Quotas for Blacks: The Public Works Administration and the Black Construction Worker." *Labor History* 16 (1975): 37–49.

Kuhn, Cliff. "Reminiscences: Interviews with Atlanta New Deal Social Workers." *Atlanta Historical Journal* 30 (1986): 107–16.

Kuklinski, James H., Michael D. Cobb, and Martin Gilens. "Racial Attitudes and the 'New South.'" *Journal of Politics* 59 (1997): 323–49.

Landes, Ruth. "A Northerner Views the South." *Social Forces* 23 (1945): 375–79.

Langford, David L. "Going Back Home to the South." *Crisis* 101 (April 1994): 26, 35, 40.

Lawson, Steven F. "Civil Rights." In *Exploring the Johnson Years*, edited by Robert A. Divine. Austin, Tex., 1981.

———. "'I Got It from The New York Times,' Lyndon Johnson and the Kennedy Civil Rights Program." *Journal of Negro History* 67 (1982): 162–69.

———. "Mixing Moderation with Militancy: Lyndon Johnson and African-American Leadership." In *The Johnson Years, Volume 3: LBJ at Home and Abroad*, edited by Robert A. Divine. Lawrence, Kans., 1994.

Lawson, Steven F., and Mark I. Gelfand. "Consensus and Civil Rights: Lyndon B. Johnson and the Black Franchise." *Prologue* 8 (1976): 65–76.

Lee, David D. "The South and the American Mainstream: The Election of Jimmy Carter." *Georgia Historical Quarterly* 61 (1977): 7–12.

Leemhuis, Roger P. "Olin Johnston Runs for the Senate, 1938 to 1962." *South Carolina Historical Association Proceedings* 56 (1986): 57–69.

Leff, Mark. "Revisioning U.S. Political History." *American Historical Review* 100 (1995): 829–53.

Lemmon, Sarah McCulloh. "Governor Eugene Talmadge and the New Deal." In *Studies in Southern History*, edited by J. Carlyle Sitterson. Chapel Hill, N.C., 1957.

———. "The Ideology of the 'Dixiecrat' Coalition." *Social Forces* 30 (1951): 162–71.

Leuchtenburg, William E. "The Pertinence of Political History: Reflections on the Significance of the State in America." *Journal of American History* 73 (1986): 585–600.

———. "The Presidents Come to Chapel Hill." *Carolina Comments* 42 (1994): 52–63.

———. "The Twentieth-Century Presidency." In *Perspectives on Modern America: Making Sense of the Twentieth Century,* edited by Harvard Sitkoff. New York, 2001.

———. "The White House and Black America." In *Have We Overcome? Race Relations since* Brown, edited by Michael V. Namorato. Jackson, Miss., 1979.

Levine, Lawrence W. "Clio, Canons, and Culture." *Journal of American History* 80 (1993): 849–67.

Lewis, Peirce. "Defining a Sense of Place." *Southern Quarterly* 17 (1979): 24–46.

Lewis-Beck, Michael S., and Tom W. Rice. "Localism in Presidential Elections: The Home State Advantage." *American Journal of Political Science* 27 (1983): 548–56.

Linenthal, Edward Tabor. "'A Reservoir of Spiritual Power': Patriotic Faith at the Alamo in the Twentieth Century." *Southwestern Historical Quarterly* 91 (1988): 509–31.

Little, Stuart J. "More than Race: Strom Thurmond, the States' Rights Democrats, and Postwar Political Ideology." *Southern Studies* 4 (1993): 113–29.

Lively, Robert A. "The South and Freight Rates: Political Settlement of an Economic Argument." *Journal of Southern History* 14 (1948): 357–84.

Lomax, Louis E. "A Negro View: Johnson Can Free the South." *Look,* March 10, 1964, 34–38.

Lord, Guy Paul. "Mississippi Republicanism and the 1960 Election." *Journal of Mississippi History* 40 (1978): 3–48.

Lotchin, Roger W., and David R. Long. "World War II and the Transformation of Southern Urban Society: A Reconsideration." *Georgia Historical Quarterly* 83 (1999): 29–57.

Lubell, Samuel. "Has Truman Lost the South?" *Look,* October 24, 1950, 129–38.

Maney, Patrick J. "Hale Boggs: The Southerner as National Democrat. " In *Masters of the House: Congressional Leadership over Two Centuries,* edited by Roger H. Davidson, Susan Webb Hammond, and Raymond W. Smock. Boulder, Colo., 1998.

Marcello, Ronald E. "Senator Joseph Bailey, Harry Hopkins, and the WPA: A Prelude to the Conservative Coalition." *Southern Studies* 22 (1983): 321–39.

Marrs, Suzanne. "'The Huge Fateful Stage of the Outside World': Eudora Welty's Life in Politics." In *Eudora Welty and Politics: Did the Writer Crusade?* edited by Harriet Pollack and Suzanne Marrs. Baton Rouge, La., 2001.

Martin, Charles H. "Negro Leaders, the Republican Party and the Election of 1932." *Phylon* 32 (1971): 85–93.

———. "Southern Labor Relations in Transition: Gadsden, Alabama, 1930–1943." *Journal of Southern History* 47 (1981): 545–68.

Marty, Myron. "America Revising." *History Teacher* 15 (1982): 545–63.

Maverick, Maury. "Let's Join the United States." *Virginia Quarterly Review* 15 (1939): 64–70.

———. "The South Is Rising." *Nation*, June 17, 1936, 770–72.

Maverick, Maury, Jr. "The Hill Country of Lyndon Johnson." *New Republic,* March 14, 1964, 12–13.

Mayo, Selz C. "Social Change, Social Movements and the Disappearing Sectional South." *Social Forces* 43 (1964): 1–10.

McElvaine, Robert S. "New Deal Cultural Programs." In *Encyclopedia of Southern Culture,* edited by Charles Reagan Wilson and William Ferris. Chapel Hill, N.C., 1989.

———. "Old Times There Are Not Forgotten: A Personal View of the 'New South.'" *Midwest Quarterly* 19 (1978): 238–50.

McGill, Ralph. "Will the South Ditch Truman?" *Saturday Evening Post,* May 22, 1948, 15–17, 88–90.

McKinney, John C., and Linda Brookover Bourque. "The Changing South: National Incorporation of a Region." *American Sociological Review* 36 (1971): 399–412.

Mead, Howard N. "Russell vs. Talmadge: Southern Politics and the New Deal." *Georgia Historical Quarterly* 65 (1981): 28–45.

Meinig, D. W. "The Continuous Shaping of America: A Prospectus for Geographers and Historians." *American Historical Review* 83 (1978): 1186–1205.

Meyerowitz, Joanne. "History and September 11: An Introduction." *Journal of American History* 89 (2002): 415.

Mezerik, A. G. "Dixie Inventory." *Nation,* January 10, 1948, 41–43.

Minchew, Kaye Lanning. "Shaping a Presidential Image: FDR in Georgia." *Georgia Historical Quarterly* 83 (1999): 741–57.

Montgomery, Michael. "The Southern Accent—Alive and Well." *Southern Cultures* (Inaugural Issue, 1993): 47–64.

Moore, A. B. "One Hundred Years of Reconstruction in the South." *Journal of Southern History* 9 (1943): 153–80.

Moore, Glen. "An Analysis of Georgia's 1938 Senate Race." *Proceedings and Papers of the Georgia Association of Historians* 6 (1985): 87–95.

Morris, Willie. "A Sense of Place and the Americanization of Mississippi." *Southern Quarterly* 17 (1979): 3–13.

Morton, Ward M. "Report on Arkansas Politics in 1948." *Southwestern Social Science Quarterly* 30 (June 1949): 35–41.

Mothner, Ira. "The Texanization of Washington." *Look,* April 6, 1965, 30–34.

Moynihan, Daniel P. "The President and the Negro: The Moment Lost." *Commentary* 43 (1967): 31–45.

Murphy, Reg. "Not since Jefferson and Madison. . . . " *Saturday Review,* n.s. 3, September 4, 1976, 8–11.

Nelson, Lawrence J. "New Deal and Free Market: The Memphis Meeting of the Southern Commissioners of Agriculture, 1937." *Journal of Southern History* 40 (1981): 225–38.

———. "Welfare Capitalism on a Mississippi Plantation in the Great Depression." *Journal of Southern History* 50 (1984): 225–50.

Nelson, Michael. "History, Meet Politics." *American Prospect* 12 (June 18, 2001): 36–37.

Nettl, J. P. "The State as a Conceptual Variable." *World Politics* 20 (1968): 559–92.

Newton, Milton B., Jr. "Settlement Patterns as Artifacts of Social Structure." In *The Human Mirror: Material and Spatial Images of Man,* edited by Miles Richardson. Baton Rouge, La., 1974.

Nixon, H. Clarence. "Farm Tenancy to the Forefront." *Southwest Review* 22 (1936): 11–15.

———. "The New Deal and the South." *Virginia Quarterly Review* 19 (1943): 321–33.

Nixon, Ron. "The Dixiefication of America." *Southern Exposure* 24 (1996): 18–22.

Norrell, Robert J. "Labor at the Ballot Box: Alabama Politics from the New Deal to the Dixiecrat Movement." *Journal of Southern History* 57 (1991): 201–34.

Nuechterlein, James A. "The Politics of Civil Rights: The FEPC, 1941–46." *Prologue* 10 (1978): 171–91.

O'Brien, Michael. "C. Vann Woodward and the Burden of Southern Liberal-ism." *American Historical Review* 78 (1973): 589–604.

Odum, Howard W. "Regionalism vs. Sectionalism in the South's Place in the National Economy." *Social Forces* 12 (1934): 338–54.

——. "Social Change in the South." *Journal of Politics* 10 (1948): 242–58.

Parker, Roy, Jr. "Roosevelt's Enduring Legacy in the South." *Fayetteville (N.C.) Times,* January 30, 1982.

Patenaude, Lionel V. "The New Deal: Its Effect on the Social Fabric of Texas Society, 1933–1938." *Social Science Journal* 14 (1977): 51–60.

——. "Vice President John Nance Garner: A Study in the Use of Influence during the New Deal." *Texana* 11 (1973): 124–44.

Patterson, James T. "Americans and the Writing of Twentieth Century His-tory." In *Imagined Histories: American Historians Interpret the Past,* edited by Anthony Molho and Gordon S. Wood. Princeton, N.J., 1998.

——. "The Failure of Party Realignment in the South, 1937–1939." *Journal of Politics* 27 (1965): 602–17.

Patterson, Samuel G. "The Political Cultures of the American States." *Journal of Politics* 30 (1968): 187–209.

Peet, John. "A Survey of the American South." *The Economist* 10 (December 1994), Supplement: 1–18.

Pepper, Claude. "The Influence of the Deep South upon the Presidential Elec-tion of 1952." *Georgia Review* 6 (1952): 125–37.

Percy, Walker. "Mississippi: The Fallen Paradise." *Harper's* 230 (1965): 166–72.

Persky, Joseph. "Regional Colonialism and the Southern Economy." *Review of Radical Political Economics* 4 (1972): 70–79.

Petrocik, John R. "Realignment: New Party Coalitions and the Nationalization of the South." *Journal of Politics* 49 (1987): 347–75.

Phillips, Leon C. "A Southern Democrat Renounces the New Deal Party." *Manufacturers' Record* 112 (August 1943): 32–33, 60.

Pierce, Robert M. "Jimmy Carter and the New South: The View from New York." *Perspectives on the American South* 2 (1984): 181–94.

Pleasants, Julian M. "Claude Pepper, Strom Thurmond, and the 1948 Presi-dential Election in Florida." *Florida Historical Quarterly* 76 (1998): 439–73.

Polenberg, Richard. "The Decline of the New Deal, 1937–1940." In *The New Deal: The National Level,* edited by John Braeman, Robert H. Bremner, and David Brody. Columbus, Ohio, 1975.

————. "Roosevelt, Carter, and Executive Reorganization: Lessons of the 1930s." *Presidential Studies Quarterly* 9 (1979): 35–46.

Price, Edward T. "The Central Courthouse Square in the American County Seat." *Geographical Review* 58 (1968): 29–60.

Pycior, Julie Leininger. "From Hope to Frustration: Mexican Americans and Lyndon Johnson in 1967." *Western Historical Quarterly* 24 (1993): 468–94.

Rable, George C. "The South and the Politics of Antilynching Legislation, 1920–1940." *Journal of Southern History* 51 (1985): 201–20.

Raper, Arthur F. "Is There 'A New South'?" *New Republic,* August 18, 1952, 9–11.

————."The Southern Negro and the NRA." *Georgia Historical Quarterly* 64 (1980): 128–45.

Raper, Arthur F., and Ira DeA. Reid. "Old Conflicts in the New South." *Virginia Quarterly Review* 16 (1940): 218–29.

Rauh, Joseph L., Jr. "The Role of the Leadership Conference on Civil Rights in the Civil Rights Struggle of 1963–64." In *The Civil Rights Act of 1964: The Passage of the Law that Ended Segregation,* edited by Robert D. Loevy. Albany, N.Y., 1997.

Ray, Joseph M. "The Influence of the Tennessee Valley Authority on Government in the South."*American Political Science Review* 43 (1949): 922–32.

Reading, Don C. "New Deal Activity and the States, 1933–1939."*Journal of Economic History* 33 (1973): 792–807.

Reed, John Shelton. "The Banner That Won't Stay Furled." *Southern Cultures* 8 (2002): 76–100.

————. "For Dixieland: The Sectionalism of I'll Take My Stand." In *A Band of Prophets: The Vanderbilt Agrarians after Fifty Years,* edited by William C. Havard and Walter Sullivan. Baton Rouge, La., 1982.

————. "The Same Old Stand?" In *Why the South Will Survive,* by Fifteen Southerners. Athens, Ga., 1981.

————. "Southerners." In *The Harvard Encyclopedia of American Ethnic Groups,* edited by Stephan Thernstrom. Cambridge, Mass., 1980.

Reed, John Shelton, James Kohls, and Carol Hanchette. "The Dissolution of Dixie and the Changing Shape of the South." *Social Forces* 69 (1990): 221–33.

Reed, Merl E. "The FEPC, the Black Worker, and the Southern Shipyards," *South Atlantic Quarterly* 74 (1975): 446–67.

————. "FEPC and the Federal Agencies in the South." *Journal of Negro History* 65 (1980): 45–56.

———. "The Nashville Convention of the Southern Conference for Human Welfare, 1942." *Alabama Review* 37 (1984): 52–59.

Reichard, Gary W. "Democrats, Civil Rights, and Electoral Strategies in the 1950's." *Congress and the Presidency* 13 (1986): 59–81.

Reissman, Leonard. "Social Development and the American South." *Journal of Social Issues* 22 (1966): 101–16.

Rhoads, William B. "Franklin D. Roosevelt and the Architecture of Warm Springs." *Georgia Historical Quarterly* 67 (1983): 70–87.

Riccards, Michael P. "Rare Counsel: Kennedy, Johnson and the Civil Rights Bill of 1963." *Presidential Studies Quarterly* 11 (1981): 395–98.

Richards, Miles S. "The Progressive Democrats in Chicago, July 1944." *South Carolina Historical Magazine* 102 (2001): 219–37.

Riley, Michael J. "Constituting the Southwest, Contesting the Southwest, Reinventing the Southwest." *Journal of the Southwest* 36 (1994): 221–41.

Robertson, David Brian. "The Return to History and the New Institutionalism in American Political Science." *Social Science History* 17 (1993): 1–36.

Robertson, Robert J. "Congressman Jack Brooks, the Civil Rights Act of 1964, and the Desegregation of Public Accommodations and Facilities in Southeast Texas: A Preliminary Inquiry." *Texas Gulf Historical and Biographical Record* 35 (1999): 18–31.

Roche, Jeff. "The Emergence of a Conservative Ideology: Texas Panhandle Politics in the Sixties." *Mid-America* 81 (1999): 233–62.

Rodgers, Daniel T. "Regionalism and the Burdens of Progress." In *Region, Race, and Reconstruction: Essays in Honor of C. Vann Woodward,* edited by J. Morgan Kousser and James M. McPherson. New York, 1982.

Roebuck, James. "Virginia and the Election of 1948: Prelude to Massive Resistance." *Valley Forge Journal* 6 (1992): 89–105.

Rogers, William Warren, Jr. "The Death of a President, April 12, 1945: An Account from Warm Springs." *Georgia Historical Quarterly* 75 (1991): 106–20.

Rohde, David, W. "The Inevitability and Solidity of the 'Republican Solid South.'" *American Review of Politics* 17 (1996): 23–46.

Roland, Charles P. "The Ever-Vanishing South." *Journal of Southern History* 48 (1982): 3–20.

———. "The South, America's Will-o-the-Wisp Eden." *Louisiana History* 11 (1970): 101–19.

Rovit, Earl. "The Region versus the Nation: Critical Battles in the Thirties." *Mississippi Quarterly* 8 (1960): 89–98.

Rowan, Carl. "Was LBJ the Greatest Civil Rights President Ever?" *Ebony* (December 1990): 76–82.

Rubin, Louis D., Jr. "An Image of the South." In *The Lasting South: Fourteen Southerners Look at Their Home,* edited by Rubin and James Jackson Kilpatrick. Chicago, 1957.

Rustin, Bayard, and Tom Kahn. "Johnson So Far: Civil Rights." *Commentary* 39 (1965): 43–46.

Salmond, John. "Aubrey Williams: Atypical New Dealer?" In *The New Deal: The National Level,* edited by John Braeman, Robert H. Bremner, and David Brody. Columbus, Ohio, 1975.

———. "'Aubrey Williams Remembers': A Note on Franklin D. Roosevelt's Attitude Toward Negro Rights." *Alabama Review* 25 (1972): 62–77.

———. "Postscript to the New Deal: The Defeat of the Nomination of Aubrey W. Williams as Rural Electrification Administrator in 1945." *Journal of American History* 61 (1974): 417–36.

Sancton, Thomas. "White Supremacy—Crisis or Plot?" *Nation,* July 24, 1948, 95–98; July 31, 1948, 125–28.

Sanders, Charles L. "LBJ and Civil Rights: An Interview with Lady Bird Johnson." *Ebony* (March 1974): 154–61.

Sanders, Elizabeth. "Industrial Concentration, Sectional Competition, and Antitrust Politics in America, 1880–1980." *Studies in American Political Development* 1 (1986): 142–214.

Sarantakes, Nicholas Evan. "Lyndon Johnson, Foreign Policy, and the Election of 1960." *Southwestern Historical Quarterly* 103 (1999): 146–72.

Schmidt, William T. "The Impact of Camp Shelby in World War II on Hattiesburg, Mississippi." *Journal of Mississippi History* 39 (1977): 41–50.

Schnell, J. Christopher, Richard J. Collings, and David W. Dillard. "The Political Impact of the Depression on Missouri, 1929–1940." *Missouri Historical Review* 85 (1991): 131–57.

Schrag, Peter. "A Hesitant New South: Fragile Promise on the Last Frontier." *Saturday Review,* February 12, 1972, 51–57.

Schreiber, E. M. "Where the Ducks Are: Southern Strategy versus Fourth Party." *Public Opinion Quarterly* 35 (1971): 157–67.

Schwarz, Benjamin. "The Idea of the South." *Atlantic Monthly* (December 1997): 117–26.

Shannon, J. B. "Presidential Politics in the South: 1938, I." *Journal of Politics* 1 (1939): 146–70.

————. "Presidential Politics in the South: 1938, II." *Journal of Politics* 1 (1939): 278–300.

————. "Presidential Politics in the South." *Journal of Politics* 10 (1948): 464–89.

Shapiro, Edward. "The Southern Agrarians and the Tennessee Valley Authority." *American Quarterly* 29 (winter 1970): 791–806.

Shepard, Paul. "Place in American Culture." *North American Review* 262 (fall 1977): 22–32.

Shoutmatoff, Elizabeth. "FDR: The Last Photo." *American Heritage* 38 (1987): 102–3.

Shuman, Howard. "Senate Rules and the Civil Rights Bill: A Case Study." *American Political Science Review* 51 (1957): 955–75.

Silbey, Joel. "The State and Practice of American Political History at the Millennium: The Nineteenth Century as a Test Case." *Journal of Policy History* 11 (1999): 1–30.

Sillitoe, Alan. "A Sense of Place." *Geographical Magazine* 47 (1975): 685–89.

Simpson, George L. "Howard W. Odum and American Regionalism." *Social Forces* 34 (1955): 101–6.

Sindler, Allan. "The Unsolid South: A Challenge to the Democratic Party." In *The Uses of Power: 7 Cases in American Politics*, edited by Alan F. Westin. New York, 1962.

Sitkoff, Harvard. "Harry Truman and the Election of 1948: The Coming of the Age of Civil Rights in American Politics." *Journal of Southern History* 37 (1971): 597–616.

Skates, John Ray. "From Enchantment to Disillusionment: A Southern Editor Views the New Deal." *Southern Quarterly* 5 (1967): 363–80.

————. "World War II as a Watershed in Mississippi History." *Journal of Mississippi History* 37 (1975): 131–42.

Skocpol, Theda. "Bringing the State Back In." *Items* 36 (1982): 1–8.

Smith, C. Calvin. "The Politics of Evasion: Arkansas' Reaction to *Smith v. Allwright*, 1944." *Journal of Negro History* 67 (1982): 40–51.

Smith, Helena Huntington. "Mrs. Tilly's Crusade." *Collier's*, December 30, 1950, 28–29, 66–67.

Smith, Nancy Kegan. "Private Reflections on a Public Life: The Papers on Lady Bird Johnson at the LBJ Library." *Presidential Studies Quarterly* 20 (1990): 737–44.

Smith, Peter H. "Political History in the 1980s: A View from Latin America." *Journal of Interdisciplinary History* 12 (1981): 3–27.

Sosna, Morton. "More Important than the Civil War?: The Impact of World War II on the South." *Perspectives on the American South* 4 (1987): 145–61.

Spalding, Phinizy. "Georgia and the Election of Jimmy Carter." *Georgia Historical Quarterly* 61 (1977): 13–22.

Sparks, Randy J. "'Heavenly Houston' or 'Hellish Houston'?" *Southern Studies* 25 (1986): 353–66.

Spencer, Thomas T. "Bennett Champ Clark and the 1936 Presidential Campaign." *Missouri Historical Review* 75 (1981): 197–213.

Starr, J. Barton. "Birmingham and the 'Dixiecrat' Convention of 1948." *Alabama Historical Quarterly* 32 (1970): 23–50.

Steele, John L. "A Kingmaker or a Dark Horse?" *Life,* June 25, 1956, 111–24.

Stearns, Peter N. "Social and Political History." *Journal of Social History* 16 (1983): 3–5.

———. "Social History Present and Future." *Journal of Social History* 37 (2003): 9–19.

Stern, Mark. "Lyndon Johnson and the Democrats' Civil Rights Strategy." *Humboldt Journal of Social Relations* 16 (1990): 1–29.

———. "Lyndon Johnson and Richard Russell: Institutions, Ambitions and Civil Rights." *Presidential Studies Quarterly* 21 (1991): 687–704.

Stoker, Kevin. "Liberal Journalism in the Deep South: Harry M. Ayers and the 'Bothersome' Race Question." *Journalism History* 27 (2001): 22–33.

Stone, R. Phillip, II. "A Battle for Their Rights: Race and Reaction in South Carolina, 1940–1945." *Proceedings of the South Carolina Historical Association 1999:* 29–44.

Swain, Martha H. "The Lion and the Fox: The Relationship of President Franklin D. Roosevelt and Senator Pat Harrison." *Journal of Mississippi History* 38 (1976): 333–59.

———. "A New Deal for Mississippi Women, 1933–1943." *Journal of Mississippi History* 46 (1984): 191–212.

———. "Pat Harrison and the Social Security Act of 1935." *Southern Quarterly* 15 (1976): 1–14.

Sweeney, James R. "The Golden Silence: The Virginia Democratic Party and the Presidential Election of 1948." *Virginia Magazine of History and Biography* 82 (1974): 351–71.

———. "A New Day in the Old Dominion: The 1964 Presidential Election." *Virginia Magazine of History and Biography* 102 (1994): 307–48.

———. "Revolt in Virginia: Harry Byrd and the 1952 Presidential Election." *Virginia Magazine of History and Biography* 86 (1978): 180–95.

———. "'Sheep without a Shepherd': The New Deal Faction in the Virginia Democratic Party." *Presidential Studies Quarterly* 29 (1999): 438–59.

———. "Whispers in the Golden Silence: Harry F. Byrd, Sr., John F. Kennedy, and Virginia Democrats in the 1960 Election." *Virginia Magazine of History and Biography* 99 (1991): 3–44.

Thelen, David. "The Practice of American History." *Journal of American History* 81 (1994): 933–68.

Thomas, Mary Martha. "The Mobile Homefront during the Second World War." *Gulf Coast Historical Quarterly* 1 (1986): 55–75.

Tindall, George B. "The Benighted South: Origins of a Modern Image." *Virginia Quarterly Review* 40 (1964): 281–94.

———. "The 'Colonial Economy' and the Growth Psychology: The South in the 1930's." *South Atlantic Quarterly* 64 (1965): 465–77.

———. "The Significance of Howard W. Odum to Southern History: A Preliminary Estimate." *Journal of Southern History* 24 (1958): 285–307.

———. "The Status and Future of Regionalism—A Symposium." *Journal of Southern History* 26 (1960): 22–24.

Vaughan, Philip H. "President Truman's Committee on Civil Rights: The Urban Implications." *Missouri Historical Review* 66 (1972): 413–30.

———. "The Truman Administration's Fair Deal for Black America." *Missouri Historical Review* 70 (1976): 291–305.

Veysey, Laurence R. "Myth and Reality in Approaching American Regionalism." *American Quarterly* 12 (1960): 31–43.

Vorse, Mary Heaton. "The South Has Changed." *Harper's* 199 (1949): 27–33.

Walker, Melissa. "African Americans and TVA Reservoir Property Removal: Race in a New Deal Program." *Agricultural History* 72 (1998): 417–28.

Walker, Stanley. "Is Texas 'South,' 'West,' Both or More?" *New York Times Magazine,* April 12, 1959, 35–36.

Watson, Denton L. "The Papers of the '101st Senator': Clarence Mitchell Jr. and Civil Rights." *Historian* 64 (2002): 623–41.

Webb, Melody. "Lyndon Johnson: The Last Frontier President." *Journal of the West* 34 (1995): 73–82.

Webster, Gerald R. "Demise of the Solid South." *Geographical Review* 82 (1992): 43–55.

Wechsler, James A. and Nancy F. "The Road Ahead for Civil Rights: The President's Report One Year Later." *Commentary* 6 (1948): 297–304.

Weill, Susan. "The Dixiecrats and the Mississippi Daily Press." *Journal of Mississippi History* 64 (2002): 259–81.

Westbrook, John T. "Twilight of Regionalism." *Southwest Review* 42 (1957): 231–34.

Whatley, Larry F. "The Works Progress Administration in Mississippi." *Journal of Mississippi History* 30 (1968): 35–50.

White, Theodore. "Texas: Land of Wealth and Fear." *Reporter,* May 25, 1954, 10–17; June 8, 1954, 30–40.

White, William S. "Who *Is* Lyndon Johnson?" *Harper's* 216 (1958): 53–58.

Wilentz, Sean. "On Class and Politics in Jacksonian America." *Reviews in American History* 10 (1982): 45–63.

Williams, David C. "The Legend of Lyndon Johnson." *The Progressive* 21 (1957): 20–23.

Williams, Raymond. "Decentralism and the Politics of Place." In *Resources of Hope: Culture, Democracy, Socialism,* edited by Robin Gale. London, 1989.

Williams, T. Harry. "Huey, Lyndon, and Southern Radicalism." *Journal of American History* 60 (1973): 267–93.

Wilson, Thomas D. "Chester A. Franklin and Harry S. Truman: An African-American Conservative and the 'Conversion' of the Future President." *Missouri Historical Review* 88 (1993): 48–77.

Winks, Robin W. "Regionalism in Comparative Perspective." In *Regionalism and the Pacific Northwest,* edited by William G. Robbins, Robert J. Frank, and Richard E. Ross. Corvallis, Ore., 1983.

Woods, Randall Bennett. "Dixie's Dove: J. William Fulbright, the Vietnam War, and the American South." *Journal of Southern History* 60 (1994): 533–52.

Woodward, C. Vann. "The Great Civil Rights Debate: The Ghost of Thaddeus Stevens in the Senate Chamber." *Commentary* 24 (1957): 283–91.

———. "Hillbilly Realism." *Southern Review* 4 (1939): 676–81.

———. "Look Away, Look Away." *Journal of Southern History* 59 (1993): 487–504.

Woolfolk, Sarah Van V. "Alabama Attitudes toward the Republican Party in 1868 and 1964." *Alabama Review* 20 (1967): 27–33.

Wright, Fielding L., as told to Howard Suttle. "Give the Government Back to the People." *American Magazine* 146 (July 1948): 36–37, 126–27.

Wright, Gavin. "The Civil Rights Revolution as Economic History." *Journal of Economic History* 59 (1999): 267–90.

———. "The Political Economy of New Deal Spending: An Econometric Analysis." *Review of Economics and Statistics* 56 (1974): 30–38.

Wright, Lawrence. "Was Dallas a City of Hate?" *Dallas* (November 1988): 62–67, 93–103.

Wyche, Billy Hall. "Southern Industrialists View Organized Labor in the New Deal Years, 1933–1941." *Southern Studies* 19 (1980): 157–71.

Yoder, Edwin M., Jr. "Thoughts on the Dixiefication of Dixie." In *Dixie Dateline: A Journalistic Portrait of the Contemporary South,* edited by John B. Boles. Houston, Tex., 1983.

Zakaria, Fareed. "The End of the End of History." *Newsweek,* September 24, 2001, 70.

Zarefsky, David. "Subordinating the Civil Rights Issue: Lyndon Johnson in 1964." *Southern Speech Communication Journal* 48 (1983): 103–18.

Zeigler, Luther Harmon, Jr. "Senator Walter George's 1938 Campaign." *Georgia Historical Quarterly* 43 (1959): 333–52.

UNPUBLISHED ESSAYS

Aistrup, Joseph A. "The Southern Strategy and the Development of the Southern Republican Parties." Ph.D. dissertation, Indiana University, 1989.

Ashley, Frank W. "Selected Southern Liberal Editors and the States' Rights Movement of 1948." Ph.D. dissertation, University of South Carolina, 1959.

Ashmore, Susan Youngblood. "Carry It On: The War on Poverty and the Civil Rights Movement in Alabama, 1964–1970." Ph.D. dissertation, Auburn University, 1999.

Ayers, Edward L. "Why Place Still Matters." Conference paper, University of Virginia, Charlottesville, Va., June 1999.

Badger, Tony. "Southerners Who Refused to Sign the Southern Manifesto." Paper delivered at Organization of American Historians meeting, April 1997.

Balthrope, Robin Bernice. "Lawlessness and the New Deal: Congress and Antilynching Legislation, 1934–1938." Ph.D. dissertation, Ohio State University, 1995.

Banks, James G. "Strom Thurmond and the Revolt against Modernity." Ph.D. dissertation, Kent State University, 1970.

Behel, Sandra K. "The Mississippi Home Front during World War II: Tradition and Change." Ph.D. dissertation, Mississippi State University, 1989.

Berman, Larry. "Lyndon Johnson's Presidential Leadership: Paths Chosen and Opportunities Lost." Paper delivered at conference on leadership in the modern presidency, Princeton University, April 1987.

Borsos, John E. "Support for the National Democratic Party in South Carolina during the Dixiecrat Revolt of 1948." M.A. essay, University of South Carolina, 1987.

Brooks, Jennifer Elizabeth. "From Hitler and Tojo to Talmadge and Jim Crow: World War II Veterans and the Remaking of Southern Political Tradition." Ph.D. dissertation, University of Tennessee, Knoxville, 1997.

Brown, Deward Clayton. "Rural Electrification in the South, 1920–1955." Ph.D. dissertation, University of California, Los Angeles, 1970.

Burns, Gladys King. "The Alabama Dixiecrat Revolt of 1948." M.A. thesis, Auburn University, 1965.

Burran, James Albert, III. "Racial Violence in the South during World War II." Ph.D. dissertation, University of Tennessee, 1977.

Cann, Marvin Leigh. "Burnett Rhett Maybank and the New Deal in South Carolina, 1931–1941." Ph.D. dissertation, University of North Carolina at Chapel Hill, 1967.

Carney, Carolyn Ann. "The 'City of Hate': Anti-Communist and Conservative Attitudes in Dallas, Texas, 1950–1964." M.A. essay, University of Texas at Arlington, 1994.

Carpenter, JoAnn Deakin. "Olin D. Johnston, the New Deal and the Politics of Class in South Carolina, 1934–1938." Ph.D. dissertation, Emory University, 1987.

Cobb, James C. "Eugene Talmadge and the Purge: The Georgia Senatorial Campaign of 1938." M.A. essay, University of Georgia, 1972.

———. "Politics in a New South City: Augusta, Georgia, 1946–1971." Ph.D. dissertation, University of Georgia, 1975.

Cravens, Chris. "Edwin A. Walker and the Right Wing in Dallas, 1960–1966." M.A. essay, Southwest Texas State University, 1991.

Crawley, William Bryan, Jr. "The Governorship of William M. Tuck: Virginia Politics in the 'Golden Age' of the Byrd Organization." Ph.D. dissertation, University of Virginia, 1974.

Crownover, A. Blair. "Franklin D. Roosevelt and the Primary Campaigns of the 1938 Congressional Election." Senior thesis, Princeton University, 1955.

Dayhuff, Travis. "The 1938 'Purge' Campaign in South Carolina and Southern Political Culture in the New Deal Era." M.A. essay, University of Tennessee, Knoxville, 1994.

Dunar, Andrew J. "Truman on Civil Rights: A Post-Presidential Perspective." Paper delivered at Southern Historical Association meeting, November 1995.

Dunn, James William. "The New Deal and Florida Politics." Ph.D. dissertation, Florida State University, 1971.

Dyer, Stanford. "Lyndon B. Johnson and the Politics of Civil Rights, 1935–1960: The Art of 'Moderate' Leadership." Ph.D. dissertation, Texas A & M University, 1978.

Ethridge, Richard Calvin. "Mississippi's Role in the Dixiecratic Movement." Ph.D. dissertation, Mississippi State University, 1971.

Faggart, Luther Brady. "Defending the Faith: The 1950 U.S. Senate Race in South Carolina." M.A. essay, University of South Carolina, 1992.

Fagin, Vernon Allen. "Franklin D. Roosevelt, Liberalism in the Democratic Party, and the 1938 Congressional Elections: The Urge to Purge." Ph.D. dissertation, University of California, Los Angeles, 1979.

Ficken, Robert Edwin. "The Democratic Party and Domestic Politics during World War II." Ph.D. dissertation, University of Washington, 1973.

Field, Betty Marie. "The Politics of the New Deal in Louisiana, 1933–1939." Ph.D. dissertation, Tulane University, 1973.

Flanagan, Beth K. "The Use of the Myth of the American West in the Political Campaigns of Lyndon Johnson and Ronald Reagan." Term paper, Morse College, Yale University, 1988.

Fleming, Douglas Lee. "Atlanta, the Depression, and the New Deal." Ph.D. dissertation, Emory University, 1984.

Fossett, Roy Edward. "The Impact of the New Deal on Georgia Politics, 1933–1941." Ph.D. dissertation, University of Florida, 1960.

Garcia, Elvia. "Lady Bird Johnson's Whistle Stopping through the South." Senior thesis, University of Texas, 1986.

Gardner, James B. "Political Leadership in a Period of Transition: Frank G. Clement, Albert Gore, Estes Kefauver, and Tennessee Politics, 1948–1956." Ph.D. dissertation, Vanderbilt University, 1978.

Gaskin, Thomas M. "Lyndon B. Johnson and Senator Richard B. Russell:

Death of a Friendship." Paper delivered at Southern Historical Association meeting, November 1989.

Germany, Kent Barnett. "Rise of the Dixiecrats: Louisiana's Conservative Defection from the National Democratic Party, 1944–1948." M.A. essay, Louisiana Technical University, 1994.

Green, George N. "The Far Right Wing in Texas Politics, 1930s–1960s." Ph.D. dissertation, Florida State University, 1966.

Grothaus, Larry Henry. "The Negro in Missouri Politics, 1890–1941." Ph.D. dissertation, University of Missouri at Columbia, 1970.

Hales, Troy Kenneth. "Josephus Daniels and the Department of the Navy: A Southern Progressive in National Administration." M.A. essay, University of North Carolina at Chapel Hill, 1991.

Hall, Alvin LeRoy. "James H. Price and Virginia Politics, 1878 to 1943." Ph.D. dissertation, University of Virginia, 1970.

Hasting, Ann Celeste. "Intraparty Struggle: Harry S. Truman—1945–1948." Ph.D. dissertation, St. Louis University, 1972.

Hayes, Jack Irby, Jr. "South Carolina and the New Deal, 1932–1938." Ph.D. dissertation, University of South Carolina, 1972.

Hayes, Robert Edward. "Senatorial Voting Behavior with Regard to the 'Southern Interest.'" Ph.D. dissertation, University of Colorado, 1964.

Henriques, Peter R. "John S. Battle and Virginia Politics, 1948–1953." Ph.D. dissertation, University of Virginia, 1971.

Herndon, Jane Walker. "Eurith Dickinson Rivers: A Political Biography." Ph.D. dissertation, University of Georgia, 1974.

Heyer, Val. "Expression of a National Conscience: Harry S. Truman's President's Committee on Civil Rights and Its Report." Term paper, University of Richmond, 1994.

Hilliard, Elbert Riley. "A Biography of Fielding Wright: Mississippi's Mr. States' Rights." M.A. essay, Mississippi State University, 1959.

Holden, Anna. "Race and Politics: Congressional Elections in the Fifth District of Georgia, 1946 to 1952." M.A. essay, University of North Carolina at Chapel Hill, 1955.

Holley, Steven Dwight. "The Dallas *Morning News* and the *Times-Herald* and the Image of Dallas in the Decade after the Kennedy Assassination." M.A. essay, University of Texas, 1974.

Hopper, John Edward. "The Purge: Franklin D. Roosevelt and the 1938 Democratic Nominations." Ph.D. dissertation, University of Chicago, 1966.

Houghton, Jonathan. Draft, Ph.D. dissertation on the Republican Party in North Carolina, University of North Carolina at Chapel Hill.

Janeway, Michael C. "Lyndon Johnson and the Rise of Conservatism in Texas." Senior thesis, Harvard University, 1952.

Johnson, Carolyn M. "A Southern Response to Civil Rights: Lyndon Baines Johnson and Civil Rights Legislation 1956–1960." M.A. essay, University of Houston, 1975.

Johnson, Karen Kalmar. "Lyndon Johnson and Richard Russell: Southerners at War over the Great Society." Paper delivered at Southern Historical Association meeting, November 1989.

Kabat, Ric A. "From New Deal to Red Scare: The Political Odyssey of Senator Claude D. Pepper." Ph.D. dissertation, Florida State University, 1995.

Kane, Peter Evans. "The Senate Debate on the 1964 Civil Rights Act." Ph.D. dissertation, Purdue University, 1967.

Keadey, Stephen C. Draft of Ph.D. dissertation on Lyndon B. Johnson and civil rights, 1965–68, University of North Carolina at Chapel Hill.

———. "Sound Government and the Silent South: Business Progressivism and the University of North Carolina, 1919–1940." M.A. essay, North Carolina State University, 1994.

Kinsella, Dorothy C., O.S.F. "Southern Apologists: A Liberal Image." Ph.D. dissertation, St. Louis University, 1971.

Kirkendall, Richard S. "Truman and the South." Paper delivered at Southern Historical Association meeting, October 1969.

Klimmer, Richard. "Liberal Attitudes Toward the South: 1930–1965." Ph.D. dissertation, Northwestern University, 1976.

Koehler-Shapley, Thomas. "Robert Mc C Figg, Jr.: South Carolina's Lawyers' Lawyer." M.A. essay, University of South Carolina, 1994.

Kruse, Kevin M. "North Carolinians' Reaction to Truman's Civil Rights Program (1947–1948)." Senior honors thesis, University of North Carolina at Chapel Hill, 1994.

Landrum, Clarence Ervin. "The States' Rights Democratic Movement of 1948." M.A. essay, Wofford College, 1950.

Leary, William Henry. "Race Relations in Turmoil: Southern Liberals and World War II." M.A. essay, University of Virginia, 1967.

Leigh, Marvin. "Burnett Rhett Maybank and the New Deal in South Carolina, 1931–1941." Ph.D. dissertation, University of North Carolina at Chapel Hill, 1967.

Lofton, Paul Stroman. "A Social and Economic History of Columbia, South Carolina, during the Great Depression, 1929–1940." Ph.D. dissertation, University of Texas, 1977.

Lovell, E. Thomas. "Houston's Reaction to the New Deal, 1932–1936." M.A. essay, University of Houston, 1964.

MacLean, Nancy. "From the Benighted South to the Sunbelt: The South in the Twentieth Century." Paper delivered at the Twentieth Century Conference, University of New Hampshire, April 17, 1999.

McClain, David H. "The Politics of Freedom: Conflicts between Lyndon Johnson and James Farmer during the 1964 Presidential Campaign." Term paper, University of Texas, 1989.

McEvoy, James, III. "The American Right in the National Election of 1964." Ph.D. dissertation, University of Michigan, 1968.

McLaurin, Ann Mathison. "The Role of the Dixiecrats in the 1948 Election." Ph.D. dissertation, University of Oklahoma, 1972.

McMillen, Neil R. Commentary on "The Death of a Friendship: Richard Russell and Lyndon Johnson." Southern Historical Association meeting, November 1989.

Melton, Thomas R. "Mr. Speaker: A Biography of Walter Sillers." M.A. essay, University of Mississippi, 1972.

Melton, Thomas Rand. "The 1960 Presidential Election in Georgia." Ph.D. dissertation, University of Mississippi, 1985.

Miller, Anthony Barry. "Palmetto Politician: The Early Political Career of Olin D. Johnston, 1896–1945." Ph.D. dissertation, University of North Carolina at Chapel Hill, 1976.

Moltke-Hansen, David. "Regional Frameworks and Networks: Changing Identities in the Southeastern United States." Paper delivered in Germany, 1997.

Moore, Winfred Bobo, Jr. "New South Statesman: The Political Career of James Francis Byrnes, 1911–1941." Ph.D. dissertation, Duke University, 1975.

Nelson, Justin. "Drafting Lyndon Johnson: The President's Secret Role in the 1968 Democratic Convention." Senior essay, Yale University, 1997.

Ness, Gary Clifford. "The States' Rights Democratic Movement of 1948." Ph.D. dissertation, Duke University, 1972.

Newberry, Anthony Lake. "Without Urgency or Ardor: The South's Middle-of-the-Road Liberals and Civil Rights, 1945–1960." Ph.D. dissertation, Ohio University, 1982.

Nitschke, Marie Morris. "Virginius Dabney of Virginia: Portrait of a Southern

Journalist in the Twentieth Century." Ph.D. dissertation, Emory University, 1987.

Olinger, James M., Jr. "The Congressional Career of John W. Flannagan, Jr." M.A. essay, East Tennessee State College, 1954.

Pack, Lindsy Escoe. "The Political Aspects of the Texas Tidelands Controversy." Ph.D. dissertation, Texas A & M University, 1979.

Parker, Daniel P. "The Political and Social Views of Harry S. Truman." Ph.D. dissertation, University of Pennsylvania, 1951.

Patton, Randall Lee. "Southern Liberals and the Emergence of a 'New South,' 1938–1950." Ph.D. dissertation, University of Georgia, 1990.

Pope, Robert Dean. "Senatorial Baron: The Long Political Career of Kenneth D. McKellar." Ph.D. dissertation, Yale University, 1976.

Potenziani, David Daniel. "Look to the Past: Richard B. Russell and the Defense of Southern White Supremacy." Ph.D. dissertation, University of Georgia, 1981.

Pritchard, Robert Louis. "Southern Politics and the Truman Administration: Georgia as a Test Case." Ph.D. dissertation, University of California, Los Angeles, 1970.

Raper, Arthur. Talk to History Honor Society. University of North Carolina at Chapel Hill, January 29, 1974.

Ratliff, Sarah F. "The Career of Thomas Lowry Bailey." M.S. essay, Mississippi State College, 1952.

Reinhart, Cornel Justin. "FEPC During the Truman Era." M.A. essay, University of South Dakota, 1968.

Roebuck, James Randolph, Jr. "Virginia in the Election of 1948." M.A. essay, University of Virginia, 1969.

Rosenstein, Joel. "Lyndon B. Johnson and the 1964 Civil Rights Act." Senior honors thesis, University of North Carolina at Chapel Hill, 1993.

Rosenzweig, Allen. "The Influence of Class and Race on Political Behavior in New Orleans: 1960–1967." M.A. essay, University of Oklahoma, 1967.

Ruby, Roy H. "The Presidential Election of 1944 in Mississippi: The Bolting Electors." M.A. essay, Mississippi State University, 1966.

Scott, Carole E. "The Economic Impact of the New Deal on the South." Ph.D. dissertation, Georgia State University, 1969.

Secrest, Andrew McDowd. "In Black and White: Press Opinion and Race Relations in South Carolina, 1954–64." Ph.D. dissertation, Duke University, 1971.

Semes, Robert Louis. "The Virginia Press Looks at the New Deal, 1933–1937." M.A. essay, University of Virginia, 1968.

Shaw, Harmon Dean, Jr. "Mississippi and the Election of 1932." M.A. essay, Mississippi State University, 1965.

Shouse, Sarah Newman. "Herman Clarence Nixon: A Biography." Ph.D. dissertation, Auburn University, 1984.

Simon, Bryant. "A Fabric of Defeat: The Politics of South Carolina Textile Workers in State and Nation, 1920–1938." Ph.D. dissertation, University of North Carolina at Chapel Hill, 1992.

———. "Rumors of Eleanor Clubs: Windows into the Wartime Fears of White Southerners." Paper delivered at the Southern Historical Association meeting, November 1997.

Sistrom, Michael Paul. "Authors of the Liberation: The Mississippi Freedom Democrats and the Redefinition of Politics." Ph.D. dissertation, University of North Carolina at Chapel Hill, 2002.

Smallwood, James M. "Texas Public Opinion and the Supreme Court Fight of 1937." M.A. essay, East Texas State University, 1969.

Stayer, James M. "A History of the Presidential Campaigns of 1948." M.A. essay, University of Virginia, 1958.

Steiner, Michael Clark. "The Regional Impulse in the United States, 1923–1941." Ph.D. dissertation, University of Minnesota, 1978.

Stephenson, Charles W. "The Democrats of Texas and Texas Liberalism, 1944–1960: A Study in Political Frustration." M.A. essay, Southwest Texas State College, 1967.

Stern, Mark. "Lyndon Johnson and the Democrats' Civil Rights Strategy." Paper delivered at the American Political Science Association meeting, 1989.

Strobel, Marian E. "FDR and the Nation's 'No. 1 Economic Problem': 1938." M.A. essay, Duke University, 1971.

Sullivan, Patricia. "Gideon's Southern Soldiers: New Deal Politics and Civil Rights Reform, 1933–1948." Ph.D. dissertation, Emory University, 1983.

Sweeney, James Robert. "Byrd and Anti-Byrd: The Struggle for Political Supremacy in Virginia, 1945–1954." Ph.D. dissertation, University of Notre Dame, 1973.

Tate, Roger D., Jr. "Easing the Burden: The Era of Depression and New Deal in Mississippi." Ph.D. dissertation, University of Tennessee, Knoxville, 1978.

Thurber, Timothy. "'The Politics of Consensus': Hubert Humphrey and Civil Rights, 1952–1957." M.A. essay, University of North Carolina at Chapel Hill, 1991.

———. Draft, Ph.D. dissertation on Hubert Humphrey and Civil Rights, University of North Carolina at Chapel Hill.

Tolleson, William Jean. "The Rift in the Texas Democratic Party, 1944." M.A. essay, University of Texas, 1953.

Tuggle, John Anthony. "The Dixiecrats as a 'Stepping-Stone' to Two-Party Politics for Mississippi." M.A. essay, University of Southern Mississippi, 1994.

Vance, Sandra Stringer. "The Congressional Career of John Bell Williams, 1947–1967." Ph.D. dissertation, Mississippi State University, 1976.

Vaughan, Philip H. "Urban Aspects of Civil Rights and the Early Truman Administration." Ph.D. dissertation, University of Oklahoma, 1971.

Vincent, Martha Kennedy. "The States' Rights Movement of 1948 in South Carolina: South Carolina Bolts the National Democratic Party." M.A. essay, University of South Carolina, 1971.

Walker, Emma Jean. "The Contemporary Texan: An Examination of Major Additions to the Mythical Texan in the Twentieth Century." Ph.D. dissertation, University of Texas, 1966.

Wallace, Harold Lew. "The Campaign of 1948." Ph.D. dissertation, Indiana University, 1970.

Wells, Raymond B. "The States' Rights Movement of 1948: A Case Study." M.A. essay, Mississippi State University, 1965.

Westerhoff, Arjen. "Politics of Protest: Strom Thurmond and the Development of the Republican Southern Strategy, 1948–1972." M.A. essay, Smith College, 1997.

Wilkerson-Freeman, Sarah. "Women and the Transformation of American Politics: North Carolina, 1898–1940." Ph.D. dissertation, University of North Carolina at Chapel Hill, 1995.

Williams, Elizabeth C. "The Anti-Byrd Organization Movement in Virginia, 1948–1949." M.A. essay, University of Virginia, 1969.

Williams, Kenneth H. "Mississippi and Civil Rights, 1945–1954." Ph.D. dissertation, Mississippi State University, 1985.

Wolfe, Donald Thomas. "Southern Strategy: Race, Region, and Republican Presidential Politics, 1964 and 1968." Ph.D. dissertation, The Johns Hopkins University, 1974.

Wolfe, Jonathan James. "Virginia in World War II." Ph.D. dissertation, University of Virginia, 1971.

Young, Roy Earl. "Presidential Leadership and Civil Rights Legislation, 1963–1964." Ph.D. dissertation, University of Texas, 1969.

INDEX

Page numbers followed by *n* refer to endnotes.

Carmichael, Stokely, 337, 339, 346, 517*n*–18*n*

Caro, Robert, 330

Carpenter, Elizabeth, 231, 235, 317

Carson, Kit, 154

Carter, Billy, 390, 403

Carter, Dan, 116

Carter, Hodding, III, 418, 472*n*

Carter, Jimmy
  cabinet and advisers, 388
  domestic policy, 397
  election of 1976 and, 386–87, 390, 397, 402, 405
  election of 1980 and, 396
  family of, 314, 390, 403, 405–6
  as governor, 405
  on LBJ, 324
  Northern views on, 386–87, 390, 391–92
  racial attitudes of, 390
  as Southerner, 1, 385–89, 390, 391–92
  Southern views on, 387, 388, 389–90, 390–91, 391
  views on government, 14, 19, 392

Cash, W. J., 21, 46, 119

Castel, Albert, 148

Cater, Douglass, 256

Catledge, Turner, 51, 84

Cayton, Horace, 57

CCC. *See* Civilian Conservation Corps

Censorship, in South, 142

Central Georgia Railroad, 126

Chapel Hill regionalists, 107–8

Charleston News and Courier (newspaper), 101, 175, 288

Charlotte Observer (newspaper), 88, 286, 315

Charlton, Louise, 452*n*–53*n*

Chattanooga Free Press (newspaper), 201

Chattanooga News (newspaper), 51, 111

Cherry, R. Gregg, 185, 190

Chicago Defender (newspaper), 162, 206, 263, 332

Chicago Herald American (newspaper), 160

Chicago machine, 83

Chicago Tribune (newspaper), 285

A Childhood (Crews), 6

Child labor, ending of, 74, 75

Chiles, Jim Crow, 151, 463*n*

Christian Science Monitor (periodical), 155

CIO. *See* Congress of Industrial Organizations

The Citadel, 400

Civil Aeronautics Administration, 214

Civilian Conservation Corps (CCC)
  Black employment in, 62, 70, 435*n*
  director of, 46
  impact on South, 353, 354, 363
  racial discrimination in, 56, 61

Civil rights (*See also* Discrimination; Segregation; White supremacy)
  Eleanor Roosevelt's activism in, 57–58, 60, 63–64, 114–15, 122, 126, 130–31, 133, 176, 458*n*
  federal defense of, as concept, 171

LBJ and
  Civil Rights Act of 1960, 268–71, 275, 300
  Civil Rights Act of 1964. *See* Civil Rights Act (1964)
  on civil rights movement, 409
  as Congressman, 245–47, 305
  Fair Housing Act, 336–37, 521*n*
  historians on, 345–46
  Howard University Speech, 335
  "Nigra, Nigra, Nigra" speech, 320–22
  Northern views on, 376
  as President, 297–98, 300–303, 303–9, 327–38, 343–46
  pressure to act, 258–60
  as Senate leader, 251–52, 256–65, 267–71
  as Senator, 247–50
  Southern views on, 222, 258, 265, 269–71, 276, 307–8, 313–15, 337, 343–44, 495*n*–96*n*, 516*n*–17*n*
  strategies, 378–81, 379
  underlying motivations, 261–62, 267, 302, 305
  urgency felt by, 257–58, 268–69
  as Vice President, 293–95

Morse, Wayne, 251

Moses, George, 456*n*

Mount Rushmore, 19

Mowry, George, 47

Moyers, Bill, 257, 299–300, 307, 320, 325, 343, 345

Moynihan, Patrick, 338

Murphy, Charles, 37

Murphy, Frank, 63

Murphy, Reg, 407

Murray, Albert, 6, 382–83

Murray, Alfalfa Bill, 196

Murray, Pauli, 435*n*

Museum of the Confederacy, 400

Myrdal, Gunnar, 68, 114

NAACP. *See* National Association for the Advancement of Colored People

Napoleon I (Napoleon Bonaparte), 17

Nashville agrarians, 113

Nashville Banner (newspaper), 178

Natchez Democrat (newspaper), 45

The Nation (periodical), 105, 108

National Airport, desegregation of, 214

National Association for the Advancement of Colored People (NAACP)

anti-lynching activism, 57–58

appeal to UN, 169

on civil rights bill of 1957, 264

on FDR, 54

Goldwater and, 309, 311, 509*n*

on LBJ, 247, 251–52, 282, 335

legal challenges by, 176

on New Deal, 56

on PCCR, 166

on Reagan, 395

Southern views on, 275

staff of, 62, 65, 225

Truman and, 153, 156–57, 171–72, 367

National Association of Broadcasters, 300

National, as term, 23

National Council of Negro Women, 59

National Defense Advisory Commission, 65

National Emergency Committee Against Mob Violence, 165–66

National Emergency Council (NEC), 357 (See also *Report on Economic Conditions of the South*)

National Industrial Recovery Act, 73–74, 80, 441*n*

National Labor Relations (Wagner) Act, 74, 84, 441*n*

National Labor Relations Board, 353

National Manufacturers' Association (National Association of Manufacturers), 82

National Museum of American History, 12

National Negro Congress, 64

National Old Trails Association, 154

National Recovery Administration (NRA), 56–57, 66, 120, 125

National Security Council, 342

National Urban League, 301, 309

National Youth Administration (NYA), 62, 63, 233, 335, 355, 487*n*

NEC. *See* National Emergency Council

Nelson, Michael, 12

Neustadt, Richard, 177

Nevada, New Deal aid to, 50

New Deal

and African American political power, 437*n*

agricultural reforms, 66–67

aid to South under, 49–51, 61–62, 71–72, 86, 431*n*, 433*n*

and civil rights

anti-discrimination efforts, 60–69

failures to act, 55–60

impact of, 84

White reaction, 121–34

Congressional resistance to, 87

dismantling of, 397, 417

FDR's role in, 18, 20, 32

impact on disadvantaged, 70–75